THIRD ARTICLE THEOLOGY

A Pneumatological Dogmatics

THIRD ARTICLE THEOLOGY

A Pneumatological Dogmatics

Edited by **MYK HABETS**

Fortress Press
Minneapolis

THIRD ARTICLE THEOLOGY
A Pneumatological Dogmatics

Cover image: Gian Lorenzo Bernini - Dove of the Holy Spirit (ca. 1660, stained glass, Throne of St. Peter, St. Peter's Basilica, Vatican) by Dnalor 01
Cover design: Joe Reinke
Interior design and typesetting: PerfecType, Nashville, TN

Library of Congress Cataloging-in-Publication Data
Print ISBN: 978-1-4514-8886-9
eBook ISBN: 978-1-5064-1691-5

The paper used in this publication meets the minimum requirements of American National Standard for Information Sciences — Permanence of Paper for Printed Library Materials, ANSI Z329.48-1984.

Manufactured in the U.S.A.

Dedication

This volume is dedicated to Professor D. Lyle Dabney, for his theological guidance and for allowing the rest of us in on what God is up to at the moment. Lyle and Janet, this one is for you.

CONTENTS

PART 1: THEOLOGY PROPER

PART 2: HOLY SCRIPTURE

PART 3: CHRISTOLOGY

PART 4: ANTHROPOLOGY

ACKNOWLEDGMENTS

Originality is an ability reserved for children and geniuses. I am no longer a child and have never been a genius, and so I make no claims to originality. This volume on Third Article Theology is no exception. A series of seminal essays delivered by a then little-known Methodist theologian (and genius) to a small audience of Australian scholars contained the genesis of what today is known as Third Article Theology. Professor D. Lyle Dabney, from Marquette University, delivered the annual Theology Today Lectures (which were subsequently published in 2001, where I read them for the first time) in which he issued a prophetic plea for the church to grow up and act its age, the hallmark of which is to start with the Spirit. I have taken his call to heart and have developed this way of thinking after God and of doing theology over a number of works, but most comprehensively here in this volume, assisted by many friends. The volume is dedicated to Lyle for this reason. (Lyle also generously examined a thesis of mine and in so doing, saved me from a multitude of errors. The thesis subsequently went on to become a book, *The Anointed Son*.)

Editorial work is no walk in the park and no scholar I know does it for fun (and if they do then they need to get a life). I edit works for a number of reasons, most important of which is that many of the projects I work on seek to draw together scholars from across a range of contexts and speak to a doctrine (the *filioque*, for example), or one of the loci of theology (the Spirit, for example), or an issue of enduring significance (gender, for example), where I believe new insights are required that can encourage the church to think differently and act more faithfully. With this volume I wanted to go beyond a partial approach and develop a way of doing theology that was orthodox and yet distinctive, biblical and yet constructive, traditional and yet contemporary. Having been turned to a Third Article Theology, I have wanted to work on a wholesale pneumatological dogmatics. Yet, I knew the time was not right for me to complete this task alone; I needed help. Drawing up a wish list of contributors, I have managed to get most of them to commit to this project, and their essays await your careful consideration. While you cannot adjudicate the worth of their proposals, not having read them yet, I can, and they are outstanding. I want to thank each contributor for bringing their considerable expertise to this task and for delivering brilliant essays. They were a joy to read and work on.

I would next like to thank Michael Gibson and the team at Fortress Press for once again doing an outstanding job of publishing seminal works in theology. My thanks also go to my now long-term formatter and subeditor, Sarah Snell, for fast, efficient, and cheerful service.

My thanks also go to Carey Baptist College, its staff, and the principal—Charles Hewlett—for making our workplace a deeply Christian and stimulating environment in which to teach, write, and play. It was a research study leave to Fuller Theological Seminary that allowed me to complete the editing of this volume.

Finally, as always, my family are a constant source of deep encouragement and love. Thank you Odele, Sydney, and Liam, for your love of the author, even if you don't really read his books.

Myk Habets
Doctor Serviens Ecclesiae
Fuller Theological Seminary, Pasadena,
2015

FOREWORD

KIRSTEEN KIM

Third Article Theology is a new, exciting, and ambitious project. It attempts nothing more and nothing less than to reflect upon the whole of Christian theology from the perspective of pneumatology. We have become accustomed to theologies of the Holy Spirit—although just fifty years ago these were novel and somewhat daring. The Third Article has been scrutinized in various ways for what it reveals about the Spirit: the Spirit's co-equality with the Father and the Son, salvific authority, life-giving quality, prophetic voice, manifestation in the church, and forgiving, restoring, and divinizing power. We have used biblical sources to discuss the baptism in/of or fullness of the Spirit; the Spirit's gifts and fruit; empowerment and liberation by the Spirit; the Spirit of reconciliation, truth, accompaniment, and unity; Spirit in creation; and so on. We have mined the church fathers and the mystics for insight and we have examined contemporary manifestations of the Spirit, especially in Renewal movements. We have explored the meaning of "spirit," the quality of holiness, the role of the Spirit in the Trinity, the most appropriate gender terms to use for the Spirit, the relationship of the Holy Spirit to other spirits, and the Spirit's relation to culture, religion, and nature.

There is plenty more pneumatology to be explored, but Third Article Theology is not only pneumatology. It is an attempt to redo the whole of theology, beginning with what we understand about the Holy Spirit. Instead of starting with God the Father, Third Article Theology will cover the Creed backwards. In the economy of God, we do in any case begin that way. Since the Spirit is life itself, we living beings are bound to start there. Moreover, the incarnation itself began with the Spirit's overshadowing Mary. In our Christian experience, we are moved by the Spirit, who leads us to Christ, who reveals the Father.

However, since the development of ideas about the immanent Trinity, theology has been approached from the other direction—as the Creed shows. And at least since Aquinas, we have begun with God as one, and only after that have we considered the processions—first of the Son and then of the Spirit. The Spirit, apparently the last, applies to us all that has been revealed and then finishes the job. Karl Barth famously departed from the traditional pattern when he began with the Word of God or Christology and constructed his Second Article Theology. Despite what some critics suggested, his works were not merely an extended Christology but covered the whole of theology. Tantalizingly, at the end of his life, Barth suggested that he could do it all again beginning with the Spirit. More recently Lyle Dabney of Marquette University has proposed Third Article Theology and others have followed suit. Now there is a network for the task and Myk Habets is to be congratulated on bringing together the first of what, it is hoped, will be many works of Third Article Theology.

The chapters in this volume deal with the method of Third Article Theology, philosophical considerations, and biblical sources, before approaching different subdisciplines—anthropology, spirituality, ecclesiology, and public theology—through the lens of the Third Article. Christology is central to the book and pivotal to this endeavor. This is because of the logic of the Trinity: if the three persons are a unity, then Third Article Theology will be intimately related to Christology. In fact, as Habets points out, Spirit Christology could be regarded as the first achievement of Third Article Theology. Its recent development from ancient sources, especially as I see it by Asian theologians, is a reminder that not everyone approaches theology from the immanent Trinity. The refreshing approach taken here is most welcome and I am sure it will stimulate many further investigations in this new field.

LIST OF CONTRIBUTORS

Raniero Cantalamessa, OFM Cap. Former Ordinary Professor of the History of Ancient Christianity and Director of the Department of Religious Sciences at the Catholic University of Milan, Preacher to the Papal Household since 1980 under Pope John Paul II, Pope Benedict XVI, and Pope Francis.

David Coffey. Professor Emeritus of Theology, Department of Theology, Marquette University, Milwaukee, Wisconsin, and of the Catholic Institute of Sydney, Australia.

Marc Cortez. Associate Professor of Theology, Wheaton College, Wheaton, Illinois.

Andrew K. Gabriel. Assistant Professor of Theology, Horizon College and Seminary, Saskatoon, Canada.

Joel B. Green. Dean of the School of Theology and Professor of New Testament Interpretation, Fuller Theological Seminary.

Tom Greggs. Marischal Chair of Divinity, University of Aberdeen.

Kirsten Laurel Guidero. Visiting Scholar of Religion, Southwestern College, Winfield, Kansas.

Myk Habets. Head of Carey Graduate School, Director of the R. J. Thompson

Centre for Theological Studies, Senior Academic in Systematic Theology, Carey Baptist College and Graduate School, Auckland, New Zealand.

Scott Harrower. Lecturer in Christian Thought, Ridley College, Melbourne, Australia.

Veli-Matti Kärkkäinen. Professor of Systematic Theology, School of Theology, Fuller Theological Seminary, and Docent of Ecumenics, University of Helsinki.

Kirsteen Kim. Professor of Theology and World Christianity, Leeds Trinity University, UK.

Cornelis van der Kooi. Professor of Western Systematic Theology; Chair of the Department of Dogmatics and Ecumenics, Director of the Centre for Evangelical and Reformation Theology, Faculty of Theology, Vrije Universiteit Amsterdam.

Gregory J. Liston. Lecturer in Systematic Theology, Laidlaw College, New Zealand, and Pastor, Mt Albert Baptist Church, Auckland, New Zealand.

Frank D. Macchia. Professor of Christian Theology at Vanguard University of Southern California and Associate Director of the Centre for Pentecostal and Charismatic Studies at Bangor University, Wales (UK).

Joseph McGarry. Independent scholar and Adjunct lecturer in theology, Carey Baptist College, Auckland, New Zealand.

Keith A. Quan. Independent scholar.

Eugene F. Rogers Jr. Professor of Religious Studies, Faculty in Women's & Gender Studies, University of North Carolina at Greensboro.

Leopoldo A. Sánchez M. Werner R. H. and Elizabeth R. Krause Professor of Hispanic Ministries, Director of the Center for Hispanic Studies, Concordia Seminary, St. Louis, Missouri.

Jason S. Sexton. Lecturer in the Honors Program of California State University, Fullerton, and Visiting Fellow at UC Riverside's Center for Ideas and Society.

John A. Studebaker Jr. Lecturer in Religion, Hillsdale College; Executive Director, BMI Oasis, Richland, Michigan.

Steven M. Studebaker. Associate Professor of Systematic and Historical Theology, Howard & Shirley Bentall Chair in Evangelical Thought, McMaster Divinity College, Hamilton, Ontario, Canada.

Wolfgang Vondey. Reader in Contemporary Christianity and Pentecostal Studies, Director of the Centre for Pentecostal and Charismatic Studies, Department of Theology and Religion, University of Birmingham.

Amos Yong. Director of the Center for Missiological Research and Professor of Theology and Mission, School of Intercultural Studies, Fuller Theological Seminary.

ABBREVIATIONS

ACO	*Acta Conciliorum Oecumenicorum.* Edited by Eduard Schwartz. Berlin: de Gruyter, 1914–84
ACW	Ancient Christian Writers
ANF	*Ante-Nicene Fathers*
CCSL	Corpus Christianorum: Series Latina
CSEL	Corpus Scriptorum Ecclesiasticorum Latinorum
EDOT	*Evangelical Dictionary of Theology.* Ed. Walter Elwell. Grand Rapids: Baker, 1984.
FC	Fathers of the Church
GCS	Die griechischen christlichen Schriftsteller der ersten [drei] Jahrhunderte
LW	*Luther's Works: The American Edition.* Edited by Jaroslav Pelikan and Helmut T. Lehmann. 55 vols. St. Louis: Concordia; Philadelphia: Fortress, 1955–86.
NIDNTT	*New International Dictionary of New Testament Theology.* Edited by Colin Brown. 4 vols. Grand Rapids: Zondervan, 1975–78

NPNF[2] *Nicene and Post-Nicene Fathers*, Series 2

para(s). paragraph(s)

par(r). parallel(s)

PG Patrologia Graeca. Edited by Jacques-Paul Migne. 162 vols. Paris, 1857–86

PL Patrologia Latina. Edited by Jacques-Paul Migne. 217 vols. Paris, 1844–64

TDNT *Theological Dictionary of the New Testament*. Edited by Gerhard Kittel and Gerhard Friedrich. Translated by Geoffrey W. Bromiley. 10 vols. Grand Rapids: Eerdmans, 1964–76

ThWAT *Theologisches Wörterbuch zum Alten Testament*. Edited by G. Johannes Botterweck and Helmer Ringgren. Stuttgart: Kohlhammer, 1970–

WA *D. Martin Luthers Werke: Kritische Gesamtausgabe*. 50 vols. Weimar: Hermann Böhlau, 1883–2007.

CHAPTER 1

Prolegomenon

On Starting with the Spirit

MYK HABETS

The rich and capacious narrative of Holy Scripture is suffused from beginning to end and back again with the presence of the triune God in creating, speaking, saving, transforming, and perfecting creation; in ordering all that is not divine into fellowship with the God of Abraham, Isaac, and Jacob; in bringing everything under the authority of the risen and ascended Lord Jesus Christ; and permeating all things, animate and inanimate, with "the Holy Spirit, Lord and Giver of life" (the third clause of the Nicene Creed). God's economic activity is made manifest as a coherent, ordered, and triune work in which the Almighty fructifies his creation. In the traditional language of conciliar theology, the Father creates, the Son sustains, and the Spirit perfects. While prone to static and modalist interpretations, such orthodox usage supports neither interpretation. Instead, it is witness to the unity of God's economic action, summarized in the Latin phrase *Omnia opera Trinitatis ad extra indivisa sunt* (the external operations of the Trinity are undividedly the work of the entire Trinity). Such a rule does not imply, however, that each person of the Trinity ceases to have its own particular subsistence, and hence certain work is appropriated to one or another of the divine persons. Manifestly evident in the scriptural account of God's economic work is the unction of the Spirit upon the world and its creatures, creating, sustaining, and perfecting them, bringing order out of chaos, turning lament to praise, transfiguring humans into gods.

While occluded, oppressed, or consigned to the margins by a christomonistic myopia, the Holy Spirit has often suffered at the hands of Christian theologians. Older textbook accounts of systematic theology had little time for pneumatology, often dealing with the topic as a short subsection of the more important doctrine of God (theology proper), or reserving the work of the Spirit to applying the benefits of the atonement to believers and thus consigning the Spirit to perpetual servitude or bonded labor to the work of Christ. Western Trinitarian theology, following Augustine's profoundly important and influential work, has explicitly constructed a Trinitarianism in which the Spirit is the fruit of a prior and superior relationship that exists between the Father and the Son.[1] The Spirit then has the role of being the bond of union between Father and Son, or that which flows from or is the result of their relationship. Eastern Trinitarianism, especially that of an Athanasian and Cappadocian flavor, has several "models" of the Trinity—namely, the monopatrist (the Father as sole source), the perichoretic (social-personal-relational), and the apophatic (essence-energies)—that mitigate the implicit subordination of the Spirit. But even so there remains a regnant relegation of the Spirit to the periphery in standard Orthodox accounts (more acute in certain doctrines than others).

Beyond a Theology of the Third Article

Third Article Theology (TAT) is proposed as one way to address this less-than-Trinitarian articulation of the faith. While a new initiative on the theological scene, TAT is not a novel enterprise, if by "novel" is meant something created de novo. Dogmatics is about faithful witness, not poetic creation. TAT owes its name and initial conception to Methodist and Pentecostal theologian D. Lyle Dabney. In a series of seminal essays,

1. The legacy of Augustine on this question has, of course, been complexified by the work of Lewis Ayres in his *Nicaea and Its Legacy: An Approach to Fourth-Century Trinitarian Theology* (Oxford: Oxford University Press, 2004); and *Augustine and the Trinity* (Cambridge: Cambridge University Press, 2010).

Dabney set forth a proposal for identifying several pathologies in what he called First and Second Article theologies following the Nicene Creed, before offering an insight and a call for a theology of the Third Article, one which starts with the Spirit.[2] Garnering biblical, philosophical, sociological, and theological support, Dabney called for the church to grow up and "act its age," arguing that "Christian theology should begin its task, that is to say, with an account of the Spirit; and thus that should now be *first* which has traditionally been *last*."[3] Dabney referred to such a program as a "theology of the third article."

While this account takes its impetus from Dabney's own theological program, it exhibits its subtle but important differences. TAT has to be distinguished from dogmatic accounts that are simply pneumatological, something more appropriately termed a theology of the Third Article. TAT, by contrast, is not simply a study of pneumatology but is, rather, a conscious and considered approach to conceiving of theology and witnessing to God's self-revelation in Word and works, from the perspective of the Spirit where questions of pneumatology set the agenda and control the trajectory of the dogmatic enterprise, rather than pneumatology being the sole focus. As such, TAT is a specific and technical name for a method of theology. It seeks to articulate the contours of a Christian theology in a Trinitarian fashion, but one that starts with the Spirit.

On the Way Toward a Third Article Theology

Across the Christian traditions, calls for a pneumatological enrichment of the received tradition are mounting. Despite the fact that TAT has been self-consciously employed by very few theologians to date, and thus it is something of a pioneer theology, a growing number of works contribute to such an approach. A brief overview of these provides the context for the contributions of the present work.

In his justly famous chapter "Concluding Unscientific Postscript on Schleiermacher," Barth reflected on his own christological

2. See especially the four essays by D. Lyle Dabney in *Starting with the Spirit: Task of Theology II*, ed. Stephen Pickard and Gordon Preece (Hindmarsh, SA: Australian Theological Forum, 2001): "Starting with the Spirit: Why the Last Should be First" (3–27); "Naming the Spirit: Toward a Pneumatology of the Cross" (28–58); "The Justification of the Spirit: Soteriological Reflections on the Resurrection" (59–82); and "The Nature of the Spirit: Creation as a Premonition of God" (83–110).

3. Dabney, "Starting with the Spirit," 4.

program and made the astounding comment that all his theological investigations could have been pursued from the perspective of pneumatology. In his words:

> What I have already intimated here and there to good friends, would be the possibility of a theology of the third article, in other words, a theology predominantly and decisively of the Holy Spirit. Everything which needs to be said, considered, and believed about God the Father and God the Son in an understanding of the first and second articles might be shown and illuminated in its foundations through God the Holy Spirit, the *vinculum pacis inter Patrem et Filium*.[4]

The great christocentrist was advocating the possibility of a thorough TAT, one which would complement his Second Article Theology of the *Church Dogmatics*: a christological program pursued from a Trinitarian perspective, highlighting the mutual relations between the Son and the Spirit in the incarnation. Many have directly or indirectly followed Barth's suggestion. Eastern Orthodox, Roman Catholic,[5] Pentecostal,[6] and Protestant theologians are taking up the challenge of a pneumatically oriented dogmatics—something now known as a TAT.

Similarly to Barth, Pope John Paul II famously issued in 1996 the encyclical *On the Holy Spirit in the Life of the Church and the World*, in which he encouraged believers to be attentive to the Spirit of God as they prepare for the third Christian millennium.[7]

4. Karl Barth, "Nachwort, or Concluding Unscientific Postscript on Schleiermacher," in *The Theology of Schleiermacher: Lectures at Göttingen*, trans. Geoffrey W. Bromiley (Grand Rapids: Eerdmans, 1982), 278.

5. See especially David M. Coffey, "Spirit Christology and the Trinity," in *Advents of the Spirit: An Introduction to the Current Study of Pneumatology*, ed. B. E. Hinze and D. L. Dabney (Milwaukee: Marquette University Press, 2001), 315–38; and Ralph Del Colle, *Christ and the Spirit: Spirit-Christology in Trinitarian Perspective* (New York: Oxford University Press, 1994).

6. Notably Veli-Matti Kärkkäinen, *Toward a Pneumatological Theology: Pentecostal and Ecumenical Perspectives on Ecclesiology, Soteriology, and Theology of Mission*, ed. A. Yong (New York: University Press of America, 2002); Kärkkäinen, *A Constructive Christian Theology for the Pluralistic World*, vol. 1, *Christ and Reconciliation* (Grand Rapids: Eerdmans, 2013), 196–209; and Amos Yong, *Beyond the Impasse: Toward a Pneumatological Theology of Religions* (Grand Rapids: Baker, 2003).

7. See the full text at: http://www.vatican.va/holy_father/john_paul_ii/encyclicals/documents/hf_jp-ii_enc_18051986_dominum-et-vivificantem_en.html.

Pope John Paul II rehearsed the efforts in Roman Catholicism to reclaim a pneumatological focus, as seen in several encyclicals and of course the focus of Vatican II. He then asserted:

> In our own age, then, we are called anew by the ever ancient and ever new faith of the Church, to draw near to the Holy Spirit as the giver of life. In this we are helped and stimulated also by the heritage we share with the Oriental Churches, which have jealously guarded the extraordinary riches of the teachings of the Fathers on the Holy Spirit. For this reason too we can say that one of the most important ecclesial events of recent years has been the Sixteenth Centenary of the First Council of Constantinople, celebrated simultaneously in Constantinople and Rome on the Solemnity of Pentecost in 1981. The Holy Spirit was then better seen, through a meditation on the mystery of the Church, as the one who points out the ways leading to the union of Christians, indeed as the supreme source of this unity, which comes from God himself and to which St. Paul gave a particular expression in the words which are frequently used to begin the Eucharistic liturgy: "The grace of our Lord Jesus Christ and the love of God and the fellowship of the Holy Spirit be with you all."[8]

While less than a call for a TAT, this does provide significant impetus for such a program by others. More recently in 2013, Pope Francis reflected upon the work of the Spirit in the life of the church and has exhorted the faithful to

> . . . let ourselves be imbued with the light of the Holy Spirit, so that He introduces us into the Truth of God, who is the only Lord of our lives. In this Year of Faith let us ask ourselves if we have actually taken a few steps to get to know Christ and the truths of faith more, by reading and meditating on the Scriptures, studying the Catechism, steadily approaching the Sacraments. But at the same time let us ask ourselves what steps we are taking so that the faith directs our whole existence. Do not be a "part-time" Christian, at certain moments, in certain circumstances, in certain choices, be Christian at all times! The truth of Christ, which the Holy Spirit teaches us and gives us,

8. Ibid., paragraph 2.

> always and forever involves our daily lives. Let us invoke him more often, to guide us on the path of Christ's disciples.[9]

Roman Catholicism

An invoking of the Spirit in theology has been heeded by a number of significant Roman Catholic scholars working toward a TAT, each in their own way. Yves Congar produced a survey of pneumatology from the early church into the twentieth century, and along the way provided thick descriptions of theological positions such that his was a contribution to post-Vatican II theology and twentieth-century pneumatology more generally, almost unrivalled in its scope and perception.[10] Heribert Mühlen developed a proto-Spirit Christology before applying such insights to the doctrine of the Trinity, and then to ecclesiology, suggesting with idiosyncratic force that the Spirit is the "we," the unity of "I" and "thou." The leitmotif of Mühlen's work may be summarized by his assertion: "The doctrine and person of the Holy Spirit is not one doctrine among others, but a fundamental doctrine and reality in the Church."[11] Ralph Del Colle and David Coffey were colleagues at Marquette University (with D. Lyle Dabney) and together they forged a formidable contribution to Spirit Christology and, by means of such, a reevaluation of how to conceive the doctrine of the Trinity along more relational and pneumatological lines.[12] Del Colle's work *Christ and the Spirit* establishes for modern theology the integrity and orthodoxy of a Trinitarian Spirit Christology and situates it among his Catholic interlocutors, while Coffey's work is more speculative, developing what he calls a "mutual-love" doctrine of the Trinity.[13] In both attempts we find a partial but significant

---

9. General audience catechesis, Wednesday, May 15, 2013, http://www.catholicworldreport.com/Blog/2260/pope_francis_reflects_on_the_work_and_power_of_the_holy_spirit.aspx#.Urd6SI2IppM.

10. Yves Congar, *I Believe in the Holy Spirit*, trans. D. Smith (New York: Crossroad, 2000).

11. Heribert Mühlen, *Una Mystica Persona: Die Kirche als das Mysterium der heilsgeschichtlichen Identität des Heiligen Geistes in Christus und den Christen; Eine Person in vielen Personen* (Paderborn: Ferdinand Schöningh, 1967), 5; translated by Wolfgang Vondey in *Heribert Mühlen: His Theology and Praxis* (Dallas: University Press of America, 2004), xv.

12. The fruits of a 1998 conference at Marquette University on a pneumatological approach to theology can be found in Hinzey and Dabney, *Advents of the Spirit*.

13. See especially David Coffey, *Deus Trinitas: The Doctrine of the Triune God* (New York: Oxford University Press, 1999); and Coffey, "The Holy Spirit as the Mutual Love of the Father and the Son," *Theological Studies* 51, no. 2 (1990): 193–229.

contribution to the rise of a TAT in ways that are influential on others.

Pentecostalism

In addition to Barth and calls for a TAT from Roman Catholics, Pentecostalism too is joining the chorus. Arguably the most significant theological movement of the twentieth century, Pentecostalism brought a renewed emphasis to the work of the Spirit, the fruits of which are being enjoyed in theology and practice today. Among recent Pentecostal labors one finds a renewed sense of impetus and imagination for dogmatics fueled precisely by starting with the Spirit.[14] A representative example here is James Smith, the Pentecostal philosopher who argues in his *Thinking in Tongues* for a distinctly "spiritual" way to think, worship, and speak.[15] The work is replete with testimony, a theology from below to above, and is suffused with an approach compatible with what we term a TAT. Smith's work makes compelling claims about the community locus of mediated authority, for spirited readings of inspired texts, and for an articulation of a worldview by which the strength of the lens is not measured by diopter, but the presence of the Holy Spirit.

While largely positive, Pentecostal theology in some quarters is tending to dislocate the work of the Spirit from the work of Christ in such a way that their respective missions are conceived as *separate* operations, each with its own integrity and ends, rather than as distinct but coordinated missions.[16] Contemporary Pentecostal scholarship is divided over an understanding of the economic activity of God, with many positing a freedom of the Spirit from Christ such that any catholic

14. Older works of theology by Pentecostals show little sustained focus on or integration of the work of the Holy Spirit throughout a dogmatics, as seen, for example, in J. Rodman Williams, *Renewal Theology: Systematic Theology from a Charismatic Perspective*, 3 vols. (Grand Rapids: Zondervan, 1988–92); or Larry D. Hart, *Truth Aflame: Theology for the Church in Renewal* (1999; repr., Grand Rapids: Zondervan, 2005). Even the work of the Reformed Charismatic theologian Wayne Grudem gives little time to developing a Third Article perspective on theology, relegating any meaningful discussion of the Spirit to soteriology (sanctification), spiritual gifts, and a traditional Western discussion of the Trinity (*Systematic Theology: An Introduction to Biblical Doctrine* [Grand Rapids: Zondervan, 1994]).

15. James K. A. Smith, *Thinking in Tongues: Pentecostal Contributions to Christian Philosophy* (Grand Rapids: Eerdmans, 2010).

16. The clearest statement of this may be found in Steven M. Studebaker, *From Pentecost to the Triune God: A Pentecostal Trinitarian Theology* (Grand Rapids: Eerdmans, 2012), 176–85, especially his appeals against any forms of "christocentrism."

notion of the Trinity has to be abandoned for a version of a social doctrine of God, or for an implicit tritheism. In either case, the notion of the *Omnia opera Trinitatis ad extra indivisa sunt* is abandoned and God's missions lack any coordination with God's processions. A Trinitarian theology shorn of its christological center threatens to distract theologians and derail dogmatics from a Christian enterprise into religious studies or a theology of religions. For some, admittedly, this is an invitation and not a challenge; for others, this spells the end of catholic theology and the beginning of a novel turn to a sub-Christian discourse. The view of Veli-Matti Kärkkäinen is more conducive to a TAT when he states, "Whereas traditional theology, not only Western scholasticism but also contemporary Eastern Orthodox tradition represented by Vladimir Lossky, quite categorically distinguishes the two 'missions' of the Son and Spirit in the one divine economy, it is more useful to speak of christological and pneumatological dimensions of the one divine economy."[17] In a terse summary he rightly contends, "'Christocentrism' and the turn to the Spirit cannot be considered as alternatives."[18]

17. Kärkkäinen, *Christ and Reconciliation*, 206.
18. Ibid., 209.

Another key voice in Pentecostal theology today, Frank Macchia, argues in his work *Justified in the Spirit* for a Pentecostal "solution" to what I am here calling a First Article Theology (represented most fittingly by Roman Catholicism) and Second Article Theology (represented most fittingly by Reformational theology), and looks to baptism in the Spirit as a Pentecostal metaphor to do so.[19] Macchia argues neither for a moral and anthropological notion of justification (Roman Catholicism) nor for a purely forensic account (Reformed Protestantism), but rather for a participatory account wherein the Spirit grants sinners access to the divine *koinōnia*; and thus righteousness is creative and not cooperative (First Article Theology) or merely declarative (Second Article Theology). While deeply Pentecostal, Macchia's account also anticipates a TAT in many ways by highlighting how in the tradition accounts of justification have looked to the Spirit for their establishment and yet, to date, have failed to adequately develop the intuition. In his words,

> The declaration of extrinsic righteousness from Protestant pulpits and the infusion

19. Frank D. Macchia, *Justified in the Spirit: Creation, Redemption, and the Triune God* (Grand Rapids: Eerdmans, 2010).

> of virtues in the creature's cooperation with grace assumed in traditional Catholic settings has required a developed appreciation of the baptism in the Spirit to link and anchor them both. Though relatively undeveloped, this metaphor came to prominence through the Pentecostal movement in the twentieth century.[20]

Taking this a step further and developing a soteriological account that does not rely on Spirit baptism as defined by Pentecostalism, but rather offers an account of justification that is pneumatologically driven, will be the task of a TAT, but Macchia has shown the way, as it were, opening the door for others to enter.

Protestantism

Protestants of all stripes are seeking to "re-enchant" theology and work from more robustly pneumatological perspectives. The late Clark Pinnock, a Baptist scholar, stands out for special mention in this regard, with his bold and insightful survey of theology in 1996 that was, in brief, a pneumatological approach. It is unique, as far as I am aware, in being an attempt to think through several major theological *loci* from a pneumatological perspective. "Far from being an incidental or isolated topic in theology," argued Pinnock, "Spirit is a major theme, supplying a standpoint, in fact, for surveying the whole vista of Christian truth."[21] Pinnock's working hypothesis is that "though we speak of the Spirit as a third person, from the standpoint of experience Spirit is first, because it is Spirit that enables us to experience God's flying by and drawing near."[22] Working not from a systematic theological perspective but, rather, with what he calls a "nondeterministic theology,"[23] Pinnock reconceives the theological task in terms more precisely articulated by James Smith as a "storied epistemology,"[24] wherein knowledge is not antirational but is antirationalist, where cognitivism is critiqued and an affective understanding is prioritized. Over seven chapters, Pinnock moves from the Trinity to creation, Christology, ecclesiology, soteriology, religions, and missions;

20. Ibid., 318.

21. Clark H. Pinnock, *Flame of Love: A Theology of the Holy Spirit* (Downers Grove, IL: InterVarsity Press, 1996), 10.

22. Ibid., 14.

23. Ibid., 18. For a comprehensive account of this approach, see Thomas F. Torrance, *Theological Science* (London: Oxford University Press, 1969). The following essay by Alan J. Torrance is also worth consulting: "Analytic Theology and the Reconciled Mind: The Significance of History," *Journal of Analytic Theology* 1 (May 2013): 30–44.

24. Smith, *Thinking in Tongues*, 48–85.

at each point his focus is on a pneumatologically construed account of God's ways in the world. The details of Pinnock's theology are open to critique (for example, his social doctrine of the Trinity, implicit universalism, and the move to a form of religious pluralism); however, his commitment to a TAT is consistently worked out and highly suggestive at key points—the relational ontology of the Godhead, Spirit Christology, *theōsis*, and ecumenism—such that it sets an agenda, even a manifesto, for others. Not without good reason Pinnock styled his a "pilgrim theology."[25]

Liberation Theologies

While not using the language or the self-conscious conceptuality of TAT, a number of feminist, liberation, and majority world theologians are adopting an implicit TAT approach to dogmatics, especially in the doctrine of the Trinity. Roman Catholic feminist theologian Elizabeth Johnson turns to the priority of the Spirit in her book *She Who Is* to order her account of the triune God and apply that to womanist concerns.[26] While endorsing theological themes not conducive to orthodox Christian belief, Johnson's feminist reading of Scripture and interpretation of experience lead her to start her theologizing at "the juncture where the dialectic of God's presence and absence shapes life in all its struggles."[27] That juncture is neither the unity of the divine nature nor the person of the Father, but the Spirit. In Johnson's words, "What results is a theology of the triune God that sets out from the experience of the Spirit."[28] In contrast to Johnson, a TAT locates the fundamental human experience of the Spirit in the life of Christ and only then accepts Johnson's point that this approach "allows a starting point more closely allied to the human experience of salvation, without which there would be no speech about the triune God at all."[29] While Johnson's journey takes her onto theological paths more orthodox pilgrims will certainly not want to traverse, it is her starting point and reasons for it that advocates of a TAT might want to share.[30]

---

25. See Clark H. Pinnock, "A Pilgrim on the Way," *Christianity Today*, February 9, 1998, http://www.ctlibrary.com/ct/1998/february9/8t2043.html.

26. Elizabeth A. Johnson, *She Who Is: The Mystery of God in Feminist Theological Discourse* (New York: Crossroad, 1992).

27. Ibid., 121.

28. Ibid., 122.

29. Ibid.

30. Similarly critical of Johnson's feminist and revisionary theology, Luke Timothy Johnson agrees that her starting with the Spirit is an inspired move allowing an enrichment of the tradition rather than requiring a wholesale revision ("Something

Elizabeth Johnson speaks for most advocates of a TAT when she expresses her concern about the relative absence of the Spirit in traditional theological discourse. She asks what has gone wrong: "For despite the pervasiveness of the dialectic experience of the Spirit, theological articulation about the Spirit has traditionally lagged considerably behind reflection on God unoriginated source of all and God incarnate, classically named Father and Son respectively. The history of doctrine shows that the Spirit, while the first and most intimate way God is experienced, was yet the last to be named explicitly divine."[31] She goes on to note that even when this was achieved at Constantinople in 381 the Spirit did not receive attention commensurate with this confession. While the possible causes for this situation are many, Johnson concludes, "For whatever reasons, theology of the Spirit remained in an embryonic state."[32] Johnson then proceeds to catalogue the ways in which the Spirit has remained in such a state throughout the Western theological tradition in both its Roman Catholic and Protestant guises. Johnson points to the inability of Aquinas to identify a proper name for the Spirit and thus his inability to name the processions that follow, the pervasive privatization of the Spirit within Pietism, Barth's insistence on describing the Spirit as the subjective side of the event of revelation, Pentecostal enthusiasm, the tendency of post-Tridentine Catholicism to bind the Spirit to ecclesiastical structures, and the tendency of Catholic piety to displace the work of the Spirit onto the pope, the cult of the Blessed Sacrament, or the Virgin Mary. Johnson's assessment, correct in my opinion, is that "[t]he cumulative effect of this meagre Western pneumatological tradition has been that the full range of the reality and activity of God the Spirit has been virtually lost from much of Christian theological consciousness."[33] A TAT accepts all of these criticisms and offers a new perspective for dogmatics capable of addressing such concerns.

In similar fashion to Johnson, but with a more orthodox feminist theology, Anglican theologian Sarah Coakley provides a comprehensive and perceptive account of the priority of the Spirit in dogmatic accounts of

Fundamental is Afoot," *Commonweal* 120 [January 29, 1993]: 17–22).

31. Johnson, *She Who Is*, 128.

32. Ibid.

33. Ibid., 130. For my own account of some of these pneumatological ailments, see Myk Habets, "*Veni Cinderella Spiritus*," *Journal of Pentecostal Theology* 10 (2001): 65–80.

the Trinity, Christology, prayer, asceticism, ministry, and worship in the first volume of her project in systematic theology. Coakley's self-styled *théologie totale* has much in common with the approach of TAT, most especially in her provocative remarks regarding the doctrine of the Trinity.[34] Coakley argues for an "incorporative trinitarianism" whereby the Spirit is more than a bonding agent (*vinculum amoris*) but is constitutive of the triune relations, following the pattern of Romans 8, linking that to the concept of desire, gender, prayer, and asceticism. Her doctrine of God propels her to the conclusion that "there can be in God's trinitarian ontology no Sonship which is not eternally 'sourced' by 'Father' *in the Spirit* (in such a way, in fact, as to query even the usual and exclusive meanings of Fatherly 'source' . . .)."[35] Grasping the fact that all theology is integrated, Coakley concludes volume 1 of her theology with a vision for the future of theology once it genuinely, in my terms, starts with the Spirit.

> [W]e must start afresh with our celestial number system, and allow the Spirit's primary propulsion to allow us to rethink, even now, trinitarian number in God, and just as much, and correctively, number in the human realm of gender. It has been the daring invitation of this book to make the problematic 'third' in God the 'first' in human encounter, not because the Spirit is thereby jostling *competitively* with the Father to be the primary ontological source, but because we humans have to cleanse our hearts and minds of any suggestion that the paternal divine 'source' could ever involve that sort of rivalry: 'source' here has become ecstatic goal as much as ecstatic origin, propelled inherently towards the transformative appearance of the God/Man. If, finally, we make this mind-shift, then everything changes.[36]

What is true of her account is shared by those advocating a TAT; when we make this shift, everything changes.

34. Sarah Coakley, *God, Sexuality, and the Self: An Essay 'On the Trinity'* (Cambridge: Cambridge University Press, 2013), especially 1–65.

35. Ibid., 332. In a footnote (34) Coakley acknowledges her broad concurrence with the similar proposal of Thomas G. Weinandy, *The Father's Spirit of Sonship: Reconceiving the Trinity* (Edinburgh: T&T Clark, 1995). In this her proposal is also conducive to my own—Myk Habets, "Getting beyond the *Filioque* with Third Article Theology," in *Ecumenical Perspectives on the Filioque for the Twenty-First Century*, ed. Myk Habets (London: Bloomsbury/T&T Clark, 2014), 211–30.

36. Coakley, *God, Sexuality, and the Self*, 333–34.

Eastern Orthodoxy

Eastern Orthodoxy too deserves mention, in that it has always had an innate ability to fine-tune theology with pneumatological insights. The Orthodox doctrines of *theōsis* are one of the clearest examples of how the Spirit is constitutive across the spectrum of the theological enterprise, from *protos* to *telos*, a theme developed later in this volume. With *theōsis* as the architectonic key to Orthodox dogmatics, all doctrines take their cue from the presence of the triune God. While not necessarily accepting Palamite and neo-Palamite emphases within the Orthodox tradition, such as the radical essence-energies distinction or its Neo-Platonism, the Basilian theme of the creating and perfecting Spirit is present throughout the Orthodox vision, the transcendent determination of the cosmos for communion with God in Christ by the Spirit is evoked across the dogmatic spectrum, and the graced relation of humanity to God from creation through to eschaton is a central theme.[37] Each of these moves is conducive to a TAT, offering insights from across the broad range of the tradition that today are being adopted, adapted, and—in terms of the topic of this volume—being recommended to the theological community as a constructive dogmatics for our time. Slowly but doggedly the foundations for TAT are being developed across the ecclesiological spectrum and across the theological *loci*.

Far and away the most work to date on TAT has been completed in the area of Christology, specifically calls to reclaim a robust and Trinitarian Spirit Christology.[38] That Spirit Christology is the area of most study and the first theological *loci* to find an articulation of a TAT is not surprising, given that even in a TAT Christology occupies the center. Accounts of the Trinity that are not simply speculative must work from God's self-revelation in Christ through to an account of the immanent Trinity;

---

37. As but one example, the theology of Romanian Orthodox theologian Dumitru Staniloae stands out. See his *Orthodox Dogmatic Theology*, vol. 1, *Revelation and Knowledge of the Triune God: The Experience of God*, trans. and ed. Ioana Ionita and Robert Barringer (Brookline, MA: Holy Cross Orthodox Press, 1994).

38. For the most comprehensive account, see Myk Habets, *The Anointed Son: A Trinitarian Spirit Christology* (Eugene, OR: Pickwick, 2010). The definitive Catholic account is Del Colle, *Christ and the Spirit*. There is also an Indian account (Christina Manohar, *Spirit Christology: An Indian Christian Perspective* [Delhi: ISPCK, 2009]) and an Hispanic account (Sammy Alfaro, *Divino Compañero: Toward a Hispanic Pentecostal Christology* [Eugene, OR: Pickwick, 2010]).

ecclesiology has as its foundation Jesus the Messiah, the Head of the church; eschatology is the revelation of the Lord Jesus Christ, and so here too a TAT is developed in connection with Christology. This turn to Spirit Christology in a robust Trinitarian context is welcome and has produced an increasing amount of suggestive and significant works. However, it is also, I suggest, a discipline come of age, and with that, it is poised to move from its preoccupation with definition and methodology—that is, with prolegomena—to constructive and systematic integration. In other words, it has moved from investigation of an individual doctrine (Spirit Christology) to immersion in a full theological program (TAT). Hence the need for a constructive account of what such a theology might look like.

Methodological Theses

This volume represents the first major work that is self-consciously a product of TAT and a constructive and dogmatic attempt to establish TAT as a distinct theological discipline. The exact means by which TAT is to be developed, however, requires comment. In several earlier publications I have sought to outline a criteriological map of what TAT entails in its broadest contours.[39] As TAT is as much a methodology as it is a theology, the rudiments or contours of such a methodology deserve consideration. The following ten criteria begin to establish the methodological concerns of TAT.[40]

1. TAT starts with the Holy Spirit. Pneumatological considerations are not left to a postscript or conclusion but are, rather, incorporated into theological discourse right from the beginning. Questions of the Spirit will no longer act as an "edifying appendage to the doctrine of God."[41]

39. Initial attempts at establishing methodological criteria for doing TAT may be found in Habets, *Anointed Son*, 232–33. Taking his impetus from Ralph Del Colle and my own work, Andrew Grosso presents rudimentary criteria for a TAT in "Spirit Christology and the Shape of the Theological Enterprise," in *A Man of the Church: Honoring the Theology, Life, and Witness of Ralph Del Colle*, ed. Michel René Barnes (Eugene, OR: Pickwick, 2012), 206–22.

40. The following ten criteria are a development of those first suggested in Myk Habets, "The Surprising Third Article Theology of Jonathan Edwards," in *The Ecumenical Edwards: Jonathan Edwards and the Theologians*, ed. Kyle Strobel (Farnham, UK: Ashgate, 2015), 197–99.

41. Heribert Mühlen, "The Person of the Holy Spirit," in *The Holy Spirit and Power*, ed. Kilian McDonnell (Garden City, NY: Doubleday, 1975), 12.

2. TAT looks *through* the Spirit rather than simply looking *at* the Spirit; thus it is a "Third Article Theology" and not a "theology of the Third Article" (which would simply be pneumatology). This does not mean, as the further criteria make clear, that the Spirit remains "nameless" and "faceless."[42] Rather, the Spirit's person and work are fully parsed in a Trinitarian context.
3. TAT should precede First and Second Article Theology, as the most consistent way of coordinating the *ordo salutis*, from which we derive the *ordo cognoscendi* and come to know the *ordo essendi*—from the Father, through the Son, to the Holy Spirit, and back by the Holy Spirit, through the Son, to the Father.[43] This point is rooted in the way God works in the world (economic Trinity) and the way humanity is created and drawn into a re-creation by the Spirit, through Christ, to the Father. Johnson's words here are apt:

> What is most baffling about forgetfulness of the Spirit is that what is being neglected is nothing less than the mystery of God's personal engagement with the world in its history of love and disaster; nothing less than God's empowering presence dialectically active within the world in the beginning, throughout history and to the end, calling forth praxis of life and freedom. Forgetting the Spirit is not ignoring a faceless, shadowy third hypostasis but the mystery of God closer to us than we are to ourselves, drawing near and passing by in quickening, liberating compassion.[44]

42. Walter Kasper notes how the Spirit is "faceless" in theological accounts of God (*God of Jesus Christ*, trans. Matthew O'Connell [New York: Crossroad, 1984], 198, 223), while Aquinas finds the Spirit "nameless" (*Summa theologiae* I, q. 36, a. 1).

43. A comprehensive argument for this priority of TAT can be found in Dabney, "Starting with the Spirit," 24–26. Grosso independently shares this conviction when he writes, "In other words, participation in the *ordo salutis* of God's work in Christ and the Spirit is the point of entry into the *ordo cognoscendi* of theological reflection, both of which are grounded in the *ordo essendi* of the new life of the risen Christ" ("Spirit Christology," 217–18). Or again, according to Thomas F. Torrance: "Therefore, there can be no true *ordo cognoscendi* (order of knowing) which is not based upon an *ordo essendi* (order of being) conceived entirely as grace, and the *ordo essendi* reaches its true destiny in the *ordo cognoscendi*" (*Theology in Reconstruction* [Grand Rapids: Eerdmans, 1965], 116).

44. Johnson, *She Who Is*, 131.

4. TAT complements and thus does not compete with First and Second Article Theologies. As such it is a contribution to a fully Trinitarian theology. This point is well illustrated by David Coffey's remarks on the relationship between Logos Christology (a species of Second Article Theology) and Spirit Christology (a species of TAT): In Logos Christology "no appeal is made to the Holy Spirit, for in such a Christology any and all activity of the Holy Spirit relative to the person and the ministry of Christ is understood as *subsequent* to the constitution of the hypostatic union. Therefore a Spirit Christology that successfully incorporates Logos Christology will be superior to a Logos Christology *tout court*."[45] By extension, a TAT will be superior to either First or Second Article Theology *tout court* precisely because it is Trinitarian from start to finish in ways that do not overlook the full contribution and significance of the Spirit, not "watered down" or "half-known."[46]

5. TAT recognizes that the Spirit continues to speak today to the church in a retroactive movement of triune discourse. This retroactive hermeneutic is first applied to Scripture and then to the communicative acts of the church empowered and inspired by the Spirit of the resurrected Christ.[47] Such a move places TAT within the developing discipline of pneumatic hermeneutics on the one hand, and the theological interpretation of Scripture on the other hand, and in the process challenges a number of widely held assumptions around biblical interpretation, namely, historical-critical approaches, historical-grammatical approaches, and reader-response approaches.[48]

45. Coffey, "Spirit Christology and the Trinity," 317–18.

46. Wolfhart Pannenberg speaks of the Spirit as "watered down" from its biblical fullness (*The Apostles Creed: In Light of Today's Questions*, trans. Margaret Kohl [Philadelphia: Westminster, 1972], 130), while Yves Congar has spoken of the Spirit as the "half-known" God of theology (*I Believe in the Holy Spirit*, 3:5).

47. A full articulation of this retroactive hermeneutic can be found in Myk Habets, "Developing a Retroactive Hermeneutic: Johannine Theology and Doctrinal Development," *American Theological Inquiry* 1 (2008): 77–89.

48. See, for example, the suggestive insights from the Renewal tradition in Kevin L. Spawn and Archie T. Wright, ed., *Spirit and Scripture: Examining a Pneumatic Hermeneutic* (London: T&T Clark, 2012). On theological interpretation of Scripture, see J. Todd Billings, *The Word of God for the People of God: An Entryway into the Theological Interpretation of Scripture* (Grand Rapids: Eerdmans, 2010); and Matthew Levering, *Participatory Biblical Exegesis: A*

6. TAT unfolds the story of the Trinitarian mission of God in the world.[49] In an academic context driven by overspecialization, a TAT reminds us that the church does not exist for itself, that the academy exists to serve its wider constituents, and that the missionary God is at work in the world ushering in the kingdom of God through creaturely media. Starting with the Spirit allows theology to recalibrate and reorient itself in line with the *Creator Spiritus*, *Spiritus vivificans*, and *missio Spiritus*. Thus any theology today claiming to be systematic has to include what might be called applied theology, including ethics, worship, and mission.[50]

7. TAT finds its focus in the center of that story—in the life, death, and resurrection of Jesus Christ. A TAT is no less Christocentric and crucicentric than the Gospel. This is both a consequence of and a stimulus for Spirit Christology, given that TAT is birthed out of such a Christology, following a critical acceptance of Rahner's *Grundaxiom* that "the 'economic' Trinity is the 'immanent' Trinity."[51] TAT is thus not a speculative theology, if by that is meant a dogmatics devoid of exegetical foundations.

8. TAT highlights the eschatological nature of God's Trinitarian mission in the world and proleptically incorporates such eschatology throughout its pneumatological dogmatics, whereby the mission of God in Christ remains the center of the divine drama.[52] An emphasis upon the eschatological

---

Theology of Biblical Interpretation (Notre Dame, IN: University of Notre Dame Press, 2008).

49. The formula of James B. Torrance is germane at this point: "When we see that the worship and mission of the church are the gift of participating through the Holy Spirit in the incarnate Son's communion with the Father and the Son's mission from the Father to the world, that the unique center of the Bible is Jesus Christ, the apostle and high priest whom we confess (Heb 3:1), then the doctrines of the Trinity, the incarnation, the atonement, the ministry of the Spirit, Church and sacraments, our understanding of the kingdom, our anthropology and eschatology, all unfold from that center" (*Worship, Community and the Triune God of Grace* [Downers Grove, IL: InterVarsity Press, 1996], 9).

50. Examples are many, but see Amos Yong, "Primed for the Spirit: Creation, Redemption and the *Missio Spiritus*," *International Review of Mission* 100 (2011): 355–66, which traces the implications of pneumatology for theology of mission, in relationship to the doctrines of creation, redemption, and the eschaton.

51. Karl Rahner, *The Trinity*, trans. Joseph Donceel (New York: Crossroad, 1997), 23. Rahner's rule is not accepted here without critical modification; for an assessment, see Scott Harrower, *Trinitarian Self and Salvation: An Evangelical Engagement with Rahner's Rule* (Eugene, OR: Pickwick, 2012).

52. This point too has been independently mentioned by Grosso, "Spirit Christology," 220–21.

ministry of the Spirit comes with at least two corollaries, one christological, the other ecclesiological. Christologically, it is Christ's resurrection, ascension, and current session that render the ministry of the Spirit effective and cosmic. It is in Jesus' words, works, and continuing ministry that the presence of the Spirit is most keenly felt. The Spirit is about proclaiming and bringing in the kingdom of God, of which Christ is the King. Ecclesiologically, the eschatological work of the Spirit is even now being progressively realized in and through the church, the body of Christ and temple of the Holy Spirit. "Thus, in a fundamental sense, the Spirit is both present—already having introduced the coming reign of God—and yet also absent—not yet fully having established the righteousness of God,"[53] writes Amos Yong. On this basis Yong helpfully speaks of a "pneumatological prolepsis," whereby the inclusion of a *missio Spiritus* will result in "an enriched patrology and christology, while simultaneously comprehending the full scope of God's redemptive work, both across space (cosmic) and across time (diachronic)."[54]

9. TAT emphasizes the sanctifying work of the Spirit, who moves believers into further holiness or christification—thus it is existentially viable and apologetically effective in today's postmodern milieu.
10. TAT is a thoroughly ecumenical theology.[55] "Ecumenical" is used here in two senses: first, it indicates a commitment to the ecumenical creeds and confessions of Christendom; and second, it indicates the potential for doctrinal unity among the currently divided traditions of Christianity. The present volume thus draws from theologians across the Christian traditions, bringing together that which should not have been rent asunder. TAT is not a Catholic, Protestant, Orthodox, or Pentecostal theology; it is a Christian dogmatics, constructed from the tradition for the church.

These criteria form a very general locus of agreement around which all of the essayists in this volume concur to a greater or lesser extent. At certain points contributors hold strong disagreements with a specific criterion; at others they offer strong assent. Within

53. Yong, "Primed for the Spirit," 363.
54. Ibid., 364.
55. Criteria 1, 6, 7, and 10 are suggested and developed by Dabney, "Starting with the Spirit," 24–26.

these broad criteria, however, each contributor is committed to developing their topics in variegated ways, given the spaciousness of the criteria, the nature of the project, and the very character of TAT, not to mention the many ecclesial contexts of the various contributors. It is hoped this work will be received in the spirit with which it is presented.

With this pneumatological dogmatics, the contributors submit to the academy a partial and incomplete recommendation for how we may go about doing and thinking theologically from and in the Spirit. There is no apology, therefore, for the partial nature of this enterprise. The pneumatological dogmatics presented here lays no claim to being comprehensive; this is not an exhaustive compendium of theology in the traditional sense of the term. Rather, this is a contribution to dogmatics from a particular perspective and place. The present contribution highlights those *loci communes* that a TAT can further illuminate and for which it can provide additional insights in ways that, to date, have not been the case. For this reason the following should be read as an addition to existing theologies in the hope that a fuller and more comprehensive view of dogmatics is the result. With this prolegomenon now at an end, it remains to provide the evidence for the many claims being made here for a TAT. As Clark Pinnock once remarked, "The Spirit challenges theology at numerous points—this may partly explain our neglect. But let the challenges stimulate growth in us as hearers of the Word of God. Let us ask what light is shed on our central Christian doctrines when they are considered from the standpoint of the Spirit."[56]

56. Pinnock, *Flame of Love*, 11.

CHAPTER 2

The Method of Third Article Theology

DAVID COFFEY

As reported by Myk Habets in the introductory chapter of this book, the call of D. Lyle Dabney for a Third Article Theology to correct and complete the accomplishments of the theologies of the First and Second Articles (of the Nicene Creed) deserves a sympathetic response from theologians. As Habets says, this theology would be a reconceiving and reworking of the subject matter of theology "from the perspective of the Spirit where questions of pneumatology set the agenda and control the trajectory of the dogmatic enterprise." This statement encompasses a twofold task: in the first instance a critical examination of the theological method used, and in the second the achievement of new results from the application of the revised method. In the ideal order this is how Third Article Theology should proceed. But in my own case—and I believe there are others like me—it is not what actually happened. Certainly, I had an appreciation of the fact that a new, and at least different, method was needed; and I even had a rough idea of what it was. These insights came not from my own efforts but from the revelatory (to me) words of Edward Schillebeeckx:

> From the Council of Nicea onwards one particular Christological model—the Johannine—has been developed as a norm within very narrow limits and one direction; and in fact only this tradition has made history in the Christian churches. For that reason the course of history has never done justice to the possibilities inherent in the synoptic model; its peculiar dynamic was checked and halted and the model relegated to the "forgotten truths" of Christianity.[1]

Once I had read this, I picked up the idea and ran with it, refining it as I went.

On Method and Content

At the start, Schillebeeckx's suggestion remained relatively undifferentiated in my mind, and it was only slowly that it crystallized for me into a clear distinction of method and content, in that order. My explicit concern, though, was with content, actual results. It can be argued that this is a normal modus operandi for the human spirit. Over time what we need to do is not so much subject our results to an increasingly critical examination—though this may be necessary too—but to probe and deepen the foundations on which we build them, and these will inevitably include method. A method thus examined and justified is clearly superior to one resting on intuition, however inspired the latter may be.

Habets, for his part, emphasizes method. "As such," he says, "Third Article Theology is a specific and technical name for a method of theology." He is right in the sense that method logically precedes content. And he is right also in the sense that method largely determines content, for by its nature method is selective. It will choose for study subjects to which it is particularly suited, tending to avoid or pass over those less congenial to it. The full truth, therefore, is that no single method will be ideal for the whole of theology, but it is entirely proper that Third Article method as defined above be allowed its day, particularly as it has been neglected hitherto. But if the proof of the pudding is in the eating, the ultimate test of method will be the quality of its results. This chapter, then, will take up the challenge implicit in Habets's words and offer in response a higher degree of specification of Third Article method than has been proposed so far. It will do this in the course of addressing the two following questions. First, what is the

1. Edward Schillebeeckx, *Jesus: An Experiment in Christology*, trans. Hubert Hoskins (London: Collins, 1979), 570.

relevance of Christology to theology in general, and therefore of Third Article Christology to Third Article Theology in general? And second, presuming a response of high relevance, how significant for the present discussion is the distinction of "Christology from below" and "Christology from above"? The treatment of these questions will permit and perhaps require discussion of some important related issues, as we shall see in the course of our presentation.

Does TAT Signal an Age of the Spirit?

At the outset we should deal with a question bound to be raised: Does this talk of Third Article Theology presume the dawning of a third age, the age of the Spirit, as foretold by that prophetic and controversial figure of almost a millennium ago, Joachim of Fiore? Joachim had predicted that the successive ages of the Father (the age of the laity, the "married") and the Son (the age of the "clerics") would be superseded by the age of the Spirit, the age of the "monks," contemplatives, spiritual men and women.[2] In this scenario the status of the revelation brought by Christ is not entirely clear. Does it remain final and definitive, as has been supposed hitherto, or is it swept aside by the onrush of the Spirit? Joachim's answer is ambivalent: the gospel of Christ is "spiritualized" in the new age. Understandably, history has been harsh in its judgment of Joachim and his vision, but Saint Bonaventure, a Franciscan, accepted aspects of it, and even held that Saint Francis of Assisi was in some ways an anticipation of Joachim's expectations. (The present-day significance of this identification will not be lost on the reader.) Saint Thomas Aquinas, on the other hand, was, in the words of Yves Congar, "resolutely, severely and radically critical of Joachim's teaching," regarding him "as a lout playing with theology."[3] Congar points out that for Thomas there could be no further age after the New Testament. "The *status* or the régime of the New Testament," he says, "is that of Christ and the Spirit together. It is a definitive *status*, and no other age can be expected to follow it."[4] For my own part, I take Thomas's point, but at the same time confess to a certain sympathy for Saint Bonaventure. In other words, I think that Third Article

2. See Yves Congar, *I Believe in the Holy Spirit*, trans. David Smith (New York: Seabury, 1983), 1:126–37.

3. Ibid., 1:127.

4. Ibid., 1:128.

Theology may well prove to be part of theology's contribution to the renewal of life and thought that the Holy Spirit seems to be working throughout the church at the present time. But this qualified approval does not necessarily mean that the Joachimite vision should be embraced in its entirety.

It emerges from this that it is necessary to apply the distinction between method and content to pneumatology itself, and so to distinguish pneumatology as method from pneumatology as content. In retrospect we can see that Joachim was concerned not so much with method as with content. Dabney, on the other hand, appears to be doing no more than commending pneumatology under the aspect of method. In this he is not suggesting that pneumatology should replace Christology as the center and heart of theology. Rather, he appears as a true disciple of Karl Barth, for whom the centrality of Christology was the linchpin of theology. He said as much in the *Church Dogmatics*, in his treatment of "Jesus Christ the Mediator."[5] Yet he advocated in his "Concluding Unscientific Postscript on Schleiermacher," quoted by Habets in his introduction, the adoption of an uncompromising Third Article Theology, without seeing it as in any way inimical to the centrality of Christ (a comment endorsed by Habets as well). This is possible only on the supposition that Barth embraced the distinction of method and content within pneumatology, and was confining his remarks to pneumatology as method.

If Barth was correct in this, as I believe he was, it has implications for the question of the relation of the mission of the Holy Spirit to that of Christ. So, for example, Saint Irenaeus's oft-repeated statement that Christ and the Spirit are the two "hands of God,"[6] though true, would need to be rendered more precise to make it clear that, though the mission of the Holy Spirit exists in its own right, the primary mission remains that of Christ, with the mission of the Spirit in a certain sense subordinate to it. Any attempt to vaunt the mission of the Spirit would come at the expense of the mission and therefore the status of Christ as the Father's definitive and abiding Word to, and Savior of, the world.

5. See Karl Barth, *Church Dogmatics* IV/1, ed. T. F. Torrance and G. W. Bromiley, trans. G. W. Bromiley (Edinburgh: T&T Clark, 1957–75), 122–28.

6. See, for example, Irenaeus, *Adversus haereses*, Book IV, Preface, no. 4.

What has Christology to do with TAT?

Let us turn now to the first of our two questions, which begins as a question of theology in general, the question of Christology in relation to the whole of theology. Barth's treatment of this matter in the *Church Dogmatics*, to which I have just referred, consists of seven pages of rhetorical argumentation that do not readily lend themselves to effective direct quotation. Hence I will be satisfied here to present a brief summary in my own words. He complains about a tendency he notices in theology to separate Christology from the rest of theology, as though it were just one component among several. This falsifies the nature of both Christology and the rest of theology, for Christology is, in itself, the whole of the event of the atonement, consisting as it does in the whole truth of God acting and of humanity receiving, in the person of Christ the Mediator, "middle point" of God and humanity. If for pedagogical reasons it is necessary or desirable to make some separation of Christology from the rest of theology (as Barth himself does in this very work), great care should be taken to preserve this connection or nexus (as he calls it). This is a valid and important point, and all theologians should heed it. Allow me to present just two instances from my own oeuvre, in which this point can be seen at work.

The first is the theology of revelation.[7] The true starting point of this theology is not Christ the Word of God, the Revealer, for Christ is more than a conduit through which the revelation of God is passed on to human beings. Before being Revealer he must be, in his humanity as mediator and so by virtue of the incarnation, the *recipient* of divine revelation; and in the first instance the revelation he receives is not a body of ready-formed words that later come to be written down in the Gospels, but the ineffable and preconceptual human experience of the incarnation itself. The only way in which, as a human being, he can understand this experience, together with its implications, for himself and express it for and to others is by having recourse to what he already knows, what he has learned and/or thought out for himself in his life up to that point. This means that he invokes and reshapes the Jewish religious tradition that

7. The theology outlined here is my own appropriation and development of that of Gabriel Moran in his book *Theology of Revelation* (London: Burns & Oates, 1967); see particularly pages 63–71. This book was a major influence on the formation of my whole approach to theology.

produced and educated him, so that it will now provide for him the words by which he can express, at least in some manner—however inadequate—the meaning of this experience that otherwise would remain concealed from us. And thus we have the teaching and witness of Jesus as recorded for us in the Gospels. Only this starting point allows us to attain a truly plausible theology of divine revelation, one that avoids charges of arbitrariness and myth making, one that provides for us a paradigm of our own religious experience, which is nothing but a participation in, and an echo of, his.

The other instance is the theology of grace.[8] As with revelation, so here: the starting point is not Jesus as bestower, but Jesus as *recipient*. Before Jesus is the sender of the Holy Spirit at Pentecost, he is the recipient of the Holy Spirit as Spirit of Sonship at the moment of conception. This reception is not to be understood in an adoptionist way as though he were already in existence as a human being before receiving the Holy Spirit. Rather, in the one divine act the Father, through the Holy Spirit, creates the sacred humanity, sanctifies it in what Catholic theology calls the created grace of union, and unites it in person with the Son, the Second Person of the Holy Trinity. "The Holy Spirit will come upon you, and the power of the Most High will overshadow you; therefore the child to be born will be called holy, the Son of God" (Luke 1:35). The order—creation, sanctification, and union—is logical only, not chronological, but these three realities—createdness, sanctification, and union—are really, not just logically, distinct. Each is as radical as it could possibly be, for Jesus is no ordinary human being: his createdness is like that of all creatures, *creatio ex nihilo*; but his sanctification is unique to himself in the hypostatic union, different in kind, not just degree, from the highest holiness of any other human being; and he alone is united in unity of person with the preexistent divine Son. A theology of grace and justification (for other human beings) can be understood only as a derivation from and participation in the grace of Jesus himself, who is graced in the incarnation itself and thus constituted Mediator between God and human beings.

Barth's argument makes a convincing case for the centrality of Christology in the whole of Christian theology. This centrality will hold firm even if the method changes

8. See my book *Grace: The Gift of the Holy Spirit*, 2nd ed. (Milwaukee: Marquette University Press, 2011).

from a Second Article Theology to a Third Article Theology. It is my contention in this chapter that a change to Third Article method, theology "from the perspective of the Spirit," far from diminishing Christology, serves to *bolster* it. What I have in mind here is the fact that my own Christology, "Spirit Christology," along with that of Jonathan Edwards,[9] is richer in content than a Second Article Christology could ever be, for the simple reason that it, with Scripture, assigns a key role to the Holy Spirit in the incarnation itself, a move that the limitations of Second Article Theology simply preclude it from making. This role is that the Spirit, having participated with the Father and the Son in the creation of the sacred humanity, sanctifies it and unites it in person with the preexistent Son, according to the Third Article Theology of the Trinity, in which the Holy Spirit, as the mutual love of the Father and the Son, unites with the Son whatever spiritual being outside the Trinity becomes the object of the Father's love. Comparison should be made between the kind of union (with the Son) that the Spirit effects in the case of Christ and that of others. In the precise language of Neo-Scholasticism as used by Maurice de la Taille, the former is a "substantial" grace, while the latter is a "habitual" or "accidental" grace, and the union itself is "substantial" as distinct from "habitual."[10] Despite its obvious limitations, this terminology enables us to see both the likeness and the nonlikeness of the two kinds of union. They are alike in that both are unions with the Son; they are unalike in that the one is substantial and the other accidental, and the difference between substance and accident is a difference of kind, not of degree. In this theology, therefore, the difference between Christ and Christians is not a mere difference of degree as some have declared in misguided criticism. The cash value of this talk of substantial and accidental grace is that the former alone is the *incarnation* of the divine Son (in the human nature of Jesus), whereas the latter is simply the *indwelling* of the same Son (in Christian persons).

In the application of this Third Article method a new and more basic role for the Holy Spirit emerges, namely, that of the

9. See Steven M. Studebaker, *The Trinitarian Vision of Jonathan Edwards and David Coffey* (Amherst: Cambria, 2011), especially chapter 3, "Edwards, Coffey, and Spirit Christology," 83–112.

10. See Maurice de la Taille, "Created Actuation by Uncreated Act," trans. Cyril Vollert, in *The Hypostatic Union and Created Actuation by Uncreated Act* (West Baden Springs, IN: West Baden College, 1952), 34–35.

Spirit of Christ as "entelechy." Here the term means "directive principle," Christ being the goal or end to which it directs. I will now give only the sketchiest account of what this entails, and for a full account I refer the reader to my 2008 response to Peter Phan, which I suspect will be my last word on this subject.[11] As coming immediately from Rahner, the term means that first and foremost the Spirit, sent by the Father, "seeks out" Christ in the world: it prompts, guides, and forms the people of God of old in their destiny to produce the Savior of the world. It inspires the messianic prophecies of the Old Testament (1 Pet. 1:10–11). Before that, it is active in the creation of the world, and is the directive principle of the process of its evolution toward Christ the Omega Point. To this day it is the Spirit of God active in the world of human beings, whether they be Christian or not, to seek Christ, and if they find him, to intensify their union with him throughout life. In the person of Christ it is the Spirit who brought about the incarnation and then was progressively appropriated by Jesus in his life and mission, the Spirit in whom eventually he offered himself to the Father on the cross (Heb. 9:14). On the acceptance of this offering, Jesus at Pentecost pours out this same Spirit, now the obverse of his self-gift to the Father in the Spirit, and so poured out as the Spirit of Christ sent by him upon the infant church, the Spirit imbued with his personality, including the message of the gospel. (This happens according to the anthropological and theological principle of the unity in distinction of the love of God and love of neighbor.)[12] This "incarnation" of the Holy Spirit in the person of Christ (as I have called it elsewhere[13]) culminates in Pentecost, but the fundamental role of the Spirit remains constant: he is always and everywhere, even in the person of Christ, the entelechy of Christ, and then—beyond Christ—of the Father. Rahner expressed the first part of this truth clearly when he wrote, "Since the universal efficacy of the Spirit is directed from the beginning to the zenith of its historical mediation, which is the Christ event (or in

11. David M. Coffey, "A Trinitarian Response to Issues Raised by Peter Phan," *TS* 69 (2008): 859–65; also Coffey, "The Spirit of Christ as Entelechy," *Philosophy and Theology* 13 (2001): 363–98.

12. See Karl Rahner, "Reflections on the Unity of the Love of Neighbour and the Love of God," in *Theological Investigations* 6, trans. Karl-H. and Boniface Kruger (London: Darton, Longman & Todd, 1969), 231–52.

13. See David Coffey, "The 'Incarnation' of the Holy Spirit in Christ," *Theological Studies* 45 (1984): 466–80.

other words the final cause of the mediation of the Spirit to the world), it can truly be said that this Spirit is everywhere and from the beginning the Spirit of Jesus Christ, the incarnate divine Logos."[14]

Great confusion has been caused in theology by a signal failure to distinguish between the two related senses of "Spirit of Christ," that is, Spirit of Christ as entelechy and therefore as sent by the Father upon the world and directed *to* Christ and then beyond Christ back to the Father, and Spirit of Christ as sent directly *by* Christ upon the church at Pentecost. The second of these senses has therefore been made to bear the whole burden of what Scripture means when it speaks of the Spirit of Christ or its equivalent, a burden that it cannot bear. The Pentecostal Spirit (let us so call it) represents the full flowering and appropriation, in the historical life of Jesus, of the fundamental, perennial, and universal role of the Spirit, that is, Spirit of Christ as entelechy. Spirit of Christ as Pentecostal Spirit represents the perspective of descending Christology, while Spirit of Christ as entelechy represents that of ascending Christology. Thus is explained the noncontradiction of the two senses: it is a matter of which perspective one freely chooses to adopt. Note that this very important result is a fruit of the application of the method of Third Article Theology, and in itself amply justifies the existence and use of this method.

Habets, in his introductory chapter in this book, cited the remarkable text of Barth in which the latter favored the adoption of a Third Article Theology, at least in regard to method. Habets tells us elsewhere that Barth wrote that text for lectures delivered in 1923–24.[15] He would still have been in this thirties when he wrote it, a relatively young man. Rahner wrote something in the same vein, but at the very end of his long life. I quoted it in my article in response to Phan,[16] but it will be useful to reproduce it here.

> Perhaps an Eastern theology will one day reverse this perspective [which awarded hegemony to Christology]. Because of the universal salvific will of God and in legitimate respect for all the major world religions outside of Christianity, it may perhaps make a pneumatology, a

14. Karl Rahner, "Jesus Christ in the Non-Christian Religions," in *Theological Investigations* 17, trans. Margaret Kohl (London: Darton, Longman & Todd, 1981), 46.

15. Myk Habets, *The Anointed Son: A Trinitarian Spirit Christology* (Eugene, OR: Pickwick, 2010), 2.

16. Coffey, "Trinitarian Response," 860.

> teaching of the inmost, divinizing gift of grace for all human beings (as an offer to their freedom), the fundamental point of departure for its entire theology, and then attempt from this point—and this is something that might be achieved only with considerable effort—to gain a real and radical understanding of Christology. For a theology of this kind John 7:39 ("There was no Spirit as yet because Jesus had not been glorified") will perhaps be less suitable and intelligible than scriptural passages which extol the universal salvific will of God, let the Spirit speak through all the prophets, and know that the Spirit has been poured out on all flesh.

First we need to situate this text in its proper context. This shows that by "Eastern theology" Rahner meant a non-European, Christian theology, and that he included in "all the prophets" not only those of Judaism and Christianity but those of other religions and perhaps even those of none. As in his earlier writings, Rahner showed an awareness that in the twentieth century all theology needed to have an ecumenical dimension (the day of "preaching to the choir" was over); here he prophetically anticipates that in the twenty-first century all theology would need to have an interreligious dimension. In an interreligious dialogue it does nothing for Christianity that the Christian participant should immediately confront the dialogue partners with the centrality of Christ. From every point of view it is preferable to begin with the universal action of the Spirit in the world. This is the point of Rahner's remark about gaining "a real and radical understanding of Christology." For him, be it remembered, the Spirit is always the Spirit of Christ as entelechy, including when it is the Pentecostal Spirit. He is by no means abandoning the centrality of Christ or of Christology. Rather, he is talking about the most fruitful method of approaching it. And this method is Third Article Theology.

Our first question, then, is sufficiently answered. The New Testament itself is clear: Jesus Christ is the sole Mediator between God and humankind and therefore the one to whom we must defer for answers regarding our relationship with God. He is the arena on which the whole drama of salvation is played out. This makes Christology not only the centerpiece of theology, but also the fountain from which the rest is derived and the focal point to which it must refer. The question of method is important too, because method affects outcome. The recent calls to approach theology in a new way, "from the perspective of the Spirit," that of Third Article Theology, should be heeded, because early applications of the method are already yielding promising results, most notably Spirit Christology itself. And there is an additional reason for starting with the Spirit, namely, that of the three persons of the Trinity the Spirit is the first contact with human beings and the mediator of contact with the other two. And it makes good sense to start with the point of contact. We have seen that Barth and Rahner, arguably the two most representative theologians of the twentieth century, were prophetically agreed: the time is ripe for such a method in theology.

Is Christology from Above or Below Appropriate?

We move on now to our second question, which assumes the form: To which of the two basic types does Third Article Christology conform, descending or ascending, that is, Christology "from above" or Christology "from below"? In his essay on the two basic types, Rahner observes that in practice they usually exist in "mixed form," which makes it difficult to distinguish them.[17] But as each exists precisely by virtue of its distinction from the other, the "mixed form" must consist in a constant, unconscious switching back and forth between them rather than in a consistent "hybrid form," to which he also makes reference, in passing.[18]

First of all, a word must be said to those who question the validity of maintaining a distinction of two basic, contrary types at all. In what is arguably the most important paragraph of the essay, Rahner justifies the existence of these two types because they constitute and respectively correspond to "the two poles of our basic understanding of humanity," namely, "the transcendentality and the historicity of man."[19] To take the second of these first, historicity means that every human person, as spirit in the *world*, is embedded forever in his or her own particular history, from which they should never even try to escape. It remains for each person the permanent reference point for whatever metaphysical flights his or her spirit might embark

17. Karl Rahner, "The Two Basic Types of Christology," in *Theological Investigations* 13, trans. David Bourke (London: Darton, Longman & Todd, 1975), 213.

18. Ibid.

19. Ibid., 219–20.

on. And transcendentality means everyone's field of aspiration as *spirit* in the world, each person's need and attempts to situate the self and one's understanding within the totality of all that exists. If I was right in my earlier remark that no single method will be ideal for the whole of theology, I would now like to push the point a little further and say that no single method will be ideal for the whole of Christology either, even for the whole of Spirit Christology, and the mixed form as defined above will need to be invoked. Our question then bifurcates: Does Third Article Theology belong *predominantly* to one basic type rather than the other, and if so, to which one?

Thus put, the question is readily answered. Since Third Article Theology is theology "from the perspective of the Spirit," the question asks about the role of the Spirit in the life of Jesus. And the Synoptic tradition reveals that the Spirit played a prominent role in this context: the Spirit, by inspiring the messianic prophecies, prepared the people of God of old to produce the Christ; Jesus is conceived by the power of the Spirit; the Spirit descends on him at his baptism and "remains" on him, with the result that he is "full of the Holy Spirit"; the Spirit "drives him out" into the wilderness, whence he "returns in the power of the Spirit into Galilee"; his association with the Spirit marks him as a "prophet";[20] thus he sees himself, thus he acts, and thus he is identified, "a prophet mighty in deed and word before God and all the people" (Luke 24:19). Above all, he offers himself to the Father "through the eternal Spirit" on the cross. But he is more than a prophet: he is the eschatological prophet, whose role is to usher in the final age. After his death, resurrection, and ascension, he is made "Lord of the Spirit," and authoritatively sends the Holy Spirit upon the fledgling church at Pentecost.

That the method here is predominantly ascending is shown by the fact that its starting point is not transcendence, but history, the observed experience of Jesus and his identification as a prophet, a role with a clear prehistory in Judaism. As reflection became more penetrating, the "low" Christology crept ever higher, but it remained ascending until a new starting point, a new launching pad, as it were, was reached, in transcendence. This came only with the perception of the preexistence of Jesus; but note, it was the preexistence of *Jesus*, not of a disembodied spirit. It has long been my contention that nowhere

20. For Scripture references in this paragraph apart from Luke 24:19, see my article "Spirit of Christ as Entelechy," 365–66.

does the New Testament attain the concept of a purely spiritual "Son of God" who enters into hypostatic union with a human nature.[21] It was Pierre Benoit who first pointed out for me that "incarnation," being-made-flesh, is not the same as being-made-human. In the prologue of the Fourth Gospel, the word "flesh" in the statement "the Word became flesh" has to be interpreted over against its biblical opposite, "spirit"; and the contrast of flesh and spirit is not the same as that of man and God.[22] The incarnation of the Word of God in the prologue does not surpass, in theological content, the descent of the Son of Man in the body of the Gospel. This denoted the preexistence of a heavenly man without any overtone of a pure metaphysical divinity. I am convinced that the transition to a metaphysical interpretation and understanding took place only after New Testament times in the period of increased Hellenization. In fact, the question became for me: Who was the first church writer to interpret the prologue in a clearly metaphysical sense? And in *Deus Trinitas* I tentatively propose for this honor Justin Martyr, a position I will hold until someone can point out to me an earlier text that demonstrably requires to be interpreted in this sense.[23]

The concept of preexistence is sufficient to provide a new starting point, namely, in transcendence. At this point the method becomes descending. Whether it be the preexistent Son of Man or the preexistent Logos who descends to the world of human beings and shares in their history, preexistence is what is needed for a descending Christology, and it is to be found in the New Testament itself. Hence Rahner's statement that both basic types of Christology are to be found in the New Testament.[24] In other words, it is not necessary to begin with the concept of the Logos as a purely spiritual, metaphysically divine being. Preexistence on its own, as denoting belonging to the sphere of the transcendent God, as does the heavenly man

21. See my article "The Pre-Existent and Incarnate Word," in *Faith and Culture: Contemporary Questions*, ed. Margaret Press (Sydney: Catholic Institute of Sydney, 1983), 62–76.

22. At this point I am constrained temporarily to abandon inclusive language, because it is too difficult to maintain without loss of meaning. Unfortunately, English does not yet possess the necessary vocabulary to cover the present context (among some others).

23. See David Coffey, *Deus Trinitas: The Doctrine of the Triune God* (New York: Oxford University Press, 1999), 14.

24. See Rahner, "Two Basic Types," 213.

of the Fourth Gospel, is enough to establish a descending Christology.

The very term "incarnation" is indicative of the descending Christology that lies behind it, because it means, by definition, the "becoming flesh" of something or someone who previously was not flesh, and which (or who) was therefore purely spirit. In the Hellenistic world and culture of Justin this could only have been God. Such a development—for development it truly was—was entirely justified, particularly within a "catholic" ecclesiology, which recognizes tradition along with Scripture as constituting an essential element of divine revelation, which, be it remembered, cannot be rightly called such unless it is received (by human beings in *their* way) as well as given (by God). This I say not to divide my readers, but, in part, to help them understand why not all Christian readers will be able to endorse my remark about development made above. But to continue the discussion of this point here would take us beyond our present subject on to a new area, namely, that of ecclesiology.

I say "in part" because the principal reason for making the present point is to justify the further point that an ascending Christology is, by nature, unable to convey a complete Christology such as is possessed by almost all Christians—of whatever church persuasion—today. The reason for this is that its starting point, namely, the history of Jesus, can never be left behind in favor of a new starting point in transcendence, which would necessarily give rise to a descending Christology. In other words, an ascending Christology on its own can never attain the full concept of the divinity of Jesus, which requires the incarnation of the preexistent divine Word, whose divinity is the same, *homoousios*, as that of God the Father. For this, a fresh start has to be made, and indeed from the standpoint of the Chalcedonian dogma, which lies beyond the New Testament but which interprets it in what I claim is an entirely justifiable way.

The best way I can illustrate this is to give an account of a recent development in my own thought. In 1970, Rahner had written, "Transcendental theology can make the 'idea' of the God-man intelligible, as the climax, at least asymptotically and hypothetically, of the movement of the [human] spirit, as its drive towards God carries it beyond itself."[25] This statement is certainly correct

25. Karl Rahner, "Transcendental Theology," *Sacramentum Mundi* 6 (London: Burns & Oates, 1970), 289a.

as far as it goes, but it does not provide—nor was it meant to provide—a complete statement of the reality of the incarnation. What Rahner is talking about here is fundamentally a human reality, no matter how exalted by grace it might be. It speaks of transcendence, but it is a transcendence that falls short of the transcendence of God that Jesus possessed by virtue of the incarnation, for this transcendence is not a human reality at all but is strictly proper to God. Of itself, the human reality of which Rahner speaks is something that the human mind can grasp, but the transcendence of God so surpasses the power of the mind that it cannot be understood at all except by recourse to analogy. It cannot therefore be the product of an ascending Christology such as Rahner espouses here, but requires a descending Christology that takes its point of departure not from history or the experience of Jesus as witnessed to in the Gospels, but from the transcendence expressed in the Chalcedonian dogma when it speaks of the "divine nature." In my most recent article I felt able, in the light of my researches, and with the help of Aquinas and the clear-sighted Maurice de la Taille, to express the exact nature of the transcendence of which Rahner speaks: it is the "created" grace of union, last disposition and first effect of the "uncreated" grace of union, which is the divine Word himself in his full untrammeled transcendence.[26] The created grace of union is unique and is proper to Jesus, and it expresses the limit of possibility of an ascending Christology. I identify it as that to which exegetes, including non-Catholic ones like Wolfhart Pannenberg, rightly refer when they speak of the divine Sonship of Jesus in the Gospels as a characteristic—indeed the principal one—of his graced humanity (rather than as a product of an "incarnation" strictly so called).[27]

---

26. See David Coffey, "De la Taille on the Grace of Union," *Irish Theological Quarterly* 79 (2014): 197–218. There is much to be explained here, but I refer the reader to the article itself for this purpose. There is one thing, though, that I need to explain here, namely, the difference between "uncreated" and "created" grace. The former is simply God, or one of the persons of the Trinity, in self-gift to humanity; the latter is the effect that this self-gift has on the human person or persons who receive it. The created grace of union, therefore, is the effect of the incarnation on the humanity of Jesus. This is what it is primarily, but it can also be spoken of as disposition, in the sense that it is the condition of humanity necessary to sustain the hypostatic union, provided it be understood as achieved not by human striving but as an element of the self-gift in the incarnation itself.

27. For references, see ibid.

Joachim of Fiore had a Point!

We conclude that across-the-board Third Article Theology, which is primarily a theological method, will take its cue directly from Spirit Christology, and will start from the Spirit, seeing everything from that perspective. Predominantly it will be an ascending method, but it will be obliged to make occasional use of the descending method, particularly in regard to the crucial issue of the full divinity of Jesus, which lies beyond the scope of the ascending method. This descending method will conform to Second Article Theology and will draw on Chalcedon. In the last analysis, therefore, Third Article Theology will provide an instance of what Rahner called a "mixed" theology. And there is a further conclusion, namely, that Schillebeeckx's advocacy of a Synoptic over a Johannine Christology, referred to at the beginning of this chapter, is really only another way of calling for a Third Article Christology beyond a Second Article one, for what principally distinguishes the Synoptic from the Johannine Christology is that the former has Jesus as a man of the Spirit, whereas the latter has him as the Word made flesh. Schillebeeckx's name therefore should be added to Barth's and Rahner's as another twentieth-century theological giant calling for a Third Article Theology. There is no objection against this theology's spread across the whole field of theological knowledge, as opposed to Christology and pneumatology alone, provided only that it maintains its original manifest connection to Christology. Indeed, extended exercises in the method have already begun to appear. It seems that a new age of the Spirit has dawned. Joachim of Fiore would doubtless be surprised at its nature, but not, I think, displeased.

Part 1

Theology Proper

CHAPTER 3

Pneumatological Insights for the Attributes of the Divine Loving

ANDREW K. GABRIEL

In an effort to help correct a pneumatological deficiency within the doctrine of the divine attributes, this essay integrates pneumatology into a fully Trinitarian doctrine of the divine attributes. I build on my work in *The Lord Is the Spirit* by entering into a constructive dialogue with Karl Barth's doctrine of God and offering pneumatological insights for theology proper as a complement to Barth's christological emphases. Following Barth's emphasis that God is the one who loves in freedom, he divides his doctrine of the divine attributes into two primary sections: the perfections (Barth's preferred term for divine "attributes") of the divine loving and the perfections of the divine freedom. Recognizing the limitations of this essay, and considering that Barth discusses a total of fourteen attributes in his doctrine of God, I focus on the attributes of divine love.[1] My aim is not to explicate Barth's doctrine. Rather, I take Barth as a dialogue partner as I explore what a Trinitarian doctrine of the divine attributes might look like when integrating insights from pneumatology. I aim, then, for this chapter to be exploratory, and

1. My previous work in Andrew K. Gabriel, *The Lord Is the Spirit: The Holy Spirit and the Divine Attributes* (Eugene, OR: Pickwick, 2011) focuses more on the perfections of divine freedom.

this conversation illustrates the fecundity of pneumatological insights for a Trinitarian doctrine of the divine attributes. Nevertheless, I offer a modest thesis statement: pneumatological insights into the doctrine of God complement Karl Barth's christological emphasis in the doctrine of the divine attributes and confirm that God is the one who loves in freedom.

A Pneumatological Deficiency in Current Trinitarian Theology

Integrating pneumatology into the doctrine of God assists one to be thoroughly Trinitarian within one's explication of the divine attributes. Beyond the simple fact that God is triune, it is important for a doctrine of the divine attributes to be Trinitarian, because the doctrine of the Trinity provides an explanation regarding the identity of God. It provides the answer to the question "Who is God?" When one asks about the attributes of "God" without exploring the identity of who that God is, there is a latent philosophical presupposition regarding the meaning of "God."[2] Rather than starting a doctrine of God with a general concept of divinity in mind, it would be more expedient to begin with the actual identity of God in mind as one seeks to understand the attributes of God. The words of John Calvin provide an important caution in this respect: "Unless we grasp these [three persons], only the bare empty name of God flits about in our brains, to the exclusion of the true God."[3] Hence, each of the divine persons should be considered when formulating a Trinitarian doctrine of the divine attributes, including the Holy Spirit. However, while Trinitarian theologians rightly critique the history of Christian doctrine on the attributes of God for being insufficiently Trinitarian, Trinitarian theologians today have still not developed a thoroughly Trinitarian approach to the doctrine of the divine attributes, inasmuch as they tend to be christologically focused and tend to neglect exploring implications from pneumatology for the doctrine of the divine attributes. This is evidenced in Barth's doctrine of God where reflection from a pneumatological perspective is relatively lacking.

There is no doubt that Barth takes a Trinitarian approach to the doctrine of the divine

2. Wolfhart Pannenberg, *Systematic Theology*, 3 vols., trans. Geoffrey W. Bromiley (Grand Rapids: Eerdmans, 1991, 1994, 1998), 1:393.

3. John Calvin, *Institutes of the Christian Religion*, ed. John T. McNeill, trans. Ford Lewis Battles (Philadelphia: Westminster, 1960), 1.13.2.

perfections. Barth intentionally discusses the doctrine of the Trinity before the doctrine of the divine attributes since, according to him, beginning with "God's being in general" before a discussion of God's triune nature constitutes "the fundamental error of the whole earlier doctrine of God."[4] Barth wants to build his doctrine based upon God's revelation, and God has certainly revealed Godself as triune. Hence, one of Barth's concerns throughout his doctrine of God is to show that the divine perfections are true of God's eternal triune being (rather than only in relationship to creation).[5] So, for example, Barth notes how God is not only omnipresent because God is present to all of creation, but God is also eternally omnipresent since, as God is three persons, God is able to be present to another in eternity.[6]

In addition to observations based on the triune nature of God (in general), since God reveals Godself in Christ, Barth offers many christological insights into the doctrine of God. Similar to comments regarding Barth's whole theology (for which he is regularly accused of "christomonism"), Don Schweitzer speaks of Barth's doctrine of God specifically as a "christologically focused Trinitarian doctrine of God."[7] In contrast to this emphasis on Christology, one has to search hard to find pneumatological reflections regarding the divine perfections in Barth (below I highlight those that do exist). Certainly, Barth makes numerous blanket statements claiming that in speaking of the being of God one *must* always be speaking of Father, Son, and Holy Spirit.[8] However, Barth seems not to follow this fully in practice.

The neglect of pneumatology in Barth's doctrine of the divine attributes might seem strange, given his prominence as a *Trinitarian* theologian. However, when considered in the light of his wider doctrine, the reason for the absence of the Spirit in his doctrine of God becomes understandable. Throughout the *Church Dogmatics*, Barth's pneumatology has a decidedly noetic function.[9] That

4. Karl Barth, *Church Dogmatics* II/I, ed. T. F. Torrance and G. W. Bromiley (Edinburgh: T&T Clark, 1957–1975), 348, cf. 329. (Hereafter cited as, Barth, *CD* followed by the volume number, part number, and page number).

5. Barth, *CD* II/1, 260, 324, 327, 344–45, and at various places as he discusses specific attributes.

6. Ibid., 463.

7. Don Schweitzer, "Karl Barth's Critique of Classical Theism," *Toronto Journal of Theology* 18 (2002): 241.

8. Consider Barth, *CD* II/1, 261 and 659.

9. Philip J. Rosato, *The Spirit as Lord: The Pneumatology of Karl Barth* (Edinburgh: T&T Clark, 1981), 133, 161, 172, and 182.

is, Barth generally relegates the work of the Holy Spirit to revealing Christ to the believer and enabling the corresponding affirmation (Barth's "Yes") that the believer gives to the person and work of Jesus Christ. This view of the Spirit begins at the very beginning of the *Church Dogmatics* where the Holy Spirit is the "Revealedness" that helps people grasp the "Revelation," who is Jesus Christ. In this context, the Holy Spirit is the "subjective reality of revelation" and the "subjective possibility of revelation."[10] Accordingly, Robert Jenson suggests, "It appears that, for Barth, an act of the Spirit would not transcend the subjectivity of our hearing." The result, Jenson continues, is that "his doctrine of Trinity, when thus *used*, often seems rather to be a doctrine of binity," ignoring the various activities of the Holy Spirit.[11]

With respect to Trinitarian theology in general, it is no secret that Barth has had an important role in the revival of Trinitarian theology. His importance for thinking about the doctrine of the divine attributes specifically is also apparent since he has had a significant influence on almost all Trinitarian doctrines of the divine attributes written after his. As a result of his influence, those who follow Barth also have a minimal place for pneumatology within their doctrines of God. Among Trinitarian theologians, Wolf Krötke exhibits an overall concern to describe God as a concrete reality who "comes to the world in Jesus Christ."[12] Accordingly, in *Gottes Klarheiten* (*God's Clarities*) each of Krötke's

10. Barth, *CD* I/1, 295, and 449; and *CD* I/2, 203 and 242.

11. Robert W. Jenson, *Systematic Theology*, 2 vols. (Oxford: Oxford University Press, 1997, 2001), 1:154. Cf. Jenson, "You Wonder Where the Spirit Went," *Pro Ecclesia* 2, no. 3 (1993): 296–304; and Eugene F. Rogers, "The Eclipse of the Spirit in Karl Barth," in *Conversing with Barth*, ed. John C. McDowell and Mike Higton, Barth Studies (Aldershot: Ashgate, 2004), 173–78. Travis Ables, "The Grammar of Pneumatology in Barth and Rahner: A Reconsideration," *International Journal of Systematic Theology* 11 (2009): 210–16, rightfully challenges the notion that Barth presents a depersonalized doctrine of the Spirit; however, the function of the Spirit is clearly still decidedly noetic in Barth and, furthermore, pneumatological reflection is clearly lacking in his doctrine of the divine perfections.

12. Wolf Krötke, *Gottes Klarheiten: Eine Neuinterpretation der Gottes 'Eigenschaften'* (Tübingen: Mohr Siebeck, 2001), 14. Regarding Krötke's christological emphasis, see Philip P. Ziegler, *Doing Theology When God Is Forgotten: The Theological Achievement of Wolf Krötke*, Issues in Systematic Theology 14 (New York: Lang, 2007), 11, 12, and 226; and Christopher R. J. Holmes, *Revisiting the Doctrine of the Divine Attributes in Dialogue with Karl Barth, Eberhard Jüngel and Wolf Krötke*, Issues in Systematic Theology 15 (New York: Lang, 2007), 156, 158, and 209.

chapters on an attribute of God include a section on "the mystery of the parable of Jesus' humanity," but with no corresponding section reflecting on each of the attributes from a pneumatological perspective. Thomas Torrance exhibits a similar christological emphasis in his doctrine of God. He writes that "*all authentic knowledge of God* is derived and understood in accordance with the incarnate reality of God's self-revelation in Jesus Christ, and is formulated in doctrinal coherence with Christology."[13] Eberhard Jüngel, too, clearly displays a christological emphasis, particularly on the passion and death of Christ. Hence, similar to his observations regarding Barth, Colin Gunton senses in Jüngel "a question of the under-determination of the place of the Spirit, and therefore a weakness in conceiving the manner of the presence of God to the world."[14] One might expect the situation to be different in Jürgen Moltmann's doctrine of God, particularly given his critique of Barth's pneumatology and Moltmann's own emphasis on the full personhood of the Holy Spirit.[15] However, in Moltmann's critique of the doctrine of impassibility in *The Crucified God*, we again find a christological emphasis and that the Spirit is inconspicuous.[16]

13. Thomas F. Torrance, *The Christian Doctrine of God: One Being Three Persons* (Edinburgh: T&T Clark, 1996), 17 (emphasis added).

14. Colin E. Gunton, "The Being and Attributes of God: Eberhard Jüngel's Dispute with the Classical Philosophical Tradition," in *The Possibilities of Theology: Studies in the Theology of Eberhard Jüngel in His Sixtieth Year*, ed. John Webster (Edinburgh: T&T Clark, 1994), 22. Cf. Christopher R. J. Holmes, "Eberhard Jüngel and Wolf Krötke: Recent Contributions toward a Trinitarian Doctrine of God's Attributes," *Toronto Journal of Theology* 22 (Fall 2006): 160. The primary writings under discussion include Eberhard Jüngel, *God as the Mystery of the World: On the Foundation of the Theology of the Crucified One in the Dispute between Theism and Atheism*, trans. Darrell L. Guder (Grand Rapids: Eerdmans, 1983); Jüngel, *God's Being Is in Becoming: The Trinitarian Being of God in the Theology of Karl Barth*, trans. John Webster (Grand Rapids: Eerdmans, 2001); and Jüngel, "Theses on the Relation of the Existence, Essence and Attributes of God," trans. Philip G. Ziegler, *Toronto Journal of Theology* 17 (2001): 55–74.

15. Jürgen Moltmann, "'The Fellowship of the Holy Spirit': On Trinitarian Pneumatology," in *History and the Triune God: Contributions to Trinitarian Theology*, trans. John Bowden (New York: Crossroad, 1991), 57–69; also Moltmann, *The Spirit of Life: A Universal Affirmation*, trans. Margaret Kohl (Minneapolis: Fortress, 1992), 289–309.

16. Andrew K. Gabriel, "Beyond the Cross: Moltmann's *Crucified God*, Rahner's Rule, and Pneumatological Implications for a Trinitarian Doctrine of God," *Didaskalia* 19 (2008): 105–6. Moltmann later speaks of the suffering of the Spirit in light of the cross in Jürgen Moltmann, *The Way of Jesus Christ: Christology in Messianic Dimensions*, trans. Margaret Kohl (San Francisco: HarperSanFrancisco, 1990), 174; and Moltmann, *Spirit of Life*,

At this point in time, Trinitarian theologians continue to focus on developing the doctrine of God from a christological perspective. Though Trinitarian theology rightly affirms the divinity of the Spirit, it still has much work to do in considering the implications of the Spirit's economic activity for the doctrine of the divine attributes.[17] A pneumatological deficit remains in the doctrine of the divine attributes, as pneumatological insights regarding the attributes of God are infrequent. Heribert Mühlen is correct in his observation that the doctrine of the Holy Spirit "is almost inevitably seen as a pious addition, an edifying ornament, but never as the [or even 'a'] most basic proposition of the teaching on God."[18]

In order to develop a Trinitarian doctrine of God, a doctrine of God must include adequate consideration of pneumatology. In making this assertion I am not suggesting that there are any Spirit-specific attributes. I am also not suggesting that pneumatology will produce radical changes in one's doctrine of the divine attributes (although it might, depending on one's theology). Nevertheless, integrating pneumatology into the doctrine of the divine attributes will certainly enrich one's understanding of God, and possibly even correct some misunderstandings. Certainly, to neglect the Spirit is (to our peril) to neglect one of the ways God exists—to neglect one of God's "modes of being" (to use Barth's preferred designation for the divine persons).[19]

In an effort to overcome Barth's (and others') pneumatological deficiency within the doctrine of the divine attributes, I turn now to offer pneumatological insights for the doctrine of the divine loving as a complement to Barth's christological insights in an effort to move toward a thoroughly Trinitarian doctrine of the divine attributes. Barth himself reached for such pneumatological insights when he wrote (near the end of his life) that he dreamed of "the possibility of a theology of the third article, a theology where the Holy Spirit would dominate and be decisive.

60–65. However, here Moltmann draws an implication regarding pneumatology (i.e., that the Spirit suffers) on the basis of Christology, more so than a pneumatological insight regarding the doctrine of God.

17. F. LeRon Shults, *Reforming the Doctrine of God* (Grand Rapids: Eerdmans, 2005), 205–93, has made particular strides toward integrating pneumatological insights into his doctrine of God.

18. Heribert Mühlen, "Holy Spirit as Person," in *The Holy Spirit and Power: The Catholic Charismatic Renewal,* ed. Kilian McDonnell (Garden City, NY: Doubleday, 1975), 13.

19. Barth, *CD* I/1, 355–60.

Everything that one believes, reflects, and says about God the Father and God the Son in understanding the first and second articles would be demonstrated and clarified basically through God the Holy Spirit."[20]

The Perfections of the Divine Loving

As with all of the divine perfections, Barth insists that when speaking of God's love, one cannot begin with a general, presupposed idea of love, but rather specifically with the love of God in Jesus Christ.[21] The result is that God is "the One who loves" in the sense that God seeks to create fellowship. "He wills as God to be for us and with us who are not God" (274). As triune, God is love eternally as "He wills and completes this fellowship in Himself" (275). In relation to creation, despite our weakness and unworthiness, God gives us Godself in the Son (276), with the result that nothing "will be able to separate us from the love of God, which is in Christ Jesus our Lord" (Rom. 8:39). Although the emphasis is on Christ, Barth does well here and includes a brief reference to the Spirit as the love of God that is poured out in believers' hearts (Rom. 5:5) (277). One may add that, just as in Christ, God loves as God seeks by the Spirit to create fellowship with people, as it is only by the Spirit that one can confess "Jesus is Lord" (1 Cor. 12:3). This is no doubt an instance of what Paul refers to as "the love of the Spirit" (Rom. 15:30).

Turning to consider specific divine attributes, Barth observes that the divine love "consists and confirms itself" in God's grace, holiness, mercy, righteousness, patience, and wisdom (351). Following Barth, I begin with the discussion of God's grace.

Grace

Grace, for Barth, is not a thing that God gives us. Rather, it is a description of God's being and action. In seeking and creating fellowship, God's love is grace. Barth affirms that God is eternally gracious in Godself, but how this is the case is "hidden from us and incomprehensible" (357). Nevertheless,

20. Karl Barth, "Nachwort," in *Schleiermacher-Auswahl*, ed. Heinz Bolli (Munich: Siebenstern-Taschenbuch, 1968), 311, as translated in Kilian McDonnell, *The Other Hand of God: The Holy Spirit as the Universal Touch and Goal* (Collegeville: Liturgical Press, 2003), 209. Compare Eberhard Busch, *Karl Barth: His Life from Letters and Autobiographical Texts*, trans. John Bowden (Philadelphia: Fortress, 1976), 494.

21. Barth, *CD* II/1, 276, 352. In-text citations refer to this volume.

the mystery of God's eternal grace has been revealed. God's grace is an act of condescending to one who is unworthy. God's grace is free in that it is not only unconditioned (we would never be worthy of it) but also not hindered by sin (353–56). God's grace is, in Paul's words, "the grace of the Lord Jesus Christ" (2 Cor. 13:14), which Barth understands to mean that it is "the grace which dwells and is manifest, knowable, effectual and imparted in the person of Jesus Christ" (*CD* II/1, 353). The incarnation is, therefore, "the archetypal form of God's gift of grace" (354).

Just as God has shown God's grace through Jesus Christ, one can add that the Spirit is "the Spirit of grace" (Heb. 10:29). Eugene Rogers and Frank Macchia have both observed how, historically, in many instances a doctrine of grace has replaced a doctrine of the Spirit.[22] Indeed, it is through the Spirit that God's grace—love as unconditioned and unhindered—takes sinners and gives them freedom (2 Cor. 3:17). In the Spirit, the grace of God is lavish as the Spirit is "enfolding human beings in grace" (to use the words of Denis Edwards), always and everywhere offering God's love to people.[23] This is often referred to as "common grace." The church, as a sign of grace, also evidences the grace of God inasmuch as the Spirit births the people of God, drawing people from alienation to the communion of the saints.[24] A pneumatological perspective on God's grace also brings an emphasis that God's grace empowers people for ministry. Because the apostles had received the Holy Spirit, Luke could report that "God's grace was so powerfully at work" (Acts 4:33) in the early church. Likewise, the gifts that the Spirit gives come only "according to the grace given to each of us" (Rom. 12:6, cf. 1 Pet. 4:10). As Father, Son, and Holy Spirit, God is gracious as God condescends to those who are unworthy.

Holiness

Barth affirms that the love of God is also holy. In God's holiness, God seeks fellowship as God "distinguishes and maintains His own will as against every other will" (*CD* II/1,

22. Eugene F. Rogers Jr., *After the Spirit: A Constructive Pneumatology from Resources outside the Modern West* (Grand Rapids: Eerdmans, 2005), 216–19, 222; and Frank D. Macchia, *Justified in the Spirit: Creation, Redemption, and the Triune God*, Pentecostal Manifestos (Grand Rapids: Eerdmans, 2010), 18, 20.

23. Denis Edwards, *Breath of Life: A Theology of the Creator Spirit* (Maryknoll, NY: Orbis Books, 2004), 50.

24. Frank D. Macchia, *Baptized in the Spirit: A Global Pentecostal Theology* (Grand Rapids: Zondervan, 2006), 156.

359). Rather than viewing holiness solely as something that separates God from people, Barth insists that God's holiness is God's love as God overcomes their resistance to God's will. As God "overcomes and destroys this resistance" (360), holiness forms a unity of judgment (including wrath) and grace as it both condemns and annihilates sin (364). God's opposition to sin is not ultimately bent on destruction, however. Rather, it is a positive opposition, ultimately aiming at our salvation.[25] Barth writes that holiness can mean "separate," but "primarily and fundamentally [it is] that which singles out, blesses, helps and restores, and only in this positive connexion does it have that other significance" (361). God is the Holy One eternally (though "there is no sin which He has first to resist") in that God is "the purity of life of the Father, Son and Holy Spirit" (368). Barth does not include extensive christological reflection on the attribute of holiness, but he does affirm that God is Holy as God redeems people through Christ and as God condemns sin in the Son (Rom. 8:3).[26]

25. Ron Highfield, *Great Is the Lord: Theology for the Praise of God* (Grand Rapids: Eerdmans, 2008), 180.

26. The brief christological focus comes particularly in Barth, *CD* II/1, 363, 364, and 367.

Barth does well to also recognize God's holiness in the Holy Spirit. The Spirit is the one who perfects fellowship between God and humanity as the Spirit convicts of righteousness, judgment, and sin (*CD* II/1, 363–64). Beyond this, as the Spirit overcomes our resistance to God's will, the Spirit not only convicts but also overcomes sin as the Spirit renews and sanctifies the believer. John Webster writes, "God the Holy Spirit is the one who completes this work of making holy, perfecting the creature by binding the creature's life into that of Christ and so realizing *in* the creature what has been achieved *for* the creature. The Spirit's holiness is thus known in his work of sanctifying."[27] One may add that the Spirit is holy in his regenerating work (that is, not just in applying the work of Christ).[28] Truly, God's love is holy as God creates and seeks fellowship with humanity by overcoming their resistance to God's will.

27. John Webster, *Holiness* (Grand Rapids: Eerdmans, 2003), 52, cf. 48.

28. Steven M. Studebaker, "Beyond Tongues: A Pentecostal Theology of Grace," in *Defining Issues in Pentecostalism: Classical and Emergent*, ed. Steven M. Studebaker, McMaster Theological Studies Series (Eugene, OR: Pickwick, 2008), 46–68, emphasizes that the Spirit has a key role in salvation, not just as the one who applies what Christ has already done.

Mercy

Barth continues to describe the divine love as he turns to discuss the mercy of God. "The mercy of God lies in His readiness to share in sympathy the distress of another" (369). In Barth's understanding of divine mercy, he explicitly rejects the doctrine of impassibility. God, Barth says, "is not impassible. He cannot be moved from outside by an extraneous power. But this does not mean that He is not capable of moving Himself" (370). Indeed, God's mercy includes compassion and pity for the sinner. God even "suffers pain because of our sin and guilt" (373). God's mercy, therefore, impels God to take the initiative to be gracious toward us. Once again, Barth affirms that this divine perfection is true of God in Godself inasmuch as mercy is a disposition of God's heart (375). Barth's brief christological reflection on this doctrine comes along with a (likewise brief) pneumatological observation. Barth observes that it is due to "the power of the divine mercy" that we receive "a living hope through the resurrection of Jesus Christ from the dead" (1 Pet. 1:3) and that "according to His mercy" God has saved us "by the washing of regeneration and renewing by the Holy Spirit" (Titus 3:5) (*CD* II/1, 373).

In his rejection of the doctrine of impassibility, Barth has not adequately recognized how impassibility has served well historically as an apophatic qualifier, that is, as a means of distinguishing divine passion from human passion and as a means of denying that God has morally problematic emotions.[29] In addition, Barth has (unfortunately) concentrated his understanding of mercy on God's *sympathy or readiness* to be gracious. In contrast, many biblical texts speak of God's actions themselves as displaying God's mercy, as God not only forgoes punishment but also comes to one's aid (for example, Isa. 55:7; Mic. 7:18; Luke 1:50). Nevertheless, pneumatology does confirm Barth's insight that God's mercy includes compassion and even suffering.[30] In God's mercy, the Holy Spirit grieves from human sin. Scriptures that

29. Paul Gavrilyuk, *The Suffering of the Impassible God: The Dialectics of Patristic Thought*, Oxford Early Christian Studies (Oxford: Oxford University Press, 2004), 16. Cf. Daniel Castelo, *The Apathetic God: Exploring the Contemporary Relevance of Divine Impassibility*, Paternoster Theological Monographs (Milton Keynes: Paternoster, 2009), 2. It is also important to emphasize that God is impassible in God's actions. That is, God is not inhibited by God's suffering—God is not ruled by God's passions and, therefore, God remains in control of God's actions. Castelo also emphasizes that God suffers only voluntarily and for the purpose of redemption (128).

30. For additional pneumatological reflections on the doctrine of divine passibility, see Gabriel, *Lord Is the Spirit*, chapter 5.

refer to the Spirit as grieving (Isa. 63:10 and Eph. 4:30) explicitly note that sinners are the external cause for this grief.[31] The passion of the Spirit is also evident as the Spirit groans, in relationship to humans and creation. Paul writes of times when believers do not know how or what to pray. At these times, he says, "the Spirit Himself intercedes for us with groanings too deep for words" (Rom. 8:26). A few verses earlier Paul wrote that believers "who have the firstfruits of the Spirit groan inwardly" (8:23). There is a clear connection here between the groans of the Spirit and the groans of humanity. This divine groaning also happens in association with the groaning of all of creation (Rom. 8:22). Like a mother giving birth to her child, God the Spirit groans that there might be new birth. Barth is correct that in God's mercy God is moved with passion.

Righteousness

The divine love is also found in the righteousness of God. In God's righteousness, God wills fellowship with creation and acts in a manner worthy of Godself as God asserts God's worth and causes God's worth to prevail (*CD* II/1, 376–77). God's righteousness is God's will and action to maintain God's covenant with humanity and to make the creature righteous and justified. In Jesus Christ, "God reveals and does what is worthy of Himself" (390). Barth observes how, in God's condemnation of Jesus Christ, God reveals both God's righteousness (including judgment) and mercy (including compassion) (384, 390, 393, 395, and 398–404). As the righteous one, God is the righteous judge who condemns sin. This condemnation of sin, nevertheless, remains an act of mercy. "It is as God forgives sins in His mercy that He judges" (382).

God is not only righteous as God justifies the sinner through Christ, for God also justifies through the Spirit. In the Old Testament, God's righteousness aims at "rightwising" creation (rather than any Protestant idea of covering up guilt), and the Old Testament looks forward to the fulfillment of the promise of righteousness with the future gift of the Spirit.[32] We are justified, then, not only "in the name of the Lord Jesus Christ" but also "in the Spirit of our God' (1 Cor. 6:11).

31. Therefore, Thomas G. Weinandy, *Does God Suffer?* (Notre Dame, IN: University of Notre Dame Press, 2000), 169, is incorrect to interpret divine grief as a metaphor where "grief" has no external cause.

32. Macchia, *Justified in the Spirit*, 123–27.

Justification and the gift of the Spirit are functional equivalents in Galatians, as both the Spirit and justification are received by faith (Gal. 3:1–8).[33] "By the washing of regeneration and renewing by the Holy Spirit" we are "being justified" by God's grace (Titus 3:5, 7). Justification is not completed with the work of Christ, for it is "through that Spirit" that we "are waiting for the hope of righteousness" (Gal. 5:5; cf. Rom. 14:17). Frank Macchia is certainly correct, therefore, in his assertion that "there can be no justification apart from the fullness of life in the Spirit."[34] Given that the ascended Christ pours out the Spirit on all flesh, one understands that Christ "was raised because of our justification" (Rom. 4:25). The result is that the righteous God makes God's creation righteous. This justification through the embrace of the Spirit includes both a divine judgment and the renewal of life (eventually culminating in the resurrection and glorification).[35] Consistent with Barth's assertion that God's righteousness is concerned with maintaining God's covenant with humanity, Macchia notes that God's righteous act of justification in the Spirit brings people into the divine *koinōnia*.[36] This is a fulfillment of God's righteousness as God is both "just and the justifier" (Rom. 3:26).

Patience

Divine love is expressed further through the patience of God. Barth describes patience as giving space and time to those with freedom with the purpose and expectation of a response (*CD* II/1, 408). All of the attributes of the divine loving indicate that God seeks to create fellowship. This is also true of God's patience, for the intention of God's patience is to summon people to faith—to give opportunity for sinners to repent and turn to God (Rom. 2:4; *CD* II/1, 413, 415, 419). (Accordingly, God's mercy depends on God's patience.) For example, "God waited patiently in the days of Noah while the ark was being built" (1 Pet. 3:20). This patience is also found true in "the factual and concrete revelation of God in Jesus Christ" (*CD* II/1, 409). Barth adds that God's patience is not a weakness—it is a strength. In God's patience,

33. Ibid., 196 and 197.

34. Ibid., 4.

35. It comes as no surprise then that Macchia believes that "regeneration, sanctification, and justification are overlapping metaphors of new life in the Spirit, each with its own unique theological nuance" (ibid., 208).

36. Ibid., 306; cf. 173.

God allows the existence of the other and does not destroy it, but rather "sustains it and allows it to develop in freedom" (410). For example, Barth notes that in the story of Cain, God saves the murderer despite Cain's unworthiness (412–13). This patience seen in divine providence is a christological reality, for God sustains all things by God's Word (Heb. 1:3)—the Word of God's Son, by whom God has spoken and "through whom also he made the universe" (Heb. 1:2). Barth affirms, "By this His Word in his Son Jesus Christ, He upholds all things and upholds them with power" (*CD* II/1, 417).

I want to build further on Barth's description of God's patience by emphasizing that just as it is true that God is not weak in his patience (which Barth emphasizes), it is also true that God is not passive in his patience. God does not just sit idly by waiting patiently in the hope that sinners will (cross your fingers!) repent and turn to God. Rather, God is active in patience. As Barth himself notes, God is actively sustaining creation, giving freedom. Further, Barth writes, "God's patience does not leave man to his own devices" (418). As God patiently gives freedom, space, and time to God's creatures, God continues to actively pursue fellowship. Although Scripture does not explicitly make this pneumatological claim, one can imagine that while God patiently waited in the days of Noah, like other Spirit-inspired prophets, Noah too could be considered a Spirit-inspired prophet who called people to repentance before their looming judgment. Aside from Noah, God's patience is certainly active as God calls people to fellowship through the prophets. One reads in Neh. 9:30, "For many years you were patient with them. By your Spirit you warned them through your prophets." As God seeks to draw people to fellowship with God by the Spirit, it is certainly true that "our Lord's patience means salvation" (2 Pet. 3:15).

We also see the patience of God in the action of sanctification. Consider the fruit of the Spirit (Galatians 5). I do not have in mind that patience itself is a fruit of the Spirit, but rather the manner in which God is active in producing "fruit" in us by the Spirit. Not only does growing fruit take time—sometimes it seems like *too much* time—but also, in producing the fruit of the Spirit, God's patience still allows freedom. One might think of the growth of fruit as not involving freedom—fruit does not grow by itself. However, to see the fruit of the Spirit cultivated in one's life, one must, Paul writes, "keep in step with the Spirit" or allow oneself to be "led by the

Spirit" (Gal. 5:16, 18, 25). This, of course, implies that one could freely choose not to keep in step with the Spirit. In this process of moral transformation, we see God patiently taking time, making space for the creature's freedom, maintaining the creature, but also actively transforming the creature so that the aim of the divine patience might be fulfilled.

Wisdom

To conclude his section on the divine love, Barth affirms divine wisdom—God's love is wise. According to Barth, wisdom refers to the fact that God's will has reason, purpose, and intention. It is the opposite of saying that God acts capriciously, impulsively, or irrationally. In making this observation, Barth desires to reaffirm that there is no paradox between God's grace and holiness and God's mercy and righteousness. God's wisdom is the rationality of divine love. In his discussion of divine love, Barth pairs divine wisdom with patience because biblically wisdom is seen as creating and maintaining the world. On account of God's wisdom, God is patient—that is, God "can allow time, space and existence to another beside Himself without uncertainty, danger or infidelity, as the Lord of this other, and to the praise of His own glory" (*CD* II/1, 427).

Barth, of course, recognizes that Christ is "the wisdom of God" (1 Cor. 1:24). The "manifold wisdom of God" was God's eternal purpose and "accomplished in Christ Jesus our Lord" (Eph. 3:10–11). In every passage where divine wisdom is expressed in relation to Jesus, it is clear, Barth observes, "wisdom is nothing more nor less than God Himself turning to man in grace and mercy, God in His love but also in His freedom, in the fullness of His love but also in the fullness of His freedom" (*CD* II/1, 439).

Just as Scripture associates Jesus with wisdom, Scripture also associates the Spirit with wisdom. Typically the idea is that as one receives the Spirit, they might also receive wisdom (Exod. 31:3; 35:31; Dan. 5:11, 14; Acts 6:3, 10; 1 Cor. 2:13; Col. 1:9). Although the result is humans acting in wisdom, this does point to the wisdom of God, for the source of this wisdom is God. The Spirit can only bring wisdom because the Spirit has the wisdom of God. This Spirit is none other than "the Spirit of wisdom" (Deut. 34:9; Isa. 11:2). And as with all of the attributes of divine love, the divine wisdom aims at fellowship with God. With the presence of the "Spirit of wisdom," Paul expects that "you may know him [God] better" (Eph. 1:17).

Conclusion

Following Barth's christological emphasis in his doctrine of God, many attempts to develop a Trinitarian doctrine of the divine attributes have been pneumatologically deficient. A Trinitarian doctrine of the divine attributes should take adequate account of the person and work of the Holy Spirit. A Trinitarian doctrine of God reveals that in God's grace, the Son and the Holy Spirit condescend to those who are unworthy in order to create fellowship with God. In God's holiness, through the Son and the Spirit, God overcomes people's resistance to God's will. In Christ we see God's mercy—God's readiness to turn to be gracious—and in the Spirit we see that God's merciful compassion moves God to be gracious. Through both the Son and the Spirit, God is righteous as God justifies the sinner in faithfulness to the covenant. As an expression of divine patience, the Son sustains all things and the Spirit actively pursues fellowship with people as God gives space and time for humanity to respond to God in repentance. And in wisdom, God directs the divine love in turning to humanity in Christ and in bringing knowledge of God through the Spirit of wisdom. I conclude, therefore, that integrating pneumatological insights with Barth's christological focus in his doctrine of God leads one closer to a Trinitarian doctrine of the divine attributes and confirms that God is indeed, as Barth emphasizes, the one who loves in freedom. The doctrine of the divine attributes is, therefore, truly good news—gospel.

CHAPTER 4

Theology Proper

The Lordship of the Holy Spirit

JOHN A. STUDEBAKER JR.

In Acts 8 we encounter the story of Simon the magician. Some had referred to Simon as "the Great Power of God" (8:10).[1] Tradition holds that he or his companion Helena claimed to *be* the Holy Spirit.[2] When Simon witnessed the power of the Spirit associated with the ministry of Peter and John, he offered them money, saying, "Give me this authority as well, so that everyone on whom I lay my hands may receive the Holy Spirit" (8:19). Peter rebuked Simon for his blatant attempt to *control* the Holy Spirit (8:20–23), and from this point forward Luke intentionally portrays the Spirit as *uncontrolled*. The Spirit immediately instructs Philip to join a chariot and, as a result, an Ethiopian official is converted to Christ (8:29–38). After the chariot stops we read "the Spirit of the Lord snatched Philip away" (8:39). In the remaining story of Acts the Spirit is seen as the director of the unfolding drama—expanding the church, telling the disciples where to go and what to say, and governing the church's affairs (see Acts 10:19; 11:12; 13:2–4; 16:6; and 21:11).

1. All Biblical quotations are taken from *The New American Standard Bible* (The Lockman Foundation, 1995).

2. Stanley M. Burgess, *The Holy Spirit: Ancient Christian Traditions* (Grand Rapids: Baker, 1990), 17.

Third Article Theology intentionally builds on the doctrine of the Holy Spirit's "Lordship." Indeed the Spirit is referred to as "Lord" or "Spirit of the Lord" at least thirty times in the Old Testament (OT)[3] and at least six in the New Testament (NT).[4] Reflecting upon such scriptural texts, the Council of Constantinople (381 CE) proclaimed in the Third Article of their Creed:

> And [we believe] in the Holy Spirit,
> the Lord, and the Life-giver
> who proceeds from the Father,
> who with the Father and the Son is worshiped and glorified,
> who spoke through the prophets.

This statement may come as a surprise, especially upon reading the *Second* Article of this Creed: "And [we believe] in one Lord, Jesus Christ. . . ." If "Lord" is the usual term given in reference to Christ in the NT (over 140 times), is it not problematic to also endow the Holy Spirit with the title "Lord"?[5]

As we shall see, Augustine, Basil, and other prominent theologians feel such a reference to the Spirit as "Lord" to be quite appropriate. In the fifteenth century, Martin Luther surprises those who thought he had neglected the Holy Spirit with the hymn "Come Holy Spirit, God and Lord":

> Come Holy Spirit, God and Lord!
> Let all thy graces be outpoured.
> On each believer's mind and heart;
> Thy fervent love to them impart
> Hallelujah, Hallelujah!
>
> Lord, by the brightness of thy light,
> Thou in the faith dost men unite
> Of ev'ry land and ev'ry tongue;
> This, to thy praise, O Lord, be sung.
> Hallelujah, Hallelujah![6]
>
> Lord, by Thy p'wer prepare each heart
> And to our weakness strength impart,
> That bravely here we may contend,
> Through life and death to Thee, ascend.
> Hallelujah, Hallelujah![7]

3. Twice in Numbers (11:25 and 29), seven times in Judges, eight times in Isaiah, seven times in Ezekiel, and four times in the Minor Prophets.

4. Luke 4:18; Acts 5:9; 8:39; 2 Cor. 3:17–18 (three times).

5. James D. G. Dunn lists twenty-eight commentators who identify *pneuma* in 2 Cor. 3:17–18 with the Lord Jesus Christ rather than the Holy Spirit ("2 Corinthians 3:17—The Lord Is the Spirit," in *The Christ and the Spirit* [Grand Rapids: Eerdmans, 1998], 1:115).

6. J. N. D. Kelly, *Early Christian Creeds*, 3rd ed. (London: Longman, 1972), 97–98.

7. James F. Lambert, *Luther's Hymns* (Philadelphia: General Council Publication House, 1917), 12.

In the twentieth century Karl Barth attempted to theologically shock those "liberal" theologians whom he deemed had substituted a human "spirit of love" for the Holy Spirit, calling the substituted spirit an "evil spirit."[8] He exalts the Spirit's Lordship in creation, reconciliation, and redemption, and asserts that the Spirit is "God the Lord in the fullness of Deity, in the total sovereignty and condescension, in the complete hiddenness and revealedness of God."[9]

Perhaps most surprising, however, is that the "Lordship of the Holy Spirit," declared to be an essential doctrine in 381 CE, continues to be essentially undefined within systematic theology. Some difficult questions that have remained unanswered include: Can such a doctrine be derived from Scripture and theology? Can divine Lordship be designated specifically to the person of the Holy Spirit? How is the Spirit's Lordship distinct from Christ's Lordship?

Defining "Lordship"

The word "Lord," whether found in Scripture or classical literature, always carries a sense of supremacy, power, or authority *over* some aspect of the world, along with possession of certain things *in* the world.

In the OT, the eternal *ʾĕlōhîm* technically becomes the "Lord" at the creation of the universe (Gen. 2:4; Pss. 24:1–2; 104:24). YHWH is commonly referred to as "Lord" of those people he has redeemed, claiming legal authority over them by virtue of being their redeemer (Exod. 3; 6:7; 19:3–5; Deut. 4:20).[10] In his introduction to Moses (Exod. 3:1–15), YHWH presents himself as both *transcendent* (eternal and sovereign over the world; illustrated in the bush that is not consumed) and *immanent* (present and personal; YHWH speaks to Moses, proclaiming, "I am the God of your father, the God of Abraham, the God of Isaac, and the God of Jacob" [3:6]). YHWH is thereby portrayed in the OT as the transcendent "Lord" who has "come down" to his people, redeeming them

8. Karl Barth, *The Holy Spirit and the Christian Life: The Theological Basis for Ethics* (Louisville: Westminster, 1993), 25.

9. Ibid., 3.

10. Kaiser et al. clarify that while *ʾĕlōhîm* refers to God as a transcendent Being who stands above (and exists prior to) the world, "the name *Yahweh* is used when the Bible wishes to present the personal character of God and his direct relationship with those human beings who have a special association with him" (Walter C. Kaiser Jr., Peter H. Davids, F. F. Bruce, Manfred T. Brauch, *Hard Sayings of the Bible* [Downers Grove, IL: InterVarsity Press], 87–88). See also H. Bietenhard, "Lord," in *NIDNTT*, 2:512.

from bondage and bringing them into a covenantal bond with himself (see Gen. 12:1–8; 15:1–18). Peter Toon makes a strong case for YHWH being depicted in the OT as a "plurality in unity" who incorporates, and sends forth, his Spirit for various purposes.[11]

In the NT the Greek word *kyrios* also carries the idea of supremacy or authority, and is most often used as a title for Christ to express his supreme status as "Lord." Saying "Jesus is *Kyrios*" (for example, 1 Cor. 12:3) became a way of proclaiming Jesus' exalted status and authority over the world and all its powers—especially the Roman emperors—and as a way of declaring his victory over sin and death.[12]

John Frame rightly defines Lordship as "covenant headship"—"Lord" is God's name as head of the Mosaic covenant and is also the name given to Jesus Christ as head of the New Covenant.[13] God's Lordship involves control ("God's sovereign power"), authority ("God's right to be obeyed"), and presence ("covenant solidarity" or "nearness").[14] Thus, in order to be considered "Lord," God must be present to us, not only sovereign over us. Divine Lordship reveals the transcendent attributes of God to us immanently. It is the *immanence* of Lordship that is highlighted with respect to the Holy Spirit.

The Lordship of the Holy Spirit in Ancient Theology

In developing their doctrine of the Holy Spirit, the early church fathers first sought to affirm the Spirit's status as a divine person. Athanasius was not only a chief defender of the divinity of Christ at the Council of Nicaea; he was likewise a leading elaborator of the Spirit's divinity after Nicaea. Here he found many converts from Arianism, such as the followers of Serapion, who had accepted the logic of Nicene Christology (the *homoousios* of the Son with the Father) but continued to view the Spirit as a creature.[15] In response, Athanasius applies *homoousios* to the Holy

11. See Peter Toon, *Our Triune God* (Wheaton, IL: Bridgepoint, 1996), 95–112.

12. Herod the Great, Agrippa I and II, and even some Roman governors were referred to as *Kyrios*. See W. Foerster, "kyrios," *TDNT* 3:1049.

13. John M. Frame, *The Doctrine of the Knowledge of God: A Theology of Lordship* (Phillipsburg, NJ: Presbyterian and Reformed, 1987), 13.

14. See Frame, *Doctrine of the Knowledge of God*, 15–16.

15. Arius denied *homoousios* regarding both Son and Spirit, and held that the Spirit is really an angel, created by the Son, and one of the spirits ministering to God in heaven. See Arius, as quoted by Athanasius, *Orations against the Arians*, 1.6.

Spirit: "And if the Son, because he is of the Father, is proper to his essence, it must be that the Spirit, who is said to be from God, is in essence proper to the Son."[16] His most famous defense of the Spirit's divinity contrasts Gen. 1:1–23 with 1 Cor. 2:11–12—the former demonstrates that creatures are created from nothing and come into being at a particular time; the latter shows that the Spirit is not created but emerges directly from God.[17]

Other church fathers, building on Athanasius's logic, form arguments for the Spirit's divinity from a different tack. They seem to fear that aligning the Spirit too closely with the created world would in some way "sell out" to human or unholy "spirits." They begin to portray the Spirit as "Lord"—demonstrating from Scripture that the *transcendent* attributes of God remain evident as the Spirit works *immanently* within creation, providence, and redemption, thereby displaying a *transcendent immanence.*

Gregory of Nazianzus wrestled with the Arians in this way. He begins with the Spirit's transcendent place in salvation. The light that is received by the creature must be true God in itself—for if the Spirit in whom the light comes to us is not God, how can we be saved? Gregory states, "If [the Spirit] is ranked with me, how can he divinize me?"[18] He then speaks of the Spirit's immanent works that retain transcendence: "For He is the maker of all these, filling all with His Essence, . . . sanctifying, not sanctified; measuring, not measured; shared, not sharing; filling, not filled; containing, not contained."[19]

Basil of Caesarea, in his essay entitled "Proof from Scripture That the Spirit Is Called Lord," argues that several uses of "Lord" in the NT must refer to the Spirit. For example, he examines 2 Thess. 3:5 ("the Lord direct your hearts into the love of God and into the patient waiting for Christ") and asks,

> Who is the Lord that directs into the love of God and into the patient waiting for Christ for tribulations? Let those men answer us who are for making a slave of the Holy Spirit. For if the argument had been about God the Father, it would certainly have said, "the Lord direct you into His own love," or if about the Son, it would have added "into His own

16. Athanasius, *First Letter to Serapion,* trans., C.R.B. Shapland, (London: Epworth Press, 1951), 1.25.

17. Athanasius, *Third Letter to Serapion* 2.28.

18. Gregory of Nazianzus, *On the Holy Spirit*, trans., Charles Brown and James Swallow (Edinburgh: T&T Clark, 1894), 325.

19. Ibid., 325–26.

> patience." Let them then seek what other Person there is who is worthy to be honoured with the title of Lord.[20]

Notice that, according to Basil, some were attempting to make the Spirit a "slave"—someone commonly bought and sold at will by a human "master"—by denying that the Spirit is a divine "person" who performs sanctifying work (to "direct our hearts into the love of God").

The Council of Constantinople recognized the logic of Athanasius's arguments for the Spirit's divinity; however, because of their fear of a tumultuous reaction from the newly excommunicated Arians, they were reluctant to refer to the Spirit as "God." Instead, following Gregory and Basil, their expansion of the Nicene Creed settled on a *via media*: "[We believe] in the Holy Spirit, the Lord and the Life-giver . . . ."

In the sixth century, John of Damascus would lead the Greek fathers to explicate the Spirit's Lordship even more deeply.[21] His *De fide orthodoxa* refers to 1 Spirit as "Lord of all creation, and not under any Lord."[22] Though remaining distinct from the world, the Spirit is the "Lord" who springs forth from the Father to create the world and to allow the creation to participate in the movement of the triune being.[23]

The Lordship of the Spirit in Relation to the Lordship of Christ

Even before Constantinople, Tertullian spoke of Christ as sending the Holy Spirit to be his "Vicar."[24] Properly speaking, a "Curate" is one charged with the "cure" or care of souls; his "Vicar" is essentially his deputy who takes his place when he cannot be there.[25] As Christ's "Vicar," the Holy Spirit takes the place of Christ after his departure from the earth.

After Constantinople, Augustine developed a more extensive exposition of the

20. Basil, "Letters and Select Works," *NPNF*[2] 8:33.

21. John of Damascus popularized the use of the term *perichoresis*, which implies that each member of the Trinity functions in vital correspondence and involvement with the other two while retaining their distinct personage in every respect. See Charles C. Twombly, *Perichoresis and Personhood: God, Christ, and Salvation in John of Damascus* (Eugene, OR: Pickwick, 2015).

22. John of Damascus, *Exposition of the Orthodox Faith*, trans. S. D. F. Salmond, in *NPNF*[2] 9:8.

23. See Alasdair Heron, *The Holy Spirit* (Philadelphia: Westminster, 1983), 85.

24. Tertullian, *De praescr.*, trans. Peter Holmes, in *ANF* 3,:1.

25. See Leon Morris, *Spirit of the Living God* (London: InterVarsity Press, 1973), 55.

Trinity. He actually begins with the economic Trinity, with the "temporal missions" of the Son and Spirit as they are sent from the Father into this world. Augustine asserts that we initially know the Son because we experience his redemption and that we initially know the Spirit through our experience of the Spirit as a divine gift.[26]

Augustine also explores the Scriptures in an attempt to discern the nature of the relationship between Christ and the Spirit. He concludes that, since the Holy Spirit is the *vinculum caritas* ("bond of love") between the Father and the Son, the Spirit must proceed from both.[27] In this procession the Spirit brings both the Father and the Son to us, so that we might actually know them in our contemplation and in our experience.

Augustine adds that, in particular, the Spirit has been sent so that we might experience the continuing effects of Christ's mission. For example, the Spirit comes to us with perceptible signs (such as the speaking in tongues at Pentecost). These signs "show that the whole world and nations with their variety of languages were going to believe in Christ by the gift of the Holy Spirit."[28]

Augustine states that, since the Son and the Spirit are inseparable in their divine nature, they indeed *act* inseparably as well.[29] Thus the Son and the Spirit, along with the Father, act inseparably when they come to us as "the Lord." Specifically, Augustine implies that the Son, who is now referred to as the exalted "Lord," came to reveal the divine Lordship through his redemptive mission; so the Spirit, who is now referred to as "Lord and life-giver," continues to reveal the divine Lordship through the Spirit's revelatory mission.

How does Scripture describe the Spirit's mission, particularly in relation to Christ's mission? The Gospels of Luke and John magnify the early histories of this relationship and in doing so provide two complementary starting points for our investigation. Luke is typically thought of as communicating a

26. See Augustine, *On the Trinity*, trans. Edmund Hill (Brooklyn: New City Press, 1991), 4.29 (127). This illustrates Augustine's famous saying "faith seeking understanding." See also Keith E. Johnson, *Rethinking the Trinity and Religious Pluralism* (Downers Grove, IL: InterVarsity Press, 2011), 55–63, 73–79, 101–19.

27. Augustine, *On the Trinity* 4.7–9.

28. Augustine, *On the Trinity* 6.29 (175).

29. Augustine, *On the Trinity* 1.19 (79). Augustine builds on the Cappadocian theologians by locating the divine unity in the Father, and adds that the actions of the three persons, in either creation or redemption, are inseparable within the essence of God. See Johnson, *Rethinking the Trinity*, 115.

"Spirit Christology," where the Spirit essentially superintends over Jesus' earthly ministry. The Spirit is involved in the conception of Jesus (Luke 1:35), anoints him for ministry (3:22), and guides him through critical stages of his earthly ministry (see, for example, Luke 4:1–14, 18).

The Gospel of John, however, presents a "Logos Christology," with Jesus portrayed as the divine "Logos" four times and the "Lord" forty times. John stresses Jesus' role in sending the Holy Spirit after his departure. In chapters 14, 15, and 16, Jesus explains to the disciples the specific way that he, as their "Lord" (14:8), will "come to you" (14:18) by personally "sending" the Holy Spirit (14:26; 15:26; and 16:7).

This future sending is first described in John 14:26, where Jesus states that the Father "will send" the Spirit "in my name." C. K. Barrett asserts that "in my name" means "to act in relation to me, in my place, with my authority."[30] This implies that Jesus will impart to the Spirit an aspect of his own authority—his Lordship—as part of the sending activity.

In John 15:26, Jesus further specifies that he "will send" the Spirit "from the Father" and that the Spirit "proceeds" from the Father. Here the Father appears as the eternal source from whom the Spirit "proceeds." The Son may well be the secondary source of the Spirit's procession (as indicated by John 16:15, "All things that the Father has are Mine").[31] However, the main clause of this verse lies at the end: "he [the Spirit] will testify about me." According to Morris, this verse indicates that the Spirit has the authority to "conduct Christ's case for him before the world."[32] The Spirit will show the world—primarily through the vehicles of the church and the Scriptures—that Jesus Christ is still alive and is actually "Lord" of the universe.

In John 16:13–14, Jesus describes three specific ways the Spirit will continue his own mission in the world after his resurrection and ascension. First, "the Spirit of truth . . . will guide you into all the truth" (16:13a).

30. C. K. Barrett, *The Gospel according to St. John* (London: SPCK, 1955), 390. George Beasley-Murray surmises that this is a remarkable declaration that binds the Spirit closely to Jesus (*John* [Waco, TX: Word, 1987], 261).

31. According to Donald Carson, "['Proceeds'] refers here to the mission of the Spirit (as opposed to some ontological 'procession' or even to the nature of the relationship of the Spirit to the Father)" (*The Gospel according to John*, Pillar New Testament Commentary [Grand Rapids: Eerdmans, 1999], 529). Both Eastern and Western theologians agree that in some way the Father and the Son participate in "sending" the Spirit.

32. Morris, *The Gospel according to John*, 607.

Earlier Jesus was proclaimed "the truth" (14:6); now the "Spirit of truth" will lead people to acknowledge that Jesus is still "the truth," and will lead disciples into a fuller understanding of the truth of Jesus.[33]

Second, "He will not speak on his own initiative, but whatever He hears, He will speak" (16:13b). The Spirit will not repeat what he hears verbatim but rather will speak in complete accordance with the voice of the Father and of the Son.[34] According to Adam Clarke, "As Christ is represented as the ambassador of the Father, so the Holy Spirit is represented as the ambassador of the Son, coming vested with his authority, as the interpreter and executor of his will."[35]

Third, Jesus proclaims that the Spirit "will glorify Me," for the Spirit "will take of mine and disclose it to you" (16:14).[36] The Spirit will reveal the fullness of Jesus' character and work to the world. "Disclose" implies that all the revelation bound up in Jesus' person and mission are pressed home to the disciples.[37] According to Beasley-Murray: "[This verse] suggests that the revelatory work of the Spirit . . . has a special relation to the *redemptive* work of Jesus, wherein the revelation of God in Christ reaches its apex."[38]

To summarize these "sending" passages, the Spirit has been "sent" as the executor of Christ's continuing mission and particularly as the "Lord of revelation" of Jesus' person and redemptive work. Neill Hamilton comments, "[T]he Spirit so effectively performs His office of communicating to men the benefits of the risen Christ that for all intents and purposes of faith the Lord Himself is present bestowing grace on His own. The Spirit brings the ascended Lord to earth again."[39]

Precisely how does the Spirit as "Lord of revelation" come to bear as an actual authority in the world and especially in the church in a practical sense? Bernard Ramm addresses this question in his classic book *The Pattern of Authority*. Ramm holds that divine authority comes to bear on us through a designated

33. The Spirit as guide appears in several OT texts as well (i.e., Isa. 63:14; Ps. 143:10).

34. See Morris, *The Gospel according to John*, 700.

35. Adam Clarke, *Christian Theology* (Salem, OH: Schmul, 1990), 157.

36. "Glorify" involves "the manifestation of a person, with special stress on the impression this creates on others" (S. Aalen, "Glory," *NIDNTT* 2:45).

37. Carson, *Gospel according to John*, *NICNT* (Grand Rapids: Eerdmans, 1995), 541.

38. Beasley-Murray, *John*, 284 (emphasis original).

39. Neill Q. Hamilton, *The Holy Spirit and Eschatology in Paul* (Edinburgh: Oliver & Boyd, 1957), 6.

pattern incorporating Christ (who is the exalted Lord and thus the focus of all authority), the Holy Spirit (who reveals the authority of Christ *to us* through the prophets and apostles), and the Sacred Scriptures (which are inspired by the Holy Spirit and are thereby the objective document of authority for faith and life).[40] This pattern thus combines both the subjective force and the objective content of authority. In addition, the Spirit has the authority to illuminate the canonical Scriptures, enabling people to perceive and respond to the words of Scripture, thereby making them efficacious in their lives.

The fulfillment of Jesus' "sending prophecies" in John 14–16 is subsequently described in the book of Acts and the letters of Paul. After Pentecost the Scripture writers begin to portray Christ as possessing an *exalted* Lordship, highlighting transcendence, and the Spirit as possessing an essentially *executorial* Lordship, highlighting immanence.[41]

A potential weakness should be noted, however, of any theology based entirely upon John's Logos Christology, especially if the Holy Spirit is described as *only* an executor of the Father and the Son. In such a case there is the tendency to reduce the Holy Spirit to an inferior or purely functional role "under" Christ and, as a result, to diminish the Spirit's "own" personhood and Lordship. Augustine's view of the Spirit as the "bond of love" between the Father and the Son may inadvertently create this sort of reduction. Gerald Bray asserts that "if the Holy Spirit really is a person in his own right, we ought to avoid language that calls him the 'bond of love' between the Father and the Son, even if there is a sense in which this is truth, because the language itself has a depersonalizing effect."[42]

Nevertheless, a denial of Logos Christology seems to open the way to a sort of dual authority structure that may easily neglect Christ's present-day authority, "as if the mission of the Son and that of the Spirit were two separate and distinct movements sent

40. Bernard Ramm, *The Pattern of Authority* (Grand Rapids: Eerdmans, 1957), 36.

41. An *executor* may not have complete authority to act on behalf of an executive; however, someone with an *executorial authority* certainly does. The ancient feudal system of the Roman Empire allowed for many coexisting "feudal lords" or "liege lords" who governed their own territories under the final authority of the emperor.

42. Gerald Bray, "The Double Procession of the Holy Spirit in Evangelical Theology Today: Do We Still Need It?," *Journal of the Evangelical Theological Society* 41 (1998): 423.

forth from God to men."[43] If the *filioque* was configured to mean that the Spirit obtains his *authority to act*—that is, his executorial Lordship—from the Son as well as from the Father, this might prove more palatable to both Eastern and Western theologians.

Colin Gunton proposes a complementary "balance" that confirms both the Spirit's "freedom" and the Spirit's role in executing Christ's mission: "Any attempt to identify the Spirit must show that there is a way of God's action towards us and his world which is not *separable* from his action in Christ, but not *reducible* to it either."[44] The Spirit's executorial Lordship serves to make Christ's person and work real and existential in the lives of individual believers, in the church body, and even in the unbelieving world. This task is not carried out mechanically but in freedom.[45] Gunton clarifies: "The freedom of the Spirit is incompatible with the Spirit being simply an impersonal principle, a medium or dimension; rather, the freedom of the Spirit presupposes the relative independence of the Spirit."[46]

The Lordship of the Spirit—Three Critical Realms

In this section we will examine the Lordship of the Holy Spirit in three important realms: as Lord of Creation, as Revealer and Executor of the new covenant, and as Governor of the church.

Lord of Creation

Theologians have traditionally held that the Father desired the world to be created and is its ultimate source; the Son was the mediator of creation, designing it with wisdom, order, and beauty; the Spirit actualized and perfected creation, bringing it into existence.

Genesis 1:2 introduces the biblical reader to the Holy Spirit's *transcendent immanence* with respect to the created world. A contrast is set forth between the impersonal "darkness" and the personal "Spirit of God" (who will bring forth "light" in 1:3). "Moved over" (or "hovered over") communicates transcendence

43. George S. Hendry, *The Holy Spirit in Christian Theology* (Philadelphia: Westminster, 1956), 46.

44. Gunton, *Theology through the Theologians* (Edinburgh: T&T Clark, 1996), 112.

45. Some NT metaphors that provide a glimpse of the Spirit's freedom include "the wind" in John 3:8 (which "blows where it wishes") and "living water" in John 4:9–11 (which is superior to well water).

46. Gunton, *Theology through the Theologians*, 211. See also Bray, "Double Procession of the Holy Spirit," 425–26.

over the unformed world, while "the surface of the waters" communicates immanence and presence. Meredith Kline holds this to be a "Glory-cloud" manifestation of the Spirit that would later appear to Moses on Mount Sinai and would hover over the Jews in the exodus.[47] This verse may have been intended as a polemic against the Egyptian sun god Amun-Ra, referred to as "Lord of truth, father of the gods, maker of men, creator of all animals, Lord of things that are, creator of the staff of life."[48]

Bruce Waltke asserts that in Gen. 1:2 the Spirit of God is "waiting for the proper moment to begin history by the creation of heaven and earth through the Word."[49] Then Gen. 1:3–31 explains the way the *rûaḥ 'ĕlōhîm* powerfully forms the earth, installing goodness, design, purpose, and order into each aspect of creation. In this way the Spirit is the "Lord" of all creation. In Gen. 2:7 we witness the Spirit breathing life into the first human, thereby endowing him with the capacity to "rule over" the earth as a reflection of the divine rulership.[50]

Psalm 104 is a creation psalm that further illuminates the Spirit's Lordship in creation.[51] "You take away their spirit, they expire" (v. 29) is contrasted with "you send forth your Spirit, they are created" (v. 30).[52] This evokes a sharp discontinuity between the human *rûa⊠* (which is fragile) and the divine *rûa⊠*[53] (who is eternal) and implies that all breathing things are utterly dependent on the Spirit for their very life. Thus the psalmist eliminates any possible blurring of the divine Spirit with the human spirit. According to Derek Kidner, this contrast of the divine Spirit to the

47. Meredith Kline, *Images of the Spirit* (Grand Rapids: Baker, 1980), 17–21.

48. E. A. Wallis Budge, *An Introduction to Egyptian Literature* (Mineola, NY: Dover, 1997), 214.

49. Bruce K. Waltke, *Creation and Chaos* (Portland, OR: Western Conservative Baptist Seminary, 1974), 52. Likewise, Calvin holds this passage to declare the Spirit's ability to sustain all of creation (John Calvin, *Institutes of the Christian Religion*, ed. John T. McNeill, trans. Ford Lewis Battles [Philadelphia: Westminster, 1960], 1.13.22).

50. Here "the Spirit-Archetype actively fathered his human ectype" (Kline, *Images of the Spirit*, 23).

51. See Alfons Deissler, "The Theology of Psalm 104," in *Standing before God* (New York: KTAV, 1981), 32–35.

52. This passage forms a chiasm, with obvious parallelism to Gen. 2:7. Joseph Addison Alexander asserts, "'Their breath' [is] the vital principle [of life] imparted by the Spirit of God (Gen 2:7), which is the God of the spirits of all flesh, i.e. the author of all life whatsoever" (*The Psalms: Translated and Explained* [Grand Rapids: Zondervan, 1964], 427).

53. A. A. Anderson, *Psalms 100–150* (Grand Rapids: Eerdmans, 1981), 724; cf. Lev. 17:10; 20:5; Deut. 31:17; Ezek. 7:22.

human spirit "deepens our accountability" before YHWH.[54]

The Spirit of YHWH will also "renew the face of the ground" (v. 30). This implies a redemption of the physical world, perhaps after the flood.[55] Thomas Oden sees in such renewal activities the "general operations" of the Spirit—the Spirit's managerial supervision of the created order that includes offering, supporting, nurturing, continuing, strengthening, and guiding life, whether plant, animal, or human life. The Spirit's Lordship in creation even extends to the political order, restraining the capacity for humanity to destroy itself. "By the Spirit the enormous diversity of creation is brought into a single meaningful whole. Even the sins of the fallen, for which God is not responsible, are in time made serviceable to the whole."[56] The Spirit dispatches redemptive themes into each major sphere of human thought and culture, including art, science, media, family, education, government, recreation, and even religion.[57] Elihu exclaims that the *rûaḥ* of God gives him understanding (Job 32:8). Sinclair Ferguson remarks, "Rich, varied and remarkable capacities and abilities are therefore present in the human race, because the Spirit continues his work as the executive of God in relation to the created order."[58]

Reductions of the Spirit's Lordship in creation, subtle as they may be, can effect a "selling out" of one's essential pneumatology and, in turn, one's submission or obedience to the Spirit as *Lord*. Contemporary reductions have emerged from those who espouse panentheistic worldviews, which tend to remove an ontological distinction between God and the world.[59] Jürgen Moltmann, for

54. Derek Kidner, *Psalm 100–150* (Downers Grove, IL: InterVarsity Press, 1975), 372.

55. See Alexander, *Psalms*, 427.

56. Thomas C. Oden, *Life in the Spirit* (San Francisco: HarperSanFrancisco, 1992), 3:34–35. Oden adds that such "general operations" are shared with the Father and the Son and display divine sovereignty. See also Job 33:4; 34:14–15.

57. Sinclair Ferguson points out that older conservative theology finds little or no room for an interaction between the Holy Spirit and the cosmos (*The Holy Spirit* [Downers Grove, IL: InterVarsity Press, 1996], 244–55).

58. Ibid., 247.

59. Theism holds that God is self-existent, the *first cause* for all created things (see Num. 23:19; Pss. 29:10; 102:25–27; James 1:17). "The incomparable divine transcendence involves a radical dualism between God and the world that ought not be blurred by a resurgent monism and pantheism. Although made like God and in the divine image, mankind is not (like Christ) begotten of God or an emanation from God of the same divine nature. The ultimate goal of salvation is not reabsorption into the being of God but unbroken fellowship with God" (G. R. Lewis, "Attributes of God," *EDOT*, 459).

example, does speak of the Spirit as "lord, as mother, and as judge,"[60] and as "[the one] through which the future that is hoped for enters into history."[61] However, Moltmann's theology is essentially panentheistic, oriented around "the world in God and God in the world."[62] He describes the Spirit in almost entirely immanent terms: the Spirit is God's presence "as community" and allows people to "exert an influence on him, just as he exerted an influence on them."[63] In these assertions Moltmann essentially equates the Spirit with human community and the Spirit's influence with human influence. The prophet Isaiah seems to confront such heresy when he states, "Who has directed the Spirit of the LORD, or as His counselor has informed Him? With whom did He consult and *who* gave Him understanding?" (Isa. 40:13–14).

60. Jürgen Moltmann, *The Spirit of Life*, trans. Margaret Kohl (San Francisco: Harper & Row, 1992), 270.

61. Moltmann, *The Church in the Power of the Spirit* (New York: Harper & Row, 1977), 34.

62. Moltmann, *Spirit of Life*, 98, 103. Referring to the mystical theologians, Moltmann asserts that we "find in many of them a panentheistic vision of the world in God, and God in the world" (ibid., 211).

63. Ibid., 217–18.

Lord over the Revelation and Execution of the New Covenant

Perhaps the most critical passage in our entire discussion of the Spirit's Lordship is 2 Cor. 3:9–18. Paul first contrasts the old covenant, highlighted by Moses's ministry, with "the surpassing glory" of the New Covenant, brought forth by the Spirit (3:9–11).[64] Paul speaks of the "veil" that was over Moses's face (mentioned in Exodus 34), which he wore so that the Israelites would not see the glory of God fading from his face (2 Cor. 3:13). Paul then explains that this veil represents the Old Covenant, which continues to dull the minds and hearts of the Jews (3:14–15). This veil is only removed by "the Lord" (3:16)—an obvious reference by Paul to Exod. 34:34, when Moses removed his veil upon entering his tent and speaking directly to the Lord.

In 2 Cor. 3:17 Paul declares, "Now the Lord is the Spirit." Paul is essentially saying, "Now 'the Lord' of whom Exodus 34:34 speaks, 'the Lord' who removes the veil, is

64. Dunn holds that this passage shows "the contrast and replacement of the Old Covenant of *gramma* with the New Covenant of *pneuma*" and serves as a "Christian midrash" or "interpretive homily" on Exod. 34:29–35 ("2 Corinthians 3:17," 119). See also Ralph P. Martin, *2 Corinthians*, Word Biblical Commentary 40 (Waco, TX: Word, 1986), 63.

the Holy Spirit."[65] Dunn explains the thrust of this verse: "It is the *pneuma* who opens peoples' eyes to the bondage and fear of the Old Covenant and brings them into the liberty and boldness of the new."[66] On this verse Basil is also insightful: "He, then, who in the reading of the Law takes away the letter and turns to the Lord—and the Lord is now called the Spirit—becomes moreover like Moses, who had his face glorified by the manifestation of God."[67]

The New Covenant was described by the OT prophets as a new messianic age when the Lord will "put My Spirit within you and cause you to walk in my statutes" (Ezek. 36:27) and will "put My law within them and on their heart I will write it" (Jer. 31:33). The Spirit is currently revealing this future messianic kingdom, bringing it into the present age in a spiritual sense. Thus "the Lord"—typically thought of in terms of the resurrected Christ—is now experienced as the Spirit.[68]

Earlier I mentioned that Frame defines Lordship as "covenant headship." In this passage the Spirit is given "headship" to reveal and execute the New Covenant, particularly one's experience of its "liberty." And this is exactly what we discern in 2 Cor. 3:18. The New Covenant is now being "unveiled" so that believers can continually "behold . . . the glory of the Lord." This use of "Lord" is actually a reference to the resurrected Christ. Believers who behold the glory of Christ are now "being transformed" into his image. "Transformed" reflects the total transformation of creation that will occur at the coming

65. Paul confirms this in the following clause: "the Spirit of the Lord." A debate exists over whether "the Lord" in 3:17 refers to God, Christ, or the Spirit. Fee explains: "The Lord in [Exod. 34:34] is now to be understood (not literally but in an analogical way) as referring to the Spirit—not because this is the proper identification of the Lord in the Exodus text but because in this argument that is the proper way to understand what happens to those who, as Moses, now 'turn to the Lord'" (Gordon D. Fee, *God's Empowering Presence: The Holy Spirit in the Letters of Paul* [Peabody, MA: Hendrickson, 1994], 311–13). John Chrysostom provides an excellent defense for such an interpretation: Saint Chrysostom: "Homilies on the Epistles of Paul to the Corinthians," *NPNF*[1] 12:313-315.

66. Dunn, "2 Corinthians 3:17," 119.

67. Basil, "Letters and Select Works," *NPNF*[2] 8:33.

68. Paul Thorsell asserts that, within the present era of the church, there is "a partial and preliminary fulfillment of the New Covenant in anticipation of a complete fulfillment in the eschaton (and thus) within the Pauline corpus the presence and activity of the Holy Spirit among believers demonstrates that the New Covenant is currently operative, albeit in a partial and preliminary way" ("The Spirit in the Present Age: Preliminary Fulfillment of the Predicted New Covenant according to Paul," *Journal of the Evangelical Theological Society* 41 [1998]: 397–98).

of the messianic kingdom (see Isa. 32:15; 35:6–7; Ezek. 36:25–30).[69] Yet an initial transformation is taking place now, and this is being accomplished "by the Lord, who is the Spirit." The Spirit is currently superintending over the initial form of this kingdom, bringing forth transformation, "from glory to glory"—that is, moving us closer and closer to the image of Christ and the blueprint of the future, glorious kingdom. How can "Lord" be used here for both Christ and the Spirit? Dunn explains: "This does not mean that they are identical in all their functions (far less their 'beings'), as though, for example, the Spirit has been crucified and raised from the dead. It only means they are identical in experience."[70]

Earlier we saw that Martin Luther's hymn "Come Holy Spirit, God and Lord" refers to the Spirit as the "Lord" who pours out the grace of the New Covenant.[71] Until recently, Luther was regarded by modern scholars as having somewhat depreciated the Holy Spirit in his theology. Regin Prenter countered this notion, unearthing Luther's view of the Spirit as the one who brings about *conformity* to Christ (*Christum forma*) rather than simply a scholastic kind of *imitation* of Christ (a lofty, distant ideal).[72] More recently, Simo Peura notes that Luther's doctrine of justification contains a mystical conception (a form of *theōsis*), incorporating the notion that a Christian must be caught up (*raptus*) in Christ through the Spirit.[73]

Luther held that this Lord of grace has distinct functions, which include the application of Christ's redemption, the unification of believers, and sanctification. Luther credits the Spirit with guiding sinners into the New Covenant through the entire process of repentance and salvation—from awakening sinners to grace to assuring believers that the crucified and risen Christ is present, standing

69. See Willem A. VanGemeren, *Interpreting the Prophetic Word: An Introduction to the Prophetic Literature of the Old Testament* (Grand Rapids: Zondervan, 1996), 221.

70. Dunn, "2 Corinthians 3:17," 124–25.

71. James Packer likewise holds one of the six belief-and-behavior principles of Evangelicalism to be: "Acknowledging the lordship of the Holy Spirit in the entire life of grace, which is the life of salvation expressed in worship, work, and witness" ("A Stunted Ecclesiology? The Theory & Practice of Evangelical Churchliness," *Touchstone* 15 [December 2002]: n.p.).

72. Regin Prenter, *Spiritus Creator*, trans. John M. Jenson (Philadelphia: Muhlenberg, 1953).

73. See Simo Peura, "Christ as Favor and Gift (*donum*): The Challenge of Luther's Understanding of Justification," in *Union with Christ: The New Finnish Interpretation of Luther*, ed. Carl E. Braaten and Robert W. Jenson (Grand Rapids: Eerdmans, 1998), 42–69.

by their side forever, sharing with them his grace, purity, and power.[74]

Governor of the Church

In what way might the Holy Spirit be called "Lord" in the church? A salient passage in this regard is 1 Cor. 12:4–13. Here Paul refers to the "same" or "one" Spirit six times—at the beginning and end of the passage and four times along the way. This creates an *inclusio*, communicating that the Spirit governs the church—that is, the Spirit owns and distributes all the spiritual gifts listed here that structure the church body.

Paul first speaks of a variety of "gifts," "ministries," and "energies" granted to the church body by the Spirit, the Lord Jesus, and God the Father, respectively (12:4–6). However, only the Spirit is personally manifest to each believer, and this "manifestation" is given "for the common good" (12:7). Believers are responsible for bringing their unique gifts (listed in 12:8–10) into the body as a benefit to all.

Then Paul uses three verbs to further explain the Spirit's sovereignty with respect to the church (12:11). First, the same Spirit "works" (ἐνεργεῖ) all the gifts and manifestations listed. A critique we sometimes hear today is that a particular church is "dead." According to this verse, the Spirit brings life and energy into the body through these gifts. That is, beyond the church's preaching, outreach, missions, community, and sacraments lies a suprahuman element, a divine energy not completely explained through words. Next, the Spirit is "distributing" (διαιροῦν) these gifts to "each one." The Spirit apportions and personalizes these gifts, providing a proper "fit" for each member. The Spirit appears as a coordinator who deftly matches persons with their proper place for maximum effectiveness. Hans Urs von Balthasar states that only the Holy Spirit "can close the tragic breach between person and role in mission."[75] Third, the Spirit distributes these gifts "as [the Spirit] wills" (καθὼς βούλεται). The Spirit remains sovereign as he structures the church (see also Heb. 2:4). Miroslav Volf comments,

> The Spirit works, first, *as* the Spirit chooses; no church, neither an entire (local) church nor any structure in the church, can prescribe which gifts the

74. See Stanley M. Burgess, *The Holy Spirit: Medieval Roman Catholic and Reformation Traditions* (Peabody, MA: Hendrickson, 1997), 147–49.

75. Hans Urs von Balthasar, *Theo-Drama: Theological Dramatic Theory* (San Francisco: Ignatius Press, 1998), 1:646.

> Spirit is to bestow upon which members. Furthermore, the Spirit works *when* the Spirit chooses; the church cannot determine at which time the Spirit is to bestow its gifts. This clearly reveals that the church lives from a dynamic not drawing from itself. . . . It is not the church that "organizes" its life, but rather the Holy Spirit.[76]

This verse is therefore a strong charge for trusting the Spirit to govern the church—to organize the church and each person's "place" within. Only the Spirit possesses these gifts, activates them, and fine-tunes them for the church community. And only the Spirit fosters a true diversity, one that respects the "otherness" of each believer's gift.[77]

Verse 13 is pivotal, adding that the "one Spirit" unifies all through his "baptism." Spirit baptism brings each new believer into the "one body," and should be thought of as an initial identification with the eschatological kingdom of God.[78] The end result is that each member has been "made to drink of one Spirit"—that is, given the capacity for a deep, personalized interaction with the Spirit in every part of one's humanity.[79]

Two major themes can be drawn from this study of 1 Corinthians 12. First, though the NT does not deny a vital *connection* between the Spirit and the church, the NT is clear to never *confuse* the Spirit (and the Spirit's work) with the church (and her diverse "works of ministry," including preaching, sacraments, organization, and so on). The Spirit's distinction from the church allows the Spirit to enter the church body and bring forth true "liberation" (2 Cor. 3:17). As the church relinquishes her concern for establishing her own "authority" in the world, she becomes "free" to be structured and guided by the Spirit. Hans Küng suggests,

76. Miroslav Volf, *After Our Likeness: The Church as the Image of the Trinity* (Grand Rapids: Eerdmans, 1997), 231–32.

77. According to Colin Gunton, 1 Corinthians 12 challenges the modern world's tendency toward homogeneity because by the Spirit's action human beings are constituted in their uniqueness and particular networks of relation (*The One, the Three and the Many* [New York: Cambridge, 1993], 183–84).

78. Jesus clarified this in Acts 1. His central teaching regarding the kingdom of God, after his resurrection, was that he would soon "baptize you in the Holy Spirit" (Acts 1:5). The disciples' response further confirms this (1:6). Jesus then explains that the future kingdom of God is coming to them now in the form of the Holy Spirit and his "power" (1:8).

79. "Drink" is sometimes used of irrigation or saturation, and suggests the thought of abundant supply (Leon Morris, *1 Corinthians*, Tyndale New Testament Commentaries [Grand Rapids: Eerdmans, 1975], 170–71).

> A Church which distinguishes between itself and the Holy Spirit can face up to sin and failure in the Church soberly and humbly, but also with the liberating hope of those already justified that they will be forgiven anew. . . . [T]he Church which humbly distinguishes itself from the free Spirit of God is for all its undeniable weakness strong, and for all its apparent unfreedom ultimately free.[80]

This distinction ensures the Spirit's rightful place as moral sanctifier of the church. Exodus 25–40 illustrates the Spirit's moral authority in the creation of the tabernacle (and of the temple that appears later).[81] The tabernacle was structured with precise dimensions and specifications in preparation for the Spirit's holy presence; some of these instructions, if disobeyed, were punishable by expulsion or death (Exod. 28:35, 43; 30:34–38). Such temple imagery is picked up by Paul in 1 Cor. 3:16–17: "Do you not know that you are a temple of God and that the Spirit of God dwells in you? If any man destroys the temple of God, God will destroy him, for the temple of God is holy, and that is what you are." The Spirit has now replaced the ritual holiness of the temple with an indwelling holiness, a Lordship conferring divine presence and moral purity.[82]

Each era of theological history seems to have found ways of "domesticating" the Spirit within the church. Some contemporary pneumatologies blend the Spirit's "energy" with the church's fellowship; others show more regard for the Spirit's "pluralism" than for the "one Spirit." Michael Welker, for example, develops his pneumatology against the background of "postmodern sensitivities," which abandon the assumption of a "unity of reality" and instead "assume a reality that consists of a plurality of structural patterns of life and of interconnected events."[83] His admirable goal is to grant personal access to the Spirit without sliding back into "modern" theologies that, in adhering to a single theological method, attempt to put God and God's power at our disposal.

80. Hans Küng, *The Church* (New York: Sheed & Ward, 1967), 175.

81. "Throughout the OT, the Spirit is present in some form during all sacred construction projects, be it the creation of Eden, the Mosaic tabernacle, or the Solomonic or exilic temple" (Wilf Hildebrandt, *An Old Testament Theology of the Spirit of God* [Peabody, MA: Hendrickson, 1995], 47).

82. See Fee, *God's Empowering Presence*, 113.

83. Michael Welker, *God the Spirit* (Minneapolis: Fortress, 1994), 37–38.

Welker's approach, however, results in a "Spiritology from below,"[84] one that begins with human experience. Welker often refers to the Spirit as a "force field" that liberates people from powerlessness, oppression, and bondage.[85] Thus, in using terms borrowed from electromagnetism, the Spirit seems to have been reduced to a functional power within the world—a power to liberate pluralistic communities. Welker holds that the Spirit is no longer "above" the world but rather influences and transforms the world through "intersubjective contexts."[86] According to Nancy Dallavalle, "one might ask how Welker allows for the transcendence of this very public and concrete Spirit, particularly in his assertion that the Spirit brings the gift of the 'clear knowledge of God.'"[87] Gunton warns of such reductions within the church: "[I]f we cannot conceive of the Spirit as the free Lord, then we may succumb to the temptation of identifying him with some immanent causal force: with our ecclesiastical or political institutions, or with some private experiences and beliefs."[88]

A second major theme emerging from 1 Corinthians 12 is that the Spirit expresses his own Lordship in the church and the world through specific "callings." By granting "gifts," "ministries," and "effects" to believers "for the common good" (12:7) the Spirit seeks to create "holy callings" that affirm each believer's distinct "mission" and that show forth the power of the Spirit in practical ways. Each mission is grounded in a spiritual gift and is designed to assist in meeting essential human needs that exist within the church.[89]

Church leaders possess a special "calling" as part of the Spirit's administration of the local church body (see Acts 13:2). The Spirit grants leaders a "functional authority" (rather than a "personal" one)[90] for the purpose of

84. This is Donald Bloesch's assessment of Welker (Bloesch, *The Holy Spirit* [Downers Grove, IL: InterVarsity Press, 2000], 260).

85. Welker, *God the Spirit*, 228–29.

86. This is Peter Hodgson's summary of Welker's pneumatology (Hodgson, *Winds of Spirit: A Constructive Christian Theology* [Louisville: Westminster John Knox, 1994], 282).

87. Nancy Dallavalle, review of *God the Spirit*, by Michael Welker, *Theological Studies* 56 (1995): 796.

88. Gunton, *Theology through the Theologians*, 189.

89. The seven spiritual gifts of Romans 12:5–8 are granted because "each member belongs to all the others": "Prophecy" meets spiritual needs; "serving," practical needs; "teaching," intellectual needs; "encouragement," psychological needs; "giving," material needs; "leadership," functional needs; "mercy," emotional needs.

90. "Functional authority" is granted to servant-leaders to minister the Word and to use the gifts of the Spirit. John Thiel explains, "[A]uthority in the Church is mediated by the Spirit who, as both

"equipping the saints for the work of ministry" (Eph. 4:12). This implies that leaders are to assist in the activation of the Spirit's gifts so that believers might find and fulfill their unique callings in and through the church. Church leaders are responsible for leading the church in a way that the Spirit might be recognized as her true Governor. James Elder Cumming asserts:

> The actual Rule of the Holy Ghost within the Church, which is under His control . . . at once opens up regarding what we might call the Business of the Church. There is, for one thing, the question of its government . . . . "He gave some to be apostles; and some, prophets; and some, evangelists; and some, pastors and teachers" (Eph. 4:8–12). All these are "governments" set over the Church by the authority and decision of the Holy Ghost.[91]

Church leaders also need to trust the Holy Spirit with the growth, structure, and guidance of the body. William Smalley sees in Western churches the need to replace "paternalism" (for example, a pattern of control over the Spirit) with the Spirit's Lordship: "We are treating [the Holy Spirit] as a small child with a new toy too complicated and dangerous for him to handle. Our paternalism is not only a paternalism toward other peoples; it is also a paternalism towards God."[92]

Church leaders and laity find common ground in their need to submit to the Spirit as the Governor who is present and active, working to enliven the church and to activate her gifts. This can be a bit unsettling at first, particularly for church bodies that have operated according to rigid procedures and methods. It may result in a certain level of unexpected disorder, temporary excesses,

divine communication and the power of believer's commitment, *is* the 'how' of responsibility toward God. In other words, how authority dwells in the Church, how it is exercised, and how it is evaluated and questioned are in large measure a matter of determining how believers are responsible to the Spirit who enables their belief and action" (*Senses of Tradition: Continuity and Development in the Catholic Faith* [New York: Oxford University Press, 2000], 165–66).

91. James Elder Cumming, *Through the Eternal Spirit* (Minneapolis: Bethany Fellowship, 1985), 100.

92. William A. Smalley, "Cultural Implications of an Indigenous Church," in *Perspectives on the World Christian Movement: A Reader*, ed. Ralph D. Winter (Pasadena, CA: William Carey Library, 1983), 502. According to Stephen Bevans, church leaders that respect the Spirit's Lordship "can avoid the danger of preaching the Gospel as if one controlled its message, or as if that message could be exhaustively expressed in objective, rational categories" ("God Inside Out: Toward a Missionary Theology of the Holy Spirit," *International Bulletin of Missionary Research* 22 [1998]: 104).

abuse of gifts, and exposure of immaturity—the same problems that were encountered by Paul in Corinth. James Packer's warning at the conclusion of his treatise on the Spirit also serves well at the conclusion of ours:

> The Corinthian disorders were due to an uncontrolled overflow of Holy Spirit life. Many churches today are orderly simply because they are asleep, and with fears that it is the sleep of death. It is no great thing to have order in a cemetery! The real and deplorable carnality and immaturity of the Corinthian Christians, which Paul censures so strongly elsewhere in the letter, must not blind us to the fact that they were enjoying the ministry of the Holy Spirit in a way in which we today are not.[93]

93. James I. Packer, *Keep in Step with the Spirit* (Grand Rapids: Baker, 1984), 249.

CHAPTER 5

Pneumatology from the Perspective of the Spirit

A Historical and Theological Assessment

WOLFGANG VONDEY

Pneumatology is a theological discipline concerned fundamentally with the nature and person of the Spirit of God, a concern that has now emerged in Christian systematic theologies as a theological discussion in its own right. The renaissance of pneumatology in the West has alerted theology to the importance of the Spirit across the theological spectrum. In the past, often subsumed under the discussions of Christology, soteriology, Trinitarian theology, or ecclesiology, the doctrine of the Holy Spirit has moved from last to first place in many theological conversations. A perspective of the Spirit has become the methodological view of choice for biblical, historical, theological, and interdisciplinary conversations. However, while the perspective of the Spirit has come to define contemporary theology in significant ways, the same cannot be said for the study of the Spirit proper, the person and nature of the Holy Spirit *as* spirit. At the heart of the discipline, pneumatology itself is still carried out largely within the domain of other theological perspectives, that is, *not* from the perspective of spirit.

Pneumatology from the perspective of spirit is initially confronted with the theological notion of spirit itself. A noteworthy biblical application of this perspective is offered by Jesus' statement that "God is spirit" (John 4:24). A metaphysical reading of this affirmation, which would suggest that God by nature is spirit, has been neglected as a theological theme in its own right in the articulation of pneumatology. Articulations of the doctrine have tended instead to favor a theologically oriented hermeneutic, which emphasizes a Trinitarian perspective on the divine person of the Holy Spirit without accounting also for "spirit" as a term for the divine nature. In the contemporary renaissance of pneumatology, the foundational Johannine testimony that "God *is* spirit" has played no significant role for an understanding of the nature and person of the Spirit.

As a foundational pneumatological statement, the metaphysical hermeneutic of saying, "God is spirit," finds historical expression in efforts to reconcile the tension between identifying the Spirit either with the divine nature *or* with a divine person. The first option leads to a pneumatology from the metaphysical perspective of spirit, the second to a pneumatology from the theological perspective of the Spirit. In this essay I suggest that the two positions have not been reconciled. While this distinction is somewhat artificial, it serves to highlight the problems associated with the notion of spirit as a root metaphor for contemporary pneumatology. In order to confirm these concerns, this essay traces the roots of the distinction between spirit and the Spirit in early Christian theology and pneumatology. I then examine the continuing conversation in the history of the definition of personhood and conclude with a contemporary theological appropriation of this historical conversation. This narrative suggests a general neglect of the unfolding of the full perspective of the notion of spirit from the history of pneumatology and illustrates that the root of this neglect is found in a theological focus on the person of the Holy Spirit that does not draw from a metaphysical identification of the divine nature.

The Perspective of the Spirit in Early Christian Theology

A theology of the Holy Spirit as a doctrine in its own right was not widely pursued during the first centuries.[1] Nonetheless, the central

1. See Michel René Barnes, "The Beginning and the End of Early Christian Pneumatology," *Augustinian Studies* 39 (2008): 169–86; R. P. C. Hanson, *The Search for the Christian Doctrine of God:*

questions of Christian pneumatology during these early years focused on what exactly is meant by "spirit" and how this designation could be applied to God.[2] In general, the notion of spirit was widely understood as an indication of the divine presence, a metaphysical conceptualization of the divine nature, typically expressed in contrast to the material and corporeal world. In early patristic pneumatology, the determination that God by nature is spirit and that "spirit" is equally shared by the divine persons eventually met the demand to identify with the term "spirit" primarily, if not exclusively, the person of the Holy Spirit. The works of Irenaeus and Tertullian illustrate this challenge in both its conceptual demands and historical origins in East and West.

Among the Greek patristic writers, the thought of Irenaeus of Lyons is widely acknowledged as one of the earliest developed approaches to the doctrine of the Holy Spirit.[3] Arguably his most well-known contribution, Irenaeus identified the Spirit as one of the two hands of God. This metaphor expressed Irenaeus's dual conviction that the Spirit is divine, and thus distinct from humanity by virtue of the divine nature identified in John 4:24 as "spirit," and that the Spirit is cocreator, and thus distinct from the Son (as the other hand of God).[4]

The distinction of the Spirit from creation is made on the basis of ontological difference: all created beings "are inferior to, and later in existence than, the Word of God and His Spirit"[5] because God produced "the substance of matter,"[6] and as created matter the human being "is a compound being" while "God is . . . all active spirit . . . and always exists one and the same."[7] Yet, not

The Arian Controversy, 318–381 (London: T&T Clark, 1988), 741.

2. See Wolf-Dieter Hauschild and Volker Henning Drecoll, *Pneumatologie in der alten Kirche*, Traditio Christiana 12 (Bern: Lang, 2004); Franz Dünzl, *Pneuma: Funktion des theologischen Begriffs in frühchristlicher Literatur* (Münster: Aschendorff, 2000); Henry B. Swete, *On the Early History of the Doctrine of the Holy Spirit with Especial Reference to the Controversies of the Fourth Century* (Cambridge: Cambridge University Press, 1873).

3. See Anthony Briggman, *Irenaeus of Lyons and the Theology of the Holy Spirit* (Oxford: Oxford University Press, 2012); Hans-Jochen Jaschke, *Der Heilige Geist im Bekenntnis der Kirche: Eine Studie zur Pneumatologie des Irenäus von Lyon im Ausgang vom altchristlichen Glaubensbekenntnis* (Münster: Aschendorff, 1976).

4. See Briggman, *Irenaeus of Lyons*, 38.

5. Irenaeus of Lyons, *Against Heresies* 2.28.2 (*ANF* 1:399).

6. Ibid., 401.

7. Ibid., 400.

only "all material things, such as the heaven, and the whole world which exists below it"[8] but also all "spiritual things" and "spiritual creatures . . . were produced by a spiritual process of birth"[9] attributed to the work of God. For Irenaeus, this creation of spiritual things could only be attributed to a spiritual being: "This Being, therefore, also made spiritual things . . . ; and He is truly the Spirit of God . . . otherwise He should never have created spiritual things."[10] In this conclusion, Irenaeus goes far beyond any existing pneumatology of the time.[11] With the reference to the "Spirit of God," he did not refer to the Holy Spirit as one of the hands of God but to God as spirit in a metaphysical sense.[12] As creator, the God who produces material and spiritual beings must by nature be a spiritual being; as spirit, God produces all that is spiritual and material. The identification of God with spirit allowed Irenaeus to affirm that all things are created by one God.[13]

At the same time, the distinction of the Spirit from the Son is made on the basis of functional difference. By identifying the Spirit as one hand of God, Irenaeus attributes to the Holy Spirit a particular function in the creative activity of God different from the Son. However, that means, for Irenaeus, "spirit" designates both the divine nature and one of the hands of God.[14] This overlap of the dimensions of the Spirit may be considered a foundation for Irenaeus's theology of the Spirit as wisdom and the one who anoints Christ and the church—typically considered central aspects of his pneumatology—and yet they are abandoned in the subsequent history of pneumatology.[15] While Irenaeus did not explicitly state this dual interpretation, the instrumentality of the Holy Spirit as one hand of God is the result of the essential property of the Holy Spirit *as* spirit, which in Irenaeus's thought represents at once the essence of God's nature and thus source of divine activity and the actualization of that activity in Word and Wisdom. The tension between these two dimensions remained unresolved in Irenaeus and in early Christian pneumatology.

8. Ibid., 405.
9. Ibid.
10. Ibid., 405–6.
11. See Briggman, *Irenaeus of Lyons*, 44–45.
12. A. Rousseau, L. Doutreleau, and C. Mercier, eds., *Contre les hérésies*, Livre V, Tome I, Texte et traduction, Source chrétiennes 152 (Paris: Cerf, 1969), 317, 332.
13. Briggman, *Irenaeus of Lyons*, 38.
14. See ibid., 126–47.
15. Cf. ibid., 204–15.

In the Latin West, Irenaeus's ideas found parallel expression in the writings of Tertullian. Amid the challenges of modalism and monarchianism of the first centuries, Tertullian indicated that the dominant problem of Trinitarian thought was the tension of reconciling the monarchy of God with God's manifestation in the economy of salvation.[16] He argued that a comprehensive understanding of the divine monarchy required its redefinition through an economic model of the divine nature itself.[17] The unique dimension of this perspective is the interpretation of the divine economy ontologically through the notion of the divine substance.[18] Tertullian's work is generally identified as the first systematic use of the term "person" in the development of the doctrine of the Trinity.[19] Yet, his approach to divine personhood through the notion of divine substance "was apparently ignored and forgotten; it never reappeared in the whole course of subsequent theological development."[20]

Tertullian's reinterpretation of the divine monarchy in terms of the divine substance illustrates the difficulties of reconciling the doctrine of God with the emerging doctrine of the Holy Spirit. Theologically, Tertullian wished to attribute the divine substance in unity to the Father, the Son, and the Holy Spirit while distinguishing in this unity an order of origin and distribution.[21] Hence, the Son and the Spirit "are so closely joined with the Father in His substance" that they "are naturally members of the Father's own substance."[22] Nonetheless, the exact substance of the Father is not identified.

> All are of One, by unity (that is) of substance; while the mystery of the dispensation is still guarded, which distributes the Unity into a Trinity, placing in their order the three Persons—the Father, the Son, and the Holy Ghost: three, however,

16. Th. Verhoeven, "Monarchia dans Tertullien. Adversus Praxean," *Vigiliae Christianae* 5 (1951): 43–48.

17. Kevin B. McCruden, "Monarchy and Economy in Tertullian's Adversus Praxeam," *Scottish Journal of Theology* 55 (2002): 325–37.

18. R. A. Markus, "Trinitarian Theology and the Economy," *Journal of Theological Studies* 9 (1958): 89–102.

19. Bernd Jochen Hilberath, *Der Personbegriff der Trinitätstheologie in Rückfrage von Karl Rahner zu Tertullians "Adversus Praxean,"* Innsbrucker Theologische Studien (Innsbruck: Tyrolia, 1986).

20. G. L. Prestige, *God in Patristic Thought* (London: SPCK, 1952), 111.

21. Wolfgang Bender, *Die Lehre über den heiligen Geist bei Tertullian* (Munich: Max Hueber, 1961), 56–100.

22. Tertullian, *Against Praxeas* (*ANF* 3:599).

> not in condition but in degree; not in substance, but in form; not in power, but in aspect; yet of one substance, and of one condition, and of one power, inasmuch as He is one God, from whom these degrees and forms and aspects are reckoned, under the name of the Father, and of the Son, and of the Holy Ghost.[23]

The difficulty in using language of "substance" with regard to both the divine nature and the three persons is striking. Tertullian placed the origin of the divine nature in the Father, yet equated that divine nature with the notion of spirit: "By His [the Father's] word were the heavens established, and all the powers thereof by His Spirit—that is to say, by the Spirit (or Divine Nature) which was in the Word."[24] While the Father, Son, and Holy Spirit differ in degree, form, and aspect as to their substance, God is one in substance because "God is spirit."[25] Tertullian could say at the same time "that the Word is a certain substance, constructed by the Spirit" and that "Spirit has a bodily substance of its own kind, in its own form."[26] On the one hand, spirit as the unity of the divine substance protects the oneness of God, while on the other hand, the Spirit "guards"[27] the distinction of the divine persons. For Tertullian this unity-in-distinction by means of the distribution of the divine substance explained how "the connection of the Father in the Son, and of the Son in the Paraclete, produces three coherent Persons, who are yet distinct One from Another. These three are one *essence*, not one *Person* . . . in respect of unity of substance."[28] The Spirit of God is therefore "Declarer of the One *Monarchy of God*" (in substance), "but at the same time the Interpreter of the *Economy*"[29] (as person). Tertullian clearly distinguished the concept of divine nature from the notion of substance,[30] albeit without clarifying how the two concepts relate to the notion of person, in general, and to the subsistence of the three divine persons, in particular. With the neglect of this aspect of Tertullian's thought in subsequent theology, the notion of substance ceased to be of central importance to the articulation of pneumatology. This hindsight, that the pneumatological advances of

23. Ibid., 598.

24. Ibid., 602.

25. Ibid. See also Bender, *Die Lehre über den heiligen Geist*, 56n5.

26. Tertullian, *Against Praxeas*, *ANF* 3:602.

27. Ibid., 603.

28. Ibid., 620.

29. Ibid., 627 (emphasis original).

30. James F. Bethune-Baker, "Tertullian's Use of Substantia, Natura, and Persona," *Journal of Theological Studies* 4 (1903): 440–42.

both Irenaeus and Tertullian with regard to the identification of God as spirit were neglected in Christian thought, may explain the subsequent difficulties associated with the term "spirit" in Trinitarian thought.

Spirit as Person and Divine Essence in Early Trinitarian Theology

The pneumatological conversation before the formulations of the Nicene and Constantinopolitan Creeds (325 and 381 CE respectively) echoes the difficulties to distinguish a metaphysical affirmation of "spirit" from other uses of the term.[31] Select examples must suffice as evidence that the distinctions of Irenaeus and Tertullian were not taken to their theological conclusions but that pneumatology in the context of Trinitarian thought returned to the primary conceptual emphasis on the divinity of the Spirit. Athanasius consequently insisted that the Holy Spirit is never "called 'spirit' without qualification"[32] in relation to creation, since the Spirit is immutable, unchangeable, and omnipresent. Especially in his Trinitarian arguments, Athanasius understood the Spirit's divinity as an expression of God's omnipresence, which must be distinguished from creation itself. Hilary of Poitiers argued succinctly that the uncreated quality of spirit expresses negatively that "God is invisible, incomprehensible, immeasurable," and positively that God "is omnipresent in space and time" because "the Spirit cannot be shut up."[33] John Chrysostom concluded that with the statement in John 4:24, Jesus declared "nothing else than His incorporeal Nature."[34] Theodore of Mopsuestia stated that as spirit, "God is incorporeal in nature and cannot be circumscribed into any place" but that God "is everywhere."[35] As a metaphysical notion, "spirit" was applied to "God" as a synonym for the divine nature and with the implication that a theology of divine omnipresence also

31. Gérard Verbeke, *L'évolution de la doctrine du pneuma, du stoicisme à s. Augustin: Étude philosophique* (Paris: D. de Brouwer, 1945).

32. Athanasius, "Letters to Serapion on the Holy Spirit, Letter 1," in *Works on the Spirit: Athanasius and Didymus*, trans. Mark DelCogliano, Andrew Radde-Gallwitz, and Lewis Ayres, Popular Patristics Series 43, ed. John Behr (Yonkers, NY: St. Vladimir's Seminary Press, 2011), 53–105 (57).

33. Hilary of Poitiers, *On the Trinity* 2.31 (*NPNF*[2] 9:60); see also ibid., 73.

34. John Chrysostom, "Homily 33 [on the Gospel of John]" (*NPNF*[1] 14:116).

35. Theodore of Mopsuestia, *Commentary on the Gospel of John*, trans. Marco Conti, Ancient Christian Texts, ed. Joel C. Elowsky (Downers Grove, IL: InterVarsity Press, 2010), 42.

accounts at the same time for a theology of the person of the Holy Spirit. The metaphysical notion of spirit served to draw an analogy between the visible, material world and the invisible, immaterial one, both to ascertain that God by nature is present in this world and to affirm that God by nature differs from creation. This difference, however, is manifested not in the divine nature as such but in the manifestation of spirit in the divine persons. The identification of the divine essence as spirit with the person of the Holy Spirit represented an unresolved problem.

In his books on the Holy Spirit, Ambrose states that "the Holy Spirit is also the Author of the grace of the Spirit,"[36] seemingly distinguishing two uses of "spirit." And yet he interprets John 4:24 elsewhere first as reference to the Father,[37] and then to both the Father and the Son.[38] The well-known treatise of Basil of Caesarea on the Holy Spirit states succinctly that the title "Holy Spirit" designates "everything that is incorporeal, purely immaterial, and indivisible"[39] and that the Spirit is by nature equal to and inseparable from the Father and the Son. Yet, Basil's exposition of the Holy Spirit as a third hypostasis, addressing objections to the divinity of the Spirit, does not reconcile the personhood of the Spirit with the divine nature. The unity of divine nature is established by the procession of the Spirit as person and not by the substance of the divine nature as spirit.[40] Gregory of Nyssa, similarly, advocated that in the oneness of the divine nature "the power of the Spirit [is] . . . included with the Father and the Son in the life-giving power," so that the Spirit "has an inseparable association with them in all the attributes ascribed in a sense of a special excellence."[41] He provides no explanation as to the nature of that distinctive. Elsewhere, Gregory speaks in the same breath of the "peculiar attributes" of the Holy Spirit, who is "to be regarded separately in certain distinctive properties," and of "an exact identity" with the Father and the Son.[42] Yet, in his subsequent elaboration on the identity of the divine nature, the Spirit is again distinguished from the divine essence.[43] The advocacy of the Spirit's divinity

36. Ambrose of Milan, "Three Books of St. Ambrose on the Holy Spirit" (*NPNF*² 10:122).

37. Ibid., 145.

38. Ibid., 107.

39. Basil of Caesarea, *On the Holy Spirit* (*NPNF*² 8:15).

40. Ibid., 29.

41. Gregory of Nyssa, *On the Holy Trinity, and of the Godhead of the Holy Spirit* (*NPNF*² 5:327).

42. Gregory of Nyssa, *On the Holy Spirit: Against the Followers of Macedonius*, in ibid., 315–16.

43. Ibid., 317 (emphasis mine).

shifts the conversation continually between the property of the Holy Spirit as person and the identity of the divine nature as spirit.

The contemporary work of Didymus the Blind illuminates a principal conflation of the divine nature in favor of the personhood of the Spirit. In his commentary on John, he contrasts "the Spirit spoken of here" (John 4:24) to the air and wind in motion in the world, and by identifying "spirit" with the unconfined nature of the divine essence, defines God with the term "spirit" as "an incorporeal and life-giving Being."[44] The implications of this equation are made explicit in his letters on the Holy Spirit, where Didymus distinguishes formally between "the designation 'Holy Spirit' and the substance which is indicated by this designation."[45] Initially, the pneumatological designation "indicates the underlying essence that is associated with the Father and the Son."[46] Like his contemporaries, Didymus defines this essence in contrast to creation as well as apophatically: the Spirit "does not have a circumscribed substance" but is "impassible and indivisible and immutable."[47] However, he asserts that the Father, Son, and Holy Spirit share a single activity, and therefore must "also have a single substance."[48] As a designation for the divine substance, the term "spirit" applies equally to the Father, Son, and Holy Spirit, "because a single nature possesses a shared name."[49] Consequently, Didymus treats Jesus' declaration that "God is spirit" as a reference to the Father, to the Son, to the Holy Spirit, *and* as a synonym for the entire Trinity.[50] Effectively, "spirit" is a designation for both the divine nature and the person of the Holy Spirit (albeit without being a distinctive property of the Holy Spirit as person).

Little distinction is made between the nature of God *as* spirit and the property of the divine persons conceptualized by the term "spirit" or the particular person of the Holy Spirit. While the early construct of the doctrine of the Trinity alerted the patristic writers to the need to develop a technical vocabulary for the doctrine of God, this demand did not immediately force the articulation of a pneumatological perspective. As a result, the

44. Didymus the Blind, "Fragments on John 3," in *Johannes-kommentare aus der griechischen Kirche*, ed. Joseph Reuss (Berlin: Akademie Verlag, 1966), 178.

45. Didymus the Blind, "On the Holy Spirit," in *Works on the Spirit*, 143–227 (143).

46. Ibid., 146.

47. Ibid., 150 and 155.

48. Ibid., 168.

49. Ibid., 216.

50. Ibid., 216, 221, 251.

monarchian notion of God, particularly in its Sabellian expression, confounded the use of the term "spirit" by designating both the divine nature and the person of the Father, who extends himself by virtue of being spirit into the Son and the Holy Spirit.[51] The formula "three persons, one substance" tended to introduce a distinction precisely between the two dimensions it was intended to join: the unity of substance and the relation of the divine persons.[52] Similarly, the divine nature of Christ and the concept of the incarnation are repeatedly described as "the Spirit" or the "Spirit of God," both as existing eternally and in taking on human form.[53] Yet, the theological conversation on the two natures of Christ is dedicated wholly to the theology of the Son with no substantive contributions from pneumatology.[54]

With the dominance assumed particularly in the West by Augustine's psychological model for the Trinity, the property of the Holy Spirit as person identified as the mutual love between the Father and the Son could no longer be distinguished from love as the essential property of the divine nature.[55] Conversation about the Holy Spirit remained in a state of uncertainty, oscillating between the notions of personhood and divine substance. The Holy Spirit is the "bond" between the Father and the Son by virtue of the Spirit's identity with the divine love.[56] As person, however, neither the procession of the Holy Spirit nor the relations of the Spirit to the Father and the Son are thus clearly identifiable.

> The Trinity can be called, in its entirety, the Holy Spirit, according to that which is written, "God is a Spirit," because both the Father is a spirit and the Son is a spirit. . . . Therefore, since . . . God is a spirit, the Trinity can be called also the Holy Spirit. But yet that Holy Spirit, who is not the Trinity, but is understood as in

51. Athanasius, *Against the Arians* 4.25 (*NPNF*[2] 4:443).

52. Cf. Ludwig Hermann, "Ambrosius von Mailand als Trinitätstheologe," *Zeitschrift für Kirchengeschichte* 69 (1958): 197–218.

53. Hanson, *Search for the Christian Doctrine of God*, 738; Swete, *On the Early History*, 15.

54. Hanson, *Search for the Christian Doctrine of God*, 760–72.

55. Michael Schmaus, *Die psychologische Trinitätslehre des heiligen Augustinus*, Münsterische Beiträge zur Theologie 11 (Münster: Aschendorff, 1927), 387. Cf. Lewis Ayres, *Nicaea and Its Legacy: An Approach to Fourth Century Trinitarian Theology* (Oxford: Oxford University Press, 2004); and Ayres, *Augustine and the Trinity* (Cambridge: Cambridge University Press, 2010).

56. See Augustine, *On the Trinity* 8.10 (*NPNF*[1] 3:124).

the Trinity, is spoken of in His proper name of the Holy Spirit relatively, since he is referred both to the Father and to the Son, because the Holy Spirit is the Spirit of both the Father and of the Son. But the relation is not itself apparent in that name. . . . Therefore the Holy Spirit is a certain unutterable communion of the Father and the Son.[57]

The recognition of the distinct personhood of the Holy Spirit met with the idea of also designating as "spirit" the divine nature, without articulating how the divine nature relates to the divine persons in a way that protects the term "spirit" for both entities. Pneumatology in subsequent centuries did not clarify the distinction between person and nature with regard to the Holy Spirit. In this context, pneumatology from the perspective of spirit became identified with pneumatology from the perspective of the Holy Spirit. This equation, however, is responsible not only for the neglect of the notion of spirit in the historical unfolding of the doctrine of God but also for a flattening of pneumatology to a theology of the Third Article at the expense of severing the person of the Spirit from conversations on the unity of the divine essence.

57. Ibid., 93.

The Perspective of Spirit in the History of Personhood

The problematic task of reconciling the Holy Spirit as person with the designation of the divine nature as spirit is well illustrated in the history of the terminology of "person." Generally considered a milestone in this development is the definition of Boethius. Taken as a basis for the continuing theological conversations of the Middle Ages, Boethius's identification of "person" as "the individual substance of a rational nature"[58] connected personhood explicitly with the notion of substance. Significantly, Boethius linked substance with subsistence and defined the ontological reality of person as "subsistences which acquired substance . . . which supplies to other things . . . a substrate enabling them to be."[59] He thus connected a possible identification of divine persons not merely with the particularity of substance in its own right but with the subsistence (of substance) that forms its ontological ground

58. Boethius, "A Treatise against Eutyches and Nestorius," in *Boethius: The Theological Tractates*, trans. H. F. Stewart, E. K. Rand, and S. J. Tester, Loeb Classical Library 74 (Cambridge, MA: Harvard University Press, 1973), 85.

59. Ibid., 89.

of being.[60] However, Boethius did not show how this definition accounts for divine personhood: (1) what exactly the divine substance is; (2) whether the divine substance is identical with rational nature; and (3) if divine personhood is necessarily defined by that identity.[61] The difficulty of applying Boethius's definition to the two natures in the one person of Christ is well established.[62] The pneumatological consequences drawn from the definition are typically subsumed under a Trinitarian perspective and not made explicit. If spirit is the divine substance and thus identical with the rational nature (which Boethius did not claim!), then the Holy Spirit would in subsistence (as person) be identical with the divine substance (as spirit). In other words, while the divine substance in the strict sense of the definition must be applied to each of the divine persons individually (that is, in their subsistence), it is only the Holy Spirit to whom the individual substance of spirit can be applied as property of person (lest the three divine persons are equally spirit as person). That means, if all three divine persons are spirit in substance, this would sufficiently define the singular divine substance as only one person unless that substance subsists differently in each person and in a particular way in the Holy Spirit. Boethius consequently reinterpreted the divine persons as subsistences of the one divine substance (effectively identical with the rational nature), yet without clarifying how the single divine nature can be present differently in each person and thereby define the persons as individual substances of the same nature. What exactly Boethius means by "individual" and how this individuality can be applied to each divine person remained undefined. Attempts to resolve this problem in subsequent history have abandoned the notion of substance in favor of the mode of existence. A pneumatology from the perspective of spirit was thus effectively transferred to a discussion of personhood without an ontological foundation in the divine substance.

Boethius's definition was corrected in the twelfth century by Richard of St. Victor, who questioned its applicability to the divine persons. The fact that the triune God is of one substance denied the possibility that an individual substance could be the basis for divine personhood, since that would either divide

60. Michael Elsässer, "Das Person-Verständnis des Boethius" (DPhil diss., University of Würzburg, 1973), 76–78.

61. Ibid., 78.

62. See Hilberath, *Der Personbegriff*, 110–12.

God into three substances or attribute to the single substance only a singular personhood.[63] Richard, in turn, identified divine personhood by existence rather than substance, that is, by "what is the principal thing in a substance" or more precisely "what has being in itself and what possesses being from another source."[64] Significant to his definition is not the mode of being but the mode of origin.[65] Hence, the notion of individuality was understood in terms of the "incommunicable existence of a divine nature,"[66] which defines the property of each divine person. With this view of the three persons, there exists for Richard "in the divine nature both an existence common to plural persons and an existence appropriate for one person alone."[67] Nonetheless, he excludes the common existence of the divine persons from the definition, since it is communicable, and elevates in its place the notion of the divine processions, which indicate the origin of each person and hence identify their incommunicable existence. The distinction of divine persons is attributed to the mode of procession: the Holy Spirit is the only person who proceeds from two persons.[68] The Spirit is thus identified as person by the relation to the other divine persons (who in turn are identified by their relations to each other). The notion of substance is here important only for the attribution of divinity but no longer for the identity as person, since in relation to the Father and the Son "the Spirit of God is certainly consubstantial and wholly equal" and thus the nature of spirit "refers to some similitude of his own property."[69] Hence Richard can state that "the Father is a spirit, and the Son is a spirit, just as we have learned from the Gospel: *God is Spirit*."[70] Investigating how the term "spirit" is a designation for all three divine persons but is the proper name of only one person leads Richard to suggest that the Spirit as person "has a much greater resemblance to the divine property."[71] With this he refers to

63. Richard of St. Victor, *On the Trinity* 5.21, in *Trinity and Creation*, Victorine Texts in Translation 1, ed. Boyd Taylor Coolman and Dale M. Coulter (Tornhout: Brepols, 2010), 286–87.

64. Ibid., 288.

65. Heinz Robert Schlette, "Das unterschiedliche Personverständnis im theologischen Denken Hugos und Richards v. St. Viktor," in *Miscellanea*, ed. Martin Grabmann and Ludwig Hödl (Munich: Huber, 1959), 55–72.

66. Richard of St. Victor, *On the Trinity* 4.22, in *Trinity and Creation*, 287–88.

67. Ibid.

68. Ibid., 304.

69. Ibid., 327.

70. Ibid., 328.

71. Ibid.

the divine nature, so that spirit proceeds as spirit; yet with regard to the person of the Holy Spirit, Richard is clear that the divine property as spirit exists differently in the three divine persons: possessing and giving the divine plenitude is the property of the Father and the Son, whereas "possessing and not giving it to another is the particular property of the Holy Spirit."[72] The notion of spirit now identifies the property of the divine substance and the possession of that property in an incommunicable way by each person. For the identification of the Holy Spirit, however, the identity of the divine substance as spirit is of no consequence to the property of the Spirit as person.

In a subsequent modification of the definition, Thomas Aquinas acknowledged Boethius's definition and sought to explain the individuality of the divine persons by distinguishing between two definitions of substance: "In one sense it is the ultimate subject which is not predicated of another: and this is the individual in the genus of substance: while in another sense it is the form or nature of a subject."[73] The divine persons thus share a common substance and each person possesses that divine essence by the principle of individuation lest that person be identical with the divine nature. The designation of the divine nature as "spirit" is therefore shared by the three persons, yet it does not indicate sufficiently in their designation as persons "the mode of subsistence which belongs to particular substances."[74] Person is defined as "a subsistent individual of a rational nature,"[75] and the mode of subsistence, as for Richard, can be defined in God "only by relation of origin"[76] and is therefore incommunicable.[77] Each divine person signifies a relation as subsisting by way of the divine substance, and this relation is a subsistence in the divine nature, "although in truth that which subsists in the divine nature is the divine nature itself."[78] As with his predecessors, Thomas thus struggled with the identity as persons held in common by the Father, Son, and Holy Spirit by way

72. Ibid., 329.

73. Thomas Aquinas, *De potentia Dei* 9.1c, in *On the Power of God*, trans. English Dominican Fathers (Westminster, MD: The Newman Press, 1952), 98–99.

74. Thomas Aquinas, *Summa theologiae* I, q. 29, a. 1, *ad* 3, in *Summa Theologica*, trans. Fathers of the English Dominican Province (New York: Benziger Bros., 1947), 351.

75. Ibid., I, q. 29, a. 3, 354.

76. Ibid., I, q. 29, a. 4, 357.

77. Thomas von Aquino, *Das Geheimnis der Person (Summa Theologica 29, 1, 1–3)*, ed. and trans. Alfons Hufnagel (Stuttgart: Klett, 1949), 35–38.

78. Aquinas, *Summa Theologica*, I, q. 29, a. 4, 357.

of the unity of the divine essence, and their subsistence as persons by way of their opposite relations. As for Richard, the Holy Spirit is person by the Spirit's procession "from another, or from others."[79] Whereas paternity constitutes the Father as person, and filiation constitutes the Son, procession is the personal notion attributed only to the Holy Spirit.[80] Procession, however, is a designation of the relation of persons to one another, not of person to substance. Although he insists that "in God relation is really the same as the essence,"[81] Thomas does not explain how each divine person subsists distinctly in the divine nature by virtue of the relation, in general, and in the particular case where the name for the divine substance and the person are identical. He indicates vaguely that "spirit" as a name for the divine person indicates "something in common with the other Persons . . . for the Father also is a spirit, and the Son is a spirit."[82] At the same time, echoing the history of pneumatology, the designation "Holy Spirit . . . is applicable to the whole Trinity: because by 'spirit' the immateriality of the divine substance is signified."[83] Thomas does not attempt to reconcile these inconsistencies except to reference "that the divine simplicity requires that in God essence is the same as . . . person,"[84] even though relation does not differ from essence but only by the opposition as persons. The theology of the Holy Spirit distinguishes the Spirit as person from the other divine persons on the basis of procession, since the divine substance offers in his perspective no information on the particular mode of existence. The name "Spirit" is consequently absent from Thomas's discussion of the essential names of God. Although it is consistent with his thought to argue that Spirit "sometimes stands for the essence," as when we say "God is spirit" (John 4:24), and "sometimes it stands for the person,"[85] as in the name for the Holy Spirit, pneumatology from the perspective of the Spirit proceeds in principle exclusively on the basis of personhood. The focus of pneumatology thus shifts from the divine essence as the principle of union to the divine relations as "the principle of distinction"[86] for each divine person. Pneumatology on the basis of personhood,

79. Ibid., I, q. 32, a. 3, 385.

80. Ibid.

81. Thomas Aquinas, *On the Power of God* (*De potentia Dei*) 9.4c, 114–16.

82. Thomas Aquinas, *Summa Theologica*, I, q. 36, a. 1, 412.

83. Ibid.

84. Ibid., 434.

85. Ibid., 440.

86. Ibid., I, q. 40, a.2, 457.

however, has no need of pneumatology of the divine essence insofar as substance constitutes personhood, in general, but not the individual persons in the case of the divine Trinity.[87] The Spirit is constituted as person by way of procession, although it is entirely unclear how the Spirit participates in this procession as person in a manner that is constitutive of the Spirit's own personhood and how this personhood is to be distinguished from the divine nature.

The Holy Spirit as Person in Contemporary Theology

It is not until the twentieth century that we find an explicit study of the personhood of the Holy Spirit in the work of Heribert Mühlen.[88] From Mühlen's perspective, Thomas had expanded the definition of Boethius to a new form of thought on the person by referring to the singularity of the individual, or the principle of individuation, as that which distinguishes a person as a self-existent being.[89] This emphasis suggested with regard to the Trinity that the term "person" could not be universally applied to all three divine persons, since they are persons in different modes of existence. Following the further modification of Thomas's definition by John Duns Scotus, Mühlen concluded that a divine person had to be identified not merely by subsistence in itself but also by a relative subsistence over against another.[90] For Duns Scotus, being as actual existence was possible only in a relation of person to person, which beyond Richard's emphasis on the relation of origin led to a more direct view of personhood. Four essential requirements were thus posited by Mühlen for the identification of the Spirit as person: pneumatology had to express the intellectual nature of the Spirit, the incommunicable existence of the Spirit, the Spirit's

87. See Gilles Emery, *The Trinitarian Theology of St. Thomas Aquinas* (Oxford: Oxford University Press, 2007), 219–97.

88. Heribert Mühlen, *Der Heilige Geist als Person: Beitrag zur Frage nach der dem Heiligen Geiste eigentümlichen Funktion in der Trinität, bei der Inkarnation und im Gnadenbund* (Münster: Aschendorff, 1963). See Wolfgang Vondey, *Heribert Mühlen: His Theology and Praxis; A New Profile of the Church* (Lanham, MD: University Press of America, 2004), 49–98.

89. Mühlen, *Der Heilige Geist als Person*, 35–36; Heribert Mühlen, *Das Vorverständnis von Person und die evangelisch-katholische Differenz: Zum Problem der theologischen Denkform* (Münster: Aschendorff, 1965), 42.

90. Heribert Mühlen, *Sein und Person nach Johannes Duns Scotus: Beitrag zur Grundlegung einer Metaphysik der Person* (Werl: Dietrich-Coelde-Verlag, 1954), 78–94.

relation of origin, and the person-to-person relations of the Spirit in the Trinity. He concluded that "in place of the univocally used word 'person' one should properly have three different words at one's disposal, in which is expressed both the personhood of each person as well as its distinction from the other two persons."[91] Mühlen's search for potential vocabulary found in Scripture the particular use of the personal pronouns "I," "thou," and "we" as expressions of a proper distinction of each divine person as well as of their relation to one another. His reading of Scripture suggested that it was possible to designate the Father as the inner-Trinitarian "I" and the Son as the "Thou." Furthermore, their relations take the form of two fundamental modes: the I-thou encounter and the we-union; the former exists in the mode of reciprocity, the latter as a consequence of a common act, of two persons. The relationship of the Father and the Son could thus be understood analogously as an I-thou relation and the procession of the Holy Spirit from the Father and the Son as a we-union.[92] The Holy Spirit, Mühlen concluded, could be called the "we in person" between the Father and Son.

Mühlen found support for his argument in the Augustinian emphasis on the procession of the Holy Spirit from the reciprocal love between the Father and the Son and the traditional declaration that the Spirit proceeds from the two persons in only one common act of spiration (*duo spirantes, sed unus spirator*).[93] The first emphasis accentuates that the Spirit proceeds from two *persons*, while the other underscores that the Father and the Son are not two principles of the Holy Spirit but numerically identical with the one divine *nature*. From the perspective of persons, the Father and the Son are two necessary and independent partial principles of the one spiration.[94] From the perspective of the divine nature, although the Father and the Son are two spirating persons, they together possess only one spirative power. Active spiration could therefore be understood as the we-union between the Father and the Son, who bring forth the Holy Spirit in a common we-act. From this perspective, the one

91. Mühlen, *Der Heilige Geist als Person*, 105. All translations of Mühlen's *Der Heilige Geist als Person* are my own.

92. Vondey, *Heribert Mühlen*, 72–79.

93. See Heinrich Denzinger, *Enchiridium symbolorum definitionum et declarationeum de rebus fidei at morum*, 38th ed., ed., rev., and trans. Peter Hünermann and Helmut Hoping (Herder: Freiburg, 1999), 527, 850, 1300.

94. Mühlen, *Der Heilige Geist als Person*, 149–51.

divine nature appears as a relation, that is, the common relation of the Father and the Son to the Holy Spirit, and the natural aspect of spiration embraces in this respect the plurality of divine persons.[95] The divine nature, consequently, should from the beginning be conceived as a relational structure, the form of a we, which then "develops" through the divine processions into a Trinity of persons.[96]

However, since active spiration in the theological tradition does not constitute a person, the Holy Spirit is said to be in the Father and the Son by virtue of the Spirit's relation to both in the act of passive spiration.[97] It is this relation to two persons, not the relational structure of the divine nature, that constitutes the Holy Spirit as person. In other words, the Holy Spirit is "one person in two persons" or "the subsisting we-act between the Father and the Son" and thus "the 'WE' IN PERSON, that is, the inner-Trinitarian we-relation."[98] The we-ness of the one divine nature is for Mühlen the foundation for the *perichoresis* of the divine persons begun in the generation of the Son and completed by the Holy Spirit: the union of the Father and the Son "becomes" person in the Holy Spirit.[99] The Father and the Son are united in the person of the Holy Spirit as the bond between them. The Holy Spirit, in turn, is the *persona media* out of and in the two persons of the Father and the Son by virtue of the relational divine nature.[100]

In his later work, Mühlen explored the relational nature of being-in-we, yet without developing concrete implications for the divine personhood.[101] He acknowledged that the word "we" does not actually stand for a person in the proper sense.[102] The difference of the Spirit as "we" in person to the "I" of the Father and the "Thou" of the Son is in Mühlen's view not ontological but what he terms "hemeisal"—that is, it is designated by a belonging of persons (belonging-to-we).[103] This belonging-to-we is not mere intersubjectivity but originates from an already existing

95. Ibid., 152–56.

96. Vondey, *Heribert Mühlen*, 77.

97. Mühlen, *Der Heilige Geist als Person*, 157–58, 164.

98. Ibid., 157.

99. Ibid., 166.

100. Ibid., 157–58.

101. See Vondey, *Heribert Mühlen*, 263–96.

102. Heribert Mühlen, "Die Wir-Philosophie als dritte Thematisierungsstufe in der abendländischen Denkgeschichte," *Theologie und Glaube* 84 (1994): 1–36.

103. Heribert Mühlen, "Der direkte Zugang zum Wir-Geschehen: Hemeislogische Grundlegung der Wir-Philosophie," *Theologie und Glaube* 85 (1995): 433–57.

we-order. Nothing is prior to the facticity of being-in-we.[104] The Holy Spirit as we in person is, in this sense, factually prior to the identity of the Father and the Son, to use Mühlen's terminology, unless by the existing we-order he meant the relational divine nature in logical distinction from the we-as-person. For a hemeisal construction of person, however, Mühlen rejected any ontological approach from the concept of nature (and hence a metaphysical approach from the notion of being) as inadequate for the articulation of personhood in communion.[105] Consequently, the procession of the Spirit is an act of persons in which the divine substance is not articulated. This rejection does not deny the possibility of designating both the divine nature and a divine person as "spirit." It is possible to designate in Mühlen's terms the Spirit as person as the coming to person of the divine nature. Yet, Mühlen's discussion of the divine nature consistently avoids the notion of substance. The reinterpretation of the divine nature in relational terms also does not identify the divine substance as spirit in this regard. Hence, Mühlen's seminal definition of the Spirit as person avoids entirely the metaphysical interpretation of the statement that God by nature is spirit. It is then impossible to say how the Spirit as the we in person originates from or relates in existence to the divine substance as spirit. Hence, in his subsequent work Mühlen identified the Spirit in the church from the perspective of person(s) without thereby drawing significant consequences for the human participation in the divine nature.[106] The theological perspective of the Spirit has effectively closed the door to a metaphysics of spirit.

Conclusion

The preceding narrative covers more territory than permissible in the confines of a brief essay. Undoubtedly, the argument requires more nuances in the articulation of the history of the theological tradition. If the basic direction indicated above is correct, however, then pneumatology from the perspective of the Spirit has come to disqualify pneumatology from the perspective of spirit. While the articulation of a theology of the Holy Spirit makes of necessity reference to both the

104. See Heribert Mühlen, *Im-Wir-Sein: Grundlegung der Wir-Wissenschaft; Beitrag zu einer wirgemäßen Lebens-und Weltordnung*, ed. Wilhelm Maas (Paderborn: Schöningh, 2008).

105. Ibid., 314–15.

106. See Vondey, *Heribert Mühlen*, 99–229.

divine nature and personhood, the characterization of the Spirit has never fully reconciled the realm of substance and nature with the reality of personhood and relationality. In the discussion of pneumatology, substance and existence are intricately linked. The mode of being and the mode of origin reflected in the nature and person of the Holy Spirit can shed light on their interconnectedness in God and creation. The postulate of contemporary theology that the definition of person has to overcome a substance metaphysics consequently needs to be replaced by a mediating ontology of relationality.[107] This revision would suggest that pneumatology from the perspective of the Spirit can be carried out only from the perspective of spirit. Spirit is then neither ontic union without relations nor divine relationality without divine substance. Rather, a revision of pneumatology from the perspective of the Spirit as the divine we brings with it also a revision of divine and human personhood. "We" designates the Spirit both as person and as divine substance, albeit with differences of perspective that have not yet been articulated theologically. The charismatic dimension of spirit may prove fruitful in further clarifying this articulation. Pneumatology will have to answer how the spirit as a designation of the divine substance is present in the Father and the Son in a manner different from the Spirit as person. Put differently, the personhood of the Holy Spirit stands in immediate correlation to the presence and power of God as spirit.[108] In turn, the presence and power of God, although manifested differently in the other divine persons and in creation, is essentially a manifestation of the Spirit as spirit. As a mandate for the future, this dimension demands a pneumatology from the perspective of the Spirit that is also pneumatology from the perspective of spirit.

107. See Hilberath, *Der Personbegriff*, 312–27.

108. Ralph Del Colle, "The Holy Spirit: Presence, Power, Person," *Theological Studies* 62 (2001): 322–40.

CHAPTER 6

A "Third Article" Proposal about the Third Person of the Trinity[1]

SCOTT HARROWER

The search for a more robust account of the person of the Holy Spirit within the eternal unity of God the Trinity is an ongoing quest in Western Trinitarian theology. This chapter works toward this constructive goal by highlighting source-related and methodological issues that contribute to a major stumbling block in the way of this endeavor, namely, the issue of inner-Trinitarian sequentialism. The problem will be outlined first. The problem is embedded in the dominant Western account of God's eternal life. This is the Trinitarian sequentialism that only offers minimal personal individuation for the person of the Holy Spirit relative to the Father and the Son. That is, there is a prominent and logically prior relationship between the Father and the Son from which the person of the Spirit is sourced. This means that only the Father and the Son are construed as active subjects within God whose actions relative to each other and the Spirit establish their fundamental and particular personal properties. The Spirit does not

1. This title deliberately trades on the title and spirit of Thomas G. Weinandy, "The *Filioque*: Beyond Athanasius and Thomas Aquinas; An Ecumenical Proposal," in *Ecumenical Perspectives on the Filioque for the Twenty-First Century*, ed. Myk Habets (London: Bloomsbury T&T Clark, 2014), 185–97.

have a comparable inner-Trinitarian action nor a relational/personal impact relative to the Father and the Son. Because the Spirit lacks a particular and particularizing action and hence relative relations to the Father and the Son, the Spirit's personhood is relatively truncated from a systematic point of view.

The theological issue presented by Trinitarian sequentialism reflects two methodological problems that must be addressed. The first is a failure regarding the sources for Trinitarian theology: it is the relative neglect of the logic and content of the Synoptic Gospels relative to the use of John's Gospel. The second is a methodological problem of inconsistency regarding the selective use of the norm that aligns Trinitarian relations in the economy of salvation with eternal processions in God.

This essay addresses the source and methodological issues at hand, and finally offers a thought experiment that points out the latent potency for Trinitarian theology that is to be found in source and methodological consistency. The account offered here is for those who wish to strictly align Trinitarian relations in the economy of salvation with eternal processions in God. The proposal is a strong rendering of the person of the Holy Spirit and the Spirit's inner-Trinitarian impact relative to the Father and the Son. This is achieved by undertaking a theological interpretation of a select pattern of economic Trinitarian relations that are found in Luke-Acts with respect to Jesus' ascension and session at the right hand of God the Father.[2] The pattern is "God the Son is seated alongside God the Father by God the Spirit." If interpreted as a mirror-like reflection of the inner life of God, this economic pattern of relations would indicate that within the inner life of God (1) the Spirit establishes the Son and Father alongside one another, (2) the Father receives the quality of fatherliness toward the Son due to the Spirit's action, and (3) the Son receives the quality of Sonship by means of the Spirit's action. This proposal offers a salutary and necessary complement to the classical Trinitarian model because it accords to the Spirit that which is fundamental to full Trinitarian

2. On the usefulness of and distinction between theological judgments in the text and theological concepts that arise from these, see David S. Yeago, "The New Testament and the Nicene Dogma: A Contribution to the Recovery of Theological Exegesis," in *The Theological Interpretation of Scripture: Classic and Contemporary Readings*, ed. S. E. Fowl (Oxford: Wiley-Blackwell, 1997), 87–102; C. Kavin Rowe, "Biblical Pressure and Trinitarian Hermeneutics," *Pro Ecclesia* 11 (2002): 295–312; Rowe, *Early Narrative Christology: The Lord in the Gospel of Luke* (Berlin: Walter de Gruyter, 2006).

personhood: establishing personal onto-relations in the same way as the Father and the Son. Hence, the Spirit is as particularly personal within the life of God as the Father and the Son are. Now to make good on such claims, starting with the Western context.

The Received Tradition and Contemporary Trinitarianism

Thomas Aquinas and his heirs took the missions of God in salvation history to be analogues of eternal relations of *procession*. Furthermore, these relations were taken to be the basis for describing *relations of opposition* between persons of the Trinity.[3] A circular logic was henceforth enshrined when the missions of God in the economy of salvation, the incarnation, and the sending of the Spirit were taken to be based upon processions within God.[4] In Aquinas's thought, "A divine person admits of being sent in the sense that . . . this implies procession of origin from the sender."[5] Hence, in "the invisible mission as well as in the visible mission, the person is sent by the one from whom he proceeds." It is important to note Aquinas's assumption that "[t]he eternal relation of origin is included in the mission itself; the person is sent according to his personal property."[6] For Aquinas, "pro-

3. Aquinas set out two possible ways by which one may arrive at and articulate the knowledge of God from Scripture and tradition. One procedure begins with *theologia* (theology proper), where the starting point is who God is in himself. The other moves forward by beginning with the *dispensatio*, with God's historical revelation of Godself in space and time. In his biblical commentaries, however, Aquinas lays out his doctrine of the Trinity according to the path of *theologia* (as described above) in tandem with the second procedure, which is according to the *dispensatio*. See Aquinas, *Lectura in Iohannis evangelium* 1:1, cited in Gilles Emery, "Theologia and Dispensatio: The centrality of divine missions in Thomas's trinitarian theology," 519-20. Hence, for Aquinas, one approach to the doctrine of God takes the divine persons as its starting point, the other takes the scriptural account of the incarnation as its point of origin. See Aquinas, *Summa theologiae* (*ST*) III, q. 2, a. 6, *ad* 1 (cited in Emery, "Theologia and Dispensatio: The centrality of divine missions in Thomas's trinitarian theology," 518.

4. There are visible and invisible missions. The visible missions are the incarnation of the Word as the Christ and the coming of the Spirit through physical means such as in the transfiguration and at Pentecost. The invisible missions refer to the sending of the Son and the Spirit into the inner life of the believer. See Aquinas, *ST* I, q. 43, a. 7 (cited in Emery, "Theologia and Dispensatio: The centrality of divine missions in Thomas's trinitarian theology," 520.

5. Aquinas, *ST* I, q. 43, a. 1 (cited in Emery, "Theologia and Dispensatio: The centrality of divine missions in Thomas's trinitarian theology," 520-21.

6. Emery, "Theologia and Dispensatio: The centrality of divine missions in Thomas's trinitarian

cessions" refers to eternal processions, which are "the coming forth (*origo*) of a person from another."[7] These are "the eternal generation of the Son from the Father, and the eternal procession of the Holy Spirit from the Father and Son."[8] For Aquinas, the intra-Trinitarian processions, or "origins," must be understood as person-constituting onto-relations: they are "the drawing out of a reality that has issued from a principle," a "relation of emanation."[9]

The positive aspect of Aquinas's proposals is that those Trinitarian relationships address the issue of the oneness and threeness of God's being. Namely, they are the basis for his understanding of the individuation of Trinitarian persons and of their relations to one another within the unity of God. As he writes:

> In God essence is not really distinct from person; and yet . . . the persons are really distinguished from each other. For person signifies relation as subsisting in the divine nature. But relation as referred to the essence does not differ therefrom really; but only in our way of thinking; while as referred to an opposite relation, it has a real distinction by virtue of that opposition. Thus there are one essence and three persons.[10]

The outworking of this account of Trinitarian persons and their inner-Trinitarian relations is clear in the *Summa theologiae.* Here, Aquinas chose the divine persons as his point of departure for Trinitarian theology. This decision determined the logic of his Trinitarian account along a sequence of intrinsic relations and personal properties: "processions, relations, the concept of person, the persons 'in particular' (Father, Son, Holy Spirit), and the persons in reference to the divine essence, to properties, to acts, and to one another."[11] The important point to note is that these personal distinctions followed a set pattern whose logic was determined by an

---

theology," 520. St. Thomas believed his view comported with the biblical text. See his commentary on John 20:22 in *Lectura in Iohannis evangelium*, 20:22, cited in Emery, "Theologia and Dispensatio: The centrality of divine missions in Thomas's trinitarian theology," 539.

7. Emery, "Theologia and Dispensatio: The centrality of divine missions in Thomas's trinitarian theology," 519-20.

8. Ibid.

9. Ibid.

10. Thomas Aquinas, *ST* I, q. 39, a. 1, as cited by Douglas F. Kelly, *Systematic Theology: Grounded in Holy Scripture and Understood in the Light of the Church*, vol. 1, *The God Who Is: The Holy Trinity* (Fearn: Mentor, 2008), 491–92.

11. Emery, "Theologia and Dispensatio: The centrality of divine missions in Thomas's trinitarian theology," 548-49.

approach to the economic missions of God as a way to resolve the threeness-in-oneness "problem." It sought both affirmation of the consubstantiality of three persons as one God, and the personal distinction of each person. As we read, "Since these processions occur within the Godhead, and since the person who proceeds remains within the person from whom he proceeds, such processions or 'origins' account for both the con-substantiality of the three (i.e., their being one single God) and their personal distinction (by virtue of the personal relations founded on the processions themselves)."[12]

There is much to be said for tightly aligning the divine processions and the historical missions. In this view, the visible missions reveal the divine persons as they are in their eternal personal particularity. In the invisible missions, believers experience the divine persons as they are without remainder, ignorance, or restraint. "The Son is sent by the Father just as he is begotten by the Father; the Holy Spirit is sent by the Father and the Son insofar as he proceeds from the Father and the Son. Under this first aspect, the invisible mission carries in it the eternal procession of the divine person who is sent. The person sent is the begotten Son and the proceeding Holy Spirit. The Son and the Holy Spirit are sent into hearts in accordance with what they are."[13] The value of this proposal also includes theological confidence that God has revealed Godself as God is in Godself, and a sense of fittingness where God's work in salvation corresponds to who God is eternally. As Emery concludes: "Saint Thomas's doctrine of the divine missions also accounts for the relationship that believers have with each divine person in his personal distinction."[14] In sum, Aquinas understood that God is internally constituted and differentiated in precisely the same manner in which God is revealed in God's relationship to history and to believers.[15]

This approach received fresh impetus in the twentieth century from both Roman Catholics (for example, Karl Rahner) and Protestants (for example, Karl Barth). Karl

12. Emery, "Theologia and Dispensatio: The centrality of divine missions in Thomas's trinitarian theology," 520.

13. Emery, "Theologia and Dispensatio: The centrality of divine missions in Thomas's trinitarian theology," 526.

14. Emery, "Theologia and Dispensatio: The centrality of divine missions in Thomas's trinitarian theology," 550.

15. *ST* 1, q. 45, a. 6 (cited in Emery, "Theologia and Dispensatio: The centrality of divine missions in Thomas's trinitarian theology," 552.

Rahner strictly identified the Trinitarian relations evident in the economy of salvation with the eternal relations and distinctions within the immanent Trinity. In his classic work *The Trinity*, Rahner penned his now famous axiom: "*The 'economic' Trinity is the 'immanent' Trinity and the 'immanent' Trinity is the 'economic' Trinity.*"[16] Though he preceded Rahner, Barth reflected Rahner's approach. To cite one example, he wrote, "God is precisely the One He is in showing and giving Himself."[17]

As beneficial as this approach and its classical expressions may be, it is beset by a fundamental problem: Trinitarian sequentialism and its attendant minimal personal properties and hence individuation of the Holy Spirit. This is outlined below.

The Problem

Thomas Weinandy, writing from a Roman Catholic perspective, has recently called for an alternative paradigm for the personal individuation within the Trinity, particularly dealing with the Holy Spirit. He identifies "inner Trinitarian sequentialism" (ITS) as the stumbling block that a new paradigm must overcome. His understanding of "Trinitarian sequentialism" within the Western tradition is that "the Father is logically and conceptually prior to the Son since he actively begets the Son. The Father and the Son are logically and conceptually prior to the Holy Spirit who proceeds from them as their act of love for one another."[18] For Weinandy, the consequence of this sequentialism as far as the person of the Holy Spirit is concerned is that ITS "deprives

16. Rahner, *Trinity*, 22. (italics are Rahner's). It has become known as Rahner's Rule. This essay will adopt Rahner's language of "immanent" and "economic," though equivalents, such as "essential" for "immanent," will be used to avoid tedium. We will take Graham Cole's definitions of the immanent and economic Trinity. The economic Trinity "[r]efers to the various roles of the members of the Trinity in the administration (economy) of the plan of salvation." The immanent (or essential) Trinity is the "Trinity's own eternal, internal, life as Father, Son and Holy Spirit," Cole, *Holy Spirit*: 286–87.

17. Karl Barth, *Church Dogmatics* I/1, ed. T. F. Torrance and G. W. Bromiley (Edinburgh: T&T Clark, 1957–75), 382 (hereafter cited as Barth, *CD*, followed by the volume number, part number, and page number). A different depiction of Barth, of course, can be seen in the work of George Hunsinger and Paul Molnar on Barth and the Trinity. See, for example, Hunsinger, *Reading Barth with Charity: A Hermeneutical Proposal* (Grand Rapids: Baker Academic, 2015); Hunsinger, *Evangelical, Catholic, and Reformed: Doctrinal Essays on Barth and Related Themes* (Grand Rapids: Eerdmans, 2015), 1–55; Molnar, *Divine Freedom and the Doctrine of the Immanent Trinity: In Dialogue with Karl Barth and Contemporary Theology* (London: T&T Clark, 2002).

18. Weinandy, "*Filioque*," 192.

the Holy Spirit of any endowed action distinctively his own, since he is purely passive amidst the sequential acts of the Father and the Son."[19]

This is explained in the two points below. First:

> the Father and the Son are active personal subjects. The Father begets the Son and the Father and his begotten Son, as one, actively bring forth the Holy Spirit who proceeds from them as their one reciprocal love. These acts metaphysically constitute their distinct subjective identities as persons—as Father and as Son. Unlike the Father and the Son there is no comparable act performed by the Holy Spirit that metaphysically constitutes and corroborates his subjective identity as a distinct person.[20]

Second:

> The Holy Spirit is merely passive within the Trinity—the love shared through the paternal and filial actions of the Father and the Son. Because the Holy Spirit performs no subjective ontological act within the Trinity, his distinct personhood is jeopardized.[21]

Weinandy believes this is a long-standing problem in Christian theology that was enshrined in Aquinas's methodology and theology proper.

Importantly, Weinandy is but one representative of a broader search for a more consistent and coherent Trinitarianism with respect to the person of the Holy Spirit, which at the same time remains rooted in Scripture and the creedal tradition.[22] A Protestant representative of this search is Myk Habets. He articulates the core of the problem within Western Trinitarianism. He writes that Western theology "has explicitly constructed a trinitarianism in which the Spirit is the fruit of a prior and superior relationship that exists between the Father and the Son. The Spirit then has the role of being the bond of union

19. Ibid. Weinandy writes the following on Aquinas: "The basis of my criticism is found within Aquinas' own exposition. Aquinas notes that the Father and the Son both act—the Father 'begets' the Son and the Father and Son 'spirate' the Holy Spirit, but the Holy Spirit does not act 'as no other person proceeds from him' (S.T., I, 32, 3). Unsurprisingly this is traditionally known as 'passive' spiration or procession. See also, S.T., I, 28, 4" (Weinandy, "*Filioque*," 189).

20. Ibid., 192.

21. Ibid.

22. The recent work edited by Habets, *Ecumenical Perspectives on the Filioque for the Twenty-First Century*, reveals the breadth of the efforts toward a revised Trinitarianism. The number and range of prominent Trinitarian theologians in the world who have contributed is impressive. Perhaps a "second wave" Trinitarian revival is at hand.

between Father and Son, or that which flows from or is the result of their relationship."[23] The perspectives offered by Weinandy and Habets highlight a significant problem needing to be resolved.

One of the methodological assumptions behind this paper is that Third Article Theology (TAT) offers both methodological and substantive avenues for addressing this issue because of its conviction that the breadth of Scripture is relevant to systematic theology and its emphasis on methodology.

The Ascension and Session of Christ in Luke–Acts

The Gospels emphasize God's active participation in the development of Jesus' life and ministry as the Messiah.[24] Luke–Acts, however, uniquely fills out this picture by way of pneumatology. Luke is especially attentive to the Spirit's work in shaping the person and the messianic ministry of Jesus. The author achieves this both explicitly and implicitly. In terms of explicit references to do with the person of Jesus, the conception of Jesus stands out. The Holy Spirit "overshadows" Mary and she is with child (Luke 1:35). Mary's child, Jesus, is presented as more closely related to the Spirit than even John the Baptizer, who is himself powerfully influenced by the Spirit (1:15), as are John's mother (1:41) and father (1:67). The implicit work of the Spirit with respect to Jesus' development as a child and teenager is also an important aspect of Luke's account. In Luke 2:52, Jesus' increase in wisdom and stature is implicitly attributed to the continuing work of the Holy Spirit in his life. Aside from the work of the Spirit in Jesus' life from conception, the account of Jesus's authoritative and amazing teaching at the

23. This situation has only been prolonged in the West by theologians via their general disinterest in the Holy Spirit. See the comments of Myk Habets in his introductory chapter. Eastern Trinitarianism does not escape this charge either as Habets claims it is also pneumatologically weak: "there remains a regnant relegation of the Spirit to the periphery in standard Orthodox accounts" (ibid.).

24. For example, in Matthew, Jesus' identity as Messiah is headlined in the opening verse of the Gospel (1:1). He is "Jesus the Messiah, the son of David, the son of Abraham." God's active participation in his life is communicated in that he is conceived by the Holy Spirit (1:18, 20), his life is protected by God's angelic warning to Joseph (2:13), at his baptism his identity as God's "beloved Son" is assured by the divine voice from heaven and the presence of the Spirit (3:17), he is lead into the wilderness by the Spirit (4:1), his identity as "the Christ the Son of the living God" is revealed by God to Peter (16:17), he is revealed to be the "beloved Son" by the voice from the cloud at the transfiguration (17:5), and is raised from the dead by God (28:2–7).

temple, for example, would be liable to the charge of being a creation of Luke's fancy. Furthermore, in this case Jesus' awareness of God as his unique "Father" and the temple as his "Father's house" would lack a firm foundation, and in turn would lead to the conclusion that these claims were sourced from Jesus' or Luke's imagination. As I have argued elsewhere, "in Luke–Acts a pneumatological undercurrent must be assumed for those spheres of divine action where a full explanation of divine instrumentality with reference to Jesus is not provided."[25] The Spirit's development of Jesus' person extends to his fittingness for ministry as the Son of God and the way in which he carries this out. Elizabeth Groppe has rightly argued that such is the significance of the Spirit upon Jesus' life, ministry, death, and resurrection that we can say that Christ is "constituted" as messianic by the Spirit.[26]

One way in which the Spirit's constitution of Jesus as the Messiah is evident is in the way that the Holy Spirit leads others to recognize Jesus as the Messiah. For example, the Spirit reveals to Simeon that Jesus is God's "salvation"—the Messiah (Luke 2:27–32). John the Baptist proclaims that Jesus will be the one through whom people will be baptized by the Holy Spirit (3:16). It is at the Spirit's descent upon Jesus (3:22) that Jesus is identified as the "beloved Son" with whom God is pleased. The baptism and anointing narrative (3:21–22) is a pivotal moment in this Gospel, as it makes the point that the entirety of Jesus' upcoming ministry is carried out "in the sphere of the Holy Spirit."[27] In the words of Joseph Fitzmyer, Jesus' ministry takes place under the "reign" of the Spirit.[28] Likewise, Sinclair Ferguson accents the influence of the Spirit upon Jesus' ministry by characterizing it as taking place under the "lordship" of the Spirit.[29]

---

25. Scott Harrower, *Trinitarian Self and Salvation* 130.

26. Elizabeth T. Groppe, *Yves Congar's Theology of the Holy Spirit* (Oxford: Oxford University Press, 2004), 57. Groppe draws together the elements of a Spirit Christology, which includes the dynamic connection between the personhood and works of the Spirit and the Son: "The Spirit who wrought the *kenōsis* of Incarnation, baptism, and death is also the Spirit of Christ's glorification—a glorification not of dominion but of communion. Jesus Christ exercises his divine Sonship precisely by giving the Spirit to others such that they, too, may become sons and daughters of God" (ibid.).

27. Joel B. Green, *Luke*: 853.

28. Fitzmyer, *Luke*: 1:229, 479–83.

29. "Jesus was baptized with the Spirit and lived under his lordship" (Sinclair B. Ferguson, *The Holy Spirit* [Downers Grove, IL: InterVarsity Press, 1996], 46). Commenting on Luke 3:23 ("Jesus was about thirty years old when he began his work"), Calvin states that with reference to his human

The power of the directional relationship that the Holy Spirit has upon Jesus is compounded in the temptation narrative (Luke 4:1–13). There Jesus is described as "full of the Spirit" (4:1).[30] This is expressed with reference to Jesus as "full of the Holy Spirit" on his return from the Jordan (4:1a), as well as his being subsequently "led by the Spirit" into the wilderness to be tested by the Devil in the wilderness (4:1b). Jesus overcomes these temptations and proceeds to Nazareth where he declares, "The Spirit of the Lord is upon me" (4:18). In this way, Jesus publicly acknowledges what became clear to him in his baptism and temptations: his ministry as the Messiah is dependent upon the work of the Holy Spirit.[31] Robert Yarbrough writes that, after Jesus' anointing with the Spirit at his baptism, "[f]rom then onward Jesus' life is characterized by the power and the presence of the Holy Spirit at work in him."[32] Hence, the Spirit is the source of authority and power for Christ's ministry.[33] The Spirit also has an affective influence on Jesus, who "rejoiced in the Holy Spirit" (ESV) over the success of the in-breaking of God's kingdom through his ministry (10:21).[34]

---

nature, "When Christ was preparing to preach the Gospel, he was introduced by Baptism into his office; and at the same time he was endued with the Holy Spirit . . . that he comes as a godlike man . . . in whom the power of the Holy Spirit reigns" (Calvin, *Harmony*, 1: 1:204).

30. Luke Timothy Johnson, *The Gospel of Luke* (Collegeville, MN: Liturgical Press, 1991), 81.

31. Significantly, the "finger of God" in Luke's Gospel has normally been interpreted as a referent to the Holy Spirit. Although see Edward Woods, who attributes this, and the work of the "finger of God," to God the Father in a "non-instrumental sense, because the Holy Spirit is already involved in miracle through the authoritative word of command and release" See Woods, *The 'Finger of God,' and Pneumatology in Luke-Acts*, 223–25. Woods writes: "With the 'finger of God' expression, God the Father is acting with power and mercy through Jesus his spirit-anointed Son (Acts 2:22; cf. Lk. 8:39). . . . [T]he phrase 'finger of God' at Luke 11:20 refer[s] to God the Father himself in a non-instrumental sense, because the Holy Spirit is already involved in miracles through the authoritative word of command and release" (ibid., 225).

32. Walter A.Elwell and Yarbrough, *Encountering the New Testament : a historical and theological survey*, 90.

33. Calvin is right to state that these words indicate that Christ "does nothing by the suggestion or advice of men, but everything by the guidance of the Spirit of God," Calvin, *Harmony*, 1: 1:228).

34. Jesus also speaks of the gift of the Holy Spirit for those who ask for the Spirit from the Father (Luke 11:13); he also promises that those who acknowledge him will receive the Holy Spirit, who in turn will aid their ministries (12:12). Implicit material in Luke regarding the close relationship between Jesus and the Spirit includes the attribution of Jesus' increase in wisdom and stature to the continuing work of the Holy Spirit in his life (2:52).

In sum, the Spirit's influence upon Jesus ensures that he is the Son who reflects God's character, concerns, and mission. This work by the Spirit, which confirms Jesus as the God-pleasing Son, ensures his fittingness to be the Son whom the Father receives at his right hand via Jesus' ascension and session. In his session, Jesus enters into full power and authority (Acts 2:33; cf. 7:56–57), and can be present to the world and empower mission through the donation of his Spirit (1:9–10; 2:33). Hence, in Luke's Gospel there is a continuum of pneumatological activity that undergirds, directs, and shapes Jesus' life and ministry as the Messiah.

The Spirit and the Ascension and Session of the Christ

The Spirit's influence on Jesus' person and ministry was unbroken through his crucifixion, death, resurrection, ascension, and session. We can take this as the case for four reasons. First, there is no evidence to the contrary.

Second, Jesus' passion and glorification are consistent with his ministry as the Messiah, who is the Spirit-anointed deliverer. The resurrection of Jesus is necessary to his work as the Messiah. This is because the cross is tied to the resurrection in Luke's passion predictions. The resurrection is thus the transition between Jesus' state of humiliation and his return to a state of glory. The resurrection event can be attributed to the work of the Holy Spirit because it is the necessary extension of the Spirit's direction of Jesus' life and ministry through death to his ministries as the ascended king. The ascension is clearly part of Jesus' messianic vocation; it has many theological functions within Luke–Acts. These functions include (but are not limited to) Jesus giving a blessing to his disciples following the OT pattern of blessing (Luke 24:50), his glorification as the completion of the resurrection event. Jesus' session is his entering into fuller power and authority (Acts 2:33; cf. 7:56–57), and it makes possible his worldwide presence and mission empowerment through the donation of his Spirit (1:9–10; 2:33), as exemplified in his appearance to Paul (9:4–6; 22:7–10; 26:14–18). In tandem with this gift of the Spirit, perhaps the most significant aspect of the ascension and session is that they are the grounds for the confession that Jesus is Lord and Christ (2:36), the one who can now convey forgiveness of sin (2:38).

Third, the material nature of ministry as God's Spirit-led, obedient Son continues through to, and including, his establishment as the ruling king. Three testing stories in particular reveal the strength of Jesus' obedience to his Father: the temptation in the wilderness, the testing on the Mount of Olives, and the temptation on the cross. These are particularly important because they demonstrate the extent of Jesus' faithfulness as he transitions through various phases of ministry through to his continuing ministry as the ascended and seated Messiah. These stories are concrete evidence of the Spirit's continuing work, which determined his earthly life and ministry. This is evidenced by his faithfulness to God. Indeed, Jesus' obedience as God's faithful Son is perhaps the central feature of the NT's basis for faith in Jesus as Messiah.[35][36]

Fourth, the death, resurrection, and session of Jesus are organic to Jesus' Spirit-led predictions of his own glorification and his own sending of the Spirit upon his people. Luke establishes this contrast between the passion of Jesus and the glory that he will enter in Luke 9:22, whereby Jesus' suffering is held in tension with the confession that he is the "Christ of God" (9:20). The second passion prediction (9:44) immediately follows people being "astounded at the greatness of God . . . and amazed at all he [Jesus] was doing," as well as the transfiguration account, which speaks of both Jesus' glory and his "exodus." The third passion prediction (18:31–34) begins the transition from the time of Jesus' miracles to the time of his temptations and passion. This transition is highlighted in 19:37a, where the disciples praise God for Jesus' miraculous work, yet shortly thereafter Jesus' own suffering occurs at that very place (22:39–53).[37]

From these four points it is reasonable to claim that the Spirit's leadership of Jesus' earthly ministry is continuous with Jesus' ministry to the point of his being seated as ruling Messiah. Hence, the Spirit may be said to direct the establishment of Jesus as the seated Son and Lord alongside the Father. From this position as seated Messiah, Jesus in turn sent his Spirit upon his people.

35. For a definition of obedience when used of Christ, see Graham A. Cole, *God the Peacemaker: How Atonement Brings Shalom* (Downers Grove, InterVarsity Press, 2009), 115-17. See also Longenecker, "The Foundational Conviction of New Testament Christology: The Obedience/Faithfulness/Sonship of Christ," 475.

36. Cole, *God the Peacemaker*; 115–17.

37. Helmut Flender, *St Luke: Theologian of Redemptive History*, trans. Reginald H. and Ilse Fuller (Philadelphia: Fortress, 1967), 31–32.

The Ascension and the Immanent Trinity

A number of economic Trinitarian relations can be discerned from the ascension and session of the Spirit-led Messiah, relations that in turn have implications for an account of the immanent Trinity. One economic pattern in particular may provide a basis from which to address the issue of inner-Trinitarian sequentialism. This pattern is: *God the Son is seated at the right hand of God the Father by God the Holy Spirit.*

Missions and Processions

A strict realist approach to this pattern of relations, such as Aquinas's or the more recent strict reading of Rahner's Rule, would align these missions in history with inner-Trinitarian processions.[38] Though not all theologians follow this approach, there is value in applying this norm and subsequently assessing its fruitfulness.[39] Adopting the missions-processions methodology could lead to the adoption of the following points from the economy of salvation to the inner life of God. Namely, that within the eternal life of God:

1. The Spirit uniquely establishes the Son's personal relation alongside the Father.
2. The Father receives the Son alongside himself, and hence the fullness of his quality of being fatherly toward the Son by way of the Spirit's operations and relations.[40]
3. Hence, the establishment of the Son alongside the Father by the Spirit also yields a number of theological proposals regarding the passive and active relational realities between the Father, Son, and Spirit. That is, drawing upon the work of Athanasius, we can say that the Spirit establishes the Son as "the image of the Father." This sequentialism must be understood as an atemporal series.[41]

---

38. For a description of Rahner's theology and his development of his axiom, see Harrower, *Trinitarian Self and Salvation* 26–72.

39. I survey the landscape of evangelical and nonevangelical approaches to Rahner's Rule (including the strict realist reading of it as a norm) in Harrower, *Trinitarian Self and Salvation* 1–25. My own position is summarized on pages 155–58 of the same work.

40. On the basis of the Spirit's economic relationship and works directly upon the Son, it may also be possible to argue that "the Spirit conforms the Son such that he has the qualities of the righteous Son of the Father." This will be explored in a forthcoming work.

41. "The issue is simply that there is a sequence, even if it is an eternal sequence. Such Trinitarian sequentialism . . . , does not provide an accurate and acceptable metaphysical account of the Trinity" (Weinandy, "*Filioque*," 189).

Below we shall focus on propositions 2 and 3 in particular.

Such a manner of conceiving the immanent Trinitarian relationships would speak to the personal impact of the Spirit upon the other persons of the Trinity. This would be an act of will within God that is focused on the hypostasis of the Spirit. As such it offers necessary conditions for viewing the Spirit in the same way as the Father and the Son. Furthermore, it offers an individuating property for the Holy Spirit. This is the property of "establishing the Son alongside the Father" and "establishing the Father in a relationship of alongsidedness and full fatherliness with the Son." This model also highlights the equal status of each person of the Trinity by way of speaking of the "alongsidedness" of persons with respect to one another.[42] This is a way of speaking of God's divine life along a horizontal vector, rather than a classic, vertically oriented one based upon causation or emanation. In this way, our proposal goes some way toward avoiding inner-Trinitarian subordination or gradation of any kind. In short, it relativizes the ontological consequences of Trinitarian sequentialism, which has plagued Western Trinitarianism. Accordingly, the paradigm proposed above overcomes the problem of Trinitarian sequentialism, which offers only minimal personal individuation for the person of the Holy Spirit within the Trinity.

In sum, what is being proposed is an account of the inner-Trinitarian impact and the individuating properties of the Spirit, which yields a strong view of the Spirit's personhood, individuation, and full divinity.[43] These are articulated in terms of the Spirit's relations of opposition or, in alternative language, of "establishing alongsidedness."

"Establishing Alongsidedness": A Complementary Paradigm?

By means of this proposal, we hope to complement the historically dominant idea of inner-Trinitarian personal derivation with the notions of alongsidedness and dependent complementary relatedness. When added to the classical model of processions, these proper and defining relations between the Father, Son, and Holy Spirit strengthen their personal particularity within the divine life.[44]

42. Najeeb Awad develops his own notion of *alongsidedness* from Cappadocian theology. See Awad, *God Without a Face?*: 134–39, 212, 221, 238, 278, 280.

43. Awad, *God Without a Face?*, 134.

44. Weinandy "*Filioque*," 193.

Further research will bear out the extent of the complementarity of the view outlined here with classic Western Trinitarianism. For example, is it coherent and noncontradictory to hold the active aspect of the Spirit's onto-relations (above) in a complementary manner with the view that the Spirit is also a gift within the Father-Son relationship?

Conclusion

This essay is an example of what a pneumatologically aware theological method could yield for the doctrine of God. I have followed Luke's Trinitarian relational dynamics regarding the ascension and session of the Son at the right hand of the Father by the Holy Spirit. If these are interpreted theologically via a missions-processions model, they yield a fresh claim to the dominant paradigm for ontotheology. The ontological claim is: "God the Son is seated at the right hand of God the Father by God the Holy Spirit." Taken together with the classical Western model, we could say: "God is the Father, Son, and Spirit in whom nontemporal acts individuate the persons and establish relations of opposition. These acts and relations include the Spirit establishing the Son alongside the Father, and the Father's reception of the Son." This provides a model of the Trinitarian life that is focused on the Spirit, the Son, and the Father, and the horizontal life of the Trinity. The uniqueness of this model is that the divine persons are not established by actions of the Father or the Father and the Son in a vertical manner alone as in the classical model. Rather, the Spirit contributes to establishing the Father and the Son as particular persons in relation.[45] A way to sum this up is to say that the Spirit has the property of "conforming alongsidedness" with reference to the Father and the Son.

In our view, the paradigm proposed above overcomes the problem of Trinitarian sequentialism, which offers only minimal personal individuation for the person of the Holy Spirit within the Trinity. If this is the case in God's eternal life, the relationship-generating actions of the Spirit provide the Spirit with a similar warrant for full particular personhood, as is the case with the Father

45. This active aspect of the Spirit's being and action is complemented by the Spirit being understood as a gift within the Father-Son relationship. Once our model takes into account the Son receiving the Spirit as the gift of the Father and sending the Spirit into the world, we can add the following: "the Father gifts the Spirit to the Son, whom the Son receives."

and the Son. Hence, this may be a powerful contribution to Trinitarian theology, as the divine personhood, individuation, and relations of opposition of the Spirit are not solely the result of the Spirit's origination from the Father (and the Son), but of the Spirit's impact upon the other persons of the Trinity *and the Spirit's necessary existence for constituting the Trinity to be who the Trinity is.* The theological and ecumenical implications of this model are profound, as they require a fuller Trinitarian paradigm.

CHAPTER 7

The Spirit of Life

Toward a Creation Pneumatology

FRANK D. MACCHIA

I look upon a photograph of a star nursery that my wife and I purchased from a local planetarium. It is a sight to behold. The rich colors and brilliant lights depict the emergence of bursting energy and stunning beauty, life in the making, our natural home, or the place from which God made us. Running through my mind as I gaze upon it are verses like Psalm 33:6: "By the word of the Lord the heavens were made, their starry host by the breath of his mouth."[1] The divine "breath" is the chief metaphor for the Spirit of God in the Bible, and this Spirit has its home address here in the cosmos.[2] One could easily attach this text to the reference of Gen. 1:2 to the Spirit of God hovering over the "deep" at creation, transcending the darkness and emptiness and giving birth to something filled with light, energy, and beautiful form. The same divine breath that brings the starry hosts into existence creates us, tying us to the earth and the larger cosmos (Gen. 2:7). We are, after all, made of stardust. The

1. Biblical quotations are from the NIV.

2. Lloyd R. Neve rightly interprets the dominant metaphor as divine "breath" rather than mere wind or storm (*The Spirit of God in the Old Testament* [Cleveland, TN: CPT, 2011], 11–12).

animals share such origins as well. Psalm 104:30 says to God: "When you send your Spirit, they are created, and you renew the face of the ground." We are indeed connected to all living things by the creative breath or Spirit of God. "In his hand is the life of every creature and the breath of all humankind" (Job 12:10). The core of our very existence as spiritual beings depends on the Spirit of God: "The Spirit of God has made me, the breath of God gives me life" (Job 33:4). One is reminded of how God gave Adam and Eve their existence as living souls through this breathing into them (Gen. 2:7). All human wisdom and other capacities essential to our humanity come from the breath of God (Job 32:8). The artisans of the tabernacle, for example, were filled with the Spirit of God in the skillful exercise of their craft (Exod. 35:31).

The wisdom literature of the Old Testament in particular places a heavy accent on the Spirit of God as the Spirit of life, of human, animal, and cosmic life. In the New Testament we find the same message, though it functions there as more of an undercurrent than a dominant theme. John the Baptist "became strong in spirit" (Luke 1:80) and Jesus "grew in wisdom and stature" (2:52) as he developed toward maturity. The same Spirit that hovered over Mary's womb to bring the Son of God into flesh (1:35) and later rested upon him at the waters of the Jordan (3:22) also worked "from below" through the natural process of human development to cause Jesus' life to flourish. In addition, Paul quotes an ancient Greek philosopher/poet, Epimenides, to the effect that our mortal breath comes from God and that in God we all live and move and have our very being. He then quotes another philosopher/poet, Aratus, that we are all God's "offspring" (Acts 17:24–28). Not only chemistry ties us to one another and to the stars, but also the very Spirit of God who created and sustains us, and causes us to flourish.

Such texts aside, it becomes abundantly clear when looking at the New Testament that the primary home address for the Spirit's work is not creation but rather resurrection. One is compelled to look at pneumatology primarily from the blinding light of Christ's victory over sin and death in his resurrection from the dead. The Spirit at work in the "big bang" of the original creation is now highlighted in the new life that burst forth at Jesus' resurrection and his outpouring of the Spirit upon all flesh, the "big bang" of the new creation, so to speak! Jesus overthrew the dark forces and inaugurated the reign of

God in the world by the Spirit (Matt. 12:28) and he was raised from the dead "according to the Spirit of holiness" (Rom. 1:4). He is raised as the "life-giving spirit" to pour forth the Spirit in service to the liberating reign of God in the world (1 Cor. 15:45). The kingdom of God is now "righteousness, peace, and joy in the Holy Spirit" (Rom. 14:17). One must view the Spirit's work in the New Testament from the vantage point of the new creation, which is still "beyond" the reach of natural processes ("flesh and blood cannot inherit the Kingdom of God," 1 Cor. 15:50). Pneumatology is now to be located within that which can only be termed "apocalyptic." How does this new home address for pneumatology alter the creation pneumatology introduced in the Old Testament? Is there a way of arriving at a theology of the Spirit of creation within the apocalyptic framework necessitated by Christology? This is the overriding concern of this essay.

A Tension between the Testaments

In drawing our attention to the Spirit of life in the Old Testament, John Levison starts critically with the supernatural work of the Spirit highlighted in the New Testament. To do this, Levison looks at Hermann Gunkel's slender work, *Wirkungen des Heiligen Geistes.* Confirmed in the pages of Gunkel's book was a picture of New Testament pneumatology that accented miraculous signs and wonders.[3] New Testament pneumatology thus points to an experience of the Spirit that is beyond the reach of natural life and, therefore, "subsequent" to natural life and its God-given capacities. The arena of the Spirit's work in the New Testament may be described by such terms as "regeneration," "sanctification," and "glorification" rather than "natural life" and its "flourishing," which is the major arena of Old Testament pneumatology for Levison. What was the major dividing line in this difference? The risen Christ! In the New Testament, Christology becomes central to the relationship between pneumatology and the Jewish doctrine of creation in order to reorientate pneumatology from creation to new creation or immortality.[4] The primary home address of pneumatology consequently shifts from creation to new creation.

This shift from the Spirit of creation to the Spirit of immortality even influenced

3. John R. Levison, *Filled with the Spirit* (Grand Rapids: Eerdmans, 2009), 3–13.

4. Ibid., 253–365.

how one came to read the Old Testament on the Spirit. Most reflections on Old Testament pneumatology that I had surveyed at the time I read Gunkel's book as a graduate student in the 1980s seemed to largely line up behind Gunkel. The Spirit in the Old Testament was typically viewed as the power of God's mighty breath blown forth from the divine "nostrils" so as to part the waters of the Red Sea (Exod. 15:8), or to suddenly possess someone like Saul with the gift of prophecy, something that seemed to transform him into an ecstatic prophet (1 Sam. 10:6). Even those places in the Old Testament where the divine Spirit inspired vitality, wisdom, or virtue were interpreted in ways that conformed to the power and suddenness of charismatic gifting by the Spirit of God from beyond human capacities. These images of the mighty and mysterious Spirit of God from the Old Testament seemed to set the stage well for the sound of a violent wind at Pentecost and the amazing effects produced by the Spirit's power in the ecstatic tongue-speaking and prophesying among the earliest Christians. In the meantime, the unique accent of the Old Testament on the Spirit of creation remained largely unappreciated. The extraordinary quality of the Spirit's work in the New Testament is not necessarily problematic in itself, but, if overemphasized, can leave open the question of continuity with the Spirit of creation as the breath of Yahweh that gave life to creation and still sustains it and causes it to flourish.

In contrast, Levison wishes to highlight the neglected uniqueness of Old Testament pneumatology as creation pneumatology. In so doing, he shows us that there is in the Scriptures a deep tension in relation to the issue of "subsequence." Being filled with the Spirit in the Old Testament is not a "subsequent" endowment from above that is detached from natural capacities but rather the *expansion* of the Spirit of life given to all humans from the beginning (Gen. 2:7) and even present in some sense in all flesh or creaturely life (Gen. 6:17). Flourishing under the shadow of death, human life experiences still manage in the Old Testament to triumph in lavish ways from below or as emerging from capacities granted by the Creator. Tied to the crucified and risen Christ (and, I would add, rooted in a more devastating estimate of the human "fall" into captivity to sin and death), the filling of the Spirit in the New Testament is a "subsequent" gift supernaturally given to natural human life. There seems to be in the light of Levison's analysis a profound difference between the pneumatologies of the two

Testaments, a difference that caused him to raise the question concerning the degree to which the pneumatology of the New Testament is *biblical*!

It is important to note, however, that Levison does not wish to overplay the contrast between the Testaments. He finds especially in Paul "a richly scriptural dimension" in his use of the risen Christ "to put death squarely in its place—in the shadow of life."[5] In the New Testament, new life triumphs decisively over death by turning the Old Testament "life flourishing under the shadow of death" into a death that now stands under the light of life. Genesis 2:7 is "radically revised" in this reordering of the relationship between life and death.[6] In other words, the Spirit of new life in the New Testament—in terms of its future fulfillment—is no longer viewed as hemmed in by death, flourishing merely by keeping death at bay but still lived out in death's shadow. In the glow of Christ's resurrection, death is defanged and conquered, cowering under the glow of life. Following Eugene Rogers, my own way of saying the same thing in the light of Levison's discussion is to note that the Spirit of immortality through faith in Christ is *excessive*, exceeding the boundaries of death and fulfilling the lavishness of the Spirit of life that previously flourished within the limitations imposed by death.[7] Levison's goal is thus to allow both Testaments to stand in a relationship of a tense "mutual illumination."[8]

Levison surely has a valid point to make. One who is heavily invested in "subsequence" or the experience of the supernatural Spirit as Levison defines it will read Old Testament pneumatology in this light. The Spirit in the Old Testament can thus be read as a fleeting and inadequate foretaste of the supernatural Spirit given through Christ's death and resurrection, punctuated by momentary and noteworthy endowments, but generally experienced within a situation of relative spiritual dearth while awaiting the fullness of the Spirit that came through Christ. The possibility that one may have overlooked in the Old Testament a rich understanding of spiritual fullness that is not well represented in the New Testament should give one pause to think. After all, one does not need to

5. Ibid., 315.

6. Ibid., 316.

7. Eugene F. Rogers Jr., *After the Spirit: A Constructive Pneumatology with Resources outside the Modern West* (Grand Rapids: Eerdmans, 2005), 33–39.

8. Levison, *Filled with the Spirit*, xxvi.

denigrate the work of the Spirit from below in order to highlight the same Spirit that comes to us from above or beyond! Certainly the promise-fulfillment relationship of the two Testaments allows room for such insights.

In thinking about Levison's book theologically, one is tempted to utilize the distinction between "common grace" (the flourishing of natural life) and salvific or sanctifying grace (a subsequent gift supernaturally granted). Though helpful, this is precisely the kind of distinction that Levison is convinced can only be anachronistically applied to the Old Testament. In the Old Testament, according to Levison, even extraordinary gifts expand lavishly precisely from the spiritual potential granted to natural life from birth and from the symbiosis of divine and human initiative available to all from the beginning of life. In other words, in the Old Testament Levison sees human nature, though dust, as graced from birth with extraordinary capacities from God.[9] What a contrast with the dominant New Testament assumption that one must be born anew by faith in Christ in order to receive the Spirit that sanctifies and to be endowed with extraordinary capacities in the Spirit. Levison thus implies that we have in the Old Testament not a mere foreshadowing of the fullness of the Spirit witnessed to in the New Testament but rather a different way of viewing this fullness! We do not just have a promise-fulfillment relationship between the pneumatologies of the two Testaments; we have to some degree complementary pneumatologies!

Implied in Levison's treatment of New Testament resurrection (or apocalyptic) pneumatology is a contrast with a creation pneumatology rooted especially in the Old Testament wisdom tradition. Martin Buber gives us an even more critical appraisal of New Testament apocalypticism in the light of the Old Testament prophetic tradition. In a provocative essay, "Prophecy, Apocalyptic, and Historical Hour," Buber contrasts Jewish apocalyptic that comes later to dominate the New Testament with the prophetic tradition's support of creation's natural propensity for freedom and the element of the unexpected.[10] Of course, creation follows natural laws. But the prophetic tradition supports the openness of creation to free participation in God's will for the world. As Buber writes: "It was here understood as the intention of creation, therefore, that the world should become an

9. Ibid., footnote 12.

10. Martin Buber, "Prophecy, Apocalyptic, and Historical Hour," *Union Seminary Quarterly Review* (March 1, 1957): 9–21.

independent seat of free decision out of which a genuine answer of the creature to his Creator can issue."[11]

For Buber, humanity was made uniquely with the power to choose, "suited to be God's partner in dialogue in history."[12] Buber elaborates: "The mystery is that of the creation of man as a being that has the power of actually choosing between the ways, and ever again and even now has the power to choose between them; for only such a being is suited to be God's partner in dialogue in history."[13]

Creation struggles for transcendence, for that which opens up new and surprising possibilities. This reach is especially true of humanity. Prophecy declares that humanity is uniquely "created to be a center of surprise of creation."[14]

The prophet is filled with the very Spirit of God in service to humanity's free openness to God and God's ongoing will for humanity.[15] He or she is on the cutting edge of humanity's struggle for transcendence and in his or her embodied life becomes a symbol of the message of hope: "The spirit moves him, and as his organs of speech, so the whole man is taken up into the service of the spirit. The body and life of the man become a part of this service and by this a symbol of the message."[16]

Only in conversation with God can the uncharted waters of the history of humanity and of the entire creation be discovered. Indeed, "one does not learn the measure and limit of what is attainable in a desired direction otherwise than through going in this direction."[17] The dialogue with God and the resultant transformation is the result of what one might call grace. Buber writes, "one cannot produce genuine dialogue, but one can be at its disposal."[18]

The thrust of apocalyptic, on the other hand, is familiar with the struggle of humans down in the core of their very soul for transcendence, for dialogue with God, but affords this struggle "no elemental significance."[19] There is no significance given to the turning of the individual or of the community toward a new historical future in conversation with God. For Buber, "the apocalyptic knows nothing of an inner transformation of man that precedes the transformation of the world and cooperates

11. Ibid., 16.
12. Ibid., 14.
13. Ibid.
14. Ibid.
15. Ibid., 16.
16. Ibid.
17. Ibid., 20.
18. Ibid., 21.
19. Ibid., 16–17.

in it."[20] To the contrary, apocalyptic regards creation as on a fixed course toward destruction and insignificance. In fact, the creation is regarded as done for, in "old age," or past any possibility for a new and hopeful direction. Creation in its true essence is thus being denied in apocalypticism. "The world, to be sure, is no longer called creation, but its irremediable old age is accepted as self-understood."[21]

The prophetic spirit that stirs history in the fullness of decision at every historical moment is absent in apocalyptic. In apocalyptic there is no stirring of the Spirit that gives rise to new possibilities, fresh possibilities for hope. Apocalyptic imposes rather an element of fatalism and hopelessness, "the existential mistrust of all against all" that "prevents any meaningful negotiation over the real differences of interest" when it comes to the possibility of dialogue over the issues of the day.[22] There are no pregnant moments in the history of creation that can give birth to something new. The creation has basically run its course and is dying out. It awaits its predetermined destruction.

Buber blames the survival of Jewish apocalyptic on "Jesus and in like manner his emissaries."[23] Indeed, Albert Schweitzer concluded his monumental *Quest of the Historical Jesus* with the idea that Jesus was centrally an apocalyptic prophet who threw himself upon the wheel of history only to be crushed beneath it.[24] Buber was not motivated by Schweitzer's analysis, but there is a certain parallel here. Like Schweitzer, Buber does not locate the problem associated with Jesus' apocalypticism in any assumption of resurrection by Jesus or his followers but rather in the apocalyptic worldview that undergirded that eventual assumption. And Buber does not so much focus on the wisdom tradition's Spirit of creation, as does Levison, but rather on the prophetic tradition's anointing for the reception of new beginnings. But Buber still assumes with Levison that Christology stands in tension with the Spirit's role in the natural realm, in the natural flow of human life, to be open to God and to converse with God toward a new future for the world.

20. Ibid., 19.

21. Ibid.

22. Ibid., 20.

23. Ibid., 21.

24. Albert Schweitzer, *The Quest of the Historical Jesus* (Mineola, NY: Dover, 2005), 261–83.

The Spirit of Creation and Resurrection

How do we deal with the doctrine of creation pneumatology so as to connect it creatively and constructively with the gift of immortality granted by the risen Christ? How do we integrate the Spirit of creation with the Spirit of the resurrection? Both Levison and Buber offer us helpful hints for addressing this challenge, even as they expose tensions between the pneumatology of the Old Testament and the apocalyptic implications of the New Testament. Levison helpfully discerns a shift from the flourishing of life under the shadow of death in the wisdom tradition to the breaking through this barrier in the resurrection of Jesus. The fist of protest raised against death in the Old Testament is fulfilled in the New Testament. The flourishing of life under the shadow of death in the Old Testament becomes the anticipated cowering of death under the light of the Spirit of resurrection in the New Testament. The Spirit at the resurrection of Jesus is excessive, eschatologically fulfilling the reach for life implied in the Old Testament by bursting through the barrier of mortality and alienation.

Buber is helpful here as well. Indeed, I can accept his insight into the prophetic tradition of the Old Testament as supporting a view of the historical moment of the creature as pregnant with new possibilities that transcend the old or that which can be predicted or calculated from that which had gone before. Creation is made for transcendence and for liberation, for an unpredictable conversation with God that bursts through old developments and opens up new and unforeseen possibilities for history. Jürgen Moltmann, among others, has noted that this is where the prophetic tradition of the Old Testament and the apocalyptic tradition of the New Testament overlap.[25] Apocalypticism rooted in the resurrection of Jesus does not leave the old creation behind, no more than the embodied life of Jesus was left behind by his resurrection. The transcendence of life beyond mortality and alienation from God that takes place in the cross and the resurrection is the ultimate surprise of creation, the ultimate unexpected turn to God and God's will for the world!

This ultimate transcendence does not simply arise from creaturely capacities. This is the apocalyptic insight. But, then again, Buber

25. I see this as the major thrust of Moltmann's seminal work, *Theology of Hope* (Minneapolis: Fortress, 1993).

himself notes that the dialogue with God is not something we produce; it is an event of grace: "one cannot produce genuine dialogue, but one can be at its disposal."[26] The empty tomb is the ultimate end of this conversation, a reality from beyond that takes creaturely yearning and groaning (in the Spirit) up into an unforeseen conversation that breaks through our slavery to sin and death. It is a conversation we cannot produce. But we can be at its disposal in our yearning and reaching for life by the very Spirit of God that made us!

There are three issues to discuss in going beyond the hints that Levison and Buber helpfully provide for us. The first issue concerns the overcoming of any dualism between God's Spirit and the material realm. In the ancient world this dualism was supported by the gnostic heresy; in modernism by the "God of the gaps," which reduces God to a border at the furthest reaches of human knowledge. Dietrich Bonhoeffer's seminal remarks about the God "of the gaps" are instructive. As is well known, Bonhoeffer wrote from prison, "Weizsäcker's book, *Zum Weltbild der Physik*, is still keeping me very busy. It has again brought home to me quite clearly how wrong it is to use God as a stopgap for the incompleteness of our knowledge. . . . God is no stopgap; He must be recognized at the center of our life, not when we are at the end of our resources."[27]

By reading C. F. von Weizsäcker's book on physics, Bonhoeffer came to appreciate the reality of God as at the very "soul" of the cosmos. Bonhoeffer was made to reflect on how theologically unfruitful it is to think of God as at work at the boundary of human discovery, as though God only makes sense in the context of inexplicable events detached from natural processes. The problem with this effort to find a "place" for God at the boundaries of science is that this divine habitation will keep shrinking as the reach of science expands. Such a dualism between God and the natural realm is devastating to pneumatology, since, as we have seen, the cosmos is in the Old Testament especially the "home address" of the Spirit's work. Within such a dualism, the Spirit gets confined to the realm of revelation or gnosis; in the modern era, the area of theological cognition or epistemology. The preoccupation with the incarnation in Christology and the consequent sacramental

26. Buber, "Prophecy, Apocalyptic, and Historical Hour," 21.

27. Dietrich Bonhoeffer, "Letter to Eberhard Bethge, May 29, 1944," in *Letters and Papers from Prison* (New York: Simon & Schuster, 1997), 310–12.

theology helped to keep the work of the Spirit anchored in its cosmic home base, though the sense of immediacy of the Spirit's work in the context of Baptism or the sacred meal was neither well understood nor cultivated. Tom F. Driver, for example, laments the fact that sacramental theology has historically not grasped well the reality that being "filled with the immediate presence of the deity" is essential to the sacramental act.[28] Moreover, what the Spirit means for the totality of life requires greater breadth and depth of understanding.

The work of theologians like Jürgen Moltmann in expanding the boundaries of pneumatology beyond the area of "revelation" to include all of creation and its renewal granted breathing room for a greater appreciation of the Spirit as the Spirit *of life*.[29] Both Bonhoeffer and Moltmann replace the God of the gaps with a divine presence that is at the *center* of all of life, sustaining it, causing it to flourish, groaning and travailing with it in its reach for redemption, and providing for its renewal through the power of the cross and the resurrection. The potential of life that is hidden in the cross, at the place of ultimate abandonment and alienation, explodes at the resurrection with all of the possibilities that God had always willed for creation.[30] Through Christ, the Spirit entered the depths of creaturely despair and need for God in order to bring the creature into the realm of faith, hope, and love, the virtues of life in the Spirit.[31]

The second issue to address is what Levison says about "subsequence." Is the Spirit of the resurrection and of immortality "subsequent" to the Spirit of life at work in all of creation? The use of the term "subsequence" accents the discontinuity between the Spirit at work "from below" through natural processes and the "supernatural" gift of the Spirit "from beyond" given at the resurrection (and penultimately in the new birth) and that flesh and blood is helpless to inherit. The apocalyptic impulse

28. Tom F. Driver, *The Magic of Ritual: Our Need for Liberating Rites That Transform Our Lives and Our Communities* (San Francisco: HarperSanFrancisco, 1981), 209.

29. Jürgen Moltmann, *The Spirit of Life: A Universal Affirmation*, trans. Margaret Kohl (Minneapolis: Fortress, 1992), 5–10.

30. This idea of the Spirit as the hidden potential for life at the cross is taken from D. Lyle Dabney, "Naming the Spirit: Towards a Pneumatology of the Cross," in *Starting with the Spirit*, ed. Stephen Prickard and Gordon Preece, Task of Theology Today 2 (Hindmarsh, Australia: Australian Theological Forum, 2001), 28–58, especially 58.

31. See how I deal with the atonement in the light of pneumatology in Frank D. Macchia, *Justified in the Spirit: Creation, Redemption, and the Triune God* (Grand Rapids: Eerdmans 2010), 155–85.

accents this discontinuity. The ultimate gift of immortality does not evolve teleologically from within the natural propensities granted to creation by the Spirit of life. The cross shatters all such pretentions. The cross is the place where all human possibilities, all creaturely strivings, crash against the rocks of alienation from God and ultimate despair. At the resurrection, immortality is granted as a new beginning, eschatologically "from beyond."

Yet, the discontinuity is not the entire story. Jesus offered himself on the cross "by the eternal Spirit" (Heb. 9:14) so that Jesus conquers at his resurrection by way of "an indestructible life" (Heb. 7:16). The Spirit of life is the hidden potential of life and hope at the cross, a potential promised to all in their abandonment and suffering. Moreover, as Levison notes, creation is an extraordinary work of the Spirit too. Natural life is created with an extraordinary capacity to yearn for God and even, as Buber noted, converse with God toward new beginnings. Indeed, as Paul wrote, Abraham "believed—the God who gives life to the dead and calls into being things that were not" (Rom. 4:17b). The implication is that an analogous relationship exists between the extraordinary work of the Spirit in giving rise to natural life "out of nothing" (out of "things that were not") and the gift of immortality granted at the resurrection. It is not as though one is natural and the other supernatural. They are both supernatural, though one is granted from below or through the flourishing of natural capacities and processes and the other is granted from above. They both orientate creation toward God in extraordinary ways, for, as Buber noted, creation is graced, at the disposal of dialogue, made for unexpected turns and surprises. Though creation follows natural laws, the Spirit of the living God keeps it open to the unexpected. Predictability has its limits, a point that quantum physicists have discovered.

So there is continuity between the Spirit of creation and the Spirit of resurrection after all. Henri de Lubac accented this continuity, noting that all human existence is constituted in the Spirit by the prophetic call of God (note the potential here for responding to Buber). As de Lubac explains: "God's call is constitutive. My finality, which is expressed by this desire, is inscribed upon my very being as it has been put into this universe by God. And, by God's will, I now have no other genuine end, no end really assigned to my nature or presented for my free acceptance under any guise, except that of 'seeing God.' "[32]

The eschatological finality lifted up by apocalypticism is not extrinsic to humanity but rather "a destiny inscribed in a man's very nature, directing him from within, and which he could not ontologically escape."[33] How could it be otherwise, when creation is itself brought into being and continuously sustained by the eschatological Spirit that raised Jesus from the dead? De Lubac notes that our entire being is constituted by the Spirit "of finality." "For it is a gift totally interior to me; nothing is left out of it, and nothing of myself is without it."[34] In creation, God gives us, and continues to give us ourselves as gift, in the sense that we have no existence apart from this gift.[35] The result is that refusing God constitutes a radical denial of oneself that threatens one's own reason for being at its very core. By claiming that Jesus and New Testament apocalypticism denied the existential significance of the prophetic tradition, Buber raised an important issue, but ended up misunderstanding New Testament apocalypticism in the process.

It is important to note, however, that the discontinuity is not thereby discounted by the continuity. De Lubac explains carefully:

> Between nature as it exists and the supernatural for which God destines it, the distance is as great, the difference as radical, as that between non-being and being: for to pass from one to the other is not merely to pass into "more being," but to pass to a different type of being. It is a crossing by grace into an impassible barrier. One does not merely need extra strength, such as an actual grace would give: one needs a new principle, that principle of divine life, which we call "sanctifying grace."[36]

The two modalities of grace, natural and sanctifying, are continuous, since creation is made and sustained by the supernatural Spirit to exist from a call to divine purposes, but the relationship between call and fulfillment is also discontinuous, because one cannot naturally pass teleologically from one to the other, any more than one can naturally pass from death to life.

32. Henri de Lubac, *The Mystery of the Supernatural* (Chestnut Ridge, NY: Crossroad, 1998), 54–55.

33. Ibid., 68–69.

34. Ibid., 77.

35. Ibid.

36. Ibid., 83.

De Lubac still affirms subsequence and does not assume, as Levison does in his reading of the wisdom tradition of the Old Testament, that sanctifying grace is part of the Spirit's work in all of creation. Yet, the doctrine of subsequence *is still qualified* in such a way as to open up a dialogue between the two pneumatologies (Old Testament and New Testament) as described by Levison. One may conclude that, though the gracing of creation by the Spirit is not sanctifying in the sense of the new birth (the gift of new life through the resurrection of Jesus), creation graced by the Spirit still inherently reaches for this sanctification and is constituted by that reach as well as the divine call at the core of it. Is this reach not in some seminal and analogous sense "sanctifying" as well? Are we not dealing in this revised subsequence doctrine with a tension between the work of the *Spiritus Vivicans* and *Spiritus Sanctificans*, one that allows for both continuity and discontinuity?[37]

The third and last issue to discuss is how best to describe the divine action in moving creation toward redemption. An entire chorus of theologians has recently weighed in against the metaphor of "intervention." God is not to be viewed as "intervening" into the created order to enact redemptive events like the exodus or the resurrection of Jesus from the dead. Indeed, the God who raised Israel up from Egypt raised Jesus from the dead.[38] If there are *both* continuity and discontinuity between creation as graced of the Spirit and God's act to grant creation immortality, then "intervention" would not be a helpful term to use. The reason is that "intervention" sounds like God is breaking in from the gaps, so to speak, or from that which is not natural, in order to bring about a result that has no basis whatsoever in (no continuity at all with) the natural realm. The Spirit that raised Jesus from the dead would be cut off from the breath of Yahweh active throughout all of creation. Rather than divine "intervention," a better word would be divine "transformation" or "conversion" of creation from that which is alien to that which belongs to the creature redemptively by the Spirit of life. Such terms preserve both elements of discontinuity and continuity.

All three issues point to the fact that the creation lives from the Spirit and reaches by

37. See Moltmann, *Spirit of Life*, 9.

38. As Robert Jenson notes in "The God of Israel and the Fruits of Trinitarian Theology," in *Another Reformation: Postliberal Christianity and the Jews*, ed. Peter Ochs (Grand Rapids: Baker Academic, 2011), 63–92, especially 68–69.

the Spirit for the Spirit's own perfection of creation in the image of the risen Christ. This reach defines the very core of the creation's being, for the creation was made by God as the dwelling place of the Spirit with this call toward transcendence, toward the risen life of the Son, as essential to its very reason for being. The raising of life from the deep in Genesis 1:2 connects in the Spirit to the raising of Jesus from the depth of alienation, sin, and death. One must understand this connection in order to understand the full expanse of the Spirit of creation.

The Spirit of Creation as the Spirit of Immortality

Can we really understand this expanse? When Lawrence Krauss wrote his provocative book, *A Universe from Nothing: Why There Is Something Rather Than Nothing*, he had no idea that he would provoke a significant pushback from philosophers of religion.[39] Philosophers, not all of whom have any faith commitment, noted that Krauss was using the term "nothing" in a way that actually implied "something," namely, a quantum vacuum. The philosophical problem of why there is something (being) rather than nothing (nonbeing) (or how something can arise from nothing), however, refers to "nothing" in some unimaginably absolute sense. Krauss claimed to have tackled an ancient philosophical problem through the lens of science but ended up sidestepping the problem in the process, or at least so redefining it that he failed to understand and to directly deal with it.[40]

Krauss's response to this challenge is indeed interesting. He pushed back just as hard claiming that he was actually clarifying the problem of "something" arising from "nothing," or redefining it so that it might make some kind of sense. Viewing "nothing" as some unimaginable "nonbeing" is an "idealized" notion of nothingness that makes no sense, since it has no concrete point of reference that we can discuss rationally or talk about in relation to the real world as we know it.[41] Reframing the problem of why and how there is something rather than nothing in the context of a quantum vacuum redefines

39. Lawrence M. Krauss, *A Universe from Nothing: Why There Is Something Rather Than Nothing* (New York: Free Press, 2012).

40. See David Albert, "On the Origin of Everything: A Universe from Nothing by Lawrence M. Krauss," *New York Times*, *Sunday Book Review* (May 23, 2012), n.p.

41. Krauss, *Universe from Nothing*, xviii–xiv.

the problem in terms accessible to science. In other words, the quantum vacuum is about as close to "nothing" as one can get while still making some kind of sense. Otherwise, the problem is discussed using terminology that is nonsensical.

The nonsensical nature of "something" arising from "nothing" in an absolute sense is precisely the point in this ancient philosophical discussion, and shifting the term "nothing" to refer to "something" accessible to science causes one to miss the point entirely. Of course, Krauss is free to say that the philosophical category of nonbeing is nonsensical and that the presence of reality as we know it is simply a brute fact with which one is stuck as the framework from which to discuss philosophical problems connected with the reality of being. But this is not what he attempts to do. He really imagines himself to be answering the problem of how being came from nonbeing. He is not doing this, no matter how loudly he might protest to the contrary.

The category of nonbeing is supposed to be unimaginable because it refers to the deeper question of being in relation to that which excludes it. It is precisely here that the traditional theology of creation by the Spirit *ex nihilo* (out of nothing) has its place. This theological framing of the ancient problem of being and nonbeing does not imply the God of the gaps, because we are dealing with a divine reality in the Spirit that cannot in principle be the object of rational investigation and manipulation (regardless of the state of scientific advances). One cannot understand creation from nothing by the breath of Yahweh any more than one can understand the resurrection of Jesus according to the Spirit of holiness. According to Paul, Abraham's faith implies just such a connection, for Abraham "believed the God who gives life to the dead and calls into being things that were not" (Rom. 4:17b). Krauss scratches his head when looking at the classical problem as to why there is being rather than nonbeing and says, "I don't understand that." Precisely. He has at that point understood the problem. When he translates the term "nonbeing" into the scientific idiom of "quantum vacuum," he has fundamentally changed the problem into something else.

Here's the point: if the work of the Spirit of creation is analogous to the work of the Spirit of resurrection, then creation from the beginning is earmarked for resurrection, absolutely extraordinary and inexplicable in its ultimate place of origin in God. This connection between the Spirit's work in creation and in resurrection means that the creation is made to be the dwelling place of the Spirit in the image of the risen Christ. Paul implies as much in 2 Corinthians 5:4–5a: "For while we are in this tent, we groan and are burdened, because we do not wish to be unclothed but to be clothed instead with our heavenly dwelling, so that what is mortal may be swallowed up by life. *Now the one who has fashioned us for this very purpose is God*" (emphasis added).

In other words, according to the above text, God fashioned us for the very purpose of bearing the "heavenly dwelling" or the body of the resurrection. All of creation groans for the liberty of embodied immortality according to Paul (Rom. 8:18–23). Like bound slaves who were created for freedom, the cosmos groans for the freedom from the chains of sin and death. It all groans for the freedom of risen materiality, the freedom of the breath of Yahweh. The breath of Yahweh created form from emptiness in order that this form may be fashioned in the image of immortal and glorious embodiment. And in reaching for transcendence, for the call of God, creation reaches for its own destiny as the free creature, the creature free from that which is alien to it: mortality, sin, and death.

Conclusion

A theology of the Spirit of creation is not superseded or laid aside by the "subsequent" gift of immortality; neither is it contradicted by the earmarking of creation for dialogue with God, a dialogue that keeps the creature free to turn toward God in new and unexpected ways. The work of the Spirit of creation is rather fulfilled in the work of the Spirit of resurrection. But the reality of the cross shows us that one cannot move in an uninterrupted way from that divine call that defines the creature, who lives by the Spirit, to the gift of immortal embodiment. Nevertheless, the Spirit of creation is not snuffed out at the cross but remains the hidden capacity for life in the midst of all that contradicts it (Heb. 9:14), an enduring promise to all those who seem overwhelmed by the realities of suffering and death. There is both continuity and discontinuity between the work of the Spirit in creation and in resurrection.

The preservation of the discontinuity helps to protect us from unbridled utopian enthusiasm. More importantly, however, the continuity of redemption theology with the Spirit of creation helps us develop an ecotheology that respects creation as earmarked for God and for the freedom won by Christ, rather than for humanity's greed, exploitation, carelessness, and self-destructive habits. It helps us to dismiss all dualisms and to affirm a theology close to the heartbeat of human life and breath, human sexuality and wholeness, human relationships and community. The Spirit of creation shatters all illusions of creaturely autonomy or of God's detachment from the world and reaches for a vision of reality as living from God and reaching for God, even to the point of groaning in travail for the liberty of the Spirit. It helps us see the cross as the place where the Spirit of creation has not totally dimmed, no matter how horrific the abandonment or oppression, but endures as the hidden potential of a new beginning, a beginning that is connected to the creature's most essential yearnings but that exceeds these in directions only graspable by unimaginable grace, a grace as unimaginable as the original creation itself. We can no more reach the reality of the empty tomb as we can have within ourselves that original eruption of light from darkness, form from void. Indeed, even the discontinuity serves to preserve the continuity, for both origins and renewal are all by grace, all by the Spirit of life.

Part 2

Holy Scripture

CHAPTER 8

Scripture

A Pneumatological Retrieval of Neglected Dimensions of the Doctrine of Scripture

KEITH A. QUAN

Current work on the doctrine of Scripture follows well-established paths, whether divine freedom, the incarnational analogy, inspiration, inerrancy, or the doctrine's proper dogmatic location. A Third Article Theology (TAT) approach—such as Myk Habets's proposal in the introductory essay to this volume—opens up a fresh direction; it suggests starting from the Spirit's identity, not letting other concerns set the trajectory or making pneumatological considerations a postscript.[1] As many theologians recognize, starting points, whether modern epistemology or the Trinity, shape dogmatic accounts of Scripture.[2] Thus by looking at the doctrine of Scripture through the lens of Trinitarian pneumatology, this

1. Although differing from TAT proponents, John Webster models a comparable approach with his account of illumination as "a theological meditation on the economy of the Spirit," an economy that itself "rests upon a theology of the deity and personality of the Spirit" ("Illumination," *Journal of Reformed Theology* 5 [2011]: 327–28).

2. See, for example, Stephen E. Fowl, "Scripture," in *The Oxford Handbook of Systematic Theology*, ed. John Webster, Kathryn Tanner, and Iain Torrance (New York: Oxford University Press, 2007), 345–51.

chapter highlights underdeveloped dimensions of the doctrine.[3]

I will not, however, attempt a complete articulation of the Spirit's relationship to Holy Scripture. Instead, sacrificing breadth for depth, I will concentrate on one question as a test case: Can Scripture's *telos*, communion with the triune God, be more deeply and thoroughly integrated into a theological construal of Scripture if it begins with the Spirit's distinct personal identity?[4] Suggestive here is Glen Scorgie's appraisal of evangelical hermeneutics:

> God is readily acknowledged as the original supervising author of the text, and his aid is now solicited to empower the exegetical miner to do his or her investigative job well. The need for guidance in making edifying connections between text and application is readily acknowledged as well. But for all of this God is essentially the "behind the scenes" source of empowerment rather than a direct and personal dialogue partner with the reader.[5]

One might address this charge only at the level of interpretive practice, perhaps by retrieving *lectio divina*. Yet the resonance between Scorgie's description of God as a behind-the-scenes empowering force and TAT's concern about the diminishment of the Spirit's personhood hints at a more profound response;[6] creative retrieval at the level of theology proper—specifically pneumatology—may

3. While plenary verbal inspiration appears to begin with the Spirit, many would contend that here inspiration functions merely as a means to an ultimately (modern) epistemological end, namely, securing an infallible foundation of theological propositions. For instance, see Darren Sarisky, *Scriptural Interpretation: A Theological Exploration*, Challenges in Contemporary Theology (Malden: Wiley-Blackwell, 2013), 84.

4. Expressing this *telos* of Scripture, Kevin J. Vanhoozer speaks of "communicative action for communion" in "Triune Discourse: Theological Reflections on the Claim That God Speaks (Part 2)," in *Trinitarian Theology for the Church: Scripture, Community, Worship*, ed. Daniel J. Treier and David Lauber (Downers Grove, IL: InterVarsity Press, 2009), 51; cf. Sarisky's argument in *Scriptural Interpretation*, and Fowl, "Scripture," 349.

5. Glen A. Scorgie, "Hermeneutics and the Meditative Use of Scripture: The Case for a Baptized Imagination," *Journal of the Evangelical Theological Society* 44, no. 2 (June 2001): 273–74.

6. Many TAT advocates are concerned that in the Western tradition the Spirit is a mere "bonding agent," both "faceless" and "nameless" (Habets, "Prolegomenon: On Starting with the Spirit," chapter 1 of the present work), and that the Spirit lacks a proper mission (David M. Coffey, "A Proper Mission of the Holy Spirit," *Theological Studies* 47 [1986]: 227). Cf. Robert W. Jenson, "You Wonder Where the Spirit Went," *Pro Ecclesia* 2 (1993): 296–304.

revitalize an emphasis on the *viva vox Dei* that will, in turn, promote the "sweet conversation" of reading Holy Writ embodied in practices such as *lectio divina*.[7]

I begin by sketching the Spirit's personal identity vis-à-vis the Father and the Son through a fresh redeployment of classical Trinitarian resources in dialogue with recent critiques of the Western tradition. After tracing the expression of this identity in the Spirit's teaching economy, I then propose supplementing traditional terminology (*inspiration*, *illumination*) with Nicholas Wolterstorff's concept of presentational discourse, to more fully order the doctrine of Scripture according to this pneumatological grammar. Even though I begin with the Spirit, however, the result is fully Trinitarian; emphasizing the identity of the "supreme judge," the "Holy Spirit speaking in the Scripture," leads to an emphasis on Holy Scripture as the "ongoing rapport between heaven and earth, between Christ and his church, between God and his children."[8]

7. Mariano Magrassi, *Praying the Bible: An Introduction to* Lectio Divina, trans. Edward Hagman (Collegeville, MN: Liturgical Press, 1998), 16.

8. Westminster Confession of Faith 1.10; Herman Bavinck, *Reformed Dogmatics*, ed. John Bolt, trans. John Vriend (Grand Rapids: Baker Academic, 2003–8), 1:385.

The Spirit's Personal Identity as Witness

The Spirit's personal identity is manifest in the distinctive pattern of relating to the Father and the Son *within* the eternal Trinitarian life and its economic *extension* in the Spirit's inclusion of rebellious sinners in that life: "*the Spirit descends from the Father to rest and remain upon the Son so that, through the Son, he may come to rest and remain upon Jesus' disciples as well.*"[9] Among the many Johannine parallels between the Father-Son and Father-disciples relationships, the chief parallel, the one that encompasses the others and marks the Son *as* Son, is the Spirit who *remains* upon the Son and now also his siblings, the children of God who share in Jesus' filial relationship with the Father (John 1:12, 32–34; 14:16–17; 20:17).[10]

9. Andreas J. Köstenberger and Scott R. Swain, *Father, Son and Spirit: The Trinity in John's Gospel*, New Studies in Biblical Theology (Downers Grove, IL: InterVarsity Press, 2008), 136 (italics in original).

10. Each parallel, whether in the Father's action (loves, abides in, sanctifies, seals, sends) or in the Son-disciples' response (speaking God's words, doing God's work, glorifying God, bearing fruit), is associated with the Spirit's work in the Johannine corpus or the broader canon. Moreover, John the Baptist testifies to Jesus' identity as the Son of God

This pattern encourages pneumatological attentiveness to the Old Testament sons of God; for insofar as the sonship of Adam, Israel, and David-Solomon prefigures the eschatological Son of God, it thereby also witnesses to the identity of the eschatological Spirit. Thus Adam's[11] reception of the breath of life (anticipatory of the life-giving Spirit) parallels his creation in the *imago Dei* that marks him as son (Gen. 1:26–27; 2:7; 5:1–5; Luke 3:38).[12] This image entails a royal and priestly task: to rule over the serpent by naming it unclean, thereby guarding the garden sanctuary through filial obedience to the divine command (Gen. 1:26–27; 2:15–20). But instead of attaining illumination, wisdom, and life (2:17; 3:22), Adam's disobedience opens their eyes to shame (3:7–8) and leads to death (3:23; 5:1–31).[13] Each potential "escalated blessing"—illumination, life, wisdom, and clothing—is linked to the Spirit later in the canon, which suggests that this fuller filial-royal endowment typifies the eschatological Spirit.[14]

Similarly, in the exodus, YHWH redeems Israel, his firstborn son (Exod. 4:22–23), so that they might be his own possession, a kingdom of priests, through filial obedience to all that YHWH speaks at Sinai (19:5–8; cf. Mal. 3:17).[15] Despite the substantial allusive continuity with Adam in Genesis (Exod. 1:7, 12, 20), Israel's postlapsarian sonship includes waiting and groaning (2:23–24).[16] Further, Israel's narrative identity as firstborn progresses through a geographical itinerary marked by the Spirit's theophanic presence—the burning bush at Horeb (3:1–3),

based upon seeing and recognizing him as the one upon whom the Spirit remains (John 1:31–34).

11. My focus on Adam alone here is guided by the New Testament's Adam-Christ typology.

12. On this relationship of Genesis 2 to the *imago* see Catherine Leigh Beckerleg, "The 'Image of God' in Eden: The Creation of Mankind in Genesis 2:5–3:24 in Light of the *mīs pî*, *pīt pî* and *wpt-r* Rituals of Mesopotamia and Ancient Egypt" (PhD diss., Harvard University, 2009).

13. William N. Wilder, "Illumination and Investiture: The Royal Significance of the Tree of Wisdom in Genesis 3," *Westminster Theological Journal* 68 (2006): 51–69.

14. Greg K. Beale, *A New Testament Biblical Theology: The Unfolding of the Old Testament in the New* (Grand Rapids: Baker Academic, 2011), 33–46. Potential escalated blessings would also explain why Genesis 2 only partially parallels Beckerleg's list of elements in cultic-image creation rituals ("'Image of God' in Eden," 187–244).

15. On the filial nature of the service required of YHWH's own possession, see Peter J. Gentry and Stephen J. Wellum, *Kingdom through Covenant: A Biblical-Theological Understanding of the Covenants* (Wheaton, IL: Crossway, 2012), 315–18.

16. Mitchell M. Kim, "The Blessing of the Curse: Fulfilling Genesis 1:28 in a Context of Suffering" (PhD diss., Wheaton College, 2010), 74–97.

the pillar of cloud-fire to Sinai (13:21–22), and the tabernacle glory-cloud to the promised land (40:34–38; cf. 16:7, 10).[17] Indeed, it is the dynamic Spirit that guides Israel's filial journey into maturity and inheritance, dividing the waters of the sea to bring forth dry land, leading through the wilderness, endowing the builders with wisdom, and filling the tabernacle.[18] Canonically, then, the eschatological Spirit and his work is again prefigured by the signs and goal of sonship: (1) circumcision—the distinguishing mark of Israel's firstborn at Passover (4:22–26; 12:7, 13, 24–49)—anticipates circumcision of the heart (Deut. 30:6);[19] (2) the sprinkling of blood that ratified the Sinai covenant (Exod. 24:8) looks to the ratification of the new covenant; and (3) the land, both given as Israel's inheritance and conditioned upon obedience as YHWH's inheritance (Deut. 4:14–21; 9:29), is an "expression" and "locus" of the filial relationship that is fulfilled in the new creation.[20]

Israel's sonship narrows to David and Solomon, who embody the nation, especially through filial Torah obedience (2 Sam. 7:8–16; Ps. 89:26–37).[21] Once again the Spirit marks David's royal-priestly status by coming upon him mightily (and departing from Saul) as Samuel anoints David (1 Sam. 16:13–14) in an ascension narrative with a clothing motif (17:38; 18:4; 24:4)—all signifying

17. On the association of the cloud with the Spirit, see Isa. 63:7–14; Neh. 9:19–20; B. J. Oropeza, *Paul and Apostasy: Eschatology, Perseverance, and Falling Away in the Corinthian Congregation*, Wissenschaftliche Untersuchungen zum Neuen Testament 2/115 (Tübingen: Mohr Siebeck, 2000), 90–102.

18. Pentateuchal and canonical intertextuality makes the resolution of breath/wind/Spirit debates unnecessary here, since a divergence in the descriptions (and understanding) of two authors does not preclude having the same referent.

19. Given the interplay between Israel's firstborn and Israel as firstborn (Exod. 4:22–26; 13:1–16), it is as if the plagues constituted corporate Israel's circumcision—at the very least, like circumcision it distinguished them as YHWH's (8:22–23; 9:4, 26; 11:7; 33:16).

20. J. G. Millar, "Land," in *New Dictionary of Biblical Theology*, ed. T. Desmond Alexander, Brian S. Rosner, D. A. Carson, and Graeme Goldsworthy (Downers Grove, IL: InterVarsity Press, 2000), 623–24. Note that the themes of circumcision, land, and inheritance all convey covenantal mutuality. For example, obedient Israel is YHWH's inheritance, and, ultimately in canonical perspective, I would argue that YHWH is Israel's true inheritance.

21. Gentry and Wellum, *Kingdom through Covenant*, 422–23. On the canonical trajectory of king as ideal Torah keeper (Deut. 17:14–20; 31:23–26; Josh. 1:1–9; Pss. 1–2), see Jamie A. Grant, *The King as Exemplar: The Function of Deuteronomy's Kingship Law in the Shaping of the Book of Psalms*, Academia Biblica (Atlanta: Society of Biblical Literature, 2004).

divine investiture.[22] Thus Israel's rest (Deut. 12:9–12) comes through David's God-given rest from his enemies (2 Sam. 7:1–16), so that Solomon, a man of rest and wise builder, may prepare YHWH's resting place and Israel's true inheritance (1 Chron. 22:9–10; 2 Chron. 6:41)—the glorious Spirit-filled temple (2 Chron. 7:1–3).

Climactically, Jesus, the last Adam, treads upon the satanic serpent (Luke 4:10–11; 10:18–19; cf. Ps. 91:12-13; Gen. 3:15) through tested filial obedience to the will of the Father (Luke 3:22, 38; 4:3, 9, 41), even unto death (4:2, 13; 22:3–6, 42; Phil. 2:8). Therefore God raises Christ from the dead, opening the way to Edenic eternal life (Luke 23:43; Rom. 5:12–21) and exalting him to the Davidic throne (Acts 2:24–36), that all things might be subject to him—enemies, powers, and even death (1 Cor. 15:20–28; Phil. 3:21). Christ, in his exaltation, does not merely bear the curse and attain the Adamic escalated blessings; he exceeds them, sitting at the right hand of God and sharing "the name which is above every name" (Phil. 2:9–11), YHWH, both "a redemptive-historical expression . . . of what is perennially true of his eternal person."[23] Yet now he reigns also *as* the obedient Adamic and Davidic Son who fulfilled all righteousness *for* the disobedient son, Israel, by exiting Egypt, passing through the baptismal waters of the Jordan, and proving faithful in the wilderness—and ultimately on a cursed tree (Matt. 2:13–15; 3:13–4:11; 11:16–19; Deut. 21:18–23).[24] Jesus' entire identity is, moreover, inseparable from the Spirit who marks him as the eternal—and now incarnate—Son, both as Adam (Luke 1:35; 3:38–4:1) and Israel (Matt. 2:15; 3:16–4:1), and from conception, growth, baptism, testing, anointing, ministry (Luke 4:14–21), and self-offering (Heb. 9:14)

22. David M. Howard, "The Transfer of Power from Saul to David in 1 Sam 16:13–14," *Journal of the Evangelical Theological Society* 32 (December 1989): 473–83; Gordon P. Hugenberger, *Marriage as Covenant: Biblical Law and Ethics as Developed from Malachi*, Biblical Studies Library (Grand Rapids: Baker, 1994), 198–99.

23. Lane G. Tipton, "Christology in Colossians 1:15–20 and Hebrews 1:1–4: An Exercise in Biblico-Systematic Theology," in *Resurrection and Eschatology: Theology in the Service of the Church*, ed. Lane G. Tipton and Jeffrey C. Waddington (Phillipsburg, NJ: Presbyterian & Reformed, 2008), 190. He fulfills all the promises as the eschatological Son precisely because he is the archetypal Son (note that the Johannine "I AM" motif precedes Jesus' hour of glory).

24. See Brandon D. Crowe, *The Obedient Son: Deuteronomy and Christology in the Gospel of Matthew*, Beihefte zur Zeitschrift für die neutestamentliche Wissenschaft 188 (Berlin: de Gruyter, 2012).

to resurrection (Rom. 1:4; 8:11) and vindication (1 Tim. 3:16).[25]

Just as the firstborn Son's identity is inseparable from the Spirit who raised him from the dead, so also the Spirit of God's Son is the identifying mark of his many siblings. Having been baptized with Jesus into his death-exodus (Rom. 6:3; Luke 9:31) and freed from slavery to sin by his blood (Rom. 6:12–23), the adopted υἱοί too are led by the Spirit in a wilderness of suffering and groaning (Rom. 8:14–27; 1 Cor. 10:1–13)—and yet, in a radical rupture of narrative sequence, the eschatological Spirit is even *now* fructifying the desert (Gal. 5:16–24) and awakening in us the Son's own filial cry, "Abba," "the entrée into the Godhead's own discourse" (4:6).[26] Indeed, the Spirit of adoption is the fulfillment of everything that signifies or constitutes divine filial status and investiture in the Old Testament: the Spirit seals the heirs of God through the removal of the body of the flesh in the *circumcision* of the heart (Rom. 2:29; Eph. 1:13; Col. 2:11),[27] sanctifies them unto obedience and the *sprinkling* of Jesus' blood of the covenant (1 Pet. 1:2; cf. Exod. 24:7–8), and will ultimately *clothe* them with immortality (Rom. 8:11; 1 Cor. 15:42–54). As the ἀρραβών, the Holy Spirit is building them together in love into a *holy temple* (Rom. 5:5; Eph. 2:21–22; 3:14–21; 4:16), even as the Spirit now already fills them with all *wisdom* (Eph. 5:15–21; Col. 1:9–12),[28] a foretaste of their *inheritance* in the Son and guarantee of their redemption as *God's own possession* (Eph. 1:11–14).

This sketch of the Spirit's identity, however, needs refinement in light of three TAT concerns about Western pneumatology.[29]

25. On the Spirit's resting upon the incarnate Son as a temporal extension of what is true eternally, see Eugene F. Rogers Jr., *After the Spirit: A Constructive Pneumatology from Resources outside the Modern West*, Radical Traditions (Grand Rapids: Eerdmans, 2005), 69; Matthias Joseph Scheeben, *The Mysteries of Christianity*, trans. Cyril Vollert (St. Louis: Herder, 1946), 154n3.

26. Ivor J. Davidson, "Salvation's Destiny: Heirs of God," in *God of Salvation: Soteriology in Theological Perspective*, ed. Ivor J. Davidson and Murray A. Rae (Burlington, VT: Ashgate, 2011), 169; Beale, *New Testament Biblical Theology*, 583–88.

27. Tucker S. Ferda, "'Sealed' with the Holy Spirit (Eph. 1, 13–14) and Circumcision," *Biblica* 93 (2012): 557–79.

28. Robert L. Foster, "'A Temple of the Lord Filled to the Fullness of God': Context and Intertextuality (Eph. 3:19)," *Novum Testamentum* 49 (2007): 85–96; Timothy G. Gombis, "Being the Fullness of God in Christ by the Spirit: Ephesians 5:18 in Its Epistolary Setting," *Tyndale Bulletin* 53, no. 2 (2002): 259–71.

29. The resemblance to the Western tradition should be evident: the trajectory of everything

First, when articulating the Spirit's identity in relation to the Son's, *inseparability* can easily slide into *absorption*, making the Spirit "superfluous."[30] But if—perhaps analogous to a crown or signet ring—the Spirit *marks* Jesus *as* the beloved Son then their identities remain distinct;[31] for just as a father and son mutually imply one another conceptually yet with a definite *taxis* (or order), so also a royal heir and crown mutually imply one another conceptually, yet a scion is crowned *because* she is heir.[32] The Father gives the Son the Spirit without measure *because* the Son is the beloved Son *by nature*—though with respect to God's children *by adoption* the gift of the Spirit is more constitutive of their filial identity, conforming them to the preeminent Son.[33]

Second, rather than tacking the Spirit on at the end or construing the Spirit solely in functional terms as applying Christ's work,[34] Western Trinitarianism may, ironically, hold the key to a maximal reading of the Spirit's work: "Identifying the Spirit's relationship to Jesus and his disciples enables us to detect the Spirit's distinctive personal activity even in places where he remains otherwise unnamed. The principle is this: when you see an analogy between the Son and his brothers, assume that the Spirit is the author of the analogy."[35] Similarly, Augustine, Aqui-

---

given to mark divine filial status and covenantal *mutuality*.

30. More pithily: "Anything the Spirit can do, the Son can do better" (Rogers, *After the Spirit*, 33).

31. The theological tradition is full of comparable language (stamp, seal, crown, pledge, and kiss). See, for instance, Scheeben, *Mysteries of Christianity*, 94, 112, 154–61.

32. That two terms of a relation mutually imply one another does not preclude an irreversible order. Accordingly, I see no basis for augmenting or revising traditional Trinitarian taxis. See Gilles Emery, *The Trinitarian Theology of Saint Thomas Aquinas*, trans. Francesca Aran Murphy (New York: Oxford University Press, 2007), 240; Rogers, *After the Spirit*, 144; Bruce D. Marshall, "*Ex Occidente Lux*? Aquinas and Eastern Orthodox Theology," *Modern Theology* 20 (January 2004): 40–41.

This solution is Christ centered without falling into christomonism. If the Son is identified as the one marked by the Spirit, then the Spirit can only be self-effacing, not anonymous; for the Spirit cannot reveal the Son as Son without also indirectly revealing his own identity as the one who marks the Son as Son. Cf. Bruce D. Marshall, "The Deep Things of God: Trinitarian Pneumatology," in *The Oxford Handbook of the Trinity*, ed. Gilles Emery and Matthew Levering (New York: Oxford University Press, 2011), 411.

33. Consider how someone could give a girl a signet ring *in order to* adopt her as a daughter. We could also further imagine a scenario in which a natural son, having received a signet ring from his father, gives it in concert with his father to another, thereby adopting her.

34. Habets, "Prolegomenon."

35. Köstenberger and Swain, *Father, Son and Spirit*, 147, cf. 176–77 where they read John 17

nas, and Jonathan Edwards use Trinitarian theology as an interpretive rule to "discern" and "understand" the Holy Spirit even in "binitarian" passages where the Spirit is not explicitly mentioned.[36] This maximizing pneumatological grammar should help us to discern the self-effacing Spirit not only *within* the full sweep of the scriptural text—including the Old Testament sons that prefigure Christ (see above)—but also *in front of* the text.[37] Whenever the children of God honor the Son *today*, joyfully holding fast to their confession amid suffering, they discern the same Spirit of glory who marked Christ throughout his ministry *now* resting upon them (1 Pet. 4:12–14), and in *every* heartfelt cry to the Father and resemblance to the Son they exult in the Spirit given to them (Rom. 5:1–5; 8:15–17, 29–30), the pledge of divine love and assurance of their full inheritance.

Third, imagery of a passive gift and inanimate *vinculum caritatis* seems to be a reduction, if not rejection, of the Spirit's fully hypostatic identity. Such language by itself, unaugmented and undisciplined, can have a depersonalizing effect; nevertheless, depersonalization is no more inevitable here than with christological language (for example, door, bread, and Word).[38] The key is a name that is related to the impersonal language and yet also irreducibly personal—in this case, "witness."[39] A witness can fulfill the epistemological dimensions of a seal, mark, or gift: announcing, assuring, or guaranteeing one person's identity, relationship, status, or affection relative to another person. And if, following John Owen, we hold together Scripture's active pneumatological language (the Spirit comes, falls on, or departs) with the passive (the Father gives, sends, pours out) then we also honor the Spirit's voluntary agency in self-giving, "the concord of the given and the

according to this principle.

36. Emery, *Trinitarian Theology*, 241–42; Robert W. Caldwell, *Communion in the Spirit: The Holy Spirit as the Bond of Union in the Theology of Jonathan Edwards*, Studies in Evangelical History and Thought (Eugene, OR: Wipf & Stock, 2006), 47, 65, 196–97, 199.

37. Attentive to the canonical trajectory of the Old Testament sons of God, this pneumatological grammar recognizes that the significance of explicit references to the Spirit exceeds the quantity, thereby balancing a more exclusive focus on the prophetic Spirit.

38. Ben Witherington III and Laura M. Ice, *The Shadow of the Almighty: Father, Son, and Spirit in Biblical Perspective* (Grand Rapids: Eerdmans, 2002), 129, 131.

39. Rogers, *After the Spirit*, 9, 85, 140–41.

givers."[40] Indeed, for all the disputes stemming from the polyvalence of רוח and πνεῦμα, the one common interpretive thread of both biblical scholarship and theological commentary is dynamic agency and movement.[41] We can now, therefore, redescribe the above pneumatological terrain accordingly:[42] whenever the children of God persevere in their witness to the Son, they discern the same Spirit who raised Jesus from the dead testifying with them (Acts 5:32), and in every cry of "Abba" and Christlikeness the υἱοί exult in the Spirit who testifies to them (Rom. 8:15)—lest they grieve and blaspheme the παράκλητος who sanctifies, strengthens, fructifies, builds, and fills, leading them into maturity and keeping them unto the day when he clothes them in glorious incorruptibility.

The Spirit as Witness in His Teaching Economy

In his teaching ministry, the "Spirit acts in conformity with the property of his person," a point evident in two strands of the biblical-theological sketch: exodus and temple.[43] To begin with, every stage of Israel's exodus itinerary is characterized not only by the Spirit's theophanic presence but also by divine discourse, both spoken and written—the revelation of the Tetragrammaton from the bush, the divinely engraved tablets of the law and reproclamation of the name on Sinai (Exod. 24:9–12; 34:1–9), and instruction from the tabernacle (25:22; 33:7–11; Num. 7:89). The collocation of the guiding cloud-tabernacle with YHWH's commands in the Exodus-Numbers narrative (Exod. 40:34–38; Num. 9:15–23), moreover, "serves especially to highlight the point that keeping Yahweh's verbal commands is essentially the same as following the divine cloud," a correlation later reinforced through parallelism with the good gift of the Spirit's instruction

40. Kelly M. Kapic, "The Spirit as Gift: Explorations in John Owen's Pneumatology," in *The Ashgate Research Companion to John Owen's Theology*, ed. Kelly M. Kapic and Mark Jones (Burlington, VT: Ashgate, 2012), 128–29.

41. Richard E. Averbeck, "Breath, Wind, Spirit, and the Holy Spirit in the Old Testament," in *Presence, Power, and Promise: The Role of the Spirit of God in the Old Testament*, ed. David G. Firth and Paul D. Wegner (Downers Grove, IL: InterVarsity Press, 2011), 25–37; Emery, *Trinitarian Theology*, 224, 229, 242–43, 247–48.

42. This does not invalidate what has already been said, however. Maintaining the impersonal language (seal, for example) is crucial to recognizing continuity with the Old Testament sons of God, which then shapes the personal language of witness.

43. Emery, *Trinitarian Theology*, 260.

(Neh. 9:19–20).[44] When read with Deuteronomy (8:5–17), we see that the Spirit's wilderness school was to train Israel in filial obedience—to walk in YHWH's instruction (Exod. 16:4)—as preparation for inheriting the land: "The Spirit of the LORD gave them rest" (Isa. 63:14).[45] This didactic ministry of the Spirit is fulfilled in the new exodus in (at least) three ways: (1) the mighty growth and multiplication of the Spirit-accompanied word in its triumphant advance from Jerusalem to the ends of the earth (Acts 6:7; 12:24; 19:20; cf. Exod. 1:7, 12, 20);[46] (2) the redeemed υἱοί of God who are led by the Spirit and walk by the Spirit that they might inherit the kingdom of God (Gal. 4:4–7; 5:16–25);[47] and (3) the "finger of God" writing now not upon tablets of stone but fleshly hearts (2 Cor. 3:3; Matt. 12:28; Luke 11:20; Exod. 31:18; 8:19).

The temple theme, too, conveys the Spirit's work of teaching. For as the dynamic word comes, bears fruit, and increases (Col. 1:6, 10; 2 Thess. 3:1), the church is being built together (ἐποικοδομηθέντες; also οἰκοδομὴ, συνοικοδομεῖσθε) by the Spirit into a holy temple, the dwelling of God (Eph. 2:19–22). This building up (οἰκοδομὴν, 4:12, 16), furthermore, comes through the various ministers of the gospel (4:11), who equip the saints for the work of service (4:12, 16)—a work that includes speaking the truth in love (4:15), using only edifying (οἰκοδομὴν) words (4:29), and speaking to one another in psalms, hymns, and spiritual songs (5:19).[48] Nevertheless, this entire teaching and speaking ministry that builds the church is from God (Eph. 4:15–16; Col. 2:19), the working of the same power that raised Christ from the dead (Eph. 1:19–20; 3:7, 16, 20; Col. 1:29). As the Spirit

44. Jason Clay Condren, "Yahweh in Their Midst: A Discourse Analysis of Numbers 1:1–10:10 and Its Relationship to the Theme of Divine Presence in the Pentateuch" (PhD diss., Trinity Evangelical Divinity School, 2005), 107, 205; W. Ross Blackburn, *The God Who Makes Himself Known: The Missionary Heart of the Book of Exodus*, New Studies in Biblical Theology (Downers Grove, IL: InterVarsity Press, 2012), 78, 133–34.

45. Youtaek Kang, "God as Teacher: Studies on Deut 5–8 and Exodus 16" (PhD diss., Durham University, 2002), 99–105.

46. David W. Pao, *Acts and the Isaianic New Exodus*, Biblical Studies Library (Grand Rapids, Baker Academic, 2000), 147–80; Keith A. Quan, "The Word of the Living God: Presentational Discourse as a Model for Contemporary Divine Address Through Scripture" (PhD Diss., Southwestern Baptist Theological Seminary, 2014), 113–20.

47. William N. Wilder, *Echoes of the Exodus Narrative in the Context and Background of Galatians 5:18*, Studies in Biblical Literature 23 (New York: Lang, 2001).

48. Foster, "Temple of the Lord," 95.

filled the builders of the tabernacle, Bezalel and Oholiab, giving wisdom to teach (Exod. 35:31–35; Eph. 3:19; 5:18), so the eschatological temple is ultimately made without hands: "'Not by might nor by power, but by My Spirit,' says the LORD of hosts" (Zech. 4:6).[49]

Each aspect of the Spirit's didactic ministry—spreading the gospel, leading the υἱοί, writing upon hearts of flesh, and building the temple—is achieved through apostolic proclamation (2 Cor. 3:12–4:6; Gal. 3:2–3; Eph. 2:20). This applies even to the participation of all believers in the eschatological building project. For Paul concludes his eschatological instruction by exhorting the Thessalonians to "comfort one another with these words" (1 Thess. 4:18), and then repeats the pattern, ending further eschatological teaching by telling them to encourage one another and build one another up (οἰκοδομεῖτε, 5:11)—presumably via the preceding words again (note διὸ). Therefore, though both the apostle Paul and other believers teach and admonish with all wisdom (Rom. 15:14; Col. 1:29; 3:16), doing so according to the working of the same power (Eph. 3:7, 20; 5:18–19), Christians are to admonish one another with *Paul's* apostolic instruction (2 Thess. 5:14–15).

Finally, this ministry of the Spirit extends to the *written* witness, the canonical Scriptures. Indeed, following Jesus' own teaching (Luke 24:25–27), the apostolic proclamation of the gospel is inseparable from the Old Testament Scriptures (Rom. 1:1–4; 1 Cor. 15:3–4). Thus the very Spirit-wrought, persevering hope that Paul writes *about* (Rom. 5:1–5)—and later expands upon in terms of the Spirit-led υἱοί (Rom. 8:1–37)—is to be wrought *through* his own epistle; for his citation of the perseverance-and-hope-producing Scriptures (Rom. 15:4, 9–12) is enclosed by two prayers in which he asks the God of perseverance and hope to make the saints in Rome "abound in hope by the power of the Holy Spirit" (Rom. 15:5–6, 13; cf. 1 Cor. 10:1–31). Likewise, the same Spirit whose distribution constituted divine testimony to so great a salvation (Heb. 2:4), now testifies to that salvation *in* and *through* the Epistle to the Hebrews by reuttering (λέγει) the living Old Testament word (Heb. 3:7; 10:15), exhorting the υἱοί to heed the example of the wilderness generation and learn obedient

49. The contrast between the golden calf's human origin and the tabernacle's divine origin (Exod. 24–40) points toward the contrast between temples χειροποιήτοις (Acts 17:24) and the ποίημα of God—the church (Eph. 2:10).

perseverance through fatherly discipline like the Son (Heb. 5:8–9; 12:1–11).[50]

Whenever the inscripturated prophetic and apostolic word grows and multiplies and believers teach and admonish one another with that same edifying word, the children of God discern the Spirit testifying with them, building and filling the eschatological temple; and in every hope-filled "Abba" and Scripture-sustained perseverance in filial obedience, the υἱοί exult in the Spirit who testifies to them—lest like the wilderness generation they grieve, blaspheme, and spurn the παράκλητος who leads and instructs them, keeping them unto the day when he clothes them in the same glorious incorruptibility as Christ.

A Terminological Gap in Divine Agency

What remains is to offer a brief meditation upon what it would mean for theology proper to govern our doctrine of Scripture, in particular, to order the locus according to the Spirit's distinct personal identity as witness vis-à-vis the Father and Son. As a way into the current state of the locus in dogmatics, consider some of what occurs prior to and in the process of me reading my copy of Plato's *The Republic*. Presumably thousands of years ago Plato writes the work and, culminating some long and messy transmission, Grube translates, Reeve revises, and Hackett publishes it. As a classic, Barnes and Noble carries it, and, for some reason (maybe a class), I purchase the book from them. Then one day I pull it off my shelf to read—perhaps remembering a poignant line, watching *The Matrix*, or answering a student's question. Once opened, everything from intellectual skill and command of Plato scholarship to personal experiences, philosophical views, and reasons for looking at the book now influences my reading. These factors, among others, shape what portions I read, what I notice and grasp, and even how it affects me.

Because scriptural reading also occurs within a creaturely writing-reception sequence, what makes this *lectio* different—indeed sui *generis*—is the divine agency that directs and permeates this sequence, and the principle task of a dogmatic account of Holy Scripture is to delineate the character and scope of this agency. Yet if terminology

50. For more on the inscripturation of the apostolic witness, see Beale, *New Testament Biblical Theology*, 827–32; Keith A. Quan, "The Inscripturated Word: The Fourth Gospel as the Continuing Speech of the Incarnate Word," *Journal of Theological Interpretation* 5 (2011): 49–67.

is indicative of the focus of scholarly energies within a discipline, the two unquestionably preeminent terms for divine agency with respect to Scripture, *inspiration* and *illumination*, indicate a doctrinal history skewed toward the two ends of the writing-reception sequence, that is, the act "of producing this work" and "whenever it is read and received with understanding."[51] And while historical-critical methods and postmodern reading strategies might enrich accounts of the creaturely processes at these two end points (composition, transmission, and personal experience), a significant terminological gap in divine agency remains with everything that it takes to get the book to a particular individual (the bookstore and class) and impetuses for particular readings (the remembrance or student question).[52]

Far from a deity who, having once intervened to inspire the Bible, now stands afar off waiting for someone to happen to open its pages before intervening again to illumine, only a divine agency of *maximal* scope accords with our pneumatological grammar; for while the metaphors of sealing, circumcising, and writing on hearts are punctiliar images, only a "perennially present and ubiquitously 'speaking'" divine author can do justice to the dynamic images of growing and multiplying, journeying, and building—especially in light of the Old Testament background.[53] What is truly remarkable, moreover, is the specificity of the Spirit's all-encompassing presence in Acts. The Spirit inaugurates every mission by designating and sending witnesses, and the Spirit not only furnishes them with the power, boldness, and "'content' of their proclamation," but also "guides the geographical itinerary of the word by directing human proclaimers to unanticipated regions, sometimes forbidding them from traveling to specific locales."[54] Whether through dreams and visions, the execution of providentially orchestrated divine coincidences (like with the Ethiopian eunuch and Cornelius), or authenticating signs and wonders, the Spirit

51. Vanhoozer, "Triune Discourse," 64; Quan, "Word of the Living God," 7, 126–28.

52. Determining how reflective terminology is of substance is beyond the scope of my argument—though consider how much of the tradition's vocabulary is Trinitarian and christological, loci central to the faith.

53. Mark Bowald, "The Character of Theological Interpretation of Scripture," *International Journal of Systematic Theology* 12 (2010): 168.

54. This section is indebted to Juhwan Joseph Kim, "'What Is This Word?': An Early Christian Narrative of the Universal Spread of the Spirit-Accompanied Word" (ThD diss., Harvard Divinity School, 2009), 276.

spearheads the totality of the word's expansion, "to facilitate and ensure" its advance.[55] Indeed, as far as I can tell, with *every* positive response to the word of the gospel in Acts, more than just opening hearts (16:14), the triune God "frequently introduces that word" and "brings it to people"—precisely the point in the writing-reception sequence where the theological tradition is terminologically deficient.[56] Thus the Spirit's oversight "of the entire historical course of the creaturely reality"[57] of Scripture encompasses not only production, preservation, and canonization, but also everything up to and including the "culminating step," the Spirit's administration of that word in preaching.[58]

Divine Presentational Discourse

It is here, with this terminological *lacuna*, that Wolterstorff's distinction between authorial and presentational discourse can aid us in constructing a pneumatologically ruled account of Scripture.[59] Roughly, presentational discourse is when one presents a previously authored text in order to perform a new speech act. So when, for instance, a mother hands her son a note to clean his room after she had already left that same note on the computer screen on which he is playing games, she can rightly say that she has told him twice. Unlike if the son happened to glance at the note again on his own initiative, the mother's act of re-presenting the note constitutes a distinct speech act in which she overtly retakes the same illocutionary stance toward the same content—though conceptually neither the force nor content need remain the same.[60]

---

55. Ibid.; see also Quan, "Word of the Living God," 116–17.

56. Bavinck, *Reformed Dogmatics*, 4:449, 459.

57. John Webster, *Holy Scripture: A Dogmatic Sketch*, Current Issues in Theology (New York: Cambridge University Press, 2003), 10, 24, 26–27; cf. Quan, "Word of the Living God," 129–32.

58. Cornelis Trimp, "Preaching as the Public Means of Divine Redemption," trans. Nelson D. Kloosterman, *Mid-America Journal of Theology* 10 (1999): 63–65.

59. Nicholas Wolterstorff, *Divine Discourse: Philosophical Reflections on the Claim That God Speaks* (New York: Cambridge University Press, 1995), 54–56, 71, 131–32, 188–89.

60. For prior theological applications of presentational discourse and related concepts, see James Robson, *Word and Spirit in Ezekiel*, Library of Hebrew Bible/Old Testament Studies 447 (New York: T&T Clark, 2006), 74–77; Daniel J. Treier, "Speech Acts, Hearing Hearts, and Other Senses: The Doctrine of Scripture Practiced in Hebrews," in *The Epistle to the Hebrews and Christian Theology*, ed. Richard Bauckham et al. (Grand Rapids: Eerdmans, 2009), 339–40; Anthony C. Thiselton, "Reader-Response Hermeneutics, Action Models, and the Parables of Jesus," in *The Responsibility of*

The proposal, then, is not that the Spirit reinspires Scripture again and again since the textual composition has ceased, yet it nonetheless posits a *divine* activity, what I call presentational discourse. Divine presentational discourse instead complements inspiration and illumination insofar as God's agency in Scripture's dissemination—the relatively neglected stretch of divine agency—complements God's activity in its production and reception. This "re-revealing" and re-announcement of the inspired scriptural word is a "public reiteration" that takes diverse forms.[61] Thus Scripture "does not remain dead and dormant in the memory or understanding" but rather "the Spirit of God brings it into remembrance" (John 2:17, 22; 12:16; 14:26);[62] for, according to Karl Barth, "while there is recollection and tradition from the standpoint of the action of the community, objectively and in fact He Himself is the acting Subject who lifts the barrier of yesterday and moves into today, making Himself present, and entering in as Lord."[63] Likewise, in preaching, "though the voice is on earth, the speaker is in heaven"; it is "the echo of God's vocal presence with us in Scripture."[64] That God "does not avail Himself of an angel" but pastor, parent, and even neighbor, Martin Luther observes, often blinds us so that we "fail to recognize God, who is conversing with" us through them.[65] Consequently, whether the medium is memory or magazine, pastor or neighbor, it is the triune God that "causes that word to go forth to people,"

Hermeneutics, ed. Roger Lundin, Anthony C. Thiselton, and Clarence Walhout (Grand Rapids: Eerdmans, 1985), 108, 112–13.

61. Donald A. Carson, "Challenges for the Twenty-First Century Pulpit," in *Preach the Word: Essays on Expository Preaching in Honor of R. Kent Hughes*, ed. Leland Ryken and Todd A. Wilson (Wheaton, IL: Crossway, 2007), 176; John Webster, *The Domain of the Word: Scripture and Theological Reason* (New York: T&T Clark, 2012), 22, 26.

62. Adolph Saphir, *The Hidden Life: Thoughts on Communion with God* (New York: Gospel, 1877), 98, 123.

63. Karl Barth, *Church Dogmatics* III/2, ed. G. W. Bromiley and T. F. Torrance, trans. Harold Knight, G. W. Bromiley, J. K. S. Reid, and R. H. Fuller (New York: T&T Clark, 1960), 470; cf. the discussion of Owen and Jonathan Edwards in Quan, "Word of the Living God," 66–70, 209–12.

64. Angus Paddison, *Scripture: A Very Theological Proposal* (New York: T&T Clark, 2009), 113; Thomas Boston, *An Illustration of the Doctrine of the Christian Religion with Respect to Faith and Practice upon the Plan of the Assembly's Shorter Catechism*, vol. 1 of *The Whole Works of the Late Reverend Thomas Boston*, ed. Samuel McMillan (Aberdeen: George and Robert King, 1848), 428–29.

65. Martin Luther, *Luther's Works*, vol. 22, *Sermons on the Gospel of St. John: Chapters 1–4*, ed. Jaroslav Pelikan, trans. Martin H. Bertram (St. Louis: Concordia, 1975), 527.

presenting it as an *admonitio*: "God *breathes* that Word to me."[66]

Presentational discourse is commensurate not only with the maximal scope of the Spirit's economy of teaching but also with the Spirit's fully hypostatic character as witness. While illumination is arguably distinct from speech and conceptually open to an impersonal interpretation, presentational discourse is as irreducibly personal as a witness—only persons can discourse presentationally and witness.[67] Presentational discourse, therefore, also coheres with the tradition's consistent—even if predominantly christological—confession about proclamation. For when John Calvin says that in preaching Jesus "calls us to himself as though he spoke with open mouth, and that we see him personally before us," and Luther compares it to "an opportunity to hear God speak in person," both Reformers attest to contemporary divine speech in the most robust and unambiguous of terms.[68] Similarly, the documents promulgated by the Second Vatican Council declare that Christ is "present in His word, because it is He Himself who speaks when sacred scripture is read in the Church."[69]

Yet such christological confidence regarding proclamation is inseparable from pneumatology; for just as Calvin calls the teaching of the Lord's doctrine a "sure and infallible sign" that Jesus Christ "holds out his arms to receive us," so also, in like context, he says that no "good and faithful teacher" can "know how to speak one word to the glory of God, except it is given him, and that the Holy Ghost govern his tongue."[70] As the liv-

66. Bavinck, *Reformed Dogmatics*, 4:449; John Woodhouse, "The Preacher and the Living Word: Preaching and the Holy Spirit," in *When God's Voice Is Heard: Essays on Preaching Presented to Dick Lucas*, ed. David Jackman and Christopher Green (Leicester: InterVarsity Press, 1995), 59. On *admonitio* in Augustine, see Frederick E. Van Fleteren, "Augustine's Ascent of the Soul in Book VII of the Confessions: A Reconsideration," *Augustinian Studies* 5 (1974): 36–41. We might say Scripture is breathed out (inspiration), to (presentational discourse), and in (illumination).

67. Wolterstorff, *Divine Discourse*, 27, 72–73; Quan, "Word of the Living God," 65–71, 112n105, 167n73.

68. John Calvin, *John Calvin's Sermons on Ephesians*, trans. A. Golding (London: Banner of Truth Trust, 1973), 368; Luther, *Sermons* 526–27.

69. *Sacrosanctum Concilium*, 7 (promulgated December 4, 1963). Online: http://www.vatican.va/archive/hist_councils/ii_vatican_council/documents/vat-ii_const_19631204_sacrosanctum-concilium_en.html.

70. Calvin, *Sermons on Ephesians*, 363, 368; cf. Kapic, "Spirit as Gift," 139; Richard Baxter, *The Life of Faith*, vol. 12 of *The Practical Works of Rev. Richard Baxter* (London: Mills, Jowett, & Mills, 1830), 496; Augustine, *Confessions*, F. J. Sheed (Indianapolis: Hackett, 1993), 280.

ing one walks among the seven golden lampstands—raising up the minister, "com[ing] out with him, directing him, instructing him, exciting him"—the preacher is called to drive home what the Spirit *is* saying to *this* church in bringing *this* prophetic and apostolic word to them at *this* moment (Revelation 1–3).[71]

Whether in a child's voice chanting, "*Tolle lege, tolle lege*," or the blindingly mundane admonition of a neighbor, the children of God discern the presentation of the Spirit of God's Son in every Christ-glorifying public reiteration and re-revelation of the scriptural word, and they exult in the παράκλητος who witnesses with and to them, leading, multiplying, building, and engraving.

Conclusion

While every dogmatic account of Holy Scripture is inescapably epistemological, by starting with the Spirit rather than modern epistemology, this probative TAT exercise was undertaken with the divine economy as the epistemological framework, which, in turn, yielded a perspective on Scripture that thoroughly integrated that economy's telos, communion with the triune God. For though the correlation between the Spirit as the identifying mark of the Son and υἱοί and the Spirit as witness with and to them is decidedly epistemological, it is an epistemology of filial relation and communion; and the Spirit's *opus proprium* in and through Scripture is not only to teach sinners *about* the triune God, but also to acquaint them with "the Trinitarian life, *moving* them from an external to an internal relation, teaching them to say 'Father,' to take on the identity of the Son, to join in the Spirit's own celebration."[72]

If we seek, moreover, a dogmatic account faithful to the scriptural witness and that witness appropriates the most relevant dynamic imagery—multiplying, building, leading, writing, propelling—to the one whose very name, רוח and πνεῦμα, bears congruence with the *actus purus* common to the Godhead, then pneumatology was an optimal lens through which to view the locus of Holy Scripture for our purposes.[73] The retrieval of a maximal reading of the Spirit's agency that

71. Boston, *Illustration of the Doctrine*, 429.

72. Rogers, *After the Spirit*, 14.

73. On appropriation as congruence, see Emery, *Trinitarian Theology*, 312–37. Aquinas focuses on what appropriation teaches about the *propria*, but, given such congruence, neglect or depersonalization of a divine *hypostasis* would seem to threaten to neglect or depersonalize the corresponding parts of the economy.

honors the Spirit's full hypostatic density as witness reinvigorated the corresponding aspects of our delineation of Scripture within the divine economy. Thus, in accordance with TAT, a fully adequate doctrine of Scripture will, I suggest, take care to maximize pneumatology in particular "and relativize (but not minimize or abolish) ecclesial action and its ordered forms" in its theological articulation of Scripture's historical and creaturely course.[74] Because at no point in building the temple made without hands is the Spirit's agency "consequent rather than initiatory," the biblical interpreter is confronted not merely with syntactical and historical decisions but ultimately with the παράκλητος who is *now* speaking.[75]

Such pneumatological reinvigoration of interpretive and dogmatic practice (discerning the Spirit even when unnamed and rectifying terminological deficiency, respectively) does not exclude its spiritual dimension—indeed, it cannot. In every scripturally sustained, persevering hope that calls forth that filial cry of trust, "Abba," the children of God may, even ought, to "meet with the Comforter" in every instance of the Spirit's manifold presentation of the scriptural witness, rather than "lying in the dark [as] to their author"; they exult in the Spirit who leads them throughout their pilgrimage—lest they grieve him by failing to glory in his presence, "without which glorying Christianity itself does not stand."[76] The rule of inseparable operation, however, gives us not only this added joy of recognizing the self-effacing Spirit but also applies in reverse. Whenever the children of God glory in the Spirit's witness in a reiteration of Scripture, they may, even ought, to meet with the Father and Son in whose "archetypal love" they partake, an adoptive share "within the circle of that love."[77]

74. John Webster, *Word and Church: Essays in Christian Dogmatics* (New York: T&T Clark, 2001), 198.

75. Webster, *Domain of the Word*, 6.

76. John Owen, *Of Communion with God the Father, Son, and Holy Ghost*, vol. 2 of *The Works of John Owen*, ed. William H. Goold (London: Banner of Truth Trust, 1965), 44–45, 267–68; John Calvin, *Calvin: Institutes of the Christian Religion*, ed. John T. McNeill, trans. Ford Lewis Battles, The Library of Christian Classics (Louisville: Westminster John Knox, 2001), 3.2.39. *Homoousia* requires *homotimia*. See John L. W. James, "An Examination of *Homotimia* in St. Basil the Great's *On the Holy Spirit*, and Contemporary Implications," *Westminster Theological Journal* 74 (2012): 257–76.

77. Scott R. Swain, *The God of the Gospel: Robert Jenson's Trinitarian Theology*, Strategic Initiatives in Evangelical Theology (Downers Grove, IL: InterVarsity Press, 2013), 202.

More than merely a perfecting cause who illumines scriptural propositions and brings about perlocutionary effects, the Spirit is ubiquitously re-presenting Scripture, a voice that echoes throughout the temple; the Spirit circumcises the fleshly hearts of the children of God and leads them through proven filial obedience into their inheritance of the new creation—all things that witness to covenantal mutuality, "a creaturely counterpart to God's fellowship with himself."[78] In reading and hearing Holy Scripture, our hearts are "deluged with love" as we meet with the Father, Son, and Holy Spirit, communion with the triune God who is our inheritance.[79]

78. Davidson, "Salvation's Destiny," 170. Because the land was the locus and barometer of filial relationship and obedience, the Spirit and the Spirit's fruit constitute a foretaste of the new creation.

79. "Deluged with love" is the chapter title inspired by Jonathan Edwards in Swain, *God of the Gospel*, 194–207.

CHAPTER 9

Spiritual Hermeneutics

JOEL B. GREEN

Seminarians and divinity students who encounter critical biblical studies for the first time are often flummoxed by what is for them alien (and alienating) interests and protocols. My favorite reaction, which I have heard repeatedly over the past three decades of teaching, is this description of what academic study does with the Bible: "After they kill it, they lay it on the table and dissect it." Not surprisingly, then, for many, biblical studies is identified largely for its antipathies toward worship and proclamation, toward the work of constructive theology, and, indeed, toward the church more generally.

Such responses are not altogether misguided, given the priorities of biblical studies in the modern era. Two of these are particularly telling. The first priority is *distantiation*—that is, the need to craft a mental and religious space separating the contemporary reader from the ancient text. Depending on the commitments of the interpreter, the biblical text may or may not have significance for twenty-first-century readers; if it does, though, the path to its significance is indirect, requiring an often circuitous and time-consuming detour through the past in order to determine what the text might originally have meant back then in its own sociohistorical context. If God is to speak in and through the biblical text today, God can do so only after history has first spoken—and, indeed, after history has first set boundaries around what God might be able to say, or what the church might say about God. The second priority is the importance of *technique*. If readers of biblical texts no longer have direct access to the words of the Bible, but must take one or more of the roads offered them by historical study, then they need training in how to traverse these new paths. If the significance of biblical texts resides in the past, then interpreters need new charts, new skills, and new gear for traversing the foreign country of the past. If the modern exercise of biblical studies is shaped by these two priorities, distantiation and technique, then perhaps it is not surprising that those who are inducted into these interests and protocols find themselves more and more reading about the Bible (rather than immersing themselves in the text of Scripture itself), and less and less sure of the immediacy of the Bible's message for their lives and the life of the church.

One way to characterize modern biblical studies brings into sharper focus our concern in this essay. Biblical studies is concerned with "hearing voices." Various forms of historical inquiry listen for voices in the past—for example, the voice of a redactor and the redactor's community, or the voice of a reconstructed historical figure, like King David or Jesus. Various forms of literary inquiry listen for voices within the text—for example, what (the textually constructed figure of) Moses has to say about (the textually constructed figure of) God. What do we hear as we tune our ears to the voice of the implied author or the narrator, or to the echo chamber of the text, with its reverberations of earlier texts and earlier voices? Various forms of "interested" reading might construe the text as an instrument of power, giving voice to the voiceless or silencing voices, for example. Engaging in some forms of autobiographical or reader-response inquiry might assist us in hearing our own voices as these are reflected in or animated by the text before us. According to this metaphor, modern biblical studies is concerned with "hearing voices." For those of us interested in the role of the Holy Spirit in biblical interpretation, however, the primary voice is conspicuously absent from the typology of approaches I have just sketched. Academic study of the Bible has not concerned itself with how those who study the Bible might hear God's own voice speaking in and through Scripture. In the opening chapters of the book of Revelation, the Living

One instructs the seven churches: "If you can hear, listen to what the Spirit is saying to the churches."[1] How to hear what the Spirit is saying to the church—this is typically not in the syllabus students follow in their introductory biblical studies courses.

The question that confronts us, then, is what role the Holy Spirit might or ought to have in biblical interpretation. Alternatively, we can inquire into the difference it might or ought to make that we read the Bible as people of the Spirit. Before taking up these questions, allow me two additional words about modern biblical studies. First, in spite of my characterization of biblical studies thus far, its contribution to the church need not be as deleterious as my observations might suggest, nor as ghastly as students sometimes experience it. If one of the chief aims of teaching students to read biblical texts closely is to slow down the process of interpretation so as to encourage reflection on the capacity of these texts to speak to and over against its interpreters today and to cultivate a basic disposition of respect for its character as "other," then biblical studies today has much to offer. In this sense, disciplined attention to Scripture can only benefit the church. Second, globally, even in the West and in parts of the Eastern and Southern Hemispheres influenced by the West, the priorities of modern biblical studies have not decimated the church's theological interests in and commitments to Scripture. A great deal of theological work with Scripture continues in all sorts of venues—sermons, prayer, hymnody, and Bible studies among them. Some of this interpretive work is seasoned by the disciplined study of the Bible sponsored by academic biblical studies, and some of it would benefit from being seasoned in this way. At the end of the day, though, theological work with Scripture—listening to what the Spirit is saying to the church in and through Scripture—finds its home in the church and not in the university. Listening for God's address in Scripture is an ecclesial practice that, ultimately, does not and cannot depend on academic accreditation.

My agenda in this essay, then, is to inquire into the difference it might make that we read the Bible as people of the Spirit. I begin with a brief introduction to some contemporary scholarship concerned with the role of the Spirit in biblical hermeneutics. I then turn to consider two texts in the Acts of the Apostles where the significance of the

1. Rev. 2:7; cf. 2:11, 17, 29; 3:6, 13, 22. Unless otherwise indicated, translations of biblical texts follow the Common English Bible.

Holy Spirit in reading Scripture is on display. Finally, drawing together some of these observations, I sketch some features of Spirit-imbued interpretation.

The Holy Spirit in Theological and Pentecostal Hermeneutics of Scripture

Undoubtedly, many Christians would affirm the role of the Spirit in reading the Bible, even if such affirmations generally come in the form of abstract statements that do little to provide an account of the Spirit's work. In a sense, this is only to be expected since, to paraphrase John 3:3, it is one thing to discern the evidence of the Spirit's work but quite another to explain it. Moreover, some hermeneuts might resist an appeal to the Holy Spirit in the disciplined work of biblical interpretation, since it is far easier to say that the Spirit teaches such and such than it is to demonstrate that such a teaching actually derives from the Spirit's prompting and carries the Spirit's imprimatur. Who is to say whether God's Spirit guides and/or authorizes this reading and not that one—and on what basis? Predictably, then, academic manuals for biblical interpretation, irrespective of whether these were written with the university department of religion studies or the seminary in mind, render the work of biblical study mostly, if not entirely, in anthropological rather than pneumatological terms. Only rarely might the question be raised: What role does the Holy Spirit have in biblical interpretation? Only rarely are we led to consider whether, and how, reading the Bible as people of the Spirit might look different or follow different protocols than reading the Bible apart from faith commitments and communities of the faithful.

In the past two decades, discussion of the role of the Spirit in biblical interpretation has found renewed energy among two overlapping groups of practitioners. The first comprises those who are committed to the recovery of theological interpretation of Scripture, with its decidedly ecclesial home, its concern with encountering the God who stands behind and is mediated through Scripture, and its emphasis on the role of Scripture in the faith and formation of persons and ecclesial communities. Simply put, if we recognize theologically that our capacity to attune our ears to God's address is essentially divine work, then we must also admit that we need more than what human beings contribute to the study of Scripture—and this presses theological interpreters to reflect on, and embrace, the role of the Holy Spirit in our work with Scripture.[2] The second includes those concerned to articulate and practice Pentecostal hermeneutics, a sustained and in many ways exemplary attempt by Pentecostal scholars both to lay their theological cards on the table of biblical interpretation and to subject their interpretive tradition to critical scrutiny. In this section, I will briefly sketch the contributions of two people from each of these two movements.

Stephen E. Fowl's book, *Engaging Scripture*, first published in 1998, is a seminal study for theological interpretation—a volume that identified many of the concerns that would come to occupy the field.[3] In a chapter entitled "How the Spirit Reads and How to Read the Spirit," he explores in what ways Christian convictions about the Holy Spirit might play out on issues of interpretation. He responds with two emphases—first, the centrality of the Spirit in the process of understanding; and second, the importance of practices of recognizing and bearing witness to the work of the Spirit in others' lives, particularly as these practices are nurtured through friendships. By way of developing these claims, Fowl discusses Jesus' Farewell Discourse in John 13–17, "the most extensive account of the role of the Spirit in the New Testament."[4] Here we learn that the Spirit speaks in unison with the Father and the Son (thus providing a Trinitarian grounding for further reflection on the work of the Spirit in interpretation), and that the Spirit's primary role is to enable disciples to make sense of Jesus' words and, indeed, the past, from the perspective of Jesus' death and resurrection. Turning then to Acts 10–15, Fowl urges that Peter's friendship with Cornelius led Peter to recognize the Spirit at work with Cornelius (and his household); that Barnabas and Paul's testimony concerning the work of the Spirit among uncircumcised gentiles, together with Peter's witness, led those in Jerusalem to recognize that God had poured out the Spirit

2. I identify these characteristic foci of theological interpretation of Scripture in Joel B. Green, *Practicing Theological Interpretation: Engaging Biblical Texts for Faith and Formation*, Theological Explorations for the Church Catholic (Grand Rapids: Baker Academic, 2011), 2–5; cf. Green, "Response: Theological Interpretation on Display; Trajectories and Questions," in *Ears That Hear: Explorations in Theological Interpretation of the Bible*, ed. Joel B. Green and Tim Meadowcroft (Sheffield: Sheffield Phoenix, 2013), 253–57 (especially at 255–56).

3. Stephen E. Fowl, *Engaging Scripture: A Model for Theological Interpretation* (London: Blackwell, 1998; Eugene, OR: Wipf & Stock, 2008).

4. Ibid., 99.

on gentiles apart from the requirement of circumcision; and that this recognition led James and the Jerusalem consultation to read Scripture so as to open the door to the inclusion of gentiles sans the need for circumcision. On the basis of this reading, Fowl concludes that the judgment of the Jerusalem consultation exemplifies how "interpretation of scripture is guided by the testimony about the Spirit's work, rather than the other way around."[5] From his vantage point, then, as the church cultivates the practices of discerning the work of the Spirit in others, of testifying to the Spirit's work, and of listening wisely to those testimonies, so the church nurtures its ability to engage in practices of scriptural reasoning in ever-changing circumstances.

A second perspective on the work of the Spirit comes from J. Todd Billings, whose book *The Word of God for the People of God* promises "an entryway to theological interpretation of Scripture."[6] Impetus to examine the role of the Spirit in this interpretive process comes from two interrelated concerns. The first arises from the inevitable cultural conditioning of all interpretation, which might lead to the conclusion: to each people their own interpretation. The second arises from recognition of the Spirit's work in indigenizing God's word in Scripture in various contexts in ways that invite God's people, wherever they may be found, to live in the new reality of God's Spirit. Both invite spiritual discernment as a dimension of faithful reception of the Bible: "reading Scripture as the church, yet submitting as the church to the life-giving word of the Spirit through Scripture." Billings develops this act of spiritual discernment under three headings: "the insufficiency of direct appeals to 'experience' as a criterion for discerning the Spirit's work in Scripture," "the guidance provided by the Spirit's work in community for discerning the Spirit's work in Scripture," and accounting for "the constructive role of suspicion toward one's own cultural captivities in scriptural interpretation, even as this is combined with a trust in the Spirit's power to speak through Scripture."[7] In a basic sense, what Billings proposes is an elaborate set of checks and balances, with the Spirit's work with respect to scriptural interpretation complementary to the Spirit's work in tradition, creeds, experience, and culture. This is not to say that the

5. Ibid., 114.

6. J. Todd Billings, *The Word of God for the People of God: An Entryway to Theological Interpretation of Scripture* (Grand Rapids: Eerdmans, 2010).

7. Ibid., 109.

Spirit's activity could be reduced to tradition, creeds, and the rest. It is rather to take seriously the past and ongoing role of the Spirit in and through the church as the Spirit both indigenizes the message of Scripture for the church in all cultures and nations and at the same time has a transformative influence on the church in all cultures and nations. The Spirit thus generates a church notable for its bounded diversity, with those boundaries ultimately constituted by Jesus Christ himself. "Therefore," Billings writes, "we must maintain a great paradox: the incarnate Word speaks through Scripture so that our faith can become our own, amidst all of our cultural particularity; yet the incarnate Word calls his disciples to a continuing conversion, wherein the Spirit uses Scripture to reshape God's people into God's image."[8]

Among contemporary biblical scholars committed to articulating and putting into play a Pentecostal hermeneutic, John Christopher Thomas deserves special mention for the way he wants to foreground the role of the Holy Spirit. "For Pentecostals," he writes, "it is indeed one of the oddities of modern theological scholarship that across the theological spectrum approaches to Scripture have little or no appreciation for the work of the Holy Spirit in interpretation." By contrast, he urges, "such a hermeneutical component is of no little interest to Pentecostals."[9] Like Fowl, Thomas develops his understanding of the role of the Spirit in biblical interpretation via a close reading of Acts 15 (though they read this text differently). Thomas notes how, once everyone is gathered in Jerusalem in Acts 15, the experience of the missionary church is in the spotlight. Only after hearing testimonies regarding God's activity in accepting gentiles apart from circumcision do we find appeals to Scripture. Why does James turn to Amos 9 as he moves toward a decision regarding gentile

8. Ibid., 126. In this important sense, Billings's proposal is christocentric (and Trinitarian), a point that may not be sufficiently recognized in the more Barthian analysis of Christopher R. J. Holmes, "Revelation in the Present Tense: On Rethinking Theological Interpretation in Light of the Prophetic Office of Jesus Christ," *Journal of Theological Interpretation* 6 (2012): 23–42.

9. John Christopher Thomas, "Reading the Bible from within Our Own Traditions: A Pentecostal Hermeneutic as Test Case," in *Between Two Horizons: Spanning New Testament Studies and Systematic Theology*, ed. Joel B. Green and Max Turner (Grand Rapids: Eerdmans, 2000), 109. See Thomas's related essays, "Women, Pentecostals and the Bible: An Experiment in Pentecostal Hermeneutics," *Journal of Pentecostal Theology* 5 (1994): 41–56; "Women in the Church: An Experiment in Pentecostal Hermeneutics," *Evangelical Review of Theology* 20 (1996): 220–37.

inclusion among God's people? For Thomas, this interpretive move makes good sense in light of Luke's already well-established interest in demonstrating from the Scriptures that God had fulfilled God's promises to David in Jesus and, therefore, that those promises concerned the nature of the church. From his overview of Acts 15, then, Thomas identifies a hermeneutic with three primary components: Scripture, the interpretive community, and the Holy Spirit who prepares the community to read its Scriptures. Though he articulates them as primary components, Thomas does not in fact refer to them so discretely. Indeed, his reading of Acts 15 already demonstrates how these components are in concert. The community is the place of the Spirit's activity, the place where testimony to the Spirit's activity is given and received, and the place for serious discussion and discernment regarding the Spirit's work and the meaning of Scripture. Moreover, Scripture is not static in terms of its significance, but dynamic. Accordingly, "for Pentecostals, the Holy Spirit's role in interpretation cannot be reduced to some vague talk of illumination, for the Holy Spirit creates the context for interpretation through his actions and, as a result, guides the church in the determination of which texts are most relevant in a particular situation and clarifies how they might best be approached."[10] In all of this, he insists, a Pentecostal hermeneutic prioritizes the authority of Scripture, since the church's experience must be judged in relation to the Bible.

Kenneth Archer extends Thomas's work in his book, *A Pentecostal Hermeneutic for the Twenty-First Century*,[11] turning in his con-

---

10. Thomas, "Reading the Bible," 119.

11. Kenneth Archer, *A Pentecostal Hermeneutic for the Twenty-First Century: Spirit, Scripture and Community*, Journal of Pentecostal Theology Supplement 28 (Bloomsbury: T&T Clark, 2004; repr., Cleveland, TN: Centre for Pentecostal Theology Press, 2009). Someone like L. William Oliverto Jr. might complain that, by representing the work of Thomas and Archer, I have constrained too tightly my representation of Pentecostal hermeneutics (see his *Theological Hermeneutics in the Classical Pentecostal Tradition: A Typological Account* [Leiden: Brill, 2012]). Oliverto's concerns with the Thomas-Archer trajectory are twofold. First, he thinks that Archer has too easily moved away from an interest in the historical referents of biblical texts—though Oliverto's claims in this regard rest on an understanding of history that is problematic both theologically and philosophically (see Joel B. Green, "Rethinking 'History' for Theological Interpretation," *Journal of Theological Interpretation* 5 [2011]: 159–74). Second, and more importantly, Oliverto is interested in a more general theological hermeneutics rather than a theological hermeneutics *of Scripture* (similarly, cf. Amos Yong, *Spirit – Word – Community: Theological Hermeneutics in Trinitarian Perspective* [Eugene,

structive proposal to the triadic negotiation of Scripture, church, and Spirit. Working with well-known categories in philosophical hermeneutics, Archer posits a text-centered, reader-oriented approach—one that prioritizes the relative stability of Scripture, yet opens wide the gate to allow for the pneumatological convictions of the Pentecostal church. It is not difficult to sense a certain tension in this characterization of the interpretive task, since Archer's proposal rests on the Spirit's voice both in community discernment and in undergirding the clarity of Scripture. The point, of course, is that the Spirit is dynamically present in and through both Scripture and the Christian community.

> The Spirit's voice is not reduced to or simply equated with the biblical text or the community, but is connected to an[d] interdependent upon these as a necessary means for expressing the past-present-future concerns of the Social Trinity. The Holy Spirit has more to say than Scripture, yet it will be scripturally based. The community must read and discern the signs and the sound of the Spirit amongst the community in dialogical relationship with the Scriptures.[12]

The term "dialogical" (or dialectical) is key: experience of the Spirit shapes a community's reading of Scripture, yet Scripture provides the lens through which the community perceives the Spirit's work.

Though differing in some key ways, these four voices share a common commitment to the dynamic character of scriptural interpretation animated by the Spirit. None of these theologians struggle with the role of the Spirit in our grasping, say, what Paul said to the Corinthians or Peter to Christ followers on the Anatolian Peninsula. If we cast the chief obstacle to understanding the Bible as historical distance, then the help we need is methodological, not pneumatological. If, however, we cast the chief obstacle in theological terms—that is, to borrow Archer's words, how the church is to understand "the present meaningfulness of Scripture"[13]—then, these theologians agree, we need an account of the hermeneutical work of the

OR: Wipf & Stock, 2002]); accordingly, he carries the conversation well beyond our more limited interests.

12. Kenneth J. Archer, "The Spirit and Theological Interpretation: A Pentecostal Strategy," in *The Gospel Revisited: Towards a Pentecostal Theology of Worship* (Eugene, OR: Pickwick, 2011), 132.

13. Archer, *Pentecostal Hermeneutic*, 182.

Spirit. Depending on their own ecclesial and institutional locations, these theologians have developed their accounts in contrast to what they regard as problematic positions—against unbridled subjectivism and/or relativism in biblical interpretation, for example, or against an over-determined understanding of biblical texts as possessing a singular meaning in the past.[14] By way of providing at least a partial antidote to or prophylactic against those interpretive excesses, they situate Scripture and discernment within the church, understood as a hermeneutical community guided by and subject to the Spirit's activity.

Reading Acts, Reading the Spirit

From voices in the contemporary conversation about the role of the Spirit in reading Scripture, we now turn to two Lukan texts that encourage our thinking pneumatology and biblical interpretation together.

Reading the Scriptures at Pentecost (Acts 2)

Given the triad identified by Thomas and Archer in their discussion of Pentecostal hermeneutics, we might not be surprised to find that Luke's Pentecost account epitomizes a careful weaving together of the Spirit's work and the interpretation of Scripture, all in the context of the community of Jesus' followers engaged in mission. In the three sections comprising Acts 2, Luke narrates the promised outpouring of the Spirit (2:1–13; cf. Luke 3:16; 24:49; Acts 1:4), interprets the outpouring of the Spirit christologically and eschatologically (2:14–41), and speaks to the quality of the community of the Spirit (2:42–47).[15] Similarly, Luke draws on Israel's Scriptures as he recounts the outpouring of the Spirit, then portrays Peter as a Spirit-empowered hermeneut who knits together the Pentecostal phenomena with Jesus' story and the witness of Israel's Scriptures. And Acts 2 begins with Luke's portrait of Jesus' followers in solidarity with

14. I have discussed this problem for the Wesleyan and Pentecostal traditions in Joel B. Green, "Contribute or Capitulate? Wesleyans, Pentecostals, and Reading the Bible in a Postcolonial Mode," *Wesleyan Theological Journal* 39 (2004): 74–90.

15. On this last point, see especially Matthias Wenk, *Community-Forming Power: The Socio-Ethical Role of the Spirit in Luke-Acts*, Journal of Pentecostal Theology Supplement Series 19 (Sheffield: Sheffield Academic Press, 2000).

each other,[16] then emphasizes their social arrangement in the form of an egalitarian community marked by unpretentiousness and the democratization of the experience of the Holy Spirit.

"What does this mean?" (2:12)—this question drives forward the narrative development of Luke's Pentecost account. Even spectacular incidents such as those Luke reports in 2:1–13 are not self-interpreting. "Mystified," "surprised," "amazed," and "bewildered"—these responses characterize those who witness the Pentecostal phenomena (2:7, 12), and why not? These are strange events, after all. The sounds of raging winds, dozens of flame-like tongues, a cacophony of languages—anyone constrained by ordinary meaning-making categories would struggle to make sense of these marvels. In fact, one group attempts a this-worldly explanation—"They're full of new wine!"—but their attempt to make sense is immediately dismissed as nonsensical (2:13, 15). The coming of the Spirit at Pentecost thus sparks a hermeneutical exercise, one that demonstrates as a nonnegotiable starting point for faithful interpretation a people who are formed by the Scriptures and whose minds have been opened by their encounter with the risen Lord (cf. Luke 24:45). The events of this day are quickly recited; the rest of Luke's account is given over to the work of scriptural interpretation. Let me sketch how this work progresses.

First, the Spirit enables among Jesus' followers, then Peter in particular, "inspired speech."[17] We turn to Peter's address momentarily. With regard to the former case, contrary to a popular reading of the Pentecost story, what Luke portrays actually is not foremost an instance of missionary proclamation articulated in the native languages of those gathered—as if they could not have understood the good news presented in Aramaic or Greek (as it would be by Peter in 2:14–36).[18] At this time, some three centuries after the

16. The phrase ἦσαν πάντες ὁμοῦ ἐπὶ τὸ αὐτό ("they were all together in one place," 2:1) recapitulates notions of unity signaled already in 1:14–15.

17. The term ἀποφθέγγομαι appears in Acts 2:4, 14; 26:25; in the LXX the term is used with reference to fortune-telling (e.g., Mic. 5:11; Zech. 10:2) and prophetic speech (1 Chron. 25:1; Ezek. 13:9, 19).

18. I have developed this point more fully, and discussed its significance, in Joel B. Green, "'In Our Own Languages': Pentecost, Babel, and the Shaping of Christian Community in Acts 2:1–13," in *The Word Leaps the Gap: Essays on Scripture and Theology in Honor of Richard B. Hays*, ed. J. Ross Wagner, C. Kavin Rowe, and A. Katherine Grieb (Grand Rapids: Eerdmans, 2008), 198–213.

military exploits of Alexander the Great, everyone present would have trafficked in Greek, and, as a predominately Jewish crowd, they would likely have known Aramaic as well. Simply put, if "linguistic competence" is all that is required, then tongues-speaking was unnecessary. Nor is this primarily missionary speech. The phrase "mighty works of God" is reminiscent of the Psalms, where we find it in the context of doxology (see Pss. 106:2; 145:4, 12), though God's mighty acts figure prominently in praise elsewhere too (for example, Exodus 15; Judges 5; 1 Samuel 2). As in the Lukan birth narratives, so here, being filled with the Spirit leads to praise.[19] What astonishes these Jerusalemites, then, is that those doing the speaking are Galileans and that these Galileans are praising God in languages that, far from representing the vernacular of Galilee, are native to their own homelands.

Why the Spirit enables this language miracle begins to emerge by means of important allusions in Acts 2 to another language miracle, the story of Babel. We should note that Genesis 11 does not present the confusion of languages simply as divine punishment. Rather, God accomplished at Babel what God had purposed from the beginning, namely, the scattering of the human family so that they might fill the whole earth (see Gen. 1:28; 9:1; 10:32; 11:8). What had frustrated this human vocation, purposed by God? The insidious nature of the idolatrous plan comes into focus in the opening reference to "one language and the same words" (Gen. 11:1)—an ancient cipher for the imperial subjugation and assimilation of conquered peoples. People of Luke's world would have understood the power of linguistic domination as an imperial instrument, living as they did in the wake of the conquest of "the world" by Alexander the Great and the coercive efforts that followed in the service of the Greco-Roman vision of "one people." God's scattering the people at Babel was a gracious act, therefore; ironically, God's intervention in Genesis 11 to thwart humanity's common building project actually opened up renewed potential for human flourishing. Luke's account of Pentecost draws on and embraces this history in order to allow those possibilities again to blossom.

Accordingly, in Luke's narrative we find no hint of a return to a single language (as if that would be a divine blessing). Like Babel,

19. See Luke 1:46–55, 67–79; 2:25–32; Leo O'Reilly, *Word and Sign in the Acts of the Apostles: A Study in Lucan Theology*, Analecta Gregoriana 243 (Rome: Pontifical Biblical Institute, 1987), 54–57.

Pentecost concerns the divine enabling of languages, but with a twist. Acts 2 begins and ends with Luke's report of the unity of human community (2:1, 42–47), but this *koinōnia* is not the consequence of political domination; this unity is not established through obliterating human differences. *Koinōnia* is experienced not through a single, repressive language, nor by the dissolution of multiple languages, nor by the disintegration of social and regional distinctives in the formation of cultural homogeneity. Spirit-inspired speech in these other languages serves actually to embrace human difference, with the result that *koinōnia* arises from the generative activity of the Spirit who is poured out by Jesus (2:33). This *koinōnia* finds its rallying point in the invitation to call on the name of the Lord and to be baptized in the name of Jesus Christ (2:21, 38).

Second, Peter interprets the Pentecostal phenomena by means of the prophet Joel, whom he quotes in Acts 2:17–21. As a Spirit-imbued hermeneut, Peter discerns the affinity of Joel's prophecy with his contemporary situation and community and identifies the wonders experienced at Pentecost as nothing less than the wonders of which Joel had spoken (2:16). Four motifs are central. (1) Joel provides a timetable within which to make sense of recent events (from the crucifixion through the outpouring of the Spirit) and the mission set in motion by the reception of the Spirit. These are the days of Israel's restoration, even if the "day of the Lord" (2:20) remains a future expectation. (2) Peter's citation of Joel gives pride of place to prophecy, and thus characterizes God's people as a community of prophets who access God's counsel and serve a destabilizing role in the world on account of their unyielding faithfulness to God. (3) Peter emphasizes the universal mission and promise of salvation, allowing for no restrictions apart from response to the call to discipleship itself: "all people . . . everyone who calls on the name of the Lord" (2:17–21). (4) If calling "on the name of the Lord" has salvific significance, then who is this Lord? For readers of Joel, the answer is obvious: Yahweh. Within the Roman world, the answer is equally clear: the emperor, giver of divine blessings. For Acts, these answers merge in Jesus, who, through his exaltation, has been installed as God's coregent, who shares in God's identity, and through whom divine beneficence is available (2:29–36).

This last point deserves a bit more development, given the emphatically christological focus of Peter's speech. Granted, the speech's theocentricity undergirds all else,[20] but for Peter God's purpose, promise, and work have a christological conclusion. God's words, expressed in the first person, "I will pour out my Spirit" (2:17), thus reemerge in the third person with reference to the exalted Jesus: "He poured out this Spirit" (2:33). For Peter, scriptural witness, Jesus' story, and the Spirit's work combine to show that the exalted Jesus is Lord of the Spirit. The Spirit is so identified with Jesus that Luke will later refer to the Holy Spirit as "the Spirit of Jesus" (16:6–7). This last phrase draws out what is already implicit in Peter's speech: with Jesus identified as the Lord, the more familiar phrase "Spirit of the Lord" or "Lord's Spirit" (for example, Luke 4:18; Acts 5:9; 8:39) can reappear as "Spirit of Jesus." Accordingly, as the Spirit served as God's agent, so the Spirit is the exalted Jesus' agent.

Generated by the Pentecostal Spirit, the church now embodies and broadcasts the interpreted Scriptures. Their minds having been opened by the risen Lord to understand the Scriptures, and now, recipients of the Spirit, they are empowered by the Spirit both to fathom the significance of these dramatic events and to communicate their significance in ways that draw those events into the scriptural witness to God's ancient purpose. They weave together Pentecostal phenomena, Jesus' story, and Israel's scriptural witness.

Reading the Scriptures at the Jerusalem Consultation

Like Fowl and Thomas, I regard Acts 15 as a useful narrative account for thinking about the church's reasoning when faced with what was for them an unprecedented challenge. Having already summarized their views, I will now sketch my own—noting my broad agreement with Thomas over against Fowl.

As an important exemplar of the process of discernment around the Scriptures, Acts 15 opens with the question of whether gentiles must undergo circumcision according to the custom or law of Moses in order to be saved (15:1, 5). Within the Lukan narrative,

20. Thus the citation from Joel is presented as God's speech (2:17), in which God repeatedly declares what "I" will do; God accredited Jesus by working signs and wonders through him (2:22), raised Jesus up (2:24, 32), exalted Jesus to God's own right hand (2:33), gave Jesus the promised Holy Spirit (2:33), and made Jesus both Lord and Christ (2:36); God swore an oath to David (2:30); God summons people to salvation (2:39–40); and, throughout, Israel's Scriptures witness to God's will and speak of what God has done and would do. Indeed, what has happened with Jesus has served "God's established plan and foreknowledge" (2:23).

I take the language of "salvation" as a reference to inclusion with and participation in the end-time community of God's people, restored through God's Messiah, Jesus, and generated by the Spirit. Must gentiles be circumcised in order to be full members of this community?

When the apostles and elders gather to take up this question, they hear first from Peter, through whom God had testified to gentile inclusion apart from circumcision "by giving them the Holy Spirit, just as he did to us. He made no distinction between us and them, but purified their deepest thoughts and desires through faith. . . . On the contrary, we believe that we and they are saved in the same way, by the grace of the Lord Jesus" (15:8–11). They then hear from Barnabas and Paul, whose testimony Luke summarizes only briefly, having just devoted two entire chapters to their Spirit-empowered mission and to the Spirit's presence among the gentiles (Acts 13–14). Note the summary Paul and Barnabas give to the church in Antioch—from which they had been sent "by the Holy Spirit" (13:1–4) and to which they return: "they . . . reported everything that God had accomplished through their activity, and how God had opened a door of faith for the Gentiles" (14:27).

When James takes the stage, he does so by affirming that Peter and the prophets of old speak with one voice: "The prophets' words agree with this. . ." (15:15).[21] That is, as James considers the testimony of Scripture alongside this contemporary witness to the Spirit's work, he finds only harmony or mutuality.[22] He summarizes the prophetic Scriptures by citing Amos 9, the message of which coheres with the good news known to readers of Luke's narrative as far back as the birth narratives of Luke 1–2 where, citing Isaiah 49, the Spirit-empowered Simeon carves out space for the gentiles within God's restored people (Luke 2:25–32). In other words, James engages in biblical interpretation not by contravening the Scriptures, not by finding in their pages a new meaning, and not by subjecting them to an esoteric or mystical reading, but—having been shaped by the gospel disclosed in Jesus' Spirit-empowered mission (Luke 4:18–19) and influenced by testimony to the Spirit's work in the church's mission—by attending to aspects of the biblical

21. συμφωνέω, "to speak with one voice," "to be of one mind," "to agree."

22. Luke can use the term "prophets" as a general reference to the Scriptures or to some large part of the Scriptures (Luke 1:70; 18:31; 24:25; Acts 3:18, 21, 24–25; 10:43; 13:27; 26:27).

message that had been moved into the shadows of the faith and life of God's people. The Spirit's work thus prompted a second look at the witness of the Scriptures, the very Scriptures that have as their source God's Spirit (as Luke tells us from time to time—Acts 1:16; 4:25; 28:25). On this basis, those gathered could write, "The Holy Spirit has led us to the decision that . . ." (15:28).

Acts and the Spirit

Admittedly, we have been able to comment only briefly on two narrative accounts in the Acts of the Apostles, so that any generalizations we might reach should come with appropriate caveats. These two accounts are nonetheless suggestive, both for our purposes in this essay and for the promise of a more thoroughgoing inquiry into Luke's theological hermeneutics. Perhaps most importantly, we have witnessed the significant degree to which Luke has woven together the Spirit's work and the interpretation of Scripture in the context of the community of Jesus' followers. This is true to such a degree that it would be problematic to imagine that these could be segregated from each other. The Spirit's agency undergirds both Scripture and church; the Scriptures are constitutive of the church, which is constituted by the Spirit. Static or dormant—these words do not describe the Scriptures; rather, in the hands of Spirit-empowered hermeneuts, the Scriptures are dynamically contemporary, not least when their role is to provide the overarching, divine narrative into which the church is inscribed and within which the church finds its character and mission. For Luke, Scripture and Spirit are one in their service as agents of God, whose agenda is the eschatological restoration of his people, both Jew and gentile, for mission. Moreover, Scripture and Spirit are agents of God's coregent, the Lord Jesus, whom they serve. The Scriptures and Christ are mutually interpretive, the Spirit is Jesus' mouthpiece, and the Spirit animates Scripture's contemporary significance by means of a christologically determined interpretive path. Is not reflection on these texts thus fertile for a theological hermeneutic committed to the Spirit's work in enlivening Scripture for the church and its vocation in the world?

The Spirit and Faithful Interpretation

How do we talk about the role of the Holy Spirit in biblical interpretation? What difference would it make if we were to read the Bible self-consciously as people of the Spirit?

In this concluding section, I want to tease out some of the ramifications of our reflections thus far. My aim is not to encourage our bypassing the important work of disciplined study of Scripture, though perhaps I have said enough already to call into question certain commitments and protocols characteristic of historical-critical inquiry in the modern era. Nor is my aim to deny the important sense in which the Spirit's work in biblical interpretation, as in all other realms, is beyond our ken, though I am urging that we can explore that mystery, however incompletely, by attending to certain interests and practices that follow from our ruminations thus far.[23]

In the present climate of biblical studies, it seems necessary to emphasize at the outset that to speak of the Holy Spirit's work in the interpretive process is to deny the hermeneutical autonomy of individual readers of Scripture and, indeed, to qualify the utility of "technique" in biblical interpretation. It is, instead, to affirm our dependence on the Spirit and on the community of God's people generated by the Spirit. If, as Charles Taylor puts it, modern identity in the West lies in self-sufficiency and self-determination, is apprehended in self-referential terms, and is realized through self-autonomy and self-legislation,[24] then a hermeneutical stance of hospitality toward the Holy Spirit undercuts much of what we take for granted in the stories we tell about ourselves and requires us to recognize our need for resources beyond ourselves and, indeed, to parade that recognition before others.

The entailments of this emphasis are legion, but primary among them would be our recognition that our interpretive interests find their only home in the church. The Spirit forms us as and within an interpretive community, the church of Jesus Christ, continuous through history and across the globe. This means, first, that notions of a "private" or individualized reading of the Bible are suspect; that we must resist any claim that the Bible "belongs" to a particular class of people, however well trained they may be, or to a particular segment of the church (such as the Western church or the American church or the Baptist church); and that the door is wide open for participation by the whole people

23. For what follows, I have taken my earlier ruminations on this question as a starting point; see Joel B. Green, *Seized by Truth: Reading the Bible as Scripture* (Nashville: Abingdon, 2007), 94–100.

24. Charles Taylor, *Sources of the Self: The Making of the Modern Identity* (Cambridge, MA: Harvard University Press, 1989).

of God in the interpretive task and for the role of the whole people of God, over time, in the work of authorizing some interpretations over others.[25] It means, second, that worship, preaching, prayer, Baptism, mission, and Eucharist—these and other ecclesial practices—comprise the world within which Scripture is most faithfully read and discussed. And when they do not comprise that immediate context then, surely, our engagement with Scripture is motivated by and serves such ecclesial practices. It means, third, that, just as the Spirit continues to press the church forward in its messianic identity and mission, so our work with Scripture must be seen as open-ended. Though the text of Scripture is relatively stable, the same cannot be said of the changing arenas in which the church actively seeks by the Spirit to read its sacred Scriptures. At the same time, fourth, we honor the history of biblical interpretation, the history of the effects of the church's engagement with its Scripture, and the work of interpretation taking place in areas of the globe other than our own. These represent arenas of the Spirit's work among our mothers and fathers, sisters and brothers in the faith, whose interaction with the Bible is potentially formative of ours and whose readings can pull back the curtain on how parochial our interpretive efforts can be. Fifth, we embrace the wider tradition of the church as the arena in which the Spirit has been at work and, so, as the context within which we discern the shape and substance of genuinely Christian interpretation. "Interpretation and realization of Scripture are ecclesiological events, and therefore the church and its tradition are integral to the handling of the Bible."[26] To proclaim the work of the Spirit in the ongoing life of the church is to recognize the importance of reading Scripture in relation to the classical faith of the church and those expressions of the church that have stood the test of time.

Accordingly, it is worth reflecting on how it matters to our reading of Scripture that we routinely recite the Apostles' Creed, that we meet each other again and again at the Lord's Table, that we speak with people who do not share our faith, that we who share a common faith in Christ eat together regularly, that we

25. Cf. Christopher Bryan, *And God Spoke: The Authority of the Bible for the Church Today* (Cambridge, MA: Cowley, 2002), 17–21.

26. D. H. Williams, *Evangelicals and Tradition: The Formative Influence of the Early Church*, Evangelical Ressourcement (Grand Rapids: Baker Academic, 2005), 101.

participate in house-building efforts for those with no home, and that we pray to Jesus as though he were God. (And what difference does it make when we do not engage in practices such as these?)

If contemporary biblical studies curricula underscore, say, the importance of philology and structure and context, those who come to Scripture as people of the Spirit highlight also the Spirit's work in readying us to read Scripture through inculcating in us dispositions and postures of invitation, openness, and availability. An integrated life of devotion to God and our willingness to participate in a repentance-oriented reading of Scripture—these dispositions and concomitant practices are the fruit of the work of the Spirit in our lives.

Negatively, this emphasis on the role of the Spirit works against certain emphases in biblical interpretation today. Attitudes of skepticism accompanying historical inquiry are eclipsed by an openness to the God who acts to liberate. Minimalist approaches to meaning are set aside in favor of an openness to the possible intentions of the divine author, and to the sometimes surprising ways a biblical text finds significance in the divine economy. Admittedly, Spirit-animated reading of Scripture may appear to take risks when compared with those forms of modern, critical study alert to what might go wrong in the interpretive process. But this is the way of pneumatological exegesis, and our taking this necessary risk is an expression of our trust in the Spirit not only to guide our interpretation but also, over time, to direct the church in its interpretation and embodiment of Scripture. As Henri de Lubac observed, "No matter what suppleness of mind is brought to determining this meaning, no matter what changes are rightly envisaged in the ways leading naturally to it, the Spirit of God cannot be omitted. It is a gift of this Spirit. In order to receive it, it is not enough, therefore, to 'press hard,' to 'seek'; it is also necessary to 'pray,' to 'implore.'" He continues, "For anyone who thinks he [*sic*] is able to do without the Spirit of God and yet uncover the Mysteries of Scripture is exactly like a man who, without a light, loses his way and has only unfamiliar walls to touch."[27]

Accordingly, we might speak of reading Scripture as self-involving (rather than dispassionate and neutral). Alternatively, not least in light of our earlier reflections on

27. Henri de Lubac, *Scripture in the Tradition*, Milestones in Catholic Theology (New York: Crossroad, 2000), 152–53.

Acts 2 and 15, we might characterize Spirit-animated scriptural reading as conversionary. From this vantage point, Scripture does not give us a set of principles awaiting application today. Instead, Scripture engages us over time in a transformative encounter by which we understand reality according to its terms and, then, come to live differently. This formation of Scripture-shaped minds that understand God and God's creation through Scripture-shaped lenses—this requires patient, deliberate reading, reading, as it were, for no good reason but for the sake of having our dispositions and reflexes shaped by the Spirit in our encounter with Scripture. Engaging with Israel's past or Jesus' parables is therefore not an antiquarian exercise as much as it is the means by which present identity is formed and contemporary vocation fashioned.

A pneumatological hermeneutic calls into question the ultimate utility often allotted to human efforts at understanding the Bible, but this does not mean that a pneumatological approach is Spirit centered. The Spirit is God's agent and, as a consequence of his exaltation, Jesus, too, is Lord of the Spirit. We hear in these words an affirmation that, as the Spirit was active in the generation of Scripture, so, in our actualization of the Scriptures, the Spirit conveys God's voice even as it points us to Christ. We also recognize a certain constraint on how we read Scripture, since we thus anticipate that Scripture (and scriptural interpretation) will never counter how God has revealed Godself in Christ.

We began this essay by inquiring into the difference it makes that we read the Bible as people of the Spirit. I contextualized this question by sketching four related perspectives from contemporary practitioners of theological interpretation of Scripture and Pentecostal hermeneutics of Scripture. I then turned to two pivotal narrative accounts in the Acts of the Apostles with an eye toward what they might say about Luke's vision of a Spirit-animated scriptural reasoning. Although much more needs to be said, it has become clear that "the difference" of a pneumatological hermeneutic is identified already in the way my question is phrased, for it weaves together this triad: Scripture, the Spirit, and the church generated and nurtured by the Spirit.

Part 3

Christology

CHAPTER 10

The Incarnation and the Mystery of the Anointing

Christology and Pneumatology in the Early Centuries of the Church

RANIERO CANTALAMESSA, OFM CAP

The main purpose of my study is to show that what we now call "Third Article Theology" is rooted in what Christians of the first centuries of the church lived and believed, and that Christology and pneumatology were once much more interconnected than in later theological systems.

The Historical Origin of the Nicene-Constantinopolitan Symbol

It is important to know first of all the historical origin of the article on the Holy Spirit in the credo from which Third Article Theology takes its name. The problem concerning the origin of this article is tied to the question of the provenance of the symbol of Constantinople in 381 CE. According to a tradition that dates back to the Council of Chalcedon (451 CE), the symbol was composed by one hundred fifty Fathers gathered for the Council of Constantinople in 381, who, however, intended only to reconfirm the Nicene Creed, inserting additions that were made necessary by successive heresies.

This idea was contested by nearly all the scholars of the nineteenth century and the first half of the twentieth century.[1] Basing themselves on the fact that there was no information whatsoever about this symbol before the Council of Chalcedon, these scholars reached the conclusion that the so-called Constantinopolitan symbol did not actually have anything to do with the Council of Constantinople in 381; it was thought to have been the baptismal symbol of a local church that was later attributed to that council—without any explanation of how or why.

The most recent research, however, has reversed that position, demonstrating that the Constantinopolitan symbol actually does go back to the council in 381, thus justifying its designation as the Nicene-Constantinopolitan symbol. According to this recent research—which I consider to be substantially sound—things happened more or less in the following way. At a certain point during the deliberations of the council in 381, at the invitation of Emperor Theodosius, there would have been a formula of faith prepared that aimed at making an agreement possible on the issue of the Holy Spirit between the orthodox party and the Macedonian party, against whom the council was united. To develop this text the Fathers who were delegated to this task would have adopted the baptismal symbol of a local church (probably the church of Jerusalem), simply adding to it the well-known statements related to the Holy Spirit.[2]

In so doing, the council Fathers could very well have believed they were not proposing a new creed but were ratifying the Nicene Creed. Throughout all of the fourth century, in fact, the phrase "the faith of Nicaea" not only meant the exact, original text from the Council of Nicaea but also every symbol of local faith that, in the meantime, was correct and complete because it contained the key elements of the definition of this council, especially the *homoousios*.[3] The symbol would thus be "Nicene," insofar as the underlying text goes back to the council of 325 CE, as well as "Constantinopolitan," insofar as it was adopted and added in its current form by the council of 381. When the goal for which the council had prepared a formulation for agreement proved unattainable because of

1. See J. N. D. Kelly, *Early Christian Creeds*, 3rd ed. (London: Continuum, 2006), 296.

2. See Adolf Martin Ritter, *Das Konzil von Konstantinopel und sein Symbol* (Göttingen:Vadenhoeck & Ruprecht, 1965), 182–91.

3. See Joseph Lebon, "Les anciens symboles dans la définition de Chalcédoine," *Revue d'histoire ecclésiastique* 37 (1936): 874 ; and Kelly, *Early Christian Creeds*, 322.

its rejection by the Macedonians, it fell into oblivion until the Council of Chalcedon in 451 brought it up again, perhaps taking it out of the imperial archives, and in their adoption of it conferred an ecumenical value on it.[4] This explains how the Council of Constantinople represents a unique case in the history of the church of a council becoming ecumenical retroactively due to the approval of a successive ecumenical council.

The Connection between the Incarnation and the Anointing in the Constantinopolitan Symbol and in the Fathers

The newest finding in Adolf Martin Ritter's research on the Council of Constantinople and its symbol has demonstrated that the symbol was composed during a particular phase of the council in an attempt to reach an agreement with the Macedonian party.[5] In reaching that conclusion, he enhanced the value of an important autobiographical testimony by Gregory of Nazianzus.[6] Gregory bitterly criticizes the formula prepared by those who were designated, ironically, as "the mediators" because they were too reticent and accommodating with regard to the Holy Spirit. The wording, in other words, did not proclaim clearly enough the divinity and the consubstantiality of the Spirit since the text lacked both the title of *theos* and *homoousios* that he was attributing to the Holy Spirit in his writings at that time.[7] In brief, the saint lamented the fact that the Council of Constantinople, in terms of the Holy Spirit, did not exercise the boldness and decisiveness that the Council of Nicaea had demonstrated regarding the Son.

We do not know if this was the only reason for Nazianzen's discontent. He also seems to allude to pressure from the emperor that would have influenced the orthodox mediators. In any case, it seems to me that there are other points in which the article on the Holy Spirit (the only one composed *ex novo* by the council) suffers from a certain haste and from the unfavorable conditions in which it was developed.

4. For the Constantinopolitan symbol at the Council of Chalcedon, see *ACO*, II, I, 2, 80 and 128; and Eduard Schwartz, "Das Nicaenum und das Constantinopolitanum auf der Synode von Chalkedon," *Zeitschrift für die neutestamentliche Wissenschaft* 25 (1926): 38–88.

5. See Ritter, *Das Konzil*, 189–91.

6. The passage in question by Gregory of Nazianzus is from *Carmina historica*, XI, vv. 1703–14 (PG 37:1148–49).

7. See Gregory of Nazianzus, *Oratio* 7.11; 21.34; 31.10 (PG 35:726, 1124; 36:144).

It seems there was no discussion *in aula* of the text, unlike what happened at the Council of Nicaea, since the report of the council's progress made by the bishops to Pope Damasus I does not give any indication of that. The point here is not to criticize the symbol—which would be senseless—but only to understand it in its historical setting for what it is.

The most obvious *lacuna*, apart from the omission of the title "God" (assuming that it was an omission), consists in the fact that in outlining the Holy Spirit's presence in salvation history, they stop at the Old Testament with the statement, "He spoke through the prophets." The Fathers before Nicaea—Irenaeus,[8] Origen,[9] and many others—had strongly emphasized the fact that the Spirit who had partially and temporarily manifested himself through the prophets of the Old Testament later wholly descended and remained on ("rested upon") Jesus of Nazareth at the time of his baptism. It was this very event that all the earlier manifestations of the Spirit pointed to as their "reality." Close to the time of the council of 381, Basil of Caesarea, in noting the workings of the Spirit in salvation history, consistently linked the Spirit's actions in the Old Testament to those related to the economy of "our God and Savior Jesus Christ" and to the "organization" of the church.[10]

This perspective could have been expressed with a very brief addition; for example, they could have added the phrase—to use biblical expressions familiar to the Fathers—"who has spoken through the prophets and descended on our Lord Jesus Christ." An allusion of this kind to Jesus' baptism would have had the advantage not only of highlighting the continuity between the Old Testament and the New Testament regarding the economy of the Spirit but also of emphasizing the relationship between Jesus and the Holy Spirit. The need to complete the affirmations of the symbol in this sense was felt very early by the church. One example is the epiclesis of the liturgy attributed to St. James used in Antioch beginning in the fourth century; the presence of the Holy Spirit in salvation history is described in it with these words:

8. See Irenaeus, *Adversus Haereses* 3.17.1–4 English trans., Irenaeus, *Against the Heresies: Book 3*, trans. Dominic J. Unger, ACW 64 (New York: Newman, 2012), 84–87.

9. See Origen, *Homiliae in Numeros* 6.3 (PG 12:608). English trans., Origen, *Homilies on Numbers*, trans. Thomas P. Scheck, ed. Christopher A. Hall, Ancient Christian Texts (Downer's Grove, IL: InterVarsity Press, 2009), 20–24.

10. See Basil of Caesarea, *De Spiritu Sancto* 16 and 19 (PG 32:137–144, 156–160; *NPNF*[2] 8:23–26, 30–31).

> Send . . . your most Holy Spirit, the Lord and Giver of life, who is seated with you, God and Father, and with your only-begotten Son; he rules with you consubstantially and coeternally. He spoke through the Law, the Prophets, and the New Testament; he descended in the form of a dove upon our Lord Jesus Christ in the Jordan River, resting upon him, and descended on his holy apostles . . . on the day of holy Pentecost.[11]

All of the above, however, has only a relative value because we know that the symbol of faith cannot contain everything, so it is necessary to place it in the perspective of those who composed it. What is interesting to me to note is that, lacking any other element in the symbol that establishes a link between the mission of the Son and that of the Holy Spirit (as for instance between Christology and pneumatology), there remains in this regard only the statement of the Second Article of the Creed: "by the power of the Holy Spirit [Jesus] was incarnate from the Virgin Mary."[12] This statement, however, was not added by the council of 381 but was simply adopted from an earlier symbol.

It is not the article of the symbol, therefore, that can help us understand the opinions of the Fathers at the end of the fourth century about the connection between Christology and pneumatology; on the contrary, it is the opinions of those Fathers themselves that can help us discover the meaning that the article had for them, or at least (since the symbol remained unknown for some time) what it meant to later theologians who were heirs to their doctrine. Now, beginning with Gregory of Nazianzus, what very soon became common in all the Fathers was the conviction that the Holy Spirit spoken about in Luke 1:35 (and therefore in the article of the symbol) does not so much indicate the Spirit sent upon Mary for her to conceive Jesus miraculously but rather primarily the Spirit sent upon the incarnate Word in view of the incarnation, that is, of the hypostatic union. In other words, it is the Spirit with whom Jesus is "anointed." The anointing of Christ is identified with his incarnation, and the Spirit by whom he is anointed is identified with the

11. See Anton Hänggi and Irmgard Pahl, *Prex Eucharistica: Textus e variis liturgiis antiquioribus selecti* (Fribourg: Éditions Universitaires, 1968), 250.

12. Heinrich Denzinger, ed., *Enchiridion symbolorum definitionum et declarationum de rebus fidei et morum*, no. 150, 43rd ed.; English ed., ed. Robert Fastiggi and Anne Englund Nash (San Francisco: Ignatius Press, 2012), 65.

Deity that unites himself to humanity. Gregory of Nazianzus writes that in the incarnation, Jesus "was anointed with divinity, and the anointing of humanity was nothing other than that of divinity itself."[13]

In this perspective in which the anointing is made to coincide with the incarnation, the mention of the Holy Spirit is retained by the appropriation and authority of Luke 1:35, but the Spirit is more often spoken of generically as "deity" (*theotes*), which thus ends up tacitly excluding the Holy Spirit, substituting the Logos himself as the anointing or chrism: "I, the Word, am the chrism, and that which is anointed by me is man."[14] The mystery of the anointing is thus reduced to a christological mystery in a strict sense (the unity of divinity and humanity in Christ) and no longer has a Trinitarian character because it does not directly involve all three divine persons insofar as they are persons.

Among the Greek Fathers this thesis is not linked to the phrase "by the power of the Holy Spirit [Jesus] was incarnate from the Virgin Mary" in the Second Article of the symbol for the simple reason that the symbol of 381 containing this phrase remained unknown until the Council of Chalcedon. In the West, on the other hand, where this article was known (being found almost exactly the same in the apostolic symbol), Augustine openly applied the interpretation just described to it. He says in *De Trinitate*,

> Nor indeed was Christ then anointed at His Baptism, when the Holy Spirit descended upon Him as a dove, for He then deigned to foreshadow His body, namely, His Church, in which those who are baptized receive the Holy Spirit in a special manner; but we are to understand that He was then anointed by that mystical and invisible anointing when the Word of God was made flesh, that is, when human nature, without any preceding merits of good works, was joined together to God the Word in the womb of the Virgin, so as to become one person with Him. *For this reason we confess that He was born of the Holy Spirit and of the Virgin Mary.*[15]

13. Gregory of Nazianzus, *Oratione* 30.2 (PG 36:105b); see also *Oratione* 10 (PG 35:832a) and *Oratione* 30.21 (PG 36:132).

14. Pseudo-Athanasius, *Contra Arianos* 4.36 (PG 26:524b): "Τὸ γὰρ χρίσμα ἐγὼ ὁ Λόγος, τὸ δὲ χρισθὲν ὑπ'ἐμοῦ ὁ ἄνθρωπος."

15. Augustine, *De Trinitate* 15.26, 46 (PL 42:1093–94). English trans., Augustine, *The Trinity*, trans. Stephen McKenna, FC 45 (Washington, DC: Catholic University of America Press, 1963), 515–16 (emphasis added).

Gregory of Nazianzus passed on this kind of explanation of the anointing to Cyril of Alexandria, John of Damascus, and Maximus the Confessor. From Augustine it passed into all of the Latin West and ended up becoming the only patristic explanation known for the connection between the incarnation and the anointing. Works like those of Petavius,[16] Thomassinus,[17] and Matthias Joseph Scheeben[18] contributed to giving it credence in modern Catholic theology.

In recent times this position in patristic theology has undergone a radical critique, whether on the part of biblical exegesis or dogmatic theology. From the exegetical point of view, Ignace de la Potterie, studying the anointing of Christ in the New Testament, came to the following radical conclusion:

> There is no text to be found in the New Testament that refers to an anointing of Christ at the time of his incarnation. Patristic and theological tradition considers the hypostatic union as a consecration of the humanity of Jesus by means of divinity, but this concept is never found in new-testamentary authors. . . . The biblical authors' point of view is different from that of the Fathers. . . . According to the New Testament, what is crucial is the moment of baptism. It is at his baptism that Jesus was anointed "with the Spirit and with power" in view of his mission, which continues that of the prophets.[19]

From the perspective of dogmatic theology, it was primarily Heribert Mühlen who made clear the intrinsic weaknesses of the theory derived from the Fathers that identifies the incarnation with the anointing. He notes that with this theory there comes an undeniable obscuring of the pneumatic dimension in Christology as well as of the true function of the Holy Spirit, which is not to unite one person (the Logos) to one nature (humanity) but rather—as it occurs within the Trinity—to unite persons. (The Holy Spirit is the personal "We" of the

16. See a large number of texts collected on the theme of Christ's anointing in Petavius [Denis Pétau], *De theologicis dogmatibus*, vol. 6, *De incarnatione Verbi*, XI, 8ff. (Paris: Ludovicus Guérin, 1869), 641–57.

17. See Thomassinus [Louis Thomassin], *Dogmata theologica*, vol. 3, *De incarnatione*, VI, 4 (Paris: Ludovicum Vivès, 1866), 679–97.

18. See, for example, Matthias Joseph Scheeben, *The Mysteries of Christianity* (1865; repr., New York: Crossroad, 2008), 331.

19. Ignace de la Potterie, "L'onction du Christ: Études de théologie biblique," *Nouvelle revue théologique* 80 (1958): 225–52 (250–51).

Father and the Son, and in the church he is "one Person in many persons.") Furthermore, in identifying the incarnation with the anointing, the two missions of the Son and of the Holy Spirit are merged together when they should instead be kept distinct, at least logically if not chronologically. And finally, such an identification is harmful to an understanding of the nature of the church and of its relationship with Christ because it does not allow an adequate distinction between the personal grace of Christ, which derives from the hypostatic union and cannot be communicated, and the *gratia Capitis* (the grace of the Head) that comes to him from the anointing of the Holy Spirit, by which he sanctifies the church and is united to the church as his body and the church to him, being the historical continuation of the anointing of Christ.[20]

20. See Heribert Mühlen, *Der Heilige Geist als Person*, 4th ed. (Munich: Aschendorff, 1980), 170; Mühlen, *Una mystica persona: Die Kirche als das Mysterium der Identität des Heiligen Geistes in Christus und den Christen; Eine Person in vielen Personen*, 2nd ed. (Paderborn: Ferdinand Schöningh, 1967). See the Italian edition, *Una mystica persona: La chiesa come il mistero dello Spirito Santo in Cristo e nei cristiani; Una persona in molte persone* (Rome: Città Nuova, 1968), 269.

The Thinking of the Earliest Fathers about the Mystery of the Anointing

The criticism by exegetes and theologians poses an embarrassing problem because it seems to put the tradition of the Fathers in irreconcilable opposition to the Bible and to contemporary dogmatics, which looks to the Bible for inspiration. I think it can be demonstrated that what is thought to be *tout court* the doctrine of the Fathers on this issue, in reality is only a thesis limited to a very specific epoch of patristics, the one following the Arian crisis, whereas earlier Fathers, at least until Basil of Caesarea, held a different position that coincides for the most part with that of the New Testament and contemporary dogmatic theology.

It is regrettable concerning this matter that the monograph of Antonio Orbe, specifically titled *The Anointing of the Word*,[21] should have gone unnoticed by biblical scholars and

21. See Antonio Orbe, *La Unción del Verbo*, vol. 3, *Estudios Valentinianos*, Analecta Gregoriana 113 (Rome: Libreria editrice dell'Università Gregoriana, 1961). Father Orbe's book certainly corresponds, at least in part, to the wish expressed by Mühlen about a monograph on the theme of the Christ's anointing in the Fathers. See Mühlen, *Der Heilige Geist*, 175–76.

dogmaticians. The research done by Father Orbe should be extended to other authors, especially, I believe, to Athanasius, Cyril of Jerusalem, Basil of Caesarea, and Ambrose. What Orbe brings to light in studying Irenaeus of Lyons is already enough to compel a substantial reconsideration of the judgment about the doctrine of the anointing in the Fathers. Until the middle of the fourth century—with the sole exception, it seems, of Origen (who, however, does not link the anointing to the incarnation but rather to Christ's preexistence)[22]—the Fathers recognized only one anointing in the life of Christ: the one received at the moment of baptism in the Jordan.[23] This is the interpretation that Jesus himself had given of his baptism when he applied Isa. 61:1–2 in the synagogue at Nazareth to himself: "The Spirit of the Lord is upon me, because the Lord has anointed me" (Luke 4:18); St. Peter takes up this same interpretation in Acts 1:37–38: "After the baptism which John preached . . . God anointed Jesus of Nazareth with the Holy Spirit and with power."[24]

For these early Fathers it was a *Trinitarian* anointing (in the sense that the whole Trinity was involved) as well as a personal anointing (in the sense that the Holy Spirit entered into the anointing as a "person" and not only as a divine nature). Irenaeus writes, "Indeed, in the name of Christ is implied He who anoints, and He who is anointed, and the ointment with which He is anointed. And so it is the Father who anoints, and the Son is anointed in the Spirit, who is the Ointment."[25] This famous statement by Ire-

---

22. See Origen, *De Principiis* 2.6.4 (GCS 22:144). English trans., Origen, *On First Principles*, trans. G. W. Butterworth (New York: Harper & Row, 1966), 111–12. See also *Contra Celsum* 6.79 (GCS 2:150–151). English trans., *Contra Celsum*, trans. Henry Chadwick (Cambridge: Cambridge University Press, 1953), 392.

23. See Irenaeus, *Adversus Haereses* 3.9.3 (ACW 64:46–47). That Irenaeus is speaking in this text of the anointing at the moment of Jesus' baptism can be deduced from the fact that the whole context is a comment on the event of the baptism ("Adhuc ait in baptismate Matthaeus") and from his citations of Isa. 11:1–4 and 61:1–2. The text of Ignatius of Antioch is also interesting in this respect (even though he is not alluding to Jesus' baptism but to his anointing at Simon's house) in *To the Ephesians* 17.1, trans. Gerald G. Walsh, in *The Apostolic Fathers*, FC 1 (Washington, DC: Catholic University of America Press, 1947): "It was for this reason that the Lord received the ointment [μύρον] on his head—that he might breathe the odor of incorruptibility into the Church [ἵνα πνέῃ τῇ ἐκκλησίᾳ ἀφθαρσίαν]" (93–94). See Orbe's comment in *La Unción*, 5.

24. Revised Standard Version, Second Catholic Edition (San Francisco: Ignatius Press, 2006).

25. Irenaeus, *Adversus Haereses* 3.18.3: "In Christi enim nomine subauditur qui unxit et ipse qui unctus est et ipsa unctio in qua unctus est; et

naeus can be found almost word for word in Basil[26] and in Ambrose,[27] an evident sign of the diffusion and the authority that this interpretation enjoyed among the earliest Fathers.

Secondly, this was a *historical* anointing linked to the concrete unfolding of salvation. The name for Jesus that is derived from the anointing, "Christ," points to an event, an action, and not to the *hypostasis*. Irenaeus says that Christ is the name of "a finished work."[28] It indicates the investiture of Jesus as the Messiah (Anointed One) by which the economy of salvation is inaugurated. The anointing creates something new in Jesus' life (something functionally new and not metaphysically new, of course). It produces spectacular and immediate effects in him: miracles, preaching with authority, the establishment of the kingdom of God, victory over demons. But unlike the powers that Jesus possessed because of the fullness of the Holy Spirit in him due to the hypostatic union (which are not transferable to others), the effects that come from the anointing at

---

unxit quidem Pater, unctus est vero Filius, in Spiritu qui est unctio." English trans, ACW 64:89. See also Tertullian, *De baptismo*, 7, 1 (CCSL 1:282): "Christus . . . quia Spiritu unctus est a Deo Patre." English trans., "On Baptism," in *Q. Septimii florentis Tertulliani de baptismo liber*, ed. and trans. Ernest Evans (London: SPCK, 1964): "[Jesus obtained the title] Christ . . . in that he was anointed with the Spirit by God the Father" (17).

26. Basil of Caesarea, *De Spiritu Sancto* 12: "For the naming of Christ is the confession of the whole [Trinity], showing forth as it does the God who gave, the Son who received, and the Spirit who is the unction. We have learned this from Peter in Acts [of the Apostles], 'Jesus of Nazareth whom God anointed with the Holy Ghost' [Acts 10:38]; and in Isaiah, 'The Spirit of the Lord is upon me, because the Lord hath anointed me' [Isa. 60:1]; and in the Psalmist, 'Therefore God, even thy God, hath anointed thee with the oil of gladness above thy fellows' [Ps. 45:7]" (*NPNF*[2] 8:18).

27. Ambrose, *De Spiritu Sancto* 1.3.44 (CSEL 79 :33): "Si Christum dicas, et Deum Patrem, a quo unctus est Filius, et ipsum, qui unctus est, Fililum et Spiritum, quo unctus est, designasti" ("If you name Christ, you imply both God the Father by Whom the Son was anointed, and the Son Himself Who was anointed, and the Holy Spirit with Whom He was anointed" [*NPNF*[2] 10:99]).

28. Irenaeus, *Epideixis tou apostolikou kerygmatos* 53 (Sources Chrétiennes 62:114). English trans., *On the Apostolic Preaching*, trans. and intro. John Behr (Crestwood, NY: St. Vladimir's Seminary, 1997): "Christ . . . [is the name] of deeds actually accomplished. For He is named 'Christ' since through Him the Father anointed and adorned all things [a cosmic anointing], and [because of] . . . His advent as man, He was anointed by the Spirit of God His Father" (75). Irenaeus believes there is an anointing prior to baptism, as does Justin Martyr, but it is identified with his preexistence and not with the incarnation. It is an anointing that the Word receives to rule over and consolidate the universe. See Orbe, *La Unción*, 67ff., 501, 630.

baptism appear destined to be communicated to the church.[29]

Thirdly, it is an *ecclesial* anointing:

> In the baptism at the Jordan, Jesus was in fact, and not merely by right, constituted the Savior of humanity. In principle the incarnate Word was the Savior from the time of his conception. Only in the Jordan was the human nature of the Word, as such, sanctified with a Spirit destined to be given to human beings. . . . This means that the Holy Spirit at the Jordan began to "connaturalize" himself to our nature on a dynamic level so that once the Spirit was "humanized" in Jesus, he could be imparted to other human beings through him. The humanization of the Spirit begins in the baptism at the Jordan and not before. The Pneuma sent by the Father sanctified Jesus in one instant and with him, *secundum primitias*, the church.[30]

Irenaeus writes, "The Spirit of God descended upon Him, the Spirit of Him who through prophets had promised that He would anoint Him, that we might be saved by receiving from the abundance of His anointing."[31]

However, in order for this impartation of the Spirit of Jesus to the church to be possible, it was first necessary that the Spirit "become accustomed" to dwelling among people and that Jesus' humanity be completely "spiritualized," so to speak, and that the triple wall of division between us and the Spirit of God (nature, sin, and death) be broken down, which happened with the death and resurrection of Christ.[32] All of the charismatic gifts and graces that are poured out on believers have as their remote source the baptism of Jesus while their proximate source is the paschal mystery. The Spirit who poured himself out at Pentecost on the apostles, then, is the same one who poured himself out on Jesus

29. Orbe, *La Unción*, 528. We can see from this that Mühlen's ecclesial understanding of the anointing is not unknown to the earliest patristic theology; see the Italian edition, *Una mystica persona*, 269.

30. Orbe, *La Unción*, 633.

31. Irenaeus, *Adversus Haereses* 3.9.3: "Spiritus ergo Dei descendit in eum, eius qui per prophetas promiserat uncturum se eum, ut de abundantia unctionis eius nos percipientes salvaremur." English trans., ACW 64:47.

32. On this point, see Nicholas Cabasilas, *De vita in Christo* 3.2–3 (PG 150:569–72). English trans., *The Life in Christ*, trans. Carmino J. deCatanzaro (Crestwood, NY: St. Vladimir's Seminary, 1974), 104–5. He is very close to Irenaeus's perspective even though he does not situate the anointing at baptism but, like all the authors of his time, at the time of the incarnation.

at his baptism. Certainly there is and can be only one Holy Spirit, but here we are dealing with something different from the substantial unity that is due to the unity of the divine person; we are dealing with a unity that is also historical. This means that the Holy Spirit does not come to us from eternity, so to speak, but from history, the history of Jesus of Nazareth. The outpouring of the Spirit described in Acts 2 presents a specific development due to the particular theological framework in which Luke places it, but it is neither unrelated to nor of a different nature from the paschal outpourings described by John (see John 19:30: "he . . . gave up his spirit"; 20:22: "he breathed on them, and said to them, 'Receive the Holy Spirit.'")

This kind of "christological" vision of the Spirit given to the church (the "Spirit of Christ"!) is confirmed by the significance that the feast of Pentecost had in the earliest days of the church. Up until the time of Athanasius, it did not primarily commemorate the descent of the Holy Spirit in the upper room but rather the presence of the risen Christ living by the Spirit in the midst of his own as an anticipation of the kingdom of heaven. It was not then the feast of the fiftieth day after Easter but rather the feast of the fifty days following Easter. It was not primarily a Trinitarian feast but a christological one; it was the feast of the Spirit of Christ or of Christ living by the Spirit.[33]

Reasons for the Shift in Interpretation of the Mystery of the Anointing

The explanation of the mystery of the anointing that I have sketched out, primarily with Irenaeus as a guide, underwent a shift for two main reasons that are linked to each other: the ontologization of Christology and the fight against heresies. An initial threat came from the gnostic heresy. According to the view of these heretics, Jesus was one thing and Christ was another: the name "Jesus" designated the man born of Mary; the name "Christ" designated the divinity that descended upon him at the moment of his baptism. In their vision of things, baptism came to negate the incarnation. Paul of Samosata and Nestorius (according to his adversaries) later arrived at a conclusion similar in part to this.

---

33. See, for example, Athanasius, *Epistulae Festales* 14.6 (PG 26:1422c). English trans., *The Festal Letters of S. Athanasius*, trans. Henry Burgess (Oxford: John Henry Parker, 1854), 111–17; see also the study by Jürgen Boeckh, "Die Entwicklung der altkirchlichen Pentekoste," *Jahrbuch für Liturgik und Hymnologie* 5 (1960): 1–45.

Added to the threat constituted by heresies was the strong tendency toward ontologization that the Fathers shared with the Greek culture of the time. In that approach, that which counts is only what exists from the beginning, the *archē* of things, their metaphysical constitution and not their historical becoming. We could say that in this perspective it is essence rather than existence that counts. From this perspective, how can the incarnate Word become something new in baptism that he was not already at the moment of the incarnation? Can we give any weight to Jesus' history and the concrete facts of his life without compromising his being the "perfect man" and the "perfect Savior" from the very beginning?[34]

Because of these and other related pressures combined, we see that little by little all the weight of Christology, from the concrete events or mysteries of the life of Jesus (he was born, baptized, suffered, died, and rose), is transferred to the moment of the incarnation. The question of the foundation for salvation (*how* the Savior *is constituted*) takes precedence over the issue of the unfolding process of salvation (*what* the Savior *does*).[35] From this new vantage point, the mystery of the baptism of Jesus retains and even increases its solemnity, especially in a Greek environment, but in an altogether different direction. Baptism now becomes a christological mystery only in the active sense (because Christ acts in it) and not in a passive sense (because of what happens to Christ in it). Christ's baptism in the Jordan becomes the feast of the institution of Christian Baptism. Gregory of Nazianzus in his sermon for that feast day established the essential theological contents of that mystery that will pass into the liturgy and the iconography of Baptism. He affirms that Jesus is baptized

> to bury the whole of the old Adam in the water. But first of all, . . . he goes up to sanctify the Jordan: as he was both spirit and flesh, he makes us perfect by the Spirit and water. . . . But now Jesus comes up out of the water. He brings the

34. The fear that the emphasis given to Christ's anointing at his baptism could lead to admitting a change in the Word can be noted in Cyril of Alexandria, *Epistola ad monachos Aegypti* 15 (*ACO* I, 3, p. 10). English trans., *St. Cyril of Alexandria, Letters 1–50*, trans. John I. McEnerney, FC 76 (Washington, DC: Catholic University of America Press, 1987), 18–19.

35. On this issue see Karl Rahner, "Chalkedon: Ende oder Anfang?," *Das Konzil von Chalkedon: Geschichte und Gegenwart*, ed. Alois Grillmeier and Heinrich Bacht (Würzburg: Echter, 1954), 3:41.

> world up with him, and sees the heavens split open, which Adam caused to be closed for himself and those who came after him, just as paradise was closed by a flaming sword. And the Spirit bears witness to his divinity.[36]

The Holy Spirit intervenes in Jesus' baptism, as we see, more to attest to the divinity of Jesus than to anoint him as the Messiah. The name "Christ" no longer designates an event or an intervention by God that affects Jesus after the incarnation (like the type of intervention with which God raised him) but designates the *hypostasis* of the incarnate Word.[37]

The determining factor in this evolution was without doubt Arianism, which emphasized the ontologization of Christology. The Arians were using the episode of the baptism, it seems, to affirm that the Word was subject to change and for this reason could not be God in the full and complete sense.[38] In responding to this objection, Athanasius does not abandon the traditional point of view up to that time that sees the anointing occur in the baptism at the Jordan. However, he emphasizes to such an extent its soteriological or active significance (Jesus anoints us) that he begins to cloud its christological or passive significance (Jesus is anointed by the Father).[39]

Basil of Caesarea and Cyril of Jerusalem[40] also operate in the ancient perspective. Basil writes,

> He [the Holy Spirit] was made an unction, and being inseparably present was

36. Gregory of Nazianzus, *In sancta lumina* [*Oratione* 29] 15–16 (PG 36:351–53); English trans., "Oration on the Holy Lights," in *Gregory of Nazianzus*, ed. and trans. Brian Daley (London: Routledge, 2012), 135–36; see also Gregory of Nyssa, "In diem luminum" (PG 46:580; *NPNF*² 5:518–24).

37. See John of Damascus, *De fide orthodoxa* 3.3 (PG 94:989). English trans., *The Orthodox Faith*, in *St. John of Damascus Writings*, trans. Frederic H. Chase Jr., FC 37 (Washington, DC: Catholic University of America Press, 1958), 271: "'Christ' will not be the name of the person but the name of the one nature [*hypostasis*]."

38. Orbe, *La Unción*, 603.

39. See Athanasius, *Contra Arianos* 1.46–47 (PG 26:105–9). English trans., *Orations against the Arians*, in *The Trinitarian Controversy*, trans. and ed. William G. Rusch (Minneapolis: Fortress, 1980), 109–11; see also the commentary by Orbe, *La Unción*, 610.

40. See Cyril of Jerusalem, *The Mystagogical Lectures* 3.1–2 (Wilhelm Karl Reischl and Joseph Rupp, *Cyrilli Opera omnia quae supersunt*, Hildesheim: Georg Olms, Repr. 2:366). English trans., *The Works of Saint Cyril of Jerusalem*, trans. Leo P. McCauley and Anthony A. Stephenson, FC 64 (Washington, DC: Catholic University of America Press, 1970), 168–70. (There would need to be a more detailed study of Cyril, however, to confirm that he holds the ancient view.)

> with the very flesh of the Lord, according to that which is written: "Upon whom thou shalt see the Spirit descending and remaining on Him, the same is . . . my beloved Son [John 1:33; Luke 5:22]" and "Jesus of Nazareth" whom "God anointed with the Holy Ghost [Acts 10:38]." After this every operation was wrought with the co-operation of the Spirit.[41]

After these authors, especially following the concise affirmations of Gregory of Nazianzus quoted above, this vision of the most ancient church fathers rapidly disappears to the point that modern authors, reading the Fathers in the light of later theories, end up considering all the texts of the Fathers (including those of Irenaeus!) as referring to the hypostatic union.[42]

This is not the place to present a critique of the new patristic concept of the mystery of the anointing that came later. (That has been done very well by Mühlen.) What is important for me to emphasize is that patristic theology—seen as a whole and once the reasons for its evolution have been explained—far from appearing opposed to the biblical perspective, constitutes, on the contrary, a coherent development and also makes a notable contribution to the tendency in contemporary theology that aims to restore to Jesus' baptism all of the enormous importance that it has in New Testament sources for understanding the work of Jesus.[43] The importance that Jesus' baptism had in early patristic thinking can also be inferred from the fact that it appears in some symbols of faith between the mention of Jesus' birth and death.[44]

What I have observed concerning the Third Article of the credo also helps us interpret the statement of the Second Article correctly: "by the power of the Holy Spirit [Jesus] was incarnate from the Virgin Mary."

41. Basil of Caesarea, *De Spiritu Sancto* 16 (PG 32:140c; *NPNF*² 8:25). See also the text quoted above (n. 25) in which the anointing is very clearly placed at the time of baptism, and the important text of *Homiliae super Psalmos* 44.8 (PG 29:405a). English trans., *Nicene and Post-Nicene Fathers*, 2nd series, vol. 8, trans. Blomfield Jackson, eds. Philip Schaff and Henry Wace (repr., Grand Rapids: Eerdmans, 1996), 25.

42. In addition to Petavius and Thomassinus cited above, see also Adhémar D'Alès, "La doctrine de l'Esprit en St. Irénée," *Recherches de science religieuse* 14 (1924): 498 and n. 8.

43. See Oscar Cullmann, *The Christology of the New Testament*, 2nd ed., trans. Shirley C. Guthrie and Charles A. M. Hall (London: SCM, 1963), 66ff.

44. See the baptismal symbol of the Armenian Church in Denziger, *Enchiridion symbolorum*, no. 6, 18. See also Ignatius of Antioch, *To the Smyrnaeans* 1 (*FC* 1:118).

The mention of the Holy Spirit here should be interpreted as referring not to the Spirit (or the Deity) that anoints Jesus at the moment of his incarnation but rather to the Spirit sent to Mary to form in her the humanity of the Savior in a miraculous way. Naturally, I do not mean by this that Jesus was not full of the Holy Spirit from the moment of his conception but simply that this "personal" and incommunicable fullness of the Spirit is not what the New Testament and the oldest patristic tradition define as the anointing that makes Jesus the "Christ."

A Reading of the Credo Backwards

I would like to complete my historical reconstruction with a general observation on the Nicene-Constantinopolitan symbol and on the usefulness of reading it "backwards," that is, from its end to its beginning, which is what the movement called Third Article Theology is proposing.

The Nicene-Constantinopolitan symbol reflects the Christian faith in its ultimate phase after all the council clarifications and definitions were completed in the fifth century. It reflects the sequential order reached at the end of the process of the dogma's formulation, but it does not, however, reflect the process itself. In other words, it does not correspond to the process by which the faith of the church was actually formed historically, nor does it correspond to the process by which someone arrives at faith today, understood as a living faith in a living God.

In today's credo one begins with God the Father and Creator and moves on from him to the Son and his redemptive work, and finally to the Holy Spirit operating in the church. In reality, the faith followed a reverse path. It was the Pentecostal experience of the Spirit that brought the church to discover who Jesus was and what his teaching was. Only with Paul and above all with John do we reach the point of ascending from Jesus to the Father. It is the Paraclete who, according to Jesus' promise (see John 16:13), leads the disciples into "all the truth" about himself and the Father.

Gregory of Nazianzus, in a famous text, synthesizes the process that led to faith in the Trinity in the following way. The Old Testament openly declares the existence of the Father and announces, in a veiled manner, the existence of the Son. The New Testament openly declares the existence of the Son and announces, in a veiled manner, the divinity of the Holy Spirit. In the church, the Spirit now grants us his manifestation distinctly, and the glory of the blessed Trinity is professed. God has measured out his manifestation, adapting it to the times and to human beings' capacity to receive.[45]

Gregory's synthesis has a serious flaw that I became aware of only when I also began to read the credo "in reverse": how it was formed and not just as a final product. The flaw is that the Father who Gregory of Nazianzus says revealed himself in the Old Testament is not the God and Father of Christians! He is other than that. He is not the "Father of our Lord Jesus Christ" (2 Cor. 1:3; Eph. 1:3), that is, the true Father of the true Son; he is the Father of Israel or the Father of the world, who is a father in a metaphoric sense. This is also the way the pagans understood a father god. The Latin name of Jove, Jupiter, is formed by two words, the first meaning "god" (*diaus* in Sanskrit, *deus* in Latin) and the second meaning "father" (*piter*). The revelation of God the Father is the absolute novelty brought to us by Christ, and only the Holy Spirit, after Easter, brings this to the awareness of the disciples, especially through the Gospel of John.

Basil of Caesarea, the author of the first treatise on the Holy Spirit, gives us a better synthesis of the development of revelation and of salvation history when he writes, "The way of the knowledge of God lies from One Spirit through the One Son to the One Father, and conversely the natural Goodness and the inherent Holiness and the royal Dignity extend from the Father through the Only-begotten to the Spirit."[46] In other words, on the level of being or the emergence of God's creatures, everything comes from the Father, goes through the Son, and reaches us through the Spirit; but in the order of conscious awareness, or of the creatures' return to God, everything begins with the Holy Spirit, passes through the Son Jesus Christ, and returns to the Father.

Sociologists have brought to light the unrepeatable character, the life and energy of a movement or institution in its *statu nascenti*, that is, at the moment of its birth. It is very appropriate that we should also make an effort at one point to understand the Christian faith in its nascent state. This does not in the least mean that the church's credo is not complete or that it needs to be reformed in line with what I have said. It cannot be other than what it is. However, what is sometimes useful to

45. See Gregory of Nazianzus, *Oratione* 31.26.

46. Basil of Caesarea, *De Spiritu Sancto* 18.47 (PG 32:153; *NPNF*[2] 8:29).

shift is the way we read it so as to retrace the path by which it was formed. There is the same difference between the two ways of approaching the credo—as a process or as a completed product—as there is between leaving St. Catherine's Monastery early in the morning to climb Mount Sinai and reading the account of someone who climbed it before us.

Today we have one more reason to do this reading of the credo "backwards" from its end to its inception. In the Pentecostal and charismatic movements this process is being revived, and people are experiencing that it is the Holy Spirit who makes us know the real Jesus, the living Lord Jesus, and it is in Jesus that we learn to say with new feeling "Abba, Father." As a scholar of the history of Christian origins, which I was for many years, it has been a surprise and a confirmation for me to see in our time a repetition of what all the evidence points to about the beginning of the church. One great scholar of the New Testament today believes that the experience of Azusa Street California in 1906, which initiated the Pentecostal movement, offers the best example we have to understand how the Christian community of the New Testament, in terms of its sociological and historical reality, began at Pentecost, that is, with "inspired mass ecstasy" brought about by the Spirit.[47]

47. Eduard Lohse, "Pentecost," *TDNT* 6:51, quoted in James D. G. Dunn, *Beginning from Jerusalem*, vol. 2 of *Christianity in the Making* (Grand Rapids: Eerdmans, 2008), 165.

CHAPTER 11

On the Identity of Jesus Christ

Spirit Christology and Logos Christology in Converse

CORNELIS VAN DER KOOI

The Christian faith points to the figure of Jesus of Nazareth as the one in whom God decisively drew near to the world, both personally and salvifically. At the beginning of the Gospel of Matthew, this good news is summarized in one name: Immanuel, God with us (Matt. 1:23). These words contain the promise of the Christian faith, which also may be considered a claim of world-historical importance: human existence, the present, and the future of this world now take place within a new horizon. God has come near to us in Christ, decisively near. That is the "new" thing for this world. The question that I want to address in this contribution is how we have to qualify the presence of God in Christ. Should we with the majority of the Christian tradition articulate the identity of Jesus in terms of the Word, and therefore by way of a Logos Christology? Or is it advisable to choose a Spirit Christology, according to which the identity of Jesus is determined by God's Spirit? Or is there the possibility for an integrated model, in which from the beginning to the end Word and Spirit cooperate? At stake here is not only the question of what is decisive for the identity of Jesus as Son of God and the possibility of a Third Article Theology, but also implicitly the question of participation of human beings. How does his appearance affect his followers?

In this brief contribution I will first give a rough sketch of the biblical basis for a Logos Christology, and subsequently the biblical basis for a Spirit Christology. In the third section I will discuss three positions regarding the relation between Logos Christology and Spirit Christology and give my own evaluation.[1]

The Word Made Flesh

In the creeds, the reality of God's life-giving and saving nearness is grasped with a concept derived from the prologue to the Gospel of John. Christ is the Word who was already in the beginning with God and who is himself God. The identity of Jesus is formulated in terms of the Word and therefore we speak of Logos Christology. The concept of the Logos in John implies a concept of preexistence. Jesus Christ comes from above, from a heavenly existence into a human existence. This preexistence is pictured in three images or conceptions: the Word is made flesh (John 1:14), the Son is sent by the Father (3:17), and the Son of Man descends from heaven (3:14). These last two conceptions suppose undoubtedly a kind of personal preexistence of Jesus Christ with the Father.[2] That means that Jesus Christ as the Son, when coming into the world, already possesses the power and dominion that belong to the Father. His identity as the Son of the Father is already set and realized. Nothing needs to be added. He has the power to lay his life down and to take it up again (10:18). It is the already existing love between the Father and the Son that will be revealed in his love for his disciples. It is this love that will endure, overcome death and darkness, and glorify the Father. It is also this love between the Father and the Son that will include and embrace the people that have been given to the Son by the Father (John 17). The divinity and identity of the Logos are there from the outset and this fixed identity became part of the christological dogma. The Logos as the Second Person of the Trinity assumes human flesh. The shadow of this

1. Some of the materials in this contribution stem from my Annie Kinkead Warfield Lectures delivered in Princeton (April 2014) under the title: "This Incredibly Benevolent Force: The Holy Spirit in Reformed Theology and Spirituality."

2. See Piet Schoonenberg, *De Geest, het Woord en de Zoon* (Kampen: Kok, 1991), 96.

glorious confession was that it became difficult to hold to the human condition of Jesus. When his identity is determined by the divine Logos, then he already possesses, for example, immediate knowledge of the Father and it is unthinkable that he will give in to sin. Then he is not only factually sinless (*impeccantia*), but—determined by the agency of the divine Logos—he also does not have the capability to sin (*impeccabilitas*). It is clear that such notions are not without tension with the picture given in other parts of the New Testament. It is these tensions that in the course of time have launched severe criticism of Logos Christology.

According to the critics of Logos Christology, the classic doctrine undermines the humanity of Jesus and even lends itself to a certain docetism. For if the eternal Logos, who always remains what he is, is the personifying center of Jesus Christ, one may be left with a humanity that seems altogether static in him. Historical development, Christ's growth, and his suffering on the cross become, we are told, difficult to grasp within the framework of a Logos Christology.[3] Historical development, growth, and suffering can only pertain to his human nature, which must in turn be considered anhypostatically. It is very difficult, however, to explain this doctrine of an "impersonal" human nature in our days. For the fact of the matter is that the word "person" makes us in modernity think right away of a being with a consciousness and a will. If then Jesus is said to have had an "impersonal" human nature, one may be left with the impression that he actually was not fully human after all! A Spirit Christology, so it is claimed, offers better perspectives for doing justice to the person of Jesus and to his humanity.

Jesus and the Spirit

Even if we leave aside for now the question of how fair this criticism really is, we must at any rate admit that the Spirit plays a fundamental role in the New Testament witness about Jesus. Regarding the relation between Jesus and the Spirit, two main lines are visible. The first line is that Jesus stems from the Spirit and is featured as the Spirit bearer. According to this line, the Spirit has priority over Jesus. Jesus is conceived by the Spirit and at his baptism he is anointed by the Spirit. The second line is from the Christ to the Spirit. Christ is described as the Giver of the Spirit. The Spirit, with which he was anointed during his life and by which he

3. Ibid., 42.

was driven and guided, also in his suffering, goes via the exalted Lord to the community around him, to his disciples. Following the Dutch theologian Piet Schoonenberg we can here distinguish between an ascending and a descending Christology. The first line is found particularly in the Synoptic Gospels, the second line is found in the Gospel of John and in the letters of Paul.

By way of example, I will make a few remarks on how this ascending Christology surfaces in one of the Synoptic Gospels, the Gospel of Mark. Mark describes Jesus as Messiah of the end time, the eschaton. In his Gospel he links up with the prophecy of Isaiah 40:3 and describes Jesus as the one who will baptize with the Spirit. Mark starts immediately with Jesus' baptism in the Jordan (Mark 1:9). The reception of the Spirit is described as something that is perceived by Jesus himself (1:10). It remains unclear which people hear the voice from heaven. Is it only Jesus, or is the voice also heard by the onlookers? The emphasis is laid on the fact that the heavenly voice is heard. Quoting Psalm 2:7, the voice proclaims that Jesus is the Son, the beloved one. Significant in this passage is that Sonship and reception of the Spirit stand in close connection to each other. Sonship and being filled with the Spirit go together. At the same time it is clear that particularly in Mark the identity of Jesus will only become public at the end of his life (Mark 14:62; 15:39). His Sonship shines out from what he does. In his life and deeds he shows himself to be connected with God, and that he may be called Son. But only at the end of this life does it become public that he is the Son and is exalted. Mark also makes crystal clear that the appearance of the Spirit of the eschaton causes resistance and confrontation.

Confrontation occurs immediately after Jesus' baptism with the Spirit. He is driven into the wilderness by that same Spirit and is tempted by Satan (1:13). In several places we read of evil spirits, who hold people captive and make themselves known loudly (1:24, 34), but the power of Jesus is too much for the evil spirits. The aspect of confrontation with devilish powers is so prominent in the Gospel of Mark that the sum of Jesus' deeds and proclamation is even thematized in terms of warfare between the Spirit of God and the evil spirits. Mark tells us that the scribes attributed his healings even to the work of Satan (3:20–30), but according to Jesus this evaluation is illogical. Everyone who, over against the evidence of deliverance and healing wrought by Jesus, argues that evil spirits—not the Spirit of the God of Israel—is at work in him, is sinning against the Spirit of the end time. Such a flat denial is unforgivable. The passage shows that the necessity of the discernment of the spirits is already acute as to Jesus' own way of acting.

In this connection one can point to another story, which in the Synoptic Gospels immediately follows the report of Jesus' baptism in the Jordan: after he has been baptized with the Spirit, Jesus is driven into the wilderness by this same Spirit and tempted there (Mark 1:12). How are we actually to conceive of his temptation? Can this account be taken seriously if the eternal Son is the personifying center in Jesus? Or did Jesus indeed have to discover his own calling and mission by a process that involved many twists and turns, doubts, and silences? According to the Epistle to the Hebrews, that was indeed the case. Jesus had to learn obedience as Son in his suffering (Heb. 5:1–9). That is exactly what sanctification in his life means. Sanctification for Christ as Son meant a process of hunger, abandonment, waiting, and discovery. Jesus did not all of a sudden just have the discernment of the spirits, but had to learn it. He had to discover his way and the will of the One whom he knew as his Father.

There is another passage in which search and discovery are prominently displayed. It is the answer Jesus gives to John's question from prison: "Are you the one who is to come, or are we to wait for another?" (Matt. 11:3).[4] This is a dramatic question in many respects, since John's entire life project is in fact at stake. Is Jesus the expected Messiah, or not? Jesus does not answer John directly, but via a quote from the prophet Isaiah: "Go and tell John what you hear and see: the blind receive their sight, the lame walk, the lepers are cleansed, the deaf hear, the dead are raised, and the poor have good news brought to them" (11:4–5). These were the signs of shalom that the prophet Isaiah had attributed to the Spirit of the eschaton. These things were happening around Jesus by virtue of the Spirit who rested upon him. And Jesus recognized these happenings as signs that the eschatological Spirit was with him. Yet this was never self-evident: "And blessed is anyone, who takes no offense at me" (11:6). People could remain blind to it. Faith and commitment were demanded from the onlookers. This very aspect, however, has not changed over time. The question of what is

4. Quotations taken from the NRSV (Oxford: Oxford University Press, 1989).

at work in Jesus, and in the community that gathers in his name, challenges us to offer our own answer and active response.

These few observations are only meant to point to biblical material that is used in contemporary debate to argue for a determination of Jesus' identity in terms of Spirit. And I want to add that systematic theological reflection should take into account that all its attempts have to do justice to this narrative. When our "constructive" theological proposals in fact function to override the deep humanity and even ambiguities in the life of Jesus, then they function wrongly as a means to tame the narrative. That being said, as a reminder to all who want to integrate Spirit Christology and Logos Christology, the following question comes up: How, then, do Spirit Christology and Logos Christology relate to each other? The following offers a contribution to answering such questions.

Spirit Christology and Logos Christology: Three Models

In what follows I distinguish three models that can be found in the contemporary debate. I have labelled them as *substitute*, *alternative*, and *complement*—though I should right away add that this distinction merely has a heuristic function.

Substitute

The first option is taken by those theologians who want to replace Logos Christology with Spirit Christology. Spirit Christology is considered by them to be the better option and is regarded as a *substitute* for Logos Christology. Sometimes this position is referred to as "post-Trinitarian."[5] It applies to a number of important nineteenth-century historical theologians like Adolf von Harnack, Reinhold Seeberg, and Friedrich Loofs, and more recently the theologians Paul Tillich, Geoffrey Lampe, Hendrikus Berkhof, James Dunn, Richard Haight, and in the Netherlands Gerrit van de Kamp and Gijs Dingemans.[6] The decisive argument in favor of this position is the charge that a Logos Christology in fact threatens the humanity of

5. Myk Habets, *The Anointed Son: A Trinitarian Spirit Christology* (Eugene, OR: Pickwick, 2010).

6. Geoffrey W. H. Lampe, *God as Spirit* (Oxford: Clarendon, 1977); Gerrit C. van de Kamp, *Pneuma-christologie: Een oud antwoord op een actuele vraag?* (Amsterdam: Rodopi, 1983). See also his reassessment of David Coffey's contribution in particular: "De pneumatologische christologie van David Coffey," *Nederlands Theologisch Tijdschrift* 66 (2012): 120–34; Schoonenberg, *De Geest, het Woord en de Zoon*; John Hick, *The Metaphor of God Incarnate* (London: SCM, 1993); G. Dijs J. Dingemans, *Het menselijk gezicht van God: Jezus als de unieke drager van de Geest* (Kampen: Kok, 2003).

Jesus. According to the proponents of a Spirit Christology, Logos Christology represents an impediment for modern people because the meaning of concepts like nature and person, which are basic to this position, has shifted, rendering them incomprehensible in the present context. From that perspective these terms do more harm than good. Already more than a century ago, Seeberg and Harnack pointed out that in the writings of the apostolic fathers the uniqueness of Jesus was not interpreted in terms of the Logos alone, but also in terms of the Spirit. The ecumenical creeds, it is therefore argued, have overshadowed and suppressed the possibility of expressing the significance of the person and work of Jesus Christ in terms of the Spirit. The doctrine of the hypostatic union of the divine and human natures in the person of the eternal Logos represents an overly static or "object-like" interpretation of the identity of Jesus. Accordingly, his human history begins to look all too much like the unraveling of a predetermined script. The critique of Logos Christology by these theologians amounted to a radical criticism of the christological and Trinitarian doctrines as such,[7] and was for a long time related to the presupposition that a "higher" Logos Christology was in fact a later development in the history of the church. In fact the particularity of Jesus Christ as not only coming from God, but also in essence being divine, was rejected.

Apart from how one may assess this criticism of established doctrine, the advantage of the pneumatological approach has to be praised. Jesus is seen first and foremost as a human being, one of us, in many ways different and higher in morality and awareness of God. But nevertheless, the idea of the life of Jesus as exemplary should not be dismissed. In early Christianity, with its emphasis on discipleship, the kingdom of God, and living according to the Sermon on the Mount, Jesus was not only redeemer, but as redeemer was also the one who has to be followed.

Given the influence of the role played in this development by the liberal camp, the term "Spirit Christology" was for long associated with a radical critique of the church's doctrine; after all, it was the very divinity of Jesus that was at stake![8] In the line of Wilhelm

7. In contrast to Myk Habets, I prefer the term "substitute" instead of "post-Trinitarian." The prefix "post" suggests a temporal order, which in the light of the contemporary renaissance of Trinitarian thought seems no longer appropriate.

8. The opinion that Logos Christology is an impediment for contemporary thought and culture

Bousset, many came to view the confession of the divinity of Jesus as a later development in an originally Palestinian or Aramaic Christianity. If I am not mistaken, this association is no longer as readily made today as it once was. The plea for a reevaluation of the pneumatological dimension of Jesus' life and therefore the reappropriation of Christology as a Spirit Christology accordingly comes also from quarters that can hardly be characterized as "liberal" and that have no interest in discarding Chalcedon. This shift in the theological landscape owes a lot to the developments in biblical scholarship. The positions have shifted considerably; the assumption that a high Christology was a "glorification" of the earthly Jesus has proved in fact to be no longer tenable.[9] This has led to greater receptivity in more orthodox environments to a Spirit-christological reflection. As a result, it is now possible to locate one's own faith *in* Jesus closer to the faith *of* Jesus.

Alternative

As a second possibility, I identify a model for which the already mentioned Dutch theologian Piet Schoonenberg once was the most important spokesperson. This model can be called *alternative.* In it, Spirit Christology and Logos Christology relate to each other as alternatives; that is, they are two parallel avenues for expressing what was so unique about Jesus Christ. They are alternatives in the sense that in the canon they indeed complement each other, but nevertheless there is a huge difference from what I label the mutual complementary model. Schoonenberg has insisted that Logos Christology and Spirit Christology are each independently able to say everything that ought to be said in a Christology. He regards Spirit Christology to be a complete Christology. Everything that needs to be said about Christ can be said within the tradition that identifies

was already put forward much earlier by Friedrich Schleiermacher. His critique of the doctrine of the two natures because of the changed meaning of the concept of nature cannot be dismissed as an attempt to transform Jesus Christ into an ordinary human being and to transpose Christology into anthropology. This interpretation of Schleiermacher by Karl Barth has determined the view of Schleiermacher for a long time—but wrongly. Schleiermacher's theology in terms of Spirit is meant to build up a Christology that in its own terms must be labeled "high."

9. See, for example, Larry W. Hurtado, *Lord Jesus Christ: Devotion to Jesus in Earliest Christianity* (Grand Rapids: Eerdmans 2003); Richard Bauckham, *Jesus and the Eyewitnesses: The Gospels as Eyewitness Testimony* (Grand Rapids: Eerdmans, 2006); and Beverly Roberts Gaventa and Richard B. Hays, eds., *Seeking the Identity of Jesus: A Pilgrimage* (Grand Rapids: Eerdmans, 2008).

Jesus as Spirit bearer. It is a Christology in which it can be confessed that Jesus Christ is the Lord and the Son of God. But this tradition also has the great advantage that it pictures Jesus as a human being, as the second Adam, who picks up the thread where the first Adam failed.[10]

Is it true? I have my doubts about this latter claim of Schoonenberg. Is it possible to express everything that belongs to a Christology in terms of the Spirit?[11]

But the goal of Schoonenberg is clear. In developing his Christology he has tried to give a proper answer to the shadow of the traditional Logos Christology, namely, the risk that the vocabulary of Logos Christology in fact favors a docetic understanding of Jesus Christ. According to orthodox doctrine, the Logos is the supporting and decisive denominator in Jesus Christ as the hypostatic union of the divine and human natures. The human nature is not thought of as a human being as such, but as the human nature. That means that the human nature must be thought to be anhypostatic. It is the eternal Logos who dwells hypostatically in and bears the human nature. It is clear that such a solution originally was meant to avoid the conclusion of a dualism in Jesus. But at the same time this bears a risk for the possibility of understanding Jesus as fully human. The person of the Son is unchanged in his distinct identity even after the incarnation. Schoonenberg tried to solve the problem by taking the human nature as the point of departure, not the eternal Logos. When Jesus is fully human, then we have to conclude that the Word or Logos cannot be fully a person in the modern way of understanding it, because "person" means in modernity a center of freedom and self-consciousness. If we think of the Logos in this way, as person, this leads to the idea of a community of three gods. Schoonenberg argued that the Logos as person can stand over against the Father only in the human consciousness of Jesus.[12] For that reason Schoonenberg sought a solution by what he called an inverted enhypostasy. He no longer wanted to see the eternal Logos as the central personalizing element in Jesus Christ, but the other way around, his humanity as the personalizing element. Therefore, Schoonenberg spoke once in his work of the divine nature in Christ as anhypostatic. It is

10. Schoonenberg, *De Geest, het Woord en de Zoon*, 41.

11. Ibid., 27.

12. Patrick Lens, "God heeft zich aan onze menselijkheid gewaagd," *Communio* 21 (1996): 366–92 (375).

the divine nature that is enhypostatic in the human nature of Jesus.[13] By entering a process of becoming, of change, and human conditions, the figure of the Logos becomes personalized. So the humanity of Christ is the supporting and bearing factor that effects an ongoing process of the Logos becoming a person. In this process the Spirit as the power of God, which in the Old Testament surfaces as Wisdom or the Spirit, is the decisive factor in the life and acts of Jesus.

What can be said of Schoonenberg's claim that this reinterpretation of the concept of Logos from the perspective of the Spirit and Wisdom allows one to say everything that must be said about Christ as Son of God? Is that true? The question can be raised as to what exactly the Logos or Wisdom is in this reinterpretation. Is it a *sphere of divinity*, a *force field* that only becomes personalized in the human self-consciousness of Jesus? Do we then still meet God in person in Jesus Christ?

Mutual Complementarity

The third and final option, which receives considerable support today, holds Spirit Christology to be a substantial complement to the Logos tradition. It means that one takes as a starting point the church's official pronouncements on the Trinity and Christology from the fourth and fifth centuries, and attempts to fill them with pneumatological elements. Instead of "Spirit Christology" it could be labeled "pneumatological Christology."[14] As one of its presuppositions, this option understands the church to have been correct when it decided to express the identity of Jesus using the phrases "true God" and "true man." The proponents of this model include such authors as Robert Jenson, Harold Hunter, and Myk Habets, as well as Roman Catholic theologians like David Coffey, Ralph del Colle, and Thomas Weinandy. In this model we can include also the work of the emeritus Pope Benedict XVI. I will make two comments.

It is first of all worth noting that there is often a typical difference between Protestant and Roman Catholic participants in this debate. It is a difference with methodological effects. Most Catholic theologians hold that we cannot go back behind the church's

13. Piet Schoonenberg, *The Christ: A Study of the God-Man Relationship in the Whole of Creation and in Jesus Christ* (New York: Herder & Herder, 1972), 87.

14. See the above-mentioned contribution of Van de Kamp, "De pneumatologische christologie van David Coffey."

doctrinal pronouncements; for them, the doctrinal determinations of the ecumenical synods are the point of departure for the church's liturgy as well as its teaching. Many Protestant theologians, in contrast, argue that these determinations do not in the first place owe their authority to the church, but are authoritative because and insofar as they are supported by Scripture or can be defended in a contemporary intellectual context. This is not to deny that there are Protestant theologians—especially in Presbyterianism—who on a practical level also take their starting point in the decisions of the church. As such they place themselves in the broader catholic and Trinitarian trajectory that a number of important Protestant confessional documents explicitly follow. The Belgic Confession states, for example, that it accepts the decisions of the early church; the Heidelberg Catechism clearly confesses the divinity of Father, Son, and Spirit, and no less clear is the statement made in this regard by the Westminster Confession. Also modern appropriations of Chalcedon, as apparent in the work of Karl Barth and many of his students, can be located on this trajectory; as modernized as it may be, it in essence comes down to being a reinterpretation of Chalcedon. The risk for this position is that Logos Christology silently remains the undisputed point of departure, and the variety of ways the New Testament pictures the identity of Jesus is not taken seriously. Nonetheless, by establishing the biblical foundation (for example, revelation itself) as the critical moment, as *norma normans*, on the center stage, one is altogether warranted to subject the church in its doctrinal pronouncements to a critical examination. And taking the contemporary attention to the variety of biblical descriptions of the identity of Jesus into account leaves Chalcedon and Logos Christology not unchanged, as is also shown in other contributions to this volume! That brings me to my second remark.

The reason why I call the third model "mutual complementarity" is that pneumatological elements in the biblical witness that were forgotten or suppressed in the course of the development of doctrine have been reintroduced in it and serve to deepen and enrich Logos Christology. However, if the pneumatological dimension of Jesus' life receives so fundamental an emphasis, such that the Logos concept also comes to be radically colored by it, we might speak rather of a "mutual complementarity." In this model, Logos Christology and Spirit Christology are understood to be two approaches that, as distinct methods of christological reflection, interpret and need each other. The mutuality is essential.

In light of the foregoing reflections, I draw the conclusion that attention to the Spirit in the life of Jesus will reinterpret and drastically correct classical Logos Christology. We are dealing with two models, one an ascending model (Synoptic Gospels) and one a descending model (John's Gospel and the Pauline Letters). The descending model, or as Coffey names it, the return model, is able at first glance to integrate the ascending model, but at the same time the ascending model keeps its own identity.

Apart from each other both models lead to one-sidedness. The best way to keep them together is to see them as complementary, but then with the notion of reciprocity or mutuality. The ascending Christology—that is, speaking of Christ as anointed with the eschatological Spirit—receives a further and decisive interpretation from the side of the descending model, because the latter articulates the unique anchoring of his Sonship in God. The descending or return model for its part also gets a radical specification from the ascending model, because this model makes undoubtedly clear that this person, the actual Jesus of Nazareth, was the Jew who lived in his times by the power of the Holy Spirit. Spirit Christology enlightens and clarifies the inner dynamics by which the Sonship of Jesus became realized.

This means that we cannot speak of the Logos or of his preexistence apart from the story of Jesus Christ. The binding of the Logos to this actual person and history implies that the concept of the Logos cannot be filled in abstraction from the drama of the salvation history of God and Israel. The Logos cannot be defined a priori by properties that are deduced from our human restrictions and boundaries, like omniscience or omnipresence.

Of course, this touches upon the theme of the cosmic Christ and preexistence. What can we say about preexistence? Not so much! It is language that points to God being the Lord over time and space. When in the Pauline Letters[15] and in the Gospel of John[16] Christ is confessed as already active in creation, in the cosmos and in all eternity, this is the language of overwhelming surprise and praise of the richness of God. Systematic theology should help the Bible reader, the preacher, and every child of God to stick to that surprise. We stand on the stage of history and are

15. 1 Cor. 8:6; Eph. 1:4; Col. 1:16.
16. John 1:1.

participants in that history; we are its recipients and do not have a place in the director's room. This means that dogmatic reflections should make way for two movements: one that walks along with the drama of the covenant and one that looks back on the drama in the light of the outcome. Or referring to the two models mentioned earlier: an ascending model and a descending or return model.

What then does this mean for preexistence and the immanent Trinity? The church's confession is that Jesus as the Son comes from God. This means that Jesus as an actual living and acting person is not alien to God, but in his deeds and person God confirms Godself. God wants to have the divine Name live on earth among God's creatures, to make Godself present, and to have justice and shalom be realized. The Old Testament pictures the encounter of God with Israel as a drama. It is a drama in which not only the people of Israel suffer by going into exile, but also God does not escape unhurt. In the mission of Jesus, God takes up the thread once more and confirms the goal of the covenant: "I will be your God and you will be my people." God confirms in the generation and mission of Jesus God's own being in a way that had not occurred until then. In Chalcedon this is expressed in terms of the assumption of the human nature: *assumptio carnis*. The meaning of the word "flesh" must be broadened after all that has been said. In the humanity of Jesus God has humbled himself, taking to himself a life in all its limitations and fragility, and has made it his own. In doing so he *confirms* his divinity. That is his glory. That is the first thing we have to say about his divinity. All other things are secondary.

By "confirmation" I mean that this movement of assumption is proper to God, it has its possibility in God himself. The appearance of this man in our history, in the time and space of this universe, finds its basic plan in God. This means that the relation of God the Father and Jesus Christ as the Son has its presupposition or anchoring in who God is in his Glory.

In the terminology of classical Christology, the mystery of Jesus is that in his life God and humanity are brought together in a way that is in our favor. This happens due to the *personal* assumption of our existence by God. It is not due to a natural susceptibility of our earthly being for divine being (*finitum capax infiniti*), but by way of God's graceful act (*infiniti capax finiti*). This assumption does not happen in a way that the order of our human being is changed or distorted, but happens *secundum modum recipientis*. The order of divine being subsists in the order of human being. Put otherwise, the divinity of Jesus is not something that stands on its own and thus as an accident, but is completely assumed and absorbed in that in which it subsists.[17]

The christological language of "assumption" is crucial here. The pneumatological language of "inhabitation," although important, falls short when it comes to the ground of being in Jesus Christ.[18] In Schoonenberg's solution the Word only becomes hypostatic in the life of Jesus.[19] Therefore Schoonenberg could speak of the anhypostatic divine nature. On modern anthropological grounds this is understandable, but in doing so, the involvement of God seems to be restricted to a sort of sphere, a divine principle or force field, in which the human being is taken up and which subsequently is personified by the humanity of Jesus. In that case "the human being Jesus is left as a nondivine subject in relation to the Father, without being himself the personal revelation of God in creational categorality."[20] The incarnation would be repeatable. At stake is the question of whether God himself enters history, or put otherwise, the question of whether Jesus Christ as person has an ontological foundation in the life of God. In the words of the Council of Constantinople (553), in Jesus Christ we encounter *unus de trinitate*. Exactly this unicity is expressed in the concept of incarnation. God has put himself into restriction, as Patrick Lens aptly formulates it.[21]

In the language of the tradition this means that the enhypostasy is in some way reversible—not in the vein of Schoonenberg, but in a sense that the human being and the divine being permeate each other. The humanity of Jesus has its center of gravity in the eternal Word, and also it should be said that the Word subsists fully in and through the humanity of Jesus. Both orders are together but in such a way that the order of humanity is not removed.[22]

17. David Coffey, "The Theandric Nature of Christ," *Theological Studies* 60 (1999): 405–31 (422).

18. Patrick Lens, "Op Hem bleef de Geest rusten," *Communio, Internationaal Katholiek Tijdschrijft* 30 (2005): 9–26 (especially 25).

19. Schoonenberg, *De Geest, het Woord en de Zoon*, 93.

20. Lens, "God heeft zich," 379 (my translation).

21. Patrick Lens, "Schoonenberg en de uniciteit van Christus," in *Verleden openen naar heden en toekomst: Meedenken met de christologie van Piet Schoonenberg*, ed. T. Merrigan and K. Struys (Averbode: Altiora, 2001), 81–98 (96).

22. Coffey, "Theandric Nature," 418.

CHAPTER 12

Spirit Christology

The Future of Christology?

MYK HABETS

Spirit Christology is becoming a dominant feature of contemporary dogmatics, yet it is not without its critics. In what follows I outline the biblical and theological *parameters* of Spirit Christology before interacting with a number of supposed *perils* this Christology presents, and then finally and briefly outlining the *promise* Spirit Christology offers. As the original impetus for and the doctrine from which a Third Article Theology (TAT) is formulated, Spirit Christology is a central feature of this volume and of this project as a whole. As with other aspects of TAT, Spirit Christology requires clear articulation, biblical evidence, and theological nuance. This essay offers a précis of the sort of Spirit Christology sponsored by TAT in dialogue with some of its critics.

In contemporary theology, the term "Spirit Christology" ranges in meaning from its most radical form, which posits S/spirit as the divine element in the person of Jesus of Nazareth, to the orthodox sense, which speaks of the reciprocal relationship between the Holy Spirit and Jesus Christ. In the former case, the displacement of Logos Christology can be seen as a proposal to reach an alternative metaphysical understanding of the operation of divinity in Jesus, one that abandons the Chalcedonian definition of one person in two natures in preference for a Christology of "inspiration." In so doing, the identity between Spirit and Word works to revise the concept of Logos from a pre-existent divine person (the eternal Son), to that of a cosmic principle of reason or order and emphasizes a more functional notion of logos as God's activity in the world (adoptionism). This model of Spirit Christology is consistently and rightly rejected by orthodox theologians. The second model of Spirit Christology is one that seeks to articulate the relationship between the "person" of the Holy Spirit and the "person" of the Son, both in the intra-Trinitarian relations and the incarnation. Hence, an orthodox Spirit Christology attempts to inform Christology with an equally important and central pneumatology, while at the same time enriching the integrity of the doctrine of the Trinity. As such, Spirit Christology is a christological construction formulated from a Spirit-oriented direction; it is a Christology that recognizes that its very constitution must proceed from a robust pneumatology. It is the latter form of Spirit Christology that a TAT articulates.

The Parameters of Spirit Christology

In an earlier work I developed a comprehensive argument for a Spirit Christology from biblical, historical, theological, and practical resources.[1] Starting from the biblical narrative and working up to dogmatics, the point was made that the earliest accounts of Jesus are laden with the Spirit, so much so that anything other than a Spirit Christology fails to adequately account for his identity and mission. From Old Testament promise to New Testament fulfillment, to the theological reflection of the Johannine community, through the Synoptic accounts, Jesus is who he is, and is known to be who he is, by means of his relationship with the Holy Spirit. Thus pneumatologically robust accounts of the identity and mission of Christ are necessary for a faithful account of the Messiah, whose name/title itself reflects this pneumatic orientation. What follows is a survey of the biblical and theological foundations of an orthodox and Trinitarian Spirit Christology as adopted by TAT.

1. Myk Habets, *The Anointed Son: A Trinitarian Spirit Christology* (Eugene, OR: Pickwick, 2010).

Messianic Kairoi

In the words of a pithy summary by Jürgen Moltmann, we might say, "In the Spirit [Jesus] knows himself to be the beloved Son. So the Spirit is the real determining subject of this special relationship of Jesus' to God, and of God's to Jesus. And it is therefore the Spirit who also 'leads' Jesus into the mutual history between himself and God his Father, in which 'through obedience' (Heb. 5.8) he will 'learn' his role as the messianic Son."[2] The long way of obedience proceeds through at least six messianic *kairoi*, or identity-disclosing episodes throughout the life of Christ, through which the Spirit is seen as *the* interpretation of Jesus' identity. The relationship of Jesus and the Spirit thus becomes crucial to understanding Jesus' identity and mission. In the briefest of summaries we might recount these as follows.[3]

First, the journey begins at Jesus' conception by the Spirit (Luke 1:26–35) and subsequent birth narrative (Luke 1–2, with the contrast between John and Jesus), events steeped in and subsequently interpreted as the fulfillment of Old Testament prophecy of the Coming One, the Suffering Servant, and so forth, but supremely, the One *smeared* with the Spirit to such an extent that he is not only endowed with the Spirit but able to dispense the Spirit as well (Matt. 11:11–12 par.). Jesus bar Joseph is actually Jesus the Messiah.

Second, in the baptism of Jesus and the wilderness temptation we listen in to the Baptist's message of the "Coming One" who would baptize with the Holy Spirit. In Luke 3:21–22 Jesus receives the Spirit again; he is anointed as the Messiah, and confirmed as the "Son" of the "Father" (John 1:34 par.). By means of three messianic indicators, Jesus is confirmed as the Christ: the descent of the Spirit as a dove (Matt. 3:16; Mark 1:10; Luke 3:22; John 1:32), the open heavens (Matt. 3:16; Mark 1:10; Luke 3:22; John 1:32), and the divine audition (Matt. 3:17; Mark 1:11; Luke 3:22; John 1:34). The temptation narrative that follows further emphasizes Jesus' messianic status as he relies

2. Jürgen Moltmann, *The Spirit of Life: A Universal Affirmation*, trans. M. Kohl (Minneapolis: Fortress, 1992), 61.

3. For detailed treatment of these messianic disclosure episodes, with full technical references, see Habets, *Anointed Son*, 118–87. This section has drawn upon that material.

upon the Spirit for the successful completion of his mission (Mark 1:12; Luke 4:14).[4]

Third, we might, for the sake of brevity, speak of the messianic vocation of Jesus and see here that his identity is clearly predicated upon his intimacy with, indwelling by, and relationship with the Father in the Spirit. Representative episodes here include John the Baptist's desperate question to Jesus about his real identity as he faces martyrdom (Matt. 11:2–19 // Luke 7:18–26; cf. Isaiah 61), and Jesus' apparently cryptic yet clearly messianic reply. A second example is Jesus' self-identification as the fulfillment of Isaiah 61:1–2 (Luke 4:16–21). Luke opens Jesus' ministry by presenting him as a Spirit-anointed healer and teacher (Luke 4:16–44). The ensuing two sections of his first teaching (4:16–30), and then stories of healing (4:31–44), are introduced similarly. Luke is clearly presenting Jesus' relationship with the Spirit as the power of his ministry and thus a key to a correct understanding of his identity. Other aspects of Jesus' ministry we could look at could include the Beelzebub controversy (Matt. 12:24–32 par.), his ministry of exorcism and healing in the power of the Spirit (Mark 1:21–34; Acts 10:38), and his works/miracles, which John summarily identifies as "signs" of Jesus' messianic status (John 20:31).[5] To the religious leaders of the day Jesus exhibited all the signs that were to accompany the Coming One. We might conclude, on such evidence,

4. The baptism of Jesus does not mark his divinization or turn him into God's Son; it does not make him divine; and neither is it his adoption into the divine family. It is an empowerment for his priestly vocation, the inauguration of his public ministry, the authentication of his messianic status, and confirmation and assurance of his Sonship. While Telford Work is careful to affirm the divinity of Jesus before, during, and after the incarnation, he insists that after his baptism Jesus "gains a *new human* relationship with the Holy Spirit. . . . He gains a *new human* relationship with the Father" ("Jesus' New Relationship with the Holy Spirit, and Ours: How Biblical Spirit-Christology Helps Resolve a Chalcedonian Dilemma," in *Christology Ancient and Modern: Explorations in Constructive Dogmatics*, ed. Oliver D. Crisp and Fred Sanders (Grand Rapids: Zondervan, 2013), 181. Rather than "new," Jesus gains a deeper intimacy, quality, and depth of relationship by means of his baptism in the Spirit. For a corrective that takes with full seriousness the conception of Jesus, see Mark L. Strauss, "Jesus and the Spirit in Biblical and Theological Perspective: Messianic Empowering, Saving Wisdom, and the Limits of Biblical Theology," in *The Spirit and Christ in the New Testament and Christian Theology*, ed. I. Howard Marshall, Volker Rabens, and Cornelis Bennema (Grand Rapids: Eerdmans, 2012), 266–70.

5. To this list we might add Jesus' identity as Prophet, Priest, and King, all of which require the Spirit for authentication and application.

that the Spirit Christology of the Gospels is not an accidental feature of the Gospel record but one of the more important interpretive keys to Christology proper; a key fashioned and shaped originally by Jesus and his historical mission, and later used effectively to open the door into a more thorough comprehension of who Jesus is and the significance of what he said and did. To separate pneumatology from Christology is to separate the ministry of Jesus from a correct understanding of that ministry and the nature of the miraculous activity as signs and pointers to the identity of Jesus. Jesus is who he is because of the Spirit. To the Jews of his day the Spirit was the definitive confirmation that this man was different, unique; he alone was the Messiah. Jesus' ministry bore the messianic stamp all over it. In an earlier work I suggested that to sidestep a Spirit Christology is to run afoul of the temptation of blasphemy against the Spirit.[6]

A fourth disclosure episode is the passion of Christ. While the death, resurrection, and exaltation of Christ have been extensively dealt with in the history of Christology, the role that the Holy Spirit plays has been grossly overlooked. What a Spirit Christology achieves is to bring the role of the Holy Spirit back into focus in all of the manifold expressions of the Spirit's relationship to Jesus and the Father. A good example of this can be seen clearly through Christ's work on the cross and beyond. Jesus would go to his death in total dependence on the same Spirit who had created, empowered, comforted, and led him throughout his life; he would go to his death in total submission to his Father's will in the power of the Spirit. As the drama reaches its climax, Mark highlights the role of the Spirit through the Gethsemane account. The prayer that ends with the Son's embracing of the Father's will, "not my will but yours" (Mark 14:36), begins with the words, which the early church identified as the witness of the Holy Spirit, that one is a child of God: "Abba" (cf. Mark 14:36; Rom. 8:15; Gal. 4:6). What began with his conception and baptism through the Spirit now ends in his passion through the Spirit. The Spirit that led Jesus into the wilderness is still beside him now in this time of trial and temptation. At his baptism God calls Jesus his beloved Son; here in Gethsemane, Jesus responds by addressing him as "Abba," "dear Father." Both the call to "life" and the response in "dying" are given "in the Spirit." Jesus goes in and through the Spirit to his death, thus fully aware that he is

6. Habets, *Anointed Son*, 160.

the messianic Son of God (Heb. 9:14). The Spirit yields Christ up to the Father to await the new nexus of his ministry, to be the Spirit of Christ poured out, first of all on the church and then eventually on all flesh. Through the "eternal Spirit" and the "indestructible life" (Heb. 7:16; 9:14) Jesus offered himself up to suffer God-forsakenness. On this basis we are compelled to look beyond Jesus' death to his rebirth from this same divine, quickening power of the Spirit.

The fifth messianic *kairos* is the resurrection of the Christ. As the one who perfects the Father's word in creation, the Spirit is the agent of the eschatological act of resurrection in the midst of time. Through the resurrection, Jesus' particular humanity becomes the basis of universal redemption. So what of the Holy Spirit? Christ offered himself up through the eternal Spirit (Heb. 9:14) and he lives in the "life-giving Spirit" (1 Cor. 15:45). He endured the sufferings and death through the power of the Spirit and was born again to eternal life by the Spirit (Rom. 8:11; 14:9; 1 Cor. 15:45; 2 Cor. 13:4), hence the pneumatological-Trinitarian paradigm. The Spirit gives birth to Christ once more, this time to eternal life, through and beyond his death. In Christ's rebirth it is the Spirit who is active, as in Christ's conception. Early Christian testimonies see the raising of Christ from the dead as the firstfruits of the end-time operation of the Spirit (Rom. 8:23; 1 Cor. 15:20, 23). Christ has been raised from the dead ahead of all others as their representative; as such the Spirit that raised Jesus is our earnest or down payment guaranteeing our future resurrection as well (2 Cor. 1:22; 5:5; Eph. 1:14). Early Christian faith in the resurrection was not based solely on Christ's appearances. It was just as strongly motivated by the experience of God's Spirit. Therefore Paul calls this Spirit "the Spirit or power of the resurrection" (Rom. 8:11; cf. 1:4). Luke follows the ascension with the Pentecostal outpouring of the Spirit: believing in the risen Christ means being possessed by the Spirit of the resurrection. In the Spirit the presence of the living Christ was experienced. The resurrection vindicates the claim that Jesus is both Christ/Messiah and Lord (Acts 2:36).

We might call the final messianic *kairos* the two-stage exaltation of Jesus, namely, ascension and Pentecost. The exaltation and enthronement of the Messiah through the ascension and Pentecost was a public display of his vindication by God, thus acting as a final chapter to his earthly history and the opening chapter of his new relationship to his kingdom as Lord of the Spirit.

The ascension acts as an important aspect of Christ's kingly office, as it is ascension to the "right hand of God" (Mark 16:19). It proclaims Christ's triumph (Eph. 4:8; Phil. 2:9; Heb. 2:9; 1 Pet. 3:22; fulfilling Psalms 8; 115; Isa. 40:28). The man of Nazareth is now Lord over all (1 Cor. 12:3; Eph. 1:22). His reign is not confined to the church but to "all things" (*ta panta*). The ascension acts as the first stage of exaltation. It is the path to the throne, the road to the destination, the antecedent to Pentecost. Pentecost is the official ceremony, the public coronation; the ascension is the final parting glimpse on earth of the Word made flesh, the light of the world, the final drama of the incarnation proper. The postresurrection ministry of the Spirit is in increasing identification with the ministry of Jesus so that the Spirit is now understood to be the messianically shaped Spirit and Jesus is now the Lord of the Spirit who will send his Spirit to reshape believers to be like him. This sending of the Spirit was initiated at Pentecost. One of the questions Pentecost answered was how the experience of salvation that Jesus came to inaugurate was to be continued and deepened when Jesus had departed. How was God to be more powerfully, self-revealingly, universally, and transformatively present among his people when Jesus was taken away? The answer: by God's Spirit who was above all God's powerful, self-revealing, and transforming presence, the Spirit of Jesus. *Kyrios* and *pneuma* belong together.

Working from Old Testament expectations, primitive Christianity understood Jesus as the bearer of the Spirit. It is clear that the community recognized, in the activity of the pre-Easter Jesus, the eschatological prophet, the New Moses, the end-time Servant of Yahweh. Yet it would take his death, resurrection, and exaltation to confirm and convince them that, in short, in Jesus they were confronted with the Messiah. The evangelists then structured their respective Gospels so as to bring out the full identity of Jesus the *Christ*. This was borne out by his conception/birth, baptism/temptation, and vocation/ministry, confirmed in his death and resurrection-exaltation, and finally lived out in the experience of the church. It was this life story that enabled the early church to make the connection between Jesus as the eschatological prophet and the title *Christos*, which at first was only used eschatologically for the function of the One who would return in power, but which was soon also connected with the earthly Jesus through the passion tradition, and could designate his whole activity.

Throughout the incarnation we have seen that the Spirit is the eschatological dimension integral to an understanding of Christology. The incarnation is a Trinitarian event that climaxes at the cross and in the exaltation of the Son to the right hand of the Father in order to be Lord of the Spirit at Pentecost.

From such biblical accounts as these, and many others we have not considered, a Spirit Christology is constructed out of God's self-revelation. Building on such testimony, a dogmatic account of Christ might now be attempted along the lines of a Spirit Christology proper.

Theological Guides

There are many ways to illustrate the provenance and orthodoxy of Spirit Christology, given its long history in the tradition and its many contemporary exponents. Despite the major works on Spirit Christology making clear its Trinitarian foundations, biblical fidelity, and historical veracity (Del Colle, Coffey, Habets, and others),[7] many today still, rather lazily, consign Spirit Christology to the category of adoptionism (Pannenberg, Baik, and others),[8] or ignore it altogether (Thiselton).[9] Perpetuating the adoptionistic interpretation of Spirit Christology is a fallacy unwarranted by a reading of its key contemporary exponents. Others want to co-opt Spirit Christology for the cause of panentheism or even process theology and to do so they appeal to a cadre of theologians whose work has been convincingly critiqued (Lampe,

7. Ralph Del Colle, *Christ and the Spirit: Spirit-Christology in Trinitarian Perspective* (New York: Oxford University Press, 1994); David M. Coffey, "Spirit Christology and the Trinity," in *Advents of the Spirit: An Introduction to the Current Study of Pneumatology*, ed. B. E. Hinze and D. L. Dabney (Milwaukee: Marquette University Press, 2001), 315–38; and Habets, *Anointed Son.*

8. Wolfhart Pannenberg, *Jesus—God and Man*, trans. Lewis L. Wilkins and Duane A. Priebe (London: SCM, 1968), 120–21, and the older textbooks such as Aloys Grillmeier, *Christ in Christian tradition*, vol. 1, 2nd ed., trans. John Bowden (Atlanta: John Knox, 1975), 53–57; Chung-Hyun Baik, *The Holy Trinity—God for God and God for Us: Seven Positions on the Immanent-Economic Trinity Relation in Contemporary Trinitarian Theology* (Eugene, OR: Pickwick, 2011), 181–82, who equates Spirit Christology with the work of Piet Schoonenberg, Roger Haight, and Geoffrey Lampe.

9. Spirit Christology does not appear in the latest voluminous work of Anthony C. Thiselton, *The Holy Spirit: In Biblical Teaching, through the Centuries, and Today* (Grand Rapids: Eerdmans, 2013), who, despite dealing with theologians such as Edward Irving, Jürgen Moltmann, Amos Yong, Frank Macchia, Veli-Matti Kärkkäinen, and others, is preoccupied with now passé discussions of renewal theology versus mainline religion, or hermeneutics and the place of Luke-Acts, than any substantive theological issues.

Haight, Dunn, Bracken, and others).[10] By examining two overlooked exemplars of Spirit Christology, one from the patristic era and the other from the development of post-Reformation Reformed theology, I hope to show the orthodoxy of Spirit Christology and to use that as a basis for addressing several objections raised against Spirit Christology.

The Blind See: Didymus on the Spirit

Didymus of Alexandria, also known as Didymus the Blind (ca. 313–98), was a disciple of his Alexandrian predecessor Origen and is thought to have succeeded Athanasius as a leading teacher of the "school" of Alexandria.[11] Jules Gross reminds us that although born before the Cappadocians, he was under their influence.[12] Didymus wrote commentaries and occasional papers on a variety of topics, but by far his reputation is as a teacher of pneumatology and *theōsis*. In terms of *theōsis*, Didymus argues that the one who deifies believers must be God, and thus *theōsis* is primarily used as an argument for the divinity of the Holy Spirit. It is Didymus's Spirit Christology that is of the most interest to us, however, as it exerted an influence over subsequent thinkers who went on to develop their own Spirit Christologies (the focus of the next section).

Didymus's *On the Holy Spirit* can be dated to 360–65 CE, which means it was one of, if not the first, full treatments of pneumatology contemporaneous with Athanasius's *Letters*

10. Geoffrey W. H. Lampe, *God as Spirit: The Bampton Lectures, 1976* (Oxford: Clarendon, 1977); Roger Haight, "The Case for Spirit Christology," *Theological Studies* 53 (1992): 257–87; Haight, *Jesus Symbol of God* (New York: Orbis, 1999); James D. G. Dunn, *The Christ and the Spirit*, 2 vols. (Grand Rapids: Eerdmans, 1998); and Joseph A. Bracken, "Trinitarian Spirit Christology: In Need of a New Metaphysics?," *Theological Studies* 72 (2011): 750–67.

11. The exact nature of the school Didymus taught at is unclear, whether it was his cell in which students learned, or was a continuation of the academy of Alexandria in imitation of his mentor, Origen. Either way, Didymus was a renowned and influential teacher in the fourth century. See Norman Russell, *The Doctrine of Deification in the Greek Patristic Tradition* (Oxford: Oxford University Press, 2004), 154–61. Due to his Origenist theology, he was condemned at the Fifth Ecumenical Council (553 CE). See the concise introduction by Andrew Radde-Gallwitz, "Introduction to Didymus's *On the Holy Spirit*," in *Works of the Spirit: Athanasius the Great and Didymus the Blind*, trans. and ed. Mark DelCogliano, Andrew Radde-Gallwitz, and Lewis Ayres, St Vladimir's Seminary Press Popular Patristics Series 43 (Yonkers, NY: St Vladimir's Seminary Press, 2011), 31–50.

12. Jules Gross, *The Divinization of the Christian according to the Greek Fathers*, trans. Paul A. Onica (Anaheim: A & C Press, 2002), 198.

to Serapion on the Holy Spirit (359–61).[13] In his *On the Holy Spirit*, Didymus deals with a number of the themes evident in any Spirit Christology, namely, a discussion of the Spirit's nature, activity, sending/procession, economic mission, and the danger of blasphemy against the Spirit. According to Lewis Ayres, however, there is one overarching or fundamental argument to the work, which is that "the Spirit is the boundless source of all sanctification in which Christians . . . participate."[14]

According to Didymus, the divinity of the Holy Spirit is proven on the following grounds: the Spirit sanctifies; the Spirit is ascribed personal activity in Scripture; the Holy Spirit most often takes a definite article in Scripture, attesting to his personal distinctness yet essential unity with God; the Father, Son, and Spirit have a single activity, indicating a single substance (*homoousion*).[15] Didymus concludes, "From these texts we conclude that the substance of the Trinity is indivisible, and that the Father is truly the Father of the Son, and that the Son is truly the Son of the Father, and that the Holy Spirit is truly the Spirit of the Father and God, and especially the Spirit of Wisdom and Truth, that is, of the Son of God. So then, this is salvation for those who believe."[16]

Didymus describes the Spirit's role in the conception of Jesus in the following way: "when the Holy Spirit came upon the virgin Mary, the creating power of the Most High fashioned the body of Christ: using it as a temple, he was born without the seed of a man."[17] He then explains further: "we have already demonstrated at length that the Holy Spirit's activity is the same as that of the Father and the Son, and that a single substance is implied by the same activity, and, vice versa, that those who are ὁμοουσια . . . do not have an activity that is diverse."[18] Still further, he identifies the presence of the Spirit as the bond of union between the

13. The precise dating of Didymus's *On the Holy Spirit* is disputed; the best current suggestion is that Didymus's treatise was "*not necessarily* written *before* Athanasius's letters, but does not offer compelling evidence that it *must* have been written *after* Athanasius's letters" (Radde-Gallwitz, "Introduction," 42 [italics in original]).

14. Lewis Ayres, "Didymus's Argument," in *Works of the Spirit*, 45.

15. Didymus of Alexandria, *On the Holy Spirit*, in *Works of the Spirit*, paras. 81–86 (168–70). All references to Didymus are to this edition of his work, cited as *Works of the Spirit* followed by paragraph and page reference.

16. Ibid., para. 103 (175–76).

17. Ibid., para. 144 (188).

18. Ibid., para. 145 (189).

two natures of Christ in reference to Psalm 117:16, 17:

> This passage is certainly the most manifest proof that this voice belongs to the person of the Lordly Man, whom the only begotten Son of God deigned to assume from the virgin because he is the right hand of God, as is written in the Acts of the Apostles. He was *descended from David according to the flesh* [Rom. 1:3] and born of a virgin when *the Holy Spirit came upon her and the power of the Most High overshadowed her* [Luke 1:35].[19]

Didymus shares much with what becomes in the Western tradition a commitment to the Trinity as a form of mutual love, before going on to make a case for the Spirit's divinity based upon his works. Common among patristic thinkers, Didymus has a form of Platonism in his theology when he adopts an understanding of God as the undiminished Giver before arguing for the inseparable operations of the Trinity. While brief, such is the implicit Spirit Christology that influenced a number of later advocates of Spirit Christology, such as John Owen, the focus of the next section.

Dear John: John Owen's Spirit Christology

While tantalizingly brief, Puritan theologian John Owen's (1616–83) explication of the functional relation between the divine and human natures of Jesus along the lines of a Spirit Christology is highly suggestive, and his influence upon successive generations of theologians should not be overlooked. Owen's pneumatic Christology was not a theological novelty, even if it was the most advanced articulation of such an approach. Owen's argument was derivative of two key influences upon him: the Reformer John Calvin and the patristic figure Didymus of Alexandria.[20] Calvin provided the immediate context of Owen's Reformed theology with a pneumatological emphasis, while Didymus provided Owen with a way to

19. Ibid., para. 227 (213) (italics in original). The editors note on this page that "though Didymus here starkly distinguishes the only-begotten Son of God and the Lordly Man such that they appear to be two agents, in *Spir.* 230 he affirms that the two natures of Christ belong to a single subject."

20. Owen refers to the work of Didymus eight times in his collected works: John Owen, *The Works of John Owen*, 23 vols. on CD-ROM (Rio, WI: Ages Digital Library, 2000), 3:69, 71, 78, 81; 4:187, 324; 11:66; and 16:132 (all references to Owen are to this edition of his works, cited as *Works* followed by volume number and page reference). Owen found in the work of Didymus a certain precedent for his own pneumatologically robust theology.

interpret the incarnation along the lines of a Spirit Christology more specifically.[21]

Owen proves to be an important case study of a Spirit Christology, given he was formulating a pneumatic Christology while holding to Nicene and Chalcedonian orthodoxy. As Oliver Crisp has stated, "By elaborating upon the role of the Holy Spirit in the ministry of Christ, as the Evangelists do, Owen is able to do justice to both the biblical and creedal poles of historic orthodoxy."[22] As such his insights can lead into a more fully informed contemporary articulation of Spirit Christology. Brandon Withrow and Stephen Holmes have both noted the connection to Owen in the work of Jonathan Edwards, for example, and through him, a host of later theologians.[23] Having examined Edwards's Spirit Christology elsewhere, I shall focus here on the account of Owen.[24]

John Owen sought to defend Christ's uniqueness as the God-man without limiting his humanity in any way (incipient docetism), a tendency to which the Western tradition was susceptible. Owen sought to present Christ as the Scriptures do, as the archetype of Christian existence, continually empowered, comforted, and sanctified by the Holy Spirit. He argued that the eternal Son of God assumed human nature into personal union with himself, but—and this was the distinctive insight of his Christology—he held that all direct divine activity on that assumed human nature was that of the Holy Spirit.[25]

---

21. Owen's usage of Didymus of Alexandria is only mentioned once in the literature, by Brandon G. Withrow, *Becoming Divine: Jonathan Edwards' Incarnational Spirituality within the Christian Tradition* (Eugene, OR: Cascade, 2011), 127n66, who merely mentions the influence as suggested to him in personal correspondence by Carl Trueman.

22. Oliver D. Crisp, *Revisioning Christology: Theology in the Reformed Tradition* (Farnham: Ashgate, 2011), 94.

23. Withrow, *Becoming Divine*, 127; and Stephen R. Holmes, *God of Grace and God of Glory: An Account of the Theology of Jonathan Edwards* (Grand Rapids: Eerdmans, 2001), 136–38. Owen's influence upon Edwards's theology as a whole is noted throughout Kyle C. Strobel, *Jonathan Edwards's Theology: A Reinterpretation*, T&T Clark Studies in Systematic Theology 19 (London: Bloomsbury T&T Clark, 2013).

24. Myk Habets, "The Surprising Third Article Theology of Jonathan Edwards," in *The Ecumenical Edwards: Jonathan Edwards and the Theologians*, ed. Kyle Strobel (Farnham: Ashgate, 2015), 195–211.

25. Alan Spence, "Christ's Humanity and Ours: John Owen," in *Persons, Divine and Human*, ed. Christoph Schwöbel and Colin E. Gunton (Edinburgh: T&T Clark, 1991), 75–76. Also see Spence, *Incarnation and Inspiration: John Owen and the Coherence of Christology* (London: T&T Clark, 2007), 52–55, and Spence, "John Owen and Trinitarian Agency," *Scottish Journal of Theology* 43 (1990): 157–73. Also see Kelly M. Kapic, *Communion with God:*

Prior to this time it was generally held that the Logos, the Son, determined the human life of Jesus directly, rather than indirectly, through the Holy Spirit. This is a crucial insight in the formulation of a Spirit Christology. Owen sought to defend this position from Scripture, marshaling extensive testimony in support.[26]

Against a rising Socinian view that the Son of God acts directly on the human nature, a view made popular at the time by John Crellius,[27] Owen identified ten operations of the Holy Spirit observable in the incarnation to prove his point.[28] Owen divided these ten operations between two main divisions: the work of the Holy Spirit as respects the person of Christ in his human nature as the immediate object, and works he performs toward others on his behalf.[29] Owen was aware of the objections to this way of thinking, objections leveled only by the Socinians—namely, that it is hard to see how the Spirit could work in between the two natures of Christ, as it were, without doing violence to them, and why the eternal Son could not simply be the immediate cause of all operations in the flesh. Similar objections are raised against Spirit Christology today, as we shall see below. Owen's argument is that the only immediate work of the Son on the human nature was the assumption of it into subsistence with himself. Owen then cites John of Damascus in support along with such texts as John 1:14; Rom. 1:3; Gal. 4:4; Phil. 2:6, 7; and Heb. 2:14, 16. This safeguards the personal union of Christ, "the inseparable subsistence of the assumed nature in the person of the Son."[30] Here Owen is being consistent with the theology of Chalcedon as well as Scripture. All other actions or operations of God in the person of the Son toward the human nature were voluntary. This safeguards a staple Reformed

---

The Divine and the Human in the Theology of John Owen (Grand Rapids: Baker, 2007), especially 84–88.

26. Graham McFarlane, *Why Do You Believe What You Believe about the Holy Spirit?* (Carlisle, UK: Paternoster, 1998), 103–6, identifies four areas especially where Owen articulated the relation between Christ and the Spirit: 1) birth, 2) sanctification, 3) power, and 4) death and resurrection. See Carl Trueman, *The Claims of Truth: John Owen's Trinitarian Theology* (Carlisle, UK: Paternoster, 1998), 177.

27. John Crellius, *Touching One God the Father Wherein Many Things Also concerning the Nature of the Son of God and the Holy Spirit Are Discoursed of* (Kofmoburg: n.p., 1665), 164, cited in Withrow, *Becoming Divine*, 129.

28. Owen, "Work of the Holy Spirit with Respect unto the Head of the New Creation—the Human Nature of Christ," in *Pneumatologia*, vol. 3, bk. 2, chapter 3 of *Works*, 199–209.

29. Ibid., 3:199–200.

30. Ibid., 3:201.

emphasis on a *communio idiomatum* and the *extra Calvinisticum*.[31]

Armed with these foundations, Owen can now make claim to a Spirit Christology in which the eternal Son acts on his human nature through the operations of the Holy Spirit. Owen states this as follows:

> The Holy Spirit is the Spirit of the Son, no less than the Spirit of the Father. He proceedeth from the Son, as from the Father. He is the 'Spirit of the Son,' Galatians 4:6. And hence is he the immediate operator of all divine acts of the Son himself, even on his own human nature. Whatever the Son of God wrought in, by, or upon the human nature, he did it by the Holy Ghost, who is his Spirit, as he is the Spirit of the Father.[32]

Lest he be misunderstood, Owen immediately makes clear that he is operating under the theological rule *Opera Trinitatis ad extra sunt indivisa*, stating: "There is no such division in the external operations of God that any one of them should be the act of one person, without the concurrence of the others; and the reason of it is, because the nature of God, which is the principle of all divine operations, is one and the same, undivided in them all."[33] Owen is clearly working within Nicene and Chalcedonian orthodoxy.

Owen then articulates ten operations of the Holy Spirit upon Jesus, operations that largely mirror the messianic *kairoi* outlined earlier in this chapter, even if the emphases are in different places. In the first place for Owen is Christ's miraculous conception by the Spirit, a fulfillment of Old Testament prophecies and a sign and announcement of God's presence to redeem. Second, the total sanctification of Christ, filling him with all grace "according to the measure of its receptivity."[34] This forms an important step in Owen's argument. As Jesus Christ was divinely conceived in the womb of the Virgin Mary by the Holy Spirit, so Jesus Christ was also filled with the Holy Spirit from conception in order that his human nature could not fall prey to the human condition—the propensity to sin (Isa. 11:1–3). Owen does not mean to say that upon conception and initial

31. Owen deals with the *communio idiomatum* in more detail earlier in Owen, *Christologia*, vol. 1, chapter 18 of *Works*, 301–3. On the *extra Calvinisticum*, see Myk Habets, "Putting the 'Extra' Back into Calvinism," *Scottish Journal of Theology* 62 (2009): 441–56.

32. Owen, *Works*, 3:202.

33. Ibid.

34. Ibid., 3:210. The language here is a direct allusion to that of Calvin.

sanctification the Son was filled with *all* grace and *all* knowledge, rather "the soul of Christ, from the first moment of its infusion, was a subject capable of a fullness of grace, as unto its habitual residence and in-being, though the actual exercise of it was suspended for a while, until the organs of the body were fitted for it."[35] Owen thus finds a robust argument to counter the Socinian question of how Jesus could grow in grace and knowledge, and yet still be God. To clarify, Owen provides a third operation of the Spirit upon Jesus—the Spirit continued to sustain and sanctify Christ throughout his life (a rejection of any Apollinarianism or docetism) as he grew in grace and wisdom (Luke 2:40). Owen is content to read Scripture at face value and to give full weight to the man Jesus, growing in grace and knowledge (Luke 2:40, 52). He writes, "his divine nature was not unto him in the place of a soul, nor did it immediately operate the things which he performed, as some of old vainly imagined; but being a perfect man, his rational soul was in him the immediate principle of all his moral operations even as ours are in us."[36] Owen is advocating here the view that Jesus Christ is *autokineton*—a self-determining spiritual principle, fully self-conscious and, as a creature, open and responsive to God, not determined by the Logos immediately. Owen's argument is that if this were not so then Christ would not be truly human.

A fourth operation of the Spirit on Christ occurs at his baptism wherein the Spirit anointed him with all the gifts and abilities required to execute his messianic vocation, especially his prophetic office. Fifth, the Spirit is the power of Christ's miracles and exorcisms. Sixth, Christ was "guided, directed, comforted, supported" by the Spirit "in the whole course of his ministry, temptations, obedience, and sufferings."[37] Seventh, Christ "offered himself up unto God through the eternal Spirit" (Heb. 9:14), who sustained and empowered Christ's offering of himself as a perfect sacrifice. Eighth, Owen argues for a special or peculiar work of the Spirit while Jesus was dead such that Jesus' soul was in the special care of the Father while his body was in the special care of the Holy Spirit such that it did not see decay (Ps. 16:10; Acts 2:31). Ninth, the Spirit is the special agent of Christ's resurrection, uniting Christ's holy soul and body (1 Pet. 3:18). Tenth, and

35. Ibid., 3:211.

36. Ibid., 3:212.

37. Ibid., 3:217.

finally, it was the Holy Spirit who glorified the human nature of Christ and made it fit for his heavenly abode at the right hand of the Father and, Owen importantly adds, "a pattern of the glorification of the bodies of them that believe on him."[38]

Such is the Spirit Christology offered by Owen. For each of the ten operations of the Holy Spirit on the life of Christ he adds further details, both biblical and theological, and applies this to the church, of which Christ is the Head. Owen concludes his treatment with one additional operation of the Spirit, not one directed upon Christ but one directed *toward* Christ, that is, the witness of the Spirit to the messianic identity and saving mission of the Son. This testifying work of the Spirit continues, Owen reminds us, to this day.[39] The contemporary articulation of a Spirit Christology would arguably be a consequence of the ongoing work of the Spirit in testifying to Christ the Head.

Owen's formulation stands in stark contrast (but not contradiction) to the long tradition received in the West through Chalcedon.[40] In the words of Holmes, Owen's Christology may be regarded as "a radicalization of the basic Reformed position, in that it introduced doctrinal innovation with the intention of defending the same point, the genuine humanity of Jesus Christ."[41] The experience of God for the man Jesus is indirect; it is through the Holy Spirit and thus is voluntary rather than natural.[42] In Christ there is both continuity with humanity and discontinuity, for after all, he is the God-man. Whence did Christ gain his source of knowledge and revelation of God the Father? As the eternal Word, he was privy to the entire council and wisdom of the Father from all ages. However, in the incarnation he restricted himself to the mediation of that knowledge and wisdom through the Spirit. Hence, he stood in continuity with the prophets of old as they were inspired by the Holy Spirit to both foretell and forthtell the things of God. What distinguishes the revelation in Christ from that of these prophets is "the infinite excellency of his

38. Ibid., 3:228.

39. Ibid., 3:228.

40. See Spence, "Christ's Humanity," 74–97. Withrow writes, "the desire to uphold the Chalcedonian definition is what fueled Owen's emphasis on the role of the Spirit in the incarnation" (*Becoming Divine*, 130).

41. Holmes, *God of Grace and God of Glory*, 136.

42. This is worked out in Owen's exegesis of Hebrews, especially Heb. 5:7. See Owen, *An Exposition of the Epistle to the Hebrews*, 7 vols., in *Works*, 20:615–44.

person above theirs,"[43] due to his person being the everlasting Son. "Though a Christian is perpetually being sanctified by the Spirit due to human imperfection, the Spirit's sanctification of Christ is that of maintaining his already perfect state, which the Spirit ensured at his conception and maintained by a *donum superadditum*."[44]

Holmes is helpful in observing three intentions of Owen in making such claims: first, to affirm the fact that Christ was made man, second, to specify an incarnational soteriology, and third, in order to apply the work of the Spirit in the life of Christ to the work of the Spirit in the life of believers.[45] In his own way Owen was able to affirm an orthodox Spirit Christology. However, due to his overriding concern for the basis of the assurance of salvation Owen did not pursue this enterprise in any greater detail or investigate the deeper Trinitarian implications of his Christology.[46]

The Perils of Spirit Christology

While appreciative of the insights that Spirit Christology offers, there are a number of theological detractors whose arguments deserve to be heard and addressed. Reformed theologian Oliver Crisp offers an appreciative critique of Owenite Christology, a critique that applies in part to any orthodox account of Spirit Christology; thus his work is especially apt to focus on in this section as it is representative of other critiques and offers the most robust critique to date. Crisp's central objection is "that it introduces a theologically damaging cleavage between God the Son and his human nature."[47] More specifically, "Owen's doctrine seems to generate a distinction between the [*sic*] God the Son and his agency 'in' or 'through' his human nature

43. Ibid., 19:37.

44. Withrow, *Becoming Divine*, 131.

45. Holmes, *God of Grace and God of Glory*, 137–38. The specific christological dogmas that Holmes shows Edwards utilizing include a denial of a Lutheran *communicatio idiomatum*, a defence and use of the *extra Calvinisticum*, and sermonic imperatives to follow the example of Christ in or by Christ's Spirit (in my opinion this was less a theology of *imitatio Christi* than a participatory soteriology centered on the vicarious humanity of Christ).

46. One attempt to articulate a commensurate divine ontology is Myk Habets, "Getting beyond the *Filioque* with Third Article Theology," in *Ecumenical Perspectives on the Filioque for the Twenty-First Century*, ed. Myk Habets (London: Bloomsbury T&T Clark, 2014), 211–30; and the contributions in the present volume from Andrew Gabriel, John Studebaker Jr., and Wolfgang Vondey.

47. Crisp, *Revisioning Christology*, 92.

at all moments after the first moment of the assumption of human nature in the very act of becoming incarnate."[48] For Crisp, this seems theologically dubious. According to Crisp's analysis, an Owenite Christology threatens the integrity of the hypostatic union, as it posits the necessary agency of the Holy Spirit in addition to that of the Son, the one who assumed the human nature, in the first place being one step removed from it.[49] Crisp considers the likely Owenite counterargument, that his endorsement of the principle *Opera Trinitatis ad extra sunt indivisa* negates the lack of proximity of the Son in the incarnation given the united work of the Trinity in all actions *ad extra*.[50] But this is not convincing either, for Crisp, for the reason that a human's actions are personal, not merely instrumental; thus the Son would have to act immediately in all incarnate actions.[51] If this is correct, then on Crisp's account "there appears to be no metaphysical room for the interposition of another divine person between the intentions of God the Son (i.e. his agency) and the intentional actions brought about in his human nature."[52] Furthermore, according to Crisp's critique, Owenite Christology amounts to a denial of the efficacy of the Son's assumption of human nature, as it appears to posit a cleavage between the immediate agency of the Son and his human nature. As such the hypostatic union itself is threatened.[53]

Crisp's central critique is that an Owenite Christology is untenable on the grounds that once the Son has assumed human nature he steps back and lets the Holy Spirit act in all future works. The direct agency of the Holy Spirit is then thought to trump the agency of the Son, and this is what is finally unacceptable in Owen's account. I concede Crisp's point here, *if* this is what Owen is suggesting. To replace the Son with the Spirit as the active subject of the person of Jesus Christ would be a denial of the incarnation of the eternal Son. And of course, Owen states that the one direct and immediate operation of the Son on the human nature is the act of

48. Ibid., 100.

49. Ibid., 100–101. Crisp uses a thought experiment to illustrate his point: the case of the relationship between astronauts and their space suits.

50. It is to be noted that Didymus also makes explicit appeal to this principle in his own version of a Spirit Christology (Didymus, *Works of the Spirit*, paras. 81–86 [168–170]).

51. Crisp, *Revisioning Christology*, 103–5, relates this to both a substance-dualist conception of being human and to a Cartesian approach to illustrate his point.

52. Ibid., 105.

53. Ibid., 107.

assumption, so he does not wish to make this move. But given his argument that all subsequent acts of the Son on the human nature are voluntary and mediated by the Spirit, is Crisp correct in his central critique?

Some contemporary proposals for Spirit Christology affirm that in the one simple being of the triune God all three persons mutually indwell the other such that the threeness of the persons is the oneness of the essence (*perichoresis*). The doctrine of personal subsistence clearly articulates the relational being of God as involving three coequal persons in one undivided (relational) substance. In the immanent Trinity the Father begets the Son in or by the Holy Spirit, and the Spirit simultaneously proceeds from the Father as the one in whom the Son is begotten.[54] The Father too is simultaneously personed in the begetting of the Son (in the Spirit) and the spiration of the Spirit (through the Son). In the economy, the missions of God are coordinated with the eternal processions such that we might be led to think that while the Son is the subject of the incarnation, this is not without the Father and the Spirit. Thus personal agency in God is more complex than it is with human creatures, and especially so when the actual human being we are considering—Jesus Christ—is unique in having two natures "unconfusedly, unchangeably, indivisibly, and inseparably" (as per Chalcedon).[55] Add to this the actual scriptural accounts of Jesus' life lived in dependence on the Spirit—his conception, baptism, vocation, passion, exaltation—and a more complex picture emerges than that of simply a Logos Christology. In fact, Christ's mission is specifically situated within the prior mission of the Spirit and can only adequately be understood in that light.[56]

54. This Trinitarian account is drawn from Thomas G. Weinandy, *The Father's Spirit of Sonship: Reconceiving the Trinity* (Edinburgh: T&T Clark, 1995).

55. Here Chalcedon has to be interpreted through the dynamic Christology of Cyril of Alexandria. The argument is too big to rehearse here, but see Anthony N. S. Lane, "Cyril of Alexandria and the Incarnation," in Marshall, Rabens, and Bennema, *Spirit and Christ*, 285–302.

56. Hermann Gunkel noted long ago that, outside of the Gospels, "the teaching regarding the πνευμα did not arise under the influence of Paul's teaching about Christ. Rather, the teaching about Christ is the peculiarly Pauline expression of what the apostle is contending for in his doctrine of the πνευμα which is borrowed from the views of the Christian community" (*The Influence of the Holy Spirit: The Popular View of the Apostolic Age and the Teaching of the Apostle Paul* [Minneapolis: Fortress, 2008], 115). Earlier Gunkel made the fascinating observation that "Paul's first pneumatic experience was an experience of the Christ" (ibid., 114). While

A contemporary Spirit Christology makes clear that the divine agency in the incarnation is that of the Son and the Spirit, in their respective ways. The Son is the active willing subject, if we might speak that way; the Spirit is the active *paraklētos*, no less personal or involved. Philip Butin writes of Calvin teaching a "perichoretic empowerment of the Son by the Spirit" in his commentary on Matthew 3:16, where Calvin writes: "in the fullness of time, to equip [Christ] for the fulfillment of the office of Redeemer, he is endowed with a new power of the Spirit. . . . He comes forth as a divine man, under the royal power of the Holy Spirit. We know that he is God, manifested in the flesh, but his heavenly power is also to be thought upon in his Person as a minister, in his human nature."[57]

It is just this kind of theology that prompts David Coffey, working out of a neoscholastic Catholic tradition, to suggest and speak of an "incarnation" of the Holy Spirit in the incarnation of the Son.[58] While the language is to my mind less than satisfactory, the intent behind it is acceptable. It is not the case that after the assumption of the human nature the Son walks away, steps back, or is not intimately involved in the incarnation. I concede that would be absurd. Human persons are infused with Spirit, they are spiritual beings. After the eternal Son takes to himself a human nature (*anhypostatic*) and becomes a *human* person (*enhypostatic*), it is the Holy Spirit who is now active in mediating human nature to the eternal Son in a *communio idiomata*.[59] If the Son acted on his human nature

Son and Spirit may have distinct missions, they are in an inseparable relationship nonetheless.

57. Philip W. Butin, *Revelation, Redemption, and Response: Calvin's Trinitarian Understanding of the Divine-Human Relationship* (New York: Oxford, 1995), 65–66, in Work, "Jesus' New Relationship," 180n32.

58. David M. Coffey, *Deus Trinitas: The Doctrine of the Triune God* (New York: Oxford University Press, 1999), 39. Admittedly, Coffey speaks of the "incarnation" of the Spirit in single quotes, but this is still too much I think.

59. A Reformed account of the *communio idiomata* differs substantially from a Lutheran account of a *communicatio idiomata*, in that in the former, the idioms of each nature are now true of the one Person of the incarnate Son, while in the latter account, attributes of the two natures are transferable across those natures. In a constructive attempt to retrieve Spirit Christology, Telford Work suggests an alternate way of interpreting Chalcedon by rejecting any notion of a *communicatio idiomata / idiomatōn koinōnia* in favor of a "concurrence of divine and human relations" ("Jesus' New Relationship," 171–83). While highly suggestive and deserving a fuller treatment, the proposal still looks to be Nestorian-like in its orientation as it posits two

immediately, then it would not be an incarnation, one would not be dealing with God *as* man but God *in* a man, as Athanasius was fond of saying.[60] In short, without this understanding of the role of the Holy Spirit in the incarnation we would simply be back to a Logos Christology, with all of its docetic entrapments. Crisp is quick to point out that such an account of Spirit Christology could imply that the Spirit is merely an interface between God the Son and his human nature, but that this was not Owen's theology. His theology is more radical, for it posits agency to the Spirit to the mutual exclusion of the Son.[61] For Crisp, this is an insurmountable objection to Owenite Christology.

But has Crisp got it right? While Owen's language might need to be tamed, it is clear from his work that he is not suggesting anything like the thought that the Son takes a backseat to the Spirit in the incarnation. He is, rather, providing an account of the incarnation in which there is dual agency at work, that of the Son and the Spirit, and both in personal ways. Ian McFarland helpfully outlines the sort of pneumatic Chalcedonianism Crisp is after, but does so in a way that is compatible with an orthodox Spirit Christology, as is being argued for here through Didymus and Owen. McFarland recognizes that Jesus has to be a genuine human, but that he is nonetheless *un*like the rest of us in some way (he is sinless, for example); and framing the Spirit's role in Chalcedonian terms does a better job of honoring the integrity of Jesus' humanity than non-Chalcedonian alternatives. In the terms of Spirit Christology, this is an account that seeks to complement Logos Christology with Spirit Christology, even if the emphasis is given to inspiration. McFarland's contention is that "an emphasis on the incarnational role of the Spirit enables this Chalcedonian insight to be developed more consistently than has often been the case by allowing Christ's humanity to be construed holistically: as a complete nature that, although at every point moved and shaped by the Spirit, remains in both being and act utterly distinct from divinity."[62]

A Chalcedonian Christology has to maintain that Christ's human nature is exactly like

person-like entities in the incarnation, and leaning toward adoptionism in that it elides the place of the conception of Jesus by the Holy Spirit in favor of his baptism being a quasi-ontological event.

60. Athanasius, *Contra Arianos* 3.29 (*NPNF*[2] 4:1002–3).

61. Crisp, *Revisioning Christology*, 107.

62. Ian A. McFarland, "Spirit and Incarnation: Toward a Pneumatic Chalcedonianism," *International Journal of Systematic Theology* 16 (2014): 144.

that of other humans; Christ fully shares our human nature, but he is a different *hypostasis*, a different person, and therein lies his uniqueness. According to Chalcedonian logic, Jesus' divine *hypostasis* is not the power behind his human attributes, something tantamount to monothelitism, a single divine will or monergism, a divine mode of activity. Whereas Crisp cannot see how the Holy Spirit can have personal agency in the human acts of Christ, it would appear that McFarland thinks this is actually necessary according to catholic Christology. The Holy Spirit, however, is not an impersonal force field through which the eternal Son acts on the human nature. Rather, the *perichoretic* being of the triune God is equally at work in the incarnation as Word and Spirit work together on the human nature. Thus the Word is the subject who wills and acts, but does so within the conditions of human nature, and that necessitates he works by or through the Holy Spirit.

Truer to Chalcedonian Christology, McFarland argues that "the confession that the Word is the *subject* of Jesus' thoughts and actions . . . must be distinguished from the claim that the Word is the *cause* of Jesus' human operations. . . . On biblical no less than Chalcedonian terms, however, it is much more profitable to ascribe this divine activity to the Holy Spirit."[63] In short, this is the claim of contemporary Spirit Christology, which is self-consciously Trinitarian and orthodox, despite McFarland's lack of awareness that this is what Del Colle, Coffey, and myself are arguing when advocating for a Spirit Christology.[64] While not discussing Owenite Christology, McFarland offers a compatible account, and a corrective to Crisp's objections, when referring to Aquinas's distinction between the grace of union (*gratia*

---

63. Ibid., 153.

64. Ibid., 154. McFarland argues that his view is in sharp contrast to Spirit Christologies both ancient and modern. The only Spirit Christologies cited in his essay, however, are the post-Trinitarian accounts of Roger Haight ("The Case for Spirit Christology," *Theological Studies* 53 [1992]: 257–87) and Paul W. Newman (*A Spirit Christology: Recovering the Biblical Paradigm of Christian Faith* [Lanham, MD: University Press of America, 1987]). This suggests McFarland only knows of post-Trinitarian Spirit Christologies and perpetuates the mistaken view that all Spirit Christologies are adoptionistic. The fact that the work of Newman is appealed to at all is evidence of a lack of awareness of recent works on Spirit Christology from an orthodox and Trinitarian perspective. Newman's work amounts to a large pamphlet, is relatively hard to access, and its influence is out of proportion to the lack of constructive theology it offers. It is influential, I suspect, merely due to the fact that it serves the purposes of perpetuating the adoptionist slur against all Spirit Christologies that many today wish to propagate.

unionis) and habitual grace (*gratia habitualis*) in Christ: "The principle of the union is the person of the Son, who took himself a human nature; and by taking a human nature this person is said to have been sent into the world. The principle of habitual grace, given as it is with charity, is the Holy Spirit; he is said to be sent when he comes to dwell in the mind by charity."[65]

With Didymus, Owen, and the growing host of contemporary advocates of a Trinitarian Spirit Christology, McFarland not only highlights the biblical fidelity of this account of the incarnation, rehearsing the messianic *kairoi* outlined earlier, but also shows the practical benefit this Christology offers, namely: "the role of the Spirit in Jesus' life is parallel with other human beings rather than something which distinguishes him from them. Whether the person in question is Jesus, the Word made flesh, or the least distinguished of the saints, it is the gift of the Holy Spirit rather than any intrinsic property of human nature that makes possible human life active in faith and love."[66] The eternal Son is the active subject of the incarnation, but he works on the human nature indirectly, through the Holy Spirit, as a real human person, Jesus bar Joseph, Jesus the Messiah. Commenting on McFarland's work, Oliver Davies makes the comment that this "opens a space for the Holy Spirit to be the dynamic presence of God within the human life of Jesus Christ himself. It is the Spirit who is the point of contact between the divine *hypostasis* and the humanity of Jesus."[67] As with other believers, Jesus' life is lived in dependence upon the Spirit of God; it is not a mere appearance of humanity.[68]

65. Thomas Aquinas, *Summa theologiae* III, q. 7, a. 13, cited by McFarland, "Spirit and Incarnation," 154. For further articulation of neoscholastic categories of grace in the context of Spirit Christology, see Del Colle, *Christ and the Spirit*, 34–63; and for a constructive critique, ibid., 64–90; and David M. Coffey, *Grace: The Gift of the Holy Spirit* (Milwaukee: Marquette University Press, 2011), whose work goes intentionally beyond neo-scholasticism. Wihout adopting this Thomistic solution I have suggested a constructive solution in Myk Habets, "The Fallen Humanity of Christ: A Pneumatological Clarification of the Theology of Thomas F. Torrance," *Participatio* 5 (2015): 18-44.

66. McFarland, "Spirit and Incarnation," 155.

67. Oliver Davies, "Holy Spirit and Mediation: Towards a Transformational Pneumatology," *International Journal of Systematic Theology* 16 (2014): 165.

68. As Crisp admits, this is where several of his own analogies for the hypostatic union break down (*Revisioning Christology*, 100–101). While the human nature the Word assumed is *anhypostatic*, once assumed it is *enhypostatic*: Jesus is the person of the eternal Son.

The Promise of Spirit Christology

Delivering upon the promise of Spirit Christology is what the current volume on Third Article Theology is about; thus this section is a brief appetizer to what can be found more fully developed throughout this volume and in other works. What is unique about Jesus is not that he is a human possessed by God (Apollinarianism and its derivatives), nor that he appears to be human but in reality his humanity is unlike ours in every respect (docetism and its derivatives), nor that in the incarnation the Word becomes two independent people—the eternal Son and Jesus of Nazareth (Nestorianism and its derivatives). Rather, as per a Spirit Christology, in the incarnation the Son who is consubstantial with God, takes to himself a human nature consubstantial with that of the rest of humanity, and as such lives a human life in humanly conscious reliance upon the Holy Spirit (through a human mind, will, and emotions). It is the Word in human flesh, the Logos operating with a human mind and will, that the Spirit anoints, empowers, and sustains. It is the theandric *person* of Christ that is unique, not his *human nature* or lack of one. As McFarland makes clear:

> Like Christ we receive the Spirit as a gift (for created human nature can only receive the Creator Spirit as a gift, even when that nature is enhypostatized by the Word) that enables us to share in God's very life; but whereas Christ receives this gift as his very own Spirit (because it is the Spirit of God, and he is God), we can receive it only in acknowledging that we have no right to it (because it is the Spirit of God, and we are not God).[69]

Christ is thus unlike the rest of humanity in his person, yet like the fallen stock of humanity as respects his human nature. What sustains, sanctifies, empowers, and perfects Christ's humanity is the Holy Spirit, *his* Spirit, now bequeathed to "all flesh." Christ is thus like and unlike us, as Spirit Christology, more than any other christological construct, is able to account for.

McFarland does not want to claim the title of Spirit Christology for his theology, as he mistakenly believes this can only mean adoptionism, and so he concludes his essay asking where one might look to find the uniqueness or divine identity of Jesus given that his humanity is the same as ours. No phenomenal capacity or property that Christ displays in his humanity shows his divinity,

---

69. McFarland, "Spirit and Incarnation," 155.

according to McFarland (miracles, resurrection, God consciousness, and so forth).[70] In lieu of any external works of Christ to show forth his divinity, McFarland says we simply have to be told this by the Father (citing such texts as Matt. 11:27; 28:18; John 5:19–24; 10:30; 17:1–5, 20–22).[71] In short, this takes a miracle of faith, by means of the work of the Spirit on the human heart. Those advocating a Spirit Christology may go further, however, and say that the incarnate Son's relationship to the Spirit, and through the Spirit to the Father, is what identifies him as unique, as the Messiah, and as the God-man. Where I do agree with McFarland is in his claim that "a pneumatic Chalcedonianism argues that *the Spirit is not what makes Christ divine, but rather what makes him human*, in that Jesus fulfills his specifically human vocation from conception to glory through the power of the Spirit."[72] Jesus then says to believers, "Follow me." Spirit Christology provides the dogmatic foundations for the actualization of this call and necessary response.

Crisp captures a key point of Spirit Christology well when he states, "advocates of an Owenite Christology can claim that his Spirit Christology has a pastoral, as well as dogmatic advantage over traditional, orthodox views that do not take with sufficient seriousness this pneumatological dimension to the life and work of Christ."[73] It is just this promise of Spirit Christology that leads McFarland to aver: "attention to the Spirit's role as that which defines the character of Jesus' humanity also gives shape to a properly Christian anthropology. Quite simply: the Spirit is what makes human beings children of God. This is as true for Jesus as for the rest of us, for while hypostatically Jesus is eternally already the Son, it is only through the Spirit that he is the Son humanly."[74] We may continue, and add,

70. For many, supernatural works of Christ, including his authority to forgive sin, are seen as proof positive of the Son's direct influence on his human nature, as, for instance, Strauss, "Jesus and the Spirit," 280–83. But as McFarland, Work, and many others point out, this is unconvincing. Jesus can act with divine authority (the Son is the active subject) while being empowered and led by the Spirit, for Word and Spirit always operate together. Strauss, to his credit, finishes his essay with: "In the end, the New Testament interpreter must admit that some questions cannot be answered through exegesis alone and that the baton must be passed to those engaged in philosophical and speculative theology" (ibid., 284). Spirit Christology replies, "Starters, take your marks."

71. Ibid., 157.

72. Ibid., 158 (italics mine).

73. Crisp, *Revisioning Christology*, 94.

74. McFarland, "Spirit and Incarnation," 158.

that on the foundations of Spirit Christology one might suitably construct a renewed doctrine of the Trinity, ecclesiology, and even eschatology. In short, Spirit Christology paves the way for a thorough Third Article Theology, one which is theologically articulate, biblically faithful, and existentially viable.

CHAPTER 13

Soteriology

A Story of the Spirit

STEVEN M. STUDEBAKER

What does it mean to be saved? A personal relationship with Jesus Christ, receiving the forgiveness of sins, and going to heaven is probably the most common way to answer that question, especially in evangelical churches. Justification is the doctrinal answer in the Catholic and Protestant traditions of theology. In both cases, the answer is christological and crucicentric. Jesus saves or justifies sinners, freeing them from the consequences of sin by his death on the cross. Everything else is auxiliary to that fundamental reality. In both cases, moreover, the Spirit has little to do with the essence of salvation.[1] Although

1. For the case that traditional soteriology subordinates pneumatology to Christology as well as the relational and transformational to legal and moral categories, see Steven M. Studebaker, "Pentecostal Soteriology and Pneumatology," *Journal of Pentecostal Theology* 11 (2003): 248–70; Studebaker, "Beyond Tongues: A Pentecostal Theology of Grace," in *Defining Issues in Pentecostalism: Classical and Emergent*, ed. Steven M. Studebaker (Eugene, OR: Pickwick, 2008), 46–68; and Studebaker, *The Trinitarian Vision of Jonathan Edwards and David Coffey* (Amherst, NY: Cambria, 2011), 167–205. This essay extends this earlier work based on the

Eastern Orthodoxy has a more prominent role for the Holy Spirit, Third Article Theology arises from within and in reaction to the Christocentric Western tradition. This proposal for a Third Article soteriology does so as well. Third Article soteriology starts with the Holy Spirit. It looks at the nature of grace and salvation from the vantage point of pneumatology.

The goal is not to replace a christological with a pneumatological overemphasis. Looking at the history of God's redemptive work from the perspective of pneumatology and identifying the place and role of the Holy Spirit in that narrative is the purpose. From the perspective of pneumatology, creation, incarnation, and Pentecost are the key moments on a continuum of redemptive history. They are not discrete and disparate economies of God's work in the world. In the incarnation, the Spirit's work that began with creation finds its fullest realization in the union of the Son with the humanity of Jesus Christ. Jesus Christ's subsequent ministry, crucifixion, and resurrection are made possible by this fundamental pneumatological condition. At Pentecost, the Spirit makes the grace of union with the Son and participation in the fellowship of the triune God universally available to all people. Beginning with creation, this essay moves to incarnation, Pentecost, and grace in order to set forth a Third Article contribution to the doctrine of salvation.

The Spirit and Creation and Redemption

This section sets out the narrative of the Spirit within the Old Testament. Although the Spirit's identity and role take on greater clarity in the New Testament, especially around the themes of incarnation and Pentecost, the Old Testament material is important because it establishes the basic features of the Spirit's work.

From the perspective of pneumatology, soteriology begins in Genesis 1:2. Creation is a work of God's Spirit and creation is redemption. The biblical story of salvation cannot be appreciated without grasping those two fundamental points. First, Genesis 1 is simply neither a creation story nor a scientific report. Before the days of creation, "the earth was formless and empty, darkness was over the surface of the deep, and the Spirit of God

---

pneumatology set forth in Amos Yong and James K. A. Smith, eds., *From Pentecost to the Triune God: A Pentecostal Trinitarian Theology*, Pentecostal Manifestos Series (Grand Rapids: Eerdmans, 2012).

was hovering over the waters" (Gen. 1:2).[2] Before the light and life of creation, an evil thrall binds the earth in a dark void. Genesis 1 reflects a cosmology common throughout the ancient Near East. Primal pandemonium preceded the present world of order and life. Genesis 1 does demythologize the Babylonian and Canaanite creation myths. Gone is the primordial battle between dragon-like chaos gods (for example, Rahab and the multiheaded Leviathan) out of which the victor brings order to the world. Nevertheless, it retains the basic narrative of ancient Near Eastern cosmology—a transition from dark abyss to fertile creation.[3] Where before all lay in darkness, God brings light. From the formless void, God crafts fields and mountains and fills them with living creatures. Creation is not a natural and neutral process. It is a transition from a place of doom to hope, life, and goodness.

Second, creation is a story of the Spirit. The Spirit of God hovering over the primal elements is the threshold of creation. The Spirit of God contrasts with the earth that stands shapeless, empty, and dark.[4] The Spirit is the catalyst of creation. The Spirit initiates the transition from primal chaos to verdant creation.[5] The habit, conditioned by traditions of Christocentrism, is to begin the creation story with the Word, "and God said" in Gen. 1:3.[6] The Spirit hovering over the abyss,

---

2. Studebaker, *From Pentecost to the Triune God*, 56–58. The Holy Bible, New International Version (Grand Rapids: Zondervan, 1991).

3. Note, however, that Ps. 74:12–17 and Job 26:12–13 retain the *Chaoskampf* characteristic of the ancient Near East. See Norman C. Habel, *The Book of Job: A Commentary* (Philadelphia: Westminster, 1985), 192. For a comparison of biblical creation stories with ancient Near Eastern alternatives, see David Toshio Tsumura, *The Earth and the Waters in Genesis 1 and 2: A Linguistic Investigation*, Journal for the Study of the Old Testament Supplement Series 83 (Sheffield: Sheffield Academic, 1989).

4. Wilf Hildebrandt, *An Old Testament Theology of the Spirit of God* (Peabody, MA: Hendrickson, 1995), 32–35. For similar interpretations, see also Tuvia Freedman, "חור םיהלא–and a Wind from God, Genesis 1:2," trans. Aviva Wolfers-Barazani, *Jewish Bible Quarterly* 24 (1996): 9–13; and John H. Sailhamer, *The Pentateuch as Narrative: A Biblical-Theological Commentary* (Grand Rapids: Zondervan, 1992), 32 and 87.

5. Psalm 33:6–7 also portrays creation as the product of God's word and spirit. For reading *rûaḥ* as Spirit of God in Genesis 1, see Studebaker, *From Pentecost to the Triune God*, 54–67.

6. Reflecting that Christocentrism, Karl Barth maintains that the Spirit hovering over the primal elements is impotent and the power of creation lies in the Word of God. See Karl Barth, *Church Dogmatics*, III/I.2, *The Doctrine of Creation*, ed. G. W. Bromiley and T. F. Torrance (Edinburgh: T&T Clark, 1958), 108. Biblical scholars are sometimes no less prone than theologians to downplay pneumatology

however, is the beginning of creation.[7] Connecting creation to the agency of not only divine *logos*, but also *pneuma* in Genesis 1 is consistent with Ps. 33:6–7: "By the word of the LORD were the heavens made, their starry host by the breath of his mouth." The Spirit of God in Gen. 1:2 is a pneumatological threshold from cosmic chaos to God's creation. At the initiative of God's Spirit, the days of creation emerge from the primal pandemonium. The biblical story portrays the Spirit of God as the divine agent that redeems the elements from that dark abyss and ushers in a world ordered for the flourishing of life.

Third, the relationship between creation and redemption and the Spirit's role in them is seamless. The psalmist describes creation as an act of salvation, declaring that "you, O God . . . bring salvation upon the earth. It was you who split open the sea by your power and broke the heads of the monster in the waters . . . you established the sun and moon . . . set all the boundaries of the earth" (Ps. 74:12–17).[8] Isaiah portrays the Spirit's redeeming work as a work that parallels creation. The coming of the Spirit transforms the "desert" into a "fertile field" and enables the people of God to live in justice and righteousness. Just as the Spirit brought life to the formlessness and emptiness of the primeval abyss, so the Spirit redeems the barren land and makes it a land of abundance (Isa. 32:15). Isaiah 42:5–7 also makes the connection between creation and redemption. Yahweh creates the heavens and the earth (Genesis 1), gives breath to its people (Gen. 2:7), calls the people in righteousness (via the exodus and formation of the people of Israel), and will take hold of their hand to lead them out of exile. Minimally, the activity of Yahweh creating means Yahweh can establish them as a people and restore them to their land—that is, because Yahweh creates, Yahweh can redeem. But the connection is deeper. The activity of creating parallels the activity of creating and restoring the people. As the primal elements were in chaos and the dirt lifeless before the breath of life, so the people of Israel faced annihilation before the onslaught of Pharaoh and now demise and obscurity in exile, but Yahweh

in the creation story—e.g., Bruce Waltke, *Genesis: A Commentary* (Grand Rapids: Zondervan, 2001), 69.

7. Thomas L. Brodie, *Genesis as Dialogue: A Literary, Historical, and Theological Commentary* (New York: Oxford University Press, 2001), 133.

8. Note that this creation account retains elements of the *Chaoskampf* characteristic of comparable ancient Near Eastern origin stories—e.g., "broke the heads of the monster in the waters."

"created"/established them as a nation and now will redeem them from exile. In other words, the creative and redemptive activities parallel one another.

The creation of human life in Genesis 2 continues the portrayal of creation as an act of redemption and of the Spirit. In Gen. 2:7, human life emerges when God breathes life into lifeless dust. Not a picture of a body that gets a soul or spirit, but rather of dirt animated by God's breath. The entirety of human life is a gift of the Spirit of God and not only its inner spiritual element. The dirt is dead until the Spirit vivifies it.[9] The breath of God brings life to the dust. By the life-giving presence of the Spirit of God the dust becomes a human being that can live in fellowship with its Creator, other human beings, and the rest of creation. Genesis 2:7 presents a pneumatological anthropology. To be human is to be a creature uniquely vitalized by God's Spirit for a unique relationship with God and creation.

The human creation story does not permit a division of life into "natural" and "spiritual." Human beings do not have a "natural" or secular existence. The Spirit gives life to them for no other reason than to live in fellowship with their God and each other. The use of the term "creation" is unfortunate because it implies its counterpart, "redemption." The inevitable result is that creation and redemption become not only binary, but also ranked categories. God creates the natural world, and then later does the more important and spiritual work of redemption. The point here is to deny neither creation nor redemption, but rather to recognize their ultimate unity. Creation, in the biblical narrative, is not a natural activity of "creation" as the traditional categories imply. Creation is an act of redemption. God redeems the primal elements from darkness and formlessness by creating an ordered world in which life thrives. Creation is the realm of God's redeeming work, but creation and redemption are not perceived in terms of natural and supernatural, respectively. Redemption is not a spiritual act that comes to a natural world, but gives creation its divinely ordered shape.

In the creation of human life in Genesis 2:7, God redeems dirt by breathing life into it. The life given to Adam is not a "natural" life to which a "spiritual" life is later added. Relationship with God is not a *superadditum*

9. John R. Levison, *Filled with the Spirit* (Grand Rapids: Eerdmans, 2009), 14–15; George T. Montague, *The Holy Spirit: Growth of a Biblical Tradition* (New York: Paulist, 1976), 5; and John H. Walton, *Genesis*, The NIV Application Commentary Series (Grand Rapids: Zondervan, 2001), 166.

of grace added to human beings otherwise living natural, secular, and nonspiritual lives. The biblical creation story does not support a "supernatural anthropology."[10] Giving Adam the breath of life created his life, but created it for no other reason than for Adam to live in this world in loving relationship with God and eventually with Eve and the rest of creation. Adam never had a "natural" existence. He was, from the beginning, created for nothing other than relationship and life with God in and for this world. Redemption does not paste a spiritual life onto a lesser natural life. Moreover, the life given by the Spirit is not for heaven, but for this world. Eden is a picture of abundant and joyful life in this world. For this reason the Old Testament prophets portray God's redemption as bringing (exodus) and restoring (from exile) the people to prosperous and peaceful life in the land of promise. Redemption is the work of God's Spirit that enables human beings to realize God's dream for them—it breathes life into lifeless dirt.

The story of Noah and the flood is creation 2.0. "The springs of the great deep burst forth, and the floodgates of the heavens were opened" (Gen. 7:12). The floodwaters kept rising until even the mountains were covered and "every living thing that moved on the earth perished . . . everything on the face of the earth was wiped out" (7:17–23). By the time the floodwaters abate, the earth lies again in the darkness of the deep. Only the creatures stowed away in Noah's ark and the sea creatures do not perish. Like creation, the flood story is a redemption story. Freeing the earth from the floodwaters redeems the earth from the abyss. The flood story is also a story of the Spirit. The agent of God's redemptive activity is pneumatological—a *rûaḥ* from God blows and frees the earth from the floodwaters.

The book of Exodus has two back-to-back accounts of the deliverance of the people of Israel from Pharaoh. Both use pneumatological imagery to describe the divine agency of their salvation. In the prose account, "the Lord drove the sea back with a strong east wind and turned it into dry land" (Exod. 14:21). The poem or the Song of Moses intensifies the personal connection of the wind that drives back the water of the sea. Exodus 15:8 and 10 declare "by the blast of your nostrils the waters piled up . . . you blew with your breath and the

10. For this term, see Craig Martin, *Capitalizing Religion: Ideology and the Opiate of the Bourgeoisie* (New York: Bloomsbury, 2014), 56. Martin argues that the separation of the spiritual and physical derives, not so much from lingering vestiges of Platonism, but from late medieval and early Reformation currents in theology (ibid., 54–56).

sea covered them." The song attributes both the act of restraining the waters for the Israelites (deliverance) and of swamping Pharaoh's army (judgment) to the *rûaḥ*/Spirit of God.[11] Both texts interpret the physical phenomenon that caused the sea to recede for the Israelites and cascade over the Egyptians as the direct intervention of Israel's God and describe that activity in pneumatological terms.[12]

Isaiah makes the connection between divine agency in redemption through the sea and the Spirit of God even more telling: "Then his people recalled the days of old, the days of Moses and his people—where is he who brought them through the sea, with the shepherd of his flock? Where is he who set his Holy Spirit among them, who sent his glorious arm of power to be at Moses' right hand, who divided the waters before them . . . who led them through the depths? [T]hey were given rest by the Spirit of the LORD" (Isa. 63:11–14).[13] Deuteronomy 32:10 connects the theophanic glory of the Exodus with the hovering Spirit of God in Genesis 1:2. The creation and exodus stories also possess parallel images. The light that shines in the primordial darkness, the division of the waters, and the appearance of dry land compares with the glory of the Lord that guides the Israelites through the darkness and the receding waters that open up the dry seabed for the Israelites.[14] In other words, pneumatology developed and became an important category for understanding God's presence and redemptive work in the history of the people of Israel. Moreover, the redemptive work of the Spirit has strong associations with the Spirit's work in creation.

Isaiah links Yahweh's creative and redemptive activity with the restoration from exile.[15] In Isaiah 32 the Spirit renews

11. Al Wolters argues that Exod. 15:8 does not refer to the deliverance of the Israelites, but that Exod. 15:8 and 15:10 both refer to the flood of water that destroyed the Egyptian forces. Although I agree with Wolters that the Song of Moses primarily showcases the destruction of Pharaoh and his army, Exod. 15:8 and 10 appear to connect the two aspects—deliverance and judgment—of the one event. See Wolters, "Not Rescue but Destruction: Rereading Exodus 15:8," *Catholic Biblical Quarterly* 52 (1990): 223–40.

12. For the connection between wind and the Spirit of God, see Studebaker, *From Pentecost to the Triune God*, 54–60.

13. See Walter Eichrodt, *Theology of the Old Testament* (Philadelphia: Westminster, 1961–67), 2:60–61.

14. Meredith G. Kline, *Images of the Spirit* (Grand Rapids: Baker, 1980), 14–15.

15. B. W. Anderson, *Understanding the Old Testament*, 3rd ed. (Englewood Cliffs, NJ: Prentice Hall, 1975), 449–50.

(re-creates) the land of promise: "Citadel and watchtower will become a wasteland forever, the delight of donkeys, a pasture for flocks, till the Spirit is poured upon us from on high, and the desert becomes a fertile field, and the fertile field seems a forest. Justice will dwell in the desert and righteousness live in the fertile field . . . peaceful dwelling places, in secure homes" (vv. 14–18). The "wasteland" echoes the desolation of the earth before creation. The arrival of the Spirit transforms the desert into a place of abundance. Thus Isaiah provides the textual and theological basis to tie together the creative and redemptive activity of God and to associate that activity with the Spirit of God.

Ezekiel's prophecies of restoration from exile also integrate pneumatology, creation, and redemption. Ezekiel promises that Yahweh will put the Spirit of God in the exiled people of Israel and that the Spirit will return them to their homeland.[16] Ezekiel uses the metaphor of the Spirit of God resurrecting a valley of dry bones to portray Israel's repatriation (Ezekiel 36–37; esp. 37:1–14). Yahweh charges Ezekiel, "Prophesy to the breath; prophesy, son of man, and say to it, 'This is what the Sovereign Lord says: Come from the four winds, O breath, and breathe into these slain, that they may live'" (37:9). The "breath," the "four winds," and the divine power that will bring new life to the people of Israel is the Spirit of Yahweh (37:14).[17]

16. See Daniel I. Block, "The Prophet of the Spirit: The Use of *RWH* in the Book Ezekiel," *Journal of the Evangelical Theological Society* 32 (1989): 27–49 (38); Paul M. Joyce, *Ezekiel: A Commentary*, Library of Hebrew Bible/Old Testament Studies 482 (New York: T&T Clark, 2007), 204; James Robson, *Word and Spirit in Ezekiel*, Library of Hebrew Bible Old Testament Studies 447 (New York: T&T Clark, 2006), 269; T. John Wright, "The Concept of *RUACH* in Ezekiel 37," in *Seeing Signals, Reading Signs: The Art of Exegesis; Studies in Honour of Antony F. Campbell, SJ for His Seventieth Birthday*, ed. Mark A. O'Brien and Howard N. Wallace (New York: T&T Clark, 2004), 142–58 (146).

17. For the ancient Near Eastern context of associating divine presence and agency with the four winds and other meteorological phenomena, see Susanne Woodhouse, "The Sun God, His Four Bas and the Four Winds in the Sacred District at Saïs: The Fragment of an Obelisk (BM EA 1512)," in *The Temple in Ancient Egypt: New Discoveries and Recent Research*, ed. Stephen Quirke (London: British Museum Press, 1997), 132–51 (136–37); Hans-Peter Hasenfratz, "Patterns of Creation in Ancient Egypt," in *Creation in Jewish and Christian Tradition*, ed. Henning Graf Reventlow and Yair Hoffman, Journal for the Study of the Old Testament Supplement Series 319 (London: Sheffield Academic, 2002), 174–78 (175); and Lászlo Kákosy, "The Ptah-Shu-Tefnut Triad and the Gods of the Winds on a Ptolemaic Sarcophagus," in *Essays on Ancient Egypt in Honour of Herman te Velde*, ed. Jacobus van Dijk, Egyptological Memoirs 1 (Groningen: Styx, 1997), 219–29. The Assyrian king Adad-nirari II arrogated

Ezekiel's use of pneumatological images to describe Yahweh's fulfillment of the promise to restore the people of Israel coheres with the Genesis creation stories.[18] The Spirit of God, the divine power that emancipates the people of Israel from their desolation in captivity and returns them to Jerusalem as the faithful covenant people of God, is the same Spirit who moved over the mayhem of Genesis 1:2 and brought forth a world teeming with life.[19] The Spirit of God breathing new life into the dead bones of exiled Israel parallels God breathing life into the dirt in Gen. 2:7.[20] In short, redemption is creation. The creation narrative of Genesis 1 and Isaiah and Ezekiel's promise of restoration to and revitalization in the land of Israel portray the Spirit as the agency of God that facilitates the transition from disrepair and despair to life and flourishing.[21] Ezekiel and Isaiah draw on the creation narratives and images to buttress faith in God's power to redeem the people of Israel. In other words, creation and soteriology are reciprocal categories.[22] The redemption from primeval chaos is a creative action. Exodus as redemption from the threat of military annihilation by the same Spirit of God who tamed the primeval waters leads to the creation of the people of Israel. Return from

to himself the sun god and likened his royal power to the "onslaught of the wind" and "the gale" (see Albert Kirk Grayson, *Assyrian Royal Inscriptions: From Tiglath-pileser I to Ashur-nasir-apli II*, 2 vols. [Wiesbaden: Harrassowitz, 1976], 2:85–86).

18. Robson, *Word and Spirit*, 269.

19. Bruce Vawter and Leslie J. Hoppe, *A New Heart: A Commentary on the Book of Ezekiel*, International Theological Commentary (Grand Rapids: Eerdmans, 1991), 166–67.

20. R. Jerome Boone, "The Role of the Holy Spirit in the Construction of the Second Temple," in *The Spirit and the Mind: Essays in Informed Pentecostalism*, ed. Terry L. Cross and Emerson B. Powery (Lanham, NY: University Press of America, 2000), 49–63 (52–53); Joyce, *Ezekiel*, 209; and John W. Yates, *The Spirit and Creation in Paul*, Wissenschaftliche Untersuchungen zum Neuen Testament 251 (Tübingen: Mohr Siebeck, 2008), 32–33.

21. George Montague does not think the pneumatological themes in the Genesis 1 and Exodus stories are related and rather sees Genesis 1 connected with the exilic and postexilic pneumatology of Second Isaiah and Ezekiel ("The Fire in the Word: The Holy Spirit in Scripture," in *Advents of the Spirit: An Introduction to the Current Study of Pneumatology*, ed. B. E. Hinze and D. L. Dabney [Milwaukee: Marquette University Press, 2001], 35–65 [39]). Without disagreeing with the historical-critical connection of Genesis 1 with exilic and postexilic pneumatology, reading the texts canonically also is appropriate. When read canonically, a theological consistency with respect to the images and activity of the *rûaḥ*/Spirit of God emerges. The Hebrew Scriptures describe God's redemptive presence in pneumatological categories.

22. See Gerhard von Rad, *Genesis: A Commentary* (Philadelphia: Westminster, 1972), 45–46; and Yates, *Spirit and Creation in Paul*, 151–54.

exile in Babylon and restoration to the land is a new exodus or re-creation of the people of Israel.

The Spirit and the Incarnation

The New Testament has two pivotal events: incarnation and Pentecost. Yet because of a tendency toward Christocentrism, the work of Christ receives most of the attention. Even Pentecostals, though accentuating the Holy Spirit in their experience, often subordinate pneumatology to Christology in their theology.[23] The solution is not to trade Christocentrism for pneumacentrism, but to recognize that Christology and pneumatology condition one another. Neither one can be understood in isolation from the other. Christ is the product of the Spirit's work. Yet at the same time and consequently, the fullest and clearest window to the nature of the Spirit's redemptive work is the life and ministry of Jesus Christ.

The Holy Spirit's work in Christ is fundamental for understanding the Spirit's identity. The Spirit's work in the incarnation, moreover, is in continuity with the Spirit's creative-redemptive work in the Old Testament. First, the work of the Spirit in the creation-redemption episodes discussed in the Old Testament is paradigmatic for the Spirit's work in the incarnation. Put more forcefully, the Spirit's work that begins in Genesis 1:2 with the redemption of creation from chaos, that is carried on further in breathing life into the dirt in Genesis 2:7, and that revivifies the valley of dry bones in Ezekiel 37:1–14, finds its historical zenith in Christ and especially his resurrection by the Spirit (Rom. 8:11). Thus the angel Gabriel comforts Mary, "Do not be afraid . . . the Holy Spirit will come upon you . . . [s]o the holy one to be born will be called the Son of God" (Luke 1:35). The angel appearing before Joseph is more direct, declaring "what is conceived in her is from the Holy Spirit" (Matt. 1:20). The Spirit hovering over the waters gave structure to the formless primordial elements. The same Spirit established the hypostatic union of the Son and the humanity of Jesus, which formed the life and

23. For a critique of this tendency, see D. Lyle Dabney, "Saul's Armor: The Problem and Promise of Pentecostal Theology Today," *Pneuma: The Journal of the Society for Pentecostal Studies* 23 (2001): 115–46 (115–17); and the references in the first footnote of this chapter. Recent exceptions to this tendency are Frank D. Macchia, *Baptized in the Spirit: A Global Pentecostal Theology* (Grand Rapids: Zondervan, 2006); Macchia, *Justified in the Spirit: Creation, Redemption, and the Triune God* (Grand Rapids: Eerdmans, 2010); and Amos Yong, *Spirit of Love: A Trinitarian Theology of Grace* (Waco, TX: Baylor University Press, 2012).

ministry of Jesus Christ. The Spirit's union of creation with Creator attains its highest possible concrete manifestation in Jesus Christ.[24]

Considering Christology from a pneumatological perspective means that Jesus is the Messiah in and through the agency of the Holy Spirit. Isaiah defines the messianic figure in terms of pneumatology. The source of the Messiah's ministry is the investiture of the Spirit. Because the "Spirit of the LORD rests on him" he will govern with "wisdom" and "justice" (Isa. 11:1–9). Isaiah 42 declares, "I will put my Spirit on him and he will bring justice to the nations . . . [a] bruised reed he will not break, and a smoldering wick he will not snuff out." Not only significant for pneumatology, these passages describe the nature of God's redemption. God desires justice, but not primarily retributive justice. God's justice aligns with contemporary notions of social or restorative justice. Not the hammer blow of penal judgment, the prophetic vision focuses on the justice that heals the bruised reed and kindles the ember into a flame. The Spirit-anointed redeemer acts on behalf of the "poor" and "needy" (Isa. 11:4), frees the captives, comforts the brokenhearted, and brings joy and abundance to those trapped in misery and austerity. Isaiah's vision is not heavenly, but earthy. The freedom, comfort, and prosperity are not "spiritual," but earthbound. The people will rebuild their cities, restore their commerce, and live in righteousness with each other and their God (Isa. 61:1–9). The justice of retribution is not absent. Isaiah 11:4 warns, "He will strike the earth with the rod of his mouth; with the breath of his lips he will slay the wicked." The focus remains, however, on social justice. The judgment visited upon the "wicked" comes because they have oppressed and exploited the poor. Rather than saving the bruised reed, they trampled it.

The Spirit constitutes Jesus the Christ. The Spirit is not the handmaiden of Christ. Traditional Christology emphasizes the Logos Christology of the Gospel of John: "In the beginning was the Word . . . and the Word became flesh" (John 1:1, 14). Yet what transpired between John 1:1 and 1:14? The Synoptic Gospels of Matthew and Luke answer that question. The transition between when "the Word was with God" and "the

24. Above and what follows contribute to the field of Spirit Christology. For background on and approaches to contemporary Spirit Christology, see Ralph Del Colle, *Christ and the Spirit: Spirit-Christology in Trinitarian Perspective* (New York: Oxford University Press, 1994); Myk Habets, *The Anointed Son: A Trinitarian Spirit Christology* (Eugene, OR: Pickwick, 2010), 188–227; and Studebaker, *From Pentecost to the Triune God*, 78–87.

Word became flesh" was an act of the Holy Spirit (Matt. 1:20; Luke 1:35). The incarnation of the Son in Jesus Christ was a result of the presence and activity of the Holy Spirit. The incarnation accounts of Matthew and Luke, therefore, support Spirit Christology.

Jesus recognized that the presence and power of the Spirit constitutes him as the Christ.[25] "Returning to Galilee in the power of the Spirit," Jesus enters the synagogue in Nazareth on the Sabbath. There he reads from the scroll of Isaiah: "'The Spirit of the Lord is on me, because he has anointed me to preach good news to the poor. He has sent me to proclaim freedom for the prisoners and recovery of sight for the blind, to release the oppressed, to proclaim the year of the Lord's favor'" (Luke 4:14–19). His subsequent ministry demonstrates that the Spirit is upon him. After self-identifying as the Spirit-anointed Messiah of Isaiah, Jesus goes forth and frees a person tormented by an "evil spirit" and heals people suffering from various physical illnesses and infirmities (4:31–5:26).

Jesus' messianic ministry, moreover, remains rooted in the Spirit. Sandwiched between the healing of the man with a deformed hand and of a man possessed by a demon that rendered him blind and mute, Matthew identifies Jesus as the Spirit-anointed Messiah of Isaiah 42: "'Here is my servant whom I have chosen, the one I love . . . I will put my Spirit on him, and he will proclaim justice to the nations . . . [a] bruised reed he will not break, and a smoldering wick he will not snuff out, till he leads justice to victory.'" Jesus, therefore, declares to the Pharisees, "If I drive out demons by the Spirit of God, then the kingdom of God has come upon you" (Matt. 12:1–28). The people healed by Jesus are concrete examples of the "bruised reed" and the "smoldering wick." Jesus' healing demonstrates that he is the Spirit-anointed Messiah.

Jesus' ministry derives from the presence and power of the Spirit in his life. The Spirit enables Jesus' life from the inception of the incarnation, to his baptism, to standing down Satan in the desert (Luke 4:1–13), and finally to his resurrection (Rom. 1:4; 8:11). In Christ, the good news had come because he was the "chosen servant," the Spirit-anointed Messiah.

---

25. James D. G. Dunn, *Romans 1–8*, Word Biblical Commentary (Waco, TX: Word, 1988), 446; Robert Jewett, *Romans: A Commentary*, Hermeneia (Minneapolis: Fortress, 2007), 106–7 and 492; Grant R. Osborne, *Romans*, IVP New Testament Commentary Series (Downers Grove, IL: InterVarsity Press, 2004), 32 and 201; and Peter Stuhlmacher, *Paul's Letter to the Romans: A Commentary*, trans. Scott J. Hafemann (Louisville: Westminster John Knox, 1994), 19 and 122.

The Spirit and Pentecost

The outpouring of the Holy Spirit on the day of Pentecost is a key event not only in the New Testament but in the entire history of redemption. Joel 2 identifies the outpouring of God's Spirit as the eschatological work of redemption. The life and ministry of Jesus Christ reflect this anticipation. Jesus' saving work does not reach its climax on the cross or even in the resurrection, but on the day of Pentecost with the outpouring of the Holy Spirit. The day of Pentecost is a decisive scene in the drama of redemption. It culminates the great movement of redemption that began with the Spirit hovering over the waters, breathing life into the dirt, and bringing about the incarnate life of Jesus Christ. Thus, Peter's Pentecost sermon identifies the outpouring of God's Spirit as the eschatological work of redemption (see Joel 2:28–32).

The baptismal narratives in the Gospels define the nature of Christ's redemptive work in terms of pneumatology—Spirit baptism.[26] Heralding the coming of the Messiah, John the Baptist also declares the nature of his salvation—"I baptize with water, he will baptize you with the Holy Spirit" (see Matt. 3:11; Mark 1:8; Luke 3:16; John 1:33). In the Gospel of Luke, Jesus indicates that the goal of his work is the gift of the Holy Spirit. In Luke 11:13, he promises that the "Father in heaven" will "give the Holy Spirit to those who ask him." Not just one among other gifts, the promise of the Holy Spirit is the gift par excellence. The Gospel of Luke closes with Jesus assuring the disciples that they will receive the promise of the Father and will be "clothed with power from on high" (24:49).

Acts 1 continues that narrative. Jesus urges the disciples not to leave Jerusalem, but to "wait for the gift my Father promised. . . . For John baptized with water, but in a few days you will be baptized with the Holy Spirit" (1:4–5). The Acts narrative (especially chapters 1 and 2) connects the inaugural promise of Jesus' ministry—John the Baptist's "I baptize with water, he will baptize you with the Holy Spirit"—with its fulfillment on the day of Pentecost. The outpouring of the Spirit of Pentecost, therefore, is eschatological. The day of Pentecost is the goal of Christ's ministry. Jesus comes as the Spirit-anointed Messiah (Luke 1:35; 4:17–19; Acts 2:33) so that the life the Spirit made possible in him can be shared with "'all people'" (Acts 2:17).

26. See Macchia, *Baptized in the Spirit*, for a Pentecostal view on the gift of the Spirit. See also Yong, *Spirit of Love*.

That all four Gospels and Acts define the goal of Jesus' ministry as baptism in the Holy Spirit is significant. It indicates that the fundamental nature of his ministry and Christian salvation is pneumatological—it is the reception of and participation in the Holy Spirit. The threshold from the Spirit's work in the life of Christ to the outpouring of that possibility on all people is the day of Pentecost. The Spirit of Pentecost makes available to all people the historical realization of the life of God with humanity that took place in Christ. But what is the consequence for traditional Christocentric understandings of grace?

The Spirit and Grace

The Spirit's work in Jesus Christ is the paradigm of the Spirit's work as the Spirit of Pentecost. The apostle Paul indicates the connection between the Spirit and the gospel of Christ. Romans 6 and 8 spotlight the parallel relationship between the Spirit's work in the life and ministry of Jesus Christ and the grace of salvation. This section showcases two ways that the Spirit's work in the incarnate life of the Christ informs the Spirit's work in grace and, therefore, a Third Article soteriology.

The Spirit of Sonship

In Romans 8:14–16, Paul connects the Sonship of Christ with Christian identity as children of God the Father: "because those who are led by the Spirit of God are sons of God. . . . For . . . you received the Spirit of sonship. And by him we cry, '*Abba*, Father.' The Spirit himself testifies with our spirit that we are God's children." Christians are children of God—that is, partakers in "sonship."[27] Their "sonship," moreover, parallels the Sonship of Christ. For that reason, they can call their Father, "Abba." That the Spirit, not Christ, is the source of their "sonship" is notable. The Spirit makes Christians children of God. Connecting the Spirit to Christian identity as children of God is not limited to Pauline theology, however.

27. I place "sonship" in quotes because that is the term Paul uses. "Sonship" sounds exclusive, but the wider context of Paul's theology makes it clear that the term is inclusive and means "children of God." In Romans, Paul emphasizes the inclusion of gentiles in God's grace. In Gal. 3:26–28, using the same image of Christians as "sons of God," Paul clarifies the gender inclusiveness of Christian identity as children of God—"There is neither Jew nor Greek, slave nor free, male nor female, for you are all one in Christ Jesus." I believe Paul uses the term "sonship" to accentuate the connection between Christ as the Son of God and the identity of Christians as children of the Father. My use of the term is inclusive and, therefore, denotes "children of God."

The prologue of the Gospel of John defines the gospel as receiving new birth as God's children: "Yet to all who received him, to those who believed in his name, he gave the right to become children of God—children born not of natural descent, nor of human decision or husband's will, but born of God" (John 1:12–13). John 3:1–8 clarifies that the Spirit of God is the source of this new birth that constitutes believers children of God.

Why is the Spirit the source of "sonship"? The Spirit's role in constituting Jesus the incarnate Son of God provides the answer. The indwelling Holy Spirit is the source of "sonship" because the Spirit constituted the Sonship of Jesus Christ—the Holy Spirit was the agent of the incarnation of the Son of God. The Spirit's work in the incarnation is the paradigm of the Spirit's work as the Spirit of Pentecost. In other words, symmetry marks the Spirit's work in the incarnation and grace. What the Spirit achieved in the life of Christ is the mission of the Spirit of Pentecost. Jesus Christ was the incarnate Son of God through the activity of the Holy Spirit. The Spirit led and enabled the life and ministry of Jesus Christ (Luke 4:1, 14). So also the Spirit constitutes believers children of God and frees their lives from sin and enables them to live in righteousness (Rom. 8:1–11).

The Spirit of Death and Life

In Romans 6:1–14, Paul parallels the Christian life with the death and resurrection of Christ.

Christ:

- died to sin (6:10)
- was raised to new life (6:4, 9, 10)

Christians:

- die to sin (6:2, 4, 5–7)
- are raised to new life (6:4–5, 11)

Paul shows that Christ's life, death, and resurrection are a paradigm for redemption. He uses Christian baptism to illustrate the death-to-sin and new-life-in-Christ pattern of salvation. Paul points out that Jesus died *to*, not only *for*, sin (Rom. 6:10). Christ died to sin because he never succumbed to temptation. But dying to sin is only half of the good news. Paul says of Christ, "the life he lives, he lives to God" (Rom. 6:10). The crucifixion was the final and absolute manifestation of Christ's ongoing life of dying to sin and living "to God." Death and new life are the negative and positive images of his comprehensive righteousness. Christ's righteousness consists not only in the absence of evil, but also in the active pursuit of God throughout his life.

Christ's death on the cross is the highest expression of his "death to sin" because death to sin becomes literal and absolute. Going down into the waters of Christian baptism symbolizes the Christians' participation in Jesus' ongoing life of death to sin and the absolute expression that takes on the cross. Rising from the waters of baptism represents the Christians' participation in Jesus' life of faithfulness and fellowship with God the Father. Taken together, they are the way Christians participate in the righteousness of Christ. That is why Paul says, "In the same way, count yourselves dead to sin but alive to God in Jesus Christ" (Rom. 6:11). What is the "same way" that Paul calls Christians to share with Christ? The previous verse answers that question: "The death he died, he died to sin once and for all; but the life he lives, he lives to God" (Rom. 6:10). Facing abandonment by his friends and agonizing death, Jesus remained faithful to the Father, neither shirking his mission to embody the righteousness of God in the world nor lashing out in vengeance toward his tormentors. The Christian life parallels the death and resurrection of Christ. Water baptism is a central rite for Christians because it publically enacts their participation in the death and life of Christ.

The from-death-to-life imagery of baptism and the historical experience of Christ's crucifixion and resurrection fit the broader canonical frame of God's redemptive work. Genesis 1 begins with "darkness over the surface of the deep." It is a place of menace and lifelessness. The hovering Spirit initiates the transition from darkness and doom to the light and life of the days of creation. The breath of God makes dust a living human being in Genesis 2. The floodwaters return the world to a murky state. God's Spirit makes the floodwaters flee from the face of the earth and restores life to its surfaces and spaces. Facing annihilation from Pharaoh's army, the Spirit of God makes a way for the people of Israel. The bleached bones lying in the valley come alive again when God's Spirit blows on them. The same Spirit of life brings forth the incarnation of the Son of God and Jesus from the tomb.

The Spirit brings life where there is death, light to dark places, hope where despair reigns, and prosperity in place of scarcity. The Spirit of God takes the world that is an empty black void and shapes it into a world full of life and vitality. The Spirit comes to human lives broken with and from sin and heals and transforms them in righteousness. The Spirit cultivates the life of Christ in "[e]veryone who calls on the name of the Lord" (Rom. 10:13). Being like Jesus is not a thin Christian moralism. It is more than tacking on spiritual disciplines to an ostensibly secular life. The essence of the Christian life is not religious calisthenics and moral asceticism. Being like Jesus is being the place where the Spirit of God brings human life into union with the eternal Son of God and fellowship with the Father. The gospel is the promise that through participation in Jesus Christ we may know the fellowship he shares with the Father ("that the love you have for me may be in them," John 17:26). A Third Article soteriology brings attention to the Spirit's place in the work of grace. The Spirit of Pentecost makes available to all people God's dream for human life that began with the Spirit's first stirring over the primeval waters and reached its fullness in the Spirit's work in the life of Jesus Christ.

Conclusion

Soteriology is a story of the Spirit. It begins with the Spirit of God hovering over the primeval abyss. It continues in the history of Israel and reaches fullness in the incarnation of Christ and the outpouring of the Spirit of Pentecost. Although different moments in the story, they are all part of one story, the story of the Spirit. A Third Article soteriology does not displace Christology, but rather shows the synergy and symmetry between Christology and pneumatology. The Spirit's work in the incarnation of Christ and as the gift of Pentecost continues and clarifies the narrative of the Spirit that begins with creation. The Spirit creates human beings to enjoy fellowship with their triune Creator and each other and for abundant life in this world. The Spirit's work in the incarnation of Christ gives this dream for human life its fullest manifestation. With the outpouring of the Spirit of Pentecost, the Spirit's work in the life of Christ achieves a universal horizon and becomes available to all people.

CHAPTER 14

The Fire in the Wine

How Does the Blood of Christ Carry the Holy Spirit?*

EUGENE F. ROGERS JR.

Christians talk very easily about "the blood of Christ." You can hear about it five times a Sunday. My introductory task will be to make blood strange. Then I make the Spirit strange; to do so, I name her often in Greek, *pneuma*; and I use the feminine pronoun "she" because "spirit," while neuter in Greek and masculine in Latin, is feminine in Hebrew and in Syriac.[1] In my thesis, the two strange things belong together: *the pneuma is in the blood.*

*I wish to thank Dean Neil Alexander and Professors Robert Hughes III and Robert MacSwain for the invitation to deliver this essay as a lecture at Sewanee on February 10, 2015. It subsequently appeared in the *Sewanee Theological Review* 58 (2016), forthcoming (used with permission).

1. Jerome, *In Isa. XI*, on Is. 40:9–11 (CCSL 73.1:459); Sebastian Brock, "The Holy Spirit as Feminine in Early Syriac Literature," in *After Eve*, ed. Janet Martin Soskice (London: Marshall Pickering, 1990); Susan Ashbrook Harvey, "Feminine Imagery for the Divine: The Holy Spirit, the Odes of Solomon, and Early Syriac Tradition," *St. Vladimir's Theological Quarterly* 37 (1993): 111–39; and Gabriele Winkler, "Further Observations in Connection with the Early Form of the Epiklesis," in *Studies in Early Christian Liturgy and Its Context,* Variorum Collected Studies Series 593 (Aldershot, UK: Ashgate, 1997), IV, 66–80, esp. 69–73, 79–80, on invocations of "the Mother, the Spirit of holiness" (69).

In an antithesis, however, I deny that blood works by magic; it is no Holy Grail. In the conclusion, I transcend both the *pneuma* in the blood and the lack of magic in the cup to suggest that the Spirit works in the blood by intention: individual, social, and divine.

Blood may be red because iron compounds make it so, but societies that see themselves as a social body draft its color and stickiness for multiple purposes of their own. We imagine individual, social, and animal bodies as securely bounded. Inside, blood carries life. Outside, it marks a body fertile or at risk. Society's work to maintain bodily integrity thus takes place in blood. It is the body's permeability that leaves us bloody-minded. The body becomes a membrane to pass when it breathes, eats, perspires, eliminates, ejaculates, conceives, or bleeds. Only bleeding evokes so swift and public a response: blood brings mother to child, bystander to victim, ambulance to patient, soldier to comrade, midwife to mother, defender to border.[2] We never fail to notice blood; but we naturalize its social role: we cease to notice how it works.

Early in my blood project, I thought I would figure out what Hebrews means by "without the shedding of blood, there is no forgiveness of sin" (Heb. 9:22);[3] I thought I would figure it out by reading Christian commentators on that verse. I found them unaccountably dull. Michael Wyschogrod, the Jewish Barthian, does something better than all the Christian commentators I consulted. He finds blood strange. If you look into Christian commentaries on "without the shedding of blood" you find either *domestication*, so that, in Aquinas, bloodshed needs no explanation; or you find *evasion*, as in Calvin, who reduces blood to "faith." Wyschogrod neither evades blood, nor does he, by repetition, disarm it even more effectively. Here is a longish sample:

> A dumb animal is to be slaughtered. . . . [It emits no] sound of terror because it does not understand . . . the instrument. It is then swiftly cut, the blood gushes forth, the bruiting begins . . . [the sound of blood rushing past an obstruction, an artery's turbulent flow.] [T]he animal's

2. I repeat this paragraph in several of my publications about blood. It first appeared in my article "The Genre of This Book" (a review of Gil Anidjar, *Blood: A Critique of Christianity*) in *Syndicate: A New Forum for Theology* 2 (2015): 152. The idea that the body is a membrane comes from Bettina Bildhauer, *Medieval Blood* (Cardiff: University of Wales Press, 2005), 1–7.

3. All Scripture citations from NRSV.

eyes lose their living sheen. The blood is sprinkled on the altar, the animal dismembered, portions of it burned, . . . [others] eaten by the priests who minister before God in the holiness of the Temple. This horror is brought into the house of God. [What bridge leads from] slaughter to the holy?

Sacrificial Judaism brings the truth of human existence into the Temple. It does not leave it outside. . . . It does not reserve sacred ground only for silent worship. Instead, the bruiting, bleeding, dying animal is brought and shown to God. This is what *our* fate is. It is not so much, as [often] said, that we deserved the fate of the dying animal and . . . have been permitted to escape [that] fate by transferring it. . . . It is rather that our fate and the animal's are the same [fate] because its end awaits us, since our eyes, too, will soon gaze . . . blindly . . . and [fix] in deathly attention on what only the dead seem to see. . . . In the Temple, therefore, it is [we human animals] who stand before God, not as [we] would like to be, but as we truly are, [realizing] that our blood will [flow soon enough]. [Thus we watch ourselves die.] Enlightened religion recoils with horror from the thought of sacrifice, preferring a spotless house of worship filled with organ music and exquisitely polite behavior. The price paid for such decorum is that the worshipers must leave the most problematic part of themselves outside the temple, [only] to reclaim it when the service is over and to live with it unencumbered by sanctification. Religion ought not to demand such a dismemberment of [the human being].[4]

Here endeth the reading from Wyschogrod. I note that it defends Second Temple Judaism from Christian supersessionism not by mishnaic means but according to the modern pattern of aligning sacrifice with solidarity rather than sin. I do not intend to do more with it, and I drop it now. I only hope it makes blood strange.

The New Testament mentions the blood of Christ three times as often as his "cross," and five times as often as his "death."[5] Blood does conceptual work according to a complex pattern, which Durkheim calls "totemism" and theologians call "analogy." The blood of

---

4. Michael Wyschogrod, *The Body of Faith: Judaism as Corporeal Election* (New York: Seabury Press, 1983), 18–19.

5. Alan M. Stibbs, *The Meaning of the Word Blood in Scripture*, 3rd rev. ed. (Oxford: Tyndale Press, 1963).

Jesus is the blood of Christ; the wine of Communion is the blood of Christ; the means of atonement is the blood of Christ; the unity of the church is in the blood of Christ; the kinship of believers is in the blood of Christ; the cup of salvation is the blood of Christ; icons ooze the blood of Christ; and the blood of Christ is the blood of God.[6] If the Holy Spirit characteristically rests on the body of Christ, how does she rest in his blood?

Spirit and blood belong together in two places: in ancient theories about how blood carries life, and in eucharistic liturgies. I take the second first. In Syriac liturgies, baptism and Eucharist both work by imparting the Spirit's Pentecostal fire paraphysically in a wet medium.

> By uttering the epiclesis [or calling down the Spirit], according to a poem by the 5th C. Syriac poet Balai, "the priest kindles fire" even in the wine.[7] Fire in the wine and in the womb:[8] if the Son ascends, it is like fire, and if the Spirit comes down, it is with fire. In Christ's image human beings may also ascend, with and therefore like fire. Indeed, they ascend to where the fire is, with the paraphysical fire-bearing elements, the water and the wine. This again reverses the fall, since the angel of death guarding the Garden of Eden held a fiery sword. "God drove out the human being; and at the East God placed the cherubim, and a flaming sword which turned every way to guard the way to the tree of life" [Gen. 3:24]. But now that Christ will not descend the cross, counting divinity nothing to be grasped, and reversing the sin of Adam who did grasp after it—now the fire too gives access to heaven rather than denying us Eden.[9]

As a gift to the Son, who took a body, the Holy Spirit also rests on matter, in holy

6. A similar paragraph appears in Eugene F. Rogers Jr., "Sociology and Theology of Creationist Objections to Evolution: How Blood Bounds the Christian Body," *Zygon* 49 (2014): 543.

7. Balai: Sebastian Brock, *The Holy Spirit in the Syrian Baptismal Tradition* (Poona, India: Anitra Printers, 1979), 29, citing *S. Ephraemi Syri . . . Balai aliorumque opera selecta*, ed. Overbeck (Oxford: n.p., 1865), 252.

8. A phrase of Ephrem the Syrian, which shows up in *The Daily Office SSF*, ed. Colin Winfred and Joyce Yarrow, 2nd rev. ed. (Rhode Island: Mowbray, 2010), 528 (canticle 65).

9. Eugene F. Rogers Jr., *After the Spirit: A Constructive Pneumatology from Resources outside the Modern West* (Grand Rapids: Eerdmans, 2005; London: SCM, 2006), 205–6, modified.

people, holy places, holy things. We cannot see the Spirit if we think only spiritually; we can see the Spirit only if we think materially.

But by what *means* does the Spirit rest on matter? Does the Spirit typically *possess* holy people,[10] take *over* holy places, and enchant holy things? In theory, of course, the Spirit *can* do that; God can do whatever God wants. Some of the "special gifts" or charismatic graces of the Spirit—prophecy, tongues—tend toward possession. So the question is not what the Spirit *can*, but what the Spirit, in giving a gift to the Son, *wants* to do: What would be fitting? I come back later to this question, under the rubric of "intention," the question of her majesty's personal *will*. What does the Spirit *want*? But the Spirit, who moves quietly and suavely, specializes in moving the wants of others.

I propose that, because the Son became human and took the form of a creature, the Spirit, in giving a gift to the Son that honors the incarnation, would prefer human means. As grace does not violate but elevates nature, so the Spirit does not magic but indwells it, leading it most courteously from the inside. The Spirit is God not by transcendent coercion but by immanent intimacy. So we should look for the Spirit to work by human means, not because they are good for God *simpliciter*, but because they are good for humans, and therefore good for the God who loves them. The idea of God's love for humanity dominates Greek Orthodox theology, which has a word for it: God's *phil-anthropia*. The Spirit, I propose, prefers human means out of *philanthropia*. In *philanthropia*, the Spirit continues to echo in us what she did in the womb of Mary, conceive God in matter. This conception does not rival the incarnation, but follows, varies, honors, and celebrates it. I got that far in 2005.

Greco-Roman *pneuma* circulates in the blood in a way that at first disturbed, then fascinated, and now comforts me. A nontranscendent *pneuma* animated blood, and because

10. As Paul Holloway pointed out at Sewanee, the same plain verb, *have* or *echei*, in English as in Greek, serves for a human being having the Spirit and the Spirit having or possessing the human being. Below we will see that sexual metaphors also attend the Spirit, and the same verb of "having" also has a sexual sense, as does the stronger word "possess." So I do not want to deny that sexual metaphors of the Spirit and possession are finally at odds; I just want to locate the ends of a range. For an interpretation of objective and subjective Spirit-possession that may be compatible with this paper, see Troels Engberg-Pedersen, *Cosmology and Self in the Apostle Paul: The Material Spirit* (New York: Oxford University Press, 2010), 44, 53–59, 203.

of blood, semen. The fact was that Paul did not have our modern notion of transcendence to go by. God had created the heavens and the earth, but plenty of principalities and powers led the way up. Not only for Arius, embarrassingly, was the line hard to draw. Richard Norris locates the invention of transcendence first in Irenaeus and then again in Athanasius, until its modern defender, Kathryn Tanner, who learned it, she says, from Norris.[11] Putting history aside, the theological problem, of course, is that lacking transcendence seems to leave the Spirit a *thing*, a *creature*. But a virtue lines this vice. Paul may have been wrong, from a modern point of view, about the transcendence of the Spirit, and yet deeply right about its immanence; and we need not require of him an anachronistic orthodoxy about how the two relate.

Shall we apply this analysis also to the wine, which is the blood of the community: *pneuma* animates blood, and therefore wine? (The spirit in the wine is not the alcohol: it comes from the blood.)

Thesis: The *Pneuma* Is in the Blood.

This is the bit that I wish most I had known before I published my Holy Spirit book: Late Antique Greek *pneuma* was a fluid *stuff*, not transcendent God, and as such it animated or circulated in blood and semen, and this has everything to do with Paul's metaphors of the Holy Spirit creating "children" of God (literally sons, or children who inherit). Skipping a millennium, even Aquinas, interpreting Rom. 8:17, makes bold where moderns may blush:

> [How we become children of God] is clear from a comparison to physical children, who are begotten by physical semen proceeding from the father. For the spiritual semen proceeding from the Father is the Holy Spirit. [*Semen autem spirituale a Patre procedens, est Spiritus Sanctus.*] And therefore by this semen some human beings are (re)generated children of God. [*per hoc semen aliqui homines in filios Dei generantur*].–1 John 3:9: "Everyone who is born of God does no sin, since the semen of God remains in him [*semen Dei manet in eo*]."[12]

11. Richard Norris, *God and World in Early Christian Theology: A Study in Justin Martyr, Irenaeus, Tertullian and Origen* (New York: Seabury, 1965), 84–86; Kathryn Tanner, *God and Creation: Tyranny or Empowerment?* (Oxford: Basil Blackwell, 1985), 46–48, 56; Tanner, *Jesus, Humanity and the Trinity* (Minneapolis: Fortress, 2001), 2.

12. "Et hoc est manifestum ex similitudine filiorum carnalium, qui per semen carnale a patre procedentes generantur. Semen autem spirituale a

Of course you will say, *semen* in Latin means both "semen" and "seed"; but Aquinas places the word without apology in its sexual context. Again, Aquinas usually genders the human soul feminine, to God's male—and then removes God from a particular gender as beyond categories and source of all. But here, quoting 1 John, Aquinas uses masculine pronouns without comment for both sides of a sexual encounter by which God regenerates, refathers, or even "breeds and seeds" gentiles. Aquinas did not have a bawdy sense of humor. Did he? In any case his account retains the spirit of Paul's desire to shock—and it puts a different spin on how to be born again in the Middle Ages. Of course semen is also another form of blood—the kind that makes children blood relatives to their fathers.[13]

In Aristotle, a child resembles mother and father for different reasons. The mother supplies the matter, but the father supplies the principles or form of movement and origin, *kinesis* and *genesis*. The father, therefore, contributes to the fetus its "shape and character."[14] Philo reports that "similarities of body and soul . . . are preserved in seminal principles (*en tois spermatikois logois*)."[15] But—and here is where adoption and natural birth come together—a Greek father has to formally accept even his biological child, admit it ritually into the family.[16] This ritual is sacrifice, the ceremonious slaughter and eating together of a large animal. The father offers a sacrifice, legitimates the child, and

Patre procedens, est Spiritus Sanctus. Et ideo per hoc semen aliqui homines in filios Dei generantur. –I Io. III, 9: 'Omnis qui natus est ex Deo peccatum non facit, quoniam semen Dei manet in eo'" (Thomas Aquinas, *Super epistolam ad Romanos lectura*. in *Super epistolas S. Pauli lectura,* 8th rev. edn, ed. P. Raphael Cai, 2 vols. (Turin: Marietti, 1953), 8:17, §636). The Greek of the passage from 1 John is *sperma*. The observation that "semen" also means "seed" and recalls (say) the parable of the sower only reinforces the connection evident elsewhere in Romans between sexual and agricultural images. For more on medieval use of sexual metaphors, see Lynda Coon, '"What Is the Word if Not Semen?' Priestly Bodies in Carolingian Exegesis," in *Gender in the Early Medieval World: East and West, 300–900*, ed. Leslie Brubaker and Julia M. H. Smith (New York: Cambridge University Press, 2004), 278–300; Caroline Walker Bynum, *Wonderful Blood* (Philadelphia: University of Pennsylvania Press, 2007), 110–69; and Rogers, *After the Spirit*, 120.

13. For more about this, see Eugene F. Rogers Jr., "How the Semen of the Spirit Genders the Gentiles," in *Aquinas and the Supreme Court: Race, Gender, and the Failure of Natural Law in Thomas's Biblical Commentaries* (Oxford: Blackwell, 2013), 289–97.

14. Caroline Johnson Hodge, *If Sons, then Heirs: A Study of Kinship and Ethnicity in the Letters of Paul* (Oxford: Oxford University Press, 2007), 94–95.

15. Quoted in ibid., 27.

16. Ibid.

gives it a name. Baptism, the ritual drowning that makes a child of God, and Eucharist, the ritual breaking that names Christians after Christ, both retain elements of accepting children by sacrifice. Similarly, in inheritance disputes, family members had to testify that heirs had been admitted at family feasts. So Apollodorus testifies: "[My adoptive father] conducted me to the altars and to the members of the extended family and the clan. With them the same law applies both when someone introduces a natural son or an adopted son: he must swear with his hand on the sacrificial animal [about] the child whom he introduces, whether his own or an adopted son."[17]

Through the ritual of shared sacrifice, even adopted children "shared blood" with their adoptive fathers and brothers:[18] "Greek texts intuit an analogy between sacrifice and men's control of childbirth because sacrifice actually effected paternal control of children."[19] "Through sacrifice, children [receive] a place in the father's lineage; through ritual, men beget their heirs."[20] Nancy Jay puts it even more starkly: male sacrifice seeks to give birth culturally, by *cultus* or, literally, cutting; men seek, in short, to "do birth better."[21] It is thus that the *pneuma* of the father gains "natural" associations with sacrifice and feasting, fire and wine: because of deeply rooted cultural (or cultic) *practices*. Those associations do not float free of embodied activities like killing and eating; they arise from them.

Here is my current problem. Paul insists that gentiles receive sonship of God by adoption (*huiothesia*, placing sons). Greco-Roman eulogies and encomiums say that adopted children resemble their adoptive *patres*: But how? Indeed, children resemble even *invented* ancestors, and they resemble adoptive ones even when everybody knows it. Thus Julius Caesar claims descent from the goddess Venus, and Cicero continues to record genealogies he recognizes as decked out with "feigned triumphs" and "too many consulships."[22] If Cicero winks at inventions even as he perpetuates them, how much more easily can the

17. Quoted in ibid., 29.

18. Ibid., 27; Nancy Jay, *Throughout Your Generations Forever* (Chicago: University of Chicago Press, 1994), 41–60.

19. Stanley Stowers, "Greeks Who Sacrifice and Those Who Do Not: Toward an Anthropology of Greek Religion," in *The Social World of the Earliest Christians: Essays in Honor of Wayne A. Meeks*, ed. L. M. White and O. L. Yarborough (Minneapolis: Fortress, 1995), 293–333 (301).

20. Hodge, *If Sons, then Heirs*, 27.

21. Jay, *Throughout Your Generations Forever*, 17.

22. Hodge, *If Sons, then Heirs*, 19, 32.

rhetoric of family resemblance accommodate the adopted who may learn their posture and character from adoptive *patres*, absorbing it, as we say in English, from the air? "The historian Diodorus of Sicily describes the heritage of Publius Scipio, who was not only born to a famous father, but also 'given in adoption to Scipio.' Diodorus goes on to cite both the birth *and* the adoptive family to prove the worth [of Publius]: 'Sprung from such stock, and succeeding to a family and clan of such importance, he showed himself worthy of *the fame of his ancestors*.'"[23] Which set of ancestors? Both. Is there a *pneuma* theory for adoption? Can it animate the air or circulate in the household? Certainly: but my application to adoption is an inference; so far I have no sources to tell me so directly. Reading Durkheim would also make you think so. According to Durkheim, societies establish facts when they entrench them in individual minds, and societies entrench facts in individual minds when they meet together in "reunions" and generate "moral effervescence,"[24] social "juice" or electricity, such as at sacrifices, Tigers' games, or the donning of the gowns. In Christianity, the social juice is the Holy Spirit—unless of course it is blood—and one of the effervescent reunions is the baptism with its extended families and fictive kin or godparents. I would like to say: Paul's adoption metaphors depend on a Greco-Roman adoption discourse according to which adopted sons resemble adoptive fathers by *pneuma*, which circulated both in the semen or blood (for biological children) and in the air or in the household (for adopted children). *Pneuma* would have circulated also in the blood and meat and community of sacrifice, as it does in the Eucharist, to leaven the bread and enflame the wine. Certainly, *Christianity* has a *pneuma* theory for adoption. It is called baptism. In it we find both sacrifice—by drowning—and birth done better, in the womb of the font. The Spirit, a fluid, extends by *krasis*, or mixing, into the water. So it extends all the more readily into that sacrifice in which the Son makes brothers by sharing his blood, into that mixed substance that modern Greek calls *krasi*, the wine: which celebrates the wedding feast that a father throws for his son, where the son says to his spouse, "this is my body, given for you."

The Spirit, I propose, is, even in antiquity, not *merely* a physical thing, but a

23. Ibid., 30, citing Diodorus, *Bibliotheca historica*, ed. and trans. Francis R. Walton (Cambridge: Harvard University Press, 1957), 31.26.4.

24. Émile Durkheim, *The Elementary Forms of the Religious Life*, trans. Joseph Ward Swain (New York: Free Press, 1965), 240–42.

*para*physical thing: one that works with and alongside but exceeds the physical. (I reclaim the notorious phrase of Romans 1 that refers to excessive gentile love of men for men or women for women, because Paul repeats it in Romans 11 to describe the excessive love of gentiles by God.)[25] Later theologians would think about the Spirit in terms of immanence and transcendence, but the ancients had no moderns to go by. Paul, as it happens, uses notably parabiological or paraphysical metaphors for the inclusion of gentiles. If Jews are God's children by nature, gentiles become God's children by adoption; they are "fellow" heirs; the Spirit must *teach* them to call God "Father," which Jews already know; in Romans 11 they make branches *grafted*, explicitly *para physin*, in excess of nature, into the unaccustomed clefts of the Jewish olive tree. Normal would be to graft sweet or oil-rich olives onto the more vigorous rootstock of a wild tree; but God does the opposite, grafting *wild*, good-for-nothing olives onto a perfectly good domestic stock. This God is no longer the sober agriculturalist of Eden but a loopy plant-fancier: this God is a giddy gardener.[26] All these metaphors are paraphysical: they *extend* even to the breaking point the metaphors of kinship. Paul's "Spirit of adoption" also works paraphysically, expanding nature according to Greco-Roman adoption theory, where the father's *pneuma* is not just "spirit," but seminal fluid. *Somehow*, it causes both biological and adoptive children to resemble him.[27]

Antithesis: The Blood Is Not a Holy Grail.

Here is where the materiality of the Spirit goes too far. I now expound a view I stand against. It is not about the Grail as such. It

25. See Eugene F. Rogers Jr., "The Spirit Rests on the Son Paraphysically," in *The Lord and Giver of Life: Perspectives on Constructive Pneumatology*, ed. David H. Jensen (Philadelphia: Westminster John Knox, 2008), 87–95, 174–76; Rogers, "Paul on Exceeding Nature: Queer Gentiles and the Giddy Gardener," in *Jewish/Christian/Queer: Crossroads and Identities*, ed. F. S. Roden (Aldershot: Ashgate, 2009), 19–33; and Rogers, *Aquinas and the Supreme Court*, 289-97.

26. These sentences first appeared to different purpose in Rogers, "Paul on Exceeding Nature," 25–26.

27. This idea first occurred to me in conversation with Stanley Stowers; it seems to be implied, but never quite stated, in Stanley Stowers, "Matter and Spirit, or What Is Pauline Participation in Christ?," in *The Holy Spirit: Classic and Contemporary Readings*, ed. Eugene F. Rogers Jr. (Oxford: Blackwell, 2009), 92–105.

is about real blood practices in high medieval Germany, detailed by Carolyn Bynum, that would make more sense if Grail legends were true—if Joseph of Arimathea had in fact captured the blood from the cross in a cup, and it had survived, red and flowing.

In the *Dauerwunder* of late medieval Germany, pilgrims regarded the substance in certain reliquaries as real, human blood miraculously kept fluid and red since the crucifixion.[28] (By the way: crucifixion needs little to no blood; it kills by suffocation. Why does blood seep in where it hardly seems to belong? But that is a question for another day.) "Fluid and red" were signal properties, because they distinguished blood from gore. In Latin as in English, "blood" was flowing and red; gore was crusty and brown.[29] If blood did not dry and oxidize, then—in the absence of modern transfusion technologies like freezing—it was staying alive outside the body, *by miracle*. Reliquary blood, flowing and red, came to rival eucharistic wine consecrated by a priest and controlled by the hierarchy. Red, flowing blood was animated, kept alive, by the Spirit. Which was the *true* blood, the blood by which the Spirit bound the community together "for real"? Was it the reliquary blood, with apparently greater claims to physicality, which bound the pilgrims ecstatically with a common experience of wonder? Or was it the institutional blood, with the acknowledged accidents of wine, which bound the church into a hierarchy with priest, bishop, pope, and even dissenter or reformer? Bynum's *Wonderful Blood* (2007) details the conflict precisely here, where instances of reliquary blood, with greater apparent claims to being physical, to having once flowed in human veins, gave up, albeit with excruciating slowness, the claim to be more real than the blood of the sacrament. Eventually the hierarchy won, and the blood that maintained the deepest connections with the *social* body retained the title "true"—the blood that best maintained the connections among the individual and society, the human being and God, the brothers and the Father, the body of Christ and the Body of Christ. It is of the greatest importance that the metaphorical blood of the Eucharist was not the less real in its conflict with putatively biological blood, but finally more real. The exception of reliquary blood proves the rule that symbolic blood—so far from contrasting with "real" blood—instead controls what counts as real. Social power makes symbolic blood more real than physical blood, just as it makes

28. Bynum, *Wonderful Blood*, passim.

29. Ibid., 17.

paper money a matter of life and death. If we today regard physical blood as more real, that is because of a powerful social practice called medicine. If we have learned that only the transfusion of biological blood of the appropriate type will heal us—and certainly not red wine—medieval Christians learned that only the drinking (or, if Communion was offered in one kind, the mere sight or proximity) of consecrated wine could save them—and certainly not biological human blood. But in deciding in favor of the wine, they put a limit on what you might call the mechanical or involuntary action of the Holy Spirit.

The personal agency of the Holy Spirit leads us away, therefore, from the idea that blood might work by magic, in the humors, or as nutrition. Thomas Aquinas, who developed transubstantiation as the feast of Corpus Christi emerged, in fact resists the idea that blood acts as a magical substance. He accords it moral, not physical effects: it produces faith and love. To draw that conclusion, Thomas models the Eucharist on the incarnation, using John of Damascus's idea that the body of Christ is God's integral instrument or organ (God's right hand). In his commentary on the Gospel of John, Thomas writes:

> even [Christ's] flesh is life-giving, for it is an organ of his divinity (*organum divinitatis*). Thus, since an instrument acts by virtue of the agent (*cum instrumentum agat virtute agentis*), then just as the divinity of Christ is life-giving, so too his flesh gives life (as Damascene says) because of the Word to which it is united. Thus Christ healed the sick by his touch. So . . . **I am the living bread,** pertained to the power of the Word; but . . . the communion of his body (*communionem sui corporis*) [pertains] to the sacrament of the Eucharist.[30]

Aquinas avoids the nutritive or humoral route also because grace requires—not as a precondition, but as an inevitable concomitant—a movement of the will. This happens because grace moves more interiorly than we are to ourselves, like romantic love: grace moves and changes our desires, so that what we do, including the movements of our will, are in accord both with our willing and with grace. Love, in short, moves the heart; and grace puts us in the position of "love God and do what you will." The trouble with nutritive or humoral theories is not that they work like

30. Thomas Aquinas, *In Johannem*, chapter 6, §959. Translation modified from Thomas Aquinas, *Commentary on the Gospel of John*, trans. James Weisheipl and Fabian Larcher (Albany: Magi Books, 1988), online at http://dhspriory.org/thomas/SSJohn.htm (bold in original).

magic—that would be a false dichotomy. The trouble is that they seem to work by human movements that are not voluntary, as digestion is not, or a shot of adrenaline is not. They bypass the will. A human action without intention is not, technically speaking, a human *act* or *actus*; it is not the having-been-done of a human agent. Aquinas distinguishes terms just here, as translators fail to do: human *actions* (*actiones*) are raw movements; human *acts* (*actus*) are intentional. Of course, acts are made up of actions, and actions unify acts, and a lot depends on how you break them up in analysis.[31] But while eating is an act, digestion is only an action. In his own terms Aquinas is right to hang the effect on eating, which is an intentional human act, as opposed to digestion, which is not.

How can the efficacy of the Eucharist depend on eating but not digestion, on drinking but not infusion? Because it depends on the *voluntary* act, not the involuntary action. *If* by grace I eat, then God takes the occasion of my eating, by a kind of divine irony, to be the cause of my salvation.

This works like intercessory prayer. God *takes* my prayer as the cause of someone else's good. God need not do so: but God can set chains of cause and effect so that my prayer counts as the cause even of what God would do anyway, because that *involves me* in charity toward others, good for both of us. Thus God draws creatures Godward.[32] (It may be that Paul's other discourse of gentile inclusion—descent from Abraham, whom God makes a "father of many nations," or of many *gentiles*—works the same way: God, like a playwright, graciously plants a cause ahead in order that the created sequence will work well later. But that is for another day.)

Similarly, it would be good if the most elemental thing we do as creatures brought our salvation: so it does. We are what we eat. *Man ist, was er isst.* It is a cosmic *convenientia* or fittingness. So Bulgakov: Just as we sinned by eating, so we are saved by eating. The tree of life *is* the bread of the Eucharist, by the cross; and the command, "in the sweat of thy brow shalt thou eat bread" (Gen. 3:19) becomes a command that saves; it narrates a

31. For more about this distinction, see Rogers, *Aquinas and the Supreme Court*, 66–68, 239.

32. Material from the sentence beginning "Aquinas avoids" appears in a different context and to support a different thesis in Eugene F. Rogers, Jr., "Tanner's Non-Competitive Account and the Blood of Christ," in *The Gift of Theology: The Contribution of Kathryn Tanner* (Minneapolis: Fortress Press, 2015), 154-55.

promise, which the bread of the Eucharist fulfills.[33]

The Spirit, as a person, works by intention. But the Spirit, as immanent, also works by the intention of others. She molds desires and arranges circumstances, as Aquinas would say, *suaviter*, sweetly.[34] She does not give the effects of Communion without molding the intention of the believer to her own. She prefers eucharistic blood to reliquary blood because eucharistic blood better engages the societal intention of the church. And, as when she conceives the Son in the womb of Mary, so she may also fulfill the intention of the Father. The fire in the wine is no magical thing; it is intention: social, individual, divine. Like the flames at Pentecost, the fire in the wine is a gift that the Spirit gives to the Son on the pattern of the incarnation. Because the Son takes a body, the Spirit too loves bodies for his sake and characteristically—by desire and intention—comes to rest on them, not in a way that violates but in a way that respects them. The Spirit shows courtesy to the body human and the social—to the individual body of Christ in the neighbor and in the collective body of Christ in the church. As the Spirit of grace builds up habits in the believer, so too the Spirit builds up rituals in the church; grace, in human beings, is always habitual, as sacraments, in the church, are always ritual. So it is too with the fire in the wine, as it was also with the lamb in the temple that was slain.

33. For more, see Rogers, *After the Spirit*, 42–43.

34. Rogers, *Aquinas and the Supreme Court*, 71.

Part 4

Anthropology

CHAPTER 15

Idols, Images, and a Spirit-ed Anthropology

A Pneumatological Account of the *Imago Dei*

MARC CORTEZ

Christian theology has long been guided by three convictions:

1. The *imago Dei* is central to a properly Christian understanding of the human person.
2. The *imago* can only be fully understood in light of the person and work of Jesus Christ.[1]
3. Jesus Christ himself can only be properly and fully understood in light of the person and work of the Holy Spirit.[2]

Taken together, these convictions would seem to lead necessarily to the conclusion that the Holy Spirit should form an important aspect of our understanding of the *imago*

1. Such a claim, of course, raises a number of important questions about the extent to which we should use NT concepts to interpret OT passages. Nonetheless, the clear NT claims about Jesus Christ being the true image of God have led most theologians to conclude that Christology is essential to any adequate account of the *imago Dei* (see Rom. 8:29; 2 Cor. 3:18; 4:4).

2. Colin Gunton thus speaks for many when he writes, "Christology which is abstracted from a discussion of the relation to it of pneumatology is not Christology rooted in the actual human career of the incarnate Lord" (*The Promise of Trinitarian Theology* [London: T&T Clark, 1997], xxx).

Dei. After all, if Christology is essential to the *imago*, and if pneumatology is essential to Christology, then it seems reasonable to conclude that pneumatology would inform the meaning of the image in some essential way.

Despite the apparent obviousness of this conclusion, however, biblical and theological studies on the image of God have generally not paid sufficient attention to the relationship between the Spirit and the image. Instead, in many such studies, there is a tendency to relate the Spirit to the image either through the Spirit's work in renewing the image and/or through some kind of reference to the Trinity. As we will see, both approaches raise significant questions regarding the extent to which we have truly integrated pneumatology into our understanding of the *imago Dei*.

The argument of this chapter, then, is that pneumatology should inform our understanding of the *imago Dei* more directly. After briefly summarizing pneumatological weaknesses in many theological interpretations of the image, we will turn our attention to two modern theologians known for having placed a greater emphasis on the role of pneumatology in theological anthropology in general: Yves Congar and Colin Gunton. Here we will see that both of these theologians offer robust frameworks for relating the Spirit to the image, but they do so in ways that raise significant questions about the adequacy of their respective approaches. Finally, the last half of this chapter will focus on a different way of relating pneumatology to the *imago Dei*, one that draws on a strong consensus among biblical scholars that has not yet received sufficient attention from systematic theologians.

Eschatological Addendum and Pneumatological Abstraction

There are two real problems with many recent treatments of the *imago Dei* and its relationship to the Spirit, which I will refer to as the *eschatological addendum* and *pneumatological abstraction* problems. The eschatological addendum problem refers to any approach to the *imago Dei* that locates the role of the Spirit primarily in the Spirit's work of restoring the image. Thus, for example, in his important text on the image Anthony Hoekema says little about the Spirit when discussing the nature and meaning of the *imago*, focusing the majority of his pneumatological reflections in a section on "The Renewed Image."[3] Similarly, in Stanley Grenz's *The Social God*

3. Anthony A. Hoekema, *Created in God's Image* (Grand Rapids: Eerdmans, 1986), 85–91.

and the Relational Self, the Spirit makes few appearances in the first half of the book, not showing up in force until Grenz discusses the Spirit's role in bringing about our eschatological transformation.[4] And F. LeRon Shults, despite referring to the Spirit extensively throughout his *Reforming Theological Anthropology*, also focuses most of his pneumatological reflections on the transformative role of the Spirit.[5]

I could multiply examples, but this suffices to establish that theologians routinely focus on the Spirit's transformative work, an understandable move given the New Testament's emphasis on the renewal of the image.[6] However, the difficulty lies in the lack of reference to the Spirit when developing the *meaning* of the image itself. Intended or not, this leads the reader toward the inevitable conclusion that the image is an essentially *non*-pneumatological concept. The Spirit simply restores something that we can and usually do understand apart from the Spirit himself. As important as the Spirit might be for the restoration of the image, he appears to be an eschatological addendum, something we add to the story of an already understood image only after we have moved into the sphere of transformation.

Some might object at this point that I am not being entirely fair. All three of the theologians I have mentioned, in addition to many more contemporary theologians, explicitly relate the *imago Dei* to the doctrine of the Trinity. We do not image just any God, but one who is eternally constituted as three persons in mutual interrelationship. The image of God thus refers to the relationality of human persons. And insofar as the Trinity is essential to the *imago* and the Spirit is essential to the Trinity, then the Spirit must be essential to the *imago* itself, not just its restoration.

Setting aside for a moment the question of how the Trinity relates to the meaning of the image, this objection leads us to our second concern: *pneumatological abstraction*. The difficulty with many such appeals is that they

4. Stanley J. Grenz, *The Social God and the Relational Self: A Trinitarian Theology of the Imago Dei* (Philadelphia: Westminster, 2001), 225–28.

5. F. LeRon Shults, *Reforming Theological Anthropology: After the Philosophical Turn to Relationality* (Grand Rapids: Eerdmans, 2003), 58–59, 77–93.

6. According to many, the NT indicates that the image was impacted in some way by the fall and in need of renewal (for example, 2 Cor. 3:18; Col. 3:10). Since the Spirit is always portrayed as the agent of renewal in the process of salvation, it seems reasonable to conclude that the Spirit's role relative to the *imago* is that of returning the image to its original state of perfection.

say little about what the Spirit in particular offers this Trinitarian understanding of the image. If the *imago* is all about relationship between persons, then would not the Father and Son alone suffice to establish the requisite relationality? To be clear, I am not saying here that these theologians have no answer to this question. Indeed, as we will see in the next section, there is a prominent tradition in Western theology that offers an explicit answer to this very question. Nonetheless, many discussions of the *imago Dei* appeal to the Trinity without offering any real explanation of precisely what the Spirit in particular contributes to our understanding of the image. Such appeals, then, are overly abstract, gesturing at the Spirit without providing any real explanatory depth.

Expanding Our Pneumatological Horizons: Yves Congar and Colin Gunton

Let us now turn to our two case studies. Yves Congar and Colin Gunton both offer theological anthropologies that avoid the addendum and abstraction problems, thus presenting the Spirit as part of the main course of the *imago Dei*. Nonetheless, we will see that the way in which they have strengthened the pneumatological content of the *imago* creates its own problems, specifically with respect to their interpretation of the image in Genesis 1.

Integrating the Eschatological Addendum

Congar and Gunton both avoided the eschatological addendum problem by relating the Spirit's transformative work to the meaning of the *imago* itself. For Congar, this occurred through his concept of the Spirit as the one who lifts up human capacities to a higher function. According to Congar, the image of God refers at least partly to the psychic capacities of the human person, particularly the intellectual capacity for knowledge and the volitional capacity for love,[7] both of which need to be oriented toward their proper end by the human capacity for free choice.[8] These are all natural capacities inherent in the human person since creation. However, Congar rejected any attempt to bifurcate nature and grace, contending that even unfallen

7. Yves M. J. Congar, "Perspectives chrétiennes sur la vie personnel et la vie collective," in *Socialisation et personne humaine—Semaines sociales de France—47ième session* (Lyons: Chronique sociale de France, 1961), 205.

8. Yves M. J. Congar, *Lay People in the Church: A Study for a Theology of Laity* (London: Geoffrey Chapman, 1985), 425.

human persons were open and receptive to divine grace, including the indwelling Spirit, from the beginning.[9] Although the natural capacities of unfallen humanity were good, they needed to be lifted up to an even greater good by the work of the Spirit.[10] Thus the soteriological work of the Spirit, which involves renewing the image by lifting up our capacities so they are again oriented toward their proper end, is a repetition of the Spirit's creational work. Rather than a mere addendum, then, the Spirit's transformative work, alongside the creational work, informs an important aspect of our understanding of the image itself: human capacities oriented by the Spirit toward their relational end.

Gunton similarly emphasized the importance of the Spirit's eschatological work for informing the nature of the image, but he did so primarily by highlighting the Spirit's role in perfecting creational realities in general. Gunton argued that God works in creation through the mediation of the Son and the Spirit,[11] and one of the Spirit's particular functions is that of bringing all of God's works to perfection.[12] The goodness of the original creation should be understood as a kind of imperfection, in the sense that it is not yet fully complete. The specific work of the Spirit is to bring all of creation toward its divinely intended end.[13] To understand creational realities, then, we have to view them in the light of eschatology, in light of their telos. As Gunton says, "it is the Spirit who enables all things to be what they are particularly created to be."[14] Accordingly, we can only understand the *imago* fully from an

9. Yves M. J. Congar, "L'homme est capable d'être appelé," *Vie Spirituelle* 120 (1969): 377–78. For Congar, the "indwelling" of the Spirit should not be understood in causal rather than spatial terms. Spatially, the Spirit is already present in all creatures. The unique "indwelling" of the Spirit involves the elevation of human life in the state of grace. See Congar, *The Mystery of the Temple: Or the Manner of God's Presence to His Creatures from Genesis to the Apocalypse* (Westminster, MD: Newman, 1962), 237; and Congar, *I Believe in the Holy Spirit* (New York: Crossroad, 2004), 2:100–101.

10. Elizabeth T. Groppe, *Yves Congar's Theology of the Holy Spirit* (New York: Oxford University Press, 2004), 95.

11. Colin E. Gunton, *The Triune Creator: A Historical and Systematic Study* (Grand Rapids: Eerdmans, 1998), 196. See also Gunton, *Father, Son & Holy Spirit: Toward a Fully Trinitarian Theology* (London: Continuum, 2003), 80.

12. Gunton, *Father, Son & Holy Spirit*, 81.

13. See esp. Gunton, *Triune Creator.*

14. Colin E. Gunton, *The Christian Faith: An Introduction to Christian Doctrine* (Oxford: Blackwell, 2002), 14.

eschatological perspective. Thus the Spirit does not merely restore an already complete image; rather, the Spirit is the one who takes that which was begun in creation and carries it to its always-intended telos.

For both Congar and Gunton, then, we avoid the eschatological addendum by providing a robust dogmatic account of how the Spirit's soteriological work informs our understanding of the image. It is not that the Spirit merely renews an image that we should understand in essentially non-pneumatological terms. Instead, we must read the story back-to-front, allowing the Spirit's eschatological work to instruct us about the meaning of the *imago* itself.

Filling in the Trinitarian Abstraction

Congar and Gunton also offer theologies of the *imago* that avoid the Trinitarian abstraction problem. Although they clearly affirm an essentially relational understanding of the image grounded in the doctrine of the Trinity, they take the extra step of explaining the precise contribution the Spirit makes to this relational framework.

Congar does this once again by appealing to the Spirit's work relative to human capacities. For Congar, the capacities that comprise the image (intellect and volition) are designed to lead us into relationship with others. As Elizabeth Groppe explains, "The human intellect and will through which we image God lead us *beyond* the self toward knowledge and love of another. We are created with the capacity to speak to another, to strive to know another, to love one another, and to receive one another in love."[15] Thus the very capacities that make us human as individuals are the same capacities that necessarily lead us toward the kind of community and relationality that truly images a triune God. Human persons are to be God's image bearers as the Spirit indwells and enlivens their natural capacities for love and knowledge such that they form societies in which people love one another with God's own love. To live in the image of God, then, is to live as both a particular individual who instantiates a common set of human capacities through the indwelling power of the Spirit, and to be led by those Spirit-empowered capacities into real community with other Spirit-indwelt humans who love and glorify God.

Gunton approaches the question from a slightly different perspective, appealing to *personhood* as the constitutive link between

15. Groppe, *Yves Congar's Theology of the Holy Spirit*, 88.

the Spirit and the image. For Gunton, the Trinity reveals that "[t]o be a person is to be distinct from other persons, and yet inextricably bound up with them: to be 'other' only in 'relation'."[16] Personhood is thus constituted in the "personal space . . . in which three persons are for and from each other in their otherness."[17] Since human persons were created to image that kind of tripersonal God, he concludes that this should also inform our understanding of the image: "Likeness to God consists in the fact that human beings are persons, while the remainder of the created world is not."[18]

If Gunton had stopped here, though, we would still have the kind of pneumatological abstraction we discussed earlier, appealing to a vague relationality in which the Spirit plays no unique role. However, Gunton also argues that it is precisely the role of the Spirit to constitute this personal space by creating an openness for the other. In his Bampton Lectures, *The One, the Three and the Many*, he frequently appeals to spirit as that which "is able to be open to that which is other than itself, to move dynamically into relation with the other."[19] Drawing on a long-standing theological tradition, he views the Spirit as the bond of love between the Father and the Son, and correlatively as the one who enables individuality *and* multiplicity in the world, establishing the possibility of real relationality.[20] Thus the Spirit plays a fundamental role in Gunton's relational *imago* precisely as the condition for its very possibility.

Both of these theologians thus avoid the Trinitarian abstraction problem as well, offering dogmatically rich accounts of the Spirit's unique role in creating the relationality necessary to their view of the image.[21]

16. Gunton, *Christian Faith*, 43.

17. Colin E. Gunton, "Trinity, Ontology and Anthropology: Towards a Renewal of the Doctrine of the Imago Dei," in *Persons, Divine and Human*, ed. Christoph Schwöbel and Colin Gunton (Edinburgh: T&T Clark, 1991), 56.

18. Gunton, *Triune Creator*, 208.

19. John Webster, "Gunton and Barth," in *The Theology of Colin Gunton*, ed. Lincoln Harvey (London: T&T Clark, 2010), 25. And this openness to the other that characterizes the human spirit is only made possible through the work of the Divine Spirit.

20. Gunton, *Christian Faith*, 14. Like Barth, Gunton finds a clear indicator of this relational *imago* in the fact that humans were created as male and female: "If, first, to be created in the image of God is to be made male and female, what is implied is that in this most central of all human relatedness is to be found a finite echo of the relatedness of Father, Son and Holy Spirit" (Colin E. Gunton, *Christ and Creation* [Grand Rapids: Eerdmans, 1992], 101).

21. Even though both integrate other views of the *imago* into their relational approach, each prioritizes the relational dynamic as the essence of the image. And it is this relational aspect that does most

An Exegetical Difficulty

The strength of such an approach, however, is also its liability. The relational view provides Congar and Gunton with a robust framework for relating the Spirit and the image, but it does so at the expense of laying itself open to objections about the exegetical adequacy of this interpretation of the image. Gunton was surely correct when he argued that the scarcity and inherent ambiguity of references to the *imago* in Scripture means that "[w]e need more than an extended exegesis of Gen. 1.26f, and in particular a broader treatment of the topic, if we are really to make more satisfactory use of the concept of the *imago Dei*."[22] Nonetheless, he also recognized that such a broader treatment must "do justice" to the specific texts involved.[23] And the difficulty with any straightforwardly relational view of the *imago* lies in the texts themselves. As J. Richard Middleton points out in his recent study of the *imago*:

> What is problematic is that most contemporary proposals of either substantialistic or relational interpretations—which tend to be found in the writings of systematic theologians—simply ignore the massive literature in Old Testament scholarship on the *imago Dei* that developed in the past century.[24]

Gunnlaugur Jónsson states the difficulty even more strongly at the end of his extensive survey of modern Old Testament research: "Were it not for the fact that a few influential OT scholars such as [James] Barr and [Claus] Westermann do not agree with this dominant understanding, we would be able to speak of a complete consensus among OT scholars on this problem."[25]

We do not have time here to rehearse all of the exegetical arguments against the relational view of the *imago*.[26] Rather than address whether the relational view does justice to the image texts, then, we will focus on another question. If the vast majority of Old

of the work in connecting the Spirit to the *imago Dei*. The Spirit is the one who creates the possibility of real image-bearing relationality.

22. Gunton, "Trinity, Ontology and Anthropology," 58.

23. Gunton, *Triune Creator*, 195.

24. J. Richard Middleton, *The Liberating Image: The* Imago Dei *in Genesis 1* (Grand Rapids: Brazos, 2005), 24.

25. Gunnlaugur A. Jónsson, *The Image of God: Genesis 1:26–28 in a Century of Old Testament Research* (Stockholm: Almqvist & Wiksell, 1988), 219.

26. See esp. James Barr, *Biblical Faith and Natural Theology: The Gifford Lectures for 1991* (Oxford: Clarendon, 1994), 161.

Testament scholars are correct and the relational view as it stands is exegetically inadequate, is there another way of relating the Spirit to the image that is more viable?

Image, Idol, and Divine Presence

Thus far I have suggested that (1) pneumatology should inform our understanding of the *imago Dei*, (2) many contemporary accounts relate the Spirit to the *imago* inadequately, and (3) even those who offer more robustly pneumatological interpretations of the image do so in ways that are liable to important exegetical objections. The task of this section, then, is to offer a different way forward. More specifically, I will suggest that understanding the image in light of concepts of idolatry and divine presence that were prevalent in the ancient Near East provides resources for linking pneumatology and the *imago Dei* in a way that is both exegetically and theologically satisfying.

Idols in the Ancient Near East

Let us begin with the clear consensus among biblical scholars that "image" (*ṣelem*) and "likeness" (*dəmût*) need to be understood as part of the semantic domain of language used to refer to idols in the ancient Near East.[27] According to David Clines, *ṣelem* and its cognates "are used predominantly in a literal sense, of three-dimensional objects which represent gods, men, or other living beings."[28] Middleton similarly concludes that *ṣelem* "primarily designates three-dimensional cult statues of various false gods," going on to state that "any Old Testament scholar worth her salt will acknowledge that the semantic range of *ṣelem* . . . includes idols."[29] *Dəmût* is a somewhat less common term for idolatry, but it too functions in that same semantic domain.[30] Although *dəmût* has occasionally been read as weakening the meaning of *ṣelem* to reduce its associations with physical idols, most biblical scholars now view the two as

---

27. See, for example, Num. 33:52; 2 Kgs. 11:18; 2 Chron. 23:17; Ezek. 7:20; 16:17; Amos 5:26.

28. David J. A. Clines, "The Image of God in Man," *Tyndale Bulletin* 19 (1968): 73. Although Clines goes on to note that *ṣelem* and its cognates can be used metaphorically, even in those contexts the notion of physical form remains prominent (ibid., 75).

29. Middleton, *Liberating Image*, 25.

30. James Barr, "The Image of God in the Book of Genesis—A Study of Terminology," *Bulletin of the John Rylands Library* 51 (1968): 11–26; Edward Mason Curtis, "Man as the Image of God in Genesis in the Light of Ancient Near Eastern Parallels" (PhD diss., University of Pennsylvania, 1984).

largely synonymous in the context of Genesis 1.[31] Thus James Barr concludes: "There is an antecedent probability that the term 'image of God' might suggest, and might therefore require some delimitation against, the then familiar use of images or idols of the divine."[32]

Although there are various lines of inquiry we might pursue in delimiting the image of God against the broader notion of idols, our purposes here require us to focus only on the idea of divine presence and how it relates to a physical idol. Here it may help if we push back on the common notion that idols were *mere* symbols of divine beings. According to common biblical rhetoric, idols are nothing but metal and wood, physical emblems with no true power.[33] An idol may "represent" a divine being in some abstract way, similar to the way a painting might be said to represent Peter Pan, but there is nothing intrinsically significant about these objects that human hands have created to worship their false gods.

Such rhetoric may be theologically justified, but it can also lead us to miss the true significance of idols in the broader theology of the ancient Near East. In that context, an idol was far more than a mere symbol; it was a real manifestation of divine presence.[34] Although the idol might appear to be of purely human origin, it became more through a ritual of consecration common throughout the region.[35] In this "washing" or "opening of the mouth" ceremony, the physical idol was imbued with the presence of a divine being such that it became a "living idol."[36] By pouring himself or herself into the idol, the divine being became so closely associated with it that actions taken against the idol were considered blasphemous and whoever had possession of the idol in some way had possession of the god's own presence.[37] José Faur thus con-

31. The fact that *dəmût* itself is often used with reference to physical form also suggests that it is not used here to weaken that aspect of *ṣelem's* meaning. See John F. Kutsko, *Between Heaven and Earth: Divine Presence and Absence in the Book of Ezekiel* (Winona Lake, IN: Eisenbrauns, 2000).

32. Barr, "Image of God," 15. See also Curtis, "Man as the Image of God"; and Kutsko, *Between Heaven and Earth*.

33. For example: Pss. 115:1–18; 135:15–18; Isa. 44:6–23; 45:20; 46:7; Jer. 10:3–16; Hab. 2:18.

34. For a good discussion of this, see José Faur, "The Biblical Idea of Idolatry," *The Jewish Quarterly Review* 69 (1978): 1–15.

35. Michael B. Dick, *Born in Heaven, Made on Earth: The Making of the Cult Image in the Ancient Near East* (Winona Lake, IN: Eisenbrauns, 1999).

36. Faur, "Biblical Idea of Idolatry."

37. Faur points out the significance this had in the ancient world for protecting your idols from being captured by your enemies (ibid., 8).

cludes, "The fundamental principle . . . was the identification of a god with his idol."[38] No mere symbol, the idol became the physical medium through which that god manifested his or her own divine presence in creation.

Idols and the Imago Dei

In the ancient Near East, then, an idol was a physical medium through which a divine being manifested its presence in the world. Consequently, if that is the proper context for understanding the image language of the Bible, we should hear the declaration that God will make humans in the divine "image" as an indication that he intends for them to be the means through which he will manifest his own presence in creation. That would in turn mean that the image is inherently pneumatological since the Spirit is precisely the one who manifests divine presence in the world throughout the Old Testament. At the beginning of Genesis we see the Spirit "hovering over the waters" (Gen. 1:2), which Middleton describes as "God's creative presence."[39] The psalmists offer some of the most explicit statements, asking, "Where can I go from your Spirit? Where can I flee from your presence?" (Ps. 139:7). And again, "Do not cast me from your presence or take your Holy Spirit from me" (Ps. 51:11). God assures Israel of his covenantal faithfulness by promising that his Spirit will remain among them (Hag. 2:5), and he routinely "sends" his Spirit into the world as an expression of his presence (for example, Ps. 104:30). Throughout the Old Testament, then, there is an inseparable link between the Spirit and the divine presence.

We may be able to find additional confirmation in the second creation narrative. Some scholars have pointed out a number of interesting parallels between the creation of the *ʾādām* in Genesis 2 and the mouth washing/opening ceremony in which idols are animated by a divine spirit. Andreas Schüle helpfully summarizes some of the points of comparison:

> Similarities occur in the general pattern—the material shaping of a body, its being brought to life, the change of environment from some desert place to the garden—but also in details like the furnishing of the garden with plants and animals and the fact that God himself is present there and joins with Adam and Eve in the early evening hours when

38. Ibid., 7.

39. Middleton, *Liberating Image*, 86. The Holy Bible, New International Version (Grand Rapids: Zondervan, 1984).

> there is a nice breeze coming in from the Mediterranean sea.[40]

If this is correct, it would mean that even though the second creation narrative does not employ explicit image language, it still utilizes the conceptual framework of idolatry to describe the creation of humanity. And this in turn would suggest that even though Genesis 2:7 does not refer explicitly to the Spirit, we are justified in understanding this as a story of God filling his designated image bearers with the Spirit of his presence.[41] Thus, despite using entirely different terminology to describe the creation of humans, the second creation narrative seems to be utilizing the conceptual framework of idol/image, strengthening the argument for seeing such a framework in the first creation account with its explicit use of idol-related terminology.

John Kutsko makes a similar argument for seeing the *imago Dei* as an important part of the theology of the book of Ezekiel.[42] Although Ezekiel does not refer explicitly to the image of God, he is fully aware of the concept and uses it actively in his polemic against idolatry. Thus Ezekiel uses the framework in order to disparage idols as images created by humans and to highlight humans as images created by God.[43] Indeed, once we have identified the root of the *imago* as God manifesting divine presence in humans through the

40. Andreas Schüle, "Made in the 'Image of God': The Concepts of Divine Images in Gen 1–3," *Zeitschrift für die alttestamentliche Wissenschaft* 117 (2005): 13. See also Catherine McDowell, "Selem ('Image') and Demut ('Likeness') Revisited: The Divine-Human Relationship Defined in Terms of Kin, King and Cult," presented at the Institute for Biblical Research, November 23, 2013.

41. This link becomes even clearer when we note the frequent biblical association of the "breath" (*nəšāmâ*) with "spirit" (*rûaḥ*)—for example: Gen. 2:7; 2 Sam. 22:16; Job 4:9; 33:4; 34:14; Ps. 18:15; Isa. 42:5.

42. Kutsko, *Between Heaven and Earth.*

43. Although Casey A. Strine agrees that Ezekiel has a robust theology of the *imago Dei*, he thinks that it is the prophet alone who is presented as being in the image of God rather than all humans ("Ezekiel's Image Problem: The Mesopotamian Cult Statue Induction Ritual and the *Imago Dei* Anthropology in the Book of Ezekiel," *Catholic Biblical Quarterly* 76 [2014]: 252–72). And Stephen Herring limits the *imago* in Ezekiel to the nation of Israel (*Divine Substitution: Humanity as the Manifestation of Deity in the Hebrew Bible and the Ancient Near East*, Forschungen zur Religion und Literatur des Alten und Neuen Testaments 247 [Göttingen: Vandenhoeck & Ruprecht, 2013]). For our purposes, though, it is enough to note that Ezekiel has a theology of the *imago Dei* in which God does in fact manifest his presence through human persons (at least one). In other words, Ezekiel confirms the essential concept of the *imago* that we have seen in this study, even if there is some difference regarding the scope of the image.

Spirit, we are equipped to see that concept functioning in any number of contexts where explicit image language itself is absent.

And although I think we can establish this understanding of the *imago* from the Old Testament alone, we should also note the ways in which it is confirmed and strengthened in the New Testament. There as well we see the motif of the Spirit enacting divine presence in the world. Indeed, this link is so strong that Gordon Fee can define the Spirit in Paul's theology simply as "God's Empowering Presence."[44] And, of course, no theology of the *imago* would be complete without looking to Jesus as the fullest expression of what it means to be made in the image of God. There we see Jesus as both the one who was uniquely filled with the Spirit and the one who uniquely manifests God's presence in creation.[45]

I think we can say with some confidence, then, that if this interpretation is correct, the *imago* is an essentially pneumatological concept. And we can make this argument without relying in any straightforward way on utilizing Trinitarian or relational concepts to understand the *imago* as it is presented in Genesis 1. As we have seen, the idea of a divine being pouring its spirit into a creaturely reality was well established in the ancient world. So, regardless of what interpretive moves we might want to make with respect to the "Let us" of Genesis 1:26, we do not need to posit some kind of proto-Trinitarianism in the creation narrative to develop a robustly pneumatological account of the *imago Dei*.

Some Objections

Before concluding, though, we need to deal with a few possible objections. First, the real "consensus" position among biblical scholars that I mentioned above has to do not with this idol framework in general, but with the idea that the *imago Dei* refers explicitly to the exercise of dominion/authority over creation. Many scholars point to ancient Near Eastern texts that also associate image language with human persons, most of which refer to kings who rule over their kingdoms as "images" of divine beings. Given that the *imago* texts also emphasize dominion (Gen. 1:26, 28), we have a clear basis for identifying this as the real meaning of the image.

In response, it is important to note that these interpretations are not exclusive. And it

44. Gordon D. Fee, *God's Empowering Presence: The Holy Spirit in the Letters of Paul* (Peabody, MA: Hendrickson, 1994).

45. See esp. the relationship between Jesus and the Spirit in the Gospel of John (1:32–33; 3:5–8, 34; 6:63; 7:39; 14:15–17; 15:26; 20:19–23).

may help to make a distinction between the primary and secondary functions of an image. What we have been discussing in this study is what we can label as the primary function: manifesting divine presence. That function holds for anything that we would call an image. But images may have more particular purposes as well: ruling, revealing, representing, and so on. Thus it may well be the case that the *imago Dei* has the primary purpose of manifesting God's presence in the world *as well as* a secondary purpose of ruling over creation. The primary function would still have a kind of logical priority—humans would exercise dominion *in virtue of* the divine presence—but in a way that still allows the secondary function to be an important aspect of the overall understanding of the image. Many studies that identify the image with dominion tend to move quickly past the notion of divine presence, focusing almost all of their attention on the dominion motif. That has the unfortunate consequence of downplaying the more fundamental aspect of the image as well as making it more difficult to locate the Spirit properly with respect to the meaning of the image.

From a different perspective, others might object that this interpretation misses the importance of relationality and community as essential to being human. What do we do with the emphasis on "male and female" in Genesis 1, the "not good" and "one flesh" of Genesis 2, and the obvious importance of persons in community that we see in the christological fulfillment of the image: the church? Such an objection, though, errs in thinking that this approach to the image is inherently individualistic. There is nothing in what we have said that precludes God from choosing to manifest his divine presence through a plurality of human persons rather than a single human individual. Indeed, it seems quite reasonable to take the command to be fruitful and multiply as a declaration that God's creational intent was to fill the world with his presence through the proliferation of his people. In the end, then, we may—and probably should—still end up with a robustly relational understanding of the image and human persons. But we will again develop this as a secondary aspect of the image. Thus, although relationality may not be inherent in the idol framework itself, we must allow a full understanding of the *imago Dei* to be informed by God's expressed intentions for his images and the narrative of his ongoing interactions with them.

A third possible objection comes from the Old Testament critique of idolatry. The biblical authors so consistently rejected any form of idolatry, that some have argued that they would never have viewed idolatry as an appropriate framework for understanding the human person.[46] As we saw with Ezekiel earlier, though, it is entirely possible to combine a strong polemic against idolatry with a clear affirmation that God manifests his presence through human persons as his images. Indeed, for Ezekiel at least, the latter was an important basis for the former.[47] The biblical critique of idolatry focused not on the question of whether humans could be images but on the specific problems associated with the worship of false gods or the idea that the physical media could be used to control or manipulate God's presence and power.

Conclusion

At the beginning of this chapter, I suggested that there is an implicit logic that should lead us to connect the Spirit and the *imago Dei*. If the *imago* is thoroughly christological, and if Jesus cannot be understood apart from the Spirit, then the *imago* should be thoroughly pneumatological. Nonetheless, we have seen that although theologians often connect the Spirit to the image, they frequently do so by presenting the Spirit as an eschatological addendum or a Trinitarian abstraction. Our two example theologians offered a more pneumatologically satisfying approach to the image, but they did so by relying on a relational view of the image that runs counter to the consensus among biblical scholars that such an approach is exegetically untenable.

Rather than relying on one of these approaches or drawing the unfortunate conclusion that maybe pneumatology has nothing to do with the meaning of the *imago* itself, I have argued that we need to understand the Bible's image language as functioning within the broader conceptual framework of idols and divine presence in the ancient

46. See especially the discussions in Richard J. Clifford, "The Function of Idol Passages in Second Isaiah," *Catholic Biblical Quarterly* 42 (1980): 450–64; and Edward M. Curtis, "The Theological Basis for the Prohibition of Images in the Old Testament," *Journal of the Evangelical Theological Society* 28 (1985): 277–87.

47. Some have also suggested that this polemical context is precisely why the biblical author chose relatively neutral terms like *ṣelem* and *dəmût* to describe the image, rather than terms more consistently used pejoratively to describe pagan idolatry. See Charles A. Kennedy, "The Semantic Field of the Term 'Idolatry,'" in *Uncovering Ancient Stones: Essays in Memory of H. Neil Richardson*, ed. Lewis M. Hopfe (Winona Lake, IN: Eisenbrauns, 1994), 193–204.

world. From this perspective, we can see that being made in the image of God suggests that human persons are the creaturely entities God has chosen as the vehicles into which he will pour his Holy Spirit and through which he will manifest his divine presence in the world. Obviously this does not mean that this is the *only* way that God manifests his presence in the world. The nature of divine presence is a complex topic that we cannot engage here, but the biblical narratives require us to say that God can be present in certain creaturely realities in a way that differs from God's presence in creation as a whole (for example, temple, incarnation, church). The image of God falls into this category. Human persons are a unique and powerful expression of God's own presence.[48] To put it simply, we are God's idols.

We have thus linked the Spirit to the *imago Dei* in such a way that pneumatology is essential to the very meaning of the image, part of the main course itself. Consequently, we have a robust framework for seeing how pneumatology is essential to the nature of humanity in general and to the person and work of Jesus Christ in particular. And we have done so in a way that seems to have ample exegetical support, while, at the same time, leaving room for many of the insights of other approaches to the *imago Dei*: particularly relational and functional interpretations.

48. See esp. Herring, *Divine Substitution.*

CHAPTER 16

Formed by the Spirit

A Third Article Theology of Christian Spirituality

JOSEPH MCGARRY

From a certain perspective, discussing Christian spirituality in a manner that thoroughly engages the fullness of both Christian history and theological methodology, and thereby presents a positive case for a specific method, is doomed from the outset. If we are not careful, either because of an overgeneralization in an attempt to interact with everyone, or because we erect convenient straw men to make the argument, the entire project collapses before it begins. Consequently, this essay will not interact at great length with specific traditions, but rather will begin with a critique of Western spiritual theologies, and then illumine the salutary aspects of a TAT methodology when considering Christian spirituality and formation in Christ.

We begin with a definition of terms, as the words "Christian spirituality" are fairly nebulous. In the introduction to *The Blackwell Companion to Christian Spirituality,* Arthur Holder notes that "any Christian understanding of that term [spirituality] must necessarily refer to the intimate loving relationship between God's Holy Spirit and the spirit (animating life force) of believers—a relationship that can be characterised both as kinship and communion."[1] Generally understood, Christian spirituality inquires after the significance of humanity's relationship with God, how that relationship is maintained, and how that relationship determines a shape of life (historically, progression into this shape has been understood in terms of Christlikeness, formation in Christ, or spiritual transformation). A theology of Christian spirituality thus identifies both formal and material aspects of the work of the Spirit in this relationship, and details how the Spirit's work results in Christian formation.[2] Formally, a theology of spirituality asks after the Spirit's work in relationship with humanity; materially, it looks at the specific means by which humanity lives in relationship with God through the Spirit. Even as the material content of Christian spiritualities—what it actually looks like to live in and from the Spirit—differs from tradition to tradition, this formal relationship between the Spirit and humanity holds across them. As Robert Davis Hughes puts it, "spirituality is simply about the Holy Spirit and her impact on the total lives of human beings."[3]

Hughes has a very helpful essay in *The Blackwell Companion to Christian Spirituality*, in which he provides an instructive critique of Western spirituality from an Eastern Orthodox position. His criticisms highlight significant issues with accounts of Christian spirituality, and thereby provide a helpful starting point for this essay's constructive proposals. Hughes notes particular problems within Western dogmatic accounts of Christian spirituality, and shows how theologians often neglect a proper appreciation of the work of the Spirit. He argues that Western theologies either emphasize the Father-Son relationship, or the Son specifically, and neglect the work of the Spirit in Christian life outright, or wrongly squeeze it alongside other theological loci. Furthermore, Western spiritualties tend to reduce the work of the Spirit to a depersonalized notion of grace.[4] As Hughes notes, such oversight results in "[a] kind of binitarianism: functions that Scripture and Eastern tradition ascribe to the Holy Spirit become appropriated to Christ (and in

1. Arthur Holder, "Introduction," in *The Blackwell Companion to Christian Spirituality*, ed. Arthur Holder (Oxford: Blackwell, 2005), 1.

2. Thus, in the Eastern tradition, there is an intricate relationship between spirituality and *theōsis*.

3. Robert Davis Hughes III, "The Holy Spirit in Christian Spirituality," in Holder, *Blackwell Companion to Christian Spirituality*, 207.

4. Ibid., 208–9.

later Protestantism, the human Jesus *per se*) or to grace used as an impersonal term, a kind of quasi-substance separate from the person and work of the Holy Spirit herself."[5]

It is helpful to appreciate the fullness of Hughes's words and the shortcomings he brings to light. Both the conflation of agencies, in which the Spirit cedes agency either to the Father or Jesus, and the objectification of grace are substantial problems.

This second aspect of Hughes's critique—the depersonalization and objectification of the Spirit's work as grace—is particularly important to grasp, as it permits us to see deeper into the issue.[6] Though unnamed, Hughes is clearly targeting traditions that emphasize moral progress—progress often dependent upon such grace—as a key element (if not the sole by-product) in Christian spirituality.[7] He concludes his criticism by saying, "Thus, these theologies became a discussion of Christian perfection or human spiritual development, not theologies of the Holy Spirit's impact on Christian lives."[8]

The problem of objectification generally presents itself within schemas that portray the moral transformation of Christians into a predetermined set of "Christ-based" virtues as a work of the Spirit. Western spirituality has often expressed this through the conceptual language of *habitus*, or through disciplines that presuppose it. On this register, a Christian spirituality begins with the experienced relationship between predetermined moral virtue that has been mapped onto the person of Christ (these moral qualities being the full definition of the term "Christlikeness," and thereby the end result of spirituality) and

5. Ibid., 209.

6. This type of objectification is perhaps most obvious in the popular work of Dallas Willard. Willard, an accomplished philosopher and Husserl scholar who extensively wrote on evangelical spirituality and spiritual transformation, likened the Spirit's grace to jet fuel saying, "If you would really like to be into consuming grace, just lead a holy life. The true saint burns grace like a 747 burns fuel on takeoff" (Dallas Willard, *The Great Omission: Reclaiming Jesus's Essential Teachings on Discipleship* [New York: HarperOne, 2006], 62).

7. See, for instance, John Calvin, *Institutes of the Christian Religion*, ed. John T. McNeill, trans. Ford Lewis Battles (Philadelphia: Westminster, 1960), 3.4; John Wesley, *A Plain Account of Christian Perfection, as Believed and Taught by the Rev. John Wesley, from 1725 to 1777* (New York: Lane & Scott, 1850), 49–60; and St. Thomas's use of *habitus* and moral virtue in the *Summa theologiae* I-II, q. 51, a. 62. Hughes himself places the initial blame at the feet of Augustine's doctrine of double predestination and use of "grace" in the anti-Pelagian texts ("Holy Spirit in Christian Spirituality," 208).

8. Hughes, "Holy Spirit in Christian Spirituality," 209.

habits that form them in people. The moral transformation is fully expressed in language at the level of being (for example, soul, nature, or essence), theologically located within sanctification, and is understood to have occurred through the grace of the Holy Spirit. This relationship between habit, being, and virtue can almost be assumed within Western spiritualities: habit forms the person, and habits that form people in accord with Christian virtue form Christians into Christlikeness. And, again, the Spirit's grace is the means by which this happens.

However, as Robert Davis Hughes has pointed out, such an approach is not without substantial issues, primarily because it lacks a necessary, formal, place for the personal work of the Spirit. When we spiritualize the human work of moral formation, and then indicate where we believe God must be alongside these efforts, the lines between human willpower and the transformative work of the Holy Spirit become blurred. Such a spirituality assigns the term "grace" to what is more appropriately understood as force of will. After all, Socrates, Plato, and Aristotle demonstrated that we can structure our lives around habits and disciplines that shape and transform our very being—even using the language of "soul"—into a certain shape of character without needing the Holy Spirit. More recently, cognitive neuroscience has illumined the redirection of neurons and the activity of neuroplasticity through the disciplines of mindfulness, attention, and repetition.[9] Thus one can identify a specific set of predefined character qualities toward which to intentionally redirect one's neurons, or (to use Aristotelian categories) establish a *hexis* through predetermined training regimine in virtue, and achieve this through a series of intentional behaviors.[10] And all of this can be done wholly apart from the necessary and required agency of God the Holy Spirit. That a spiritual theology might map the character qualities developed over a set of virtues identified with the character of Jesus, or drawn from the fruit of the Spirit in Galatians 5, is surely noble, but need not be anything more

9. See Curt Thompson, *Anatomy of the Soul: Surprising Connections between Neuroscience and Spiritual Practices That Can Transform Your Life and Relationships* (Carol Stream: Tyndale Momentum, 2010).

10. Michael Pakaluk defines Aristotle's use of *hexis* as "a stable trait, built up and established . . . through some kind of 'training'." See Michael Pakaluk, *Aristotle's Nicomachean Ethics: An Introduction*, (Cambridge: Cambridge University Press, 2005), 107–8. Pakaluk gives a fine overview of Aristotle's relationship between the soul, virtue, and *hexis* in 87–113.

than that. Humanity can grow in love, joy, peace, patience, kindness, goodness, faithfulness, gentleness, and self-control without the Holy Spirit. The Greek philosophers and modern psychology have shown how, and this is highly problematic for those types of spiritualities. When the quasi-personal force "grace" is so easily replaced by will, one is left wondering how necessary the Spirit truly is.

Fascinatingly, this tension is well known among those who think seriously about Christian spirituality and Christian formation, though—unfortunately—it is not viewed as a methodological problem, and therefore solutions perpetuate the core issues. Biola University's Center for Christian Thought focused on this issue during 2013–14, as the center's research engaged psychology and spiritual formation. The research fellows addressed, among other things, the key issue of understanding spiritual formation and the role of the Holy Spirit. The means by which a number of the researchers and clinicians spoke of spiritual formation was illuminating, because of both a complete lack of reference to the Holy Spirit, and its nonessential place in what they were describing as spiritual formation.[11] And this is by no means to criticize or reduce the importance of this work at the intersection of psychology and personal formation. Such research is absolutely crucial. Rather, it highlights the theological difficulties that arise when accounting for the phenomenon of personal change from within this type of methodology. The deeper issue regards how we understand the consequences of human willpower to be a participation in the ongoing and perpetual work of the Spirit. This seems to be the key question, and why the issue is one of methodology and systematic organization—not of practice.

Obviously Christians respond in faithfulness to the work of the Spirit, the fruit of the Spirit is genuinely the fruit of the Spirit's work in the body, and character formation is an essential element of faithful Christian life. Yet, as Hughes points out, our conceptual ordering is very important, and the types of muddied waters he criticizes highlight the significance of one's starting point; beginning with the practice of spiritual disciplines and then locating "grace" in them leads scholars

11. Curt Thompson's work is particularly emblematic of these types of issues. The Center for Christian Thought's website has a fine repository of easily accessible videos and papers of the research fellows and their various contributions to the project. See http://cct.biola.edu/resources/theme/psyc-spirit-formation/.

to form their questions incorrectly. Instead of asking, "Where is the Spirit in this process of character formation?" the better question is, "How is this human work in virtue cultivation part of the divine work of the Spirit?"

Consequently, this essay addresses the intersection of human faithfulness and the work of the Spirit within Christian spirituality. It will demonstrate that a careful consideration of Christian spirituality through a method that begins with the Spirit answers Hughes's concerns and provides a helpful way forward. Thus with these concerns in mind, we turn our attention to our constructive argument.

The Spirit's Work in the World

First, the formal aspect, and here we are best served by posing a deceptively complex question: What is the work of the Holy Spirit in creation, such that we understand faithful relationship with God as participating in it? Generally speaking, the bulk of emphasis on the Spirit's work in Christian spirituality has been on the discrete tasks of the Spirit, as testified in Scripture. The Holy Spirit convicts the world of sin, righteousness, and judgment (John 16:8); guides us into all truth (John 16:13); regenerates us (John 3:5–8; Titus 3:5); glorifies and testifies to Christ (John 15:26; 16:14); reveals Christ to us and in us (John 16:14–15); and so on. However, these activities are rarely put in relationship to a comprehensive appreciation of the Spirit's work. How are these discrete actions part of a larger whole? Put another way: What is the Spirit doing in the world, such that the things we see in the Scriptures are the means by which the Spirit accomplishes this larger task?

Dietrich Bonhoeffer's theology is particularly helpful here, as he intentionally differentiates between these categories while doing his work, and his theological priorities helpfully guide our thought. For Bonhoeffer, the Spirit is always at work actualizing reality in Christ, conforming history in accord with this reality, and thereby making Christ present in the world. God has achieved something genuinely real in the life, death, and resurrection of Jesus of Nazareth (the founding of the church and renewal of humanity), and the Spirit increasingly makes this reality actual in space and time.[12] This is, if you will,

12. Christopher Holmes, working in an intentionally Bonhoefferian mode, develops a helpful metaphor wherein Christ's resurrection establishes a "grain of the universe," structuring reality in a certain manner around himself such that humanity can live in conflict with it—against the grain—or in harmony with it. See Christopher R. J. Holmes,

the Spirit's formal task: it is the ongoing and perpetual work of the Holy Spirit to make reality in Christ present in history through the life of God's people. To explicate what he intends, Bonhoeffer deploys the conceptual differentiation between reality and actuality, thereby carving out appropriate space for the agency of both Christ and the Holy Spirit in God's work of redemption and renewal.

Bonhoeffer examines this exhaustively in his doctoral thesis, *Sanctorum Communio.* In that text, he theologically and sociologically demonstrates how and why the church is "Christ existing as church-community."[13] He describes the relationship between Christ and the Spirit by differentiating between the accomplished work of Christ and the way his completed work takes genuine form. The church is complete in reality in Christ, but it is still to be built within human history, and the Spirit accomplishes this.[14] Note the relationship between the accomplished work of Christ and the ongoing role of the Spirit in making this reality actual. Bonhoeffer writes:

> Christ is the foundation, the cornerstone, the pioneer, the master builder. But Christ is also at all times a real presence for the church, for it is Christ's body, and the people are members of this body (1 Cor. 12:2ff.; Rom. 12:4ff.; Eph. 1:23, 4:15f.; Col. 1:18), or members of Christ himself (1 Cor. 6:15; Rom. 6:13 and 19). . . . The actualisation is accomplished by the spirit of Christ and by the Holy Spirit. *What the former is for the church as a whole, the latter is for the individual. The Holy Spirit brings Christ to individuals (Rom. 8:14; Eph. 2:22) and establishes community among them (2 Cor. 13:13; Phil. 2.1).*[15]

Christ establishes the church in reality and gives himself to the community as a real presence, but these are actualized through the work of the Holy Spirit. The Spirit is the active force in the *everydayness* of life in the building of the church.[16] The Holy Spirit, and only the

---

Ethics in the Presence of Christ (London: T&T Clark, 2012), especially 81.

13. Dietrich Bonhoeffer, *Sanctorum Communio: A Theological Study of the Sociology of the Church*, ed. Clifford J. Green and Joachim von Soosten, trans. Reinhard Krauss and Nancy Lukens, Dietrich Bonhoeffer Works 1 (Minneapolis: Fortress, 2009), 121. Hereafter cited as DBWE 1.

14. Ibid., 153.

15. Ibid., 139 (emphasis mine).

16. Thus the future from which Christian possibility-to-be takes shape in any moment is called forth by the Spirit. See Dietrich Bonhoeffer, *Act and Being: Transcendental Philosophy and Ontology in Systematic Theology*, ed. Hans-Richard Reuter and Wayne Whitson Floyd Jr., trans. H. Martin

Holy Spirit, actualizes the church, con-forms creation to reality in Christ, and makes Christ genuinely present. This happens—in Bonhoeffer's language of "actualization"—through all the ways revealed in Scripture.

Establishing this allows us to address Hughes's material critique: How does faithful human relationship with the Holy Spirit actualize reality in history, and how is the church formed in Christ through it? How is the Spirit *necessary* for this formation? For Bonhoeffer, humanity is in relationship with Christ through the Spirit, and this necessarily leads to faithful discipleship, life appropriate to God's people. The Spirit brings intimacy with Christ in the hearts of Christians, and the certainty of this relationship leads to acts of visible obedience.[17] This extended quotation from the *Ethics* manuscript "Christ, Reality, and Good" (perhaps Bonhoeffer's most succinct treatment of this topic) reveals the formal aspects between Christ and the Spirit, and material aspects of its actualization via human participation. He writes:

> The place that in all other ethics is marked by the antithesis between ought and is, idea and realisation, motive and work, is occupied in Christian ethics by the relation between reality and becoming real, between past and present, between history and event (faith) or, to replace the many concepts with the simple name of the thing itself, *the relation between Jesus Christ and the Holy Spirit.* The question of the good becomes the question of participating in God's reality revealed in Christ.[18]

In faithfulness, humanity increasingly participates in Christ's reality, and, again, this participation is only possible through the Spirit.[19] This is why the ethical life of the church—life in harmony with reality in Christ—was so important for Bonhoeffer's thought, and why faithful behavior was an ever-present impulse in his writings. From Christian life *miteinander* and *füreinander* in *Sanctorum Communio*,[20] to authentic living from the future in *Act and Being*,[21] to growing in Christian character in

Rumscheidt, Dietrich Bonhoeffer Works 2 (Minneapolis: Fortress, 1996), 160. Hereafter cited as DBWE 2.

17. Dietrich Bonhoeffer, *Discipleship*, ed. Martin Kuske et al., trans. Barbara Green and Reinhard Krauss, Dietrich Bonhoeffer Works 4 (Minneapolis: Fortress, 2003), 210. Hereafter cited as DBWE 4.

18. Dietrich Bonhoeffer, *Ethics*, ed. Ilse Tödt et al., trans. Reinhard Krauss, Charles C. West, and Douglas W. Stott, Dietrich Bonhoeffer Works 6 (Minneapolis: Fortress, 2005), 49–50 (emphasis mine). Hereafter cited as DBWE 6.

19. Ibid., 64.

20. DBWE 1:178.

21. DBWE 2:157.

his lectures on theological anthropology,[22] to following in simple obedience in *Discipleship*,[23] to responsible vicarious action in the *Ethics* manuscripts,[24] and up until one of his last written works (his "Outline for a Book"),[25] Bonhoeffer is consistently asking after the shape of Christian life in faithful response to reality in Christ, because this is how the Spirit actualizes reality. Consequently, Bonhoeffer presents a very practical, nonpietistic spirituality, summed up as the church's faithful witness of Jesus Christ to the world. And, indeed, it is through the church's faithful life that the Spirit makes Christ present.

Formation in Christ in Bonhoeffer's Theology

Like all theologies of Christian spirituality, Bonhoeffer too understands Christian formation to be the product of Christian living. However, his is a very unique perspective because he understands formation in Christ as something beyond moral formation. Over and against a program of virtue cultivation or pious living, Bonhoeffer is singularly concerned about how Christ takes form among a community of faith; and though moral formation is a necessary aspect of Christian life, being formed into the image of Christ is something different altogether.[26] For Bonhoeffer, formation in Christ always and only means Christ taking form in the world through the church.[27] Furthermore, when Bonhoeffer does speak of formation, it is always as a by-product of the church's faithfulness to Christ. This is also why he begins the *Ethics* manuscript "Guilt, Justification, and Renewal" by stating, "The issue is the *process by which* Christ takes form among us."[28] Both *Discipleship* and the *Ethics* manuscripts are devoted to a certain form of Christian behavior (simple

22. Dietrich Bonhoeffer, *Berlin: 1932–1933*, ed. Carsten Nicolaisen, Ernst-Albert Scharffenorth, and Larry L. Rasmussen, trans. Isabel Best, David Higgins, and Douglas W. Stott, Dietrich Bonhoeffer Works 12 (Minneapolis: Fortress, 2009), 231. Hereafter cited as DBWE 12.

23. DBWE 4:57.

24. DBWE 6:219.

25. Dietrich Bonhoeffer, *Letters and Papers from Prison*, ed. Christian Gremmels et al., trans. Isabel Best et al., Dietrich Bonhoeffer Works 8 (Minneapolis: Fortress, 2010), 499.

26. For Bonhoeffer's emphasis on moral formation, see DBWE 12:230–32. Additionally, in *Discipleship*, Bonhoeffer links the fruit of sanctification with moral qualities, arguing that those who have encountered God's costly grace live lives worthy of that gospel—specifically understood in moral terms. See DBWE 4:268–69, and references to living a life worthy of the gospel (passim).

27. See DBWE 4:281; 6:76; 12:315.

28. DBWE 6:134 (emphasis mine).

obedience, responsible vicarious action), and in both texts Bonhoeffer dedicates space to formation as a consequential effect of the church's life.

He first treats the topic at length in *Discipleship*.[29] There, he builds upon a notion he briefly mentions in his Christology lectures, namely, that the form of Christ exists as church-community.[30] *Discipleship* develops how the Spirit conforms the disciples into the image of Christ through simple obedience, and Bonhoeffer describes an inverse relation between the purpose of discipleship and its effects.[31] Formation in Christ is developed along a strict asymmetry: disciples only follow. The Spirit alone makes Christ present. As he says, "Through the Holy Spirit, the crucified and risen Christ exists as the church-community [*Gemeinde*], as the 'new human being'."[32]

In the *Ethics* manuscript "Ethics as Formation," he again addresses formation as a consequence of faithfulness, and there highlights that Christ takes form as a by-product of the ethical life of the church.[33] There he writes, "Formation means, therefore, in the first place Jesus Christ taking form in Christ's church."[34] His point—in harmony with his thoughts in *Discipleship*—is that while the saints strive after a certain mode of being, the Spirit increasingly makes Christ present in the world. Bonhoeffer concludes the manuscript: "Ethics as formation is possible only on the basis of the form of Jesus Christ present in Christ's church. The church is the place where Jesus Christ's taking form is proclaimed and where it happens. *The Christian ethic stands in the service of this proclamation and this event*."[35]

Contra spiritualities that emphasize moral formation, Bonhoeffer's formation is not about Christ being formed *in me*, so much as it is Christ taking form *among us*. The church exists in a certain way—actualizing reality in Christ through her faithful life here and now—and, very importantly, Christ is truly present through this. Thus, having established the Spirit's formal work of conforming creation to Christ, the material way

29. DBWE 4:281–88.

30. DBWE 12:323.

31. See DBWE 4:209–10 for how the Spirit enables obedience to Christ, and DBWE 4:281–88 for how the Spirit con-forms disciples into the image of Christ.

32. Ibid., 220.

33. DBWE 6:102.

34. Ibid., 96.

35. Ibid., 102 (emphasis mine).

this occurs (through faithful ethical life), and how—through this mode of being—the form of Christ takes form through the Spirit, we can now look specifically at the content of the form of Christ.

The People of God as the Image of Christ

How does one speak of the *telos* of Christian formation, that into which Christ's disciples are formed? The biblical language and metaphors most associated with spiritual formation are those of transformation into—as well as the imitation of—Christ (for example, being clothed in Christ [Rom. 13:14; Gal. 3:27], having the mind of Christ [1 Cor. 2:16], and having Christ being formed in us [Gal. 4:19], as well as allusions to being imitators of or following Christ [1 Cor. 11:1; 1 John 2:6; 1 Pet. 2:21). However, it is crucial to acknowledge that the content of these metaphors—what it means to be an imitator of Christ, clothed in Christ, or to have Christ formed in us—is very much a matter of interpretation.

This *something* that the Spirit is forming us into—this notion of Christlikeness—is actually a very interesting issue, precisely because there are no passages that state "Christlikeness is . . ." or conclusively provide an exhaustive account of what formation in Christ means. The content of these metaphors is strikingly open to discussion. This seems to raise a very provocative line of questions regarding why we conceptualize spiritual transformation as we do. When we permit both Hughes and Bonhoeffer the full force of their arguments—Hughes regarding the dogmatic account of the Spirit and the dangers of a quasi-personal use of grace, and Bonhoeffer regarding the Spirit's work of making Christ present in the world through the faithful life of the church—a new path opens, one also at the point of contact with recent biblical scholarship.

Bonhoeffer's theological impulses show significant promise when placed alongside recent research on the Hebrew Bible and the cultic use of images in the ancient Near East (ANE). In his work, *Divine Substitution: Humanity as the Manifestation of Deity in the Hebrew Bible and the Ancient Near East*, Stephen Herring gives a detailed study that investigates a variety of ways that images functioned in Mesopotamian religious and cultic practice, and persuasively argues that divine images connoted divine presence. Ultimately, he illumines that the ANE use of images most closely parallels Catholic and Eastern Orthodox conceptualizations of transubstantiation within the Eucharist. In both contexts, he writes, "The divide between what is 'real' and what is 'representation' is not at all apparent."[36] Citing Thorkild Jacobsen, Herring notes that the Mesopotamian statue "mythically become[s] what it represents, the god, without, however, in any way limiting the god, who remains transcendent . . . the statue ceases to be mere earthly wood, precious metal and stones, ceases to be the work of human hands. It becomes transubstantiated, a divine being, the god it represents."[37]

In context, the term "image of god" was used to refer to the vehicle by which a deity's "real" presence could be made manifest in the world, whether a statue, idol, or whatever. That the scriptural authors knew of this conceptualization can be most clearly seen in the polemical rhetoric against such "living" statues (see, for example, Isaiah 44).

Yet, the divine presence experienced in this manner was not always condemned, and passages in the Hebrew Bible portray the idea that a material object could manifest the divine presence in positive terms (Gen. 1:26; Exod. 34:29–34). Within the ANE, it is a genuinely unique development that the Hebrew Bible, using cultic-image analogies, asserts that human beings—not statues or idols—are the material object by which the divine is present on earth. Andreas Schüle notes, "According the priestly telling of creation in Gen 1, 1–2, 4a, it is not lifeless matter, not a man-made statue, but *humans as living beings* that are envisioned to be indeed the true image of God."[38] In the Hebrew Bible, humanity is the image (transubstantiated presence) of God, not a statue.

Specifically, in Ezekiel 36–37 we see a fascinating parallel to the *mīs pî* (mouth-washing) and *pīt pî* (mouth-opening) rituals. Assyrian and Babylonian cults used these rituals in order to consecrate and "re-create" the statue as a god. Herring writes, "These statues, having gone through the purification, charging (*mīs pî*), and activating (*pīt pî*) ritual(s), were then effectively considered to be

36. Stephen Herring, *Divine Substitution: Humanity as the Manifestation of Deity in the Hebrew Bible and the Ancient Near East* (Göttingen: Vandenhoeck & Ruprecht, 2013), 94.

37. Thorkild Jacobsen, "The Graven Image," in *Ancient Israelite Religion: Essays in Honor of Frank Moore Cross*, ed. P. D. Miller Jr. et al. (Philadelphia: Fortress, 1987), 15–32, cited in Herring, *Divine Substitution*, 94–95.

38. Andreas Schüle, "Made in the 'Image of God': The Concepts of Divine Images in Gen 1–3," *Zeitschrift für die alttestamentliche Wissenschaft* 117 (2005): 2 (emphasis mine).

the god."[39] He draws our attention to Ezekiel 37:1–14, and notes how "the scattered bones of idolatrous Israel are repaired and provided with YHWH's own spirit in order to bring them back to life."[40] And, indeed, it is the giving of YHWH's divine spirit that transforms Israel into an obedient people. Importantly—loudly echoing the *mīs pî* and *pīt pî* rituals—Israel has been "purified, repaired, and consecrated as YHWH's divine images before being sent back to their own land."[41] The people of God, having been restored and consecrated by the Spirit of God, have become the presence of God.

This conceptualization is explicitly expanded upon by the New Testament authors, and understanding divine presence in terms of the "image" metaphor is very instructive for explaining the divine Jesus in the New Testament, specifically as the presence of God on earth (for example, Col. 1:15; cf. 2 Cor. 4:4; Heb. 1:3). Furthermore, the metaphor continues to characterize Christians as the "image" of Jesus (for example, Rom 8:29; cf. 1 Cor. 15:49; Col. 3:10), who are indwelled by the divine presence (1 Cor. 6:19). The New Testament authors make explicit what the Hebrew Bible authors first described: as beings created in the divine image, the people of God are God's genuine and actual presence on earth.

Conclusion

This essay began with a broad critique of Western spiritualities and demonstrated that significant issues within theologies of spirituality are truly issues of theological method; when theologians do not begin with the work of the Spirit, they tread into a formidable theological minefield. However, this need not be the case, and Dietrich Bonhoeffer and Stephen Herring have shown a way forward, one that begins with the work of the Spirit. Perhaps Western theologians working in Christian spirituality would be best served by understanding that formation in Christ is the process by which the Holy Spirit makes Christ truly present on earth (conforming the church to Christ's image) while she lives her faithful life of obedient discipleship. This would comport with the biblical evidence, as well as satisfy Hughes's theological critique. It would, in fact, be a very fruitful and provocative line of investigation. To revisit our original concerns: the formal aspects regarding

39. Herring, *Divine Substitution*, 27.
40. Ibid., 208.
41. Ibid.

locating the Spirit's work and maintaining appropriate agency is safeguarded. Humanity retains meaningful—necessary—work in partnership with the Spirit. Crucial aspects of human growth (for example, virtue formation and responsible action for others) remain in place. And yet, precisely because these are not transformation itself, but rather the means by which the Spirit makes Christ present, the necessity of the Spirit in this formation is also safeguarded. Furthermore, this organization provides a clear path to engage important advances in the disciplines of neuropsychology and philosophy without reducing the significance of the Spirit in Christian spirituality. Humanity can embrace the fullness of the human condition without encroaching upon the work of the Spirit. Surely such a significant reconfiguration will require additional development; however, by highlighting the centrality of theological method in addressing the issue, we avoid perpetuating past mistakes. By beginning with the work of the Spirit, then moving to the church's meaningful participation, and then illustrating how the product of formation—the genuine presence of Christ—is something absolutely impossible for humanity to achieve through force of will, we encounter fewer theological issues and have a more biblically faithful theology of spirituality.

CHAPTER 17

Sculpting Christ in Us

Public Faces of the Spirit in God's World

LEOPOLDO A. SÁNCHEZ M.

What does life in the Spirit look like? In *The Spirit of Life*, Jürgen Moltmann proposes the "formative" metaphor of *Gestalt* to speak of the "configurations of life" the Spirit impresses upon Christ's disciples in the world.[1] Moltmann suggests that without "Christ's taking form in us" (Dietrich Bonhoeffer's expression), the "energies" of the Spirit and the "spaces" of the Spirit's activity in our lives would become self-enclosed and resistant to the fullness of the experiences of God's life with and for others.[2] A *Gestalt* has the boundaries of its shape, which make it concrete and identifiable. Having such specificity is not an end in itself, but a means to a personal relation with God and neighbor.

Moltmann's formative metaphor, as well as his holistic pneumatology in general, attempts to move the discourse on the Spirit away from the self-enclosed piety of the individual soul and toward the whole person's embracing of life. It is a pneumatology with a material and social trajectory. While

1. Jürgen Moltmann, *The Spirit of Life: A Universal Affirmation*, trans. Margaret Kohl (Minneapolis: Fortress, 1992), 277.

2. Ibid., 278.

the term "spirit" often conveys the image of some airy or ethereal reality, Yves Congar reminds us that the biblical narratives—particularly in the Old Testament—portray the Spirit more in terms of "subtle corporeality" than "immateriality."[3] The contemporary move toward a pneumatology of embodiment begs the question of the Spirit's public face(s) in creation. Like a sculptor, the creator Spirit chisels people to become certain kinds of persons, giving them a public profile in church and world. If life in the Spirit does make a difference in us and in everyday life, what then are the configurations of such a life? And what is the biblical or theological basis for speaking of the Spirit's formative action in us?

Searching for the Face of the Spirit

An important contribution to the question comes from the twentieth-century revival of Spirit Christology, which asks what the presence and activity of the Spirit in the mystery of the incarnation mean for theology and life.[4] By seeing the Spirit not only *before* and *after* Jesus, but also *in* Jesus, a Spirit Christology embraces the fleshly existence of the Son as the privileged locus of the Spirit and thus avoids a flight of the Spirit away from created, incarnate, and embodied life. The Spirit is "self-effacing" and "faceless" as such, but due to "its close association with the incarnate Word," the Spirit takes form in Christ and then takes the form of Christ in his saints.[5] Jesus becomes the public face of the Spirit par excellence, the definitive receiver and bearer of the Spirit in God's world. And this means that the Holy Spirit is not afraid to "get his hands dirty," so to speak, embracing human and material means to sanctify God's creation.

Jesus, the receiver and bearer of the Spirit, also gives, pours out, or breathes his Spirit upon others whose lives are shaped after his. The Spirit is passed on from Jesus to others. The Spirit is handed over to the saints with Jesus' imprint or image on it so that they may be like Jesus for the sake of the world. We can speak of the faces of the Spirit of Jesus in us.

3. Yves Congar, *I Believe in the Holy Spirit*, trans. David Smith (New York: Seabury, 1983; repr., New York: Crossroad, 1997), 1:3.

4. Leopoldo A. Sánchez M., *Receiver, Bearer, and Giver of God's Spirit: Jesus' Life in the Spirit as a Lens for Theology and Life* (Eugene, OR: Pickwick, 2015).

5. Ibid., xiii.

Tracing the Spirit's movement from Christ to us reveals a life pattern. For Moltmann, such a christological pattern suggests our being "'conformed' to his messianic life and his healing, radiating, and loving way of living . . . to his path of suffering in our conflicts with the powers of destruction," and to his bodily resurrection.[6]

A Spirit Christology suggests that to know what life in the Spirit looks like for us in God's world, we must first look to Jesus' own life in the Spirit. This essay explores such a thesis, testing the productivity of a Spirit Christology for reflection on four descriptive models of life in the Spirit. Our proposal argues for the centrifugal or social orientation of each model, suggesting ways in which each one fosters a certain kind of public life that addresses particular issues and needs in a broken and hurting world.

On Imitation and Conformation: Sharing in the Spirit-Formed Life of Christ

A significant question in the field of Spirit Christology is the degree of continuity and discontinuity between the indwelling of the Spirit in Christ and us. When the uniqueness of the Son's divine preexistence and the unrepeatable character of his incarnation become the central issues over against the historic problem of adoptionism, Logos (or two-natures) Christology preserves the radical discontinuity between Christ and us. It does so by highlighting the Son's being of "one substance" (*homoousios*) with the Father against Arianism and the unity of the "person" (*hypostasis*) of Christ against Nestorianism. The councils' teachings are directed against an adoptive view of Jesus' Sonship that portrays him as either a mere deified man (Arius) or a man assumed by the Logos (Nestorius).

Arian Christology sees the Spirit's descent upon the created Son at the Jordan as an instance of his obedience on the way to becoming godlike. Nestorian Christology could accommodate the logical idea that the Logos assumed a Spirit-indwelt temple worthy of union with God. The ontological subordination of the Son to the immutable God in Arian Christology and the logical disjunction between the assumed man (temple) Jesus and the immutable Logos in Nestorian Christology moves the councils to stress the radical discontinuity between Christ and the saints. The Son alone is God. Not us. Jesus

6. Moltmann, *Spirit of Life*, 278.

is not a man indwelt by the Logos, but the divine Logos who acts through his own flesh. What to do with the Spirit in this already complex christological matrix?

Parallel to the development of Logos Christology, there are nonadoptionist attempts in the history of dogma to highlight how the adopted "sons" (male and female) are like the incarnate Son, what Christ shares in common with the saints. Hilary of Poitiers, who is staunchly anti-Arian, brings a Spirit-oriented dynamic into his Christology. He uses the language of Psalm 2:7 ("Today I have begotten you") to speak of the Son's four "births" for us—that is, from God in his divinity, from Mary as man, at the Jordan for mission, and at his resurrection as the firstborn among many brethren—so that we might be reborn in his glorified humanity.[7] Hilary makes room for the notion of our human sharing in the Son's exalted humanity, which the Western theologian grounds in the Son's human growth in sanctification by the action of the "Spirit" (*spiritus*) in him.[8] There is no question regarding the Son's divinity or *homoousios* with God the Father. The theologian's view of the Son's growth or perfection concerns his human economy or dispensation in God's plan of salvation for us, not his divinity. It is a matter of soteriology, not ontology.

In this early Spirit Christology, Hilary does no more than echo Athanasius's earlier argument in the East against the Arians, namely, that Jesus is not a mere man deified by God on account of his works, but rather God become flesh in order to deify the flesh. The Holy Spirit also comes into this picture of salvation. For Athanasius, the incarnate Son anointed himself with his Spirit—a reality revealed at his baptism—so that he might in turn give the deifying Spirit to others in baptism.[9] This theology of deification in the early development of christological dogma depends in turn on Irenaeus's earlier argument against the gnostics that the Son took on the flesh of Adam at his incarnation (union) and was anointed at the Jordan with the Holy Spirit lost by Adam in order to restore the race of Adam to the image and likeness of God.[10]

7. Luis F. Ladaria, *La cristología de Hilario de Poitiers*, Analecta Gregoriana 225 (Rome: Università Gregoriana, 1989). Biblical references are to the ESV.

8. For Hilary's pneumatology, see Luis F. Ladaria, "El Espíritu Santo en San Hilario de Poitiers," in *Credo in Spiritum Sanctum*, vol. 1 (Vatican City: Libreria Editrice Vaticana), 243–53.

9. Sánchez, *Receiver, Bearer, and Giver*, 21–27.

10. Ibid., 12–20.

The medieval piety of the "imitation of Christ" (*imitatio Christi*)—so popularized by Thomas à Kempis's book by the same name—stressed the continuity between Christ and his saints even if the focus laid on the individual soul's imitation of Jesus through flight from worldly distractions. Franciscan spirituality included a social trajectory, which fostered an external embodiment of the humility, poverty, and silence of the infant Jesus, the crucified Christ, and the Christ in the sacrament (Eucharist) respectively, for the sake of preaching and teaching the words of Scripture.[11] Thomas Aquinas's theology of prayer did not only speak of Christ as one whose prayer to the Father revealed to others his divine Sonship (a concern in a Logos Christology), but also portrayed Christ as our Spirit-led example and teacher of prayer.[12] While the Holy Spirit was not always mentioned, the scholastic theology of "habitual grace" (*gratia habitualis*), which for Thomas spoke of the "special holiness" of Christ as a man, necessitated an implicit pneumatology.[13] Medieval monastic piety claimed to live in the Spirit of Christ, internalizing or externalizing aspects of Christ's life—his fight against temptation, his poverty and preaching, and prayer.

The teaching on Christ's "threefold office" (*munus triplex*) linked the Old Testament offices or titles of prophet, priest, and king to their New Testament fulfillment in Christ. In medieval times, Franciscan John of La Rochelle's view of the Synoptic Gospels as portrayals of Christ's kingly power (Matthew), doctoral wisdom as teacher (Mark), and priestly role as our sacrifice (Luke) served not only as a reflection on the excellencies of Christ's humanity but also as an exhortation to imitate them.[14] In a similar vein, patristic scholar Raniero Cantalamessa shows how a Spirit Christology focused on the anointing of Jesus at the Jordan speaks to the church's present-day participation in Christ's threefold anointing with the Spirit.[15] Through her

11. Eric Doyle, OFM, and Damian McElrath, "St. Francis of Assisi and the Christocentric Character of Franciscan Life and Doctrine," in *Franciscan Christology: Selected Texts, Translations and Introductory Essays*, ed. Damian McElrath, Franciscan Sources 1 (St. Bonaventure, NY: Franciscan Institute Publications, 1980), 1–13.

12. Sánchez, *Receiver, Bearer, and Giver*, 200–208.

13. Thomas Aquinas, *Summa theologiae* III, q. 6, a. 6.

14. Girard J. Etzkorn, "John of La Rochelle's View of Christ as King, Teacher and Priest," and John of La Rochelle, "Introduction to the Four Gospels," in McElrath, *Franciscan Christology*, 40–58.

15. Raniero Cantalamessa, *The Holy Spirit in the Life of Jesus: The Mystery of Christ's Baptism*, trans.

anointing in baptism, the church shares in Christ's mission to drive out demons (kingly anointing), proclaim the good news (prophetic anointing), and pray (priestly anointing).

Luther's reaction against a certain late medieval scholastic version of *imitatio Christi*, which posited a natural or supernatural affinity between the human spirit and the Holy Spirit, was met with an emphasis on the Spirit's monergistic work of "conforming" (*conformitas*) the sinner to Christ's death and resurrection.[16] Luther's appropriation of Bernard of Clairvaux's final dying words, and the monk's thoughts on the wounds of Christ, illustrate the Reformer's shift away from *imitatio* to *conformitas* piety. Bernard's words "perdite vixi" (that is, "I have lived a sinful life") were interpreted as an example of faith, that is, "as the prime example of ultimate repentance and self-accusation in one's dying hour . . . the renunciation of human righteousness and final reliance on Christ by faith alone."[17] While late medieval piety on Christ's wounds at times focused on human cooperation with God in salvation by emulating Christ's suffering, Luther "emphasizes that it is the work of God which the believer should discern in this suffering."[18] One sees in Luther's thought the stress on the cruciform shape of the Christian life, and thus the continuity between the cross of Christ and the life of daily repentance characterized by the Spirit's work of crucifying the sinner in order to raise him or her to new life.

Toward a *Genus Habitualis* or *Pneumatikon*: Making Room for the Spirit in the Incarnation

Contemporary Spirit Christologies differ in their views of Spirit and Christ. Since post-Trinitarian approaches see "Spirit" not as a divine person per se but as one biblical symbol—among others like Logos (Word) and Wisdom—of the general presence and activity of God in the man Jesus, its proponents argue for a revisionist approach to the divinity of Christ and the Trinitarian theology of the councils.[19] The Son is said to be divine,

Alan Neame (Collegeville, MN: Liturgical Press, 1994).

16. Regin Prenter, *Spiritus Creator: Luther's Concept of the Holy Spirit*, trans. John M. Jensen (Philadelphia: Muhlenberg, 1953).

17. Theo M. M. A. C. Bell, "Luther's Reception of Bernard of Clairvaux," *Concordia Theological Quarterly* 59 (1995): 256–57.

18. Ibid., 262.

19. Roger Haight, "The Case for Spirit Christology," *Theological Studies* 53 (1992): 257, 267–68.

not in the substantial sense that he is God of God, but in the sense that he acts "divinely" or according to the power of God who dwells in him.[20] Such power is God himself in action, but not the Spirit as a personal agent in its own right. A reason for revisiting classic Logos-oriented Christology lies in the desire to see Christ more fully in terms of his humanity and thus allow for human participation in the divine life. To do so, the post-Trinitarian framework posits a difference of degree, instead of nature or kind, between Jesus and other humans. Jesus becomes the greatest instance of human openness to God's influence or grace, and our example of free human potential for fellowship with God.[21]

In contrast to the post-Trinitarian route, our thesis adopts those Spirit Christologies in a Trinitarian key that seek to complement—rather than replace—a Logos Christology with a strong pneumatological trajectory. A Trinitarian Spirit Christology distinguishes the Logos's assumption of a human nature from the Holy Spirit's indwelling of the assumed humanity.[22] A Logos Christology sees the Son as the *unigenitus*, the "only begotten" Son of God, in distinction from the adopted sons; a Spirit Christology focuses on the Son's identity as the *primogenitus* or "firstborn" among many brethren, the one who goes ahead of us through his baptism and resurrection into the eschatological realm of the life-giving Spirit, as the firstfruits of our future bodily resurrection.[23] Human participation in the Spirit-indwelt humanity of the Son does not contest his personal identity as Logos.

Notwithstanding the various ways theologians speak about the "grace" of adoption by which humans share in the Spirit-indwelt humanity of the Son, Spirit Christologies in a Trinitarian key offer a promising way to link the church's life in the Spirit to Christ's own human life and history.[24] Yet the *how* of the complementarity of Logos and Spirit Christologies remains, and I have offered an ecumenical proposal that has the potential of bringing together the strengths of Eastern-Alexandrian and Western-scholastic

20. Geoffrey W. H. Lampe, "The Holy Spirit and the Person of Christ," in *Christ, Faith and History*, ed. S. W. Sykes and J. P. Clayton (London: Cambridge, 1972), 123–24.

21. Ibid., 126.

22. Sánchez, *Receiver, Bearer, and Giver*, 94–101.

23. Congar, *I Believe in the Holy Spirit*, 3:165–73.

24. For a critical engagement with anthropologies in liberal and conservative Spirit Christologies, see Sánchez, *Receiver, Bearer, and Giver*, 186–94.

accents.[25] Eastern-Alexandrian theology highlights the Logos's communication of divine majesty to his assumed humanity—what the Lutheran dogmaticians call the *genus maestaticum*.[26] But this "genus of the majesty" does not yet deal with the Holy Spirit's communication of itself to the humanity of the Logos.

The Eastern-Alexandrian focus on the Logos as the subject of his own actions, while helpful in addressing Nestorianism, makes it difficult for the Spirit to have an active role in the Logos's humanity. There is a tendency in the Alexandrian school to speak of the Spirit as one who reveals the Son's divinity or glory to others through his human life, but not as the Spirit who dwells in, works through, or fashions the Son in his life and mission. As Boris Bobrinskoy puts it in his description of the Alexandrian influence on Gregory of Nazianzus's pneumatic Christology, the Spirit is "present but not acting" in the Word made flesh.[27] The revelatory character of the Spirit's presence in the mission of Jesus *for others* takes precedence over the Spirit's constitutive role in the life of Jesus *himself*.

A look at the Western christological tradition may open another venue for locating the Spirit's activity in the Logos's humanity. A key to unlock the West's potential lies in the scholastic notion of habitual grace which, as we saw earlier, refers to Christ's special holiness. While the holiness of the assumed humanity may be ascribed to its union to the person of the Logos, it can also be ascribed to the Holy Spirit's sanctification of the same. For instance, the Lutheran dogmatician Martin Chemnitz uses the scholastic category of habitual or "supernatural gifts" (*hyperphysica*)—or "created and finite gifts" (*gratuita dona et finita*)—to refer to passages that speak of the Holy Spirit in (or the holiness of) the humanity of Christ (for example,

25. Ibid., 167–80.

26. The *genus maiestaticum* is a "kind" (*genus*) of statement about the communion of divine and human attributes in the person of Christ, according to which the divine nature, "majesty" (*maiestas*), and power of the Logos are passed on, communicated to, or revealed (displayed) through his assumed human nature; for an illustrative example of various "kinds" (*genera*) of the "communication of attributes" (*communicatio idiomatum*), see Martin Chemnitz, *The Two Natures in Christ*, trans. J. A. O. Preus (St. Louis: Concordia, 1971), 157–69.

27. Bobrinskoy has argued that Basil and John Chrysostom, who represent salutary aspects of the Syrian and Antiochene traditions respectively, speak more openly of the Holy Spirit's active role in the humanity of Christ. See Boris Bobrinskoy, "The Indwelling of the Spirit in Christ: 'Pneumatic Christology' in the Cappadocian Fathers," *St. Vladimir's Theological Quarterly* 28 (1984): 59–65.

Luke 1:35; 2:52; Isa. 11:1–2; 61:1; Ps. 45:7; Heb. 2:17).[28] Chemnitz argues that such holiness "formed and perfected" the assumed humanity "so that it can be an instrument . . . suitable for, and properly disposed for" the divine Logos to perform his saving works.[29] The pneumatological element or trajectory of the Logos's human history is laid out if not fully developed, leaving room for what I have called a *genus habitualis* or *genus pneumatikon* in Christology.[30] Such a *genus* or kind of statement about the incarnation offers a way to account fully for the Spirit's place in the sanctification of the Logos's humanity for the sake of our salvation.

One of the advantages of positing a *genus pneumatikon* is its ability to ground Christ's giving of the Spirit to humanity in his prior receiving and bearing of the same Spirit in his humanity. For how can Christ give to the flesh what he does not have in his own flesh? The incarnate Logos, upon whom the Spirit descends and remains, baptizes others with the same Spirit (John 1:33; see also Luke 3:16). Various stories of the Spirit in Christ and in us reveal Christlike configurations of the Spirit in God's world.

28. Chemnitz, *Two Natures in Christ*, 247–55 (see also 52, 56–57); for my development of Chemnitz's ideas, see Sánchez, *Receiver, Bearer, and Giver*, 170–76.

29. Chemnitz, *Two Natures in Christ*, 248. Chemnitz asserts that "these infused gifts are not actually the essential attributes of the divine nature [of the Logos]. Rather, they are His workings outside the divine nature which are infused into the human nature of Christ in such a way that they inhere in it, as they say in the schools, formally, habitually, and subjectively, by which the very humanity of Christ in itself and according to itself is formed and perfected, so that it can be an instrument characteristic of, suitable for, and properly disposed for the deity, through which and in communion with and in cooperation with which the divine power of the Logos can exercise and carry out the workings of His divine majesty."

30. The *genus* "of habitual grace" (*habitualis*), or *genus* "of the Spirit" (*pneumatikon*), refers to a "kind" (*genus*) of statement about the incarnation "that focuses on the supernatural presence and activity of the Holy Spirit in, with, and through the human life and history of the Logos. . . . The *genus* highlights the incarnate Logos's work of salvation through his Spirit-indwelt humanity" (Sánchez, *Receiver, Bearer, and Giver*, 244); for my initial proposal of the *genus pneumatikon*, see Leopoldo A. Sánchez M., "Pneumatology: Key to Understanding the Trinity," in *Who Is God? In the Light of the Lutheran Confessions*, ed. John A. Maxfield (St. Louis: Luther Academy, 2012), 137–39.

Public Faces of the Spirit in the World: Centrifugal Models of Life in the Spirit

The identity of the incarnate Son as the receiver, bearer, and giver of God's Spirit yields a number of potential trajectories for exploring the Spirit's sculpting work in our lives. We will focus on the area of sanctification, laying out four models of life in the Spirit. In *Teología de la santificación*, I painted images of life in the Spirit that were grounded in various aspects of Christ's life.[31] I offered baptismal, dramatic, and eucharistic models of sanctification, drawing especially from sources in the Lutheran tradition.[32]

In my initial descriptions of these models, I saw the eucharistic one, which describes life in the Spirit as a sacrifice of thanksgiving to God in service to others, as the only one with a centrifugal or public orientation. The baptismal model, which deals with dying to sin and living anew, and the dramatic one, which portrays life in terms of spiritual warfare, were seen as dealing with more introspective or centripetal issues such as individual guilt (baptismal) and vulnerability to temptation (dramatic). After further reflection, however, one can see how all of these models have centrifugal trajectories and social implications for life in God's world. In what follows, I build upon and expand my work in this social direction. I also introduce a fourth configuration, which I am calling the hospitality model. Our four models describe how the Spirit marks Jesus himself, and through Jesus, marks and shapes us. These are stories of death and resurrection, vigilance and resistance, sacrifice and service, and marginality and welcome.

The Face of Renewal: Death and Resurrection

A venerable patristic tradition sees the anointing of Jesus at his baptism as a prelude to his death on the cross, and the basis in God's plan of salvation for our participation in his death and resurrection through baptismal renewal. The theme of the purification of the waters is of particular significance. Ignatius of Antioch confesses Jesus Christ as one "who was born and baptized, that by His passion He might purify the water."[33] Through his baptism unto

31. Leopoldo A. Sánchez M., *Teología de la santificación: La espiritualidad del cristiano* (St. Louis: Editorial Concordia, 2013).

32. Ibid., 75–147; for a shorter presentation, see Sánchez, *Receiver, Bearer, and Giver*, 219–37.

33. Ignatius, *Letter to the Ephesians* 18 (*ANF* 1:57).

death, Jesus makes our baptism a water of cleansing. Gregory of Nazianzus speaks of the purification of the waters by Jesus at the Jordan as a saving mystery that occurs "for my Purification, or rather, sanctifying the waters by His purification" in order to bring about "my perfection and return to the first condition of Adam."[34]

By descending into the waters of the Jordan on behalf of the sinful race of Adam, Jesus becomes the new Adam who sanctifies the waters of our baptism so that he might make us a new creation, perfecting in us the image of Adam lost in the fall. Gregory assumes Irenaeus's theology of recapitulation, in which the Son does over again the failed history of sinful Adam by taking upon himself Adam's nature. The Spirit departed from the race of Adam after the first creation, but by descending upon the incarnate Son at the Jordan, the Spirit becomes "accustomed in fellowship with Him to dwell in the human race . . . working the will of the Father in them, and renewing them from their old habits into the newness of Christ."[35] Through his incarnation and anointing, Christ, the new Adam, makes possible the return of the Spirit to the human race.

The vicarious character of the Jordan flows from its inseparable link to the mystery of the incarnation and the cross. For Cyril of Jerusalem, Christ sanctifies the waters of the Jordan with his divinity, and together with the Holy Spirit, who is God and rests on him, makes the baptized sharers in the Spirit whom Christ has by nature.[36] Cyril explains that "Jesus sanctified Baptism by being Himself baptized . . . that He might give to them that are baptized a divine and excellent grace."[37] One hears in these words echoes of Athanasius's theology of deification, which notes that humans partake of and are sanctified with the Spirit because "the giver of the Spirit, the Word Himself, had spoken of Himself as anointed with the Spirit for us."[38] Ambrose of Milan adds that God himself has robed with our human flesh and washed it in his baptism not for his benefit but for ours, so that he might cover us with his robe of joy

34. Gregory of Nazianzus, *Oration* 38.16 (*NPNF*² 7:350–51).

35. Irenaeus, *Against Heresies* 3.17.1 (*ANF* 1:444).

36. Cirilo de Jerúsalen, *Mistagógicas* 3.1, in Carmelo Granado, *El Espíritu Santo en la teología patrística* (Salamanca: Sígueme, 1987), 149.

37. Cyril of Jerusalem, *Catechetical Lectures, On Baptism* 3.11 (*NPNF*² 7:16).

38. Athanasius, *First Discourse against the Arians* 12.50 (*NPNF*² 4:336).

and cleanse our filth.[39] In light of the cross, Jesus goes down into the waters of the Jordan on behalf of sinners, leaving his robe of holiness there, so that those who are united with him in baptism might come out of the waters of the new creation covered with his robe of righteousness.[40]

Luther's baptismal rite proclaims that by the baptism of the Son, God "hallowed and set apart the Jordan and all water to be a blessed flood and a rich washing of sins."[41] In God's economy, the waters of the flood and the Red Sea are seen as instruments of judgment and death, but also as means of divine blessing and renewal for God's people. The Christian life is like a daily flood, a return to the waters of baptism, where the old Adam is drowned or dies with Christ through contrition in order to be raised out of the waters with Christ to newness of life.[42] Luther incorporates the robe image of Ephesians 4:22–24 into his baptismal catechesis of Romans 6:1–14. Through daily repentance, contrition, and absolution, baptism becomes for Christians "the daily garment that they are to wear all the time. Every day they should be found in faith and with its fruits, suppressing the old creature and growing up in the new."[43] This account of the Christian life as a return to baptism describes life in the Spirit as a cycle of death and resurrection.

By conforming us to Christ crucified and risen, the Holy Spirit shapes in us the face of renewal. The waters of baptism act as a mirror against which we see our sins, but also as a means of renewal through which we are refreshed with God's forgiveness.[44] This model of sanctification sees each day as a new day with both realism and optimism, helping us to avoid fatalistic and perfectionistic extremes in our attitude toward and engagement with God's world.[45] By calling us to die to sin daily, the renewal model prevents us

39. San Ambrosio de Milán, *De patriarchis* 4.24, in Granado, *El Espíritu Santo*, 232.

40. Kilian McDonnell, *The Baptism of Jesus at the Jordan: The Trinitarian and Cosmic Order of Salvation* (Collegeville, MN: Liturgical Press, 1996), 55–68.

41. Martin Luther, *Large Catechism* [hereafter *LC*], Baptismal Booklet, para. 14, in Robert Kolb and Timothy Wengert, eds., *The Book of Concord: The Confessions of the Evangelical Lutheran Church* [hereafter *BC*] (Minneapolis: Fortress, 2000), 374.

42. Martin Luther, *Small Catechism*, the Sacrament of Holy Baptism, paras. 11–14 (*BC*, 360).

43. Luther, *LC*, Fourth Part: Concerning Baptism, paras. 84–85 (*BC*, 466).

44. Sánchez, *Teología de la santificación*, 91–92.

45. Ibid., 92–97.

from a perfectionistic view of life that, seeing creation only as "good," sets too high a standard of holiness for people or fosters an overly realized eschatology that sets unrealistic goals for kingdom building on earth. This model acknowledges that life is not always "good," and true reconciliation with those whom we have hurt or neglected in society cannot take place without recognizing our own faults and transgressions. The Spirit's drowning of the old creature through contrition prepares the way for right or just relations.

On the other hand, by calling us to rise as new creatures from the waters, this model steers away from a fatalistic view of life. By seeing the world only as "corrupt," fatalism discourages laboring toward faithful stewardship and creative use of God's gifts to make the world a better place, or can lead to an overly spiritualized eschatology that flees from a world in need. The model of renewal recognizes the power of God's forgiveness to restore relationships and deal justly with others in the world. It takes seriously the power of the Spirit at work through God's people to bring the abundance of Christ's life wherever a culture of death is glorified. The Spirit's raising of the new creature through absolution empowers right relations.

The Spirit's conforming people to Christ's death and resurrection deals primarily with the problem of guilt, drawing attention to our complicity in sin, our need for divine cleansing, and our renewal to bear fruits of repentance. This public face of the Spirit brings to mind the church's mediating role in reconciliation tribunals, where perpetrators and victims meet face-to-face as a preliminary step for moving the work of justice forward in nations devastated by oppressive regimes and civil wars. One also thinks of instances in which mother church has asked for forgiveness—at times after a long hiatus of denial—for sins committed by her children against minors, as a preliminary step in setting things right and offering reparations. These examples offer us a glimpse into the public face of the Spirit in the renewal of God's world. Where is the Spirit leading us today to die to self, to own our complicity in sin, in order to make room for others, and move toward reconciliation and restoration?

The Face of Battle: Vigilance and Resistance

After the Spirit anoints Jesus to become our suffering Servant, Jesus is "led by the Spirit" into the desert to be tempted by the devil (Luke 4:1–2; see also Mark 1:12–13). In his sermon at Cornelius's house, Peter proclaims that Jesus was anointed with the Holy Spirit and power and healed all those who were "oppressed by the devil" (Acts 10:38). After healing the deaf mute, Jesus tells his critics that his driving out demons by the Spirit of God is a sign of the coming of God's kingdom in the midst of a creation in bondage to the evil one (Matt. 12:28). Jesus' life reveals a battle between the Holy Spirit and the evil spirit.

In his sermons on the baptism of Christ, Luther speaks of the church's participation in the desert experience of Jesus. Like Christ, the baptized suffer physical temptations, but also spiritual ones such as doubt about God's promises.[46] The Reformer shows continuity between Christ's life and ours. Drawing on the medieval rite of exorcism, Luther notes that the baptizer will command the evil spirit to leave the child at the font and pray for the Holy Spirit to dwell in the newly baptized.[47] The whole Christian life becomes a lifelong struggle and battle against the evil one.

Such life brings about "spiritual attacks" (*tentatio*) by the devil, but in Luther's cosmic vision, the Holy Spirit enters such conflict on our behalf and uses it to form us as theologians.[48] The desert becomes the playground of the evil spirit, and paradoxically the school of the Holy Spirit who forms us as stronger theologians through the struggle. Like the faithful Son in the desert, in the midst of "spiritual attack" (*Anfechtung*), God's children learn to remain firm and resolute through "meditation" (*meditatio*) or reliance on God's word and trust in God's deliverance through "prayer" (*oratio*).

Dietrich Bonhoeffer sums up the vicarious nature of Christ's temptation. God's economy of salvation is seen in terms of the "two stories of temptation," or as a sort of cosmic battle between God and the devil for the lives of God's creatures, so that "either the Adam in me is tempted—in which case we fall. Or the Christ in us is tempted—in which case

46. Martin Luther, "First Sunday in Lent (Invocavit)," in *The Complete Sermons of Martin Luther*, trans. and ed. John Nicholas Lenker (Grand Rapids: Baker, 2000), 1/2:133–47; and Luther, "Invocavit Sunday—First Sunday in Lent (1534)," in *The Complete Sermons of Martin Luther*, trans. and ed. Eugene F. A. Klug, 5:312–20.

47. "The baptizer shall say: 'Depart, you unclean spirit, and make room for the Holy Spirit,'" *LC*, Baptismal Booklet, para. 11 (*BC*, 373).

48. John W. Kleinig, "Oratio, Meditatio, Tentatio: What Makes a Theologian?," *Concordia Theological Quarterly* 66 (2002): 255–67.

Satan is bound to fall."[49] This account of life in the Spirit calls for vigilance and resistance in the face of evil. In the garden, the other place where Adam was tempted in the first creation and failed, Christ, the new Adam, defeats the evil one and entrusts his life to the Father (Mark 14:32–42).

Like the garden, the desert is a battlefield, where Jesus' disciples ought to be vigilant (Mark 16:38) and stand firm like a disciplined runner (1 Cor. 9:24–10:13) and gladiator (Eph. 6:1–10) lest they become overly confident in the contest against Satan and fall. This model of sanctification deals primarily with the problem of desensitization and bondage to evil. It presents the Holy Spirit's chiseling of the baptized to rely on the word of God ("the sword of the Spirit") and prayer as they face evil in the world. While the model can focus on confronting one's personal "inner demons"—that is to say, those areas of vulnerability or habitual struggle where one is most likely to fall—the face of the Spirit in the struggle against evil can also encompass a more social trajectory.

One thinks, for instance, of the boldness of Christians who spoke against the atrocities of Nazi Germany committed against the Jews, and at times put their own lives at risk by providing safe haven to the persecuted.[50] Of more recent memory, Archbishop Oscar A. Romero's public denunciation of abuses of human rights in El Salvador as instances of idolatry—an unveiling of systemic evil that cost him his life—serves as another example of steadfastness against manifestations of evil in society. For the archbishop, riches, private property, and national security, while not necessarily evil in themselves, had become idols in his country because the oligarchy backed by the military claimed these things in order to justify their absolute power over the majority of the impoverished nation and perpetuate a culture of fear, torture, and death.

49. Dietrich Bonhoeffer, *Creation and Fall, Temptation: Two Biblical Studies* (New York: Simon & Schuster, 1997), 115.

50. While Luther in his own time spoke no more harshly about the Jews than others, and while his comments were arguably not against the Jews as a race but rather as a religious group, Bernard Lohse has noted that Luther's harsh words should not be relativized or excused given their influential power to encourage further attacks upon an already defenseless group. See Bernard Lohse, *Martin Luther's Theology: Its Historical and Systematic Development*, trans. Roy A. Harrisville (Minneapolis: Fortress, 1999), 336–45.

The public face of the Spirit of battle against evil in the world is, for the disciples of Jesus, the way of nonviolence, which unveils idols of death in our world and speaks in favor of the dignity of all life from the womb to the grave, even as it prays "deliver us from the evil one" and holds on to God's promise of deliverance from evil at the last day. In which deserts, gardens, or battlefields are we most likely to fall? Where must we stand firm in the face of evil, denounce it, and proclaim life in the midst of death? Where have we become so desensitized and bound to the spirit of this world that the Spirit must teach us to be vigilant again in prayer and resist evil through reliance on the Word? Which idols blind us, or our community or nation, to the suffering and struggles of neighbors?

The Face of Sacrifice: Service and Sharing

The Spirit in whom Jesus is anointed to be our Servant shapes his disciples so that they do not lord it over others but become servants, who do not come to be served but to serve and to give their lives for others (Mark 16:35–45). The moral implications of the mystery of Christ's humiliation are laid out in Paul's christological hymn (Phil. 2:1–11), where the Spirit shapes the mind of Christ in us by giving us his configuration, namely, the "form of a servant" (v. 7). Through repentance and baptism in his name, the exalted Christ's outpouring of the gift of the Holy Spirit on Pentecost brings about a new community of believers, who gather around the teaching of the apostles, break bread, and share all things with one another (Acts 2:42–47). Their outward life of sharing flows from an inward unity of mind and spirit (Acts 4:32). The Spirit moves God's people toward communion, making them one in teaching and life.

The early church fathers and the monastic communities sought to emulate the life portrayed among the faithful in the book of Acts.[51] The *Didache* grounds the church's sharing of material blessings with the needy in their deeper sharing of spiritual blessings with one another: "Do not turn your back on the needy, but share everything with your brother and call nothing your own. For if you have what is eternal in common, how much more should you have what is transient!"[52] In his description

51. Nereo Silanes, *La santísima Trinidad, programa social del cristianismo: Principios bíblico-teológicos* (Salamanca: Secretariado Trinitario, 1991), 43–46.

52. *Didache* 4.8, in *Early Christian Fathers*, ed. Cyril C. Richardson, LCC 1 (Philadelphia: Westminster, 1952), 173.

of Christian worship, Justin Martyr notes the tradition, after Sunday Eucharist, of gathering a collection to care for "orphans and widows, and those who are in want on account of sickness or any other cause, and those who are in bonds, and the strangers who are sojourners among [us], and . . . all those in need."[53] Communion with Christ in the Eucharist joins us to the members of his body through a life of service and care for one another, and such love among the saints spreads into the world, making the church "the aroma of Christ" among many (2 Cor. 2:15).

Speaking of the Lord's Supper as an occasion for "thanksgiving" (*eucharistia*), Philip Melanchthon uses the language of "eucharistic sacrifice" to refer to the church's response to a gracious God for God's gifts through their works of love.[54] Such sacrifices are pleasing to God and are our "spiritual worship" because their source is the Holy Spirit, who grants us the righteousness of faith and the fruits of love that follow.[55] Reflecting on the spiritual benefit of Holy Communion, Luther argues that partaking with others in Christ's body and blood leads to an intercommunion of love among the saints. There is a social trajectory to the Lord's Supper. It is not simply my individual communion with God in splendid isolation from the rest of the community, but rather our sharing in each other's burdens and joys. Communion signifies and promises that "Christ and all his saints are coming to you with all their virtues, sufferings, and mercies, to live, work, suffer, and die with you, and that they desire to be wholly yours."[56]

Luther speaks of the mystery of the cross as a "happy exchange" between Christ and us, in which he takes on our unrighteousness in order to give us his righteousness. By becoming the body of Christ, the church also embodies a life of happy exchanges—that is to say, "a fellowship and a gracious exchange or blending of our sin and suffering with the righteousness of Christ and his saints."[57] Christ comes to us in his needy saints, so that we might make their need our own and become a compassionate Christ to them. Christ also comes to us in his merciful

53. Justin Martyr, *First Apology* 67 (LCC 1:287).

54. *Apology to the Augsburg Confession*, 24, para. 19 (*BC*, 261).

55. Ibid., 26–27 (*BC*, 262–63).

56. Martin Luther, *The Blessed Sacrament of the Holy and True Blood of Christ, and the Brotherhoods*, trans. Jeremiah J. Schindel, in *Luther's Works*, ed. Helmut T. Lehman (Philadelphia: Muhlenberg, 1960), 35:61.

57. Ibid., 35:60.

saints, so that we might receive their virtues as Christ's own gifts to us. The Spirit who unites us to Christ unites us to one another, and such unity takes on an economic form. It is an exchange of burdens and joys. I give you my sin for your forgiveness, and vice versa. I give you my grief for your joy, and vice versa. I give you my poverty for your abundance, and vice versa. The Spirit makes the church into an economy of "happy exchanges."

The public face of the Spirit in sacrifice addresses the problem of individualism with a neighbor-oriented view of vocation.[58] What the public face of service and sharing looks like here and there will depend on the face of the neighbors whom we encounter, their struggles and needs, their virtues and contributions. The self-effacing character of the Spirit appears in that the Spirit does not draw attention to its presence in the saints, but rather to the neighbors whom they are called to meet and walk with in life. This means in part that, in approaching neighbors, we avoid paternalistic models of justice that reduce life together to one-way charity, and instead move toward two-way partnerships where people enrich one another in times of plenty and lack.[59] Christian agencies that deal with effective short-term relief efforts in times of humanitarian crises, but also establish long-term partnerships with local stakeholders toward sustainable economic development, offer an ideal example of justice in a spirit of mutual exchange.

Unlike capitalist and socialist systems of exchange, the economy of the Spirit in the world seeks neither to maximize profits for gain nor to stifle the creative stewardship of resources. Instead, the Spirit promotes free exchanges without expectation of remuneration, exchanges that also adapt dynamically to the realities of neighbors around the world. This model of sanctification presents the church as a gym, where Christians exercise their love for one another, and this love then grows and overflows into the world where we also partake in the burdens and joys of others. What does the public face of sacrifice, of service and sharing, look like in our families and neighborhoods? What are the places where happy exchanges are taking place today? Where must these exchanges happen more frequently?

58. Leopoldo A. Sánchez M., "The Human Face of Justice: Reclaiming the Neighbor in Law, Vocation, and Justice Talk," *Concordia Journal* 39 (2013): 117–21.

59. Ibid., 121–25.

The Face of Hospitality: Marginality and Welcome

Even though Jesus is anointed with the Holy Spirit to bring God's kingdom to the lost sheep of Israel, two surprising things happen. First, the Spirit bearer is not welcomed, but rejected by his own people. In the power of the Spirit, Jesus proclaims good news and the favorable year of the Lord in his own hometown's synagogue, and his compatriots want to throw him off a cliff (Luke 4:14–30). Jesus drives out demons by the Spirit of God, and the religious leaders of Israel suggest he does it by the power of the devil (Luke 11:14–23; see also Matt. 12:22–30). Life in the Spirit marginalizes Jesus.

Second, Jesus, the Spirit giver, extends his Father's kingdom outside the boundaries of Israel, bringing God's compassion to characters such as the demon-possessed daughter of a Canaanite or Syrophoenician woman (Matt. 15:21–28; Mark 7:24–30). Jesus walks along "God-forsaken" areas despised by the Jews such as Samaria, promising "living water" (the Holy Spirit; see John 7:37–39) to a Samaritan woman who had nothing going for her, dealing with her shame, and empowering her to be a witness among her own people (John 4:3–42). Life in the Spirit drives Jesus toward marginalized people.

The Spirit pushes God's people toward the margins in two ways. Life in the Spirit brings about the disciples' own marginality in the world, but also pushes them toward marginal spaces. We see this dynamic at work in biblical narratives. Mexican-American theologian Virgilio Elizondo, for instance, has drawn attention to the Galilean identity of Christ and his disciples, noting that the Jerusalem Jews, who likely saw themselves as the wiser, purer, and more righteous Jews, would have seen Galilean Jews as backward, impure, and untrustworthy due to their close proximity to gentiles.[60] In Jerusalem, the privileged center of wisdom and power, Jesus only meets rejection and death on the cross. Jesus the Galilean calls his disciples out of Galilee too. And in the end, it is from Galilee, not Jerusalem, that Jesus commissions his disciples to make disciples of all nations by baptizing and teaching (Matthew 28). Surprisingly, the narrative of salvation moves from the margins of Galilee to the margins of gentile lands.

Such a suspicious attitude toward Galileans at the time might explain in part why

60. Virgilio Elizondo, *Galilean Journey: The Mexican-American Promise*, 2nd ed. (Maryknoll, NY: Orbis Books, 1983); see also Timothy Matovina, ed., *Beyond Borders: Writings of Virgilio Elizondo and Friends* (Maryknoll, NY: Orbis Books, 2000), 143–86.

the apostle Philip's exciting announcement concerning the Messiah is met by Nathanael's guarded words, "Can anything good come out of Nazareth?" (John 1:46). The implication is that God cannot work his mighty wonders from such lowly places and folks. Yet Philip invites Nathanael to "come and see" what the Lord can do from the margins (v. 46). To adopt a Johannine tone, we are likewise invited to see reality from God's perspective, that is to say, through the eyes of the Holy Spirit. In Pauline terms, we are called to see the wisdom of the Spirit in the mystery of the cross, where God shows strength through weakness and wisdom through foolishness (1 Cor. 1:18–31).

A similar dynamic is at work in other biblical stories. Jesus walks along the despised border between Samaria and Galilee, where he meets unclean lepers who are literally at the margins of society (Luke 17:11–19). After healing the ten lepers, only one returns to thank God, and surprisingly, this foreigner is a Samaritan, an enemy of God's people. The centrifugal movement of the Spirit toward odd and strange characters is also evident in the story of Philip, who serves Greek-speaking Jewish widows (Acts 6:1–6) and brings the gospel to the Samaritans (8:9–25) and an Ethiopian eunuch (8:26–39). These people are not seen as full members of the community of the righteous because of their linguistic, cultural, racial, and/or religious impurity. Are they in or out? According to human standards, they are excluded from God's kingdom. Yet the Spirit surprises us and pushes the church in Jerusalem toward Judea, Samaria, and the ends of the earth.

These are stories of marginality, but also hospitality. As a marginal community in the world, the church has a special place in her heart for marginal people. When the church over time becomes a centralized institution comfortable in her own skin, she can become somewhat guarded about the contributions of groups from her own communion who live and minister at the margins of society. She can also become less sensitive to or aware of the pains and aspirations of those outside her boundaries, and become shy about reaching out across the other side of the railroad tracks or the borders that divide us.

Yahweh's command to Israel to care for the vulnerable in their midst (for example, orphans, widows, the poor, and aliens) was embodied by Jesus in his own ministry toward outsiders and provides his disciples in all times with a guiding ethic or value to emulate. Today, people migrate more than ever due to economic exploitation and in search of dignified labor, because of political, religious, or criminal persecution, or to reunify with family members. Whatever policies nation-states propose to deal with forced migrations, the collective and tireless work of Christian agencies that advocate for refugees, immigrants, and their families, before governments and their own religious constituencies, serves as an example of solidarity with vulnerable neighbors.

This model of life in the Spirit addresses the fundamental human need for belonging. Ultimately, stories of marginality and welcome remind us of our need for acceptance and justification before others and God.[61] They remind us that God embraces the unlovable, the impure, the unworthy. These stories teach us that our inclusion in God's kingdom does not depend on socioeconomic status, language, race, culture, ethnicity, place of origin, or any other condition in life. They offer the hand of welcome and acceptance to all who have been shamed and excluded unfairly from participating in God's blessings.

61. Leopoldo A. Sánchez M., "Can Anything Good Come Out of______? Come and See!: Faithful Witness in Marginality and Hospitality," *Concordia Journal* 41 (2015): 111–23.

Conclusion

Our proposal tested the productivity of a Trinitarian Spirit Christology as a ground for exploring the relative continuity between Christ and his saints, giving pneumatology an incarnational center and ecclesial trajectory in the world. Parting from the Holy Spirit's dwelling in the humanity of Christ, and Christ's taking form in us by the sculpting work of his Spirit, we proposed four configurations of life in the Spirit. Each form yielded a different public face of the Spirit working in and through us in order to make a difference in the world. We reflected on the centrifugal or outward-oriented picture of sanctification or holiness each model offers. While these models intersect and interact with each other in real life, our essay looked at the characteristics of each one in its own right. People may identify with one model more than another, depending on what they are going through at a particular time in their lives or what is happening in their neighborhoods at home or in the global community.

The renewal model presents life in the Spirit as a cycle of death and resurrection, and addresses issues such as guilt, repentance, reconciliation, and restoration. The battle model presents the Christian life as a struggle against the evil one and the seductive power of evil in the world, and deals with the need for vigilance and resistance in the face of spiritual attacks. It also calls for the unmasking of idols that keep people in bondage to systemic evil. The model of sacrifice sees life in the Spirit as a sharing in Christ's humble service. Discipleship is a spiritual act of worship grounded in faith that, in thanksgiving to God for God's gifts, spreads the pleasing aroma of Christ in the world. As an antidote against individualism and collectivism, this form of life encourages "happy exchanges" where we share each other's burdens and joys in creative and flexible ways that honor both the needs and virtues of various neighbors.

The hospitality model looks at the Christian life as a sharing in Christ's marginality, which in turn makes her especially aware of and compassionate toward marginalized neighbors. The Holy Spirit pushes us to walk with Jesus along the forgotten borders between Samaria and Galilee, where unlovable folk make their dwelling, or to walk with Philip the evangelist as he proclaims God's word to outsiders like the Ethiopian eunuch and Samaritans who are excluded from full participation in God's kingdom. Based on God's justification of the sinner apart from human merit, this model embraces the unlovable and undesirable. It addresses the problem of shame and the need for belonging, and notes that God's acceptance and embrace is by Christ's merits alone.

No one model in itself can account for the complexity of human experience and the richness of the Christian life in all its configurations across time and space. Instead, all models work together to give us a more complete picture of life in the Spirit and of the Spirit's manifold works in God's world.

Part 5

Ecclesiology

CHAPTER 18

Where the Love of Christ is Found

Toward a Third Article Ecclesiology

GREGORY J. LISTON

The Western church is struggling. While in the global South (Asia, Africa, and South America) the church is growing rapidly, its more established counterpart is experiencing an ever accelerating loss of size, status, and significance. Historians label this phenomenon the "collapse of Christendom." Most responses simply urge the Western church to "do" better. They argue that by being more organized, more pragmatic—by utilizing some authoritative and effective technique—the church can recover its numbers, regain its respect, and reexert its influence. There are alternative responses, however. For example, Colin Gunton argues for a "greater emphasis on [the church's] constitution by the Spirit."[1] This enables us to "reappropriate an ecclesiology of the humanity of Christ."[2] He sees this as "the first and crying need if responses to the collapse of Christendom are not to take the form of new authoritarianisms, as they are indeed doing."[3] From such a perspective, the collapse of Christendom is not a tragedy,

1. Colin Gunton, "The Church on Earth: The Roots of Community," in *On Being the Church* ed. C. Gunton and D. Hardy; (Edinburgh: T&T Clark, 1989), 62.

2. Ibid., 65.

3. Ibid.

but an opportunity. Through this loss of size, status, and significance—through our weakness—we can relearn to define ourselves not by our *position* in the world, but by our *participation* in God's Trinitarian life. The church can choose again to walk by faith and not by sight, to understand itself not primarily as a player in society but profoundly and irreducibly constituted by God's Spirit.

The development of a Third Article Ecclesiology finds its motivation in such a conviction. It examines ecclesiology through the methodology of Third Article Theology (TAT), where all reality is viewed *through the lens of the Spirit*. The close relationship between the Spirit and the church is, of course, not a new recognition. The Apostles' Creed places them side by side: "I believe in the Holy Spirit, the holy, catholic church, the communion of saints."[4] But as is often noted, "the pervasive association between 'Spirit' and 'church' notwithstanding, theologians have reflected relatively little on precisely *how* the two are related."[5] This essay consequently aims first (briefly) to describe and justify how the approach of TAT can be applied to ecclesiology, and second (at slightly greater length) to demonstrate the value of such an approach.[6] Just as Spirit Christology has gained new insight by examining Christ's person and life through a pneumatological lens, approaching ecclesiology through the methodology of TAT provides similar benefits.

Approaching a Third Article Ecclesiology

Even a cursory examination of ecclesiology *through the lens of the Spirit* reveals that this doctrine cannot be viewed in isolation. For it is primarily through the Spirit that ecclesiology is connected with other theological doctrines. A comprehensive framework and methodology for a Third Article Ecclesiology

4. Jaroslav Pelikan and Valerie Hotchkiss, eds., *Creeds and Confessions of Faith in the Christian Tradition: Early, Eastern and Medieval* (New Haven: Yale University Press, 2003), 669.

5. Miroslav Volf and Maurice Lee, "The Spirit and the Church," in *Advents of the Spirit: An Introduction to the Current Study of Pneumatology* ed. Bradford E. Hinze and D. Lyle Dabney; (Milwaukee: Marquette University Press, 2005), 382. See also William R. Barr and Rena M. Yocum, "Introduction," in *The Church in the Movement of the Spirit* ed. William R. Barr and Rena M. Yocum; (Grand Rapids: Eerdmans, 1994), 1–2.

6. This essay summarizes material argued in more depth in Gregory J. Liston, *The Anointed Church: Toward a Third Article Ecclesiology* (Minneapolis: Fortress, 2015).

emerges from this recognition. Rather than looking directly at ecclesiology through the Spirit, the constituent features of a Third Article Ecclesiology are illuminated by looking *through* the lens of the Spirit *from the vantage point* of other theological loci.

To illustrate, consider the view of ecclesiology as seen from the vantage point of Christology. First, the link between the two subjects is primarily pneumatological. The church is connected historically, metaphorically, and organically with Christ, and each of these connections is pneumatologically enabled.[7] For example, just as the Spirit birthed and empowered Jesus during the incarnation, so the Spirit birthed and empowers the church. Second, the link between the two loci is analogical. The church's identity is related to but not identical with Jesus' identity. The continuities are real, but not exact, and determining the limits to which the analogy can be taken and how the analogy can best be utilized is pivotal in obtaining an accurate ecclesiological understanding. Third, the particular vantage point utilized illuminates some but not all ecclesiological features. So the link between Christology and ecclesiology illuminates the ontology of the church, but (because of Jesus' individuality) sheds little light on ecclesial relationships. Another vantage point needs to be utilized in order to clearly view this aspect of ecclesiology.

Recognizing these features leads to the conclusion that a comprehensive and systematic Third Article Ecclesiology must be developed dialogically. Working backwards, the third insight above (that each vantage point only sheds light on particular features of ecclesiology) means that a variety of vantage points will be needed to move toward a truly comprehensive understanding of ecclesiology. It is not sufficient to view ecclesiology only from the vantage point of Christology. The pneumatological perspectives from other theological loci—the Trinity, eschatology, and others—also need to be included. The second insight (that the connection between theological loci is analogical) means that a valid analogical connection needs to be established between the two doctrines. Thankfully, this "analogous" pathway has been traveled by former theological giants, on whose shoulders we can stand. For example, Karl Barth's examination of reconciliation in *Church Dogmatics* IV extensively utilizes the notion of analogy, or, as Barth more wisely

7. The church was founded by Christ (historical); the church is like Christ (metaphorical); and the church is in Christ (organic). For further discussion, see ibid., Ch. 5.

terms it, correspondence.[8] But, as the first insight affirms, the analogical connection needs to be intrinsically pneumatological, a perspective that has often been underappreciated and insufficiently utilized.

Perhaps the most instructive philosophical framework through which this approach can be categorized and understood is the dialogical approach outlined by Nicholas Wolterstorff in his seminal work *Reason within the Bounds of Religion*.[9] Rejecting foundationalism, Wolterstorff nevertheless asserts that scholars can approach a true understanding of reality through the analysis and interchange of background beliefs, data beliefs, and control beliefs. To take an illustrative example, consider the way an astronomer measures a star's position. Put simply, the optical features of a telescope are utilized to determine the star's coordinates. Indeed, astronomers usually integrate several measurements to obtain the most accurate results possible. Applying Wolterstorff's framework to this example, the star's position is the data belief—the reality the astronomer is determining. The telescope's optical features are the control beliefs—the basis on which the astronomer determines the star's position. Everything else, such as Newton's laws of motion, is simply assumed. These are background beliefs. Wolterstorff claims that scientists regularly swap the positions of the data beliefs, control beliefs, and background beliefs. So, for another experiment, the astronomer will simply assume how the telescope works (background belief) and measure a star's position (control belief) in order to test Newton's laws of motion (data belief).[10] The star's position in the sky, which was originally a data belief, becomes a new control belief.

Wolterstorff's framework provides an overall methodology for moving toward a

8. See, for example, Karl Barth, *Church Dogmatics,* trans. G. W. Bromiley and T. F. Torrance (Peabody: Hendrickson, 2010), IV.3.2 532-33. See also Kimlyn J. Bender, *Karl Barth's Christological Ecclesiology* (Aldershot: Ashgate, 2005), 5–7.

9. See Nicholas Wolterstorff, *Reason Within the Bounds of Religion* (Grand Rapids: Eerdmans, 1976). Wolterstorff does not use the word "dialogical" but the idea is implied.

10. Interestingly, this is exactly what happened when Eddington observed the relative shift of a star's position during a solar eclipse in 1919. His new control belief disproved the data belief of Newton's laws of motion, and was a confirmation of the new data belief of Einstein's general theory of relativity. Apparently, when Einstein was asked what his reaction would have been if his new data belief of general relativity had not been confirmed by the experiment, he replied, "Then I would feel sorry for the dear Lord. The theory is correct anyway."

complete and coherent Third Article Ecclesiology. There are background beliefs—Holy Scripture and the creeds—that are crucial reference points, but not the focus area of this particular research project. There are several control beliefs—specific doctrines of TAT such as Spirit Christology—that form the basis or vantage points from which the examination occurs. And finally there is the data belief—ecclesiology—that is the specific area being examined. Each of the ecclesiological views gained from the different perspectives are integrated to determine as complete and coherent a view of a Third Article Ecclesiology as possible. While such a combined ecclesiological understanding represents the ultimate goal of a Third Article Ecclesiology, it does not form the end of the theological program. As Wolterstorff's framework expounds, this ecclesiological understanding should then be utilized as a control belief—a vantage point from which other TAT loci can be examined.[11]

The remainder of this essay describes some initial steps taken along this path that will lead toward a robust, coherent, and comprehensive Third Article Ecclesiology. In particular it examines ecclesiology from the perspectives of Christology and the Trinity, through the lens of the Spirit. These vantage points have been chosen not just because they are the most developed doctrines dealt with to date by a TAT, but also because the relationship between each of them and ecclesiology is so clearly pneumatologically derived. Regarding Christology, it is the Spirit that forms the church as the body of Christ (1 Cor. 12:13). For the Trinity, it is by the Spirit that the church joins in the life of the Trinity. As James Torrance writes, we participate "by the Spirit in the Son's communion with the Father."[12] A brief final discussion explores how this research may be extended so that other vantage points such as eschatology and the world can be utilized and the views they give of ecclesiology incorporated to construct a coherent and comprehensive Third Article Ecclesiology.

11. Andrew Grosso develops a similar understanding of how a comprehensive TAT could be developed but utilizes the epistemological framework of Michael Polanyi rather than Wolterstorff. See Andrew Grosso, "Spirit Christology and the Shape of the Theological Enterprise," in *A Man of the Church: Honoring the Theology, Life, and Witness of Ralph Del Colle*, ed. Michel René Barnes; (Eugene: Pickwick Publications, 2012), 215–22.

12. James B. Torrance, *Worship, Community and the Triune God of Grace* (Downers Grove: IVP Academic, 1996), 31.

The Church as Sequel to the Incarnation—A *Christological* Third Article Ecclesiology

Two premises inform the development of Third Article Ecclesiology as seen from the vantage point of Christology. The first is that significant insight into the ontology of the church can be gained from comparison with the ontology of Christ (as compellingly worked out by Karl Barth and his utilization of the "Chalcedonian pattern"[13]). The second premise is that this correspondence cannot be adequately examined without giving the Spirit prominence (as often overlooked by Barth), for it is by the Spirit that the church forms Christ's body. The most extended biblical outworking of the body image asserts precisely this reality: "For we were all baptised by one Spirit so as to form one body—whether Jews or Gentiles, slave or free—and we were all given one Spirit to drink" (1 Cor. 12:13).[14] This key verse is not merely saying that the Spirit enables believers to embrace unity in diversity as a functional community. More profoundly, it is claiming that the Spirit *makes* the church Christ's body. Gary Badcock comments, "The church as the body of Christ cannot be considered apart from [the Spirit's presence], for the ecclesiastical 'body' of Christ is something that is mediated by the work of the Spirit, and cannot exist without the Spirit."[15] If the Bible so strongly emphasizes the pneumatological nature of this connection, then a coherent theological understanding of the union and correspondence between Christ and the church simply cannot be formed without reference to the Spirit. Pneumatological insights into how the eternal Son became human inform our understanding of how the perfect Christ indwells an imperfect church. As Veli-Matti Kärkkäinen asserts: "the only way to construe a viable pneumato-ecclesiology is to reflect very carefully on the relationship between Christ and the Spirit on the one hand, and on the relation of the Spirit to the church on the other hand, and then try and see these three as mutual entities that inform each other."[16]

---

13. George Hunsinger, *How to Read Karl Barth:The Shape of His Theology* (New York/Oxford: Oxford University Press, 1991), 185.

14. All Scriptural quotations in this chapter are taken from the *TNIV* (2005).

15. Gary D. Badcock, *The House Where God Lives: Renewing the Doctrine of the Church for Today* (Grand Rapids: Eerdmans, 2009), 85.

16. Veli-Matti Kärkkäinen, *Toward a Pneumatological Theology: Pentecostal and Ecumenical Perspectives on Ecclesiology, Soteriology, and Theology*

Prioritizing the pneumatological connection between Christ and the church reveals an important ecclesiological balancing point. Ecclesiologies traditionally aim for balance between the divine and the human aspects of the church—errors that may be termed ecclesial docetism or ecclesial Ebionism, respectively. It is equally important for the Son and the Spirit's ecclesial involvement to be balanced—both must be logically distinguished without being existentially separated. The Son's ecclesial involvement must not be subsumed into or subordinated below that of the Spirit, or the Spirit's ecclesial involvement subsumed into or subordinated below that of the Son. This insight parallels one derived in Spirit Christology, for just as traditionally Christology aims to balance the divine or the human nature of Jesus (avoiding docetism and Ebionism), so Spirit Christology has aimed for a reinforcing balance between the Son and the Spirit's involvement in the incarnation.[17]

Such ecclesiological balance is best achieved by exploring the pneumatologically inspired parallels between Spirit Christology and Third Article Ecclesiology:

- The Spirit conceives (Christ and the church)
- The Spirit sustains the communion (of Christ and the church)
- The Spirit conforms (Christ and the church)
- The Spirit directs and empowers (Christ and the church)
- The Spirit is displayed and mediated (by Christ and the church)

Examining ecclesiology in such a parallel manner enables the balances gained in Spirit Christology to be equally applied to the church.

On the basis of these parallels we are justified in characterizing the church as the *sequel* of the incarnation. Like a movie sequel's relationship with its original, the church has a clear continuity with the incarnation. Many of the same characters emerge and similar themes are explored. But (also like a sequel) the church is not simply a continuation or repetition of the incarnation. Just as disaster awaits attempts to make a movie sequel too similar to its original, so disaster awaits attempts to identify the church too closely with Christ. The church cannot add to or

of Mission (Lanham: University Press of America, 2002), 93.

17. See Gregory J. Liston, "A "Chalcedonian" Spirit Christology," *Irish Theological Quarterly* 81, no. 1 (2016): 74-93. See also Liston, *The Anointed Church*, Ch. 2.

replicate Christ's already completed work—in attempting to do so it becomes not more but less than it should be. Finally, there is a necessary asymmetry. Just as there is no movie sequel without an original, there is no church without Christ. Jesus is God's Son become human independent of what the church is or does. In contrast, the church is Christ's or it is not the church at all.

Exploring in detail the Spirit-inspired parallels arising from the church being the sequel to the incarnation allows some very fundamental questions to be asked and answered, such as:

Q: What is the church?

A: The Spirit-enabled union that exists between the incarnate Christ and the human community.

Q: Who is in the church?

A: Those humans who have been united by the Spirit to Christ.

Q: How is a church recognized?

A: By having *both* a Christ-centered orientation and an overall momentum toward Christlikeness.

Q: What does the church do?

A: The church is cruciform in shape (molded by suffering), missional in purpose, narrative in character and relational in identity.

Exploring each of these parallels and their accompanying insights in depth provides a rich, full, and—most importantly—balanced view of the church as seen from the vantage point of Christology through a pneumatological lens. The following discussion will explore just the second question, to illustrate theological balance and practical implications arising from such an examination of the Spirit-inspired parallels between Christ and the church.

The key insight required for examining and answering the question "Who is in the church?" is that the church is the *unique context* in which the Spirit unites humanity to Christ. (This recognition arises directly from our understanding of Jesus' uniqueness.) When a person is united to Christ by the Spirit, then that uniquely occurs through the transformation of that person into a member of the church. So there is, quite simply, no such thing as a lone or anonymous Christian. Friedrich Schleiermacher famously distinguished between the two major denominational streams by noting, "Protestantism makes the individual's relation to the church dependent on his relation to Christ," while Catholicism "makes the individual's relation to Christ dependent on his relation to the church."[18] Whether this statement is theologically and historically accurate or not,[19] TAT goes to neither extreme, but logically identifies one's relationship to Christ with one's membership in the church.

In this understanding, then, the church consists of those individuals who are pneumatologically united with Christ. Or, to utilize more thoroughly biblical language, it consists of those who have been baptized into the body of Christ by the Spirit (Spirit baptism). But this invisible relationship has clear and visible markers, of which water baptism is primary.[20] Spirit baptism and water baptism thus have a complementary relationship, which can be understood according to a pneumatologically conditioned version of Barth's Chalcedonian logic.[21] First, (following the Chalcedonian pattern) Spirit baptism cannot be separated from nor confused with water baptism. Second, (following the *anhypostasia/enhypostasia* formula) water baptism has no meaning beyond being a human rite without an accompanying Spirit baptism, but Spirit baptism imbues water baptism with a genuine reality. Third, water baptism corresponds to and reflects the genuine reality of Spirit baptism. It thus can be said that through baptism a person genuinely becomes united to Christ in his body the church. Just as all who are in a marriage relationship have had a wedding, all who are in the church and participate in his body have been baptized. The church is precisely the community of the baptized: those who are a part of the body

18. Friedrich Schleiermacher, *The Christian Faith* (London: T&T Clark, 1999), 103.

19. See Veli-Matti Kärkkäinen, *An Introduction to Ecclesiology: Ecumenical, Historical and Global Perspectives* (Downers Grove: IVP Academic, 2002), 11–12.

20. In utilizing the term "water baptism" the immediate question that arises is whether it is paedo or credo baptism that is being referred to. A pneumato-ecclesiology does not draw a sharp distinction between the two competing interpretations of water baptism, and both can fit within this framework. The key recognition is the correspondence between Spirit baptism and water baptism, as discussed below. Credo baptism fits perhaps more naturally with the pneumato-ecclesial perspective, as the rite of water baptism chronologically follows the event of Spirit baptism that it corresponds to and from which its significance and meaning are drawn. But paedo baptism, if considered as a proleptic anticipation of Spirit baptism, can also fit within the framework, through a pneumatologically enabled time reversal.

21. See, for example, George Hunsinger, "Baptism and the Soteriology of Forgiveness," *International Journal of Systematic Theology* 2, no. 3 (2000): 247–69.

of Christ, which is relationally connected to him through the Spirit.

This understanding, of course, requires some alteration of the "conventional" understanding of baptism. As Gunton notes, "It is not first of all the expression of the faith of an individual or some invisible inner cleansing, but it is public and communal: it is the means by which a person is brought into relation with Christ through the medium of his body, the church."[22] The clearest way to demonstrate this understanding of baptism is to recognize the potential errors it seeks to avoid. The initial two errors correspond to the classical christological heresies. An ecclesially docetic understanding of baptism excessively focuses on Spirit baptism at the expense of water baptism, reducing water baptism to merely a responsive gesture, a "public testimony to an inner spiritual transformation."[23] This is a common position espoused in certain Baptistic settings, and at the extreme can even treat baptism as a nonessential practice (for example, the Quakers or the Salvation Army). The opposite error is ecclesial Ebionism, which completely neglects any mystical aspect of water baptism, and views it merely as an initiatory rite into the human community of the church. Examples can be seen in some liberal mainline churches and nominal Roman Catholics.

But there is a balance required not just between the divine and human elements of baptism, but also between the involvement of the Son and the Spirit in the act. Subsuming the Son's involvement into the Spirit's leads to *confusing* water baptism and Spirit baptism. Many theologians of the Middle Ages, for example, claimed that baptismal regeneration occurred in and of the act itself (*ex opere operato*).[24] But the act of baptism, in and of itself, is not regenerative. Union with Christ cannot be brought about through the performance of a physical act as if by magic. Further, as Stanley Grenz notes, "Baptismal regeneration survives in some form in the contemporary expressions of the more sacramental traditions, including the Roman Catholic and Eastern Orthodox churches and also among certain Lutherans."[25] John Zizioulas's overemphasis on the Spirit at the expense of Christ in the life of the church, for

22. Colin Gunton, "Baptism: Baptism and the Christian Community," in *Father, Son and Holy Spirit: Toward a Trinitarian Theology* (London: T&T Clark, 2003), 208.

23. Millard Erickson, *Christian Theology* (Grand Rapids: Baker Book House, 1983), 1096.

24. Stanley J. Grenz, *Theology for the Community of God* (Grand Rapids: Eerdmans, 1994), 526.

25. Ibid.

example, leads directly to him holding such a position.[26] His overemphasis on the Spirit comes as a direct consequence of lacking an understanding of Christ's person external to his corporate personality in the church. According to Zizioulas, an individual's connection to Christ and to Christ's church is literally and not just logically identified, and so Spirit baptism and water baptism must also be literally identical and not just logically complementary.

The opposite error subsumes the role of the Spirit into that of the Son, with the consequence that water baptism and Spirit baptism are excessively distinguished. This view does not neglect the importance of either form of baptism, but it views them as separate and (more importantly) separable. Some argue that Barth's work trends in this direction. For example, toward the end of his *Church Dogmatics*, on the basis that Jesus Christ is the one and only sacrament of God, Barth maintains the nonsacramental nature of water baptism,[27] a claim that perplexes even his most ardent supporters. George Hunsinger writes that Barth's "argument is peculiar. Although, for Barth, Jesus Christ is the Word of God in the strict and proper sense, that did not prevent God's Word from having a threefold form. . . . A similar logic immediately suggests itself for thinking about baptism and the Lord's supper as sacraments."[28] Barth's tendency to overemphasize that the human and the divine within the church are "unconfused" results directly from his tendency to subsume the role of the Spirit in ecclesial life into that of the Son. It is perhaps in his characterization of the sacraments, and baptism in particular, that the problematic implications of Barth's tendency to subsume the Spirit in the work of the Son are seen at their clearest.

So, beyond simply not emphasizing water baptism over Spirit baptism or vice versa, a *christological* Third Article Ecclesiology also

26. John Zizioulas, *Communion and Otherness: Further Studies in Personhood and the Church* (London: T&T Clark, 2006), 80. See also Jonathan Martin Ciraulo, "Sacraments and Personhood: John Zizioulas' Impasse and A Way Forward," *The Heythrop Journal* 53, no. 6 (2012): 995–97. For more details, see the discussion in Liston, *The Anointed Church*, Chs. 4 & 6.

27. See Barth, *Church Dogmatics*, IV/4, 100–10. While it is true that Christ is the ultimate sacrament, this truth does not necessarily reduce baptism to a mere ordinance. See, for example, W. Travis McMaken, *The Sign of the Gospel: Toward an Evangelical Doctrine of Infant Baptism After Karl Barth* (Minneapolis: Fortress, 2013). For more details, see the discussion in Liston, *The Anointed Church*, Chs. 4 & 6.

28. Hunsinger, "Baptism and the Soteriology of Forgiveness," 254.

balances the tendency to merge Spirit baptism and water baptism (arising from an overemphasis on the Spirit's ecclesial role) and the tendency to excessively separate them (arising from an overemphasis on the Son's ecclesial role). Viewed through the lens of the Spirit, water baptism becomes the analogy of Spirit baptism, the human counterpart of a divine action. While this is only one of many balanced insights attained through this TAT methodology, it reveals the gains obtained from viewing the church, and this action in particular, through the lens of the Spirit. Moreover, it affirms the pneumato-ecclesial understanding of the church as the *unique context* in which a person's relationship with Christ is outworked and enabled. As Gunton rightly asserts, "the Holy Spirit is the agent of our incorporation into Christ through the medium of the community of faith."[29]

The Church as Participant in Trinitarian Life—A *Trinitarian* Third Article Ecclesiology

Viewing ecclesiology from the vantage point of the Trinity through the lens of the Spirit proves to be equally illuminating, but the approach requires significantly more nuance. In viewing the church from the vantage point of Christology, both entities being discussed "include" divinity and humanity. In comparing the Trinity and the church, this similarity no longer holds. One entity is entirely divine and the other is partially (and perhaps predominantly) human. Quite a lot of effort has been devoted recently to establishing such a coherent analogical link between the Trinity and the church. Attempts to engineer a viable bridge are often followed by theological quality-control inspectors, however, who argue that such links have flawed foundations and inadequately span the gulf between Creator and creature. This section briefly outlines an argument that TAT enables a viable analogical connection to be constructed, but results in an ecclesial understanding that is substantially different from those that utilize other connection mechanisms that do not prioritize the Spirit.

Consider first (as an important counterexample) Miroslav Volf's well-known characterization of the church as the Trinity's image or likeness.[30] The logic he uses to link the two

29. Gunton, "Baptism: Baptism and the Christian Community," 212–13.

30. Miroslav Volf, *After Our Likeness: The Church as the Image of the Trinity* (Grand Rapids: Eerdmans, 1998).

doctrines is best described as reflective. Volf considers Trinitarian characteristics one by one and determines to what extent each of these characteristics can also be considered to apply to the church. So, just as the Trinity is a relational community, with divine hypostases that cannot and do not exist in isolation from the Trinitarian community, so (in reflection) individual Christians form a relational community, and they cannot and do not live in isolation from the ecclesial community. The Trinity is an egalitarian, nonhierarchical community of persons; therefore, the church should be like this too. Volf's application of *perichoresis* is similar, although more limited. Volf argues that Trinitarian persons indwell each other as persons, while ecclesial persons merely indwell each other through the "mutual internalization of personal characteristics." He writes, "we give to each other a piece of ourselves, something of that which we have made of ourselves in communion with others, and from others we take not only something, but also a piece of them."[31]

A number of theologians, however, are voicing the opinion that Volf's reflective approach is fundamentally flawed. They maintain that a "reflective" model cannot work because the church is not an image of the Trinity at all. Perhaps the most influential voice of this group is Kathryn Tanner, who argues that "it would be better to steer attention away from Trinitarian relations when making judgments about the proper character of human ones."[32] Taking aim not just at Volf's work, but others such as Moltmann, Boff, Zizioulas, and LaCugna who adopt such a reflective methodology, she outlines four broad areas of concern.

First, she notes the decidedly ambiguous sociopolitical potential of applying Trinitarian theology to human relationships, arguing that Trinitarianism has to be interpreted quite narrowly for it to be maintained as a helpful social analogy. Think about what Trinitarianism *could* mean if indiscriminately applied to human interactions. The fact that Trinitarian persons are defined by their relationship *could* imply that people should be defined by their (often demeaning) social roles, for example. Second, she argues that making the Trinity directly applicable to social relationships involves making unjustified theological moves. For example, to have social

31. Ibid., 211.

32. Kathryn Tanner, *Christ the Key* (Cambridge: Cambridge University Press, 2010), 207–8. The following paragraph briefly summarizes Tanner's argument in this chapter.

applicability the Trinity must be viewed as equivalent to a society of human persons, with the clear implication of tritheism. Tanner's third concern centers on our limited knowledge of the Trinity's inner workings. This leads to the circular logic well documented by Karen Kilby, where something unknown in the Trinity is "filled out" from our human experience, only then to be presented as a resource to *inform* our human experience.[33] Fourth and finally, Tanner recognizes the infinite gap between creature and Creator, and she argues that to the degree that the Trinity either is or becomes like humanity, it can teach us nothing about human society, for we already know from experience what it means to be human. But to the degree that the Trinity remains distinct from humanity, we are inevitably powerless to imitate it. Humanity's finitude and sinfulness mean that Trinitarian imitation is thus reduced to an unreachable utopian goal. Tanner comments: "Turned into a recommendation for social relations, the Trinity seems unrealistic, hopelessly naïve, and, for that reason, perhaps even politically dangerous."[34] Tanner's solution to all of these problems is to replace the Trinitarian analogy with a christological one. She claims that the incarnation provides much more insight into human relationships, and is a much better analogy for human communities to aspire to.

Applied specifically to the reflective methodology of Volf and others, Tanner's concerns, critiques, and conclusions are very persuasive. Indeed they are so persuasive that several theologians argue that not just reflective analogical bridges like Volf's, but any and all analogical bridges joining the Trinity and the church are similarly flawed. For example, John Webster writes that "the connection of theology proper and ecclesiology is [not] best explicated . . . by setting out two terms of an analogy."[35] Such comments, however, go well beyond Tanner's explicit and implicit intent, and significantly too far in general, precisely because there exist viable analogical alternatives to the reflective methodology adopted by Volf and others.

What about an alternative analogical methodology that, in Gunton's words, "replaces a logical conception of the relation

33. Karen Kilby, "Perichoresis and Projection: Problems with Social Doctrines of the Trinity," *New Blackfriars* 81, no. 957 (2000): 432–45.

34. Tanner, *Christ the Key*, 228.

35. John Webster, "In the Society of God: Some Principles of Ecclesiology," in *Perspectives on Ecclesiology and Ethnography* ed. Pete Ward; (Grand Rapids: Eerdmans, 2012), 206.

between God and the world with a personal one"?[36] What about an alternative approach that, rather than looking at how the church is *like* the Trinity, examines the implications of the church being pneumatologically *in* the Trinity, participating in its very life? What if the similarities between divine and human relationships occur not because humans are somewhat like divinity, but because they are personally indwelt by the divine Spirit, and therefore united with the human Christ? If this approach is adopted, then the continuities between the Spirit's immanent identity and his ecclesial role could be utilized to inform our ecclesial understanding. And further, believers' pneumatological union with Christ would enable comparison between his identity as Son and our participatory filial role in the Trinity. Such a pneumatologically enabled but christologically conditioned approach would proceed by first determining the Trinitarian understanding that is most responsible to the biblical revelation. That understanding of the Trinity is then applied to the economy by observing how the immanent identities of the Son and the Spirit are reprised on a series of expanding stages, christologically in the hypostatic union between the human and divine natures of Christ, soteriologically in the mystical union between Christ and the church, and finally and most pertinently ecclesiologically in the ecclesial relation between individual church members. It is not too difficult to see that this kind of alternative analogical approach not only avoids Tanner's critiques and concerns, but also demonstrates that a Trinitarian perspective is needed to complement and enhance the christological analogy suggested by Tanner and exclusively commended by others.[37] The following discussion presents a brief overview of such a TAT approach to constructing an analogical bridge between the Trinity and the church, and illustrates one particularly important example of the value it provides.

As outlined in the previous paragraph, the first question to address is to which Trinity the church is analogously related. Not that there are many Trinities, but there are many doctrines of the Trinity, as evidenced for example in the disagreements about the *filioque*. Pioneers in this field of study have already argued that "Spirit Christology provides our best mode of access to the theology

36. Gunton, "The Church on Earth: The Roots of Community," 60.

37. For more detail, see Liston, *The Anointed Church*, Ch. 8.

of the Trinity,"[38] and that a Spirit Christology implies a "reconceived" understanding of the Trinity where "the Father begets the Son in or by the Holy Spirit [and] the Son is begotten by the Father in the Spirit and thus the Spirit simultaneously proceeds from the Father as the one in whom the Son is begotten. The Son, being begotten in the Spirit, simultaneously loves the Father in the Same Spirit by which he himself is begotten (is Loved)."[39] In this understanding, championed by Thomas Weinandy and Myk Habets among others, the immanent identities of the Son and the Spirit have three key features. First, both the Son and the Spirit originate from the Father in one single action with two distinguishable parts. Just as, in human speech, breath and word are logically distinguishable but existentially inseparable, so too is the Father's breathing of the Word. The immanent identities of the Son and Spirit are thus logically and chronologically synchronous. Second, each of the Trinitarian persons is truly personal, with an active and constitutive role in the Godhead. So the Father (the originating person), persons the Son (the personed person), by the Spirit (the personing person). What this leads to is a nuanced understanding of Trinitarian *perichoresis*, which is identified as the very begetting or spirating by which the hypostases are personed. And third, this personing is not a one-off activity, but an ongoing reality, which is the third feature of this "reconceived" understanding of the Trinity. There is no distinction between how the Trinity is and how the Trinity came to be; God *in fieri* is God *in facto esse*. In every moment of eternity, the Godhead is constituted and subsists as a relational ontology *through* the Father begetting the Son in the Spirit, and the Son returning the love of the Father through the Spirit of Sonship given to him.

Having determined the Trinitarian understanding to be utilized, the next stage is to apply this understanding to the economy by observing how the immanent identities of the Son and the Spirit are reprised on a

38. David Coffey, "Spirit Christology and the Trinity," in *Advents of the Spirit: An Introduction to the Current Study of Pneumatology*, ed. Bradford E. Hinze and D. Lyle Dabney (Milwaukee: Marquette University Press, 2005), 315.

39. Thomas Weinandy, *The Father's Spirit of Sonship: Reconceiving the Trinity* (Edinburgh: T&T Clark, 1995), 17. See also Myk Habets, *The Anointed Son: A Trinitarian Spirit Christology* (Eugene, OR: Pickwick Publications, 2010), 224. Habets has also extended his formulation of Weinandy's understanding Myk Habets, "*Filioque? Nein*: A Proposal for Coherent Coinherence," in *Trinitarian Theology after Barth*, ed. Myk Habets and Phillip Tolliday (Eugene, OR: Pickwick Publications, 2011), 161–202.

series of expanding stages, the first of which is Christology. So, in an analogous manner to the Father begetting the Son by the Spirit, the Father sends the Son to become human by the Spirit. And in an analogous manner to the Son returning love to the Father by the Spirit, Jesus prays and worships the Father, giving all that he is and has to the Father by the Spirit as a loving response. The simultaneous nature of the immanent Trinity is elongated and spread, for the limitations of space, time, and Jesus' changing and growing humanity bring an inevitably sequential component. Jesus must grow and develop as a human in order to increasingly experience in an actualized relationship the Sonship that is his by nature. But the overall shape of the immanent identities remains. First, the Son and the Spirit *together* are sent out from and return to the Father. In the incarnation, like in the Trinity, there is no Jesus the Son without the Spirit and no Spirit without Jesus the Son. Second, it is through the Spirit that the Son is incarnated as a human and through the Spirit the human Son returns love to the Father. So the Son and the Spirit reprise in time their immanent identities. The Son is again the personed person, or in this case the incarnated person, the Spirit is again the personing person, as the means by which the Son becomes incarnate and also the means by which the incarnate Son returns love to the Father. And following the third Trinitarian feature, this gift and return is an ongoing activity. While there is a natural elongation in the pattern so that a distinction is needed between Jesus' status and experience of Sonship, it is nevertheless true that it is only through the continuing gift of the Spirit from the Father that the incarnate Son has and retains both his status and his growing human experience of Sonship.

The second stage on which the hypostases reprise their identities is soteriology. For as the incarnate Son loves and worships the Father by the Spirit, believers participate in Christ's filial relationship. We *enjoy the status* of Sonship because the incarnate Son in his vicarious humanity has responded to God on behalf of humans. And we *appropriate this status* of Sonship as an active experiential relationship *through the Spirit*. As Paul explains in Galatians, "Because we are God's children [our status], God sends the Spirit of his Son into our hearts, the Spirit who calls out 'Abba, Father' [our experience]" (Gal. 4:6). The immanent identities of the Son and the Spirit are thus reprised not just in the hypostatic union but in the mystical union. Just as the Son was begotten in eternity *through the Spirit*; just as Christ was hypostatically united in the incarnation *through the Spirit*; so the church is adopted as sons and daughters of God in Christ *through the Spirit*. The Spirit continues to do what the Spirit has always done and will always continue to do . . . *person* sons and daughters of God in Christ. Recognizing necessary discontinuities, there are also significant continuities between the unions: what the Spirit does in eternity is what the Spirit does in the incarnation is what the Spirit does in the church. As Calvin asserts: "We are the sons of God because we have received the same Spirit as his only Son."[40] And the Son too reprises his immanent identity in the mystical union. So the Son who is begotten in eternity, who is incarnated in creation, is embodied in the church, which consequently becomes his mystical body. Again, recognizing necessary discontinuities, there are significant continuities between the Son being *personed* in the Trinity, *personed* in the hypostatic union, and most pertinently here *personed in the church*. So now it is Christ who lives his life through us (for example, Gal. 2:20). Calvin again: "we are *one* with the Son of God . . . because, by the power of the Spirit, he imparts to us his life and all the blessings which he has received from the Father."[41]

So again, in this expansion into the mystical union, the same three immanent features appear. First, the Son and the Spirit are breathed out and return to the Father together. Their roles are logically distinct but existentially inseparable. Second, the Spirit is again the personing person and the Son the personed person. It is by the Spirit that the church is personed as the mystical body of Christ, or to say the same thing in reverse, it is Christ who is embodied in the church by the Spirit. But thirdly, this embodying is not a one-off activity but is continuously repeating. Tanner comments, "Son and Spirit are sent . . . in order to enable our return to the Father. But returned to the Father we are sent out with Son and Spirit again to do the Father's work of service to the world. The return brings with it another going out because in returning we are incorporated into the dynamic Trinitarian outflow of God's own life for the world."[42]

40. John Calvin, *Calvin's Commentaries*, trans. John Pringle, 23 vols. (Grand Rapids: BakerBooks, 2009), Gal. 4:6, 23:120.

41. Ibid., John 17:21, 18:184.

42. Tanner, *Christ the Key*, 205.

While it must be emphasized that this filial participation is primarily communal, something that we as a church enjoy together, similar affirmations can certainly be made regarding the relationship between Christ and each believer as an individual. Perhaps the key biblical image by which this communal and individual reality is conveyed is that of priesthood. Jesus is our great high priest, and through his life, death, and resurrection he offers us God's grace: grace that is precisely identified as neither more nor less than union with him through the Spirit, and consequently participation in his Trinitarian Sonship. All the other aspects of salvation follow as a consequence of this union. However, the New Testament does not merely speak of Christ as the great high priest, but also speaks of each of us individually as priests, together forming a kingdom of priests, or a royal priesthood. Gerald O'Collins and Michael Keenan Jones comment, "While the priesthood of Christ is unique, it is also participated in, albeit differently, by all the baptized."[43] But if Christ's priestly gift of grace is the gift of union with him through the Spirit and therefore participation in his Trinitarian Sonship, then our participatory role as priests leads to the conclusion that we too offer others grace as we participate in Christ. Other believers' union with Christ goes not just through the Spirit, but through us. Other believers are personed not just by Christ's relationship with them through the Spirit, but by our relationship with them as well. Not only is Christ formed or personed in each believer through Christ's gift of the Spirit, but also, in a participatory way, we person each other as well. In this manner, the Trinitarian identities of Son and Spirit are not just extended *to* the church but *within* it, not just to the inter-ecclesial relationship the church enjoys in Christ with the Father, but also to the intra-ecclesial relationships between individual church members.

This ecclesial union can be characterized as follows. As a believer participates in Christ's life, they offer his love to other believers by the Spirit, and those other believers, by the Spirit given to them, return the love of Christ to the one who originally offered it. So once again in this intra-ecclesial union, the immanent Trinitarian identities are reprised. First, the work of the Son and the work of the Spirit are again inseparable but logically distinct from each other. It is only as we participate in the life of Christ that we can offer his love by

43. Gerald O'Collins and Michael Keenan Jones, *Jesus Our Priest: A Christian Approach to the Priesthood of Christ* (Oxford: Oxford University Press, 2010), 271.

the Spirit, and it is only as this love is received and returned by the Spirit that Christ is "personed" or "formed" in the receiver. Second, in this union, the Spirit again acts as the "personing person" constituting others as ecclesial persons in Christ through their receipt and response of love. And the respondent is intrinsically identified with Christ (the "personed person") for it is through the believer's response of love enabled by the offered Spirit that Christ is personed or formed in the believer, and that he or she shares Christ's ecclesial consciousness and thus participates in his life. In other words, it is through their Spirit-enabled positive response that Christ is formed in them. In the very act of reaching out with the love of Christ by the Spirit, both the one receiving the love and the one giving it are constituted as ecclesial persons. Third, this gift of the Spirit from one to another is not a single activity that is once done and then complete, but a continuing action. We are *continually* "personed" in Christ as he offers us the gift of the Holy Spirit and we return that love to him by the very Holy Spirit *continually* given to us, *and* moreover, we are continually personing *each other* in Christ as we offer the Spirit to others, and as they receive and return the love offered by the very Spirit continually given to them.

There are many and varied outworkings and implications of this ecclesial understanding. First and foremost, it enables a clear characterization of the church as existing in any and all relationships where by the Spirit the love of Christ is offered and returned. It identifies the church as being intrinsically relational, an event of intersubjectivity, characterized by mutual giving and receiving, where every believer is both mother and mothered. It recognizes the Spirit's foundational role, but argues that the Spirit does not indwell an individual but rather resides in relationship. And significantly it identifies the sacramental nature of fellowship.

Each of these points could be expanded at length.[44] But perhaps the best way to illustrate the value of this approach to developing an ecclesiology is to contrast the features of this Trinitarian Third Article Ecclesiology with that of the ecclesiology derived by Volf and his directly reflective approach. Both understandings utilize the language of Trinitarian participation, but they use the concept in profoundly different ways. As Richard Bauckham recognizes, "Volf's twin ideas of the church participating in Trinitarian life and

44. For more detail, see Liston, *The Anointed Church*, Ch. 10.

the Trinity being a model for the church are compatible only if we think of the Trinity as like a group of three friends who include us in the friendship as yet more friends. This means that the kind of relationship (i.e. friendship) enjoyed by the original group of three friends is the kind of relationship the new members of the circle have with each other, since what has happened is that the friendship circle has expanded."[45] In Volf's understanding, then, our Trinitarian participation is participation *with* the Trinity. We take on Trinitarian characteristics, and our relationship with them is similar to their relationship with each other.

In the alternative Trinitarian ecclesiology presented here the church does not participate *with* the Trinity, but rather *in* it. We do not merely take on Trinitarian characteristics, we indwell the unique Trinitarian life. The reason such an understanding is enabled is because, unlike Volf's argument, our relationships with the Trinitarian persons and their relationship with each other are uniquely and permanently differentiated. Through the Spirit (who always is and acts as the personing person), we are united with Christ (who always is and acts as the personed person), so that we share Christ's unique status and experience of Sonship. Participating *in* Trinitarian life is incompatible with an egalitarian Trinity like Volf's (or Moltmann's), which allows changing relationships between the Trinitarian persons, as Ralph Del Colle recognizes: "Out of deep respect for Professor Moltmann I implore him to consider that the divine unity is indeed a perichoretic tri-unity (as he so strongly affirms) but that this tri-unity manifests itself now and in glory in the constitutive *distinction* of persons without which our participation in the divine nature could not occur, for our very persons are birthed anew by the Spirit to manifest the Son to the glory of the Father."[46]

The implications of this difference are far-reaching indeed. Consider as just one example the ecclesial practice of prayer and worship. If, as in Bauckham's critical assessment of Volf's understanding, the church participates with the Trinity and not in it, then prayer

45. Richard Bauckham, "Jürgen Moltmann's The Trinity and the Kingdom of God and the Question of Pluralism," in *The Trinity in a Pluralistic Age*, ed. Kevin J. Vanhoozer (Grand Rapids: Eerdmans, 1997), 160–61. See also Paul S. Fiddes, *Participating in God: A Pastoral Doctrine of the Trinity* (London: Darton Longman Todd, 2000), 46–49.

46. Ralph Del Colle, "A Response to Jürgen Moltmann and David Coffey " in *Advents of the Spirit: An Introduction to the Current Study of Pneumatology*, ed. Bradford E. Hinze and D. Lyle Dabney (Milwaukee: Marquette University Press, 2005), 346.

is fundamentally a task we do. It cannot be sourced from the Trinitarian persons, because it is offered to them, and we cannot have differentiated relationships with them, for they do not have differentiated relationships with one another. Now, no doubt we need God's help to pray and worship. We do it because Jesus taught us to do it and left us an example of how to do it. But worship is ultimately what we do for God. Volf's egalitarian Trinity and reflective analogical approach do not provide any practical assistance or insight to our prayer life beyond throwing us back on our own initiative.

The picture of prayer that emerges from the Trinitarian Third Article Ecclesiology developed above could not be more different. First and foremost, prayer is not something that *I* do, but something that *we* do. Given that the church in this understanding is intrinsically relational, prayer becomes a community task, in which individual believers are trained and formed to become valuable members of the community. Much more importantly, though, in this understanding we do not pray *to* God, but *in* God. Prayer is initiated by the Father, who through the Spirit directs Christ as to how we should pray, and Christ in turn directs us as we are in him and in the Spirit. Then, because of our union with Christ, as we obediently follow the guidance of the Spirit, the Father accepts our prayers as if they were from Jesus. Essentially, Jesus takes our prayers that he has given to us from the Father and gives them to the Father as if they were his. As Marcel Sarot comments: "It is only because the Christian community in prayer is the body of the Son that it has through the Spirit access to the Fatherhood of the Father."[47]

An Integrated Third Article Ecclesiology

Christology and the Trinity have been utilized as the vantage points from which to examine ecclesiology not just because, to date, they are the most developed doctrines within TAT, but also because the relationship between each of them and ecclesiology is intrinsically and clearly pneumatological. Regarding Christology, it is the Spirit that forms the church as the body of Christ. Regarding the Trinity, it is by the Spirit that the church joins in the life of the Trinity. There are, however, other theological doctrines from which the church can be examined.

Ecclesiology, for example, can be viewed through the lens of the Spirit from the vantage point of *eschatology*. Just as there is an analogical correspondence between Christ and the

47. Marcel Sarot, "Trinity and Church: Trinitarian Perspectives on the Identity of the Christian Community," *International Journal of Systematic Theology* 12, no. 1 (2010): 44.

church (as the sequel to the incarnation), and between the Trinity and the church (as participant in the life of God) there is also a correspondence between the coming kingdom and the church (as the kingdom's proleptic anticipation). There are similarities between utilizing the christological vantage point and the eschatological vantage point, one of which is that the connective identity of the Spirit is again primary. Undergirding this is the recognition that just as the Spirit makes the church the body of Christ, it is the Spirit that makes the church the proleptic anticipation of the coming kingdom. Utilizing a pneumatological lens thus seems ideally suited to exploring the analogical link between church and kingdom. Such an analysis is hindered somewhat, because a specifically Third Article Eschatology is still awaiting development. For example, Heribert Mühlen's observation in 1964 that a book on the Holy Spirit and time had not yet been written "still holds true today."[48] The above observations, however, suggest that investigating Third Article Eschatology and the perspective it gives on ecclesiology could profitably be developed in tandem. While this avenue of research is still to be explored, an *eschatological* Third Article Ecclesiology should provide particular insight into the church as a "being transformed" institution, with a focus on *how* the church is transformed by the Spirit.

Perhaps the most obvious vantage point that has not yet been utilized is viewing the church in terms of its place in the world. The approach a TAT would take to examining this perspective differs substantially from the other three vantage points, however, because while the church is ontologically dependent on Christology, Trinity, and (in a slightly different sense) eschatology, the church is ontologically prior to the world. To explain, Henri de Lubac distinguishes between the active and passive aspects of the word *ecclesia*. The church is simultaneously "the community called together" and "the community of the called together."[49] John Dadosky extends this understanding by further distinguishing between "the nature and the mission of the church—the nature pertains to the people gathered, and its mission is to gather

48. Wolfgang Vondey, "The Holy Spirit and Time in Contemporary Catholic and Protestant Theology," *Scottish Journal of Theology* 58, no. 4 (2005): 393. See also Heribert Mühlen, *Una Mystica Persona. Die Kirche als das Mysterium der heilsgeschichtilichen Identität des Heiligen Geistes in Christus und den Christen: Eine Person in vielen Personen* (Paderborn: Ferdinand Schöningh, 1967), 279.

49. Henri de Lubac, *The Splendour of the Church*, trans. Michael Mason (London: Sheed and Ward, 1956), 69–86, especially 69–73.

others."[50] Clearly, these two aspects of the church are strongly interrelated. Perhaps, with some caution regarding overlapping terminology, one aspect may be labeled as the *immanent* church: the community of those called together, what the church is *in itself* by virtue of its relationship with God; and the other the *economic* church: the community called together, what the church is *for the world* by virtue of its relationship with God. And having introduced such terminology, it can also be affirmed that *the immanent church is the economic church and the economic church is the immanent church.*

This insight enables an analogical connection between the world and the church to be drawn. In a sense, the economic church is examined and viewed *through* an understanding of the immanent church. The economic aspect is not unimportant or unrelated, as the adapted *Grundaxiom* above affirms. It is by looking from the vantage points of Christology, the Trinity, and eschatology through the lens of the Spirit that we gain a view not just of what the church is in itself (immanently), but also of what the church is for the world (economically). For example, considering an extension of the Trinitarian vantage point beyond the immanent to the economic church enables the recognition that the church participates not just in the continual return of the Son and the Spirit *to* the Father in worship, but also in their continuing mission as they are sent into the world *by* the Father. Exploring this involves extending the immanent Trinitarian identities of the Son and Spirit beyond the hypostatic union, the mystical union, and the ecclesial union, into yet another sphere. This may be termed a missional union (or perhaps better, a missional offering), for just as the church exists wherever by the Spirit the love of Christ is offered and returned, so mission occurs wherever by the Spirit the love of Christ is offered, and salvation comes wherever that love is returned.

A comprehensive and coherent Third Article Ecclesiology will require not just observing ecclesiology through the lens of the Spirit from each of these four vantage points (Christology, Trinity, eschatology, world), but integrating the viewpoints gained and resolving any tensions that arise. It would be idealistic to believe that the ecclesial perspectives gained from each of the vantage points will integrate with each other perfectly, given the human excesses and oversights bound to

50. John Dadosky, "*Ecclesia de Trinitate*: Ecclesial Foundations from Above," *New Blackfriars* 94, no. 1049 (2013): 65.

creep into all of them. Nevertheless, there are grounds for hoping that the different TAT vantage points will complement each other more than they contradict. Note, for example, that while each of the vantage points illuminate all four ecclesial marks to a degree, early investigations suggest that they each most clearly illuminate a different mark. Christology, as already noted, particularly illuminates the ecclesial mark of oneness: the church is one because by one Spirit believers participate in Christ's one relationship of Sonship with his one Father. The Trinity particularly illuminates the mark of catholicity: as examined earlier, believers are personed not through Christ alone but also through others, as by the Spirit they offer Christ's love to each other and so share in his ecclesial consciousness. Early investigations suggest the eschatological vantage point particularly illuminates the mark of holiness: by the Spirit, believers are set apart for (and from) the future, journeying toward the eschaton and uniquely on earth carrying the foretaste of it within them. And finally, the vantage point of the world illuminates the ecclesial mark of apostolicity, although it is a "refined" understanding of apostolicity, which "must be understood in the original New Testament sense of being sent out to bear witness to the eschatological future that has broken forth in the life, death and resurrection of Jesus Christ,"[51] a "refined" definition that Cheryl Peterson notes as a natural consequence of examining ecclesiology through the lens of the Spirit. By the Spirit, we are sent into the world, following in the footsteps of those sent by Jesus.

At this point, with much research still to be done, it is of course impossible to say definitively what a truly systematic and comprehensive Third Article Ecclesiology will look like. But notwithstanding such analysis and future perception, the christological and Trinitarian viewpoints alone have yielded significant insight into the constituent features of a Third Article Ecclesiology. If Cheryl Peterson is correct in positing that "the real crisis facing the churches is one of identity,"[52] and that "to discover who the church is . . . we ought to 'start with the Spirit,'"[53] then it is hoped that the pursuit of a Third Article Ecclesiology provides a helpful step forward.

---

51. Cheryl M. Peterson, *Who is the Church? An Ecclesiology for the Twenty-First Century* (Minneapolis: Fortress, 2013), 133. For further discussion of this "refined" definition of apostolicity, see ibid.

52. Cheryl M. Peterson, "Who is the Church?," *Dialog* 51, no. 1 (2012): 24.

53. Ibid., 28.

CHAPTER 19

Communio Ecclesiology

The Spirit's Work of Salvation in the Life of the Church

TOM GREGGS

Human fallenness has a horizontal as well as a vertical dimension: the fall not only ruptures relations with God, but also (and as a consequence of this) ruptures relations between humans, and between humans and the rest of creation. Reconciliation and redemption, therefore, are not only needed for humans in relation to the vertical order (vis-à-vis God), but also in relation to the horizontal dimensions of sinfulness (in relation to the rest of creation). It is in this context that we might think most appropriately of the work of the Spirit in salvation,[1] and in this way that we might begin to understand St. Cyprian's maxim *salus extra ecclesiam non est.*[2] The Spirit is the one who opens humans up to one another, incorporating them into the body of Christ, giving them a true and fundamental identity in baptism and through the life

1. This said, it is important to attend here to the doctrine of appropriations. See Thomas Aquinas, *Summa theologiae* I, q. 39.

2. More commonly rendered, *extra ecclesiam nulla salus est*—"Outside the church there is no salvation."

of the church (which the Spirit creates), and opening them up through the church to the world. In this communion, we see redemption being worked out by God through the person of the Spirit in space and time on the horizontal plane: this is the ongoing work of salvation (salvation to life in all its fullness) in the time between the resurrection of Jesus and the consummation of all things. In the life, death, and resurrection of Jesus Christ, the God-human, reconciliation between God and humans is completed once and for all. In the time of the church (the time of God's patience),[3] this restored relationship between God and humanity begins to be worked out not only (vertically) in the praise, prayer, and confession of God's people in the life of the church, by which the Spirit orders the human toward God, but also through the work of the Spirit in creating communion *with one another* (horizontally) in the church.

This chapter will outline the essence of sin as the *cor incurvatus in se* (the heart turned in upon itself), and identify not only the vertical implications of this, but also the horizontal impacts of the fall in terms of human individualism and self-centeredness in relation to the rest of the created world. From here, the chapter will argue that it is necessary to examine the operation of God in salvation from the perspective of the effects of the fall on the horizontal plane as well as the vertical plane. The chapter will advance that through incorporation into the body of Christ the believer participates by the Spirit in the true humanity of Jesus (a humanity that is opened fully to God and fully to others), and the believer does this by receiving and sharing in the same Spirit as rested fully and intensely upon Christ in his full, perfect, and complete humanity. The Spirit incorporates the individual into the body of Christ, and creates in her the realization that humanity is cohumanity and that cohumanity is the reorientated reality that arises in space and time from God's work of salvation. The concrete form of this new life that the believer has takes shape through the continuing work of the Spirit in establishing the life of the church. The establishing of the church itself is a salvific act of God, which allows the outworking of the vertical reconciliation that God has effected in Jesus Christ to reverse the effects of the fall in time and space in both restoring the relationship of humanity to God *and, in the life of the church, restoring the*

3. See Karl Barth, *Church Dogmatics* II/1: *The Doctrine of God*, ed. Geoffrey W. Bromiley and Thomas F. Torrance, trans. T. H. L. Parker et al. (Edinburgh: T&T Clark, 1957), 406–39 (§30.3).

relations between humans and between humans and creation. This aspect of salvation is the operation of God the Holy Spirit in turning the heart turned in upon itself out toward that which is not itself in creation.

Horizontal Fallenness

The origins of sin arise from the human breaking a relationship with God through disobedience: Adam and Eve disobey the one command God gives to them in the context of God's superabundant grace in creation; they eat the forbidden fruit. But the immediate consequence and effect of this act, even before the description of the rupture in the relationship with God that follows, is that the man and woman understand themselves to be naked in front of each other, and cover themselves (Gen. 3:7).[4] Furthermore, having hidden himself from God because of his nakedness when God walks in the garden, Adam immediately seeks to divert blame away from himself and toward Eve, and indeed through this to God: it is "the woman you [God] gave to be with me" whom Adam blames for eating the fruit, which, he is clear, was given by Eve (Gen. 3:12).[5] The woman then also offers blame away from herself toward the serpent (Gen. 3:13).[6] We see disjointed and conflictual individual reality arising immediately from the fall, with the sense of separate and individualized identity, not only in relation to God, but also in relation to other humans and the rest of creation.

4. Luther reflects on both the vertical and horizontal components of this verse. See Martin Luther, *Lectures on Genesis Chapters 1–5*, Luther's Works, ed. Jaroslav Pelikan (St. Louis: Concordia, 1958), 163–69 (especially 167–69 on the rupture between human beings).

5. All Bible quotations are taken from the *New Revised Standard Version* (1989).

6. Clearly, there are significant issues here to which feminist theology rightly draws our attention, such as the potentially problematic male-female power relations of the text, specifically with regard to man's fall through woman. For an initial survey of the literature on this theme, see, for example, Carol Meyers, "Gender Roles and Genesis 3:16 Revisited," in *The Word of the Lord Shall Go Forth*, eds Carol Meyers and Patrick O'Connor (Philadelphia: Eisenbrauns, 1983); Ilana Pardes, *Countertraditions in the Bible: A Feminist Approach* (Cambridge, MA: Harvard University Press, 1992); Phyllis Trible, *God and the Rhetoric of Sexuality* (Philadelphia: Fortress, 1986); Mary Daly, *Beyond God the Father: Toward a Philosophy of Women's Liberation* (Boston: Beacon, 1973). The points made in this chapter do not seek to displace such critiques. However, this chapter seeks to focus these critiques further in relation to the issue of individualistic alterity. Feminist critique of the text presupposes the very problem that the text intends to clarify, namely, the very individual power relations that arise from a distorted alterity.

Human nature is thereby corrupted by sin, for this alters the relationship that exists not only between the human and God, but also between human beings themselves. Because the human no longer seeks to be orientated on God and to share in the good gifts of God's grace, the human shifts the focus of her orientation onto herself. There is an awareness of individual identity in a relationship of (potentially conflictual or hostile) alterity toward both God and other human beings. Indeed, to be aware of other options beyond immediate obedience is itself to be aware of one's self over and against God: no longer shared co-willing, but a distinctive will aside from that which God has. It is an act of the grace of God, indeed a participating in that grace toward that which is other than Godself in creation, for the human to be able to be orientated toward another—both God and other human beings. As soon as humanity is tempted to step outside of that relationship of grace, the consequence is that the human being ceases to participate in the grace that allows her to be orientated toward another and not herself: outside of grace, the human finds herself outside of the ability to receive and share in God's absolute, free loving-kindness, which affects her orientation toward those around her. That the myth of Genesis records that it is one individual who is tempted to behave thus, and then the other also partakes of the forbidden fruit, further underlines the degree to which the individual's self-awareness and self-orientation is key: Eve and Adam do not make the decision together initially, but apart from each other; they blame each other; the man even blames God for giving him the woman. This is a long way from the origins of man and woman recorded in the second creation myth:

> This at last is bone of my bones
> and flesh of my flesh;
> this one shall be called Woman,
> for out of Man this one was taken.
> (Gen. 2:23)

The unity and sense of identity between man and woman in the second myth (emphasized by the story of the rib taken from Adam) indicates that cohumanity was originally a (perhaps the) central feature of the creation of humanity. This is also evident in the first creation myth in which the unity of man and woman is linked with being made in the image of God:

> So God created humankind in his
> image,
> in the image of God he created them;

> male and female he created them.
> (Gen. 1:27)

Male and female are created together, and their joint creation is in the image of the gracious Creator: there is no individualism here, and human unity ("them") is related to the image of God who in creation determines Godself to be for another.[7] In the story of the fall, it is the person's *individual* identity in relation to another (both God and another human being) that begins to take center stage.

Accounts, therefore, of the restoration of creation from the fall require an account of the operation of God in restoring the relations of humans to other humans as well as humanity's relation to the rest of creation,[8] since these, too, are consequences of fallenness, along with broken relations between the divine life and the human. In general, accounts of salvation have focused upon the economy of God in the incarnation of the Second Person of the Trinity, God the Son. Salvation comes through the God-human, Jesus Christ, who mediates God to humanity and humanity to God.[9] The key concern here is that the fall is overcome, and humanity is offered salvation by restoring the relationship between God and humanity. Clearly, this is the primary concern of salvation: humans are saved by the grace of God in Jesus, who while we were still sinners died for us (Rom. 5:8); for us and for our salvation, God became human, as the Nicene Creed attests. It is only as a gift of God's grace that humans are saved, and God's merciful, free loving-kindness is such that God chooses not to be without the fallen human creature. Furthermore, for God, horizontal and vertical (or ethical and ritual) sin cannot be differentiated: all sin is a falling short of God's glory; and it is only (as we have established) by participating in the good grace of God that the human can share in being orientated away from the self and toward the other in creation. However, God does not only in God's salvific grace set right human relations with Godself (vertically); in God's economy of salvation, God also in God's grace sets right human relations to each other and to creation. This horizontal

7. See Barth, *CD* III/1: *The Doctrine of Creation*, §41; cf. *CD* II/2.

8. On this theme, see David L. Clough, *On Animals*, vol. 1 of *Systematic Theology* (London: T&T Clark, 2012), especially chapter 7.

9. We might think of the locus classicus of this view as Anselm's *Cur Deus Homo?* See "Cur Deus Homo," in Anselm, *Anselm: Basic Writings*, trans. Thomas Williams (Hackett Publishing, 2007), 237–326.

reorientation of humanity is no less a work of God's salvation than the vertical restoration.

This is no new discovery. But what might be of note is that where there is a concern to express the horizontal dimension of salvation, this again has tended to be in relation to the work of God in Jesus Christ—through a moral example,[10] through Christ's command,[11] or through an enhypostatic participation in Christ's humanity.[12] The operation of the Spirit in salvation is often somewhat overlooked or played only in a minor key.[13] The role of the Spirit in establishing the life of the church, and the church's salvific significance, can fall into the background—that is, it is not theologically explored or related to other aspects of the economy of God's salvation. Such a perspective that underplays the Spirit's work may well, however, sublate God's economy of salvation, either reducing the church negatively to a mere human structure (as simply a gathering of humans with no recognition of the salvific miracle of the church's existence),[14] or heightening human authority in the institutions of the church (without a critical approach to an overidentification of God's work with human

10. Perhaps the greatest example of such "subjective" theories of atonement—as Gustav Aulen dubbed them in his now classic *Christus Victor: An Historical Study of the Three Main Types of the Idea of the Atonement* (New York: Macmillan, 1969)—is that of Friedrich Schleiermacher, whose doctrine taught that the effects of the cross were of no real effect outside of the new community of the church (*The Christian Faith*, 2nd ed., trans. H. R. Mackintosh and J. S. Stewart [Edinburgh: T&T Clark, 1928], 425–38). This idea was carried forward by Adolf von Harnack in his "The Essence of Christianity" lectures, and later by Albrecht Ritschl in *The Christian Doctrine of Justification and Reconciliation* (New York: Scribner, 1902).

11. See Dietrich Bonhoeffer, *Discipleship*, ed. Geoffrey B. Kelly and John D. Godsey, trans. Martin Kuske and Ilse Tödt (Minneapolis: Fortress, 2003), 77; and Barth, *CD* II/2, §37.

12. See my *Barth, Origen, and Universal Salvation: Restoring Particularity* (Oxford: Oxford University Press, 2009), 32. Cf. Barth, *CD* II/2, 7; George Hunsinger, *How to Read Karl Barth: The Shape of His Theology* (New York: Oxford University Press, 1991), 114; Bruce L. McCormack, "Grace and Being: The Role of God's Gracious Election in Karl Barth's Theological Ontology," in *The Cambridge Companion to Karl Barth*, ed. John Webster (Cambridge: Cambridge University Press, 2000), 92–100.

13. This is potentially a more Protestant propensity, as there is nervousness about affording too much salvific "power" to the church: only Christ saves. However, the point of this chapter is to argue that in the life of the church there is a further salvific work not of the church as an institution but of *God* in the person of the Holy Spirit.

14. See John Webster, "'In the Society of God': Some Principles of Ecclesiology," in *Perspectives on Ecclesiology and Ethnography*, ed. Pete Ward (Grand Rapids: Eerdmans, 2012), 200–222.

structures).[15] There is a need for accounts of salvation to have a deeper degree of reflection on the Third Person of the Trinity. While attending to the doctrine of appropriations (and remembering *opera trinitatis ad extra indivisa sunt*), no doubt we would wish to affirm with the most ancient traditions that the Father creates, the Son saves, and the Spirit sanctifies the people of God;[16] we must also note that the act of sanctifying is a salvific act that reverses the effects of the fall by returning humans to communion, not only with God in Christ, but also with each other in the work of the Holy Spirit in the life of the church. To speak of the work of the Holy Spirit is to speak of the acts and events of God in the time between the ascension and return of Jesus Christ; it is to speak of the acts of God in establishing the life and work of the church by an event of the Holy Spirit. Such a work of God is a continuing work of salvation before the consummation, for in time and space God establishes returned interhuman relations, which redefine the identity of the human not as those whose hearts are turned in upon themselves in self-preserving egoism, but as those whose hearts are turned outward toward God, and—as they are turned outward toward God—turned outward toward the church (that is, as the corporate body of Christ in which the individual finds her primary and most basic identity).

Horizontal Salvation through the Spirit in the Communion of the Church

Through the life, death, and resurrection of Jesus Christ, humanity is reconciled to God. The restoration of this vertical relationship to what it was in a prelapsarian condition also involves the restoration to that condition and a reversal of the effects of the broken relationship with God and God's good grace: thereby, broken human-to-human relationships are

15. We might think of these approaches as being crudely parallel to Ebionism or docetism respectively, and may correspond to low-church and high-church self-understandings accordingly. On such characterizations of ecclesiology, see Colin Gunton, "The Church on Earth: The Roots of Community," in *On Being the Church: Essays on the Christian Community*, ed. Colin E. Gunton and Daniel W. Hardy (Edinburgh: T&T Clark, 1997), 65.

16. Classically, in the Niceno-Constantinopolitan Creed, the church confesses belief in "God the Father, Maker of heaven and earth . . . in Jesus Christ . . . [who] for us and for our salvation came down from heaven . . . [and] in the Holy Spirit . . . [who] has spoken through the prophets" and whose presence enables "one, holy, catholic, and apostolic church . . . the forgiveness of sins . . . and the resurrection of the body."

also restored, as humans are able to participate in the grace of God, and are thus orientated away from themselves and toward others (the movement that is the foundational nature of God's grace as God wills to be for another other than Godself in creation—even in its fallen state). This reorientation of humanity and restoration of human-to-human relationality is an act of the Spirit of God, who makes us participants in the body of Christ, sons and daughters of God. As Paul recounts in 1 Corinthians: "For in the one Spirit we were all baptized into one body—Jews or Greeks, slaves or free—and we were all made to drink of one Spirit" (1 Cor. 12:13). Here, difference and individual identity are relativized and reduced in relation to the one Spirit and one body into which all individuals are baptized. This body is defined by Paul later in the chapter as the body of Christ: "Now you are the body of Christ and individually members of it" (12:27). It is the Spirit (with whom Christ baptizes) in whom members of the church are baptized, and through whom they come to be members of the body of Christ.[17] To be a member of the body of Christ not only alters our relationship to God, from its broken postlapsarian state, but also alters the anthropological status of individuals who are no longer essentially understood in their individual identity, but through the Spirit's baptism in their relationship to Christ: there is no longer Jew or Greek, slave or free, male or female, since the church is one in Jesus Christ (see Gal. 3:28). In Christ, we not only share in his mediating work between God and humans, but we also recover, by the Spirit with whom he baptizes, what it means to be fully human as God eternally determined—participating in God's grace through restored vertical relations, and so enabled to be turned away from ourselves and out toward other human beings. By being a member of the body of Christ, our humanity is transformed into the humanity it was created by God to be. This is a cohumanity, rather than an individualistic humanity—a humanity whereby we do not exist by ourselves or even in groups or organizations of individuals who gather together as individuals jointly, but in which we *share in one another.* As Paul puts it in Romans: "so we, who are many, are one body in Christ, and individually we are members one of another" (Rom. 12:5). To be a member of the body of Christ is not only to aggregate together in the church, but it is also to be "members of one another"—to

17. On the distinction between water baptism and baptism by the Spirit, see Barth, *CD* IV/4, "The Foundation of the Christian Life," 30–31.

recognize that salvation makes our identity radically different. Or, put otherwise, the church is not simply a collection of individuals who come together and are dispersed; the church reveals our true and eternal identity as members of the body of Christ. We are not to think of ourselves first as individuals and second as those individuals who gather but rather as a communion of those who share in each other as we share in the body of Christ.

But what specifically has this to do with the Spirit? Is this not more Second Article than Third Article Theology? Let us parse the above argument, and begin in relation to baptism, which itself exists under the Third Article of the Creed.[18] In baptism, we are baptized into Christ, and in this we share with Christ in receiving the Holy Spirit (see Matt. 3:16 and parr.). This gift of God to humanity is not, however, a means by which we are transformed into something other than human, nor in baptism is something added to us beyond God's initial prelapsarian desire for creation. In receiving the Spirit in baptism, humanity is enabled to share and participate (both de jure and de facto) in the humanity of Christ. Christ's reception of the Holy Spirit in the baptismal narrative is not a pointer to his divine identity; this comes in the Father's announcement that Jesus is his beloved Son. Rather, it might be best to think of Christ's reception of the Holy Spirit (like his baptism itself) as a fitting sign and even fulfillment of Christ's full humanity. The reason for this might be traced to the presence of the Spirit as being constitutive of human life: the *nish'mat-ruach chayim* or the breath of life, where the two words for breath (*nishmah* and *ruach*) are used almost as synonyms or perhaps in apposition such that *nishmah* (breath) is described as the *ruach chayim* (the Spirit of life). The use of *ruach* here is significant. The Spirit (who is, as the Constantinopolitan Creed notes, the Giver of Life) gives life (breath) to humanity: it is by the Spirit that humans become living beings. Job gives us a clear image of this, linking the presence of the Spirit, breath and human life:

> If he [God] should take back his spirit to
> himself,
> and gather to himself his breath,
> all flesh would perish together,
> and all mortals return to dust. (Job
> 34:14–16)

18. The Creed should not be read as four articles, as if the discussion of the church were a separate, fourth moment: the Creed's Third Article on the Holy Spirit is the one under which we read about the identity of the church.

To be a true and real living human being involves receiving the breath (or Spirit) of God. If we are to think of the baptismal narrative as having some echoes of the creation narrative,[19] we might wish to suggest that the Spirit's resting on Jesus in his baptism is a perfection of his full humanity:[20] the Spirit who is extensively present throughout the world is fully and intensively present in the human Jesus. The receiving of the Holy Spirit by Jesus is an active recognition or even consummation of his true humanity—the humanity that other humans as yet do not possess in fullness but which they will receive in the eschaton.[21] The reception is a fulfillment of creation, an eschatological anticipation of the true humanity to which humans were eternally predestined, seen in the discussion of human existence in Scripture: the resting of the Spirit on Jesus is a confirmation of his complete and true humanity, which is caused by and drenched with or immersed in the Holy Spirit.

In short, to be wholly and truly human is to be wholly and truly open to the Spirit of God: to become more human and to increase our humanity is to be completely open to the Holy Spirit; the more the Spirit dwells with us, the more human we may become. The

19. A number of commentaries point to the reminiscence of Gen. 1:2 (the Spirit hovering over the waters of the deep) here; see, for example, C. E. B. Cranfield, *The Gospel according to St. Mark* (Cambridge: Cambridge University Press, 1963), 53–54; and Morna D. Hooker, *The Gospel according to St. Mark* (London: Black, 1991), 47. However, the connection to the presence of the Spirit in the creation of humanity does not seem to be considered, despite parallels that suggest themselves, especially in light of the Pauline idea of the first Adam becoming a living being, but the last Adam a life-giving Spirit (see 1 Cor. 15:45).

20. This is distinctive to Spirit Christology. This form of Christology, sometimes explained in distinction from (but not necessarily contradiction to) so-called Incarnation or Logos Christology, understands the work of the Spirit as integral to both Christ's identity as the Second Person of the Trinity (the Son), and Christ's salvific work as risen Lord. Specifically, Christ's baptism and mission in the Spirit, his giving of the Spirit to the church, and his objective love with the Father, which is the Spirit, are each understood as integral to his divine person. See, for a range of examples, Walter Kasper, *Jesus the Christ* (London: T&T Clark, 1976, 2011); Paul Tillich, *Systematic Theology*, vol. 2, *Existence and the Christ* (Chicago: University of Chicago Press, 1975); David Coffey, *Deus Trinitas: The Doctrine of the Triune God* (Oxford: Oxford University Press, 1999); and Ralph Del Colle, *Christ and the Spirit: Spirit-Christology in Trinitarian Perspective* (Oxford: Oxford University Press, 1997). The approach offered in this chapter seeks to associate the presence of the Spirit far more closely with what it means to speak of Christ as true human.

21. See Eberhard Jüngel, *Theological Essays II* (London: Bloomsbury, 2014), 216–40.

descent of the Spirit onto Jesus is the realization in time and completion of his true humanity; this is in part why the baptismal narrative follows the infancy narratives so closely. Since time and space are essential to created humanity, in time and space Jesus' humanity flourishes to be complete humanity, which all of humanity was determined to share in; the resting of the Spirit on Jesus is an indication of this. Yet, Jesus is not only the one who is baptized and receives the Holy Spirit; he is also the one who baptizes with the Holy Spirit. In the giving of the Holy Spirit in baptism, Jesus offers the gift of God's own self in the person of the Spirit in the economy of salvation, so as to restore humanity to the true humanity it was created to be: baptism by the Spirit is a way in which humanity is not only reconciled to God but made anew as true human beings. Paul picks up this link between Adam's creation, Jesus' baptism, and giving of the Spirit when he writes: "Thus it is written, 'The first man, Adam, became a living being'; the last Adam became a life-giving spirit" (1 Cor. 15:45). In baptism, by receiving the Spirit of God, we become human (or open ourselves to the potential of becoming human), and in this are enabled to participate both passively (by the objective reality of God's grace in salvation) and actively (through acts and behavior that correspond to that objective reality) in Christ's full humanity.[22] This true humanity is a humanity that shares in Christ and that has an identity more foundational than any individual identity each human may possess. Clearly, Jesus' is a life that shares fully (in fact, uniquely) in God's life—the God who has become in the Second Person of the Trinity this particular human, Jesus. But by an act of the Spirit we share in Jesus' humanity, for the same Holy Spirit who breathed life into humanity and rested fully on Christ is present to his people and works within us. We share in Christ's humanity such that we become adopted children of God (Eph. 1:5).

However, reception of the Holy Spirit through baptism, in making us adopted children of God, not only makes us fully human on an individual level, but also reorients us toward our *corporate and communal* identity in Christ. The first sense of this is that our primary and ontological identity is in relation to being part of the body of Christ. The Spirit who is at work in creation redeems humanity from its individualism and enables us to share in our true identity,

22. See 2 Cor. 5:17: in Christ the old has passed away and the new has come. This is a work from God, and in this God enables humanity to become righteous.

which is in its prelapsarian state "naked and not ashamed" (to quote Dietrich Bonhoeffer).[23] Through the presence of the Spirit in her life, the believer recovers the humanity that she was always to have: she becomes a new creation to herself, but this is the creation God eternally determined her to be. This humanity is not one where there is enmity between individuals, but where all are one in Jesus Christ. As Ephesians 4 reminds us:

> I therefore . . . beg you to lead a life worthy of the calling to which you have been called, with all humility and gentleness, with patience, bearing with one another in love, making every effort to maintain the unity of the Spirit in the bond of peace. There is one body and one Spirit, just as you were called to the one hope of your calling, one Lord, one faith, one baptism, one God and Father of all, who is above all and through all and in all. (Eph. 4:1–6)

The unity of the Spirit is the unity to which the believer is called. Humans are enabled to escape the effects of the fall through the work of the Holy Spirit, whose baptism enables us to share in the humanity of Christ. By this, horizontal relations are reordered, and cohumanity becomes the primary identity of the human being. Individual alterity in relation to God and fellow humans is reversed by a salvific act of God, who makes us anew by God's Spirit in baptism.

In time and space, the effects of this reorientation of horizontal relationality take form in the life of the church that the Spirit creates. The event of Pentecost, with the giving of the Holy Spirit, is the birth of the church. In the gift of the Spirit comes the capacity to be ordered not to oneself but to others. The life of the church in all of its variety provides the concrete form for the outworking in time and space of salvation on the horizontal plane. In the "other," within the life of the concrete community of the church, to whom one is united not by virtue of any other element except for unity in Christ through the baptism of the Spirit, one finds the form that the life of the redeemed in time has. In the life of the church, the other human exists as a divine gift to whom, by a work of the Spirit, the individual not only becomes ordered but through whom and with whom the individual also finds her true identity as not existing in

23. Dietrich Bonhoeffer, *Creation and Fall: A Theological Exposition of Genesis 1–3* (Minneapolis: Fortress, 2004), 82: "The human being is naked and not ashamed, speaks with, and has to do with, God as though they belong to each another."

and of herself, but as one who is in Christ and as such ordered to cohumanity. In the concrete life of the community of the church, there exist others who are enabled to be the objects of the turning out of our hearts through the work of the Spirit. These others are not those to whom we necessarily are attracted by virtue of some benefit to ourselves or by virtue of a repetition of our own identities that we see mirrored in theirs. Instead, the others within the church are genuine others who are given by the Spirit as a gift of God within the church. As Bonhoeffer puts it, it is essential that we avoid the "greatest danger":

> the danger of confusing Christian community with some wishful image of pious community, the danger of blending the devout heart's natural desire for community with the spiritual reality of Christian community. It is essential for Christian community that two things become clear right from the beginning. *First, Christian community is not an ideal, but a divine reality; second, Christian community is a spiritual [pneumatische] and not a psychic [psychische] reality.*[24]

For Bonhoeffer, there are no idealized images, no demands, no bonds of union other than the act of God in bringing the community together; and for that act and the gift of the other, the believer should be thankful.[25] The otherness of these others is a divine reality given to the believer in the life of the church. In them, we discover our truest identity (not in race, class, gender, status, and so forth), but in the true cohumanity that we share in Jesus Christ through baptism as the Spirit, which rested fully in his humanity, dwells within us and makes us human. This means that variety in the life of the church is crucial: the community needs to be a community in which there is variance between individual members such that the believer is enabled genuinely to be turned out to other humans. The church is not a community like any other in which there might be some bond of attraction between members (whether shared or aggregated interests), but is a community formed by the Spirit of God where members are joined together through the redeeming activity of God's Holy Spirit, who frees individuals from sin in relation to the horizontal order of humanity. Humans are freed to be for others and to share in the cohumanity of these

24. Dietrich Bonhoeffer, *Life Together and Prayerbook of the Bible* (Minneapolis: Fortress, 2004), 35 (emphasis original).

25. Ibid., 36.

others in Christ, and this is based on nothing other than the economy of God's salvation through the work of the Spirit, who enables humans to be saved from the *cor incurvatus in se* and to be genuinely focused on the full cohumanity of all others in Christ. In the gathering of the church, the Spirit becomes intensively present,[26] bringing together these others and saving them from their focus upon themselves in their sinful hearts turned in toward themselves. This bringing together and focus on cohumanity is a work of salvation that humans cannot achieve by themselves: in fallen sinfulness, human desire is ordered toward the self and the ego, but through the Spirit this fallenness is overcome.

The church is not, therefore, a society of like-minded people or of friends, but a community of salvation (a proleptic anticipation of redemption),[27] in which we are freed from our focus on ourselves and opened to the genuine otherness of the other in the church—the other as one who also shares in the fundamental identity that we possess by participating in the true humanity of Christ. We are able to see this in the earliest communities of the church, and in the description offered in Acts 2 of its character. Here, there are two things to note. The first is the political salvation that the giving of the Spirit brings in the gift of tongues. The passage makes the variety of nations represented by those in Jerusalem at Pentecost plainly clear: "every nation under heaven" (Acts 2:5) with a very long associated list (2:9–11). However, the differences that exist between them are overcome by an event of the Spirit, who does not suppress the otherness of those present, but (affirming this otherness) transcends it and prevents it from inhibiting genuine communication between peoples:

> All of them were filled with the Holy Spirit and began to speak in other languages, as the Spirit gave them ability. Now there were devout Jews from every nation under heaven living in Jerusalem. And at this sound the crowd gathered and was bewildered, because each one heard them speaking in the native language of each. Amazed and astonished, they asked, "Are not all these who are speaking Galileans? And how is it that

26. The language of intensity and extensity is borrowed from Daniel W. Hardy, *Finding the Church: The Dynamic Truth of Anglicanism* (London: SCM, 2001).

27. For a detailed and systematic account of proleptic anticipation, see Wolfhart Pannenberg, *Jesus—God and Man* (Westminster John Knox, 1982) and Pannenberg, *Systematic Theology*, vol. 3, trans. Geoffrey W. Bromiley (Grand Rapids: Eerdmans, 2009).

> we hear, each of us, in our own native language?" (Acts 2:4–8)

Cultural and linguistic difference and otherness are not removed, but they become the means for the work of God's Spirit: it is in each native language rather than some spiritual Esperanto that those present at Pentecost hear the disciples speak. The church's form is such that it includes difference, but the Spirit brings us together in communion in that difference: otherness is essential for the possibility of freeing our hearts from their propensity to be turned in upon themselves. This is profoundly political: one identity is not suppressed or removed for the sake of another, but various identities are not an obstacle for communication, coming together, and sociality.[28] The second point to note is the sociopolitical and economic consequences of the salvific work of the Spirit. Rather than individuals preserving the things God has given them for the sake of their own individual self-preservation, all things are held in common: the church becomes the primary identity of the believer who is so orientated toward those others within the church that she is prepared to share her individual possessions. This is clearly something that Luke finds remarkable in his recounting of the life of the first Christians: "All who believed were together and had all things in common; they would sell their possessions and goods and distribute the proceeds to all, as any had need" (Acts 2:44–45). This is as much a miraculous work of the Spirit as the more "supernatural" accompanying signs of Pentecost: the effects of the freeing of humans from hearts turned in on themselves is profound in and for the life of the church, and, if the story of Ananias and Sapphira is anything to go by, central to the identity of the redeemed spiritual community. Unity in the life of the church and a life ordered toward others is a sharing in the humanity of Christ, which is a gift of salvation of the Holy Spirit of God. In this, the horizontal effects of sin are overcome, and humans are freed to share humanity rather than seek to preserve their individual egos.[29] This is why there is no salvation outside the walls of the church.

28. See Daniel W. Hardy, "Created and Redeemed Sociality," in Gunton and Hardy, *On Being the Church*, 21–47.

29. This is something that overly individualized accounts of salvation need to recognize: salvation is not simply about an individual's relationship with God, but also following from this the individual's relationship to the rest of humanity. There the greatest command involves not only loving God but also loving neighbor.

Nonexclusive *Communio*

Since the work of the Spirit in salvation brings the human being into the humanity of Christ, which is the humanity for which humans were eternally destined (rather than the fallen humanity in which postlapsarian humans currently participate), and by this redeems the human from the horizontal effects of the *cor incurvatus in se*, the form of the redeemed humanity that the Spirit brings corresponds to the humanity of Christ in which it participates. This is a body that is turned outward toward others. There is, therefore, in the Spirit's work in salvation a double turning of the heart outward: first, out toward concrete others in the life of the church in which the believer participates; second, as the body of the church out toward the world and the concrete others who are as yet not part of the church. This orientation out toward the world reflects the movement in the narrative of Christ's life: when the Spirit is given and rests on Jesus in the baptism, Jesus begins his public ministry. The resting of the Spirit on Jesus leads him to be outward focused.

The Spirit's salvific work of orientating us toward others establishes the church as a community in which members are not only united in being focused on one another (i.e., within the church), but also united in being focused as a body on others in the world. Having been gathered together corporately, in the event of Pentecost, the church receives its true identity by being ordered outward toward the world. This is an activity of the Holy Spirit in forming humanity into the body of Christ. Just as Christ is the human for others,[30] so too his body, the church, is enabled to be ordered to other human beings through the Spirit's work.

This outwards orientation through the Spirit has a double effect. First, individuals find their true identities in the body of Christ: true identity is not the individual ego, but the life of the Spirit in which we become human by being incorporated into the true humanity of the body of Christ. Second, that true humanity is such that there is no corporate egoism to replace individual egoism; in the corporate body of the church, individuals are orientated not only on one another but also on the world. The individual *cor incurvatus in se* is not replaced by a corporate or ecclesial *cor incurvatus in se*. Since through the Spirit's work human fallenness and its horizontal

30. See Dietrich Bonhoeffer, *Letters and Papers from Prison* (Minneapolis: Fortress, 2010), 228 and 501.

propensity for individualism (whether singular or collective) are reversed by incorporation into the body of Christ, Christ's own body—by a gift of the Spirit of Christ—is reflected in the corporate body of the church; just as Christ himself is offered for and focused on others, so also the corporate body of Christ in its very communion and unity is not turned in on itself, but is opened up to the world. It is the body of Christ given *for the world*. The Spirit's work in salvation in establishing the life of the church, in which the believer is freed from focusing in on herself to focusing out to the concrete other in the community of the church, is propelled beyond the confines of the community in and of itself. The reversal of human sinfulness in the heart turned toward itself terminates on the horizontal plane in the church's existence for the sake of the world. Individual hearts are turned out toward others by the Spirit within the church, and the corporate heart of the church community is turned out toward the world. Barth makes this point emphatically:

> The work of the Holy Spirit in the gathering and upbuilding of the community (*C.D.*, IV, 1 § 62 and IV, 2 § 67) cannot merely lead to the blind alley of a new qualification, enhancement, deepening and enrichment of this being of the community as such. Wonderful and glorious as this is, it is not an end in itself even in what it includes for its individual members. The enlightening power of the Holy Spirit draws and impels and presses beyond its being as such, beyond all the reception and experience of its members, beyond all that is promised to them personally. And only as it follows this drawing and impelling is it the real community of Jesus Christ.[31]

As the community of witness to Jesus Christ, which is brought about by the Holy Spirit, the church cannot simply be an end in itself even in the individual salvific end of being freed from individualism and pointed toward the other in the life of the community. As a community, the task of the church, instead, is to be sent out to the world for which it exists. The church's orientation is not to be focused on itself even in its communion and corporeality, but out toward the rest of the world for which the church exists.

There is an important order here. The world does not exist for the sake of the church—to provide members, for self-preservation, or to

31. *CD* IV/3, 764 (cf. *CD* IV/1, §62; IV/2, §67).

bring those others who are outside its bounds within it. Corporately, the church exists for the world, to witness through the power of the Spirit to the life, death, and resurrection of Jesus Christ and to the reconciliation and redemption of humanity. The Spirit not only saves humanity from anthropological egoism through the community of the church, but also saves humanity and the church from sacral communal egoism through the work of the Spirit in the church's existence for the world. Crucially, there must be a recognition of the provisionality of the church: the church is not an end in itself but a witness to the end prepared for all creation, when God will be all in all (1 Cor. 15:28). The church's existence is not to stand aside from the world, but to stand for the world. It is not the world that is instrumental for the church, since there will be a new creation and a new heaven and new earth in the eschaton (Rev. 21:1); it is instead the church that is instrumental for the world to make clear to the world that which it already is—the world reconciled by Jesus Christ. The Spirit frees the church to exist not for itself but for the world to which the church pays this testimony. This is a communal reversal of human fallenness: on the horizontal plane the community is freed from the sin of existing for self-preservation. Instead, participating in Christ's humanity, the church corporately mediates the message of salvation to the world: it is the presence of Christ in the context of the world in the time between his ascension and return. Again, this is a work of salvation, since only by the grace of God's Spirit is the church able to participate in the divine grace that is seen in God's being for another than Godself in creation. As the community of humans who are freed by the Spirit from the effects of sin in individual self-preservation, the church is a community that also corresponds to that order of existence orientated on another.[32] Life in the

32. Bonhoeffer takes this so far that he even claims that the church exists in order to take the sins of the world onto itself. This is a fulfillment of the church's existence for the sake of the world. Bonhoeffer arrestingly writes:

> The church is today the community of people who, grasped by the power of Christ's grace, acknowledge, confess, and take upon themselves not only their personal sins, but also the Western world's falling away from Jesus Christ as toward Jesus Christ. . . . With this confession the whole guilt of the world falls on the church, on Christians, and because here it is confessed and not denied, the possibility of forgiveness is opened . . . for there are people here who take all—really all—guilt upon themselves, not in some heroic self-sacrificing decision, but simply overwhelmed by their very own guilt towards Christ. In that moment they can no longer

Spirit is life ordered toward God *and others in the world*, and by this work the Spirit frees believers from replacing individual self-preservation with collective self-preservation. The concrete life of faith is one turned outward away from the self (whether on a single or collective front) and out toward others.

Conclusion

Salvation does not exist outside of the church since the church is a work of the Spirit in which salvation is worked out in space and time in the world in the time between the ascension and return of Christ. This work of the Spirit is a further work of the economy of God, which undoes the horizontal effects of the fall by freeing humans from their individual or corporate egoism of the *cor incurvatus in se*. This reverses the effects of the fall, and restores humanity to the humanity it was eternally determined to be by God. Through sharing in the same Spirit who rests on Christ and fulfills his true humanity, human beings are freed to become genuinely human and to increase the humanity that they currently have, since human existence is a work of God breathing the Spirit into Adam. The concrete form of this pneumatologically inspired anthropology is that it is ordered not on the self (which is the effect of the fall), but on God and on others. On an individual level, the community of the church provides the divine gift of others in their otherness who are essential to the truest and deepest identity of any individual—an identity that comes only in sharing in the humanity of Jesus Christ. On a corporate level, just as the Spirit compelled Jesus to begin his public ministry following his baptism and the resting of the Spirit on him, so too the Spirit compels the church to exist for the world beyond its bounds for which it exists.

think about retributive justice for the "chief sinners" but only about the forgiveness of their own great guilt (Bonhoeffer, *Ethics*, ed. Clifford J. Green, trans. Reinhard Krauss, Charles C. West, and Douglas W. Stott [Minneapolis: Fortress, 2005], 135–36).

CHAPTER 20

Proclamation and the Third Article

Towards a Pneumatology of Preaching

AMOS YONG

James Forbes, now senior minister emeritus of the renowned Riverside Church in Upper Manhattan, wrote in his book on homiletics, "Preaching is an event in which the living word of God is proclaimed in the power of the Holy Spirit."[1] While much has been said about preaching in relationship to the Holy Spirit,[2] much less has been proffered

---

1. James Forbes, *The Holy Spirit and Preaching* (Nashville: Abingdon, 1989), 56. Forbes taught homiletics at Union Theological Seminary in New York City from 1976 to 1989, including the last five of those years as the inaugural Joe R. Engle Professor of Preaching, and then served as senior minister at Riverside for the next eighteen years until his retirement. He was not only the first African American preacher to serve in both roles but also, noteworthy for our purposes, the first to come from a pentecostal background.

2. The books are legion, a sampling of which include: J. Ithel Jones, *The Holy Spirit and Christian Preaching* (London: Epworth, 1967); Calvin Miller, *Spirit, Word, and Story: A Philosophy of Preaching* (Dallas: Word, 1989); Jay Edward Adams, *Preaching according to the Holy Spirit* (Woodruff, SC: Timeless Texts, 2000); Jim Cymbala, with Dean Merrill, *Fresh Power: Experiencing the Vast Resources of the Spirit of God* (Grand Rapids: Zondervan, 2001); Tae-Hyeun Park, *The Sacred Rhetoric of the Holy Spirit: A Study of Puritan Preaching in a Pneumatological Perspective* (Apeldoorn, Neth.: Theologische Universiteit Apeldoorn, 2005); Greg Heisler, *Spirit-Led Preaching: The Holy Spirit's Role in Sermon Preparation and Delivery* (Nashville: B&H Academic, 2007); Jeffrey Crotts, *Illuminated Preaching:*

about why and how kerygmatic proclamation is a pneumatic or pneumatological event. The intuition behind this essay is that the dynamic character of Christian preaching should be explicated not only theologically (or pneumatologically, as in this case) but also phenomenologically in terms of its orality and ontologically in terms of its audibility. I will submit throughout this inquiry, however, that both the oral and audible or sonic aspects of preaching are resonant for thinking about Christian proclamation when explored along the pneumatological register.

There will be three steps to the following thought experiment. First, we will explicate the obvious orality of preaching but do so in conversation with the oral culture of Pentecostalism.[3] This is not only the Christian tradition I know best and have worked out of the most, but the pneumatological linkages between orality and preaching—the triad of themes in this discussion—also will quickly amplify against the pentecostal backdrop.[4] Second, we will shift from the oral to the audible horizon and analyze the sonic dimension of preaching. Here we will draw at length on studies of oral culture, but, again, pneumatological resonances will guide our quest. The final section will attempt to sketch what might be called a pneumatological theology of preaching. Here our goal is both descriptive and normative: on the one hand to offer an overview of preaching as pneumatological event, but on the other hand to suggest that attentiveness to the pneumatic and the oral-audible aspects of Christian communication provides a guide to homiletical praxis relevant for the present time.

Two caveats need to be foregrounded before proceeding. First, the following ought not to be read as a pentecostal theology of preaching.[5] It is more accurately considered

The Holy Spirit's Vital Role in Unveiling His Word, the Bible (Leominster, UK: Day One, 2010); and Albert N. Martin, *Preaching in the Holy Spirit* (Grand Rapids: Reformation Heritage Books, 2011).

3. In this essay, I capitalize "Pentecostals" (believers) or "Pentecostalism" when used as nouns but not when used as adjectives.

4. Most relevant for my program in pneumatological and pentecostal theology are Yong, *Spirit-Word-Community: Theological Hermeneutics in Trinitarian Perspective*, New Critical Thinking in Religion, Theology and Biblical Studies Series (Burlington, VT: Ashgate, 2002), and Yong, *The Spirit Poured Out on All Flesh: Pentecostalism and the Possibility of Global Theology* (Grand Rapids: Baker Academic, 2005).

5. There are plenty of such books, including but not limited to: Guy P. Duffield, *Pentecostal Preaching* (New York: Vantage, 1957); Ray H. Hughes,

an outline of a pneumatological theology of preaching, perhaps even a contribution to thinking about the nature of the so-called Spirit-filled or Spirit-empowered preaching prevalent in the literature,[6] albeit one especially informed by oral-cultural analyses (of pentecostal preaching) and phenomenological considerations (regarding the nature of sound). Second, I am only at the beginning stages of thinking about orality and its theological implications and have yet to thoroughly engage the literature. Yet I am led instinctively to the interconnections between pentecostal or other forms of orality and what might be called a sonic rationality, and believe these might be productive for thinking theologically about preaching.[7] If our line of inquiry proceeds successfully, it might add to the growing discussion of pneumatological theology, a conversation in which I have been decidedly invested as a systematic theologian.[8]

Pentecostalism and Oral Culture: A New Soundscape for Spirit-Empowered Preaching?

Any literary consideration of modern pentecostal preaching, such as this essay, has to

Pentecostal Preaching (Cleveland, TN: Church of God Department of General Education, 1981); Ken Chant, *The Pentecostal Pulpit: Studies in the Art of Preaching* (Ramona, CA: Vision, 1995); Charles T. Crabtree, *Pentecostal Preaching* (Springfield, MO: Gospel Publishing House, 2003); and Aldwin Ragoonath, *Preach the Word: A Pentecostal Approach* (Winnipeg, MB: Agape Teaching Ministry of Canada, 2004).

6. From the nonpentecostal, charismatic side, see Arturo G. Azurdia III, *Spirit Empowered Preaching: The Vitality of the Holy Spirit in Preaching* (Fearn Ross-shire, UK: Mentor, 1998); cf. pentecostal scholars also on this theme: Mark L. Williams and Lee Roy Martin, eds., *Spirit-Filled Preaching in the 21st-Century* (Cleveland, TN: Pathway, 2014).

7. My cues for the so-called sonic rationality spring from Werner Kelber's reference to a "typographic . . . rationality"—see Werner H. Kelber, "The Oral-Scribal-Memorial Arts of Communication in Early Christianity," in *Jesus, the Voice, and the Text: Beyond* The Oral and the Written Gospel, ed. Tom Thatcher (Waco, TX: Baylor University Press, 2008), 235–62 (260)—a modality and frame of thinking dominated by sight, reading, and print. My question here is how thinking proceeds orally, even prior to literacy and its benefits.

8. So far, I have written books (in some cases more than one) on pneumatological theology of religions and interfaith encounter, pneumatological hermeneutics, pneumatological theology of disability, pneumatology and science, pneumatological-political theology, pneumatology of love, pneumatological missiology, and pneumatological systematics, among other less ambitious explorations in pneumatological theology. Why not trek toward a pneumatological theology of preaching? Consider this a first step in that direction.

acknowledge the struggle of shifting from an oral to a written register. From the latter perspective, much of pentecostal preaching, especially its stylistic distinctiveness, is alien, if not incomprehensible.[9] The following, however, wagers that the pentecostal preaching tradition can be comprehended more accurately when considered acoustically and resounded vis-à-vis human orality. What if its so-called emotionalism and exuberance were understood in terms of holistic embodiment instead? Might the affectivity of pentecostal preaching appear differently when rung out in oral-cultural modulation? When happens when we perceive pentecostal spirituality as oral performance rather than from a literary or textual perspective?[10]

If we consulted the recognized dean of pentecostal studies, Walter Hollenweger, we would note that of the many sources nurturing the modern pentecostal movement, what he calls the "oral root" may well be the most crucial and substantive.[11] More specifically,

9. Much has been assumed about pentecostal preaching and not all of this salutary. Pentecostal preaching has been stereotyped as being too emotional, animated, even frenzied. For all the whooping, shouting, and crying produced, such preaching, for its critics, lacks content, especially intellectual and theological substance. Hence pentecostal preaching might be effective in moving hearts and exciting bodies, but fails to feed and nourish the mind. At its worst, stirring up the emotions is misguided and can even be manipulative for preachers motivated for reasons other than the proclamation of the gospel. These characterizations, however, are oblivious to how the norms of literate cultures misapprehend oral performances, precisely part of the point of the pages to come. Anticipating the following argument will be helped if we considered a phenomenology of pentecostal preaching that situates its performativity within the broader culture of pentecostal worship; see for instance Cheryl J. Sanders, *Saints in Exile: The Holiness-Pentecostal Experience in African American Religion and Culture* (New York: Oxford University Press, 1996), chapter 3, "'In the Beauty of Holiness': Ethics and Aesthetics in the Worship of the Saints."

10. Elaine J. Lawless, *Handmaidens of the Lord: Pentecostal Women Preachers and Traditional Religion* (Philadelphia: University of Pennsylvania Press, 1988), deploys rhetorical rather than oral-cultural analysis (as a professor of English rather than of communication), but the beginnings of such a shift of perspective are evident in her work, which highlights all that critics would find problematic about pentecostal preaching (pentecostal women's preaching no less!)—its emotionality and affectivity, existentiality, narrativity, autobiographical quality, etc.—even as her deftly articulated gendered and racial-ethnic (these are southern or Bible-belt tongues speakers!) scrutiny precipitates additional sound-ways into the orality of pentecostal culture and spirituality.

11. The "black oral root" takes up over 85 percent of the first 145 pages of Walter J. Hollenweger, *Pentecostalism: Origins and Developments Worldwide* (Peabody, MA: Hendrickson, 1997). While three of the other four "roots"—he calls them Catholic, evangelical, critical, and ecumenical—occupy the

Hollenweger understands pentecostal orality in terms of its origins at the Azusa Street revival under the leadership of the black holiness preacher William J. Seymour and argues that the distinctiveness of much of pentecostal faith is informed by the black American slave experience, including but not limited to its traditions of worship, singing, and preaching. When set in a global context, such pentecostal sensibilities resonate with indigenous cultures similarly orally constituted such as Native American (not only North American) traditions, Korean shamanism, and African religious spirituality, and this might well be part of what accounts for Pentecostalism's explosive and phenomenal growth worldwide in the last century.[12]

Our focus here, however, is on preaching. Yet thinking about the orality of Christian proclamation in light of pentecostal orality might also be instructive. More pointedly, as black pentecostal homiletician William C. Turner has reminded us, "the music of black preaching can be understood as a sort of 'singing in the spirit,' for there is a surplus (*glossa*) expressed in music which accompanies the rational content (*logos*) enunciated in words."[13] Turner's pitch extends the Hollenwegerian claim about the black oral roots of pentecostal spirituality in a homiletical direction and beyond. Preaching, when heard through a black pentecostal amplifier, not only requires thinking about Christian proclamation in terms of song and music (about which more momentarily) but also invites consideration of the event of preaching to be holistically constituted, as a fully embodied experience. Much more is engaged than the intellectual dimension, as cognition is constituted by affectivity as much as by rationality.[14]

---

same amount of space combined, the "critical root" and its 135 pages actually rely (explicitly and otherwise) on and make sense only from out of the oral matrix of pentecostal spirituality.

12. Harvey G. Cox, *Fire from Heaven: The Rise of Pentecostal Spirituality and the Reshaping of Religion in the 21st Century* (Reading, MA: Addison-Wesley, 1995), discusses this global pentecostal phenomenon in light of what he calls its primal spirituality.

13. William C. Turner Jr., "Foreword," in *Sacred Symphony: The Chanted Sermon of the Black Preacher*, by Jon Michael Spencer (New York: Greenwood, 1987), ix–xii, (xi). While our focus here will be on black pentecostal preaching, this neither essentializes pentecostal preaching in its black forms nor intends to ignore the diversity of homiletical styles across the global pentecostal movement. The point is to get at the oral dimension of preaching and my wager is that attention to the black pentecostal tradition will help us just as well in this regard as other alternatives.

14. Some might be concerned that my approach risks reducing black (pentecostal) spirituality and preaching to orality and in that respect overlooks

To be sure, black pentecostal preaching is just as much black as it is pentecostal, this being, at least in part, the gist of Hollenweger's argument. Thus our consideration of pentecostal orality in conversation with Hollenweger and Turner urges focused dialogue with the black preaching tradition in general. In this vein, preaching involves not only speaking but multiple forms of vocalization: intoning, moaning, whooping, shouting, and harmonizing are all part of the African American call-and-response tradition that informs not only the preacher's performance but also the assembly's role. The latter, in turn, is not merely responsive since there are "counterpoint" moments when the congregational participation and feedback provoke the preacher's rejoinder in turn. Considered then in terms of the event that includes preacher and hearers, the robustly embodied character of Christian proclamation comes into full view: "the listeners respond percussively with hand-clapping, foot-stomping, body-tapping, and holy dancing, the resulting texture of which is contrapuntal matrix of African-like cross-rhythms . . . [and the rhythmic repetition climaxing in a shout] typically occurs in Pentecostal and Holiness churches where holy dancing is the customary expression of jubilation."[15]

Beyond this affective and kinesthetic dimension, preaching heard through black and pentecostal earphones is perceptually interpersonal and intersubjective. More than just saying "Amen!" and "Hallelujah!"—as central as these are—call-and-response, especially at those counterpoints, involves "reciprocal instruction, through which preacher and congregation commune in the spontaneous creation of spirituals," so that "the art of black preaching involves such components as skillful solicitation of dialogue, dramatic timing or 'emotional pace,' and the ability to bring about climactic congregational celebration of

---

the rich literary tradition of black homiletics; yet to focus on and unpack the oral performance of black preaching is not to deny that in some or many instances manuscripts are written out and produced. When the liturgical and dramaturgical aspects of black worship and preaching are understood, then the point is that literary modalities might be involved, but they are still dramatized or performed in order to mediate the divine presence. Harold Dean Trulear's "The Sacramentality of Preaching," in *The Landscape of Praise: Readings in Liturgical Renewal*, ed. Blair Gilmer Meeks (Valley Forge, PA: Trinity Press International, 1996), 202–10, unpacks these liturgical and dramaturgical dimensions of black worship, even as the following pages unfold its performative quality with the help of orality studies.

15. Spencer, *Sacred Symphony*, 4.

the 'good news.'"[16] This points to the heart of preaching in the black church and pentecostal traditions wherein spontaneity and improvisation are the rule, rather than the exception. As Jon Spencer puts it, "as the gospel singer's song is characterized by a freely melismatic melodizing and the jazz singer's song by a creatively syncopated sentencing, so are the preacher's spirituals distinguished by an unrestrained and extemporaneous outpouring of religious verse executed with the finesse of a poet."[17] This does not mean that pentecostal (or black) preachers do not come prepared; it just means that the delivery of the message is dynamically performed so that the final outcome depends as much on interaction with the audience as upon having internalized the details of the sermon.

The interactivity of preaching within at least these Christian traditions might be threatening to those for whom kerygmatic proclamation ought to proceed "decently and in order"; here no less an authority than the apostle Paul is often cited (1 Cor. 14:40 KJV). Yet such concerns about anarchic subjectivism do not take into account oral-cultural dynamics wherein both speakers and audiences synergistically perform and interrelate within agreed upon parameters. So, "[w]hile call and response are moderated by the talented preacher through calculated phraseology which intentionally leaves space for response, polyphonic and heterophonic (contrapuntal) dialogue is controlled by the congregation as they allow themselves to respond to spiritual repletion"; if this is the case, then even if theoretically "dissonance is the consequence of harmonies resulting polyphonically and heterophonically . . . , to those who appreciate the tradition the overall effect is consonant."[18] Through a pentecostal sound scope, this ought

16. Spencer, *Sacred Symphony*, 6–7; for more on pentecostal call-and-response, see Christine Callender and Deborah Cameron, "Responsive Listening as a Part of Religious Rhetoric: The Case of Black Pentecostal Preaching," in *Reception and Response: Hearer Creativity and the Analysis of Spoken and Written Texts*, ed. Graham McGregor and R. S. White (London: Routledge, 1990), 160–78.

17. Spencer, *Sacred Symphony*, 16. On pentecostal spirituality heard through the improvisational dynamics of jazz, see Harvey G. Cox, "Jazz and Pentecostalism," *Archives de sciences sociales des religions* 38, no. 84 (1993): 181–88; and Stephen J. Casmier and Donald H. Matthews, "Why Scatting Is Like Speaking in Tongues: Post-modern Reflections on Jazz, Pentecostalism and 'Africosmysticism,'" *Literature and Theology* 13 (1999): 166–76. See also Jared E. Alcántara, *Crossover Preaching: Intercultural-Improvisational Homiletics in Conversation with Gardner C. Taylor* (Downers Grove, IL: IVP Academic, 2015).

18. Spencer, *Sacred Symphony*, 11.

not be too surprising, as on the day of Pentecost itself, there was multilingual and polyvocal dissonance—amazement, perplexity, incredulity, and unbelief on the one hand (cf. Acts 2:12–13)—yet such was somehow also simultaneously an incomprehensible harmony: "in our own languages we hear them speaking about God's deeds of power" (Acts 2:11).[19]

Resorting to the narrative of the day of Pentecost at this juncture thrusts us into the theological nexus where scriptural interpretation meets performative application. If in some theological circles (especially those of conservative evangelical Protestantism) there are stricter lines separating scriptural exegesis (focused on deriving the original meaning of texts in their contexts) from practical application (directed to identifying contemporary significance), pentecostal hermeneutics presumes a restorationist *this-is-that* approach that overcomes the historical chasm between biblical times and the present.[20] Thus the apostolic experience (*that*) either certifies or inspires contemporary Christian life (*this*); at the very least, the scriptural narrative provides a map for trekking, both descriptively and normatively, present faithfulness. Yet this is not merely a reader-response hermeneutic, as much as such chimes with the current discussion, since the pentecostal belief proceeds more narratively and, equally important, pneumatically. If the latter pneumatic note insists that not all that is in the Bible is relevant for any or our time except that which the Spirit retrieves, the former narrativity emerges from out of the orality of pentecostal sensibilities as it imaginatively connects Christian hope with the scriptural drama.[21]

---

19. Unless otherwise noted, all scriptural references are from the New Revised Standard Version.

20. I explicate some of this in my article, "Reading Scripture and Nature: Pentecostal Hermeneutics and Their Implications for the Contemporary Evangelical Theology and Science Conversation," *Perspectives on Science and Christian Faith* 63 (2011): 1–13, esp. 4–6; see also my discussion of this-is-that in *The Dialogical Spirit: Christian Reason and Theological Method for the Third Millennium* (Eugene, OR: Cascade, 2014), 108–10.

21. In a post-oral and post-chirographic and post-typographic age—our present age of the electronic, more specifically—Alan C. Purves, *The Web of Text and the Web of God: An Essay on the Third Information Transformation* (London: Guilford, 1998), 188, puts it this way:

> Following from the idea that the individual receives the Holy Spirit or the divine inspiration directly and is thus empowered, the charismatic view coincides with the view of the reader as author or coauthor. The text is not outside but rather what I read and therefore in me. When the charismatic reads the gospel, she is highly aware that she is the reader, she is an empowered spiritual person engaging with the

Against this background, the homiletical reflections of Luke Powery, a Princeton Seminary professor who also hails from a pentecostal background, are relevant.[22] Powery's thoughts echo pertinently for us along these lines, although they can only be ever so briefly traced. First, the this-is-that methodology connects if not fuses the biblical soundscape and the historic experience especially of the black church through the ongoing work of the Spirit of God. Powery thereby highlights how scriptural themes of lament and celebration vibrate within the African American slave historical context and how the prophetic vision of resurrection life amid a valley of dry bones (Ezekiel 37) speaks to matters of life and death amid this milieu.[23] More accurately, here black preaching not only emerges from out of the fires of real life,[24] but also is unavoidably and inextricably intertwined with black spirituality, singing, and worship. "God the Spirit gave blacks these musical sermons called the spirituals; thus they may be called *spiritual preaching*, that is, Spirit-filled proclamation."[25] In other words, pneumatology provides the proclamatory content even as the spirituals shape the form of the message and the Spirit is believed to enable the preacher.

Second, Powery's pneumatological homiletic emerges, arguably, from out of the pentecostal spirituality that shapes his thinking. The hope of which he then speaks is not merely rhetorical but is theologically grounded in the pentecostal work of the Spirit. On the one hand, the "'spirituals' [are] songs of the Spirit that voice ideas of death and hope as expressions of the Spirit"; on the other hand, "[t]o preach in the Spirit includes preaching the hope of heaven for the present and future."[26] Together, both reflect recogni-

Word of God, not following what she reads as if it were a map but responding to it as it strikes sympathetic chords in her mind and soul. . . . The charismatic is also not averse to images, because the idea of the vision, the image of God in and through the Word, come together. Word and icon, image and text, are all stimuli to the religious and divine spark of knowing that is my consciousness.

22. Luke A. Powery, "The Holy Spirit and African-American Preaching" (PhD diss., Emmanuel College of Victoria University, 2006), is the doctoral dissertation that charts many of the trajectories unfolded since in Powery's homiletical works.

23. See Luke A. Powery, *Spirit Speech: Lament and Celebration in Preaching* (Nashville: Abingdon, 2009), and Powery, *Dem Dry Bones: Preaching, Death, and Hope* (Minneapolis: Fortress, 2012).

24. "Preaching in the Spirit, spiritual preaching, faces death directly as part of proclaiming hope" (Powery, *Dem Dry Bones*, 77).

25. Ibid., 54 (emphasis in original).

26. Ibid., 17, 75.

tion that oral culture needs not propositions but inspiration to undertake the task for the next week and that such teleological encouragement will need to be theologically tethered and informed to have lasting value and impact.[27]

But third and most important for our consideration, Powery proposes from out of his reflections on pneumatic preaching what he calls a "sounding the Spirit": "The spirituals, like preaching, imply pneumatology. It is more appropriate to think about the spirituals as the expressive voice of the Spirit preaching through humanity with particular words and sounds. . . . The Spirit permeates the entirety of the spiritual, even without being explicitly named; thus the content of *spiritual* preaching requires lyrical and acoustical sensitivity."[28] Such a pneumatological phonic involves not just the vocalization of the sermon but also a charismatic orchestration of "the mood" of and for the message. For Powery, then, spiritual preaching commences variously: "repetition, rhythm, antiphony, melody, body, metaphoric coded language—conjoin the other basics of preaching to help voice the mood. It will be sonic and somatic because it is pneumatic. . . . It may take groans and moans to preach the gospel and shouts of joy when there appears to be nothing to shout about."[29] Such gestures toward what we might consider a pneumatological acoustemology. Not only: "Sound says something about the presence of the Spirit and invites the Spirit";[30] but also: hearing is inherently about not audibility but pneumatology, about the "soundings" of the Spirit from and into the deep recesses of the human soul that are immeasurable in terms of decibel levels but no less effective in their affectivity.[31]

In part for this reason African American pentecostal scholars like David Daniels have talked about a "Pentecostal sensorium"

27. In this regard, Powery also writes about what might be called the kerygmatic imagination: "Imagination is not only tethered with the Spirit but vital to a hermeneutics of hope" (ibid., 127). Thus such a kerygmatic imagination is also pneumatological: it understands that the Spirit both propels the preacher and enables—illumines, inspires, empowers—the hearing and receiving congregation

28. Ibid., 55 (italics in original).

29. Ibid., 71.

30. Ibid., 72.

31. Indeed, even people with hearing impairment can "listen" through their bodies. As Don Ihde notes, "Phenomenologically I do not merely hear with my *ears*, *I hear* with my whole body. My ears are at best the *focal* organs of hearing. . . . Sound permeates and penetrates my bodily being" (*Listening and Voice: Phenomenologies of Sound*, 2nd ed. [Albany: State University of New York Press, 2007], 44 [emphasis in original]).

that includes not only oral but also audial, tactile, and other kinesthetic registers, which combine to comprise a more expansive pentecostal and, I would add, pneumatological acoustemology.[32] The full range of pentecostal spirituality—its sounds of prayer, singing, preaching, testifying, music making, cries, glossolalia, praise, worship, shouting, tarrying, clapping, stomping, silence, and so on—are heard as challenging the orality-literary binary chiefly because these multiple modalities of pentecostal faith deprivilege vision or sight, or at least balance the playing field between what is seen and what is heard and felt. While Daniels is interested at least in part in how such a pentecostal "way of knowing" might be drawn upon to eliminate hierarchies of race (not to mention class and gender),[33] our present purposes press questions regarding how to further comprehend such pneumatological and acoustemological dynamics for a theology of preaching.[34]

Orality and the Sound of the Spirit: Intoning an Acoustemological Pneumatology

In order to probe deeper into the implications of orality for a theology of preaching, I want to expand our field of analysis to include both the nature of speaking vis-à-vis vocalization and the nature of hearing in relationship to sound. The former might be considered an exercise in what Werner Kelber calls oral ontology, the latter in what Don Ihde designates ontology of the auditory.[35] Throughout, we will be in dialogue with the maestro of orality studies, Jesuit scholar Walter Ong, even as we will connect the discussion of

32. David D. Daniels III, "'Gotta Moan Sometime': A Sonic Exploration of Earwitnesses to Early Pentecostal Sound in North America," *Pneuma: The Journal of the Society for Pentecostal Studies* 30 (2008): 29.

33. Daniels, "'Gotta Moan Sometime,'" 26–29.

34. Although I will say little more about the interface of music and preaching, the preceding hints at why I think more study of pentecostal music is needed to appreciate its affective potency and popularity among oral-cultural contexts around the world. For a global overview, see Monique Ingalls and Amos Yong, eds., *The Spirit of Praise: Music and Worship in Global Pentecostal-Charismatic Christianity* (University Park: Pennsylvania State University Press, 2015). A more local albeit also transnational assessment is provided by Robert Beckford, whose *Jesus Dub: Theology, Music and Social Change* (New York: Routledge, 2006), explores Caribbean and black British pentecostal music making and its implications for pentecostal (and Christian) faith and praxis.

35. See Werner H. Kelber, *The Oral and the Written Gospel: The Hermeneutics of Speaking and Writing in the Synoptic Tradition, Mark, Paul, and Q* (Philadelphia: Fortress, 1983), 167, 185; and Ihde, *Listening and Voice*, 15.

pentecostal preaching above to our pneumatological theology of preaching to come. In effect, the following can be considered a pneumatological rendition of Ong's explorations of the oral, sonic, and auditory dimensions of the human experience.

According to Ong, there are a number of features of oral-cultural interaction that are underestimated or completely overlooked by literate cultures that rely on written modes of communication.[36] Most of us reading this essay (or hearing its presentation) presume a logical, analytical, information-based, propositional, categorical, abstract, and chronologically-and-sequentially oriented form of discursive rationality. This is based on an ontology of sight, dominated by visual observation, which presumes distance between the individual knower and the known, and focuses (notice the correlation of the verb with the optic lens) on distinctions within a field of awareness.[37] By contrast, oral-cultural communicative patterns, as prelogical, formulaic, testimonial, narratival, and proverbial, are phonologically, metrically, syntactically, and mnemonically constrained to greater or lesser degrees. But its performance presumes verbal, vocal, and aural embodiment; its environments are participatory, situational, and social; and its eventness is characterized by evanescence, dynamism, and presentness.[38]

Stereotypical pentecostal preaching can be understood along each of these registers as an oral-cultural event. Its rhetoric, repetitiousness, and rhythms engage speaker and listeners. Preachers connect existentially to congregations through patterned sets of comparative and contrastive tropes, narratives, and testimonies. The masses connect with alliterativeness, popular cultural stock, and religiously and theologically coded formulations. Last but not least, there is a personalization of the message through the preacher's gestures, vocal inflections, facial expressions,

36. The magisterial comparative study is Walter J. Ong, *Orality and Literacy: The Technologizing of the Word* (London: Routledge, 1982).

37. Thus the "preference for vision is tied to a metaphysics of objects. Vision already is on the way to being the 'objective' sense" (Ihde, *Listening and Voice*, 7).

38. I am aware of the danger of either overcontrasting the differences between seeing and hearing on the one hand or elevating, prioritizing, or hierarchically ordering the latter over the former on the other hand, both of which are cautioned against by David Chidester, *Word and Light: Seeing, Hearing, and Religious Discourse* (Urbana: University of Illinois Press, 1992), esp. 135–38. Our focus in this essay on verbal proclamation, however, warrants our analysis of the auditory dimension; nothing in what follows presumes that other modes of human perception are less or unimportant.

and other animations. Yet we have to probe deeper. What is it that connects the preacher and the audience as from deep to deep? Here we segue to a phenomenology of sound in order to understand oral-cultural dynamics.

Oral vocalizations connect human beings as subjects, from heart to heart, as it were. Ong thereby speaks about "interiority of sound"[39] in this way:

> My voice really goes out of me. But it calls not to something outside, but to the inwardness of another. It is a call of one interior through an exterior to another interior. Because presence is itself interior, it is involved in the world of sound with which we have here been concerned more intimately than in the world of space. Sound, as we have seen, reveals interiors. For man the paradigm of sound is voice, in which communication between man and man (man in the deepest of interiors) flowers as in no other sensory manifestation. Voice is alive.[40]

Think about how sounds emanate from within—as in tapping a can allows us to discern what might or might not be in it—and about how human voices represent themselves as subjects, emerging from within, and are directed to other subjects. Thus "[s]ound reveals interiors because its nature is determined by interior relationships," and "[s]ound binds interiors to one another as interiors."[41] My point is that preaching as event is thoroughly intersubjective surely because of the oral medium, and pentecostal preaching is exemplary in this regard perhaps because of its oral virtues (without ignoring its potential problems).

Now compare oral communication to what has happened in literate cultures dependent on the written word: "Writing and reading . . . are solo activities (though reading at first was often enough done communally). They engage the psyche in strenuous, interiorized, individualized thought of a sort inaccessible to oral folk."[42] So if visuality separates the knowing subject from the known object,[43] hearing binds knowers together with the

39. Ong, *Orality and Literacy*, 71–74.

40. Walter J. Ong, *The Presence of the Word: Some Prolegomena for Cultural and Religious History* (New Haven: Yale University Press, 1967), 118 and 125.

41. Ibid., 309.

42. Ibid., 153.

43. Ong notes how Kantian and Husserlian epistemologies are predicated on sight and thus presume the chasm between the phenomenon and noumenon, the manifestation/appearance and the *Ding an sich* (ibid., 74). Might modernism thus be reliant upon a visually impaired or at least constrained modality of knowing?

known. This is what makes oral communication thoroughly interpersonal and communal as well. "The word, which is essentially sound, unites not just one man and another; it forms men into groups. It is the expression and incarnation of community."[44] More pointedly, in an auditory world, "[o]ne feels knowledge as *our* possession rather than as *my* possession."[45]

Yet it is not just that oral culture presumes human communities. Beyond communal relationality, oral interactivity catalyzes an ethos, ambience, and "entire sensory apparatus as an operational complex"[46] that supports what I have called a sonic rationality. We can consider again Turner's assessment: "Music in black preaching establishes a direct link between the spirit within the preacher, the word that is uttered, and the worshiping congregation. It operates beneath the structures of logical discourse and produces a captivating effect upon the hearer."[47] What Turner is gesturing to is that oral communication is a deeply affective and embodied medium that operates bidirectionally, as preacher and congregation are constituted by a sound-filled space. As already augured, if chirographic cultures privilege the author, even the author's intention, oral cultures prioritize neither speaker nor listener but their relationship.[48] Historically, then, oral communication presumed both that the audience's background knowledge enables completion of the speaker's meaning, and that the latter is influenced by the former. Hence Ong notes, "Orally managed language and thought is not noted for analytic precision," and, "In an oral culture, the flow of words, the corresponding flood of thought, the *copia* advocated in Europe by rhetoricians from classical antiquity

44. Ibid., 310; in his later book, Ong puts it this way: "the spoken word forms human beings into close-knit groups. . . . Writing and print isolate" (*Orality and Literacy*, 74).

45. Ong, *Presence of the Word*, 233 (emphasis in original).

46. Ibid., 6.

47. Turner, "Foreword," x. Elsewhere, Turner writes about the preacher existing, living, or even gestating in what he calls "pneumatic space—space saturated by the Spirit"; he is describing the space of the preacher's preparation vis-à-vis the scriptural text, during which, where, and when "the Spirit is free to brood, hover, inseminate fecundity for the creative work that precedes preaching" (*Preaching That Makes the Word Plain: Doing Theology in the Crucible of Life* [Eugene, OR: Cascade, 2008], xvi and 21). It would be consistent to suggest, in light of the present discussion, that such pneumatic work not only *precedes* but also *constitutes and follows* the preaching event.

48. See also Werner H. Kelber and Tom Thatcher, "'It's Not Easy to Take a Fresh Approach': Reflections on *The Oral and the Written Gospel* (An Interview with Werner Kelber)," in Thatcher, *Jesus, the Voice, and the Text*, 27–43.

through the Renaissance, tends to manage discrepancies by glossing them over—the etymology here is telling, *glossa*, tongues, by 'tonguing' them over."[49] Oral communication is therefore interactive with meaning contextually emergent and communally negotiated (between speakers and hearers and vice versa), but more rather than less definitive; in contrast, written communication is closed and in that sense static, even as its meaning is open-ended because texts invite interpretation but without authorial feedback available.

Before turning from orality to the auditory, we need to make a preliminary pneumatological connection. Stephen Webb's important contribution to theology of proclamation foregrounds the spoken word in relationship to Christology: the primordial Word and voice is that of Jesus Christ.[50] The christological emphasis is not surprising given the Barthian provenance of Webb as constructive theologian.[51] Yet there is passing reference in this regard to Barth's pneumatology as including not only speech but also hearing,[52] which parallels the pentecostal understanding of the miracle of Pentecost as one of either speech or hearing. My point here is twofold: not only that the Spirit empowers proclamation and reception of the message but that the Spirit's communicative modality is from deep to deep—the "Spirit bearing witness with our spirit" (Rom. 8:16)—even from heart to heart (cf. the Johannine account and gloss of Jesus' teaching about the Spirit: "'Out of the believer's heart shall flow rivers of living water.' Now he said this about the Spirit, which believers in him were to receive;" John 7:38–39); and that the communality of preaching as an

49. Ong, *Presence of the Word*, 104.

50. See Stephen H. Webb, *The Divine Voice: Christian Proclamation and the Theology of Sound* (Grand Rapids: Brazos, 2004). Webb also writes that "the inner life is a soundscape that integrates body, mind, and emotion, all of which are revealed in the voice" (ibid., 44).

51. The interconnections between Barth's pneumatology and Christology are carefully delineated in Aaron T. Smith, *A Theology of the Third Article: Karl Barth and the Spirit of the Word* (Minneapolis: Fortress, 2014), even as there is a nice section that unfolds how Barth's robust pneumatological and christological Trinitarianism was informed by his reflections on preaching (ibid., 35–48). My only comment is that the hermeneutical circle between pneumatology and Christology so expertly woven by Smith needs to be supplemented by an equally robust hermeneutical spiral between God and creation given the material, historical, and social character through which the triune self-revelation is unfolded. If Smith's more formal theological analysis foregrounds the former dialectic, our focus on the sonic dimensions of preaching as oral proclamation invites sustained consideration of the latter interlocution, precisely what this essay attempts to explore.

52. Webb, *Divine Voice*, 174.

oral event is fundamentally pneumatological, funded indeed by "the communion of the Holy Spirit" (2 Cor. 13:13). In short, preaching understood as an oral, auditory, and sonic event resounds pneumatologically, inviting even a pneumatological ontology that comprehends, analogously, the "presence of the Spirit, in which we live, move, and have our being, [as] the space in which the infinitely full utterance of life reverberates."[53]

Such a pneumatological ontology begs for further elucidation, especially of its sonic dimensions. This leads us from orality to audibility and the auditory. We have already begun to appreciate the all-encompassing and yet intimate nature of sound. Any phenomenological analysis will perceive ephemeral sounds surrounding and penetrating. We can helpfully compare for instance experiencing a symphony on the one side with participating in a black pentecostal worship service on the other side; the musical harmonies and the call-and-response envelop, submerge, inundate, even invade the human soul from all directions. Ong puts it this way:

> Whereas sight situates the observer outside what he views, at a distance, sound pours into the hearer. . . . You can immerse yourself in hearing, in sound. There is no way to immerse yourself similarly in sight. By contrast with vision, the dissecting sense, sound is thus a unifying sense. A typical visual ideal is clarity and distinctness, a taking apart. . . . The auditory ideal, by contrast, is harmony, a putting together.[54]

This is why a sonic rationality is both fully embodied but yet environmentally constituted, interconnected, and reverberated.

At the same time, the presentness of the hearing experience means that while sounds are fleeting, they both grow and fade; they can be anticipated and felt as echoes. In that sense, there is both synchronicity and diachronicity to sound: in its transitory evanescence, the presence of sound is the moment in which we find ourselves connected with our surroundings, and the passage through which our past meets our future. Yet there is a dynamism to sound: the next moment introduces a reintonated past and a new realm of possibilities, even as we find ourselves resituated vis-à-vis others and our environment. From

53. Christopher Emerick, "Not by Bread Alone: An Ontology of Christian Proclamation in Theological Perspective" (PhD diss., Regent University School of Divinity, 2011), 203; Emerick's thesis is much more pneumatologically funded than the title suggests.

54. Ong, *Orality and Literacy*, 72.

this auditory site, the self emerges as a temporal and spatial field: "The centering action of sound (the field of sound is not spread out before me but is all around me) affects man's sense of the cosmos. For oral cultures, the cosmos is an ongoing event with man at its center. Man is the *umbilicus mundi*, the navel of the world."[55]

Yet it is precisely this dynamic, vital, and depth dimensionality of sound that intimates a pneumatologically infused world. Ong suggests that "[f]or earlier man, under the influence of oral-aural or preliterate communications media, the world tended to be vaguely animistic. . . . Economies of thought built around the study of nature are thus vaguely animistic, for *natura* means at root birth"; by contrast, the scientific and Newtonian revolution, especially with its "accompanying exaltation of the sense of sight at the expense of hearing, spelled the end of the feeling for a vitalized universe. . . . The old more or less auditory syntheses had presented the universe as being, which was here and now acting, filled with events. For the new, more visual synthesis, the universe was simply there, a mass of things, quite uneventful."[56] Any recovery, or at least appreciation, of the oral imagination therefore triggers also a pneumatological reinvigoration. "The spirit (Latin, *spiritus*)," Ong reminds us, "meant the breath, the vehicle of the living word in time."[57]

So if the modern synthesis resulted first in a deistic God, removed from human affairs—out of sight, literally, meant out of mind and out of contact—and then later in agnostic (at best) or atheistic (at worst) dispositions, the postmodern reaction prompted at least two lines of deliberation. On the one hand, it is "evident enough that in general Asian and African cultures remain to this day far more radically oral than those of the West,"[58] and this reconnects us to the prior discussion of the expansion of pentecostal spirituality across the majority world. While some anthropologists have long called attention to the "excluded middle"—the realm of ancestors, angels, and other spiritual realities

55. Ibid., 73.

56. Ong, *Presence of the Word*, 227–28. Further, Ong writes: "Early man had a true, if at the same time, confused, sense of the mystery, power, and holiness of the word. He lived by the word in its natural habitat, the world of sound, partly because he did not know how to do otherwise. He was undistracted, although at the same time he was relatively undeveloped" (ibid., 314).

57. Ibid., 138.

58. Ibid., 75.

between the human and divine planes[59]—contemporary oral cultures remain irreducibly tridimensional, to extend this metaphorical conceptualization. On the other hand, within the Western context, there is a gradual if also palpable "reenchantment" of the world that is arguably due to the influx of new spiritualities derived from global South resources due to migration.[60] My point is the pneumatological one: (re)attunement to the world of sound brings with it awareness of other presences, interiorities, and even subjects so that we may be rediscovering ourselves as in the midst of and resounding with others. If modernity produced a "devocalized, depersonalized universe,"[61] our time booms with its acoustic ebullience, potentially replenishing our cosmic habitation with ancestors, spirits, and even deities.[62]

The preceding ontological inquiries into the oral and the auditory are indicative of how sonic considerations open up toward what Werner Kelber calls a metaphysics of presence.[63] While Kelber is interested primarily in how orality makes human agents (speakers) present to one another and how sound locates human subjects in relationship to their environments, I want to take more seriously than Ong, whose language of "earlier man" might be interpreted paternalistically, how the acoustemological imagination has pneumatological implications in multiple directions. If the apostle Paul, who is generally agreed upon as operating primarily in an oral frequency,[64] speaks not only regularly about the principalities and powers but also, in the context of kerygmatic proclamation, insists that "through the church the wisdom of God in its rich variety might now be made known to the rulers and authorities in the heavenly places" (Eph. 3:10), then oral-cultural animism converges with a pneumatology of

59. See Paul G. Hiebert, *Anthropological Reflections on Missiological Issues* (Grand Rapids: Baker Books, 1994), part 3.

60. See Christopher Partridge, ed., *The Re-Enchantment of the West*, vol. 2, *Alternative Spiritualities, Sacralization, Popular Culture and Occulture* (New York: Bloomsbury, 2006).

61. Ong, *Presence of the Word*, 231.

62. Veli-Matti Kärkkäinen, Kirsteen Kim, and Amos Yong, eds., *Interdisciplinary and Religio-Cultural Discourses on a Spirit-Filled World: Loosing the Spirits* (New York: Palgrave Macmillan, 2013), unfolds, although not quite sounds out, just such a pluralistic and pneumatological cosmos in contemporary terms.

63. Kelber, *Oral and the Written Gospel*, 99–100.

64. See Joanna Dewey, "Textuality in an Oral Culture: A Survey of the Pauline Traditions," in *Orality and Textuality in Early Christian Literature*, ed. Joanna Dewey, Semeia 65 (Atlanta: Society of Biblical Literature, 1995), 37–65.

preaching in line with the present inquiry. This is not to suggest a "spirit" behind every pulpit—to spring off the common criticism of pentecostal-charismatics that they see a demon behind every tree—but it is to recognize that the context of the preaching event is multiply constituted by preacher, hearers, the Holy Spirit, and perhaps other spiritual dynamics when considered acoustemologically and pneumatologically.[65]

Our pneumatological turn might be considered too much, or at least too hazardous for our theological health, since it seems like we are asking now not only about the Holy Spirit but about the sounds of other spirits as well. I am going out on a limb, I admit, much further than even as innovative and constructive a theologian as Jeremy Begbie has gone in his efforts to provide "music therapy for theologians."[66] Begbie's project was to draw on acoustemics to reproblematize classical theological conundrums like the relationship between divine sovereignty and human freedom. When considered spatially, what emerges is a zero-sum game whereby gains on either side threaten the other. He suggests that the sound angle opens up the possibility of "two in one space" and "three in one space"—here calling to mind incarnational (divine-human) and Trinitarian (Father-Son-Spirit) logic—that allows us to see harmonization but also "interpenetration" between otherwise competing realities in order to resecure the notion of creaturely freedom without compromising divine sovereignty.[67] In this vein, I am proposing an exercise in acoustemic therapy for theologians and preachers that foregrounds orality and sound, and with that also affectivity, embodiment, intersubjectivity, and effervescence, as a way beyond the tunnel vision dominated by literary textuality and its intellectualistic rationalism, toward understanding the event of proclamation and of the good news of the gospel in a pneumatically infused cosmos.

65. For those interested in how I have carried forward—rather than demythologized in the Bultmannian sense—this complicated matter of the principalities and powers vis-à-vis pentecostal theological projects in political theology and in the theology and science dialogue, see respectively my *In the Days of Caesar: Pentecostalism and Political Theology—The Cadbury Lectures 2009*, Sacra Doctrina: Christian Theology for a Postmodern Age (Grand Rapids: Eerdmans, 2010), chapter 4; and *The Spirit of Creation: Modern Science and Divine Action in the Pentecostal-Charismatic Imagination*, Pentecostal Manifestos 4 (Grand Rapids: Eerdmans, 2011), chapter 6.

66. Jeremy Begbie, *Music, Modernity, and God: Essays in Listening* (Oxford: Oxford University Press, 2013), 142.

67. Ibid., 151, 154, and 159.

If Begbie is correct that music "is capable of evoking a space for the hearer that is, so to speak, 'edgeless', an inherently expansive space that has no close parallel in the world of the eye,"[68] then the preaching of the gospel is a sonic event that tolls out cosmic dimensions for human creatures that are historical and material, although irreducibly so.

Proclamation in/of the Spirit: Toward a Pneumatological Theology of Preaching

In this final section I have space for no more than a sketch—cursory almost to the extreme, begging expansion and further detail at every turn—of how a sonic rationality, channeled through the audioscope of pentecostal and pneumatological thought, can revitalize theology of preaching. Three schemes are interwoven: the biblical-soteriological-Trinitarian; past-future-present; and Spirit-Son-Father. The key to each register and their interrelationship is pneumatological, and pneumatic preaching advances via this triadic resonance.

First, a pneumatological theology of preaching connects the past to the present through the biblical witness. Chronologically, we might say that we have three sets of events: those behind the biblical text; those constituting the scriptural witness; and those in front of the text, receivers of its legacy and message. The integrity of each set of events, and their togetherness, can be pneumatologically understood.

The world behind the text, while inaccessible (except to scholars) apart from the text, is the salvation history of the living God. This can be understood theologically as superintended by the Spirit. For Pentecostals, the import of Scripture is specifically that it preserves the apostolic witness to these salvation-historical events. Two generations ago, C. H. Dodd brought to the fore the main lines of the apostolic kerygma.[69] Without the Spirit's outpouring on all flesh, there would be no apostolic proclamation preserved for posterity. Similarly, apart from the Spirit's hovering over the primordial waters, or coming upon Moses and the prophets, or accompanying and inspiring postexilic Israel, we would have no Hebrew canon. In these senses, then, salvation history is pneumatologically pealed, and pneumatic preaching is keen to listen to the ringing of the Spirit's work therein.

68. Ibid., 162.

69. C. H. Dodd, *The Apostolic Preaching and Its Developments* (New York: Harper & Brothers, 1936).

But further, "All scripture is inspired by God" (2 Tim. 3:16), and henceforth also by the Spirit of God (cf. 2 Pet. 1:20–21). So any reading or hearing of Scripture's witness to the mighty salvation-historical acts of God is from the beginning pneumatic, and ought to be pursued pneumatically. If "the letter kills, but the Spirit gives life" (2 Cor. 3:6b),[70] then only a pneumatic encounter with the Bible will be life-giving. This line of thinking connotes the previously understood "distance" between the words of Scripture as Spirit inspired and the reception of Scripture as Spirit illuminated.[71] Perhaps a pneumatological approach bridges also this gap, enabling hearing through the Scriptures of the world of the text. In fact the Spirit not only facilitates such engagement but the Scriptures themselves also urge us to hear what the Spirit is saying (Revelation 2–3).[72] But how do we *hear* the Spirit's message? A pneumatic hermeneutic responds: not only by reading with a visual rationality, but also by being attentive to the oral dimensions of Scripture. The narrativity of Scripture is certainly important,[73] but beyond this, also its affective aspects. Here the point is not only

70. Arthur J. Dewey, *Spirit and Letter in Paul*, Studies in the Bible and Early Christianity 33 (Lewiston, NY: Mellen, 1996), argues historically from Gal. 3:1–5; 2 Cor. 3:1–6; Rom. 2:29; and 7:6 (7:7–8:25) toward reading Paul as opposing the life-taking aspects of tradition and the law, and highlighting the life-giving aspects of the eschatological Spirit, a thesis that is congruent with the thrust of this essay.

71. This classical division of labor—between the Spirit's inspiration as productive of the biblical text and the Spirit's illumination as transformative of Scripture's readers—focuses the main lines of previous pneumatologies of preaching, especially in the Reformed tradition, on what happens with the listening congregation; this is the emphasis, for instance, in Park, *Sacred Rhetoric*, which highlights the "experimentalism" of Puritanism, which looked for the effects of the Spirit's work on the hearts and souls of those to whom the word of God was proclaimed. My point is that what happens to the listening congregation is only part of the field of the Spirit's work in the entirety of the preaching event.

72. See also Robby Waddell, *The Spirit of the Book of Revelation*, Journal of Pentecostal Theology Supplement Series 30 (Blandford Forum, UK: Deo, 2005), chapter 4, "Hearing What the Spirit Says to the Churches"; cf. Melissa L. Archer, *'I Was in the Spirit on the Lord's Day': A Pentecostal Engagement with Worship in the Apocalypse* (Cleveland, TN: CPT, 2015), chapter 4 on "Hearing the Revelation of John"; and David Seal, "Sensitivity to Aural Elements of a Text: Some Acoustical Elements in Revelation," *Journal of Biblical and Pneumatological Research* 3 (2011): 38–51.

73. Pentecostal biblical scholar Martin Mittelstadt thus argues that pentecostal orality comes more fully into its own when narrative analyses and approaches predominate (*Reading Luke-Acts in the Pentecostal Tradition* [Cleveland, TN: CPT, 2010], §3.1).

to hear Scripture read aloud (as opposed to reading it silently) but also to enter into its affective dimensions,[74] with the latter being attuned both to the affective history of God's saving works (the world behind the text) and to the affectivity of the narrative rhetoric (the text itself). Pneumatic preaching of necessity then—hopefully appropriately prompted and guided by the Holy Spirit—is affectively generated in hearing and knelling the scriptural witness in the preaching event.

My claim, however, is that a pneumatological approach to revelation not only connects the world behind the text to the text itself, but also brings both forward to the present.[75] It is the Spirit that aids our living into or out of the scriptural witness—the apostolic testimony, for pentecostal-charismatics—through sparking the oral and auditory imagination so that the scriptural message becomes potent for faithful ecclesial discipleship in any succeeding age.[76] If Hans Frei not only lamented the loss but also forged the retrieval of the narrativity of Scripture for the (post)modern or at least postliberal imagination,[77] a pentecostal and pneumatological assist accentuates the oral, sonic, and acoustic soundings

74. Leading the way among pentecostal biblical scholars in exploring affectivity in biblical criticism is Lee Roy Martin: "Psalm 63 and Pentecostal Spirituality: An Exercise in Affective Hermeneutics," in *Pentecostal Hermeneutics: A Reader*, ed. Lee Roy Martin (Leiden: Brill, 2013), chapter 15; "'Oh Give Thanks to the Lord for He Is Good': Affective Hermeneutics, Psalm 107, and Pentecostal Spirituality," *Pneuma: The Journal of the Society for Pentecostal Studies* 36 (2014): 1–24; and "Rhetorical Criticism and the Affective Dimension of the Biblical Text," *Journal for Semitics* 23 (2014): 339–53. Martin's *The Unheard Voice of God: A Pentecostal Hearing of the Book of Judges*, Journal of Pentecostal Theology Supplement Series 32 (Blandford Forum, UK: Deo, 2008), also begins but does not follow through on an auditory hermeneutic insofar as he remains concerned primarily with the literary aspects of the "voice of God" in the Judges narrative.

75. I argue this thesis in my *Renewing Christian Theology: Systematics for a Global Christianity*, images and commentary by Jonathan A. Anderson (Waco, TX: Baylor University Press, 2014), chapter 12.

76. The great homiletician Roland Allen proposes a "hermeneutic of analogy" that makes plausible present experience of the apostolic message; see Ronald J. Allen, *Preaching Luke-Acts* (St. Louis: Chalice, 2000), 20. A pentecostal-charismatic parallel is Kevin J. Spawn, "The Principle of Analogy and Biblical Interpretation in the Renewal Tradition," in *Spirit and Scripture: Exploring a Pneumatic Hermeneutic*, ed. Kevin J. Spawn and Archie T. Wright (London: Bloomsbury T&T Clark, 2012), 46–72, which replays David Tracy's analogical imagination in the oral-cultural arena of the Spirit and its attendant spiritual dimensions.

77. Hans W. Frei, *The Eclipse of Biblical Narrative: A Study in Eighteenth and Nineteenth Century Hermeneutics* (New Haven: Yale University Press, 1980).

of the biblical story line and probes into their kerygmatic implications for Christian faith in the present time. The point is that Scripture is not merely a collection of historic "facts" or mythic stories, but "is inspired by God and is useful for teaching, for reproof, for correction, and for training in righteousness, so that everyone who belongs to God may be proficient, equipped for every good work" (2 Tim. 3:16–17). Pneumatic preaching thereby thunders out the salvation-historical acts of God through the scriptural witness for contemporary inhabitation.

But this line of thought leads, *second*, to the assertion that a pneumatological theology of preaching listens to the living and *enspirited* word of God in order that others also may hear and experience divine salvation. This opens up to the teleological and eschatological vectors of preaching. Preaching toward what end? Toward experiencing the full salvation of God in the present life.[78] Let me elaborate on this soteriological arrow of preaching along three lines: the orthopathic, the orthodoxic, and the orthopraxic.

Orthopathically, salvation begins with what the Scriptures denote metaphorically as the heart. This is why preaching is never merely about cognitive content but is always affective, directed to the soul and its fears, desires, and hopes; preaching attempts to align human hearts with the heart of God and this happens when human lives are gripped with the love of God and comforted by the presence of God. Divine salvation is more than intellectualizable as it meets people in their historicity, embodiment, sociality, and environmental situatedness. In these domains, conversion is about reorientation of human concerns, aspirations, and longings toward the eschatological—present here and now through the Spirit but also coming—reign of God. Whatever else might be rightfully said in criticism of pentecostal emotionalism in preaching, their attentiveness to the dispositional and gut levels of human affectivity is pneumatically resonant. The goal is to steer away from merely being emotional for emotion's sake, or to be manipulative of the emotions of hearers, but to nurture right feelings and proper Christian piety—orthopathos—allied with the soteriological work of

78. Urged forcefully by pentecostal theologian Chris E. W. Green in his "Transfiguring Preaching: Salvation, Mediation, and Proclamation," in *Toward a Pentecostal Theology of Preaching*, ed. Lee Roy Martin (Cleveland, TN: CPT, 2015), 46–63.

God.[79] Pneumatic preaching thus hears what the Spirit is whispering to human hearts to heal them of their brokenness and rehabilitate right feelings and actions that signal the eschatological age has come.

Yet to be sure, orthopathos is impossible without orthodoxy in some fundamental sense. Here I refer to orthodoxy not as creedally defined (most Pentecostals are minimally creedal, at least with respect to the historic creeds, even as charismatics are nominally creedal or exist across the spectrum of confessions), but in terms of living into the truth of the Spirit's present outworking of the biblical narrative. Because such a pneumatological approach presumes that the works of the Spirit did not cease with the canonization of the biblical writings (as cessationists, increasingly few in number, have claimed), retrievals and reappropriations of the apostolic message will always tinkle in continuity with the salvation-historical acts of God but yet with a difference for the present time. This variance will always be disputed, but it is precisely in such contestation that we discern a mere repetition (which can be ritualized and controlled clerically or through some other authoritarian ecclesial means) from a vibrant and thereby salvific reiteration. In pneumatological amplification, for instance, such might be seen in the prophetic preaching and ministry of the Blumhardts: their charismatic leanings were by no means clearly heard in their age, but their legacy has withstood the passing of time.[80] In this way, orthodoxy understood as the truth that the Spirit always leads into confirms orthopathy heard as the affections that the Spirit fosters, and vice versa. So, pneumatic preaching listens to what the Spirit is saying to illuminate human minds of their distortions, darkness, confusions, and ignorance, and renew right thinking in accordance with the coming reign of God.

Yet orthopathy and orthodoxy also cannot stand apart from orthopraxis. The passions of

79. Pentecostals who have worked on orthopathic theologies include Steven J. Land, *Pentecostal Spirituality: A Passion for the Kingdom*, Journal of Pentecostal Theology Supplement Series 1 (Sheffield: Sheffield Academic, 1993); and Samuel Solivan, *Spirit, Pathos and Liberation: Toward an Hispanic Pentecostal Theology*, Journal of Pentecostal Theology Supplement Series 14 (Sheffield: Sheffield Academic, 1998); see also my discussion of orthopathy in Yong, *Spirit of Love: A Trinitarian Theology of Grace* (Waco, TX: Baylor University Press, 2012), chapter 5.

80. See Simeon Zahl, *Pneumatology and Theology of the Cross in the Preaching of Christoph Friedrich Blumhardt: The Holy Spirit between Wittenberg and Azusa Street* (New York: Bloomsbury T&T Clark, 2010).

the Spirit (the heart of God) and the mind of the Spirit (also the mind of Christ) are inseparable from the fruits of the Spirit (the works enabled and empowered by the Spirit). The Spirit-filled and Spirit-empowered life, after all, consists not only of right feelings and right thinking but also in right behaviors, actions, and activities in relationship to others. The telos of right feeling and right thinking is incomplete without right acting, and it is the work of the Spirit to transfigure the last so that we can be not only rightly related to ourselves and to the divine but also ethically shaped in response to others and to the world, including the spirit-filled cosmos with its principalities and powers. Preaching that is of the Spirit and in the Spirit will empower liberative praxis in an otherwise unjust world.[81] In this way, pneumatic preaching hearkens to the Spirit's voice in order to transform human deeds in their self-directedness and arouse right behaviors as harbingers of the eschatological reign of God.[82]

The work of the Spirit consequently redeems human hearts, repairs human thinking, and renews human lives. Thus does the Spirit foster a multistranded soteriological telos—that is simultaneously orthopathic, orthodoxic, and orthopraxic—as heralding the divine reign. Preaching in the Spirit hence not only looks back to the scriptural horizon but also indwells that message as precipitating the eschatological age.

In the end, however, a pneumatological theology of preaching is irreducible to the biblical message or the pronounced eschatological redemption since both inevitably involve and include encounter with the living God. This *third* strand moves us from the biblical and soteriological to the theological register. More specifically, this is not a generic theological turn but, consistent with our pneumatological reframing, an explicitly Trinitarian one. Pneumatic preaching listens to the scriptural testimony that brings divine salvation surely into the present by inviting encounter with the triune God. There are not only horizontal dimensions to the event

81. See also Vincent Beng Leoh, "Ethics and Pentecostal Preaching: The Anastatic, Organic, and Communal Strands" (PhD diss., The Southern Baptist Theological Seminary, 1990), who connects the emotivist and ethical horizons of preaching in the Spirit.

82. See also pentecostal-holiness ethicist Cheryl J. Sanders, "God's Trombones: Voices in African American Folk Preaching," in *Sharing Heaven's Music: The Heart of Christian Preaching—Essays in Honor of James Earl Massey*, ed. Barry L. Callen (Nashville: Abingdon, 1995), 151–64, who calls attention to the ethical dimensions of oral proclamation.

of preaching—wherein the past meets the future in the present or through which human lives are reformed internally (in their hearts and heads) and set right relationally with others (through their hands)—but there is also the vertical passageway. Pneumatic preaching opens up a portal between creational immanence and divine transcendence so that human lives meet and are transformed by the God of Jesus Christ through his Spirit.

This christological face, word, and voice of pneumatic preaching cannot be underemphasized.[83] Christian preaching in and by the Holy Spirit calls attention ultimately to no other name. This is not just the historical Jesus, but also the living and resurrected Christ, encountered through his Holy Spirit. Further, the scriptural witness also culminates in the incarnate, crucified, risen, and ascended Christ, even as salvation of mind, body, and soul is actualized in his name through the Spirit. Pneumatic preaching therefore has as its alpha and omega the lifting up of the name of Jesus, the explication of his life, ministry, and teachings, and the manifestation of his eschatological but no less real presence.[84]

Yet we also are saved by and meet the living Christ by his Spirit through his body, the church. Preaching is thereby "a communal event,"[85] not merely because much of it transpires within congregational worship services, but indeed because its verbalization and vocalization are communally shaped, contextually negotiated, and ecclesially interacted and interactivated. Such communality and ecclesiality might be most pronounced in the call-and-response tradition of the black (pentecostal) church (portrayed above) but we ought not to underrate the interrelationality between all ministers and preachers and their

83. Such christocentrism is most pronounced in Oneness pentecostal traditions, although a Jesus-piety is palpable across pentecostal communities as it is in other pietist forms of Christian faith. For a representative "Jesus-only" systematic theological formulation, see David Norris, *I Am: A Oneness Pentecostal Theology* (Hazelwood, MO: Word Alfame, 2012).

84. As argued in Timothy Matthew Slemmons, *Groans of the Spirit: Homiletical Dialectics in an Age of Confusion* (Eugene, OR: Pickwick, 2010), it is only through the Spirit that the gap between divinity and humanity and the crevice between past incarnation and present faith are bridged. Slemmons thus invokes a "fifth *sola* . . . : *Sola Sanctus Spiritus*. . . . For only when contemporaneity is understood in light of the role of the Holy Spirit and faith—faith as gift, as sphere, as Truth—can the preacher say with the apostle, on the one hand, that 'we are not peddlers of God's word like so many; but in Christ we speak as persons of sincerity, as persons sent from God and standing in his presence' (2 Cor 2:17)" (ibid., 77).

85. Justo L. González and Pablo A. Jiménez, *Púlpito: An Introduction to Hispanic Preaching* (Nashville: Abingdon, 2005), 57.

hearers, regardless of the outward or auditory perturbations—or lack of such—during the preaching event. One might say then that the sacrament of the word—the homily or the sermon—is the moment when the community of faith, through the preacher, echoes the voice of God in Jesus Christ by the Holy Spirit. Pneumatic preaching is ecclesial preaching in that sense because the church is not only the body of Christ and the people of God but also the fellowship of the Holy Spirit.

Last but not least, then, pneumatic preaching is an event of divine-human encounter as it mediates the presence, voice, and call of the living God. "Therefore, as the Holy Spirit says, 'Today, if you hear his voice, do not harden your hearts'" (Heb. 3:7–11; see also 3:13, 15; 4:7). Pneumatic preaching announces the call of the triune God and urges human response in the immediacy of the moment, one bursting with existential urgency and momentum because of the divine presence proclaimed by the living word of Christ. Under the authority of the Spirit of Christ, the preacher voices the saving word of God that has the capacity to redeem the past and transform the transient present in anticipation of a more kingdom-constituted future.[86]

If there can be no end to these reflections in part perhaps because their truth, if echoing at all, will persist into our future, then we can at least return to James Forbes's claim announced at the beginning: "Preaching is an event in which the living word of God is proclaimed in the power of the Holy Spirit." I have tried to sound out the eventness of preaching by audibilizing its pneumatological and oral character: the word of God arrives through Spirit-enabled acoustic and auditory forms of vocalized and verbalized speech.[87]

---

86. So if Michael Pasquarello III, *Christian Preaching: A Trinitarian Theology of Proclamation* (Grand Rapids: Baker Academic, 2006), insists that authentic Christian proclamation ought not to be anthropological but theological and even Trinitarian (on the triune God), this essay emphasizes that pneumatology is crucial not only for the *what* of Trinitarian preaching (Pasquarello's primary concern) but also for *how* Trinitarian proclamation is performed.

87. L. Susan Bond, *Contemporary African American Preaching: Diversity in Theory and Style* (St. Louis: Chalice, 2003), chapter 5, notes that Forbes's sermon is a speech-event because of the pneumatic mediation of divine presence that makes proclamation a present-tense experience. Bond's, and Forbes's, speech-event is akin to what humanities professor and art historian David Morgan (*The Lure of Images: A History of Religion and Visual Media in America* [London: Routledge, 2007], 218–22) identifies, with the help of philosopher J. L. Austin, as speech acts: "Charismatic orality is grounded in the body and understands speech as a performative action, a movement of the Spirit of God through the body and person of the inspired, anointed preacher. Face-to-face encounter is the primary register of

Our recital began with pentecostal orality and then, through attempting to listen from where the divine breath comes and discern where it goes (cf. John 3:8), we rehearsed the sound-rooms of oral ontology and the ontology of the auditory in search of clues to the dynamic event of kerygmatic proclamation. The resulting acoustemological arrangement was then oscillated across three theological registers—the biblical (world behind the text, world of the text, and world in front of the text), the soteriological (the orthodoxic, orthopathic, and orthopraxic dimensions of transformation the Spirit brings about through preaching), and the Trinitarian (wherein preaching facilitates encounter of the body of Christ and fellowship of the Spirit with the living God)—in order to articulate the contours of a theology of preaching that connects preacher and audience through the Spirit. At this point, then, I can do no better than riff off Ephraim Radner's insistence: "In my view, the less we talk about the Spirit—and simply pray in the Spirit—the better"[88]—and say, let the pneumatologizing cease and let the preaching begin![89]

---

charismatic orality, where spoken words are heard directly and such transmissions of spiritual power as the laying on of hands and spiritual anointing occur" (222). My essay can be heard as an effort to add theological and pneumatological heft to Bond's more homiletical and Morgan's more theoretical analyses.

88. Ephraim Radner, "Responses to Reviewers," *Pro Ecclesia* 23 (2014): 275—which is Radner's rejoinder (pages 274–81) to friends and critics of his recent book, *A Brutal Unity: The Spiritual Politics of the Christian Church* (Waco, TX: Baylor University Press, 2014), although his topic is far afield from ours.

89. An earlier version of this piece was published in *The Living Pulpit* (May 2015) (used with permission), and read by my new friend, Elim Pentecostal pastor, and St. Andrews postgraduate student, Tom Skelton, by my graduate assistant, Ryan Seow, and by my Fuller Seminary colleague Robert Johnston, resulting in a clearer and tighter argument. It was presented also by Skype at the American Theological Society (ATS) annual meeting at Princeton Seminary, 28 March 2015, as my travel to Princeton was prevented at the last minute; I am thankful to Kendall Soulen, James Kay, and others at ATS and Princeton Seminary for facilitating this discussion, to Cheryl J. Sanders for her incisive response to the paper, to the ATS members present there for the ensuing vigorous conversation mediated technologically, and to Dale T. Irvin for sharing important insights after the meeting—all of which was the gift to me in shaping the final form of this essay. All turbulent dissonances, clamorous clangs, and boisterous bongs over the course of the preceding electroscript remain my own responsibility.

CHAPTER 21

"In Him We Live and Move and Have Our Being"

A Theotic Account of Ethics

MYK HABETS

In Search of a Trinitarian Ethic

For two millennia ethics, or more correctly, moral theology as it is also known, has held a special place within the domain of Christian thinking. The founder of Christianity, Jesus Christ, is commonly held to be a morally good person who taught morally good principles that, when applied to life, were considered to be holy and healthy. But we must say more than this and insist that a Christian ethic concerns both *morality* and *theology*. Moral theology is theological at root, thus ethics is a constituent part of Christian dogmatics, not an addendum or optional extra. In a lovely turn of phrase Helmut Thielicke speaks of ethics falling under the "over-all suzerainty of dogmatics"; hence, ethics is not "an additional or supplementary discipline."[1] Moral theology is the specific inquiry of reconciled creatures into the ways and works of God in the world such that they may participate in Christ's vicarious ministry in ways that contribute to God's shalom and glory and, in the process, believers are caught up into fellowship with God and participate in creaturely

1. Helmut Thielicke, *Theological Ethics*, vol. 1, *Foundations*, ed. William H. Lazareth (Philadelphia: Fortress, 1966), 36 and 38.

ways in the divine being. Moral theology is thus another exercise in Trinitarian theology, and when the active role of the Holy Spirit is specifically the focus, one is contributing to a Third Article Theology (TAT).

While the Christian church has generated much literature within the field of ethics, it is my contention that it has yet to construct much in the way of comprehensive and compelling explanations of ethics that are distinctively *Christian*, which means, explicitly *Trinitarian* in intent, scope, and form.[2] This claim deserves some explanation by way of qualifying such an outrageous assertion. My claim should not imply that the great works of Christian ethics are sub-Trinitarian or anti-Trinitarian. They are not. It is, rather, to argue that few are yet comprehensively and self-consciously structured on a Trinitarian theology. In the history of Christian thought one is hard pressed, in fact, to find works that are specifically and self-confessedly "Trinitarian ethics."[3] As an incomplete argument, but a suggestive one that could have been replicated had time and space permitted, *The Oxford Handbook of Theological Ethics* offers a final section that outlines "the structure of theological ethics" by canvasing seven influential people, works, or movements that give shape to the field.[4] While admittedly idiosyncratic, none of the seven substantial chapters of this section of the work presents a moral theology that explicitly works out of a Trinitarian theology or is structured by such (hardly any even mention the Trinity!). Ethical heavyweights like Ernst Troeltsch, Anders

2. The same point is made by Roderick T. Leupp, *The Renewal of Trinitarian Theology: Themes, Patterns and Explorations* (Downers Grove, IL: InterVarsity Press, 2008), 147.

3. While there are many fine works of Christian ethics that contribute to and work out of an orthodox Trinitarian theology, my claim here is more specific. In my own (fallible) search for sources some of the works that approximate an ethics *explicitly* based upon a Trinitarian theology include: L. Gregory Jones, *Transformed Judgment: Toward a Trinitarian Account of the Moral Life* (1990; repr., Eugene, OR: Wipf & Stock, 2008); Anthony J. Kelly, "A Trinitarian Moral Theology," *Studia Moralia* 39 (2001): 245–89; Samuel M. Powell, *Participating in God: Creation and Trinity*, Theology and the Sciences (Minneapolis: Fortress, 2003), especially 163–213; William J. Danaher Jr., *The Trinitarian Ethics of Jonathan Edwards* (Louisville: Westminster John Knox, 2004); and Leupp, *Renewal of Trinitarian Theology*, 145–97. I am also aware of a lecture presented by Edwin Hui at Regent College, Vancouver, as part of "The Trinity and the Christian Life" (1992), http://www.regentaudio.com/collections/edwin-hui/products/the-trinity-and-the-christian-life. Space does not allow a critique of these works.

4. Gilbert Meilaender and William Werpehowski, eds., *The Oxford Handbook of Theological Ethics* (Oxford: Oxford University Press, 2005), 413–538.

Nygren, and the Niebuhr brothers are all accounted for, yet the ground and grammar of theology, the Trinity, is peripheral at best, and that means, of course, that any significant acknowledgment of the Spirit is sorely lacking.[5] Had one chosen Jonathan Edwards, Dietrich Bonhoeffer, and Karl Barth, for instance, the results would have been more favorable; although, even then I believe my case still stands. In what follows I present the contours of a Trinitarian ethic and argue that, whatever the final form these delineations take, at the heart of a distinctively Christian ethic stands the Trinity. In addition, I wish to ask what sort of Trinitarian ethics is apropos within TAT, and argue that a theotic account is the most fitting.[6]

John Webster outlines in sublime fashion a foundation for and vision of the Christian's hope that is centered on the triune God. In what amounts to a précis for a Trinitarian ethics, Webster writes (and I quote at length):

> This repleteness of God's life includes within itself, as an integral aspect of its perfection, a turn to that which is not God. In this turn there occurs a movement in which the fellowship of the immanent life of God creates a further object of love. This turn is free, self-caused, wholly spontaneous, original to the divine being; its necessity is purely the necessity of God's own self-determination to be in fellowship with that which is other than himself. As such, it is not a turn which completes or extends the divine life; it is a turning out of fullness, not out of lack. More simply; it is gift, love. This turning or act of love is the work of the triune God as the world's creator, reconciler, and consummator. It takes historical form in the simply yet staggeringly complex work of God's majesty in the entire scope of the economy, as

5. Christopher R. J. Holmes, *Ethics in the Presence of Christ* (London: Continuum T&T Clark, 2012), 5, points out that not only the Trinity but also Christology is largely absent from much recent work on ethics, and he rightly sees his project as one of intervention. Also see the essays in F. LeRon Shults and Brent Waters, eds., *Christology and Ethics* (Grand Rapids: Eerdmans, 2010).

6. Theotic accounts of moral theology are standard in Eastern Orthodox theology. Outside of Orthodoxy others have argued for a theotic account of moral theology, such as Danaher, *Trinitarian Ethics*; John Milbank, *Being Reconciled: Ontology and Pardon* (London: Routledge, 2004); Michael Gorman, *Inhabiting the Cruciform God: Kenosis, Justification, and Theosis in Paul's Narrative Soteriology* (Grand Rapids: Eerdmans, 2009), 105–28; and Neil Ormerod, "The Metaphysics of Holiness: Created Participation in the Divine Nature," *Irish Theological Quarterly* 79 (2014): 68–82.

God brings creaturely reality into being, redeems it and ensures that it will arrive at its perfection.

As Father, God purposes that in its abundance the divine love should be directed to bringing creation into being, bestowing upon it life, order, and direction. Because it is rooted in the Father's will, this purpose is unshakeable. That is, God's relation to what he makes is not simply an act of origination, but an act which ensures the creation's *destiny*, and therefore one which oversees, directs, and protects the creation so that it attains that destiny. As Son, God intervenes in the history of creation when, by its own perversity, the creature seeks to struggle free from the Father's purpose, refusing to be a creature, and in so doing exposing itself to mortal peril. Only as creature can the creature have life; and it is the work of the Son to reconcile, and therefore to recreate, what has brought destruction upon itself. Through the person and work of the Son, gathering created being to himself and bearing in himself its alienation from the source of its life and well-being, creation is reintegrated into the Father's purpose. Lastly, as Spirit, God acts to bring to completion that which the Father purposes and the Son secures against all opposition: namely, the identity and integrity of the creation in fellowship with God. God the Spirit perfects, bringing creaturely being and history to their completion.[7]

Here Webster is not making a case for *theōsis* or for a TAT, and yet his argument is conducive to such an account. Elsewhere Webster has asserted, "Moral theology is thus an element in faith's intelligent apprehension of the triune God, his inner perfection and his outer works."[8] I wish to draw upon Webster's remarks in order to introduce my own case for a theotic construal of Trinitarian ethics.

Creation–communion–command is the sort of sequence we might derive from Webster's work. While all God's works are triune and undivided, it is, with the tradition, appropriate to ascribe certain economic actions to one of the triune persons more specifically. Here, the Father creates in freedom creatures who conform to his image (the Son), and are

7. John Webster, "Hope," in Meilaender and Werpehowski, *Oxford Handbook of Theological Ethics*, 294.

8. John Webster, "Courage," in *A Man of the Church: Honoring the Theology, Life, and Witness of Ralph Del Colle*, ed. Michel René Barnes (Eugene, OR: Pickwick, 2012), 40.

thus able to be his representatives and cocreators on earth. The incarnate Son is the one in whom believers are united, by the Spirit, in order that his life becomes their life and their life is found within him in ways that respect the free agency of the human creature and the sovereign will of our Lord and Savior Jesus Christ. The Holy Spirit unites the believer with Christ, making one alive to God and God's will, so that they are gifted (*charismata*) with the grace of sharing in Christ's lordly work and in such work are perfected (Christification). Thus command signifies the willful service of Spirit-filled saints located in Christ and living to bring glory to God the Father. In such an account it is the vicarious humanity of Christ that forms the locus of ethical activity, not the human will, created capacity, or heartfelt desire. One might even suggest that in such an account ethics is Christian worship offered to the Father to the degree that it is a human participation in the divine life made possible by the Spirit in Christ. *Theōsis*, in other words, is the way of Christian worship, and thus of Christian ethics.

The Fourfold Ethics of *Theōsis*

In a moral theology where *theōsis* is the structuring dogma, *theōsis* occupies the intended *goal* and the *means* of ethics. In relation to a central scriptural text on *theōsis*, 2 Peter 1:3–11, Stephen Finlan asks: "How does divinization begin for Second Peter?" He goes on to answer: "The necessary preconditions are ethical character and proper belief. When these are present, divinization commences, which then results in enhancement of one's ethical character, and establishment of one in proper belief! *The means and the destination are quite alike*."[9] Putting aside here the specifics of his exegesis of this text, such an account of moral theology entails an interrelationship between four fundamental philosophical concepts in ethics: ontological ethics, deontological ethics, virtue/character ethics, and teleological ethics. When each of these frameworks is read through a Christian doctrine of *theōsis*, they become distinctly theological concepts requiring further definition.

Ontos: *"None but God Is Good"*

Ontological claims entail ethical commitments. While this relationship might be disputed in much secular postmodern

9. Stephen Finlan, "Second Peter's Notion of Divine Participation," in *Theosis: Deification in Christian Theology*, ed. Stephen Finlan and Vladimir Kharlamov (Eugene, OR: Pickwick, 2006), 46 (emphasis added).

philosophy, it is an undeniable feature of classical philosophy and ethics, and is something shared by moral theology.[10] Against cognitivist, constructivist, and emotivist understandings of ethics, Christian moral theology offers a (critically) realist account of ethics whereby moral action is performed (deontological), by moral agents (virtue), for moral ends (teleological), as creatures are empowered by the Spirit (ontological). Ontological ethics within a Christian moral theology, then, signifies the fact that the moral agents participate in God such that their actions flow out of the will and energy of God. This is based on the fundamental assumption that God is the almighty Creator and moral agents are the creation of God's good purpose. Being created in the *imago Dei* means that the "good" life can only be lived in accordance with God's good intentions and purpose for our lives, but such living (acting) is only possible when it flows from and in the power of God (being). This ultimate purpose of creation is to glorify God. We further understand that God is not the indivisible, unmoved monad of Greek philosophy but the relational and communal God of the Hebrew and Christian Scriptures (even when the doctrines of simplicity and impassibility are rightly adopted). This God is self-revealed as one being–three persons: God the Father, God the Son, and God the Holy Spirit. This means that any truly theological ethic must be a Trinitarian ethic, and by that we mean the triune God must be named and worshiped throughout any account of moral theology.

In contrast to the classical philosophical tradition of Plato and Aristotle, the church fathers rejected the thesis that ontology is predicated upon archaeology (Ideals, Forms, and so forth) in favor of an ontology of the end. Human creatures were created purposively, to be conformed to the image of the incarnate Son; human ontology is thus dynamic and not static (this Eastern teleological view of the human is in stark contrast to the Western substantive position, which is static).[11] The truth of being is thus found in

10. As but one example of the link between ethics and ontology in classical philosophy, see the argument of Christopher P. Long, *The Ethics of Ontology: Rethinking an Aristotelian Legacy* (New York: SUNY Press, 2004).

11. Substantive accounts of the *imago Dei* are proper to First Article theologies, relational and functional accounts of the *imago Dei* are proper to Second Article theologies. Anthropologies built upon First or Second Article theologies result in an ingrained dualism between body and soul, material

what creatures will become, not in what they were (innocent but immature), or are (fallen and depraved). This teleological definition of the *imago Dei* means that time and space are not accidental evils that need to be escaped. Rather, embodied temporal action is both the means and the end of creaturely being. Human creatures in the *imago Dei* find their being and action in time-space, hence the incarnation of the eternal Son becomes the centerpiece of history. John Zizioulas argues in this regard:

> There are two reasons that forced the Fathers of the Church to change thus the ancient Hellenic ontology. First, Christ is the truth of being. This means that, as St. Maximus the Confessor points out, all creation, that is to say, all the beings truly exist only within (in the relationship with) the Mystery of Christ, which is rounded (ends) in the eschaton. The Mystery of Christ, however, is impossible without the time and body, within which the freedom of the Holy Spirit is manifested. Consequently, Christology, in its pneumatological sense, obliged the Fathers to relocate the ontology from the beginning to the end, and to incorporate it in time, history and body, the three elements that the ancient Hellenic thought could [not] include in its ontology.[12]

Adopting the distinction between Hellenic and Christian ontology allows us to make clearer statements about moral theology. Whereas ontology and ethics have traditionally been seen as distinct and even separate subjects, a Christian ontology breaks down all such dualisms. If a substantive and functional view of the *imago Dei* is replaced by a teleological and christological one, then action flows out of being and being flows into action. This is what has sponsored, as we shall see, the recent discourse on virtue ethics in moral theology. But as we shall consider shortly, virtue is not defined in the same way in Christian as it is in Hellenic contexts. A doctrine of *theōsis* brings together being and act into a christological and pneumatological synthesis.

The antitheses of the Sermon on the Mount are illustrative at this point. Framed by seemingly impossible directives to exceed the righteousness of the Pharisees (Matt. 5:20) and to "be perfect, as your heavenly

---

and spiritual, time and eternity, being and action. Third Article Theology resists all such dualisms.

12. John Zizioulas, "Ontology and Ethics," *Sobornost* 6 (2012): 5.

Father is perfect" (5:48),[13] six contrasts are made whereby those in Christ are to exceed any command issued in the Old Testament; all of which look like the law on steroids. How is this possible? We find out it is not. Fallen creatures cannot obey God and cannot fulfill the law; only one man can, Jesus Christ: "With people this is impossible, but with God all things are possible" (19:26). In these same texts, again to illustrate, we have the teaching of Jesus that a mere show of mental assent does not save: "Not everyone who says to me 'Lord, Lord,' will enter the kingdom of heaven" (7:21), nor do works alone: "'Lord, Lord, did we not prophesy in your name, and in your name cast out demons, and in your name perform many miracles?" (7:22). Instead, actions as a result of being are what count: "So every good tree bears good fruit, but the bad tree bears bad fruit" (7:17); ethical agents ("a wise man") believe Christ ("hears my words") and act in the Spirit ("and built upon the rock," 7:24).

Accepting the basis of ethical action in being, *theōsis* is a means to frame and situate moral theology. Without collapsing the Creator-creature divide, in the one person of the mediator Jesus Christ, humanity and divinity exist in perfect communion. When united to the incarnate Son by the Holy Spirit, human creatures are lifted up and participate in the triune life of God in such a way that they now act out of an alternate agency and live in an alternate reality. They are not of the world as Christ is not of the world (John 17:16); if anyone is in Christ they are a new creation, the old has gone (2 Cor. 5:17); they are seated in heavenly realms in Christ Jesus (Eph. 2:6); they are in Christ (over 160 times in the Pauline Epistles alone), in the Spirit (Gal. 5:16 and many other places), adopted (Eph. 1:5), coheirs with Christ (Rom. 8:17), and live and move and have their being in God (Acts 17:28). In numerous texts moral agency is moved from the human self to Christ in the case of good works (Rom. 7:6; Gal. 2:20), while the creature remains culpable for bad works (Rom. 6:16; 7:5). Throughout Romans 8 believers are said to be in Christ and to act according to the Spirit. What is true now, as glorious as it may be, is only a foretaste of what is yet to come in the resurrection (Rom. 8:11).[14]

13. Unless otherwise indicated, biblical referneces are to the *NEW AMERICAN STANDARD BIBLE* (1995).

14. For comprehensive Pauline studies see Volker Rabens, *The Holy Spirit and Ethics in Paul: Transformation and Empowering for Religious-Ethical Life*, 2nd ed. (Minneapolis: Fortress, 2014); and

A doctrine of *theōsis* argues that the most consistent picture of moral theology Scripture gives us is that, in union and communion with Christ, we are made to act out of Christ's agency without in the process losing our own agency. Human creatures are enabled to live as God, if by that we mean to live in and as Christ, empowered by the Spirit, for the glory of the Father. Such an ethics has the eternal being as its goal, not simply a human individual's own well-being.[15] These are the fundamental ontological points of a theotic orientation to moral theology: only when creatures participate in God are they good, for none but God is good (Luke 18:19).

Deon: *"Do unto Others as You Would Have Them Do unto You"*

For many Christians, ethics can be reduced to a single word—"law." By "law" they mean either the Decalogue or the larger law of the entire Old Testament. In addition Christians would add to the Old Testament law various New Testament examples and admonitions and turn them into further laws to be obeyed no matter what. When ethics is reduced to law certain actions and attitudes come as a result. The duty to be performed takes precedence over the person to be loved; and God becomes a remote lawgiver, like some punitive judge of a petty court out to prove a point of abstract justice. This sort of God does not inspire holy living but rather strikes fear into sinful hearts. Such views are known as divine command theories and have more in common with the deontological ethics of Immanuel Kant than they do with the God of Scripture.[16]

I want to argue that this view of Scripture and of God is faulty. If we look back into the Old Testament we see that the law was not given to curtail freedom but to enhance it. The law of God is an expression of the nature of God and it is in this sense that Paul could call the law holy and right and good (Rom. 7:12). Thus the law expresses God's will, which in turn is an expression of God's nature. The law is a redeeming law, a liberating law, a law of freedom. One only has to read the preamble to the giving of the Decalogue

---

Gorman, *Inhabiting the Cruciform God*, who presents "Paul's vision of participatory Trinitarian cruciform holiness, or theosis" (128).

15. Zizioulas, "Ontology and Ethics," 6.

16. This opinion was clearly presented by Alasdair MacIntyre, *A Short History of Ethics: A History of Moral Philosophy from the Homeric Age to the Twentieth Century* (London: Routledge & Kegan Paul, 1967): "For many who have never heard of philosophy, let alone of Kant, morality is roughly what Kant said it was" (190).

to see this, where God declares his faithfulness to his covenant people before providing them with a way of life (Exod. 20:1–2). The law is an expression of covenant faithfulness, not merely a legal contract.[17] As a result of this gift of God's love believers can have a moral confidence—a confidence that God loves us (Eph. 3:20; 2 Thess. 1:11). We see this most fully expressed in the life of Christ, who lived in an atmosphere of confidence in God's providence. In expressing the love of God we become aware of being objects of such love and so our response is not like the debtor repaying the creditor but is filial—the Father who first loved us has given all so we give all back in response (2 Cor. 9:15), even our very lives.

Fidelity to God is faithfulness to the law. It is not an external mandate so much as an internal motivation and compulsion. This is the fundamental difference between secular ethics and a proper moral theology: secular ethics defines good and evil by formulating laws and precepts according to anthropocentric standards and ideals. As a result, ethics becomes what *we* do, how *we* can obey categorical imperatives, how well *we* perform according to an external code. In short, ethics is reduced to how well *we* are able to keep the law. Moral theology takes issue with all attempts by moral agents to live up to an extrinsic standard by their own efforts. The law is an expression of the love of the Father, a redeeming love that comes to fruition in the person of Jesus Christ and is made possible by the Holy Spirit. God's love is free and gratuitous, not the love of extrinsic justice, which is a relationship of exchange. God's love is a gift. Moral theology is predicated upon ontology, thus our relationship to the Father and our response to his gratuitous love is the basis for all duties. Moral theology concerns the unfolding of this gratitude and faith as responsive love to the Father who first loved us.

The love of the Father provides the occasion for moral theology and the motivation for response. But how do we express this attitude of gratitude? The biblical answer is: in Christ Jesus. From the incarnation—God's ultimate self-revelation—we learn about the Trinitarian God. One of the key things we learn is that God receives only what is united

17. For the seminal work on this distinction, see James B. Torrance, "Covenant or Contract?: A Study of the Theological Background of Worship in Seventeenth-Century Scotland," *Scottish Journal of Theology* 23 (1970): 51–76; and Torrance, "The Covenant Concept in Scottish Theology and Politics and Its Legacy," *Scottish Journal of Theology*, 34 (1981): 225–43.

to Christ. Outside of Christ there is no salvation, no ethics, and so no *theōsis*. The fundamental moral requirement of the Scriptures is to be united to Christ. This union can be developed comprehensively through the motif of union with Christ the Son. For Paul, the Christian is none other than a being in Christ. This is not the idea of fusion or absorption but relationship between the human and divine, most comprehensively represented as *theōsis*. We can see this in Paul when he uses the "in Christ" language (Rom. 6:5; 2 Cor. 5:17) we are so used to, and in John with his customary use of the Greek word *menō* or "remain," "abide" (John 14:10, 17, 25; 15:4–10, 16).

Being in Christ is more than a bond, it is a complete dependence of the Christian in/with/on Christ. It expresses the reality that there is no life apart from Christ. In Gal. 2:10 we read that we are in Christ and he is in us—a total participation. This has tremendous ethical implications. The Christian's moral life consists in living in and putting into effect this grace of the Son by means of the Spirit. This is a continuous and progressive death to sin and a life of renewal and victory.

In the West we most often speak of this as the doctrine of progressive sanctification. In the East the model of participation is summarized around the idea of *theōsis*, not osmosis, metamorphosis, or evolution—this is participation in relationship, the most intimate and abiding relationship one can think of. We see this in the triunity of God and then we see a veiled but nonetheless real example in our participation in God (John 17:21; 2 Pet. 1:4) and then in community with each other.

For John, the "in Christ" language is traded for the Greek *menō* or "abiding." In the Septuagint, *menō* most often refers to God's act: God stands, lasts, remains, endures, or abides—and always the word used is *menō*. And so we read in Ps. 116:2 that God's loving-kindness and truth *menō* (remains) the same forever (cf. Pss. 9:8; 32:11; 101:13; 110:3, 10; 111:3, 9). In John 14:10 we read that Jesus is in the Father and the Father is in him—the Father abides (*menō*) in Jesus Christ. In John 15:1–11 we have the teaching that Jesus is the vine and we are the branches and that we are to remain (*menō*) in Jesus Christ. But there is a condition: remaining steadfast (*menō*) relates to the commitment and security of God; in the Gospels we read that Jesus Christ remains (*menō*) in God—and then that believers are to remain (*menō*) in Jesus Christ. Then in 1 John 2:24 we read that the word of God is to abide (*menō*) in us and that is the condition for our abiding (*menō*) in Jesus Christ. The written word transplants the relationship between the Father and the Son into us! Further, in 1 John 2:27 and 4:14 the Spirit abides (*menō*) in us and that is also a condition of our abiding (*menō*) in Christ (2:28). So word and Spirit go hand-in-hand and when they do, ethical action follows (3:17; 4:16).

The Christian ethical ideal is only a reality in Christ; thus participation in Christ becomes the context for Christian ethics. The abiding life carries great rewards, nothing less than a divine enlightenment that leads to moral freedom (John 8:31–32). By abiding in the Son's teaching believers will remain, and by abiding in the Lord they will in turn be enabled to live out the precepts and principles of the kingdom of God, for we are free to do so. The Christian's moral strength is to be found in participation—as we remain (*menō*) in Christ—and in turn with the Trinitarian God. In Christ we will be conformed to the image of Christ (Col. 3:3). Christian morality is summed up by Paul in Philippians 1:21—"To live is Christ." This is not simply some placid statement—it is an ontologically accurate phrase that carries extensive repercussions. Morality is simply the consequence of the union or communion of our being and abiding in/with Christ and his abiding in/with us. In the helpful summary of Chris Holmes, we are speaking about "ethics in the presence of Christ." Based upon the vicarious ministry of Jesus Christ, Holmes summarizes ethics as "simply action evoked by and participant in his saving action and saving obedience."[18]

Jesus Christ is the center, focus, and standard of Christian ethics. He is the Christ, the image of the invisible God, the one who has made known the will and character of the Father. It is in reference to Jesus Christ that Christians undertake the task of living lives of discipleship and thinking about what sort of life is worth living. It is upon the confession that Jesus died and rose again that moral theology is founded—because in Jesus Christ alone God is present to humanity in a saving way. It is here that the most fundamental differences between moral theology and secular ethics arise. Christians believe that

18. Holmes, *Ethics*, 1. Or as Daniel Migliore asserts in relation to Karl Barth's theological ethics, the "Christian life is a *participatio Christi* in the active, agential, ethical sense of free and glad participation in the service of Jesus Christ and his work of reconciliation" ("*Participatio Christi*: The Central Theme of Barth's Doctrine of Sanctification," *Zeitschrift für dialektische Theologie* 18 [2002]: 291). On why Barth accepted the category of participation but not *theōsis*, see the discussion in Paul T. Nimmo, *Being in Action: The Theological Shape of Barth's Ethical Vision* (London: T&T Clark, 2007), 176–79.

the failure to live out of a center in God and not in the self is of the greatest significance. If ontological ethics has most to do with God the Father, deontological ethics has most to do with the incarnate Son who fulfilled the law in our stead and lives that we might have life and have it abundantly.

Aretē: *"The Fellowship of the Holy Spirit"*

Gratitude to the Father inspires the moral life, and the expression of that gratitude is lived out in Christ, but it still needs to be shown how this abiding is made possible—and that is where the Holy Spirit plays a major role. In addition to ontological and deontological ethics, virtue ethics is also an essential feature of a theotic account of moral theology.

As much a reaction to deontological and consequentialist ethics as it is a reappraisal of classical ethics, virtue ethics holds that an *action* is not virtuous, rather, a moral agent is, and thus action is consequent to being.[19] Virtue ethics derives from the Greek philosophers, especially Aristotle who believed that there are a series of positive characteristics or virtues that are required to allow an individual to lead the fullest possible life—to *flourish*. The virtues for any activity can be identified and taught. Once they have been assimilated the virtuous person can be left to act rightly in any given situation. For Aristotle, the four cardinal virtues are courage, self-control, generosity, and truthfulness. An Aristotelian virtue is defined as a midpoint between two vices: bravery, for example, is the virtue, with cowardliness and foolhardiness being the two extremes; temperance is the mean between indulgence and insensibility; pride is the mean between indulgence and humility; and courage is the mean between fear and aggression.[20]

Many Christian ethicists have adopted virtue ethics as *the* Christian ethic, and to good effect.[21] However, on its own, virtue

19. For a scholarly primer on virtue ethics, see Stephen M. Gardiner, ed., *Virtue Ethics Old and New* (Ithaca, NY: Cornell University Press, 2005).

20. Other Aristotelian virtues included: benevolence, fairness, reasonableness, civility, friendliness, self-confidence, compassion, generosity, tactfulness, thoughtfulness, tolerance, and moderation.

21. See, for example, Joseph J. Kotva, *The Christian Case for Virtue Ethics* (Washington, DC: Georgetown University Press, 1996), who offers a defence of virtue theory in Christian discourse and stands in continuity with other Christian virtue ethicists such as Alasdair MacIntyre, Stanley Hauerwas, and Samuel Wells. Kotva offers a teleological virtue ethic focused on the movement of who we are to who we can be.

ethics is not sufficient. One of the problems with virtue ethics is not whether moderation is the proper expression of morality, but whether it is the proper definition (or essence) of morality. Several reasons are advanced as to why it is not the very nature of what is good. First, many times the right thing is the extreme thing to do (in emergencies, in self-defense, and so forth). Even some of the virtues should not be expressed in moderate amounts: Who wants to be moderately loving, grateful, or generous? Second, there is no universal agreement on what is moderate. Third, moderation is at best only a general guide for action, not a comprehensive ethical directive. Ultimately virtue ethics in its classical guise suffers from anthropocentric accounts of what is good and can often lead to a civilized ethic rather than the radical countercultural life of the kingdom. After all, Aristotle's virtuous paragon was the soldier; Christ's is the martyr. The classical cardinal virtues were replaced in the Christian context by the "theological" virtues: faith, hope, love, and obedience (to God's commands). But this often resulted in a divine-command theory and then in deontological ethics whereby people were thrown back upon themselves to work for righteousness. Deontological ethics alone, then, cannot satisfy the demands of moral theology as it descends into a Pelagian ethic (*self*-works). Virtue ethics by itself is also not sufficient as it descends into cultural relativism (an ethics of the polis).

Despite criticisms, virtue ethics is helpful in moral theology as one of four foundations.[22] In a theotic account of ethics where being determines action, virtue and the development of character are highly conducive to the formation of ethical agents in Christ by the Spirit. As David Cunningham has written, "Christians understand the virtues to be those dispositions *God has by nature*, and in which human beings *can participate by grace*."[23] In short, *theōsis* is a participation in the virtues of the triune God such that believers image the Image of the Father (Christ) as they are filled with the Holy Spirit. This is achieved objectively in Christ Jesus, the deified man for us, and is subjectively realized in each believer as they participate by the Holy Spirit in Christ, to the pleasure of God the Father. Thus only in the Spirit will believers be able

---

22. One example of how to Christianize virtue ethics is provided by Glen H. Stassen and David P. Gushee, *Kingdom Ethics: Following Jesus in Contemporary Context* (Downers Grove, IL: InterVarsity Press, 2003), 59–68.

23. David S. Cunningham, *Christian Ethics: The End of the Law* (London: Routledge, 2008), 167 (emphasis in original).

to receive and taste *theōsis* and to reach the point of becoming like God.

In Scripture virtue is an important feature of right living. "For it is from within, from the human heart, that evil intentions come: fornication, theft, murder, adultery, avarice, wickedness, deceit, licentiousness, envy, slander, pride, folly. All these evil things come from within, and they defile a person" (Mark 7:21–23). In contrast to evil actions resulting from an evil person, Romans 8:26 holds the key to the Christian moral life—life lived in Christ made possible by the Spirit. The Holy Spirit is the special gift of the Father and the Son to all believers. The Spirit is life and strength and is the immanent dynamic agent of God. But we must not think of the Spirit simply in terms of energy or power; the Spirit is the *Holy* Spirit—and the Spirit's power is relational (Acts 1:8; Eph. 3:16). The Holy Spirit is the source of our moral life as we respond to the ongoing work of Christ on a daily basis. This movement is in gentleness (Acts 9:31) and quietness (*hēsychia*) and in order (1 Tim. 2:2)—that is why it is the Spirit of Christ. When we are filled with the Spirit we see things God's way, through the eyes of Christ, the eyes of faith as we move and respond to the Spirit's promptings (Gal. 3; 6:1). We read in Romans 8:2 about the "law of the Spirit" being in Christ, setting us free from external human laws, commands, and regulations (Rom. 8:4; Gal. 5:18). Thus it is the Spirit who becomes our moral compass, guide, judge, and convincer. External power alone is no good—that is one of the lessons of the old covenant. God's ultimate plan always included internal motivation and enabling—and this is the essence of the new covenant initiated by Christ (Jer. 31:31–34; Joel 2:28–29). For this reason we are able to cry out to God—not God the judge and lawgiver but God our Father in the words of filial relationship—"Abba Father" (Rom. 8:15; Gal. 4:6). Here we are adopted into God's family, brought into the triune communion of love in the person of Jesus Christ, and divinized. A morality of the Spirit is a morality of sanctity (2 Thess. 2:13).

In the Spirit there is no ethical tension between our will and that of the Spirit—the Spirit's work is our moral life! We are in Christ and Christ is in us, and this is made possible by the indwelling gift of the Holy Spirit (1 Thess. 4:7–8; 5:19).[24] Paul says in Romans

24. The theology of Jonathan Edwards is apropos here: "Edwards understands the realization of personhood in terms of the saint's theotic participation in God through the 'communication' and 'indwelling' of the Spirit, which distinguishes the

12:1–2 that our moral life is a spiritual sacrifice, an act of rational worship. The Christian moral life is more than a philosophically virtuous life. It is a life set apart to be holy and blameless in God's sight, a life of sacrifice and worship made possible only if we live and abide in and by the Spirit (Gal. 5). Life in the communion of the Spirit is a moral life of sanctity, of worship, of freedom (liberation from enslavement), as Romans 8:1–2 and 2 Corinthians 3:17 make clear. Freedom is the ultimate goal of the moral life—a progressive emancipation rather than a forced submission (Gal. 5:1). Jesus sets people free. Freedom is not virtue or even fruit of the Spirit. Freedom is the life of Christ himself, and his life is now our life. Precepts and laws are no longer imposed upon us from outside, something that results in enslavement to commandments. But Christians have the law of Christ, the law of the Spirit, the law of grace dwelling within them. This is the ethical implication of the new covenant. The Spirit inspires our spontaneous response and empowers us for action. Through the Spirit we are sharing in the liberty of God himself because we are sharing in God himself. But we are not lawless! No, a new law is present—the law of the Spirit. The Spirit infuses into us life—the life of the incarnate Son—a life of love and grace, which has its own power that is directive. To think lovingly, to act graciously, so life and the law of the Spirit is a law of love (Gal. 5:13–14). The demands of love constrain and control our exercise of liberty (1 Cor. 9:19). Here faith, hope, and love flourish, to name but three Christian virtues.

Christian virtues are given by the Spirit, as we see in the fruit of the Spirit: love, joy, peace, patience, kindness, goodness, faithfulness, gentleness, self-control (Gal. 5:22–23); yet these do not come to fruition outside of the cooperation of moral agents striving for holiness among the community of the faithful (Phil. 2:12). It should not be assumed that this equates to a synergistic doctrine of salvation; it does not. Cooperation in *theōsis* is consistent with doctrines of concurrence, whereby God-enabled human action is required alongside the irruption of transforming grace. The dynamic between divine grace and grace-enabled human action is seen in 2 Peter 1:3–11, where *theōsis* is the basis and consequence of moral action. Already in the prelude Peter has acknowledged the gifts of faith, righteousness, grace, peace, and

---

Christian vision of the moral life from those that pivot on individual choice or achievement" (Danaher, *Trinitarian Ethics*, 244).

knowledge in Jesus Christ (1:2–3) before providing a list of virtues now to be given and habituated in Christ Jesus as the moral means to *theōsis*.[25] Before the virtues are expounded Peter makes it clear that the moral life starts and ends in God, and is normed by God's own goodness. God's divine power has given us everything required to be like God, and it has in turn enabled an "escape from the corruption of the world" and holds out the promise of participation in the divine nature (1:4). On this basis believers "apply all diligence" to cultivate the virtues of faith, goodness, knowledge, self-control, perseverance, godliness, kindness, and love (1:5, 10). Finally, such virtues will be perfected in the eschaton (1:11).[26] As Basil stated in terms of the work of the Spirit in deifying believers:

> Thence comes foreknowledge of the future, understanding of mysteries, apprehension of secrets, distribution of graces, heavenly citizenship, the chorus with angels, unending joy, remaining in God, kinship with God, *and the highest object of desire, becoming God* [*theon genesthai*]. Such, then, are a few from the many of our thoughts on the Holy Spirit, that we have been taught by the very words of the Spirit about his greatness, his dignity, and his energies.[27]

Telos: *"Become Partakers of the Divine Nature"*

It is a commonly accepted theme in dogmatics that human nature may be considered in one of four states: primal integrity or innocence (creation), entire corruption or total depravity (fall), inaugurated re-creation in Christ (redemption), and perfect restoration in the resurrection (renewal). Moral theology is largely if not wholly concerned with the third of these four states of humanity, with the time in which Christ's completed reconciliation is being applied to and appropriated by human creatures through the renovating and re-creating work of the Spirit. In this mode of ethics the Trinitarian theology of Basil the Great provides the theological

25. See J. Daryl Charles, "The Language and Logic of Virtue in 2 Peter 1:5–7," *Bulletin for Biblical Research* 8 (1998): 55–73.

26. For a theological exposition see Wyndy Corbin Reuschling, "The Means and End in 2 Peter 1:3–11: The Theological and Moral Significance of Theōsis," *Journal of Theological Interpretation* 8, no. 2 (2014): 275–86.

27. Basil the Great, *On the Holy Spirit*, trans. Stephen Hildebrand, Popular Patristics Series 42 (Yonkers, NY: St. Vladimir's Seminary Press, 2011), 9.23 (page 54 [emphasis added]).

impetus, in his depiction of the Holy Spirit as the perfecting cause of creation.[28] In complementary fashion Calvin speaks of the differences between the divine persons such that "to the Father is attributed the beginning of activity, and the fountain and wellspring of all things; to the Son, wisdom, counsel, and the ordered disposition of all things; but to the Spirit is assigned the power and efficacy of that activity."[29] Teleology, including eschatology, thus forms the final foundation of a Trinitarian ethic.

In Acts 2:37, Peter's audience are reported to have said, "Brethren, what shall we do?" in response to his Pentecost sermon. Thielicke calls this the biblical motto of theological ethics, the answer to which sets moral theology on its journey. Peter replies in verse 38, "Repent, and be baptized every one of you in the name of Jesus Christ for the forgiveness of your sins; and you shall receive the gift of the Holy Spirit." As Thielicke makes clear,

> what they asked was simply another way of asking the other more radical question of how it might come to pass—and what contribution my conduct could make—that the resurrection of Christ attested by Peter should become an event involving me [*quoad me*]. The question is: How do I become a member of the new aeon, that aeon which came into existence through the events of Christmas, Easter, and Pentecost?[30]

For Thielicke, "theological ethics is eschatological or it is nothing."[31] Christian ethics must be seen as an "impossible possibility," as exemplified by the Sermon on the Mount's call to not just *do* differently but to *be* different—"it imposes its demand upon us as if the new aeon had already come and replaced the old."[32] Yet, Christian ethics is a necessary enterprise as believers live between the existing order and the new order to come and must find a modus vivendi.

As a way of accounting for this modus vivendi, a convergence of sorts has eventuated between literary studies, hermeneutics, theatre, and the arts. Each discipline has converged around a dominant metaphor, that of drama. Kevin Vanhoozer has written a monumental

28. Ibid., 16.38 (pages 70–71).

29. John Calvin, *Institutes of the Christian Religion* [1559], Library of Christian Classics 20–21, ed. John T. McNeill, trans. Ford Lewis Battles (Philadelphia: Westminster, 1960), 1.13.18 (pages 142–43).

30. Thielicke, *Theological Ethics*, 1:39.

31. Ibid., 47.

32. Ibid., 45.

work that picks up the theme of the dramatic and applies it to theology. According to Vanhoozer, "[T]he Father is the playwright and producer of the action; the Son is the climax and summation of the action. The Spirit, as the one who unites us to Christ, is the dresser who clothes us with Christ's righteousness, the prompter who helps us remember our biblical lines, and the prop master who gives gifts (accessories) to each church member, equipping us to play our parts."[33] In such an account the gospel is "theo-dramatic"—a series of divine entrances and exits, especially as these pertain to what God has done and is doing in Jesus Christ. Theology responds and corresponds to God's word and deeds; accordingly, theology itself is part of the theo-dramatic action. This insight leads to a first statement of the directive theory of doctrine that lies at the heart of Vanhoozer's work. "If theology is about the speech and action of the triune God and the church's response in word and deed, then doctrine is best viewed as direction for the church's fitting participation in the drama of redemption."[34] Once again, moral theology is theological.

33. Kevin J. Vanhoozer, *The Drama of Doctrine: A Canonical-Linguistic Approach to Christian Doctrine* (Louisville: Westminster John Knox, 2005), 448.

34. Ibid., 31.

When we frame ethics in terms of the dramatic we are led to ask: Whose direction counts, and why? This involves providing a theological account of the proper order in which Scripture, tradition, Christ, and the Spirit stand in relation to one another, not to mention *ontos*, *deon*, *aretē*, and *telos*. In Vanhoozer's words,

> *Sola scriptura* is not only a principle but a *practice*. Specifically, it is the Spirit-enabled practice of participating in the "canonical practices" that comprise Scripture. Canonical-linguistic theology is ultimately a matter of being apprenticed to the diverse communicative practices that make up the church's script. It is through such apprenticeship that the Spirit conforms church members to the image of God in Christ.[35]

When the category of drama is used in this helpful way, and is allied to an eschatological orientation of theology, it invites further reflection on how to construe Christian ethics around the analogy of improvisation.

> The ultimate goal of theology is to foster creative understanding—the ability to improvise what to say and do as disciples

35. Ibid., 32 (emphasis in original).

> of Jesus Christ in ways that are at once faithful yet fitting to their subject matter and setting. The church continues to perform the same text in different contexts, despite the difference of centuries, cultures, and conceptual schemes, by "improvising" with a canonical script.[36]

In terms of moral theology we walk in the momentum of creation and eschaton, of *ontos* and *telos*, of Genesis and Revelation. Here we may speak then of two grand narratives. We could say that there is, throughout Scripture and the Christian worldview, the "tick" of Genesis and the "tock" of Revelation, the "tick" of humanity in rebellion and the "tock" of humanity in reconciliation, the "tick" of humanity "in Adam" and the "tock" of humanity "in Christ." As Michael Horton, another advocate of dramatic theology, writes: "One is a narrative of pointless rebellion against a good God and his creation, leading only to frustration and death; the other is a narrative of redemption and reconciliation, consummated in everlasting life with the triune God in a restored cosmos."[37]

Another prominent exponent of this dramatic theology is Tom Wright, who has proposed a four-act play as a way to recount the drama of Scripture: 1) creation, 2) fall, 3) Israel, 4) Jesus.[38] Rightly critiqued for its lack of eschatology and the dislocation of the centrality of Christ, Wright's schema has been developed by a number of theologians, most notably for our account by ethicist Samuel Wells, who proposes a five-act play: 1) creation, 2) Israel, 3) Jesus, 4) church, 5) eschaton.[39] This schema matches up with our own account of moral theology from *ontos* to *telos* and also makes much use of the concept of improvisation as a way to characterize ethical action in the present. Believers incorporated into the body of Christ are called to indwell the story or drama of Scripture and become one of the performers. In order to perform to the best of our ability we have to learn the skill of improvisation. Improvisation in the theatre

36. Ibid.

37. Michael Horton, *A Better Way: Rediscovering the Drama of Christ-Centred Worship* (Grand Rapids: Baker Books, 2002), 53. The theme of tick-tock is not unique to me and is found often in the literature, but I have drawn upon Horton's use of it.

38. N. Tom Wright, "How Can the Bible Be Authoritative?," *Vox Evangelica* 21 (1991): 17–32. Wright has developed this scheme himself and has applied virtue ethics to it in Wright, *Virtue Reborn* (London: SPCK, 2010).

39. Samuel Wells, *Improvisation: The Drama of Christian Ethics* (Grand Rapids: Brazos, 2004), 53–57.

is a practice through which actors seek to develop trust in themselves and one another in order that they may conduct unscripted dramas without fear. Within ecclesial contexts believers are called to become a community of trust in order that it may faithfully encounter the unknown of the future without fear. Wells appeals to Gerard Laughlin:

> When a person enters the scriptural story he or she does so by entering the Church's performance of that story: he or she is baptised into a biblical and ecclesial drama. It is not so much being written into a book as taking part in a play, a play that has to be improvised on the spot. As Rowan Williams puts it, people are "invited to 'create' themselves in finding a place within this drama—an improvisation in the theatre workshop, but one that purports to be about a comprehensive truth affecting one's identity and future."[40]

When applied to the task of ethics, Wells concludes, "When improvisers are trained to work in the theatre, they are schooled in a tradition so thoroughly that they learn to act from habit in ways appropriate to the circumstance. This is exactly the goal of theological ethics."[41]

In a passage from Thomas Torrance worth citing in full we find all the essential features of a Trinitarian moral theology outlined in their eschatological dimensions:

> As such grace is the all-comprehensive and constant presupposition of faith, which, while giving rise to an intensely personal life in the Spirit, necessarily assumes a charismatic and eschatological character. Under the gracious impingement of Christ through the Spirit there is a glad spontaneity about the New Testament believer. He is not really concerned to ask questions about ethical practice. He acts before questions can be asked. He is caught up in the overwhelming love of Christ, and is concerned only about doing His will. There is no anxious concern about the past. It is Christ that died! There is no anxious striving toward an ideal. It is Christ that rose again! In Him all the Christian's hopes are centred. His life is hid with Christ in God. In Him a new order of things has come into being, by which the old is set aside. Everything therefore is seen in Christ, in the light

40. Ibid., 65, citing G. Laughlin, *Telling God's Story: Bible, Church, and Narrative Theology* (Cambridge: Cambridge University Press, 1996), 20.

41. Wells, *Improvisation*, 65.

of the end, toward which the whole creation groaneth and travaileth waiting for redemption. The great act of salvation has already taken place in Christ, and has become an eternal indicative. The other side of faith is grace, the immediate act of God in Christ, and because He is the persistent Subject of all Christian life and thought, faith stands necessarily on the threshold of the new world, with the intense consciousness of the advent of Christ. The charismatic and the eschatological aspects of faith are really one. In Christ the Eternal God has entered into this present evil world which shall in due course pass away before the full unveiling of the glory of God. That is the reason for the double consciousness of faith in the New Testament. By the Cross the believer has been put in the right with God once for all—Christ is his righteousness. He is already in Christ what he will be—to that no striving will add one iota. But faith is conscious of the essential imminence of that day, because of the intense nearness of Christ, when it shall know even as it is known, when it shall be what it already is. And so what fills the forward view is not some ideal yet to be attained, but the Christian's position already attained in Christ and about to be revealed. The pressure of this imminence may be so great upon the mind as to turn the thin veil of sense and time into apocalyptic imagery behind which faith sees the consummation of all things. Throughout all this the predominating thought is grace, the presence of the amazing love of God in Christ, which has unaccountably overtaken the believer and set him in a completely new world which is also the eternal Kingdom of God.[42]

The end of ethics is the glorification of saints, union and communion with the triune God, and the full possession of the Holy Spirit such that we can see God and be like God. Between creation and the eschaton the church is the locus within which the life of Christ in the Spirit is nurtured through baptism, the Eucharist, and good works. As Orthodox writer Christoforos Stavropoulos comments, "God the Father, before all ages, conceives of the work of salvation and theosis. He realizes it in time, in the Son. The Holy Spirit completes and perfects and adapts this work to people. In the sphere of the Church, the Holy

42. Thomas F. Torrance, *The Doctrine of Grace in the Apostolic Fathers* (1948; repr., Eugene, OR: Wipf & Stock, 1996), 34–35.

Spirit mystically sanctifies and unites the faithful with Christ, thus creating and giving life to the mystical body of the Lord."[43]

Conclusion

By way of conclusion, my theotic account of moral theology leads me to certain affirmations. First, I affirm with the Great Tradition that Scripture does contain propositional revelation, which provides the Christian community with certain laws, rules, commandments, and prohibitions to live by. While all of Scripture is contextual and needs to be interpreted before it may be applied, many of the scriptural injunctions are as applicable today as they were in their own cultural milieu. Second, I affirm with the Great Tradition that the letter of the law is dead but the law of Christ and the Spirit is life. Formalized laws can only ever offer external motivation for ethical conduct. What the new covenant means is that an internal motivation is provided—by God—so that the moral agent *wants* to do good (action) because they *are* good (being) in Christ. Third, I affirm with the Great Tradition that a truly Christian ethic must be centered on Jesus Christ, the definitive self-revelation of God. As such Christ occupies the central stage in a Christian ethic; ethics is the life of Christ lived out in those savingly united to him. Fourth, I affirm with the Great Tradition that the individual does not hold priority over the community of believers. Thus a Christian ethic must be one shaped and lived out in community. This communal aspect involves those saints who are with us today and those who have departed. Finally, a Christian ethic is another way to speak of worship, of participation in Christ, of life in the Spirit, and of the way of *theōsis*, the ultimate fellowship with God.

The Christian moral life is lived in communion with God. To be a Christian moral agent is to be a being in communion with the triune God—experiencing and living in the reality of the love of God, the grace of Christ, and the fellowship of the Holy Spirit (1 Cor. 13:14).

43. Christoforos Stavropoulos, *Partakers of Divine Nature*, trans. Stanley Harakas (Minneapolis: Light and Life, 1976), 31.

Part 6

Public Theology

CHAPTER 22

Public Theology

The Spirit Sent to Bring Good News

JASON S. SEXTON

All theology happens in particular contexts. This means that theology, if worth doing at all—whether as critical construction, ecclesial dogma, or apologetic versions—is done in and from real places. The contributions in the present volume, including this chapter, have as their stated perspective to be "thinking theologically from and in the Spirit."[1] While this viewpoint, seen in each essay, contributes to the budding of what is being called Third Article Theology, even theologies beginning with such uniformity are going to bring additional perspectives beyond thinking with an explicit precommitment "from and in the Spirit." Some of these perspectives will reflect various sensibilities, proclivities, and eccentricities of authors, whether this be the result of their ecclesial identities, some other theological or philosophical persuasions, or the part of the world they come from, their so-called contexts.[2] To refer to such a theology as

1. Myk Habets, "Prologeomenon: On Starting with the Spirit," chapter 1 of the present volume.

2. For a recent example of an approach to developing a regional theology, see Fred Sanders and Jason S. Sexton, eds., *Theology and California: Theological Refractions on California's Culture* (New York: Routledge, 2014).

contextual theology would be jejune, since all theology is done from somewhere and bears particular markings descriptive of particular settings and situations.

These considerations bring the theologian paying attention to the place where she finds an echo of the very first question asked in Scripture, a question asked by God to the first human beings: "Where are you?" (Gen. 3:9).[3] This question is not wrought in any private setting, but flies entirely out in the open, despite the human inclination to retreat in isolation and hiding (3:7–8, 10). Here our first parents are summoned to reckon with their own postlapsarian condition, and with the actual events that were carried out openly, which brought them to their mortified, ruined estate. Precisely here, in this context, God speaks. It is the place that has been profaned and would be cursed, where all creation hears the divine public pronouncement of malediction (3:14–19). Yet equally in this place a divine promise is made (3:15). It is the setting where the divine presence invades, where grace comes and God's word is clearly spoken and heard. It all happens in public. But what is "public"?

The Nature of Public Theology

Various models have been given in the extant literature attempting to describe precisely the meaning of the term "public theology."[4] I do not propose to settle any matters pertinent

3. *The New International Version* (Grand Rapids: Zondervan, 2011).

4. Definitions of "public theology" offered in recent scholarship often begin with either political or societal agendas, as noted in Max L. Stackhouse, *Public Theology and Political Economy: Christian Stewardship in Modern Society* (Grand Rapids: Eerdmans, 1987), xi, 17–35; Ronald F. Thiemann, *Constructing a Public Theology: The Church in a Pluralistic Culture* (Louisville: Westminster John Knox, 1991), 19–25; William F. Storrar and Andrew R. Morton, eds., *Public Theology for the 21st Century* (London: T&T Clark, 2004), 1–21; and Sebastian C. H. Kim, *Theology in the Public Sphere: Public Theology as Catalyst for Open Debate* (London: SCM, 2011), 3–26. See the description of Stackhouse and Thiemann alongside Abraham Kuyper in Vincent E. Bacote, *The Spirit in Public Theology: Appropriating the Legacy of Abraham Kuyper* (Grand Rapids: Baker, 2005), 40–53; and an account of Wolfhart Pannenberg's concept of a public, scientific theology in Jason S. Sexton, *The Trinitarian Theology of Stanley J. Grenz* (London: T&T Clark, 2013), 26–29. Alternatively, see the different notion of "public theology" as a "thoroughly theological and biblical analysis," in Stephen R. Holmes, ed., *Public Theology in Cultural Engagement* (Milton Keynes, UK: Paternoster, 2008), x; and an evangelical, presuppositional, apologetic method applied to constructive societal engagement in Daniel Strange, "Evangelical Public Theology: What on Earth? Why on Earth? How on Earth?," in *A Higher Throne: Evangelicals and Public Theology*, ed. Chris Green (Nottingham: Apollos, 2008), 14–61.

to the wider debate here, but I do wish to acknowledge that many of the descriptions given are quite particularist and therefore less descriptive for the wider practice of actually doing theology. Eneida Jacobsen helpfully sketches a number of models for possible appropriation in her own Brazilian context. After her survey, she ultimately finds that the kind of theology that would be found relevant and meaningful will be "anchored in the lifeworld," "mobilized by the suffering of people," and seeking "to contribute to the expansion of the communicative efforts of a society."[5] This seems relevant for theology's work in any public setting.

If these communicative efforts truly come through in the language of the people, appropriately anchored in their lifeworld, as with the aim of theologies like that of Jürgen Moltmann and liberation theologians,[6] this kind of theology will also include diverse media and forms of public expressions that come from the people. It should take the form of such things as poetry, prose, letters, and other popular, regional expressions of meaningful life in a given culture. Fred Sanders has argued that something like this should be made use of for doing theology at least in the highly problematic California context,[7] with implications for elsewhere. Various moods, tonalities, and rhythms will naturally mark a language descriptive of a reality known to the common person's experience of the world. Insofar as this is fueled by the Holy Spirit it is for "others," as Moltmann consistently emphasizes, and especially for the poor and those who have fallen victim to tyrannical pride and fear of oppressors with whom the church must resist any alliance.[8]

---

5. Eneida Jacobsen, "Models of Public Theology," *International Journal of Public Theology* 6 (2012): 22.

6. Moltmann's vision of public theology ought not to be equated with that of liberation theology, the latter often collapsing a theological vision into a political one whereas the former understands *Deus crucifixus* as a "stateless God," the church thus unable to be identified with a national community. Indeed, for Moltmann, freedom in Christ means fellowship and solidarity with the victims of political religion. He writes, "The worship of politics is a superstition, anathema to Christians. For Christians are joined with Christ crucified to speak to men of a greater freedom" ("The Cross and Civil Religion," in *Religion and Political Society*, trans. Thomas Hughson and Paul Rigby [San Francisco: Harper & Row, 1974], 46).

7. Fred Sanders, "California, Localized Theology, and Theological Localism," in Sanders and Sexton, *Theology and California*, 19–33.

8. Moltmann, "Cross and Civil Religion," 41–47. I am also grateful to my colleague Sandra M. Pérez for recently highlighting the role theology might play in the contemporary California State University as having something of a prophetic voice

With public theology's aim being for the good of the "other," following Moltmann, a corresponding question becomes precisely how this kind of theology might meaningfully serve the other in concrete ways and in public expressions that highlight the nature of its authentic witness. Pursuing this question requires further consideration of the nature of public space.

The *Oxford English Dictionary* defines "public" in this way: "Open to general observation, view, or knowledge; existing, performed, or carried out without concealment, so that all may see or hear."[9] Applying this definition to the action of the church's theology highlights Christianity as something universally verifiable, supernaturally revealed, and personally experienced. It showcases the action of the Trinity to create and work through Israel's story, coming to fruition in the incarnation, with the angelic announcements of Jesus' birth (Luke 2), brought about and into the public by the Spirit (Matt. 1:20). Beyond this, Jesus' entire public ministry is visibly manifested and inaugurated at his public baptism in the Jordan River (Matt. 3:16; Mark 1:10; Luke 3:22; John 1:32), and all the way to his crucifixion, resurrection, ascension, as well as to his promised and anticipated second advent. More will be said about the nature of Jesus' ministry in a moment, but what is interesting to note is *the public witness of embodiment* on display at each point. This leads one's watchful eyes, following the biblical arc, to the Spirit's public action in the life of the church, creating a new kind of body politic within the public sphere, having constituted the church precisely there in time and space, embodied.

Focusing these matters of the Spirit's activity in the embodied activity of redemptive history, this essay proceeds with an argument sympathetic to Wolfhart Pannenberg's approach to the matter, exhibiting a measured disdain for the privatization of religion that existed at various unfortunate times in the history of the church. Rightly rejecting religion's totalizing impulse, religious expression after the Reformation, for example, became a matter of private practice.[10] This has especially been amplified by US evangelicals at different

for responding to oppressive societal (esp. religious) power structures.

9. "public, adj. and n." *OED Online*. December 2014 (Oxford: Oxford University Press, 2014), accessed January 3, 2015, http://www.oed.com.libproxy.usc.edu/view/Entry/154052?result=1&rskey=VUMIOq&.

10. Wolfhart Pannenberg, *Faith and Reality* (London: Search Press, 1977), 137–38.

points in more recent history, where religion became cut off from other cultural issues affecting the church and society. This would happen only to then see religion roar back at different moments in the forms of reactionary movements that tend to co-opt faith for unfortunate, and sometimes both dubious and disastrous, ends.

Christianity's Public Localized Shape

Yet nevertheless and in spite of Christianity being co-opted for other ends in the public square, the truth at the heart of Christianity still holds power of transforming lives, of witnessing to the coming kingdom, of proclaiming judgment,[11] and of laboring to love inexplicably. In spite of being co-opted at times, the gospel does this insofar as it remains under the ultimate jurisdiction of the divine Holy Spirit who remains sovereign throughout the course of all matters in heaven and on earth, whether in the lives of individuals, in the life of the church, or in the affairs of the wider society.

Also worth mentioning, before accounting for how sustained public pneumatology gives way to the actual unfolding of the gospel in the world, is the nature of the contemporary world. As conversations continue about the nature of theology in public space, including how it relates to civil religion and secular society, the game may be changing faster than often realized.[12] Much of this has to do with globalization and its effects on nearly every aspect of a commonly shared global society.

Globalization is the big idea that the world has changed to become much more interconnected than it was in previous eras, and thus refers to the deeper, wider, faster, and increasing forms of interconnectedness of all of social life at every level, including the cultural, criminal, financial, and theological.[13] As such globalization affirms both the

11. Luke Bretherton, *Christianity and Contemporary Politics: The Conditions and Possibilities of Faithful Witness* (Oxford: Wiley-Blackwell, 2010), 148–49.

12. Linell E. Cady, "Public Theology and the Postsecular Turn," *International Journal of Public Theology* 8 (2014): 292–312. For more critical responses to the impulse to move beyond secularism, see Khaled Furani, "Is There a Postsecular?," *Journal of the American Academy of Religion* 83 (March 2015): 1–26; and Atalia Omer, "Modernists Despite Themselves: The Phenomenology of the Secular and the Limits of Critique as an Instrument of Change," *Journal of the American Academy of Religion* 81 (March 2015): 27–71.

13. For a brief discussion of this, see Jason S. Sexton, "Globalization," in *New Dictionary of Theology*, rev. ed., ed. T. A. Noble, Tim Grass, Martin

local, universal, and transcendent, including the significance of particular settings as meaningful places to do theology *from*. This relates precisely to an important feature of theology's essential public shape as a centrifugal movement, and where universality comes, but only through particularity.[14] It is therefore the local that comes into view as the place where the Spirit works, and from where witness continues to take expansive shape, all while in public. The Spirit's work to accomplish this has no ultimate aim other than that God be all in all, and all things be reconciled (1 Cor. 15:28). The Spirit's *testimonium* goes out, revealing in ways that are not part of the common order of things as currently situated, but pulsating with distinct rhythms and tonalities that disrupt the now common course of the created order in all of its postlapsarian bungle.

Some theologians have begun to make much of not only the church in exile, but also the church as entirely displaced, arguing this as the way mission works.[15] While there is surely something true about this, it cannot be a vision of the public life of the church (and revelation) happening in such a way that the church vanishes from public altogether, only to reappear at the beginning of apocalyptic irruption. This seems like a sure recipe for apostasy. In contrast, the church's very identity, as a divinely re-created and reconstituted thing (even amid its extant forms of disrepair), is an affront to the world, fulfilling the world's deepest longings in various ways by the power of the Spirit, and doing so as a testimony to the worldly principalities and powers. It is therefore situated, having been built with a concrete historical identity and with real human lives (*epoikodomēthentes*, Eph. 2:20), and indeed having a real operational space as the reality lived out in lives of real participants who both come from and remain living in real communities in the contemporary world. This contemporary world is thus

Davie, John McDowell, and Stephen R. Holmes (Nottingham: InterVarsity Press, 2016), 364-65.

14. For a discussion of the centripetal, centrifugal, and diasporic images of Christian mission, see Richard Bauckham, *Bible and Mission: Christian Witness in a Postmodern World* (Grands Rapids: Baker, 2003), 72–81.

15. For example, see Jonathan R. Wilson, "Aesthetics of the Kingdom: Apocalypsis, Eschatos, and Vision for Christian Mission," in *Revisioning, Renewing, and Rediscovering the Triune Center: Essays in Honor of Stanley J. Grenz*, ed. Derek J. Tidball, Brian S. Harris, and Jason S. Sexton (Eugene, OR: Cascade, 2014), 157–74; and Samuel V. Adams, *The Reality of God and Historical Method: Apocalyptic Theology in Conversation with N. T. Wright* (Downers Grove, IL: InterVarsity Press, 2015).

precisely the place where the Spirit operates to create church, wherever it may find itself and whatever the nature of its public witness, as the "new humanity" (Eph. 2:15). This means that there is an otherwise operative humanity that this new one is replacing by virtue of its relationship to Christ and new access through him to God the Father by the Spirit (Eph. 2:18). With a testimony to its real and proleptic healing, the church is locally established amid the brokenness of both the corporate community and its own members' bodies, yet while simultaneously testifying to what these will become through the Spirit's work to bring Christ's work to completion. The church's public shape then is irreducibly both local and transcendent.

Pneumatological Public Christology

An integral feature of the Spirit's action seen in Scripture (for example, John 15:26) is to witness to Christ, whose very life is bound up with the life and action of the Spirit.[16] As such, nobody can acknowledge Jesus apart from the Spirit's action. John Owen (1616–83) wrestled with this matter for those who would locate the Spirit's work exclusively in the early church. Himself locating the "extraordinary and miraculous operations" of the Spirit in that first-century moment (against the Socinians), Owen refused to confine the Spirit's entire work there. Owen believed that doing so is "plainly to deny the truth of Christ's promises, and to overthrow his church: for we shall make it undeniably evident, that none can believe in Christ, or yield obedience to him, or worship God in him, but by the Holy Ghost; and, therefore, if his communications cease, so must all faith in Christ, and Christianity too."[17] In the same discourse Owen explains,

> He who never experienced the special work of the Spirit upon him, never received any special mercy from God. How is it possible? For whatever God works in us, is by his Spirit; he therefore who has no work of the Spirit on his heart, never received either mercy or grace from God. To renounce therefore

16. The work of the Spirit and Son are also bound up with the life and work of the Father, as the well-known Trinitarian dictate goes (*opera trinitatis ad extra indivisa sunt*, "the external works of the Trinity are inseparable"), and therefore every member of the Trinity is present for and in every action.

17. John Owen, *The Holy Spirit: His Gifts and Power* (repr., Grand Rapids: Kregel, 1954), 32.

> the work of the Spirit is to renounce all interest in the mercy and grace of God.
>
> There is not anything done by us, that is holy and acceptable to God, but it is an effect of the Spirit's operation. "Without him we can do nothing"; John xv.5; for without Christ we cannot; and by him alone, is the grace of Christ communicated. By him we are regenerated; by him we are sanctified; by him we are cleansed; by him we are assisted in every good work.[18]

The expansiveness of public witness relates to the universal reach of the lordship of Christ, who possesses "all authority in heaven and on earth" (Matt. 28:18). Pneumatologically driven public theology grants this high Christology. Jesus is Lord of the cosmos, and his followers are caught up in a kind of worship-igniting enrapturement that prepares a kind of existential martyrdom posture and nurtures reliance on the Spirit's wisdom and dynamic dependence on ecclesial siblings and genuine friends in missional living; it resists the current structures, fueling witness, and testifying widely to the truth of the gospel. It testifies to the comprehensiveness of Christ, which locates this Jesus in the particularities of believers' lives, and also in the relationship Jesus has with his Father by the Spirit as seen in the biblical Gospels, highlighting a low Christology. By virtue of this movement, one of "sonship," Christ's life, death, and exaltation become the means of all participation in God.[19]

While union with Christ through the Spirit precisely denotes participation in the life of God, the very same reality is also a participation in public space, where the incarnation touches. It corresponds to the *homoousios* nature of Christ and therefore reaches into and touches the places where community brokenness exists, of abused women and children with no fathers, as well as abusers and abandoners. Personal and societal wounds in their particularities give way to the healing that the pneumatologically empowered incarnation brings in its own woundedness and atoning power.

Jesus' presence is the very divine presence and goodness. In Dietrich Bonhoeffer's

18. Ibid., 24.

19. For an argument that Jesus occupies "space" or the "normative place" within the "field of force" in God that is wisdom, and does so in such a way that his atoning work establishes him as becoming "the space for all people into which wisdom is concentrated," see Paul S. Fiddes, *Seeing the World and Knowing God: Hebrew Wisdom and Christian Doctrine in a Late-Modern Context* (Oxford: Oxford University Press, 2015), 344–46, 387–92.

terms, Christ becomes the man for us today, or the one rerealized in ever new spaces by the Spirit. This happens since Christ is what Paul Fiddes calls "the 'comprehensive space' where we have access to the inexhaustible depths and multiplicity of the divine wisdom."[20] This wisdom revealed by the Spirit (1 Cor. 2:10) enabled Christ to become wisdom for us (1:30), which grants not only fellowship with God's Son but also an understanding of "spiritual realities" (2:14). This new insight equips believers with the facilities to reckon all things as *sub ratione dei*, which renders everything in relationship to God. This leads consequently to the life of the church, the public actor established by virtue of its union with Christ, and the faith *in* Christ possessed by those participating in the life of the church.

Pneumatological Public Ecclesiology

Unlike some systematic theologies (especially evangelical ones) and various academic curricula in some theological institutions that treat ecclesiology as somewhat detached from other theological categories, and especially from theology proper, this should not be the case. Whenever the Creed is recited, in contrast, the church does not come *after* belief in the Trinity, but is rather part of what it means to believe in the Trinity today. The Third Article[21] has this: "I believe in the Holy Spirit . . . the holy catholic church, the communion of saints" [*Credo in Spiritum Sanctum, sanctam ecclesiam catholicam, sanctorum communionem*]. The presence of the cognate terms, *sanctam* and *sanctorum*, following *Spiritum Sanctum* is not insignificant. There is a holy catholic church and a communion of holy people (saints) precisely because the Holy Spirit acted to make it so. The church is therefore intimately connected to the Spirit and to the Trinity insofar as the Third Article of the Creed is part of any exposition of what

20. Ibid., 345.

21. The Creed is better understood as a threefold confession rather than a twelvefold one if it is to be shorthand for the gospel. The designation of twelve seems to be much more suitable for academic analysis and critical assessment of the Creed's features. But otherwise, the point of the Creed is to confess faith in the triune God who is reconciling the world through Christ. As Pannenberg emphasizes at the close of his Trinitarian theology: "The distinction and unity of the immanent and economic Trinity constitute the heartbeat of the divine love, and with a single such heartbeat this love encompasses the whole world of creatures" (*Systematic Theology*, trans. Geoffrey W. Bromiley [Grand Rapids: Eerdmans, 1998], 3:646).

it means to believe in God the Father, and in his Son, Jesus Christ, and in the Holy Spirit.

Hans Urs von Balthasar in perhaps less careful language takes the part of the Creed that expresses faith in the church as belief in precisely what *follows* belief in the Father, Son, and Spirit. That is, now that belief in the Trinity is established, focus turns to the redemptive work of the three divine persons.[22] But this divides the Creed unnecessarily, somewhat betraying the structure and content of the Creed as *one whole Creed*, which articulates faith in and an exposition of the life and action of the triune God, which views everything in relation to this God, the Trinity, requiring that belief in the church is an essential part of what it means to believe in the triune God, and thus in the Spirit who creates the church. Contrary to Balthasar, then, it is not that the church begins once faith in the Trinity has concluded, allowing belief to range off into other foreign directions, into foreign objects of worship or additional works of the Trinity that operate beyond our salvation, as if believers do not know and come to believe in the Trinity on the basis of and in relation to the triune action. The triune action in the salvation economy focuses particularly and primarily on the church. Belief in the Trinity means there is also a church, a holy one, by virtue of its relationship to the Holy One. As such, the church is an extension of the triune God's action and continues bearing witness to that action of the Spirit's life within the church, and also in the revelation of the church's book.

Witnesses within the Church

The special creation of the Spirit is the church, which boasts various gifts to carry out its many different ministries. Some of these gifts showed up as apostles, some prophets, some evangelists, some pastors and teachers (Eph. 4:11). Each of these gifts has a public function, but sometimes will overlap more explicitly into a public role, with a different measure of public presence, and sometimes even a different level of statesmanship. The pastor may even be a state senator, and sometimes a martyr. This is precisely the openness and vulnerability of the witness displayed in the life of the late Reverend Clementa Pinckney,[23] who along with eight others

22. Hans Urs von Balthasar, *Credo: Meditations on the Apostle's Creed*, trans. David Kipp (Edinburgh: T&T Clark, 1990), 83.

23. See the brief biography of Pinckney, the late South Carolina state senator and the pastor of the Emanuel A.M.E. Church in Charleston, South Carolina in Tom Cleary, "Clementa

was killed in Mother Emanuel Church in Charleston, South Carolina, by a racist act of terrorism after hospitably welcoming his very murderer into a small open Bible study.[24] In this way, for one, the Spirit's public action is displayed in the life of the church, empowering the church for extraordinary witness, even in the face of death. In the case of the very public slayings of Clementa Pinckney and the members of his congregation, this death bore all sorts of strange fruit, including the reflection on grace from the sitting United States president, amid his singing of the song "Amazing Grace" during his eulogy at Pinckney's funeral service.[25]

The Spirit births this kind of reality in the life of the church, giving it an embodied outlook far beyond mere public optimism, and certainly not a banal and misplaced triumphalism, which some colonialist ecclesiologies exhibit. Instead the church embodies a hope of a true renewal of all things in God. This reality has begun within the renewed community brought into union with Christ by the Spirit and living in adopted fellowship with God the Father. The Spirit calls the church into public existence, which translates into the significance of why water baptism takes place in a public setting.

The Spirit also speaks to the church, which exists in public, and thus maintains a vulnerable calling as the primary actor in the public square. Precisely in this space the Spirit offers forgiveness to all who believe, extending the same to members of the church, granting them hope in the resurrection and in everlasting life, as the Creed states. All of this is part of the public faith and witness of the church, as the Spirit sanctifies it in the very same space where it was called to life. In this way, the church has a function of hallowing space, embodying a kind of healing presence among those who do not yet believe the gospel. This can change cultures, and yet can also be abused when misappropriated by a dislocation from the derived healing presence and power that

---

Pinckney Dead: 5 Fast Facts You Need to Know," *Heavy* (June 18, 2015), accessed August 5, 2015, http://heavy.com/news/2015/06/clementa-pinckney-dead-charleston-church-shooting-victim-black-church-pastor-ame-shot-injury/.

24. See also the conversation, "In the Shadow of Charleston: Politics, Religion, & White Supremacy," *Syndicate* (July 2015), accessed August 6, 2015, https://syndicatetheology.com/symposium/in-the-shadow-of-charleston/.

25. Sarah Kaufman, "Why Obama's Singing of 'Amazing Grace' Is So Powerful," *Washington Post* (June 26, 2015), accessed August 6, 2015, https://www.washingtonpost.com/news/style-blog/wp/2015/06/26/why-obamas-singing-of-amazing-grace-is-so-powerful/.

the church both experiences and participates in through the Spirit.

Throughout all this there exists a kind of negotiability of culture that corresponds to the vulnerability of active witness, where nothing ever remains static. This also designates all cultural settings as opening up the in-between spaces where pneumatological action occurs, where life is breathed where there is none, where healing is desperately needed, and where the Spirit comes in power (1 Thess. 1:5). Among this divine action is the movement of the Spirit that created not only the church, but also the church's sacred text.

Witnesses within Scripture

The Spirit speaks in such a way as to draw believers into the heart and essence of what is spoken in Holy Scripture. The shape and forms of this speaking are not always necessarily found in Scripture, but will be more often than not in the contemporary age. The Bible is indeed "the Spirit's book" and as such is the place the Spirit has spoken God's word and will to humanity.[26] But this was not always the case.

What is now seen and commanded to be read in public (1 Tim. 4:13)—the Bible—was grounded in earlier public action. In other words, the Spirit was working in public space, in redemptive history and in the lives of participants in the redeemed community, long before Scripture was ever produced. The Spirit worked in the task of the production and will work long after the text had been produced. The text accounts for the additional witness of the Spirit's public activity, past, present, and future, as viewed through the lens of Scripture and through our lenses.

As a small sampling of the public activity of the Spirit—a kind of pneumatic public theology seen in the pages of Scripture where the Spirit redemptively sweeps up God's people to act in particular ways in the public square—consider the following. The psalmist describes the Spirit's powerful action, moving out both to create and to renew (Ps. 104:30). After David describes the inscrutability of God's knowledge, he then develops a subsequent understanding that there is no place where one might avoid the omnipresence of the Spirit, meaning that his presence is always public inasmuch as all flesh is ever before him (Ps. 139:7).

The Spirit's public activity bringing about public ministry is seen at Jesus' baptism in the Jordan River (Luke 3:21-–23), which took place before the Spirit hurled (*ekballei*) Jesus into the desert, leading him into great

26. Stanley J. Grenz, *Theology for the Community of God* (Grand Rapids: Eerdmans, 2000), 379–91.

difficulty (Mark 1:12). The Spirit empowers witness (Acts 1:8), giving the words to say (Luke 12:11–12). It is precisely there in the public arena for all to see that the Spirit transforms believers by gifts given to otherwise menial and "less honorable" members of the church (1 Corinthians 12). In this way the Spirit brings life amid cultural decay, even as one's public testimony of faith in Christ is the genuine sign of salvation wrought by the Spirit (Rom. 10:8–9; 1 Cor. 12:3).

Scripture highlights the Spirit's role in public theology, which—while done within the wider culture—can never be reduced to mere cultural description, however well developed and insightful. Stephen Holmes correctly says that a proper notion of public theology—and I would add, one that is pneumatologically driven—will never be reduced to sociology, cultural studies, or social anthropology. Instead it will shine forth as a thoroughly theological and biblical analysis, meaning that theology will show itself as what it is in its ability "to speak truthfully about all present realities."[27]

As the church's book, Scripture takes cues from the Spirit's witness and what the Spirit is saying to the churches. In this way Scripture is equally the Spirit's book. Calvin describes Scripture as where "God is truly and vividly described to us from his works, while these very works are appraised not by our depraved judgment but by the rule of eternal truth."[28] He elsewhere states that "the Holy Spirit so inheres in His truth, which He expresses in Scripture, that only when its proper reverence and dignity are given to the Word does the Holy Spirit show forth His power." He goes on to describe that by this "kind of mutual bond the Lord has joined together the certainty of his Word and of his Spirit so that the perfect religion of the Word may abide in our minds when the Spirit, who causes us to contemplate God's face, shines."[29]

The church as the primary actor in the world remains such as it is oriented to the Spirit's voice in Scripture, the Spirit's book. The church sees this authority in its own life in the same way that the church derives its very existence from the triune God as a unique creature of the Spirit, gathered around the

27. Holmes, *Public Theology in Cultural Engagement*, x.

28. John Calvin, *Institutes of the Christian Religion*, ed. John T. McNeill, trans. Ford Lewis Battles (Louisville: Westminster John Knox, 1960), 1.6.3 (1:73).

29. Ibid., 1.9.3 (1:95).

Spirit-inspired text, which charts the course of its existence in the public arena.

Public Pneumatology, Societal Religions, and Cultural Institutions

In the public arena the church exists as church, having ontological priority over the world in a very real sense and making a critical assessment of the institutions and other public-square actors that exist within the church's proximity and purview. In its engagement the church labors for the good of its members, but also for the freedom and flourishing of all—people of faith and no faith, wealthy and poor, and otherwise—within a culture that is never "neutral" in any meaningful sense, but ought to be neutral in this penultimate age. Laboring for such an emphasis, especially when power brokers and stakeholders feel cut in on, can often cost the church significantly.[30]

Empowered by the Holy Spirit, the church exists in the world with what Lesslie Newbigin described as "lenses" through which it can understand and interpret the world. In doing so, believers strive to see plausibility structures brought about which establish greater senses of neutrality so that the gospel message about what God in Christ has done to reconcile the world can be preached.[31] Some of these plausibility structures will take shape in the grammar of various institutions of healing, wholeness, and hope birthed by the church, both in the ancient and present worlds. Among these might be things like the institution of marriage, or hospitals, or academic institutions. They might also include institutions with different operational bases, including things like governments, other governance structures, or prisons, which have had the church at the center of their existence.[32]

Whatever institutional structures are erected at any given time, the task belongs to the Spirit to bring about an irruption amid the structures, especially those erected against the Spirit's lordship, as it were. The Spirit breaks through those edifices with a view to bringing life where there is none, birthing the

30. Drawing from William T. Cavanaugh, see Rowan Williams, "Convictions, Loyalties and the Secular State," in *Faith in the Public Square* (London: Bloomsbury, 2012), 43–44.

31. Lesslie Newbigin, *The Gospel in a Pluralist Society* (London: SPCK, 1989), 227–29.

32. I list government and prison because each has played significant roles within sociopolitical entities where the church has existed as part of the official government structure.

church and cultivating gospel witness. This happens also amid societal religions of particular cultures, for which the church is called to an elenctic task of mission. Appropriating a presuppositional Reformed methodology, Daniel Strange refers to the elenctic task as

> a trialogue in which the Christian enters into the already existing relationship between the non-Christian and the Holy Spirit, the dynamic relationship between divine revelation and human suppression and substitution. . . . In such a trialogue it is essential that the Christian takes time to listen compassionately and understand the religious Other to discover what they have done with God. To achieve this goal, one needs to be familiar with both a general "scientific awareness" of other religions (historically, psychologically, philosophically, and phenomenologically) and a more particular "living approach," which appreciates the individualistic nature of religious consciousness.[33]

Going further than Strange here, it seems necessary also to recognize the integrity of religions in their own development (morally, historically particular, and otherwise) and a genuine contestability of each one's truth claims in the public square. Commenting on John 16:8,[34] J. H. Bavinck states, "The Holy Spirit will convince the world of sin. The Holy Spirit is actually the only conceivable actor of the verb, for the conviction of sin exceeds all human ability. Only the Holy Spirit can do this, even though he can and will use instruments in his hand."[35]

Constituted and cultivated by the Holy Spirit amid all kinds of different societal structures at any given time, the resilience of the church shows itself by finding precisely the right places to serve and the right gaps to fill in a culture, even as it is often rebuffed by present and dominant institutional structures, including and often especially the so-called confessional ones. While no institution can always realize its goals, it is especially injurious when confessional ones do not.

Here is where difficulty may be seen in T. F. Torrance's notion of evangelizing the "foundations of culture." His identification

33. Daniel Strange, *Their Rock Is Not Like Our Rock: A Theology of Religions* (Grand Rapids: Zondervan, 2014), 278.

34. "When that helper comes he will convict the world concerning sin, righteousness, and judgment."

35. J. H. Bavinck, *An Introduction to the Science of Missions*, trans. David H. Freeman (Phillipsburg, NJ: P&R, 1960), 222, cited in Strange, *Their Rock*, 278.

of the need for transformation of human persons is one thing, and offers a correspondingly modest view of societal transformation in this age; but to assume this can be done for "the mind of human society and culture in which human beings exist" is another thing altogether. Yet Torrance thinks this is necessary if the church is to put down roots in a particular society and remain genuinely Christian.[36] Much could be said here about the early church existing during its first three centuries on the furthest societal margins, living as light in the darkness and operating in a distressed situation (1 Cor. 7:26). Furthermore, Torrance may simply be working with the notion of an established church. But even so, it doesn't seem plausible that there is, or ever has been, an actual Christian society; there are only Christians. And they belong to society within public space, to one another, and to the Lord, insofar as they participate in the lives of each.

Accordingly, there are no foundations of culture per se. There are only *people* who make culture and are shaped by the culture that others have made, and who either contribute to the health of particular cultures, or to their decay. Being negotiable at every point, all cultures exist within a constant negotiability of epistemological structures present within culture.[37] Institutions set within their cultures, as all institutions are, reflect more of the time and cultural features of their designers than any belief structures they are based on. This happens because the same belief will look different in different settings, even while some things remain the same, embodied by the same kinds of people.

In the advocacy of freedom for all in the public square, and plausibility structures more consistent with neutrality and the flourishing of all, the secular project has failed wider societies. Yet in the case of secularism, or other nonneutral cultural hegemonies, John Cobb has recently expressed the significant insight that "[t]he only justification of modern secularism is that Christendom was much worse."[38] So while resisting any so-called Christian hegemonic triumphalism, there is a genuine work that the Spirit effectually

36. Thomas F. Torrance, *Atonement: The Person and Work of Christ*, ed. Robert T. Walker (Downers Grove, IL: InterVarsity Press, 2009), 444.

37. George A. Lindbeck, *The Nature of Doctrine: Religion and Theology in a Postliberal Age* (Philadelphia: Westminster John Knox, 1984), 32–41.

38. John B. Cobb Jr., *Jesus' Abba: The God Who Has Not Failed* (Minneapolis: Fortress, 2016).

performs with the gospel's advancement into public spaces, which truly changes things.

Dynamic, Expansive, Public Exposition

Paul described early Christians as Holy Spirit–generated human letters, consisting of individual lives known by all, and publicly verifiable as to their authenticity (2 Cor. 3:2). The Spirit reshapes these lives, effecting the divine will amid common societal structures and problems. This public action is liberating, and needs no additional secretive expression. They remain public, "in the light" (1 John 1:7; 2:9–10), open to outside scrutiny, yet anticipating that day when God's glory covers the land and all flesh shall see it. The question remains how such glory might be developed, how it works out in the public arena.

First, it must be stated that efforts for legislative and judicial struggles for righteousness have never been the way of the gospel. The Spirit maintains unfathomable freedom in sovereignly bringing about whatever God wants to produce in societies. Human effort—even Christians' attempts—to bring about the kingdom is not the way of Christianity. In his rebuke of Peter at his arrest, even Jesus stated that his ways and kingdom were not of this world (John 18:36).

One intensely contested matter around the globe is the subject of marriage, a matter the gospel says very much about. Theological voices have been largely absent from the church's construction of a theological account of sexuality and marriage.[39] And yet, something has happened with the institution of marriage in common society that many evangelicals and Catholics (and Muslims . . .) find very troubling. What does a pneumatological public theology have to say about it? Whatever it might say in the freedom of conscience, it cannot remain neutral on matters that Scripture speaks to, and thus must make judgments on public and cultural phenomena. Public theology furthermore cannot remain silent about (and therefore complicit in) injustice, racism, prejudice, homophobia, and other forms of oppression, but maintains particular descriptions and assessments of each of these things, and even some things the gospel renders irredeemable.

If a public theology were robustly operative in the public square, faith would be

39. This is beginning to change, with numerous efforts underway, including the 2016 quadrennial meeting of the UK-based Tyndale Fellowship, focusing on "Marriage, Family, and Relationships."

recognized consistently by the powers of the age, leaders of Babylon, Athens, Jerusalem, or whatever contexts the church finds itself in. In the current situation, as in the past, the Spirit may indeed throw believers out into the desolate places, but so will the Spirit guide their words in the places of societal decay or power, wherever the journey may lead. Discerning the precise location of Christian witness is the ongoing task, but it cannot be done in any hegemonic ways. Even "Babylon" is a mixture of things, exuding ways that real people have made meaningful lives, and yet who are simultaneously called to find their ultimate life in Christ, as the Spirit and the bride call them (Rev. 22:7), which call remains an ever-present and public calling to all. But as the ages wax on ahead of the Lord's return, Babylon is much more likely the destination where believers will find themselves.

Christian engagement in the public square must be explicitly rooted in God's plan for the world.[40] This is the matter the Spirit is chiefly concerned with, and the manner in which the Spirit continues to dispatch grace to the world. Thereby mission becomes both the message and the posture of the church, whose existence is captured by the movement of the triune God and whose place in the public arena is the sphere in which Christian confession announces the truth of the coming kingdom's reality.

Contrary to the depiction of being the reduction of faith to "vague religiosity that serves primarily to energize, heal, and give meaning to the business of life" whose activity is shaped by factors other than faith,[41] the vision that sees theology integrating with missiology as public theology aims to make sense of things both as they are and as they ought to be, deemed thus in light of Scripture's vision of the coming kingdom, and in the way that the kingdom's transformative features are embodied by those devoted to following Jesus in the present. This is not merely "internal difference" as opposed to the liberal, postliberal, or separatist programs,[42] nor is it merely the notion of "faithful presence."[43] Instead, it views theology's outworking as a *mode* that intends

40. See Dan Strange, "Not Ashamed! The Sufficiency of Scripture for Public Theology," *Themelios* 36 (2011): 241–43.

41. See this description of the primary target for his thesis in Miroslav Volf, *A Public Faith: How Followers of Christ Should Serve the Common Good* (Grand Rapids: Brazos, 2011), 40.

42. Ibid., 84–97.

43. James Davison Hunter, *To Change the World: The Irony, Tragedy, and Possibility of Christianity in the Late Modern World* (New York: Oxford University Press, 2010), 197–286.

to address public issues and therefore as being a bit further down the line of confessing the substance of what is hoped for.

Therefore it is not only *being* a faithful witness (Acts 1:8), but also seeking ways to cultivate that witness while living life in the public square amid other competing narratives. By its very nature, Christian witness has always been public; to recap, this specific form aims "to address matters of public importance." Arising from theological reflection along with commitments and convictions rooted in the Christian tradition, the reflection viewed here "is invariably sparked off by public issues, whether global or local or both, that require exploring trajectories of faith and praxis." Yet this form of Christian witness occurs in the form of a discourse *accessible* within the framework of the very discourse operative in the public square.[44] In other words, while aware of and somewhat operative within the church-academy-society framework, the discourse flowing from the Christian witness is meant to be available to ordinary people. Public theology is then expressed through "reflection on public life in specific cultural contexts, and if its conclusions are to be communicated and understood in the public square, then it may need to be expressed in the vernacular and in dynamic interaction with cultural forms."[45] This correlates with Thiemann's notion of "faith seeking to understand the relation between Christian convictions and the broader social and cultural context within which the Christian community lives."[46] This is precisely faith actively situated within public life and expanding even further out in public.

The public mission of Christian witness, of course, is something that cannot be fabricated—the nature and existence of Christian witness are indicative (Acts 1:8). Therefore it is not something always necessarily operative in verbal form,[47] and when it is, is *never merely verbal.* The genuine engagement of public theology takes place with the whole being. It is ever opening in capaciousness to reckon

44. John W. de Gruchy, "Public Theology as Christian Witness: Exploring the Genre," *International Journal of Public Theology* 1 (2007): 40–41.

45. Kim, *Theology in the Public Sphere*, 54.

46. Ronals F. Thiemann, *Constructing a Public Theology The Church in a Pluralistic Culture* (Louisville: Westminster/John Knox, 1991), 21, cited in Kim, *Theology in the Public Sphere*, 7.

47. One of the challenges of the verbal-proclamation view is its anemic gospel for the whole people of God, including those who cannot talk. And what is the value of verbal gospel proclamation to a twenty-month-old, prematurely born child with a fatal disease and only minutes or hours to live?

with all things personal and public, and ever expansive. According to Miroslav Volf, it is

> not a matter of either speaking or doing; not a matter of either offering a compelling intellectual vision or embodying a set of alternative practices; not a matter of either merely making manifest the richness and depth of interior life or merely working to change the institutions of society; not a matter of either only displaying alternative politics gathered in Eucharistic celebrations or merely working for change as the dispersed people of God. It is all these things and more.[48]

This public engagement concerns the space (or sphere) in which God is currently working amid the present brokenness, which the church enters into in its own brokenness for the world, a brokenness shaped by the church's imperfect confession, which nevertheless courageously and humbly, with Scripture's sure voice as guide,[49] tells of the world's true hope. The distinctive Christian commitment to this gospel renders pluralism as a political project untenable,[50] itself seeming to obfuscate the special investment God has made, an investment of his life for the world by giving rise to the body of Christ, which has been called, gathered, and sent by an electing God of love. Thus God's Son came as Israel's promised king and messiah, who felt the force of sin's penalty as its verdict discoursed in a plurality of voices with contradictory worldviews who nevertheless united in realizing his crucifixion. These narratival voices he nevertheless subversively fulfills in his resurrection, ascension, and triumphal return, which is the public reality Christians witness to, and is far greater than anything else this world has to offer.

48. Volf, *Public Faith*, 97.

49. For the importance of this, see the chapter "The Bible as a Public Book" in Kim, *Theology in the Public Sphere*, 27–56; and Holmes, *Public Theology in Cultural Engagement*, 2, who claims the Bible should have "not just a place, but a central place, in public discourse."

50. See Volf, *Public Faith*, 126.

CHAPTER 23

Divine Action in the World in a Trinitarian-Pneumatological Framework*

VELI-MATTI KÄRKKÄINEN

In addition to the original work of creation and continuous creation, the Christian Scriptures—in sync with Jewish and Islamic traditions—are filled with accounts of divine acts in the world, not only in "salvation" history but also in universal history. They are so many and varied that one hardly needs to begin to compile a list. Indeed, all the way from the church fathers until the advent of modern science, the "mighty acts" of God were taken for granted. It simply was assumed that the God who had created the world in the first place, has the prerogative not only to "maintain" and guide it according to eternal divine purposes (general providence) but also to continue acting in history and nature—even to the point of responding to prayer and working out miracles (special providence).

So, what is the challenge to theology today? Philip Clayton, a leading expert in science-theology dialogue, puts it succinctly:

> Physical science, it appears, leaves no place for divine action. Modern science

*This essay is a shorter and slightly revised version of chapter 7 in my *Creation and Humanity: A Constructive Christian Theology for the Pluralistic World*, vol. 3 (Grand Rapids: Eerdmans, 2015), used with permission.

> presupposes that the universe is a closed physical system, that interactions are regular and law-like, that all causal histories can be traced, and that anomalies will ultimately have physical explanations. But traditional assertions of God acting in the world conflict with all four of these conditions: they presuppose that the universe is open, that God acts from time to time according to his purposes, that the ultimate source and explanation of these actions is the divine will, and that no earthly account would ever suffice to explain God's intentions.[1]

Not surprisingly, this dilemma became evident even to the pioneers of modern science. However, Newton and other believing scientists still felt compelled because of religious reasons to combine the mechanistic-determinist view of the world with real divine acts. Although they were willing to live with the unresolved problem, later modern scientists were not; that uneasy relationship was soon torn apart. Evolutionary theory with its focus on chance further helped make divine acts obsolete. Any notion of free agency in a world ruled by determinism and causal closure (which of course leads to reductionism) is an extremely difficult concept.[2]

Modern theology had several options in this situation; none of them, however, were satisfactory or fruitful. To simplify a complicated matter, a bifurcation emerged: whereas conservatives continued the affirmation of divine acts without concern for science, liberals virtually left behind any factual notion of divine acts as they were conceived to be merely subjective responses to religious influences (Friedrich Schleiermacher).[3] In other words, if any notion of an objective ("real") divine act entails intervention by God in the world, which is supposed to function according to the divinely set laws, it looks like the only alternative is to speak of subjective divine acts, that is, personal religious responses. That would certainly not contradict science, but then, theologically speaking, it would make

1. Philip Clayton, "The Impossible Possibility: Divine Causes in the World of Nature," in *God, Life, and the Cosmos: Christian and Islamic Perspectives*, ed. Ted Peters, Muzaffar Iqbal, and Syed Nomanul Haq (Surrey, UK: Ashgate, 2002), 249.

2. See further, Arthur R. Peacocke, *Theology for a Scientific Age: Being and Becoming–Natural, Divine, and Human*, Theology and the Sciences, enlarged ed. (Minneapolis: Fortress, 1993), 139–40.

3. For a detailed history and discussion, see Nancey Murphy, *Beyond Liberalism and Fundamentalism: How Modern and Postmodern Philosophy Set the Theological Agenda* (Valley Forge, PA: Trinity Press International, 1996).

meaningless the whole idea of God's works in nature and history. Even the neoorthodox attempt to salvage divine acts did not produce an alternative. With all their resistance to classical liberalism, they continued subscribing to the "nature-history" dualism; that is, science investigates the happenings in nature and humanities the domain of human affairs. That of course led to removing God and God's acts from the realm of the sciences.[4]

So, is there a way out of this impasse? Dissatisfied with available options, a growing group of leading theologians and believing scientists are aiming at a third alternative that, while sensitive to the necessity (for biblical-theological reasons) of affirming divine acts, wishes to do so in a way that would not contradict physical sciences. Unprecedented theological advances have been made during the past decades, particularly under the leadership of the long-term international "Scientific Perspectives on Divine Action" interdisciplinary project cosponsored by the Center for Theology and Natural Sciences (Berkeley, CA) and the Vatican Observatory (Vatican City).[5] The key theological-philosophical approach advocated by the project is known under the somewhat cumbersome nomenclature "Non-Interventionist Objective Divine Action" (NIODA).[6] That proposal seeks to "view special providence as consisting in the *objective* acts of God in nature and history to which we respond through faith *and* we can interpret these acts in a *non-interventionist* manner consistent with the natural sciences." In other words, it is able to "believe credibly that God really did do what the Bible testifies to."[7]

The current essay takes its point of departure in the promise of the NIODA project. It does so by both affirming its main intent

4. A prime example is Langdon Gilkey, "Cosmology, Ontology, and the Travail of Biblical Language," *The Journal of Religion* 41 (1961): 194–205. Other similar interpretations can be found in R. Bultmann, G. Kaufman, and M. Wiles, among others.

5. An assessment of the twenty-year interdisciplinary work on divine action with major volumes of publications is: Robert John Russell, Nancey Murphy, and William R. Stoeger, SJ, eds., *Scientific Perspectives on Divine Action: Twenty Years of Challenge and Progress* (Vatican City and Berkeley, CA: Vatican Observatory and Center for Theology and the Natural Sciences, 2008).

6. See Robert J. Russell, "Challenges and Progress in 'Theology and Science': An Overview of the VO/CTNS Series," in *Scientific Perspectives on Divine Action*, ed. Russell, Murphy, and Stoeger, 3–56; Clayton, "Toward a Theory of Divine Action," in ibid., 85–110.

7. Robert J. Russell, *Cosmology: From Alpha to Omega; The Creative Mutual Interaction of Theology and Science* (Minneapolis: Fortress, 2008), 112 (emphasis in original).

and sympathetically critiquing NIODA's liabilities and limitations. The main goal of the essay is to locate NIODA in a robust Trinitarian-pneumatological framework in order to save it from some potential problems (to be identified below) and to make it more satisfactory for (systematic) Christian theology of divine providence and continuing creation.

I will first introduce the conditions and possibility of NIODA with regard to negotiating the dilemma about divine action described above. Thereafter, I will subject NIODA to a sympathetic critical assessment by focusing on theological (rather than scientific) aspects. Finally, I will seek to offer a constructive proposal with a view toward pneumatological and Trinitarian conditions and implications.

The Conditions and Possibility of Non-Interventionist Objective Divine Acts

The goal of NIODA is to reaffirm divine acts without the fear of divine intervention. Particularly, it seeks "to speak about special divine acts in which God acts objectively in an unusual and particularly meaningful way in, with, and through events which serve to mediate God's action."[8] It main architect, the physicist-theologian Bob Russell, underlines that NIODA is not meant as an attempt to explain how exactly God acts, let alone prove that God acts. Rather, NIODA explanations seek to reconcile the conditions of non-interventionist divine acts vis-à-vis current scientific understanding. Nor is NIODA another version of the God-of-the-gaps. Rather than focusing on the gaps in our knowledge (which will probably be filled by new scientific discoveries), NIODA instead relies on what we currently know.[9]

The "Openness" of Nature

What makes NIODA possible is the radical transformation of the scientific worldview in the twentieth century as the result of the shift away from the semimechanistic and dualistic Newtonian cosmology to relativity theories, quantum theory, and related developments.[10] Rather than steady, mechanistic, and dualistic, the workings of the cosmos bespeak relationality, interdependence, dynamism, evolvement, and complexity. What quantum theory reveals is that not only at the smallest,

8. Ibid., 117.

9. See ibid., 125–29.

10. For a succinct listing, see ibid., 117–19.

subatomic level (where it primarily functions), but also at the macro level, nature reveals surprises, irregularities, and unpredictability. This is not to say that nature acts unlawfully; the laws of nature are still in place and natural phenomena are (relatively speaking) deterministic, otherwise no scientific observations would be possible. What the unpredictability means is that determinism is not ironclad and that—according to the major (Copenhagian) interpretation of quantum theory—natural processes and events are probabilistic in nature. The lack of exact results is not a matter of weakness of measurement but an inherent feature of the reality studied.[11]

This kind of world is open rather than closed in nature. In the open universe, the process of emergence is constantly at work. The basic definition of *emergence* is "that new and unpredictable phenomena are naturally produced by interactions in nature; that these new structures, organisms, and ideas are not reducible to the subsystems on which they depend; and that the newly evolved realities in turn exercise a causal influence on the parts out of which they arose."[12] A theologically and eschatologically significant observation is that "[e]mergence at all levels of being, and not just at those of life and mind, requires that nature possess an anticipatory rather than simply a cumulative character. It must be open to a domain of potentiality that makes a quiet entrance—from the future as it were—and thus opens up the otherwise unbending fabric of things to the later-and-more."[13] In other words, there is a dynamic tension between increasing entropy and the higher structuring. "In its dependence all creaturely reality is subject to the fate of destructuring, of dissolution according to the law of entropy. Because of the openness of process structures to future events, however, new structures are constantly formed, since processes take place in open rather than closed systems."[14]

11. See further, Alister E. McGrath, *A Scientific Theology*, vol. 2, *Reality* (Grand Rapids: Eerdmans, 2002), 83–85; Russell, "Quantum Physics in Philosophical and Theological Perspective," in *Physics, Philosophy and Theology: A Common Quest for Understanding*, ed. Robert J. Russell, William R. Stoeger, and George V. Coyne (Vatican City: Vatican Observatory, 1988), 343–74.

12. Clayton, *Mind and Emergence: From Quantum to Consciousness* (Oxford: Oxford University Press, 2004), vi; for the history, see chapter 1.

13. John F. Haught, *Is Nature Enough? Meaning and Truth in the Age of Science* (Cambridge: Cambridge University Press, 2006), 86.

14. Wolfhart Pannenberg, *Systematic Theology*, vol. 2, trans. Geoffrey W. Bromiley (Grand Rapids: Eerdmans, 1994), 112.

A Multifaceted and Complex Account of Divine Action

In keeping with the complexity and multi-level nature of the cosmos, NIODA's notion of divine action is multifaceted, not only because it encompasses both objective and subjective dimensions as argued, but also because it allows for divine action to happen directly (without having to perform any prior act) or indirectly (by setting into motion a sequence of events) as well as in either a mediated way (God acting in, with, and through the existing processes) or in an immediate way (*ex nihilo*).[15] The simultaneous establishment of various types of causalities is superior to the tendency to reduce it to only one type, typically the bottom-up approach, which refers to the effects of the lower on upper levels. Along with that we need to acknowledge other forms of causality and influence: "'Top-down' refers to God's action at a higher epistemic and phenomenological level than the level of the effects," such as when mind causally influences brain (and therefore the whole human being).[16] "'Whole-part' causality or constraint refers to the way the boundary of a system affects the specific state of the system," as God is the "boundary of the universe itself," leading up to certain states and processes. "Lateral" causality refers to effects at the same epistemic level as their causes, but at the end of the causal chain (as in biology, biological effects).[17]

Along with the top-down, the whole-part influence model is another way to speak of God's influence on the world without interrupting the regularities set up by the same God;[18] this is particularly important in complex systems.[19] The notion of informa-

15. Russell, *Cosmology*, 122.

16. For a thoughtful and cautious clarification and questioning of some of the premises behind Peacocke's and others' use of downward causation (and emergence), see Murphy, "Emergence, Downward Causation, and Divine Action," *Scientific Perspectives on Divine Action*, ed. Russell, Murphy, and Stoeger, 111–31.

17. All citations from Russell, *Cosmology*, 124.

18. Arthur Peacocke, "The Sound of Sheer Silence: How Does God Communicate with Humanity?" in *Neuroscience and the Person: Scientific Perspectives on Divine Action*, ed. Robert John Russell, Nancey Murphy, Theo C. Meyering, and Michael A. Arbib (Vatican City and Berkeley, CA: Vatican Observatory and Center for Theological and the Natural Sciences, 1999), 235–40 particularly; Peacocke, *Theology for a Scientific Age*, 157–60.

19. For an accessible explanation, see Nancey Murphy and George F. R. Ellis, *On the Moral Nature of the Universe: Theology, Cosmology, and Ethics* (Minneapolis: Fortress, 1996), 22–32; see also Nancey Murphy and Warren S. Brown, *Did My Neurons Make Me Do It? Philosophical and Neurobiological Perspectives on Moral Responsibility and*

tion is useful for speaking of the influence of the environment or large system on various levels.[20] What is striking is that even in dissipative systems far from equilibrium, large-scale patterns may appear in spite of random motions of the units; this is what is aptly called "order out of chaos."[21]

Theologically speaking, the model is based on the recognition that the omniscient God uniquely knows, across all frameworks of reference of time and space, everything that is possible to know about the state(s) of all-that-is, including the interconnectedness and interdependence of the world's entities, structures, and processes. Because the "'ontological gap(s)' between the world and God is/are located simply *everywhere* in space and time, God could affect holistically the state of the world (the whole in this context). . . . This unitive, holistic effect of God on the world could occur without abrogating any of the laws (regularities) which apply to the levels of the world's constituents."[22]

Divine Action and a Chastened Interpretation of Determinism

One of the openings for divine action is "ontological indeterminism"; that is, while regular, natural processes are not totally deterministic, they are rather statistical or probabilistic. Hence, pace Laplace, there is no way to fully predict all processes of nature, not only because we do not know enough but also because indeterminism describes natural processes.[23] Among science-theology scholars, both quantum theory and chaos theory have been widely investigated concerning indeterminism, that is, their capacity to provide a meaningful opening for divine action.

Quantum theory helps explain bottom-up causality as it claims (in its major Copenhagen interpretation) that events and processes at the subatomic level are to some extent indeterministic and hence probabilistic. In that sense, the future is ontologically open, "influenced but *under*determined by the factors of nature acting in the present."

Free Will (Oxford: Oxford University Press, 2007), 57–62.

20. Peacocke, "Sound of Sheer Silence," 220–29.

21. Ilya Prigogine and Isabelle Stengers, *Order out of Chaos: Man's New Dialogue with Nature* (Toronto: Bantam, 1984). "In dissipative systems order can indeed result from chaos. The requirement is that energy must enter the system in order for this to occur" (Richard Carlson, private email communication, September 7, 2013).

22. Peacocke, "Sound of Sheer Silence," 236.

23. See also Russell, *Cosmology*, 120–21.

Hence, we speak of potentialities and actualities.[24] The theologian who utilizes quantum theory is not implying that the subatomic level is the only one at which God works; recall the multifaceted nature of divine action discussed above.[25] Furthermore, the theologian must be careful not to make God a "natural cause." While deeply involved in natural processes, God also supremely transcends the created order, even in the deepest immanence.[26] And again, quantum theory is not creating another form of the God-of-the-gaps. Rather, indeterminacy has to do with what are called "causal gaps" in nature, that is, the lack of total determinism.[27] Rather than "intervening," God works in keeping with nature's indeterminacy. Finally, in order to avoid occasionalism (that is, the created order merely provides an occasion for God's works, without any true mediatory role), per our discussion above, one needs to speak also of the mediation of divine acts in cooperation with created agents.[28]

Not all scholars agree on quantum theory's compatibility with divine action.[29] Former quantum physicist John Polkinghorne has rightly reminded us that, if not careful, the employ of indeterminacy may yield an episodic account of divine action by a "hole-and-corner deity."[30] Furthermore, he has wondered as to how out of lack of order ("chaos") would come something meaningful. More importantly, he

24. Ibid., 156 (emphasis in original). See also William J. Stoeger, "Epistemological and Ontological Issues Arising from Quantum Theory," in *Quantum Mechanics: Scientific Perspectives on Divine Action*, ed. Robert J. Russell, Philip Clayton, Kirk Wegter-McNelly, and John Polkinghorne (Vatican City and Berkeley, CA: Vatican Observatory and Center for Theological and the Natural Sciences, 2001), 81–98.

25. See also Russell, *Cosmology*, 157, 159.

26. Ibid., 155, 169–70.

27. Thomas Tracy, "Particular Providence and the God of the Gaps," in *Chaos and Complexity: Scientific Perspectives on Divine Action*, ed. Robert John Russell, Nancey Murphy, and Arthur R. Peacocke (Vatican City and Berkeley, CA: Vatican Observatory and Center for Theological and the Natural Sciences, 1995), 290.

28. Murphy, "Divine Action in the Natural Order: Buridan's Ass and Schrödinger's Cat," in *Chaos and Complexity*, ed. Russell, Murphy, and Peacoke, especially 340–42.

29. An outright "global" rejection of not only quantum-theology engagement but the whole NIODA project is Nicholas Saunders, *Divine Action and Modern Science* (Cambridge: Cambridge University Press, 2002); for thoughtful responses and rebuttals, see Russell, *Cosmology*, 174–77; Wesley J. Wildman, "The Divine Action Project, 1988–2003," *Theology and Science* 2 (April 2004): 31–75.

30. John Polkinghorne, *Science and Creation: The Search for Understanding* (Boston: New Science Library, 1989), 58; more extensively and precisely in Polkinghorne, *Science and Providence: God's Interaction with the World* (West Conshohocken, PA: Templeton Foundation Press, 2005), especially 27–28.

also refers to the well-known "measurement problem" (a hugely complicated issue regarding its meaning and implications). For the sake of this discussion, let me (over)simplify what is the problem for him: when it comes to the "time development" of the wave function Ψ, it follows determinism (of Schrödinger's equation), whereas when it comes to interaction *between* quantum systems, "irreversible interaction" turns out to be indeterministic. Now, on this basis, Polkinghorne rejects the quantum principle as an aid for divine action because it would render it episodic, applying only to the moments of "measurement" and their effects in the macroworld.[31] Is that so? Not necessarily. Robert Russell has neatly argued that the "measurements" (irreversible interactions) include all kinds of phenomena ranging from "'micro-macro,' 'micro-meso,' and 'micro-micro' interactions" and "are not limited to interactions with the ordinary world around us." Therefore, only looking at those "episodic" moments when the effects of irreversible interactions cause effects at the macro level is much too limited an outlook. A comprehensive, multilevel understanding alone may yield a "ubiquitous" and "pervasive" character of divine action.[32]

Chaos theory has brought even to the popular consciousness the extremely intricate nature of natural processes, as discussed above. Particularly striking is the "extreme sensitivity to initial conditions displayed by some nonlinear dissipative systems."[33] What is ironic about chaos theory is that while the behavior can be modeled by mathematical equations,[34] because of the sheer complexity it soon generates a process whose outcome is unpredictable. Minimally it can be said that chaos theory "illustrates the insurmountable epistemic limits of any finite intelligence."[35] But not only that: "it also suggests causal relationships

31. Polkinghorne, *Reason and Reality: The Relationship between Science and Religion* (Philadelphia: Trinity Press International, 1991), 40–41.

32. Russell, *Cosmology*, 164–67 (165), 171–73. Similarly Murphy, "Divine Action in the Natural Order: Buridan's Ass and Schrödinger's Cat," in *Chaos and Complexity: Scientific Perspectives on Divine Action*, ed. Robert John Russell, Nancey Murphy, and Arthur R. Peacocke [Vatican City and Berkeley, Calif.: Vatican Observatory and Center for Theology and the Natural Sciences, 1995], 325–57, especially 340–42) supports the pervasive nature of divine actions in the quantum world.

33. Tracy, "Special Divine Action and the Laws of Nature," in *Scientific Perspectives on Divine Action*, ed. Russell, Murphy, and Stoeger, 266.

34. See Wesley J. Wildman and Robert John Russell, "Chaos: A Mathematic Introduction with Philosophical Reflections," in *Chaos and Complexity*, ed. Russell, Murphy, and Peacocke, 49–90.

35. Tracy, "Special Divine Action," 267.

where none were previously suspected."[36] So the term "chaos" has to be rightly handled; in scientific understanding it is deterministic and thus compatible with classical physics (otherwise, no equations would be possible of course). What makes it "chaotic" is that in light of our current knowledge, it relies on probabilities and statistical explanations. In that sense it represents a third alternative between classical and quantum physics, as it combines features of both.[37] Chaos theory has of course everything to do with science's better understanding of an unprecedented complexity of the universe.[38] What is also astonishing is that "chaos" is not merely a limitation to the otherwise regular process of nature; nature (as open) employs "chaos" also for creative, novel, constructive purposes.[39]

Having registered above the grave doubts expressed by Polkinghorne toward quantum indeterminacy's relevance, not surprisingly he has turned to chaos theory in search of an asset. Somewhat similarly to Peacocke's "whole-part" influence, he surmises that because chaotic systems are extensively linked with other complex processes (and of course ultimately to the whole) God's influence can be understood in terms of "input of active information" as a way of selecting between alternative paths of development.[40] There are no compelling arguments against the claim that in an "open" world, including an "open" future (without compromising the basically deterministic nature of natural processes), "there is room for the operation of holistic organizing principles, . . . for human intentionality, and for divine providential interaction."[41] Similarly to other theological claims, this kind of holistic and multifaceted divine action is hidden to scientific exploration.[42]

---

36. James P. Crutchfield, Doyne Farmer, Norman H. Packard, and Robert S. Shaw, "Chaos," in *Chaos and Complexity*, ed. Russell, Murphy, and Peacocke, 35; an accessible primer to chaos theory.

37. Russell, *Cosmology*, 130.

38. See Bernd-Olaf Küppers, "Understanding Complexity," in *Chaos and Complexity*, ed. Russell, Murphy, and Peacocke, 93–105.

39. See Prigogine and Stengers, *Order out of Chaos*.

40. Polkinghorne, "Metaphysics of Divine Action," in *Chaos and Complexity*, ed. Russell, Murphy, and Peacocke, 153–54.

41. Polkinghorne, "The Laws of Nature and the Laws of Physics," in *Quantum Cosmology and the Laws of Nature: Scientific Perspectives on Divine Action*, ed. Robert J. Russell, Nancey Murphy, and C. J. Isham (Vatican City and Berkeley, CA: Vatican Observatory and Center for Theological and the Natural Sciences, 1993), 442.

42. See Polkinghorne, "Laws of Nature," 446.

Having now clarified the challenges to theological talk about divine action (and providence) vis-à-vis the contemporary scientific worldview and the promise of NIODA in combatting those challenges, let me turn to a theological assessment of that proposal. Following that sympathetic critical account, I wish to offer a constructive pneumatological proposal.

Toward a Pneumatological-Trinitarian Theology of Divine Action and Providence

Let me emphasize that the theologically driven critical remarks on the NIODA template should not be taken as undermining, let alone rejecting, its superb achievements. Critique rather arises out of the deep desire to refine it and so make it fit for a systematic/constructive theological work.

Revising and Reorienting the Non-Interventionist Divine Action Approach

First, ironically, NIODA suffers from "dualistic" tendencies in its conception of divine action's conditions in creation. What I mean is this: when listing the scientific obstacles to divine action, the NIODA scholars tend to resort—against their better knowledge, I take it—to an outdated worldview in which "subject" (God) and "object" (world), physical and spiritual, divine and earthly are strictly taken as alternatives.

Coupled with that, second, is the tendency to make determinism (of natural processes) the default position, which has to be qualified at any cost "to make room" for God to act, instead of beginning from the current scientific understanding of the world's processes as regular and law-like, but so utterly complex and probabilistic that openness is to be taken for granted (although, of course, not openness for *divine* action). I fear at times the NIODA advocates take determinism more seriously than most scientists![43] On the other side, the whole concept of indeterminacy, while certainly related to quantum and chaos theory, may be a wider and more complex concept, and (as a default position) calls for a robust analysis.[44] That is closely linked with a

---

43. For a thoughtful reflection, see Stoeger, "Conceiving Divine Action in a Dynamic Universe," in *Scientific Perspectives on Divine Action*, ed. Russell, Murphy, and Stoeger, 240–44.

44. See further, Niels Henrik Gregersen, "Three Types of Indeterminacy," in *The Concept of Nature in Science and Theology*, part 1, ed. Niels Henrik Gregersen, Michael W. S. Parsons, and Christoph Wasserman (Geneva: Labor et Fides, 1997),

better philosophical-theological understanding of natural law: while respectful of the regularities of the world, there is no reason to consider God as prisoner to his own laws![45]

Related, third, is NIODA's almost pathological (or at least exaggerated) fear of "intervention." As N. T. Wright correctly notes, the continuous use of terms such as

> invasive, intrusive or . . . "interventionist" . . . imply, or even presuppose, a latent Epicurean framework: the divinity is normally outside the process of the world, and occasionally reaches in, does something, and then goes away again. But in biblical thought heaven and earth—God's sphere and our sphere—are not thought of as detached or separate. They overlap and interlock.[46]

Fourth, NIODA is much more sophisticated in scientific-philosophical than (systematic-) theological argumentation and approach. Indeed, the whole effort so far has been motivated so much by apologetic concerns deriving from (at times somewhat non-critically) listening to natural scientists that the constructive theological work is yet to be done. Part of the weakness is its lack of an integral Trinitarian conception of God's works in the world, its lack of Trinitarian contours.[47]

Some critics of NIODA have wondered whether its use of various kinds of approaches to "make room" for divine action, namely, whole-part/top-down causation, quantum, and chaos theory, is a liability. I disagree with this criticism and wholeheartedly underline that multiplicity of tactics is rather a great asset.[48] This is far superior to "uniformitarianism," which reductionistically thinks that "God always and everywhere does the same job of creating-and-upholding an already

---

165–86; Keith Ward, "Divine Action in an Emergent Cosmos," in *Scientific Perspectives on Divine Action*, ed. Russell, Murphy, and Stoeger, 289.

45. See "Contingency and Natural Law," in Pannenberg, *Towards a Theology of Nature: Essays on Science and Faith,* ed. Ted Peters (Louisville: Westminster John Knox, 1993), 72–122.

46. Nicholas T. Wright, "Mind, Spirit, Soul and Body: All for One and One for All; Reflections on Paul's Anthropology in His Complex Contexts," presented at Society of Christian Philosophers Eastern Meeting (March 18, 2011): n.p., accessed November 26, 2013, http://www.ntwrightpage.com/Wright_SCP_MindSpiritSoulBody.htm.

47. Russell (*Cosmology*, 192–93 and elsewhere), though, notes the need for that.

48. So also Gregersen, "Special Divine Action and the Quilt of Laws: Why the Distinction between Special and General Divine Action Cannot be Maintained," in *Scientific Perspectives on Divine Action*, ed. Russell, Murphy, and Stoeger, 181–83.

established universe," after Schleiermacher and contemporary liberals.[49]

Finally, the foundational question that has to be asked in relation to the NIODA project is whether, contrary to all its claims otherwise, it still ends up being a new form of a God-of-the-gaps theology. This has to do with its robust use of both quantum and chaos theory's alleged "openings." Although the approach avoids the old-time pitfall of the God-of-the-gaps tactics in which God is needed whenever there are epistemological gaps (because NIODA speaks of permanent, ontological gaps in an indeterministic nature), it still is the case that the divine influence is pretty thin. Clayton expresses my doubts well: "A gap for divine action that cannot be closed may represent a breakthrough for the theologian, but inserting God into this space, even if it is a permanent opening rather than a gap, may well seem like a sleight of hand to one's scientific partners" and hardly convincing at all.[50] That said, it can be counterargued (and I think Clayton would agree with me) that the whole aim of the Divine Action project is minimalist, to provide the context for theologians to speak of divine acts in a meaningful way in the context of current scientific understanding of the world. As to how much that may or may not be convincing to nonbelieving scientists is a different matter.

A Pneumatological-Trinitarian Theology of Divine Action

Trinitarian theology is a distinctively Christian framework for conceiving not only the coming into existence of the created order but also the Creator's continuous creation thereof. With the same love that the Father loves the Son, he loves the universe, his creation, by continuously providing for its life, meaning, and hope for the future. The Son as Logos and mediator of all creative work of God is the one in whom everything is held together. Through the Spirit the triune God is present in, under, above, and below, so to speak, all natural processes.[51] According to Gregory of Nyssa, "For all things depend on Him who is, nor can there be anything which has not its being in Him who is. . . . [A]ll things are in Him, and He in all things. . . . He Who holds together Nature in existence is transfused in *us*; while at that other time

49. Ibid., 184.

50. Clayton, "Toward a Theory of Divine Action That Has Traction," in *Scientific Perspectives on Divine Action*, ed. Russell, Murphy, and Stoeger, 108.

51. For a full-scale Trinitarian theology of creation, see chapter 4 in my *Creation and Humanity*.

He was transfused throughout *our nature*."[52] Astonishingly—in light of the cosmologies of his times—Gregory's thinking is so thoroughly participatory and holistic that even heaven for him does not represent merely something transcendent but rather "pervades all creation and . . . does not exist separated from being."[53] Many other theological witnesses to the same effect can be found in theological tradition.[54] The Australian Roman Catholic Denis Edwards succinctly summarizes the main thrust of a Trinitarian theology of providence: "The trinitarian God works in and through the process of the universe, through laws and boundary conditions, through regularities and chance, through chaotic systems and the capacity for self-organization."[55]

Consequently, as already emphasized, theologically we must hold on to the widest and most diverse possible account of divine action in the world, rather than, say, debating whether it takes place due to quantum or chaos indeterminacy. Furthermore, very importantly, we should not seek to reveal the "'causal joint' between divine action and created causality," simply because we cannot[56]—or else we could read God's mind! At the same time, we should of course consider scientific and theological explanations as complementary.

A key to a ubiquitous and comprehensive theology of divine action is the Trinitarian doctrine of divine omnipresence—which also entails divine omniscience: "All things are present to him and are kept by him in his presence,"[57] as classically affirmed in Psalm 139. Through his Spirit God is present everywhere and thus able to know everything. This is of course not to compromise but rather to

52. Gregory of Nyssa, *The Great Catechism*, 25, in *A Select Library of the Nicene and Post-Nicene Fathers of the Christian Church*. Second Series. 14 vols. ed Philip Schaff and Henry Wace (Edinburgh: T&T Clark, 1886-1880 (public domain; available at www.ccel.org), 5:493.

53. Gregory of Nyssa, "On What It Means to Call Oneself a Christian," in Gregory of Nyssa, Ascetical Works, trans. Virginia Woods Callahan. *The Fathers of the Church*, Vol 58 (Washington, D.C.: The Catholic University of America, 1967), 87. I am indebted to Jens Zimmermann, *Incarnational Humanism: A Philosophy of Culture for the Church in the World* (Downers Grove, IL: InterVarsity Press, 2012), 235.

54. Aquinas, *Summa theologiae* I, q. 1, a. 8; Luther, WA 23:133; *LW* 37:58.

55. Denis Edwards, "The Discovery of Chaos and the Retrieval of the Trinity," in *Chaos and Complexity*, ed. Russell, Murphy, and Peacocke, 170.

56. Edwards, "Discovery of Chaos," 172–73.

57. Pannenberg, *Systematic Theology*, vol. 1, trans. Geoffrey Bromiley (Grand Rapids: Eerdmans, 1991), 380.

establish transcendence as well: "Precisely as the one who incommensurably transcends his creation, God is still present to even the least of his creatures. As in the case of his eternity, then, there are combined in his omnipresence elements of both immanence and transcendence in keeping with the criterion of the true Infinite."[58] In this sense, the establishment of divine action with the help of quantum theory (in its ubiquitous form) points in the right direction, "reemphasizing God's operational presence in the most basic processes of nature known to us,"[59] that is, even the subatomic. Here an analogical-metaphorical use of the scientific concept of field of force is appropriate: "the presence of God's Spirit in his creation can be described as a field of creative presence, a comprehensive field of force that releases event after event into finite existence."[60]

In keeping with the scriptural teaching (Pss. 104:29–30; 139), the Trinitarian presence in the world is funded by a robust pneumatological doctrine. Moltmann's striking term "immanent transcendence" well captures this dynamic. "Through his Spirit God himself is present in his creation. The whole creation is a fabric woven and shot through by the efficacies of the Spirit. Through his Spirit God is also present in the very structures of matter. Creation contains neither spiritless matter nor non-material spirit; there is only *informed* matter."[61] In keeping with the complexity of the world—and infinity of the triune God—the presence of the Spirit is manifested in various forms in every being in the world.[62] Far from being subsumed in the natural processes or acting as yet another natural cause, the Spirit of God is transcendently immanent in all things.[63] Again, this is a theological claim and of course hidden to scientific experiments.

Colin Gunton adds the important note that whatever problems may relate to the interpretation of the Spirit of God in terms of "force-field," it has great value for the question of how to understand God's action: the idea of the Spirit's work "as interacting fields

58. Ibid., 412.

59. Gregersen, "Special Divine Action and the Quilt of Laws," 194.

60. Pannenberg, *Introduction to Systematic Theology* (Grand Rapids: Eerdmans, 1991), 49.

61. Jürgen Moltmann, *God in Creation: A New Theology of Creation and the Spirit of God*, trans. Margaret Kohl (Minneapolis: Fortress, 1993), 212 (emphasis in original).

62. Moltmann, *Spirit of Life: A Universal Affirmation*, trans. Margaret Kohl (Minneapolis: Fortress, 1992), 34.

63. Ibid., 34, 35.

of force rather than billiard-ball-like entities bumping into one another, is of extreme importance in showing that the world is open to God's continuing interaction with it."[64]

A robust Trinitarian panentheism ("Classical Panentheism"[65]) funds a dynamic, multifaceted divine action, providence, and causality. To be the Creator is far more than being the world's cause. While causality should not of course be eliminated from the theological thesaurus,[66] the main focus should be placed on the living, dynamic, creative presence of the Creator in the world:

> If the Creator is himself present in his creation by virtue of the Spirit, then his relationship to creation must rather be viewed as an intricate web of unilateral, reciprocal and many-sided relationships. In this network of relationships, "making," "preserving," "maintaining" and "perfecting" are certainly the great *one-sided* relationships; but "indwelling," "sym-pathizing," "participating," "accompanying," "enduring," "delighting" and "glorifying" are relationships of *mutuality* which describe a cosmic community of living between God the Spirit and all his created beings.[67]

Classical Panentheism also allows us to hold on tightly to both sides of the activity and relationship between God and the world: the "one-sided" creation and the "mutual" participation of creatures in preservation, perfecting, and final consummation.[68] The divinely given mandate (Gen. 1:26–27) belongs to that invitation for collaboration and vice-regency.

Unlike we humans, the triune Creator is not in a hurry with the universe. Speaking of continuous creation and divine acts in the universe, we need to be reminded of the long timeline. If, as we think currently, the universe came into being about fourteen billion years ago with extremely fine-tuned conditions, we have a lot of room, so to

64. Colin E. Gunton, *The Triune Creator: A Historical and Systematic Study*, Edinburgh Studies in Constructive Theology (Grand Rapids: Eerdmans, 1998), 175, also 176.

65. In chapter 10 of my *Trinity and Revelation: A Constructive Christian Theology for the Pluralistic World*, vol. 2 (Grand Rapids: Eerdmans, 2014) I have developed a theological alternative to the impasse between classical theism and (forms of contemporary) panentheism(s) which I call "Classical Panentheism."

66. Contra Moltmann, *God in Creation*, 14.

67. Ibid. (emphasis in original).

68. I am aware that here I modify Moltmann's citation to serve my own "less" panentheistic and more classical account of the God-world relationship.

speak, to consider the breadth and depth of divine action throughout the universe's history. In that framework, talk about the multilevel (top-down/whole part and bottom-up, among others) causality and influence is both necessary and highly useful.[69]

In light of these theological reflections, we should also be reminded in this context that in keeping with the triune God's infinite nature, including omniscience, we should be open to recognizing "the profound metaphysical point that divine causality transcends any other category of causality."[70] This is not an effort to divorce God from the world, nor to make divine action more mysterious than it is. Rather, it is to cash out the implications of God's thoroughgoing, all-pervasive presence through the Spirit in the world created and sustained in and through the Son because of the Father's overflowing love.

An important step toward a comprehensive, ubiquitous theological account of the divine action is to affirm God's exceptional acts along with regular law-like events.

69. See also Russell, *Cosmology*, 160.

70. William E. Carroll, "Aquinas on Creation and the Metaphysical Foundations of Science," *Sapientia* 54 (1999): 91; cited in Tracy, "Special Divine Action," 254.

Special Divine Action and "Miracles"

A proper way to test the theological suitability of a pneumatological-Trinitarian account of NIODA is to consider what may be appropriately called the special divine action, namely, instances when God seems to be executing a divine act that can be labeled miraculous or at least untypical. Not surprisingly these kinds of divine acts—say, a tangible answer to a specific prayer in terms of a healing of sickness, release from under a financial breakdown, or, say, an instantaneous healing of a relationship—have come under a massive suspicion among the critics of divine acts. Not only among them but even for some advocates of NIODA such as Peacocke, the divine action does not include miraculous divine action.[71] Recall that the reason why theologians such as Paul Tillich eschewed what he called the "supranaturalistic" is that he saw them as violations of nature's laws (although

71. See, for instance, Peacocke, "Prologue: Naturalism, Theism, and Religion," in Arthur Peacocke, *All That Is: A Naturalistic Faith for the Twenty-First Century*, ed. Philip Clayton (Minneapolis: Fortress, 2007), 9. Unfortunately, Peacocke mistakenly claims to find support for this antimiraculous, noninterventionist view in Eastern Orthodox theology by taking out of context a statement from Vladimir Lossky (*The Mystical Theology of the Eastern Church* [Cambridge: James Clarke, 1991], 70).

he rightly saw that if "miracles" were allowed, they should be called "sign-events," following Johannine terminology).[72]

Without being able to go into the important investigation of the ways the notions of the "miraculous" and "supernatural" have developed in the history of philosophy and theology, we can say safely that the Enlightenment-based rebuttal of the miraculous because of the alleged ironclad determinism of the world hardly calls for a sustained theological-philosophical rebuttal. The reason is simply the openness of the cosmos, discussed above. In that light, we can set aside the Humean claim for the miracle as the violation of natural laws. That claim is tied to the now-outdated Newtonian-Laplacean strict determinism and as such has lost much of its key appeal.

Against those who reject special divine action, Keith Ward rightly wonders that while believing that "God, a supernatural being, has caused, and continues to cause, the whole universe to exist . . . [h]ow plausible it is, then, to say that such a God will refuse to operate in the world in particular ways?" Furthermore, he reminds us, because of the divine omnipresence, "no part of the physical universe is ever absent from God." If so, then the personal God truly interacts with the world, including being affected by world affairs. Now comes Ward's main challenge to those who deny special divine action: if God creates the world with an intentional act (as all theists believe), then it has to be said that "[s]ince the bringing of something into being is the strongest possible causal influence upon it, it may seem unnecessary to espouse a theory that denies any particular influence of God upon the universe."[73]

I would add that in Peacocke's own deeply panentheistic, mutually conditioned theology, to suppose that something comes from "outside" to violate the natural laws seems like an odd fear. Only a deist could say so, but not a panentheist (nor even a classical theist). Furthermore, when personal beings are in mutual interaction and have causal effects, these influences are not external violations of the other person's balance, so to speak. God similarly is believed to be (analogically speaking) a person and hence intends to have a personal relationship.[74] Ward also

72. Paul Tillich, *Systematic Theology* (Chicago: University Press of Chicago, 1951), 1:115.

73. Keith Ward, "Personhood, Spirit, and the Supernatural," in Peacocke, *All That Is*, 155.

74. See Maurice Wiles, "Religious Authority and Divine Action," in *God's Activity in the World:*

makes the needed observation that unless one thinks of natural laws as reducible to a set of physical laws, the Humean fear of the violation thereof disappears. This is also supported by the simple notion that we no longer think that nature is totally deterministic (although it is "regular") and that therefore, the laws of nature "do not cover everything."[75]

Hence, the conclusion is that rather than denying the possibility of miracles, we just have to do away with the mistaken concept of miracles as "arbitrary interferences in an otherwise elegant and lawlike cosmos"—the violation of the laws of nature. Instead, we have to say that in the kind of created reality we live in, miracles have "their own form of intelligibility and rationality" as the personal God is affected by and responds to the needs, desires, and prayers of his creatures. Recall our conviction that "the divine Spirit interpenetrates the universe at every point." To call these divine "interventions" violations of laws is absurd. That natural sciences are neither able to predict nor able to fully investigate them, does not make miracles any less true.[76]

Ward rightly concludes that miracles are neither "immoral," that is, breaches of natural laws, nor "irrational," that is, "emergency-interventions" to fix what went wrong in nature. Rather, they are "law-transcending events, extraordinary events manifesting divine causality that modifies the normal regularities of nature with the purpose of manifesting the basis and goal of the physical world in a wider spiritual realm." One of the purposes of miracles is to "show the power of Spirit to relate matter to Spirit" in transcending the typical patterns of interaction.[77] The most profound Christian miracle, the resurrection of Christ, seems to point to freedom from decay and dissolution, "showing the goal of the whole physical process to be the transformation of the physical into an incorruptible vehicle of divine life."[78] Significantly the miracles in the Gospel of John are called "signs" (*semeia*). Ultimately, miracles thus receive their meaning not from the past but from the future, new creation.

The Contemporary Problem, ed. Owen C. Thomas (Chico, CA: Scholars Press, 1983), 181–94.

75. Ward, "Personhood," 157.

76. Ibid., 160.

77. Ward, "Divine Action in an Emergent Cosmos," 297.

78. Ibid. On the importance of the resurrection of Christ in this regard, see also Polkinghorne, *Quarks, Chaos and Christianity: Questions to Science and Religion*, rev. ed. (New York: A Crossroad Book, 2005), chapter 6.

Christ's resurrection as the most profound divine action known to us reveals the ultimate meaning of the miracle. Rather than going against nature, it transcends and lifts up the natural. It points to the eschatological consummation when, according to the biblical promises, creation "will be set free from its bondage to decay" (Rom. 8:21 NRSV). In resurrection even death will be defeated (1 Cor. 15:55).

In the final analysis, a theological perception of an event as miraculous is just that: *theological*. On the one hand, miracle can only be had through the eye of faith—and therefore, the "miracle does not replace faith by demonstrating the presence of God through sign language."[79] On the other hand, without faith, theological interpretation, even the strangest and most counterintuitive event can also be explained otherwise. Similarly to the Book of Nature, a "miraculous act by itself is silent" and invites diverse interpretations.[80]

A Brief Concluding Reflection

The task of this essay is simple and straightforward, namely, to establish the possibility and nature of divine action vis-à-vis those opinions that (mistakenly) believe that the rebuttal follows more or less automatically from the contemporary scientific worldview. The basic aim is not primarily apologetic. It simply is the case that for a naturalist[81] nothing that happens in this cosmos is to be attributed to God. Rather, the main aim is to make meaningful the *theological* talk about providence and divine action—whether general or special. For that purpose, a careful scrutiny of the NIODA (non-interventionist objective divine action) was conducted. While taking that proposal as the point of departure, a robust pneumatological-Trinitarian proposal was set forth as a way to correct the liabilities of that project and to advance a more coherent and comprehensive theological account of divine action.

Among the advocates of NIODA, there are differing opinions as to what might be the main avenue or platform for the establishment of the "openness" in nature to facilitate the divine action. The quantum indeterminacy and chaos theory are the main candidates. For a nonscientist such as myself, not capable of assessing the scientific ramifications, it is

79. Hans Schwarz, *Creation* (Grand Rapids: Eerdmans, 2002), 221.

80. Ibid., 225.

81. For a typology of various forms of naturalisms and their theological implications, see chapter 2 in my *Creation and Humanity*.

best not to be dogmatic. As long as leading believing scientists such as the late Peacocke (quantum theory) and Polkinghorne (chaos theory) make a compelling case for either one, the theologian hardly is able to resolve the issue. The theologian's contribution is to remind of the importance of the Spirit: through the Spirit, the divine omnipresence and omniscience fund a comprehensive account of divine action.

CHAPTER 24

"In the Unity of the Holy Spirit"

A Third Article Theology of Receptive Ecumenism

KIRSTEN LAUREL GUIDERO

Ecumenical theology's difficulties remain oft rehearsed: Christian division "characterized by centuries of stereotypes, rancor, and mutual vilification"[1] debilitates the church's testimony,[2] exemplifies "the direct opposite of the true spirit of the Church,"[3] and engenders an ecumenism of complacent coexistence rather than full union.[4] Though decades of work creating consensus, lifting various excommunications, and finding regular seats at the dialogue table were fittingly termed a "harvest"

1. Bruce Myers, "Keeping Warm: Reception in the Ecumenical Winter," *The Ecumenical Review* 65 (October 2013): 380.

2. See Anonymous Editorial, "Ecumenism: Urgency and Method," *America* 166, no. 2 (Jan. 18, 1992): 27; and *World Missionary Conference, 1910: Report of Commission VIII, Co-operation and the Promotion of Unity* (Edinburgh: Oliphant, Anderson, & Ferrier, 1910), 9.

3. Georges Florovsky, "The Doctrine of the Church and the Ecumenical Problem," *The Ecumenical Review* 2 (December 1, 1950): 152.

4. See André Birmelé, *Crisis and Challenge of the Ecumenical Movement: Integrity and Indivisibility* (Geneva: Institute for Ecumenical Research/Strasbourg: World Council of Churches, 1994), 4–5.

of worthy fruits by Cardinal Walter Kasper,[5] more recently, the rush of excitement over these possibilities has tempered. Persisting different definitions of dialogue, ecclesiology, and unity complicate efforts to craft Christian union, even when such efforts make official agreed statements their foundation.[6] Questions of what constitutes true ecumenism abound: Given the enormous breadth of theological and ecclesial disparities that persist even after the first harvest of sustained ecumenical dialogue, what will eventually yield Christian union?[7]

In response, attention has recently shifted to the notion of receptive ecumenism (RE) as an approach that can redirect the ecumenical future. The fruit of several years of study and collaboration under the auspices of the Durham Centre for Catholic Studies, RE now considers how each Christian tradition can learn from the others. In the words of Paul D. Murray, RE concerns "how ecumenical encounter, ecumenical engagement, ecumenical responsibility and calling can be privileged contexts for promoting this process of personal and ecclesial growth into more intensely configured communion in Christ and the Spirit."[8] As Paul Avis parses it in 2012, RE's promotion of an "attitude of self-searching, of self-criticism and of seeking to receive the good things

5. See Cardinal Walter Kasper, *Harvesting the Fruits: Basic Aspects of Christian Faith in Ecumenical Dialogue* (London: Continuum, 2009), as well as the excellent shorter summaries found in Birmelé, *Crisis and Challenge*, 1–22, and in Myers, "Keeping Warm," 377–80.

6. For instance, see Gillian R. Evans, *Method in Ecumenical Theology: The Lessons So Far* (Cambridge: Cambridge University Press, 1996), 182–218, which summarizes how the discordance between what the members of ARCIC-I (the Anglican Roman Catholic International Commission-I.) believed they had achieved and the various responses to their conclusions show up difficulties in ecumenical method: those who participate in a given dialogue are naturally predisposed toward finding convergence with that particular ecclesial partner, while convincing the rest of their ecclesial community remains another matter.

7. Some advocate simply promoting cooperative work between denominations while others continue to stress dialogue and formal union. Compare, for instance, Konrad Raiser's "Ecumenism in Search of a New Vision," in *The Ecumenical Movement: An Anthology of Key Texts and Voices*, ed. Michael Kinnamon and Brian E. Cope (Grand Rapids: Eerdmans, 1997), 70–77, with the perspective of the authors and signatories of *In One Body through the Cross: The Princeton Proposal for Christian Unity*, ed. Carl E. Braaten and Robert W. Jenson (Grand Rapids: Eerdmans, 2003), 23–25, §17.

8. Paul D. Murray, "Receptive Ecumenism and Catholic Learning—Establishing the Agenda," in *Receptive Ecumenism and the Call to Catholic Learning: Exploring a Way for Contemporary Ecumenism*, ed. Paul D. Murray with Luca Badini-Confalonieri (Oxford: Oxford University Press, 2008), 5–25 (7).

that God has given to the partner" thus holds the potential "to re-motivate, re-energise and redirect the ecumenical movement in our time."[9] Advocates of RE acknowledge that though the work of ecumenism must always be driven by receptivity, ecumenical processes of themselves cannot produce such a posture. Rather, RE "is a work of the Spirit which stirs both in grace-filled delight in another's beauties and in a longing awareness of a fitting match between our own particular lacks and needs and the other's particular gifts."[10]

If RE represents a crucial component enabling the future of the ecumenical movement, it warrants continued examination. If RE occurs primarily as a work of the Spirit, such an effort should include a thorough pneumatology that discerns how attention to the Spirit connects with its goals. In what follows, I attempt to outline the basis for a Third Article Theology (TAT) of RE. This approach starts with the Spirit as the person who enables those of all times and places to enter Christ's transformative mission. I then elaborate how the Spirit enables that transformation through RE's call to convert to the other.[11] I begin with Scripture as the resource that each Christian tradition can claim to hold in common with the others; I add in contemporary insights from philosophy and theology as they demonstrate ecumenical sensitivity. This meeting of TAT with the RE project identifies the heart of Christian union as *profoundly and reliably* a function of pneumatology. First, I briefly explain the contours of RE before taking up

9. Paul Avis, "Are We Receiving 'Receptive Ecumenism'?," *Ecclesiology* 8 (2012): 223–34 (226, 225).

10. Murray, "Establishing the Agenda," 16.

11. See Myk Habets, "'Justified by the Spirit'? Developing a Third Article Theology," in *The Anointed Son: A Trinitarian Spirit Christology* (Eugene, OR: Pickwick, 2010), 228–57 (232). See also D. Lyle Dabney, "Starting with the Spirit: Why the Last Should Now Be First," in *Starting with the Spirit: Task of Theology II*, ed. Stephen Pickard and Gordon Preece (Hindmarsh, SA: Australian Theological Forum, 2001), 3–27, especially 24–27; and his additional essays "Naming the Spirit: Towards a Pneumatology of the Cross," "The Justification of the Spirit: Soteriological Reflections on the Resurrection," and "The Nature of the Spirit: Creation as a Premonition of God," in Pickard and Preece, *Starting with the Spirit*, 28–58, 59–82, and 83–110, respectively. Since my focus is more on RE as a mind-set and less on ecclesiology, my take here differs somewhat from that of Denis Edwards, "The Holy Spirit as the Gift—Pneumatology and Catholic Re-reception of Petrine Ministry in the Theology of Walter Kasper," in Murray and Badini-Confalonieri, *Receptive Ecumenism*, 197–210. I hope that what follows displays consonances with Edwards's excellent piece.

concerns that a focus on the Holy Spirit actually ill-suits ecumenical theology, distracting it from union in Christ.

What Is Receptive Ecumenism?

Although they were not named as a discrete strategy until recently, the principles of RE are not new. Twenty years ago, Gillian Evans's analysis of ecumenical method emphasized the need for dialogue partners to mutually move into each other's thinking and to find new language encompassing what all parties can hold in common.[12] Even then, she admitted how rarely dialogue partners successfully implement either aspect of ecumenical method due to fears of dissolving their own community's identity.[13] Nevertheless, she contended that this very "change of attitude" about one's own role and identity provides an essential building block of ecumenical reciprocity: "where a sense of 'otherness' persists, theology cannot be done in wholeness, and the Church cannot be fully herself."[14] Ten years later, Angelo Maffeis called for ecclesial communities to go outside of themselves in order to encounter, understand, and find common ground with the other.[15] Ecumenical work does not end with agreed statements, for such do not suffice to form ecclesial union. Unity requires deeper change more along the lines of conversion than those of mere consensus.[16]

Murray, writing in 2008, highlights how the category of RE binds together such encouragements toward transformative recognition of the other and names them as the heart of ecumenical endeavors. Though related to the practice of reception, RE does not simply describe this component of ecumenism but rather comprises a strategy of developing "the prior necessary disposition to receptive transformational learning that the bilateral processes presuppose."[17] Within RE, emphasis lies on the postures and attitudes underlying all levels of ecumenical engagement.[18] Murray beautifully describes RE as

12. Evans, *Method in Ecumenical Theology*, 86–88, 89–113.

13. Ibid., 90–91.

14. Ibid., 55, 44.

15. Angelo Maffeis, *Ecumenical Dialogue*, trans. Lorelei F. Fuchs (Collegeville, MN: Liturgical Press, 2005), 79–84.

16. Ibid., 95–100.

17. Murray, "Establishing the Agenda," 14.

18. Ibid., 7, citing Thomas S. Reese, "Organizational Factors Inhibiting Receptive Catholic Learning," in *Receptive Ecumenism*, ed. Murray and Badini-Confalonieri 346–56. Reese suggests that not only is Roman Catholic reform essential for

the path to "the very core of what is required for any real effective progress to occur at all . . . the essential way forward towards the anticipated goal of organic structural unity."[19] This "transformational receptivity" reframes ecumenism as the conversion of each tradition from the inside out toward the others, rather than as mere reconciliation of language and history.[20] As such, RE entails spiritual growth, becoming "a matter of the heart before it is a matter of the head; a matter of falling in love with the experienced presence and action of God in the people, practices, even structures of another tradition and being impelled thereby to search for ways in which all impediments to closer relationship might be overcome."[21]

How can each tradition live up to this high call to recognize and fall in love with the presence and action of God in others? I believe it correct to identify such conversion to the other as the work of the Holy Spirit. But championing the role of the Spirit in ecumenical engagement is by no means an uncontroversial move. Clarifying this connection remains crucial for my argument—and so to this topic I now turn.

How Should the Spirit Best be Related to Ecumenism?

Ecumenism remains permeated by pneumatological claims. Both analyses of ecumenical work as well as agreed statements tend to stress the Holy Spirit's significance for ecumenism while often attributing their successes to the work of the Spirit. Such connections are too numerous to fully catalogue here, so I will briefly mention a few notable instances. Philip J. Rosato's 1978 piece argued that a recovered emphasis on the Holy Spirit promotes Roman Catholic advancement into ecumenical efforts by suggesting that ecclesial traits can be found wherever the Spirit works.[22] Drawing on Cardinal Kasper's work, Rosato stressed the need to situate ecclesiology within and underneath

ecumenism, but also ecumenism itself provides an essential goad toward said reform ("Organizational Factors," 354).

19. Murray, "Establishing the Agenda," 15.

20. Ibid., 14.

21. Ibid., 15.

22. Philip J. Rosato, "Called by God, in the Holy Spirit: Pneumatological Insights into Ecumenism," *The Ecumenical Review* 30 (April 1, 1978): 110–26 (110 and 112). However, he qualified this statement by noting that the Spirit's work is known in word, sacrament, and office, which restricts genuine ecclesiality to those churches that maintain all three of those elements in a form recognizable to Catholicism.

pneumatology rather than the other way around.[23] The 2002 edition of the *Dictionary of the Ecumenical Movement* includes an entry on the Holy Spirit as well as another on the Spirit in ecumenical thought; both catalogue the numerous instances of pneumatology's appearances in ecumenical documents.[24] In the same year, the Bose Consultation on the Spirit, the Church, and Christian Unity produced a number of stellar papers discussing how these theological themes might intersect with each other.[25]

However, other reflections on the relation of Spirit to ecumenism take a more pessimistic view. They sound alarms that the Spirit's work to create full union may be thwarted or that the significance of pneumatology for ecclesiology has not yet found enough common ground to provide a sturdy ecumenical foundation. Michael Root warns that "our failure to live out the unity we are given is nothing less than a frustration of the Spirit's work" to constitute and preserve the life of the church.[26] Douglas Koskela's analysis of Yves Congar's contributions to ecclesiology in light of the Spirit rings true in a wider context: though the need to subordinate church to Spirit remains a significant advance, differing conceptions of precisely how this intersection of pneumatology and ecclesiology should be framed still create ecumenical disjunction.[27] Or, as Jeremy Ber-

---

23. Rosato, "Called by God," 115, referencing Kasper's *Einführung in den Glauben* (Mainz: Matthias-Grünewald, 1973), 121. Kasper returns to this theme repeatedly. See Denis Edwards's summary of his views in "Holy Spirit as the Gift," 203–5. See also Veli-Matti Kärkkäinen, "The Ecumenical Potential of Pneumatology," *Gregorianum* 80, no. 1 (1999): 121–45; and Jeremy Bergen, "The Holy Spirit and Lived Communion from the Perspective of International Bilateral Dialogues," *Journal of Ecumenical Studies* 49 (Spring 2014): 193–217.

24. Boris Bobrinskoy, "Holy Spirit," and Konrad Reiser, "Holy Spirit in Ecumenical Thought," in *Dictionary of the Ecumenical Movement*, 2nd ed., ed. Nicholas Lossky et al. (Geneva: WCC Publications, 2002), 531–34 and 534–41, respectively.

25. See especially Mary Tanner, "Pneumatology in Multilateral Settings," and Ralph Del Colle, "The Outpouring of the Holy Spirit: Implications for the Church and Ecumenism," in *The Holy Spirit, the Church, and Christian Unity: Proceedings of the Consultation Held at the Monastery of Bose, Italy (14–20 October 2002)*, ed. D. Donnelly, A. Denaux, and J. Famerée (Leuven: Leuven University Press, 2005), 225–45 and 247–65, respectively.

26. Michael Root, "Essential Unity and Lived Communion: The Interrelation of the Unity We Have and the Unity We Seek," in *The Ecumenical Future: Background Papers for In One Body through the Cross, the Princeton Proposal for Christian Unity*, ed. Carl E. Braaten and Robert W. Jenson (Grand Rapids: Eerdmans, 2004), 123.

27. Douglas M. Koskela, *Ecclesiality and Ecumenism: Yves Congar and the Road to Unity* (Milwaukee: Marquette University Press, 2008), 159–60.

gen suggests at the conclusion of his recent treatment of the Holy Spirit in international bilateral dialogues, "[t]he question might be raised whether assertions of the Spirit's leading and blessing of dialogues is premature, given that in very few cases visible unity or lived communion has been the result. While the churches together may confess many things *about* the Spirit . . . might it not be advisable to judge the presence of Spirit amid divisions by the fruit of lived communion?"[28]

The Princeton Proposal admits that "[s]hort of a decisive intervention of the Holy Spirit, the full visible unity of 'all in each place' described in the New Delhi statement does not lie in the immediate future,"[29] but it is by no means clear that such an intervention could even be recognized or accepted by the different traditions because their senses of the Spirit and the Spirit's relation to ecumenism remain so disparate.

Perhaps it is the attempt to privilege the Holy Spirit within ecumenism that goes amiss. Some worry that an overly pliable pneumatology vitiates Christian theology of its content.[30] Along these lines, in April 2014, Ephraim Radner published an article on the Holy Spirit and unity, taking as his subtitle the rather pointed phrase, "Getting Out of the Way of Christ."[31] His goal was to argue for "a limited pneumatological definition of Christian unity," as in his view, only "a more exclusive christological explanation" brings reconciliation.[32] Radner focuses on the insufficient pneumatology of three seventeenth-century theologians, the trajectories of whose arguments misdirect contemporary discussions of unity—although he also spends time charting how aspects of earlier theological stances paved the way for these errors.[33] In particular, Radner notes that Augustine's famous naming of the Spirit as "love" can be used to reduce the Spirit into a principle of "pneumatic abstraction."[34] This potential for decoupling the Spirit from Christian particularities was originally held in check by early and medieval

28. Bergen, "Holy Spirit and Lived Communion," 215–16.

29. Braaten and Jenson, *In One Body through the Cross*, 58, §72.

30. See Habets, "'Justified by the Spirit'?," 326–28; as well as Stuart Print and Myk Habets, "A Critical Review Essay on Amos Yong, *Beyond the Impasse: Toward a Pneumatological Theology of Religions*," *Pacific Journal of Baptist Research* 3 (April 2007): 53–60 (especially 58–60).

31. Ephraim Radner, "The Holy Spirit and Unity: Getting Out of the Way of Christ," *International Journal of Systematic Theology* 16 (April 2014): 207–20.

32. Ibid., 207.

33. Ibid., 208–9.

34. Ibid., 209–10.

commitments forging the Spirit's connection to love and unity through submission to Scripture and to christological character.[35] For Radner, the modern era decouples these links, which leads astray the ecumenical movement's understandable move to set a nonmaterial arbiter of union—the Spirit—in place of various idolatrous alternatives. Therefore, if ecumenism's focus on the Spirit is maintained, it must be qualified by the acknowledgment that the Spirit demonstrates the divine priority of union—the "fact" of the divine instrument of unity—while the "form" of union remains Christ. "Nothing," Radner concludes,

> "looks like the Spirit"; the Spirit reveals all that there is that has a "look" and thus a form, and this "mind of God" is Christ himself . . . the Spirit recedes behind all these forms, for the sake of absolutizing their practical value . . . it is Christ's concreteness that emerges, as that one concrete element of God that is given to us redemptively . . . the Spirit presses him forward into our midst so that there is nothing else to be seen.[36]

There is much in Radner's analysis that I find compelling. I consider quite persuasive his arguments detailing the modern loosening of pneumatology from the form of Christ and the consequences for conceptualizing ecclesial unity. I happily accept his admonishments that unity "looks like" and ought to be defined by the character of Christ, and moreover that it is the special task of the Spirit to reveal such a form. Nevertheless, I find troubling the statement that for Christ's "concreteness" to "emerge" the Spirit would need to "recede." This almost seems to pit the divine persons against one another rather than explicate their union as the Trinity. At the same time, Radner's claim that the Spirit still holds the responsibility to "press" Christ "forward into our midst" provides a counterpoint. The Spirit remains active, then, perhaps not just a "fact" of divine union but its necessary constitution. How should this pressing forward of the Spirit be explicated? Is there a way to hold together this work of the Spirit to bring about Christian union with a dense account of the christological form of that union?

I suspect that the problems Radner detects are not as much a function of pneumatology as a function of its being *improperly conceived and underdeveloped.* His portrayal of modern pneumatology's errors seems to

35. Ibid., 209–11.
36. Ibid., 218–20, quote from 220.

support this analysis. By contrast, an accurate understanding of the Spirit cannot entail the former getting in the way of Christ because the Holy Spirit, properly understood, unites the person and the community to Christ by forming Christ in them. In other words, recoupling pneumatology to its biblical roots and to formation of Christlike character provides the antidote to modern fuzziness on the Spirit's intersection with ecclesial unity.

Reenergizing these connections enables RE to occur. Radner's own material on the hallmarks of early Christian communities suggests the way, although I hope to sharpen the point slightly: the christological shape of ecclesial union derives from the coming together of people who, only to the extent that they are open to the Spirit, recognize Christ within each other. Here, RE's proposals to develop dispositions that recognize God's presence within the other find purchase in an explicit and thoroughly grounded pneumatology. Such an RE places recognition of the Spirit forming Christlikeness within the other as the basis for acknowledging shared existence within the body of Christ, able to receive what one's own communion lacks from the gifts of the other. To get there, we must reclaim a proper understanding of the Spirit.

Which Pneumatology? Whose Spirit?

As Leopoldo A. Sánchez M. wryly notes, "[n]o one disputes that the Holy Spirit leads the church into all truth. But how does one discern the spirits?"[37] For the purposes of this article, I suggest a discernment that takes up and develops Radner's criteria, the guidance of Scripture, and the formation of christological character. I am keenly aware that this focus represents the tip of the proverbial iceberg; there is far more that needs to be said about how the identity of the Spirit relates to ecumenism. At the same time, I hope that a Scriptural foundation and an emphasis on imitating Christ can serve as two benchmarks for that discussion." discussion." I will thus begin with a scene from the Gospel of Luke, proceed to some general New Testament contributions, and then turn to Kevin Hector in order to construct a pneumatic foundation for receptive ecumenism.

37. Leopoldo A. Sánchez M., "More Promise than Ambiguity: Pneumatological Christology as a Model for Ecumenical Engagement," in *Critical Issues in Ecclesiology: Essays in Honor of Carl E. Braaten*, ed. Alberto L. Garcia and Susan K. Wood (Grand Rapids: Eerdmans, 2011), 211.

Luke's Gospel begins with an account chronicling what happens when the Spirit of God moves within human flesh to motivate recognition of Christ.[38] Such recognition prompts worship of God in the company of others. In Luke 1:39–45, the Gospel presents Mary hurrying to visit Elizabeth, who becomes "filled with the Holy Spirit" and exclaims loudly in response. Elizabeth recognizes the unborn Christ borne by Mary, publicly declares that reality, and blesses Mary for choosing to bear Christ despite the risks and costs involved. Elizabeth's public blessing of Mary and of the Christ whom Mary carries releases Mary to make her own prophetic song affirming that Jesus' salvation displays God's goodness. The Spirit enables these two women to mutually recognize the presence and work of God redeeming the world in Christ, which leads to their shared worship. Recognition of the presence of Christ, even when that presence has been physically displaced, prompts shared worship, or as Jean-Luc Marion would have it, the ability and desire to bless the Father.[39] The Gospel of Luke suggests from its start that Christ, even when he removes himself from physical proximity and availability, is known through the presence of the Spirit.[40]

Beyond Luke-Acts, the New Testament as a whole establishes the role of the Spirit as the one who enables recognition of Christ and draws his followers into shared worship. For his part, Marion considers the Gospels' depiction of the departure of the risen Christ as the opportunity for the disciples to know this presence in an even more crystallized fashion. Any who would follow Christ must be enabled to repeat his behavior by imitating his example, and only the absence of Christ from "the worldly economy of presence" can create the space for the participation of others.[41] Apart from the Spirit given when Christ ascends, the opening of the Trinitarian life to all people of all ages and places remains impossible.[42] Thus, "[t]he highest presence of Christ lies in the Spirit's action of making us, with him and in him, bless the Father."[43]

38. See David Lyle Jeffrey, *Luke*, Brazos Theological Commentary on the Bible (Grand Rapids: Brazos, 2012), 284.

39. Jean-Luc Marion, "The Gift of a Presence," in *Prolegomena to Charity*, trans. Stephen Lewis (New York: Fordham University Press, 2002), 124–52.

40. Luke-Acts as a whole concerns itself especially with recognition and reception of Christ by the Spirit. See Paul Borgman, *The Way according to Luke: Hearing the Whole Story of Luke-Acts* (Grand Rapids: Eerdmans, 2006), 7–14, 63–64, 211–12.

41. Marion, "Gift of a Presence," 131, 138–45.

42. Ibid., 146.

43. Ibid., 145.

James D. G. Dunn's volume of collected essays on pneumatology provides a thorough underpinning for these claims. He notes that:

> the Spirit for Paul has been constitutively stamped with the character of Christ. Christ by his resurrection entered wholly upon the realm of the Spirit. . . . That is to say, the exalted Christ is now experienced in, through, and as Spirit. Christ now cannot be experienced apart from the Spirit; the Spirit is the medium of union between Christ and the believer. . . . Conversely, the Spirit is now experienced as the power of the risen Christ—the Spirit now cannot be experienced apart from Christ. . . . It is because the Spirit has taken the shape of Christ that the character of Christ can and must serve as the basic criterion whereby the Spirit's activity may be discerned; only that which makes the individual or church more like Christ can claim fully to be an expression of the Spirit of Christ.[44]

Several important points can be gleaned from this paragraph and Dunn's elaborations on its substance. First, the Holy Spirit constitutes the link between each believer and the resurrected Christ. As with Marion, all benefits of believing, following, and knowing Christ are granted through the Spirit who linked Jesus to God and who now continues that work for each of Christ's followers.[45] Kilian McDonnell put it this way in 1982: "[i]t is the Spirit who realizes in us the Christ-Presence. The Spirit renders the Christ a living reality that would otherwise remain historical speculation."[46] Second, as in Marion's analysis, the Spirit's task comprises reproducing Christ's character in each person and community.[47] I will return to this aspect below. Third, the Spirit's formation of people into imitators of Christ draws them toward each other. The Spirit's presence is both "what makes the individual a member of Christ" and the impetus drawing believers together.[48] The indwelling of the Spirit shapes not just the individual but also connections between individuals: "the corporate life of Christians arises out of the shared experience of the

44. James D. G. Dunn, "Spirit and Holy Spirit in the New Testament," *The Christ and the Spirit*, vol. 2, *Pneumatology* (Grand Rapids: Eerdmans, 1998), 3–21 (16).

45. See also James D. G. Dunn, "Rediscovering the Spirit (1)," in *Christ and the Spirit*, 2:43–61 (52).

46. Killan McDonnell, "The Determinative Doctrine of the Holy Spirit," *Theology Today* 39 (July 1, 1982): 142–61 (154).

47. Dunn, "Rediscovering the Spirit (1)," 52.

48. Dunn, "Spirit and Holy Spirit," 13.

Spirit . . . [and] the continuing existence and unity of any church depends on the sharing of that shared Spirit."[49] For "the Spirit precedes the Church and stands over it . . . it is their experience of the Spirit which unites the members of the body."[50] The Spirit remains the source and guarantor of Christian unity, because such unity rests upon, builds up, and enables a shared imitation of Christ.

What constitutes the character of Christ? What marks disclose his identity and thus ratify any claim that the Spirit of Christ is present? Dunn distills the scriptural criteria for discerning an authentic expression of the Spirit in a person or community: acknowledgment of the lordship of Jesus, promotion of the character of Christlike love, and building up the entire community.[51] As the hallmark of the Spirit remains love, "the kind of love which Jesus lived out in all his ministry," relationships within any community claiming Christ as Lord must be characterized by the same disposition.[52] All character formed by the Spirit—at both individual and communal levels—remains accountable to and measured by the model of Jesus.[53] This includes the character of the suffering Christ on the cross, which is never left behind in order to experience the resurrection.[54] Interestingly, Dunn also notes that this commitment to imitating Christ means that at various points, some structures and forms of the churches may need to die so that the coming to life of Christ may continue to occur.[55]

Recovering this scriptural pneumatology offers us the chance to understand the Spirit as always the Spirit of Christ, always concerned with formation of Christlikeness within each person and community, always capable of being discerned, and always bound up with Christian unity. In fact, Dunn's analysis reveals that Christ simply cannot be known, received, or joined apart from the Spirit's work. The Spirit's presence forming Christ's character within a person and community determines whether or not that person or community can be given the title Christian.[56] Therefore, not only *can* Christians look to the Spirit in order to form union with each other, in fact they *must* do so, since the Spirit always belongs and always forms

49. Ibid., 15.

50. Dunn, "Rediscovering the Spirit (1)," 58.

51. Dunn, "Rediscovering the Spirit (2)," in *Christ and the Spirit*, 2:62–80 (71–72).

52. Dunn, "The Spirit and the Body of Christ," in *Christ and the Spirit*, 2:343–57 (349).

53. Ibid., 350.

54. Ibid., 350–51.

55. Ibid., 354–55.

56. See Dunn, "Rediscovering the Spirit (1)," 45.

others to Christ. We are now in a position to gather these threads together and suggest the contours of a TAT of receptive ecumenism.

The Unity of the Holy Spirit: Toward Receptive Ecumenism

If RE seeks to promote a posture such that the various traditions convert to each other by recognizing how others uniquely instantiate God's presence, it must begin by orienting itself to the Spirit who makes possible such formation. More than this, RE needs to understand the Spirit as enabling recognition of God's presence in the other. For this point, I turn to Kevin Hector's recent work.[57]

In a manner consonant with the points above, Hector argues that the ascension of Christ does not convert the authoritative presence of God into either Scripture or church. Rather, as with Dunn and Marion, the ascension draws us deeper into the dynamics of the Trinity via the Spirit.[58] Hector explains:

> the Spirit, on this account, is first of all the Spirit of Christ's recognition of what counts as following him, a Spirit he conveyed to those whose practices he recognized, and that they conveyed to still others. In this way, the norms according to which Christ assessed whether one was following him were passed along to others, and, since these norms are the means by which one is transformed to Christ, it follows that this account provides some

57. Kevin W. Hector, *Theology without Metaphysics: God, Language, and the Spirit of Recognition* (Cambridge: Cambridge University Press, 2011). Whether or not Hector has rendered substance-based metaphysics unnecessary falls outside the scope of this article. See his conversation with Rowan Williams in *Marginalia*, with Williams's initial review, "To Speak Truly about God," http://marginalia.lareviewofbooks.org/speak-truly-god/, and Hector's reply, "Letter to the Editors: The Rowan Williams Review," http://marginalia.lareviewofbooks.org/letter-to-the-editors-review-rowan-williams/, both accessed June 19, 2015. I find Hector's approach important because it attempts to offer the "theopneumatics" heretofore largely missing from Christian theology. In addition to note 13 above, see also Robert W. Jenson, "You Wonder Where the Spirit Went," *Pro Ecclesia* 2 (June 1993): 296–304; Eugene F. Rogers Jr., "The Mystery of the Spirit in Three Traditions: Calvin, Rahner, Florensky, or, You *Keep* Wondering Where the Spirit Went," *Modern Theology* 19 (April 2003): 243–60; John Milbank, "The Second Difference," in *The Word Made Strange: Theology, Language, Culture* (Oxford: Blackwell, 1997), 171–93; and Sarah Coakley, *God, Sexuality, and the Self: An Essay 'On the Trinity'* (Cambridge: Cambridge University Press, 2013), as well as my dissertation, "Filled with 'the Fullness of the Gifts of God': Towards a Pneumatic *Theosis*," (PhD diss., Marquette University, forthcoming).

58. Hector, *Theology without Metaphysics*, 34–35.

> explanation of one of the central works traditionally ascribed to the Holy Spirit.[59]

The Spirit enables people and communities to go on in the same ways Christ demonstrated to be revelatory of God.[60] Identifying anything as disclosing God and thus authoritative for the Christian community therefore depends upon the mutual recognition of Christ's normative Spirit indwelling believers. This means that conformity to Christ can be acknowledged even across areas of significant doctrinal difference and that discerning a shared Christian identity does not depend upon the parties becoming identical.[61] This understanding is not to be seen as oppositional to doctrine or ecclesial institutions, or as displacing their importance for Christian unity; rather, it offers an evaluative standard for them. Brian Daley notes that "the heart of the church's institutional life, the soul that animates the body, *is* the love poured out by the Holy Spirit as the gift of himself . . . the concrete manifestation of that God-given love is not simply feelings of fellowship, but functioning corporate life."[62] Therefore, a TAT of receptive ecumenism offers a way Christians can forge unity by working to recognize Christ's Spirit everywhere the Spirit may be seen and by learning to subject doctrine and ecclesial institutions to the hallmarks of the Spirit.

Recognition of Christ's Spirit in the other enables modification of unjust ecclesial forms and structures and promotes overcoming differences through the principles of ecumenical dialogue. We do not need to cast the Spirit as "receding" from Christ in our midst in order for Christ to be known, but rather to stress that where the hallmarks of the Spirit—profession of Christ's lordship, embracing cruciform character, seeking to build up the community of believers—are recognized in the other, the Spirit draws us out from insularity into the communion of Christ. We do not see only Christ and not the Spirit, but rather we ratify the Spirit constituting Christ within the other, sometimes in unexpected or surprising ways. Only thus can we know ourselves as part of Christ's body, knowing all the while that our Head is continually directing the Spirit who animates that body to bring

59. Ibid., 91.

60. Ibid., 191.

61. Ibid., 47–102, and Minna Hietamäki, *Agreeable Agreement: An Examination of the Quest for Consensus in Ecumenical Dialogue*, Ecclesiological Investigations 8 (London: T&T Clark, 2010), 209.

62. Brian E. Daley, SJ, "Rebuilding the Structure of Love," in Braaten and Jenson, *Ecumenical Future*, 104–5.

together all its members. We engage in ecumenical dialogue out of this posture of eagerness to seek and find the Spirit in the other, not just to detail consensus or difference.

Though there is still much work to be done relating TAT to receptive ecumenism, I hope this essay has gestured toward how these areas of inquiry can fruitfully inform each other. In brief, starting with the Spirit enables Christian theology to acknowledge that we live within the economy of the Spirit, who has taken up the work of Christ and will carry it on to completion within individual lives and community formation. Third Article Theology enables RE to develop as the reliable foundation for its proposed postures of receptivity and conversion the recognition of the Spirit within the other. Receptive ecumenism can thus challenge the churches to focus on the hallmarks of the Spirit as the markers of God's presence in the other, and to cast love of and union with those others as what one needs in order to fully know God. Promotion of these postures and their related practices can sow seeds for a new season of ecumenical engagement.

Finally, specific actions from ecumenists, theologians, professors, pastors, and ecclesial leaders can contribute toward prioritizing the recognition of the Spirit both within and outside of the official dialogues, thus eventually bearing fruit for ecclesial structures of unity. I close with a nonexhaustive list of recommendations for promoting an RE of the Spirit, noting that each of the following points can be considered an instantiation of the posture Elizabeth takes toward Mary. For when we choose to put on the demeanor of Elizabeth, nudged by the Spirit to see how the other is filled by the Spirit to bear Christ, RE will wondrously flower.

1. Consistently engage in acts of penance within one's worship services for the missed presence of the others from whom one's community is divided, starting with acknowledging the missed others whose presence one needs in order to be whole and including prayers for reunification.[63]

---

63. See Geraldine Smyth, OP, "Jerusalem, Athens, and Zurich—Psychoanalytic Perspectives on Factors Inhibiting Receptive Ecumenism," in *Receptive Ecumenism*, ed. Murray and Badini-Confalonieri 285–302, particularly 294–96: "We cannot free ourselves—whether through more personal effort or striving to overcome collective apathy or in the comfort zone of churchly narcissism. Reconciliation will be found not by denying that we find ourselves at a loss but in acknowledging that it is a grace within us and beyond us . . . [which] comes to us only when we accept that we have come to a dead end—incapable of tracing any secure sense of meaning, wholeness, or promise. Is this the hour in the ecumenical movement when churches must stand

2. Embrace and teach the primacy of recognizing the Spirit for Christian unity, *including over and against one's own ecclesial structures* where these would deny others acceptance based on anything other than the marks of the Spirit.
3. Work to end *any and all* of one's own ecclesial structures or practices that prioritize anything over recognition of the Spirit for forming union in Christ.
4. Work to dismantle *any and all* of one's own ecclesial structures or practices that take as their justification anything other than the formation of Christ by the Spirit.
5. Practice recognizing whoever displays the Holy Spirit as a bearer of Christ, focusing on the hallmarks of acknowledging the lordship of Christ, the desire to build up the body, and the desire to love sacrificially and cruciformly, paying special attention to how others understand themselves to be so engaged, not merely to one's own community's standards.
6. In treatments of other Christian traditions, focus not on areas that one's tradition regards as its specialty and whose lack might mark a deficiency in the other (these might include reading Scripture so as to identify Christians solely by traditions, the episcopacy, or other heritages and structures for the liturgical churches and reading Scripture so as to decry others' ecclesial traditions, structures, and heritages for the Protestant churches), but instead honor how the others form Christ in ways that one's own community lacks.
7. As much as possible, where their lives and teachings bear the hallmarks of the Spirit described above, teach the saints and heroes of other denominations as bearers of the character of Christ and thus worthy of emulation and honor.
8. And, as much as possible, receive and teach other denominations' theology, again as it displays the Holy Spirit and thus forms Christ.[64]

face-to-face in the impasse? Even at the terminus of human capacity can we make an act of faith in God's future, entrusting ourselves to the guiding power of the Spirit, and search out new paths?"

64. For their incisive comments on earlier drafts, and indeed for representing to me the very character traits I mention here—being willing to learn from and with me, as well as to share with me the riches of their traditions and thoughts—I thank D. Glenn Butner, Myk Habets, Andrew Kuzma, and, as always, my husband, Darin Allen Fawley.

SELECT BIBLIOGRAPHY

Alfaro, Sammy. *Divino Compañero: Toward a Hispanic Pentecostal Christology*. Eugene, OR: Pickwick, 2010.

Barth, Karl Barth. "Nachwort, or Concluding Unscientific Postscript on Schleiermacher." In *The Theology of Schleiermacher: Lectures at Göttingen*, translated by Geoffrey W. Bromiley, 261–79. Grand Rapids: Eerdmans, 1982.

Bracken, Joseph A. "Trinitarian Spirit Christology: In Need of a New Metaphysics?" *Theological Studies* 72 (2011): 750–67.

Coffey, David M. "Spirit Christology and the Trinity." In *Advents of the Spirit: An Introduction to the Current Study of Pneumatology*, edited by B. E. Hinze and D. L. Dabney, 315–38. Milwaukee: Marquette University Press, 2001.

Dabney, D. Lyle. "The Justification of the Spirit: Soteriological Reflections on the Resurrection." In Pickard and Preece, *Starting with the Spirit*, 59–82.

———. "Naming the Spirit: Toward a Pneumatology of the Cross." In Pickard and Preece, *Starting with the Spirit*, 28–58.

———. "The Nature of the Spirit: Creation as a Premonition of God." In Pickard and Preece, *Starting with the Spirit*, 83–110.

———. "Starting with the Spirit: Why the Last Should be First." In Pickard and Preece, *Starting with the Spirit*, 3–27.

Del Colle, Ralph. *Christ and the Spirit: Spirit-Christology in Trinitarian Perspective*. New York: Oxford University Press, 1994.

Grosso, Andrew. "Spirit Christology and the Shape of the Theological Enterprise." In *A Man of the Church: Honoring the Theology, Life, and Witness of Ralph Del Colle*, edited by Michel René Barnes, 206–22. Eugene, OR: Pickwick, 2012.

Habets, Myk. *The Anointed Son: A Trinitarian Spirit Christology*. Eugene, OR: Pickwick, 2010.

———. "*Filioque*? Nein: A Proposal for Coherent Coinherence." In *Trinitarian Theology after Barth*, edited by Myk Habets and Phillip Tolliday, 161–202. Eugene, OR: Pickwick, 2011.

———. "Getting beyond the *Filioque* with Third Article Theology." In *Ecumenical Perspectives on the Filioque for the Twenty-First Century*, edited by Myk Habets, 211–30. London: Bloomsbury/T&T Clark, 2014.

———. "The Surprising Third Article Theology of Jonathan Edwards." In *The Ecumenical Edwards: Jonathan Edwards and the Theologians*, edited by Kyle Strobel, 195–211. Farnham, UK: Ashgate, 2015.

———. "*Veni Cinderella Spiritus*." *Journal of Pentecostal Theology* 10 (2001): 65–80.

Kärkkäinen, Veli-Matti. *Toward a Pneumatological Theology: Pentecostal and Ecumenical Perspectives on Ecclesiology, Soteriology, and Theology of Mission*. Edited by A. Yong. New York: University Press of America, 2002.

Liston, Gregory J. *The Anointed Church: Toward a Third Article Ecclesiology*. Minneapolis: Fortress, 2015.

Macchia, Frank D. *Justified in the Spirit: Creation, Redemption, and the Triune God*. Grand Rapids: Eerdmans, 2010.

Moltmann, Jürgen. *The Spirit of Life: A Universal Affirmation*. Translated by M. Kohl. Minneapolis: Fortress, 1992.

Mühlen, Heribert. *Una Mystica Persona: Die Kirche als das Mysterium der heilsgeschichtlichen Identität des Heiligen Geistes in Christus und den Christen; Eine Person in vielen Personen*. Paderborn: Ferdinand Schöningh, 1967. Translated by Wolfgang Vondey as *Heribert Mühlen: His Theology and Praxis*. Dallas: University Press of America, 2004.

Pickard, Stephen, and Gordon Preece, eds. *Starting with the Spirit: Task of Theology II*. Hindmarsh, SA: Australian Theological Forum, 2001.

Pinnock, Clark H. *Flame of Love: A Theology of the Holy Spirit*. Downers Grove, IL: InterVarsity Press, 1996.

Sánchez M., Leopoldo A. *Receiver, Bearer, and Giver of God's Spirit: Jesus' Life in the Spirit as a Lens for Theology and Life*. Eugene, OR: Pickwick, 2015.

Smith, James K. A. *Thinking in Tongues: Pentecostal Contributions to Christian Philosophy*. Grand Rapids: Eerdmans, 2010.

Studebaker, Steven M. *From Pentecost to the Triune God: A Pentecostal Trinitarian Theology*. Grand Rapids: Eerdmans, 2012.

Weinandy, Thomas G. *The Father's Spirit of Sonship: Reconceiving the Trinity*. Edinburgh: T&T Clark, 1995.

Yong, Amos. *Beyond the Impasse: Toward a Pneumatological Theology of Religions* (Grand Rapids: Baker, 2003).

INDEX